STRYKE FORCE

MORGAN STRYKER, a cybernetically enhanced soldier turned mercenary, leads a team of outlaw heroes-for-hire with incredible powers on dangerous missions around the world. Always staying one step ahead of the law, Stryker and his team put their lives on the line with every mission. Sometimes for money and no glory, and sometimes because people need saving and there is no one else who can get the job done, the Strykeforce team fights the wars...

...you never even hear about.

Strykeforce and *Codename: Strykeforce*
created by **Marc Silvestri**

Strykeforce issues #1-5 written by **Jay Faerber**

Codename: Strykeforce issue #0 story by **Mike Heisler**
Codename: Strykeforce issue #1 plotted and
scripted by **Marc Silvestri**
Codename: Strykeforce issues #2-3 plot by **Marc Silvestri**
and **David Wohl**, scripted by **Marc Silvestri**

For the original editions: *Codename: Strykeforce* issues #0-3
lettering by **Chris Eliopoulos,**
Dennis Heisler and **Mike Heisler**

For the original editions: *Strykeforce* issues #1-5 lettering by
Robin Spehar and **Dreamer Design's**
Dennis Heisler and **Mark Roslan**

For this edition, book design & layout by: **Spehar, Dreamer**

ISBN #: 1-58240-471-2
Published by Image Comics®
Strykeforce Vol. 1 2005 First Printing. Office of Publication: 1942 University Ave., Suite 305, Berkeley, CA 94704. Originally published as Strykeforce issues #1-5 and Codename: Strykeforce issues #0-3 as well as Codename: Strykeforce trade paperback (1995). Strykeforce® and Codename: Strykeforce® are © 2005 Top Cow Productions, Inc. "Strykeforce" and "Codename: Strykeforce", their logos, all related characters and their likenesses are registered trademarks of Top Cow Productions, Inc. The characters, events, and stories in this publication are entirely fictional. With the exception of art used for review purposes, none of the contents of this book may be reprinted in any form without the express written consent of Top Cow Productions, Inc. **PRINTED IN HONG KONG**

To find the comics shop nearest
you call: 1-888-COMICBOOK

What did you think of this book? We love to
hear from our readers. Please e-mail us at:
fanmail@topcow.com

or write us at:
Strykeforce Letters
c/o Top Cow Productions, Inc.
10350 Santa Monica Blvd., Suite #100
Los Angeles, CA 90025

FOR
image
COMICS
Erik Larsen
publisher

Marc Silvestri—chief executive officer
Matt Hawkins—president / chief operating officer
Jim McLauchlin—editor in chief
Renae Geerlings—vp of publishing / managing editor
Scott Tucker—editor
Chaz Riggs—production manager
Annie Pham—marketing director
Peter Lam—webmaster
Phil Smith—trades and submissions
Rob Levin—editorial assistant
Jacques David—intern

visit us on the web at
WWW.TOPCOW.COM

TABLE OF CONTENTS

My work on Strykeforce started in 1996.

No, really.

In 1996, Warren Ellis took over as writer of WildStorm's *Stormwatch* series, and rebuilt it pretty much from the ground up. I was still trying to break into comics at that point, and I got the bright idea that maybe Top Cow's *Codename: Strykeforce* series could use a similar revitalization. And naturally, I figured I was just the man for the job. So, I sent a letter to the guys at Top Cow, asking if they'd be interested in such a project, and … well, nothing. No response. And who can blame them? I was, at that point, a complete nobody (I'm still a nobody – just not *completely*). At any rate, two years later I managed to sell a script to Marvel Comics, and then one to DC Comics, and the work remained fairly steady.

Fast-forward to 2003. I'd been working on various comic series since 1998, and I'd run into Top Cow's new editor-in-chief, Jim McLauchlin, a number of times over the years. Still, I was surprised to hear from him out of the blue one day. He thought it'd be fun for me to do something at Top Cow, and asked if he could send me some reference on their catalogue of characters. I pretended to be mildly interested (when I was, in fact, incredibly psyched), and said "Sure" – even though I already knew what I wanted to pitch.

I'd heard rumblings over the years of Marc Silvestri himself planning to revive *Cyberforce,* so I figured it'd be pointless to pitch that particular project. But *Codename: Strykeforce* … there was a book just ripe for an update. I suggested that to Jim, and he approved the pitch almost immediately.

Codename: Strykeforce was pretty much the perfect project to update because of its history. It didn't have much. The book didn't have a particularly long history, so there wasn't a ton of baggage attached to it. On the other hand, it *did* have an established premise, so it wasn't like I had to build something from scratch. The foundation was already there.

Over the next month or two, Jim, Scott (Tucker, the book's actual editor) and I bounced around ideas about characters, deciding who to keep from the original line-up, and what form the new characters would take. Marc himself even got involved. I'd initially only wanted to keep Stryker from the original team, but Marc suggested we use Black Anvil, as well. And it was a good call. When we announced the book, I was floored by the number of e-mails I received from Black Anvil fans. Marc also created Tia Katana, with her amazing tattoo/sword.

Then came Tyler Kirkham. He actually wasn't our first choice for the book. We'd gone through a few different people, some who were only briefly considered, and some of whom actually drew sketches of the character. Tyler was in some kind of intern program at the Top Cow offices, and hadn't really gotten a major assignment yet, but he drew the most amazing pin-up of Stryker, just for the hell of it, and showed it around the office. In no time, he was our artist. I was hoping that drawing would get used somewhere in this TPB collection and in fact it did make it into the bonus material on pg. 234.

At any rate, that's pretty much the back-story to the our 5-issue *Strykeforce* series. I had a blast writing Stryker and Anvil, and introducing Lift, Killawatt, Tia Katana, and Sly. Tyler's vision of these characters perfectly matched mine, and I think you'll agree that that symmetry comes across on every page.

So please, enjoy. We sure did.

Jay Faerber
Seattle, 2004

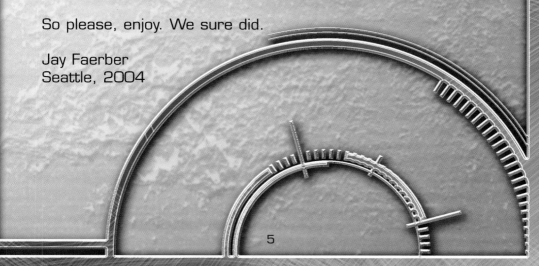

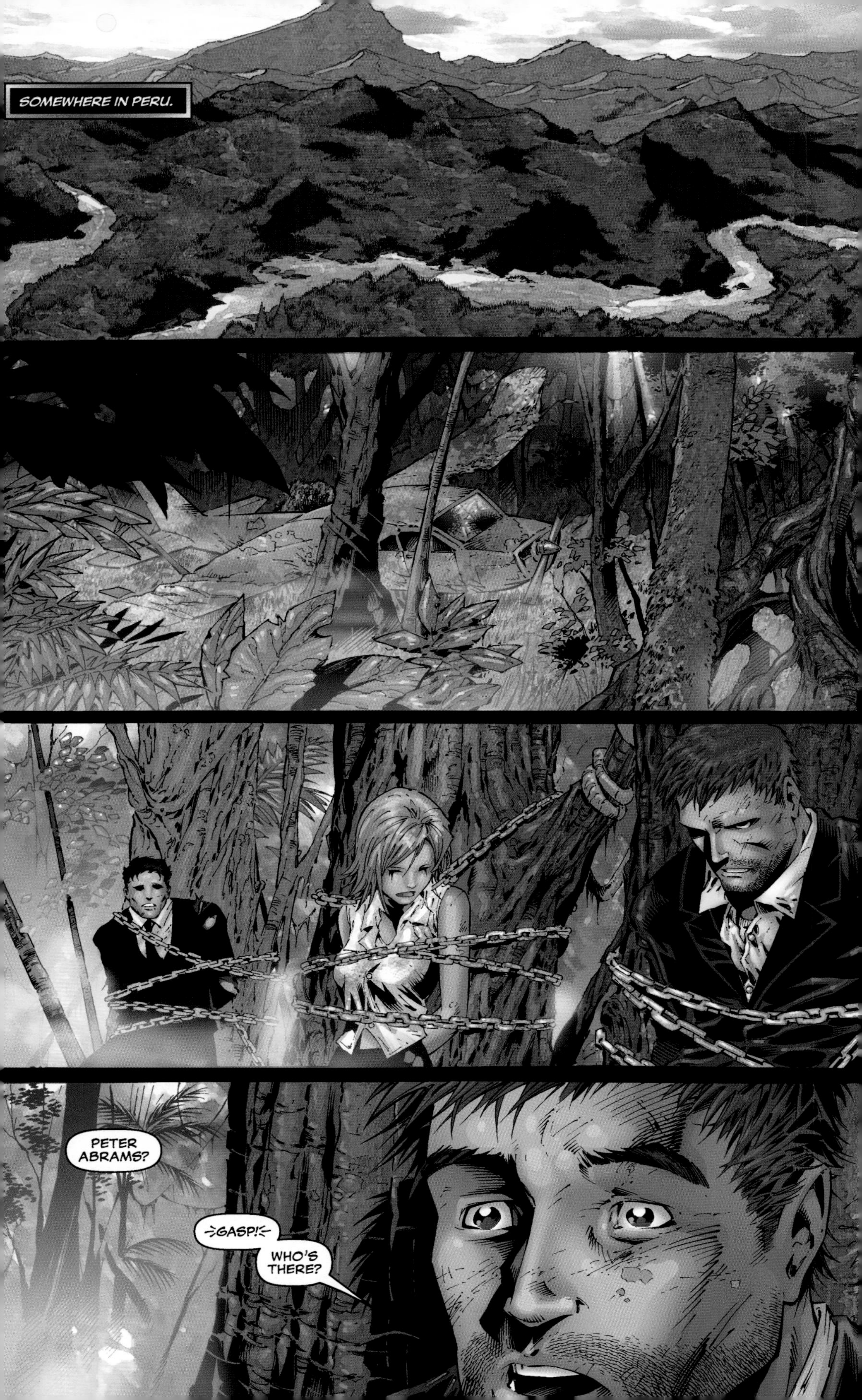
SOMEWHERE IN PERU.
PETER ABRAMS?
GASP!
WHO'S THERE?

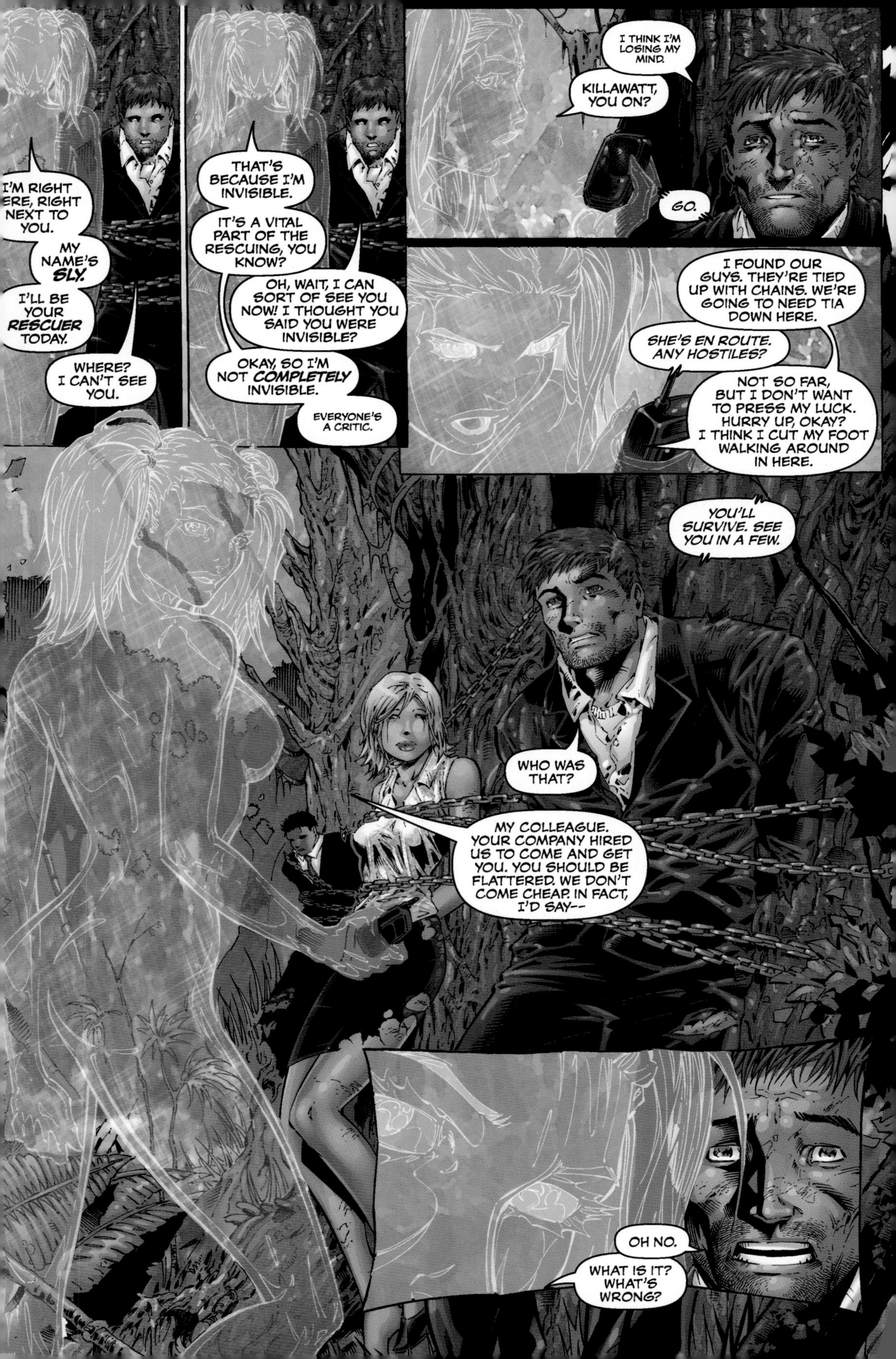
I'M RIGHT ERE, RIGHT NEXT TO YOU.
MY NAME'S SLY.
I'LL BE YOUR RESCUER TODAY.
WHERE? I CAN'T SEE YOU.
THAT'S BECAUSE I'M INVISIBLE.
IT'S A VITAL PART OF THE RESCUING, YOU KNOW?
OH, WAIT, I CAN SORT OF SEE YOU NOW! I THOUGHT YOU SAID YOU WERE INVISIBLE?
OKAY, SO I'M NOT COMPLETELY INVISIBLE.
EVERYONE'S A CRITIC.
I THINK I'M LOSING MY MIND.
KILLAWATT, YOU ON?
GO.
I FOUND OUR GUYS. THEY'RE TIED UP WITH CHAINS. WE'RE GOING TO NEED TIA DOWN HERE.
SHE'S EN ROUTE. ANY HOSTILES?
NOT SO FAR, BUT I DON'T WANT TO PRESS MY LUCK. HURRY UP, OKAY? I THINK I CUT MY FOOT WALKING AROUND IN HERE.
YOU'LL SURVIVE. SEE YOU IN A FEW.
WHO WAS THAT?
MY COLLEAGUE. YOUR COMPANY HIRED US TO COME AND GET YOU. YOU SHOULD BE FLATTERED. WE DON'T COME CHEAP. IN FACT, I'D SAY--
OH NO.
WHAT IS IT? WHAT'S WRONG?

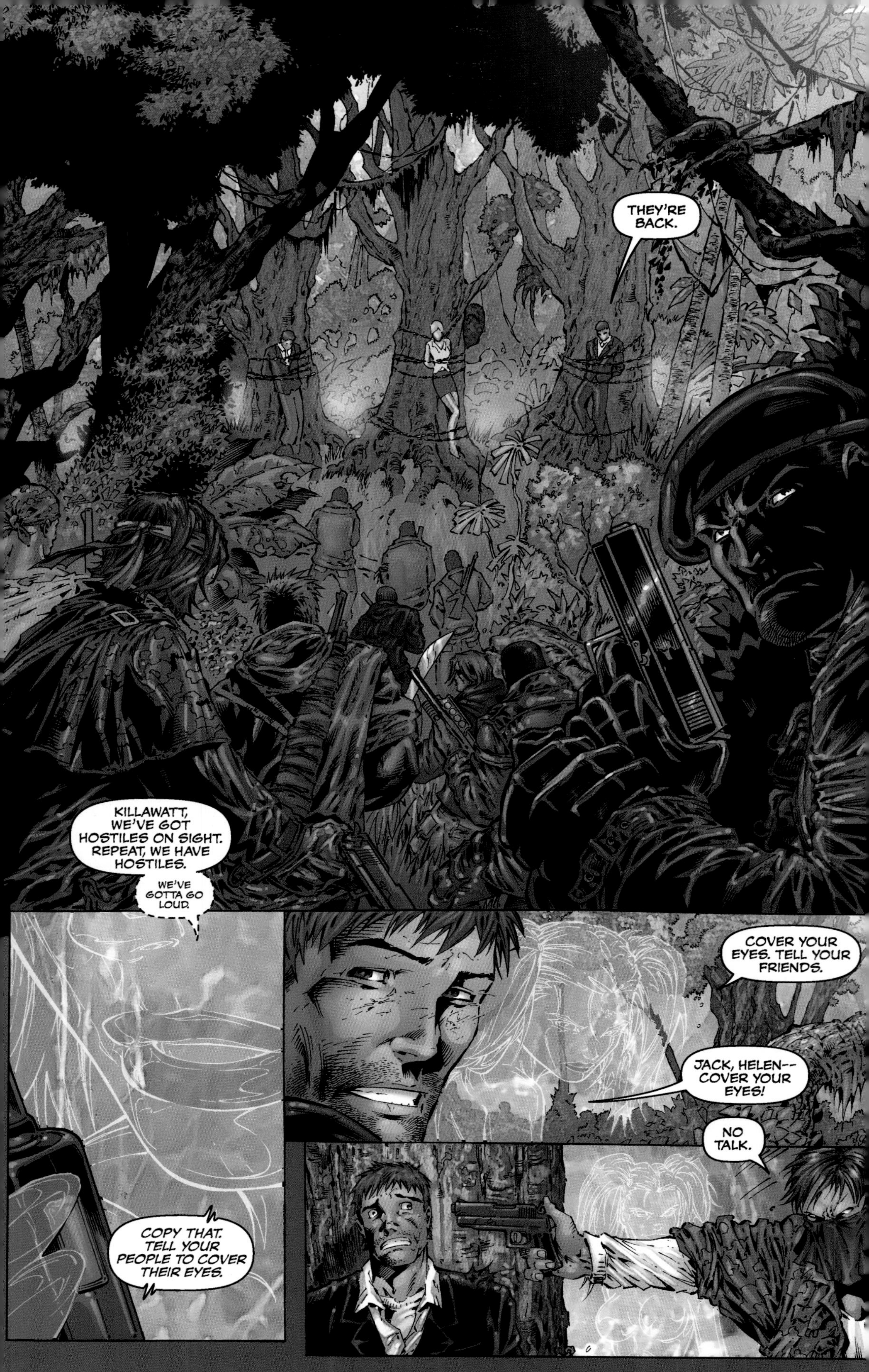
THEY'RE BACK.
KILLAWATT, WE'VE GOT HOSTILES ON SIGHT. REPEAT, WE HAVE HOSTILES.
WE'VE GOTTA GO LOUD.
COVER YOUR EYES. TELL YOUR FRIENDS.
JACK, HELEN-- COVER YOUR EYES!
COPY THAT. TELL YOUR PEOPLE TO COVER THEIR EYES.
NO TALK.

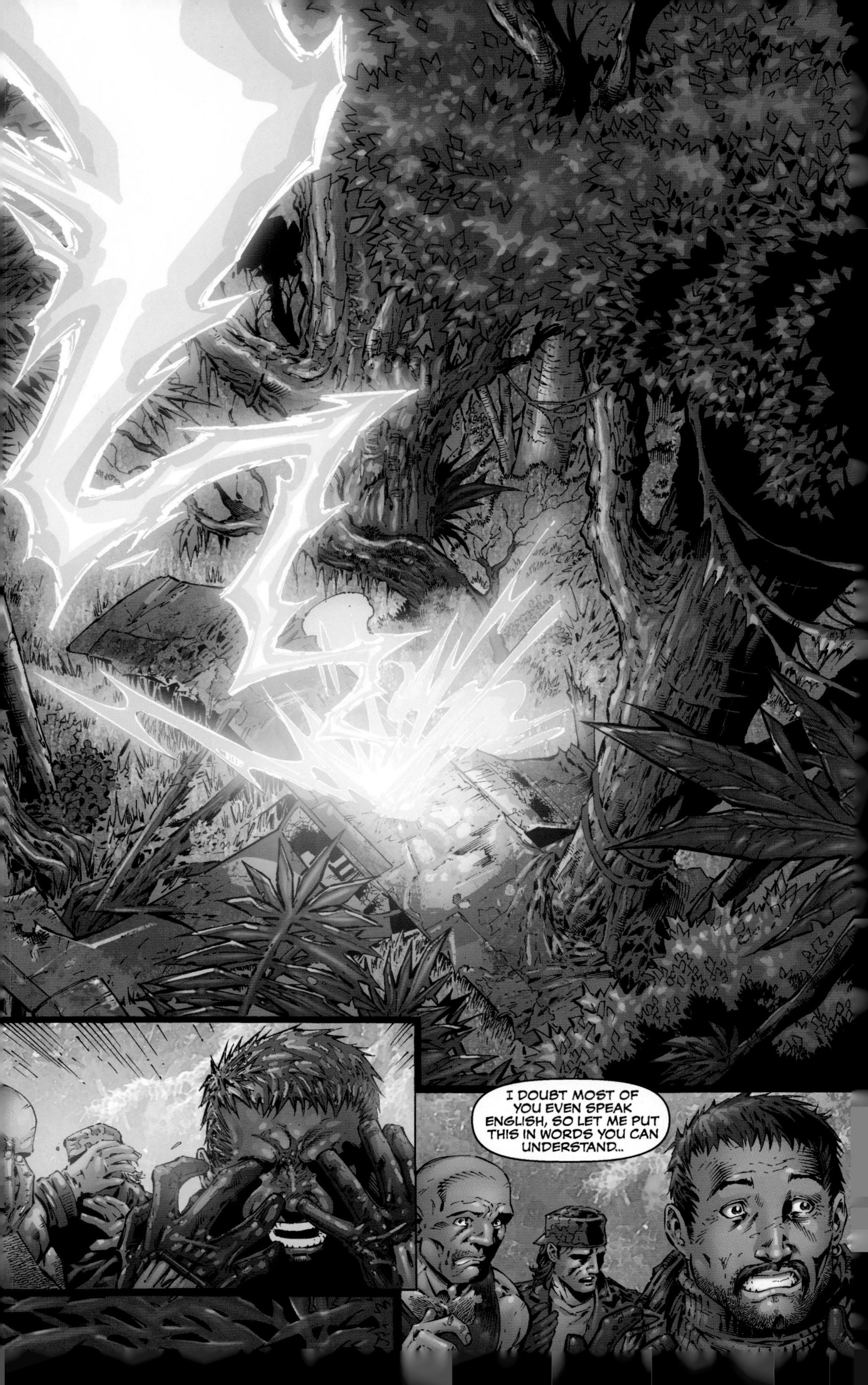
I DOUBT MOST OF YOU EVEN SPEAK ENGLISH, SO LET ME PUT THIS IN WORDS YOU CAN UNDERSTAND...

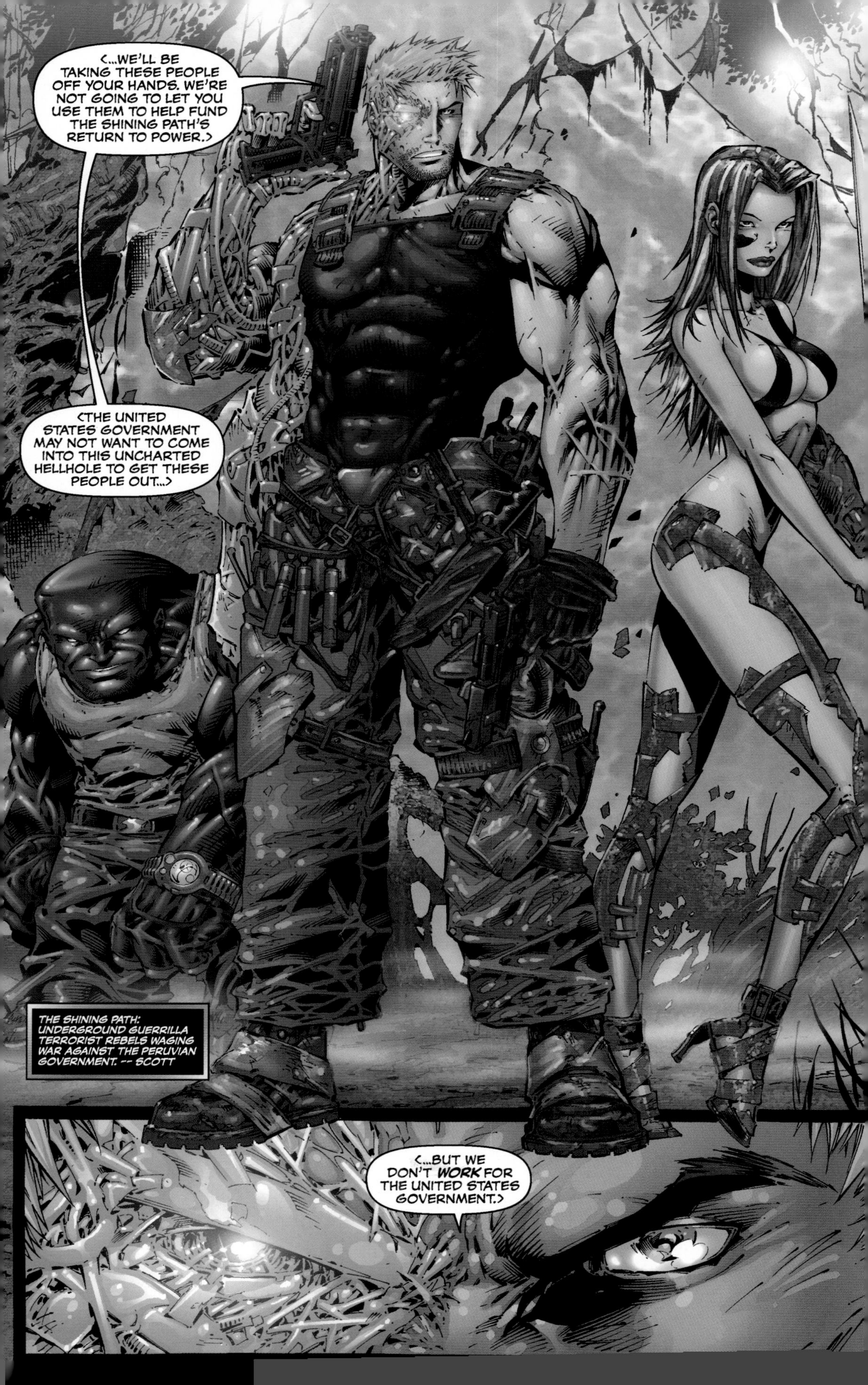

<...WE'LL BE TAKING THESE PEOPLE OFF YOUR HANDS. WE'RE NOT GOING TO LET YOU USE THEM TO HELP FUND THE SHINING PATH'S RETURN TO POWER.>
<THE UNITED STATES GOVERNMENT MAY NOT WANT TO COME INTO THIS UNCHARTED HELLHOLE TO GET THESE PEOPLE OUT...>
THE SHINING PATH: UNDERGROUND GUERRILLA TERRORIST REBELS WAGING WAR AGAINST THE PERUVIAN GOVERNMENT. -- SCOTT
<...BUT WE DON'T WORK FOR THE UNITED STATES GOVERNMENT.>

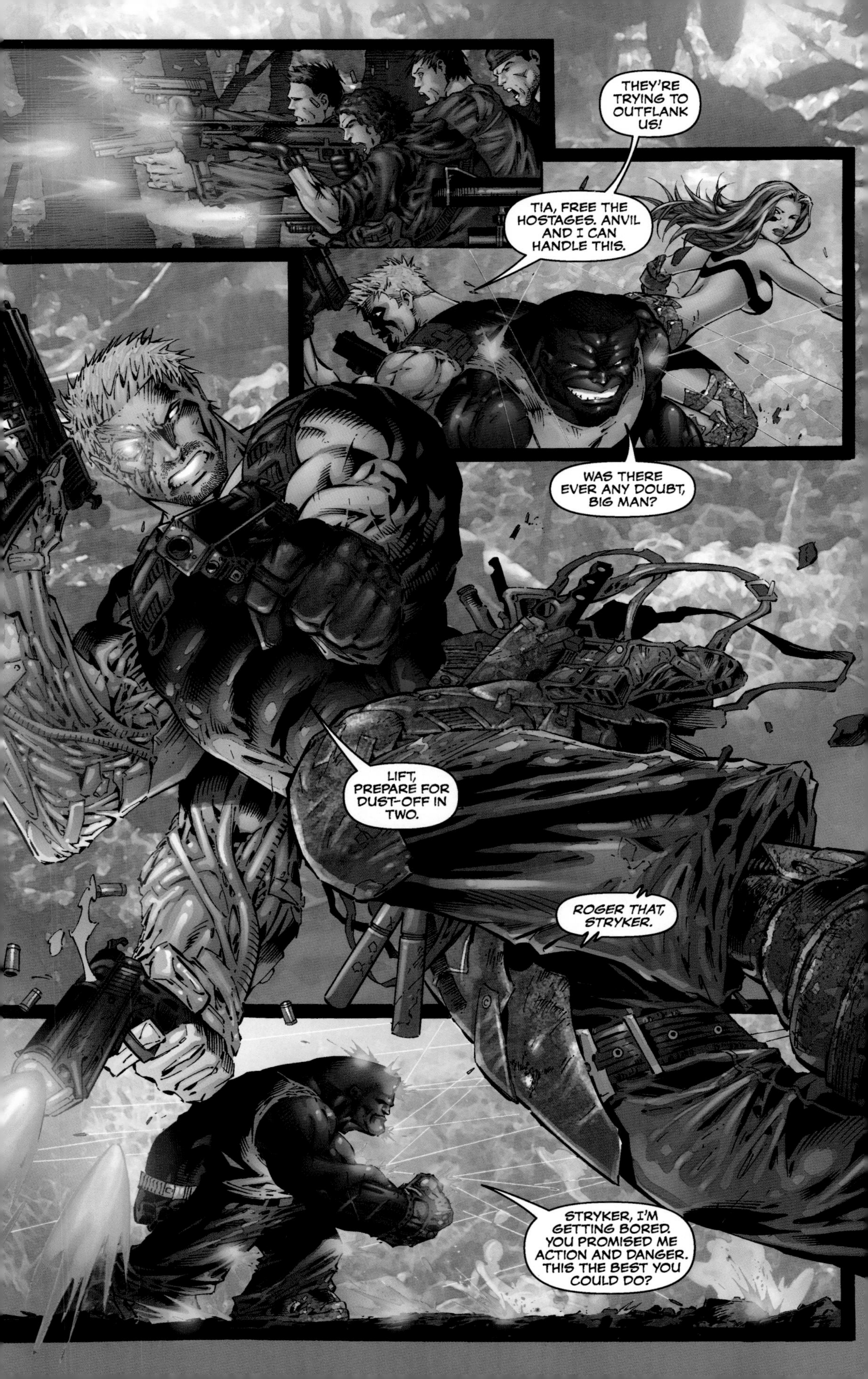
THEY'RE TRYING TO OUTFLANK US!
TIA, FREE THE HOSTAGES. ANVIL AND I CAN HANDLE THIS.
WAS THERE EVER ANY DOUBT, BIG MAN?
LIFT, PREPARE FOR DUST-OFF IN TWO.
ROGER THAT, STRYKER.
STRYKER, I'M GETTING BORED. YOU PROMISED ME ACTION AND DANGER. THIS THE BEST YOU COULD DO?

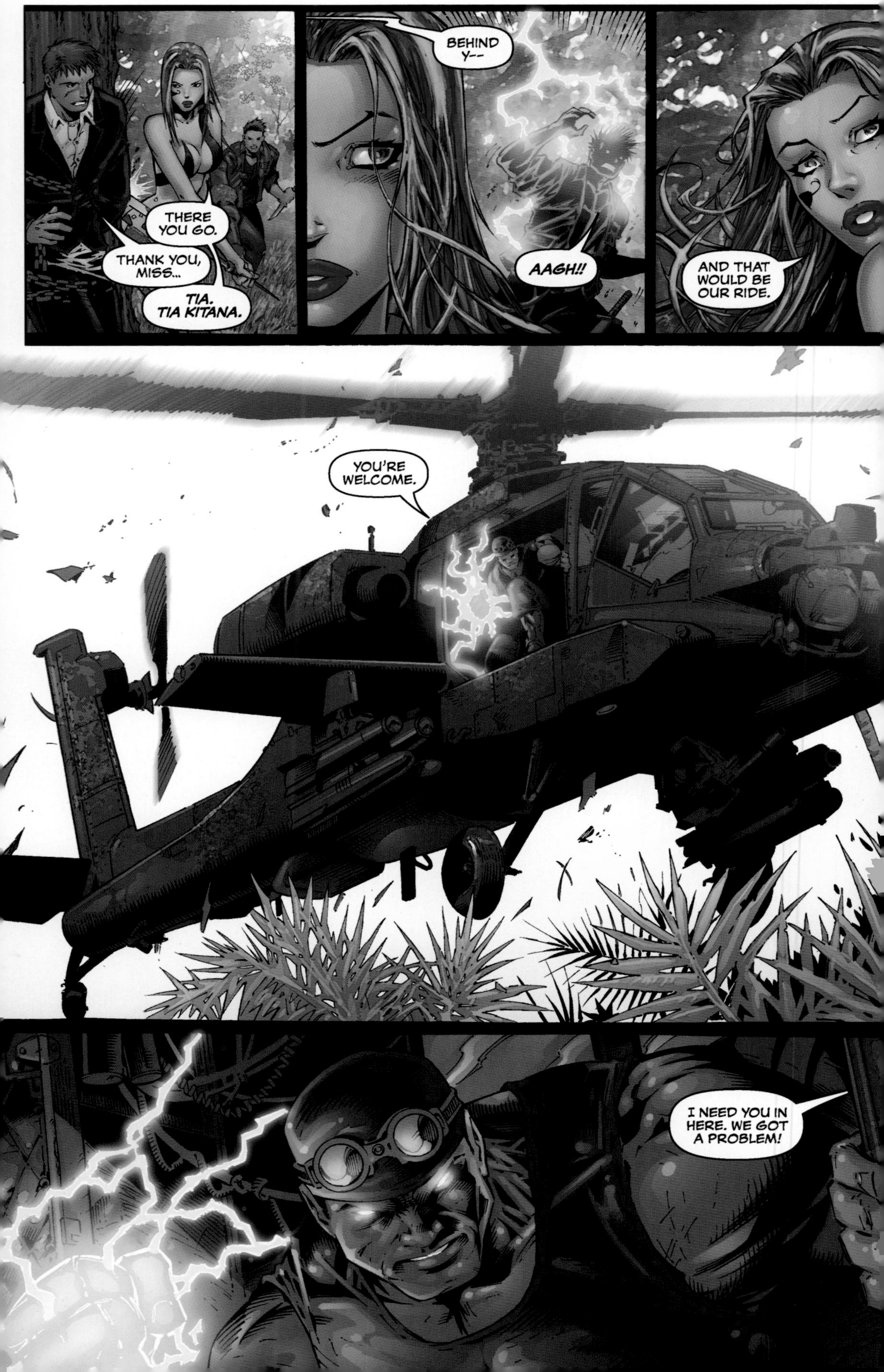

THERE YOU GO.
THANK YOU, MISS...
TIA. TIA KITANA.
BEHIND Y--
AAGH!!
AND THAT WOULD BE OUR RIDE.
YOU'RE WELCOME.
I NEED YOU IN HERE. WE GOT A PROBLEM!

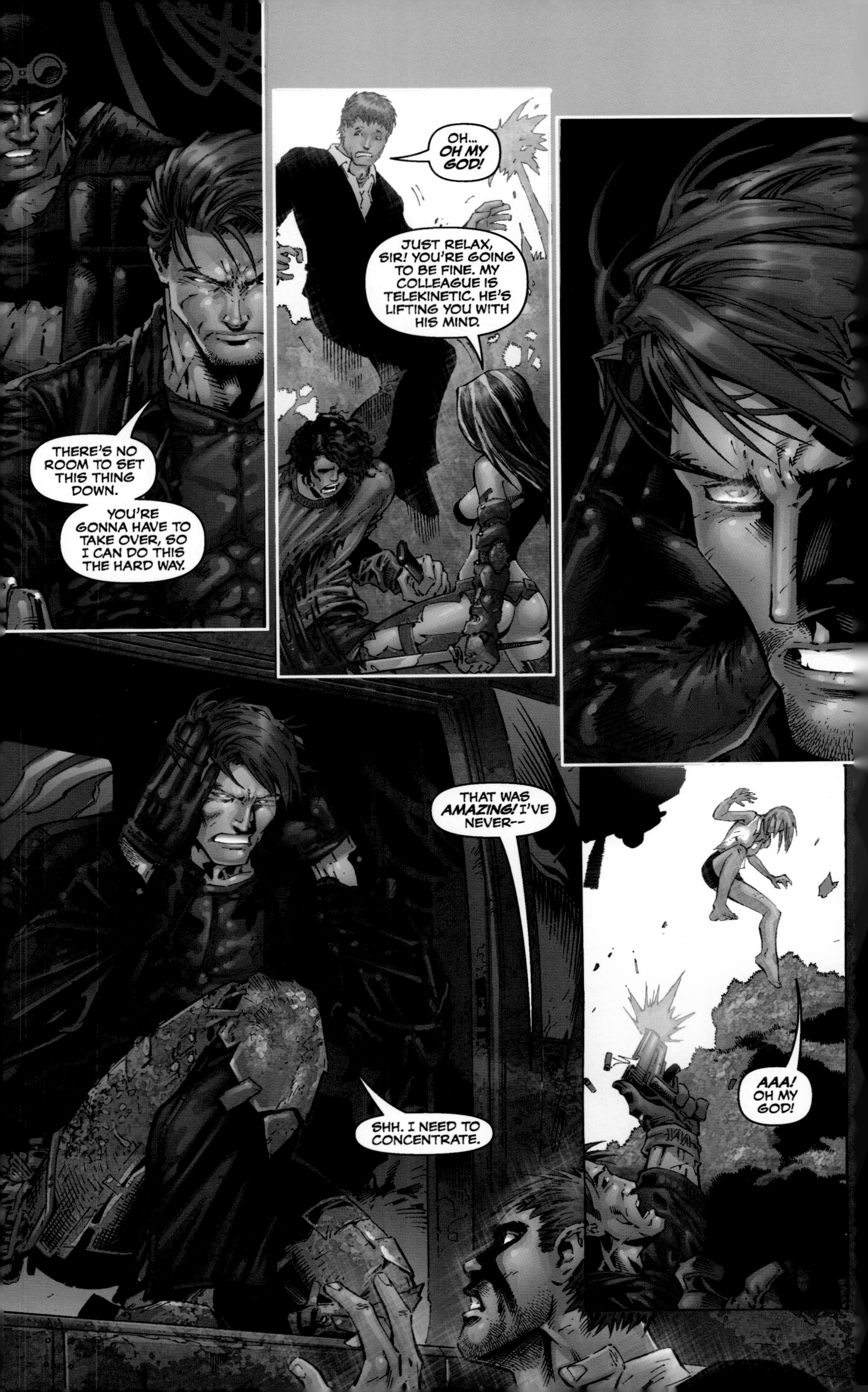

THERE'S NO ROOM TO SET THIS THING DOWN.
YOU'RE GONNA HAVE TO TAKE OVER, SO I CAN DO THIS THE HARD WAY.
OH... OH MY GOD!
JUST RELAX, SIR! YOU'RE GOING TO BE FINE. MY COLLEAGUE IS TELEKINETIC. HE'S LIFTING YOU WITH HIS MIND.
THAT WAS AMAZING! I'VE NEVER--
SHH. I NEED TO CONCENTRATE.
AAA! OH MY GOD!

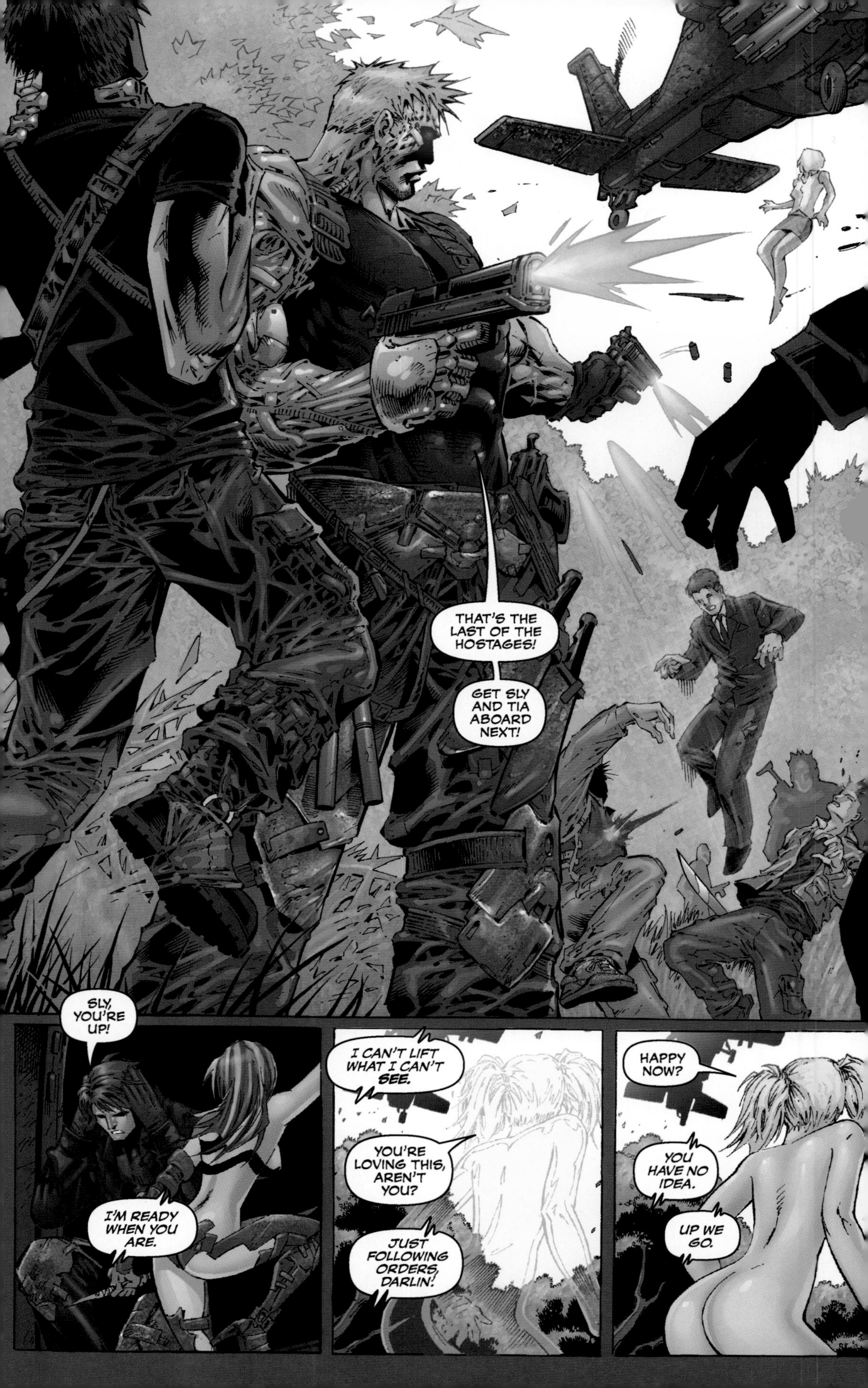

THAT'S THE LAST OF THE HOSTAGES!
GET SLY AND TIA ABOARD NEXT!
SLY, YOU'RE UP!
I'M READY WHEN YOU ARE.
I CAN'T LIFT WHAT I CAN'T SEE.
YOU'RE LOVING THIS, AREN'T YOU?
JUST FOLLOWING ORDERS, DARLIN'.
HAPPY NOW?
YOU HAVE NO IDEA.
UP WE GO.

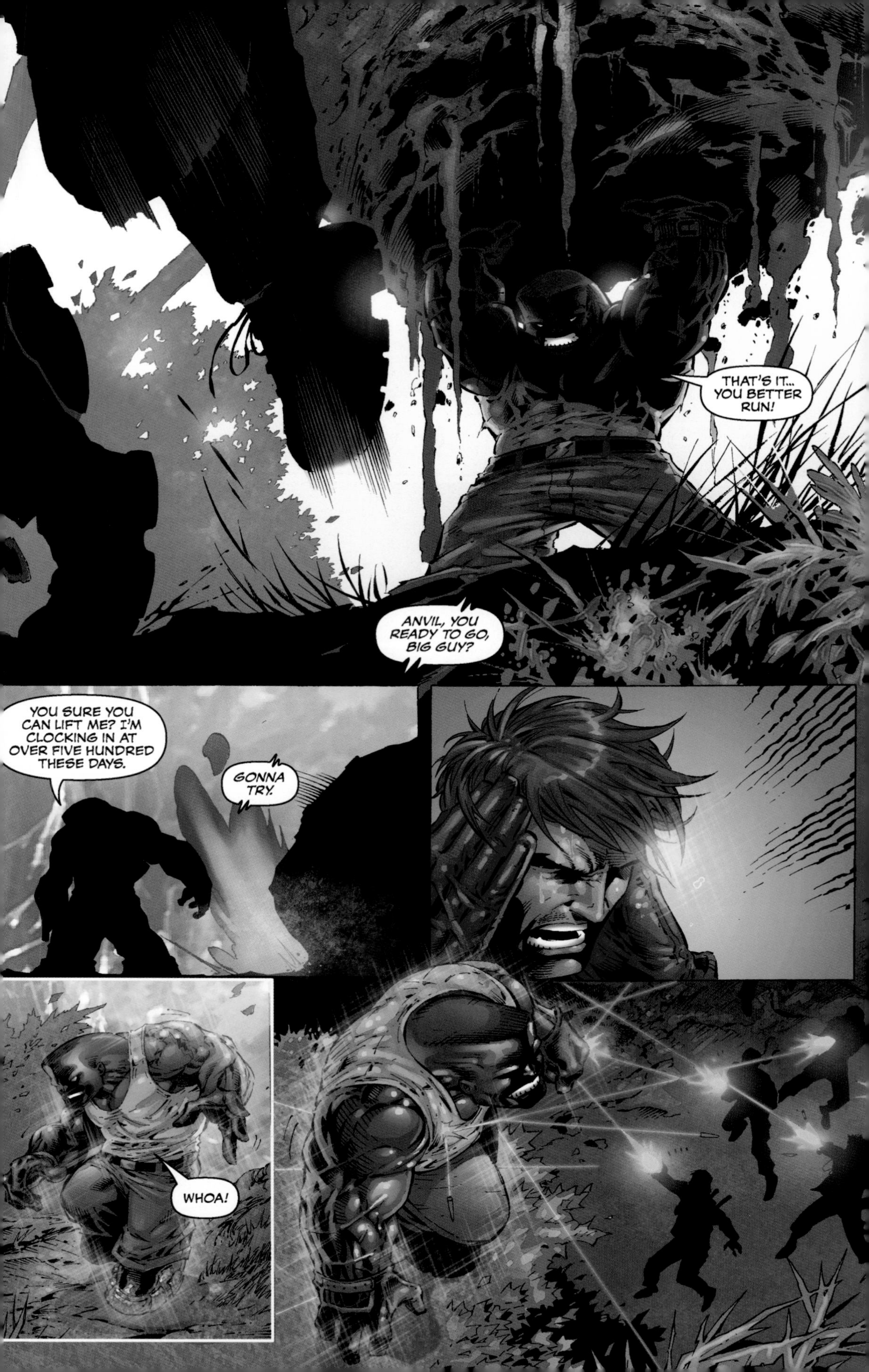
THAT'S IT... YOU BETTER RUN!
ANVIL, YOU READY TO GO, BIG GUY?
YOU SURE YOU CAN LIFT ME? I'M CLOCKING IN AT OVER FIVE HUNDRED THESE DAYS.
GONNA TRY.
WHOA!

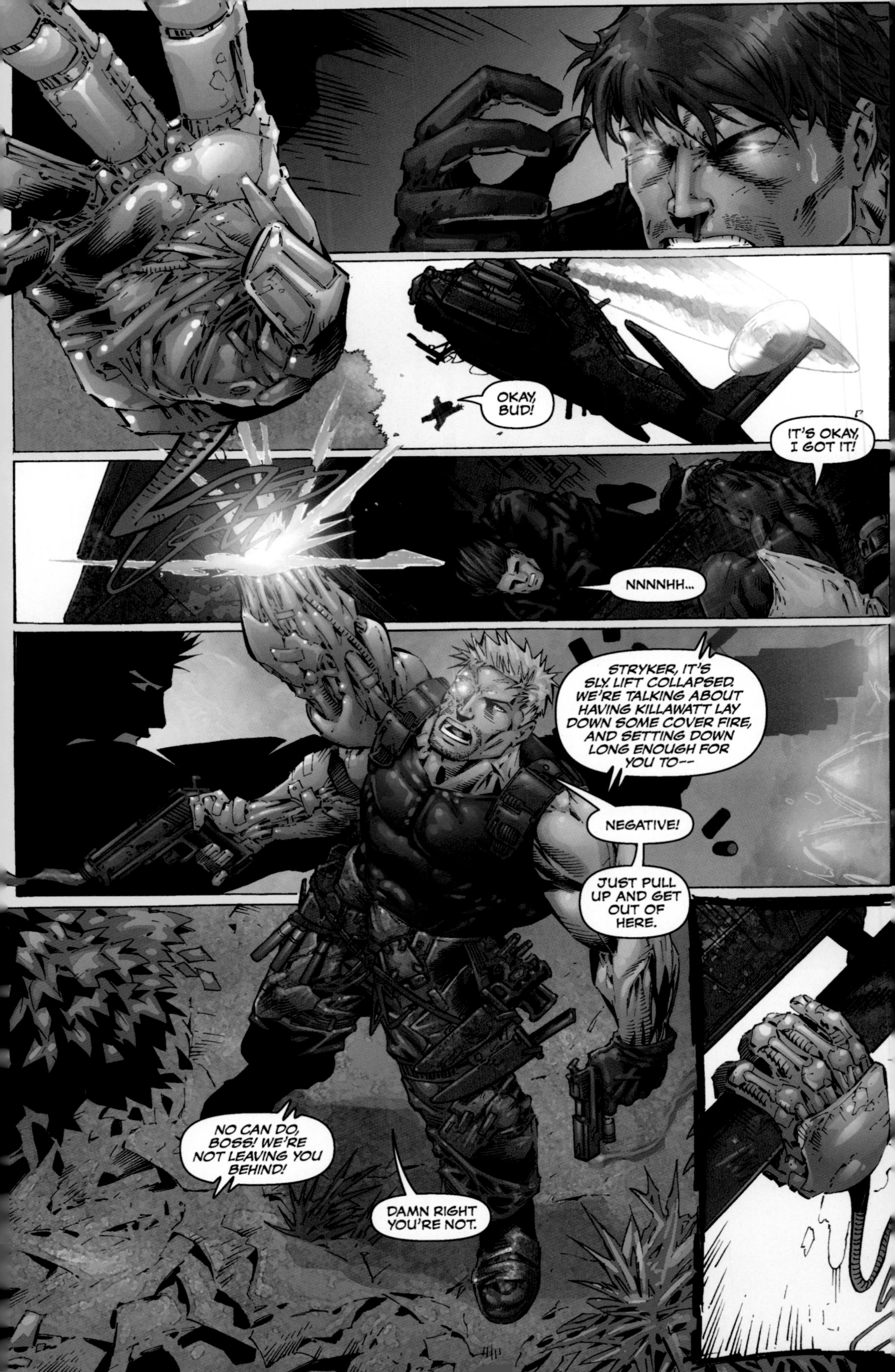
OKAY, BUD!
IT'S OKAY, I GOT IT!
NNNNHH...
STRYKER, IT'S SLY. LIFT COLLAPSED. WE'RE TALKING ABOUT HAVING KILLAWATT LAY DOWN SOME COVER FIRE, AND SETTING DOWN LONG ENOUGH FOR YOU TO--
NEGATIVE!
JUST PULL UP AND GET OUT OF HERE.
NO CAN DO, BOSS! WE'RE NOT LEAVING YOU BEHIND!
DAMN RIGHT YOU'RE NOT.

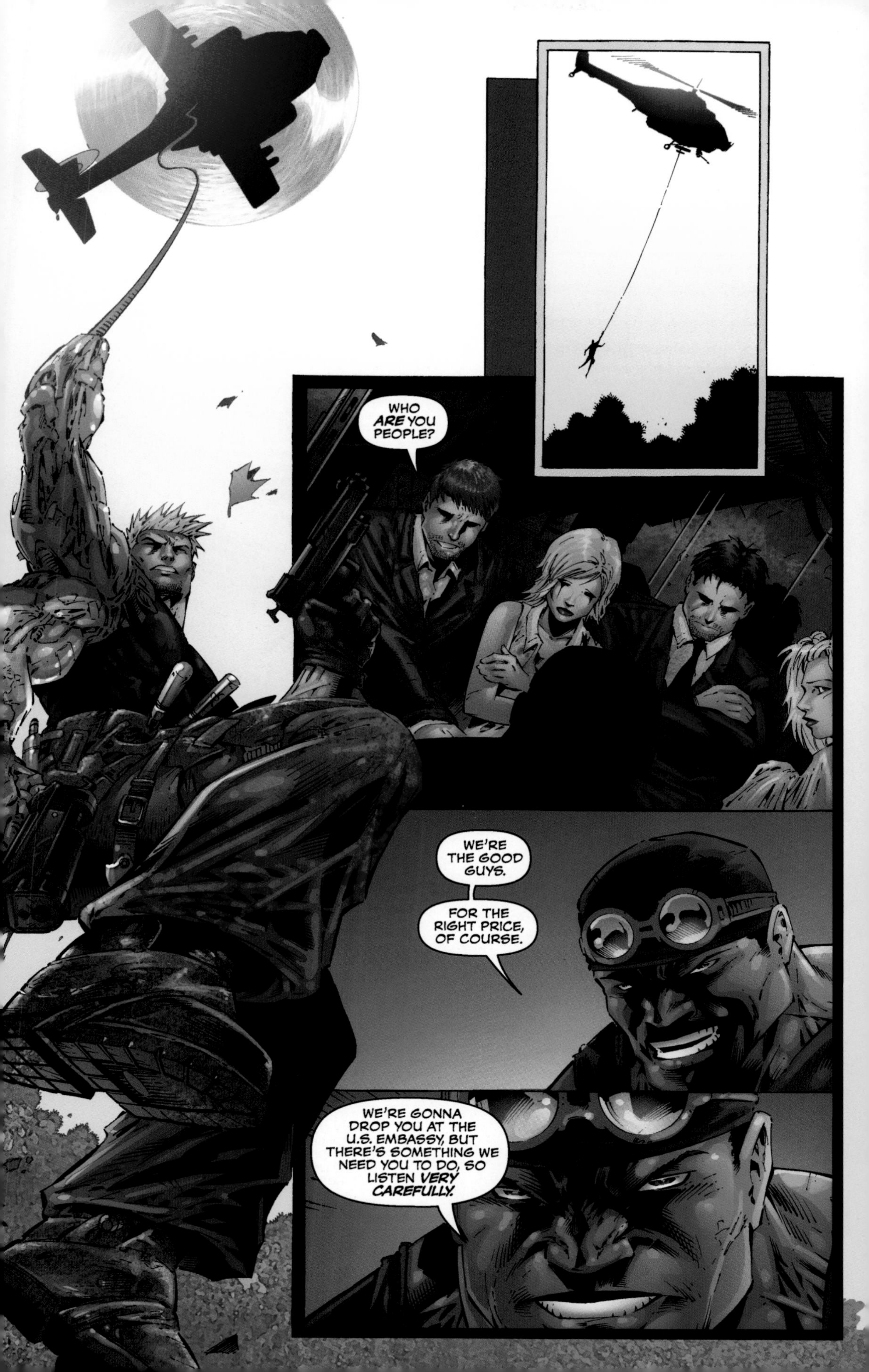
WHO ARE YOU PEOPLE?
WE'RE THE GOOD GUYS.
FOR THE RIGHT PRICE, OF COURSE.
WE'RE GONNA DROP YOU AT THE U.S. EMBASSY, BUT THERE'S SOMETHING WE NEED YOU TO DO, SO LISTEN VERY CAREFULLY.

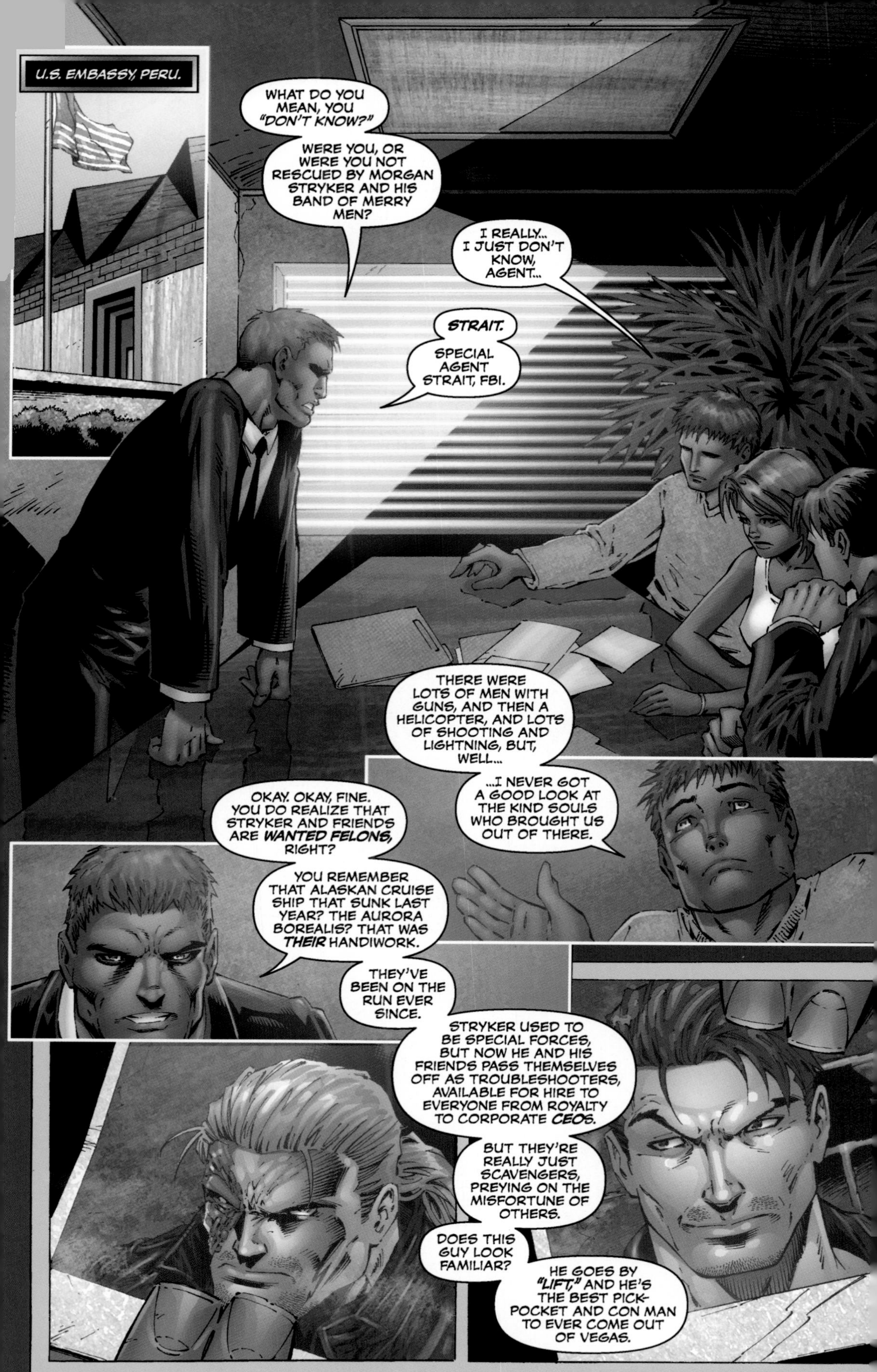
U.S. EMBASSY, PERU.
WHAT DO YOU MEAN, YOU "DON'T KNOW?"
WERE YOU, OR WERE YOU NOT RESCUED BY MORGAN STRYKER AND HIS BAND OF MERRY MEN?
I REALLY... I JUST DON'T KNOW, AGENT...
STRAIT.
SPECIAL AGENT STRAIT, FBI.
THERE WERE LOTS OF MEN WITH GUNS, AND THEN A HELICOPTER, AND LOTS OF SHOOTING AND LIGHTNING, BUT, WELL...
...I NEVER GOT A GOOD LOOK AT THE KIND SOULS WHO BROUGHT US OUT OF THERE.
OKAY. OKAY, FINE. YOU DO REALIZE THAT STRYKER AND FRIENDS ARE WANTED FELONS, RIGHT?
YOU REMEMBER THAT ALASKAN CRUISE SHIP THAT SUNK LAST YEAR? THE AURORA BOREALIS? THAT WAS THEIR HANDIWORK.
THEY'VE BEEN ON THE RUN EVER SINCE.
STRYKER USED TO BE SPECIAL FORCES, BUT NOW HE AND HIS FRIENDS PASS THEMSELVES OFF AS TROUBLESHOOTERS, AVAILABLE FOR HIRE TO EVERYONE FROM ROYALTY TO CORPORATE CEOS.
BUT THEY'RE REALLY JUST SCAVENGERS, PREYING ON THE MISFORTUNE OF OTHERS.
DOES THIS GUY LOOK FAMILIAR?
HE GOES BY "LIFT," AND HE'S THE BEST PICK-POCKET AND CON MAN TO EVER COME OUT OF VEGAS.

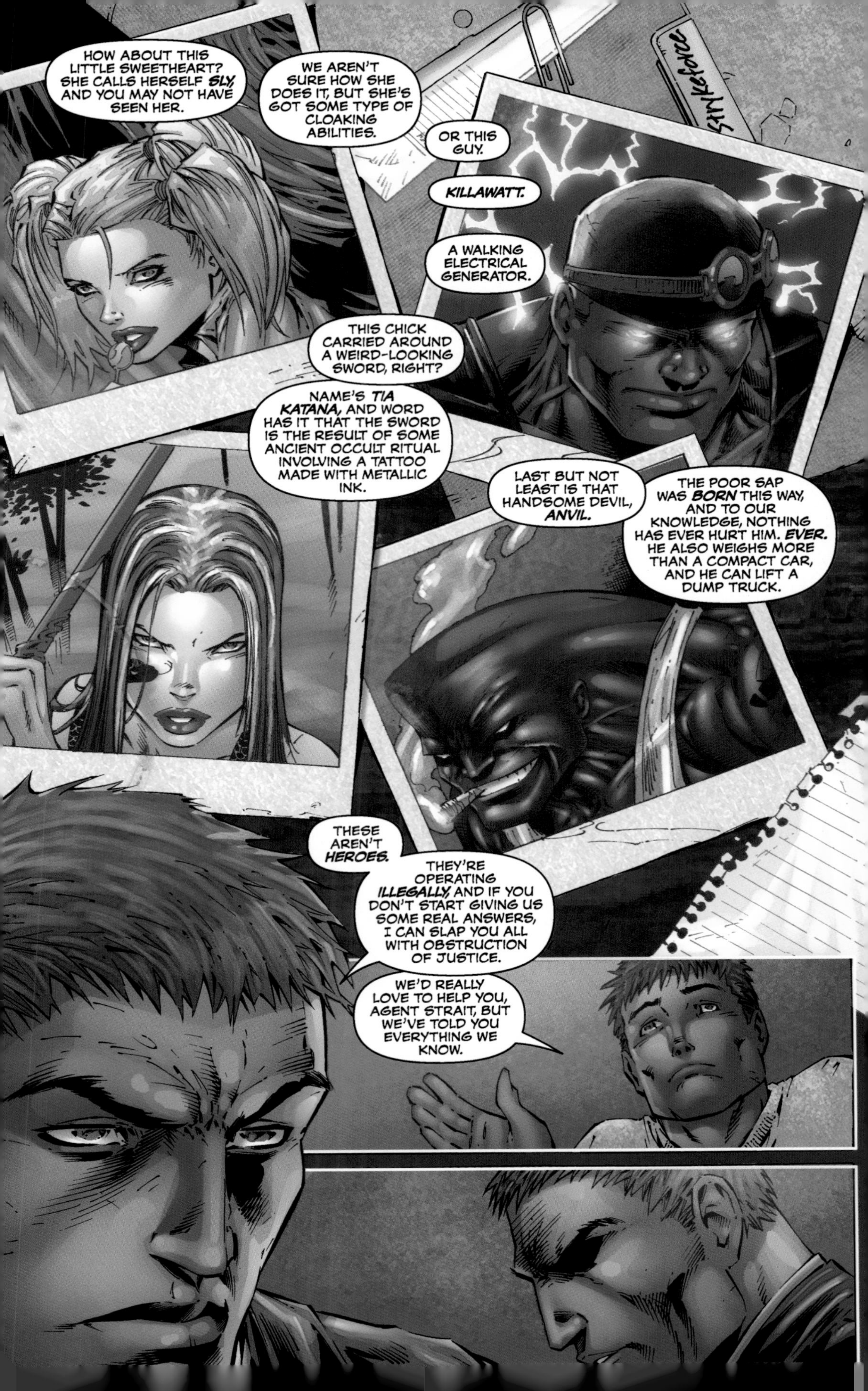
HOW ABOUT THIS LITTLE SWEETHEART? SHE CALLS HERSELF *SLY*, AND YOU MAY NOT HAVE SEEN HER.
WE AREN'T SURE HOW SHE DOES IT, BUT SHE'S GOT SOME TYPE OF CLOAKING ABILITIES.
OR THIS GUY.
KILLAWATT.
A WALKING ELECTRICAL GENERATOR.
THIS CHICK CARRIED AROUND A WEIRD-LOOKING SWORD, RIGHT?
NAME'S *TIA KATANA*, AND WORD HAS IT THAT THE SWORD IS THE RESULT OF SOME ANCIENT OCCULT RITUAL INVOLVING A TATTOO MADE WITH METALLIC INK.
LAST BUT NOT LEAST IS THAT HANDSOME DEVIL, *ANVIL.*
THE POOR SAP WAS *BORN* THIS WAY, AND TO OUR KNOWLEDGE, NOTHING HAS EVER HURT HIM. *EVER.* HE ALSO WEIGHS MORE THAN A COMPACT CAR, AND HE CAN LIFT A DUMP TRUCK.
THESE AREN'T *HEROES.*
THEY'RE OPERATING *ILLEGALLY*, AND IF YOU DON'T START GIVING US SOME REAL ANSWERS, I CAN SLAP YOU ALL WITH OBSTRUCTION OF JUSTICE.
WE'D REALLY LOVE TO HELP YOU, AGENT STRAIT, BUT WE'VE TOLD YOU EVERYTHING WE KNOW.

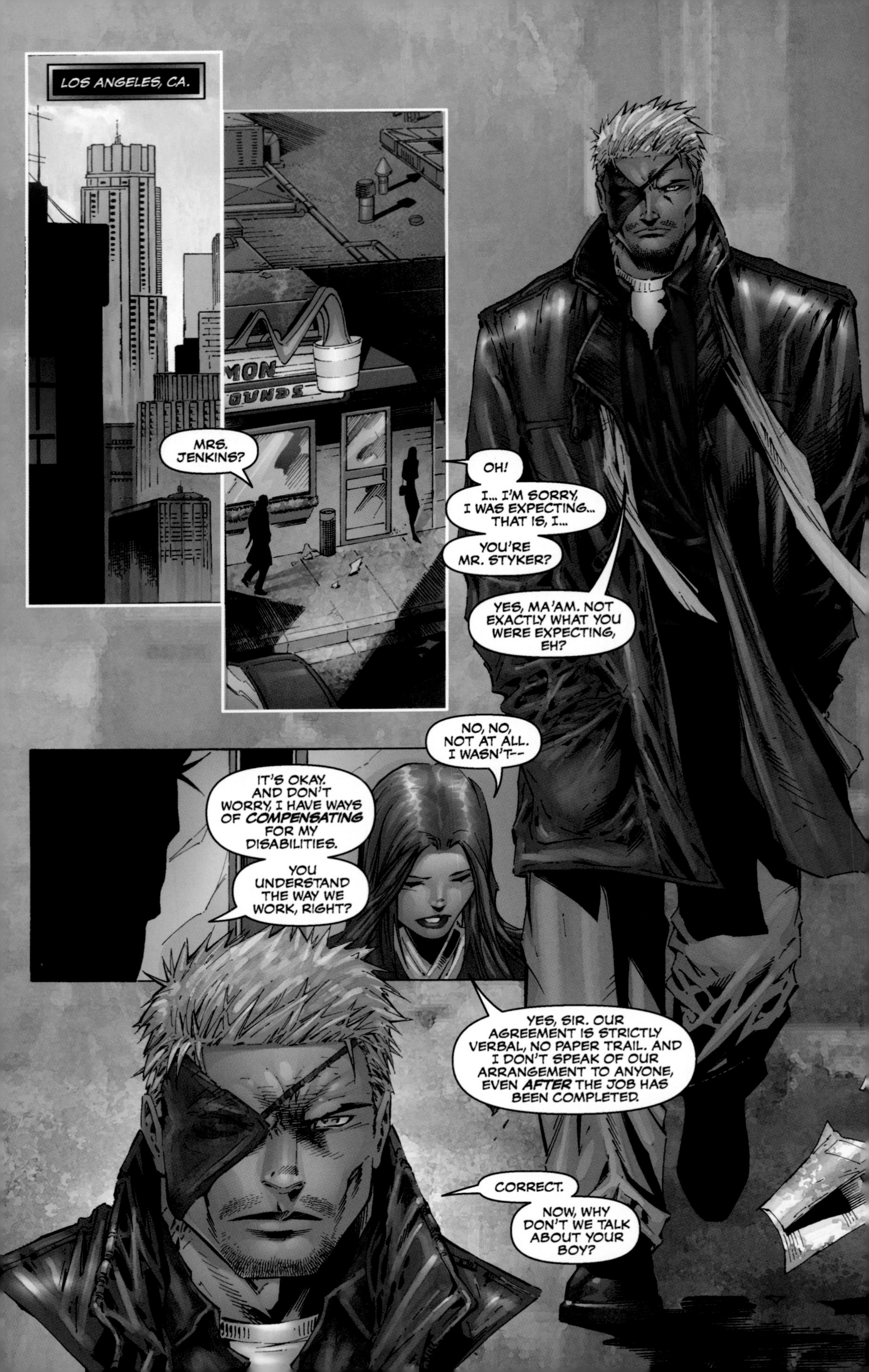
LOS ANGELES, CA.
MRS. JENKINS?
OH!
I... I'M SORRY, I WAS EXPECTING... THAT IS, I...
YOU'RE MR. STYKER?
YES, MA'AM. NOT EXACTLY WHAT YOU WERE EXPECTING, EH?
NO, NO, NOT AT ALL. I WASN'T--
IT'S OKAY. AND DON'T WORRY, I HAVE WAYS OF COMPENSATING FOR MY DISABILITIES.
YOU UNDERSTAND THE WAY WE WORK, RIGHT?
YES, SIR. OUR AGREEMENT IS STRICTLY VERBAL, NO PAPER TRAIL. AND I DON'T SPEAK OF OUR ARRANGEMENT TO ANYONE, EVEN AFTER THE JOB HAS BEEN COMPLETED.
CORRECT.
NOW, WHY DON'T WE TALK ABOUT YOUR BOY?

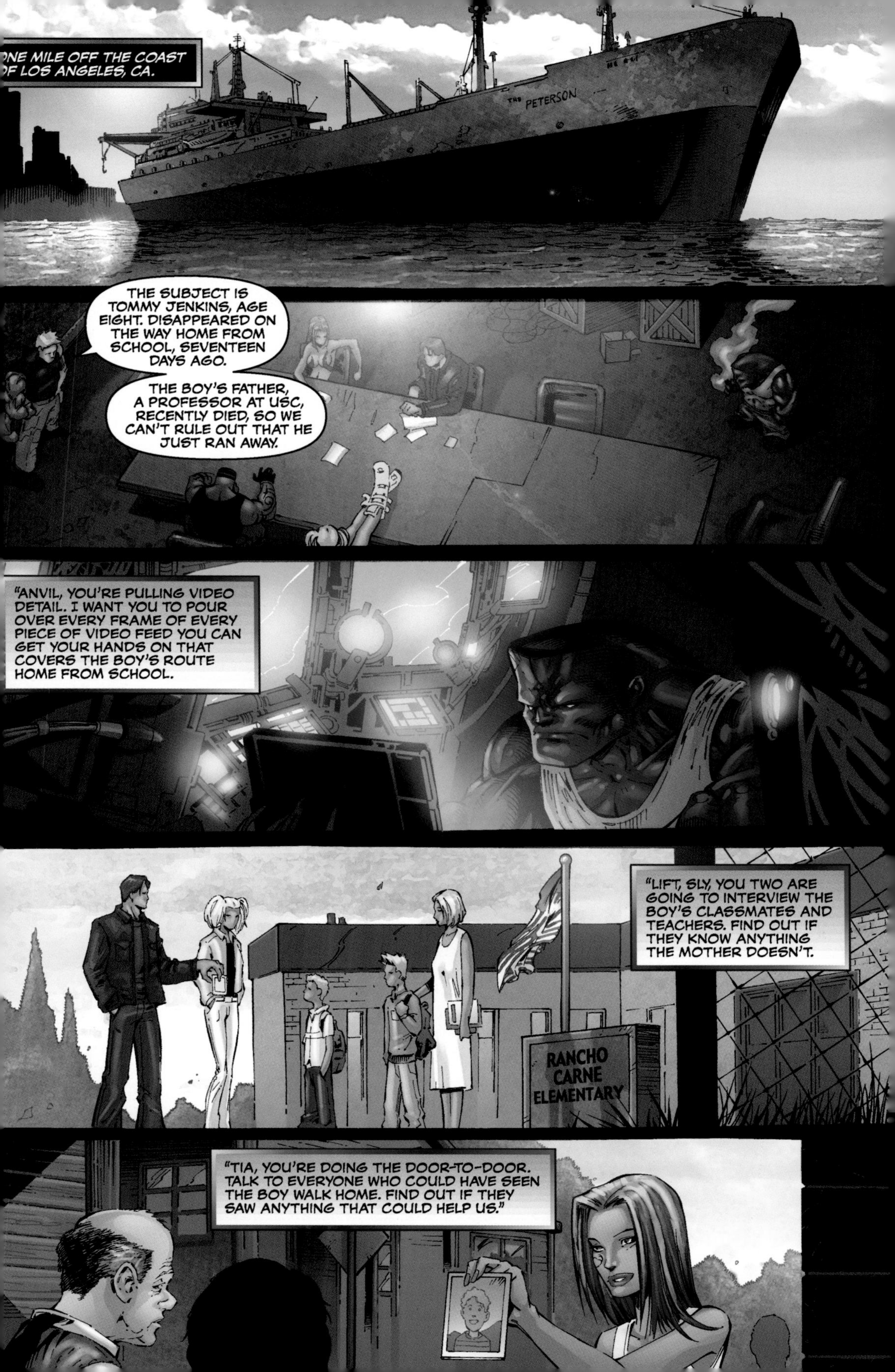
ONE MILE OFF THE COAST OF LOS ANGELES, CA.
THE PETERSON
THE SUBJECT IS TOMMY JENKINS, AGE EIGHT. DISAPPEARED ON THE WAY HOME FROM SCHOOL, SEVENTEEN DAYS AGO.
THE BOY'S FATHER, A PROFESSOR AT USC, RECENTLY DIED, SO WE CAN'T RULE OUT THAT HE JUST RAN AWAY.
"ANVIL, YOU'RE PULLING VIDEO DETAIL. I WANT YOU TO POUR OVER EVERY FRAME OF EVERY PIECE OF VIDEO FEED YOU CAN GET YOUR HANDS ON THAT COVERS THE BOY'S ROUTE HOME FROM SCHOOL.
"LIFT, SLY, YOU TWO ARE GOING TO INTERVIEW THE BOY'S CLASSMATES AND TEACHERS. FIND OUT IF THEY KNOW ANYTHING THE MOTHER DOESN'T.
RANCHO CARNE ELEMENTARY
"TIA, YOU'RE DOING THE DOOR-TO-DOOR. TALK TO EVERYONE WHO COULD HAVE SEEN THE BOY WALK HOME. FIND OUT IF THEY SAW ANYTHING THAT COULD HELP US."

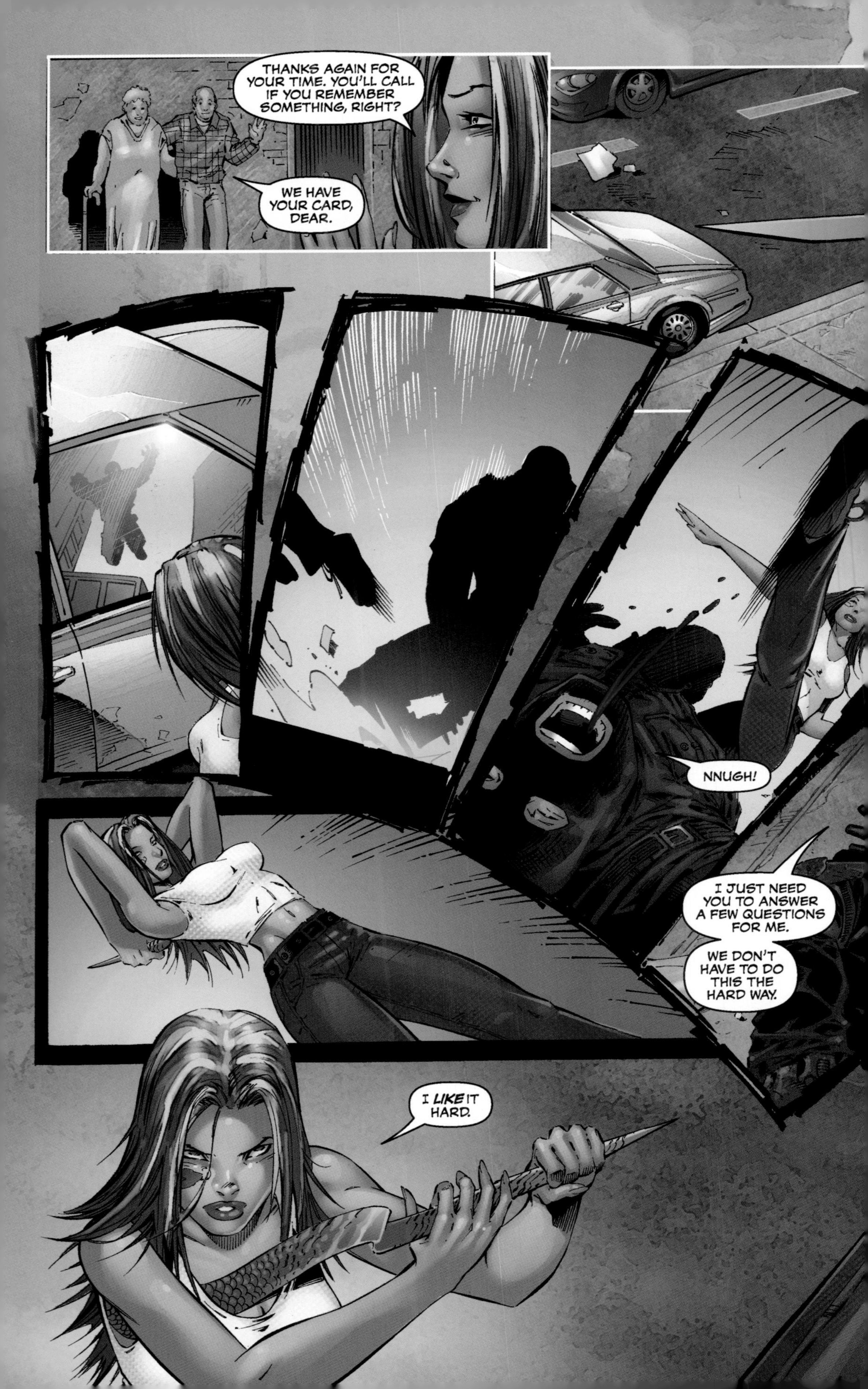
THANKS AGAIN FOR YOUR TIME. YOU'LL CALL IF YOU REMEMBER SOMETHING, RIGHT?
WE HAVE YOUR CARD, DEAR.
NNUGH!
I JUST NEED YOU TO ANSWER A FEW QUESTIONS FOR ME.
WE DON'T HAVE TO DO THIS THE HARD WAY.
I *LIKE* IT HARD.

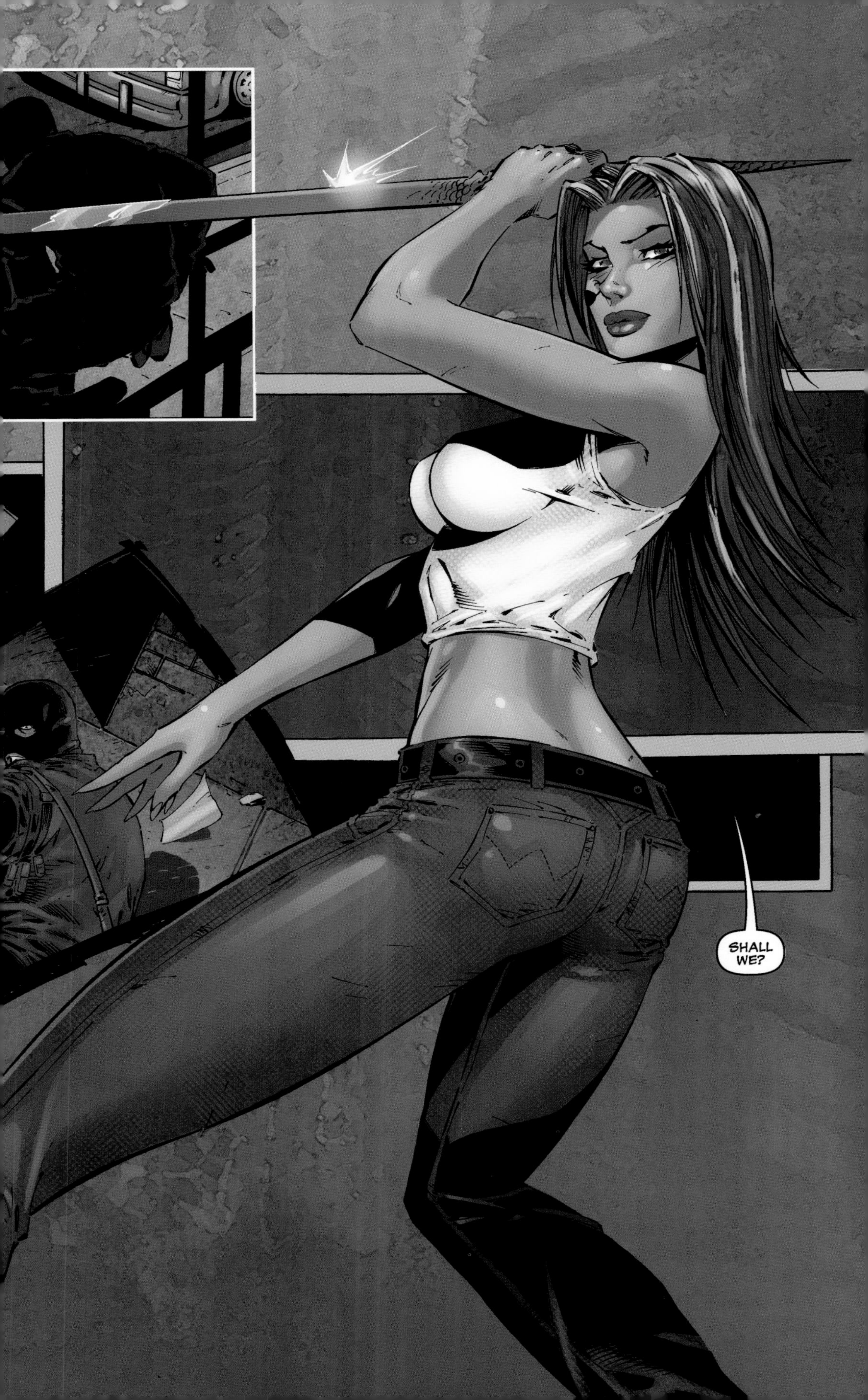
SHALL WE?

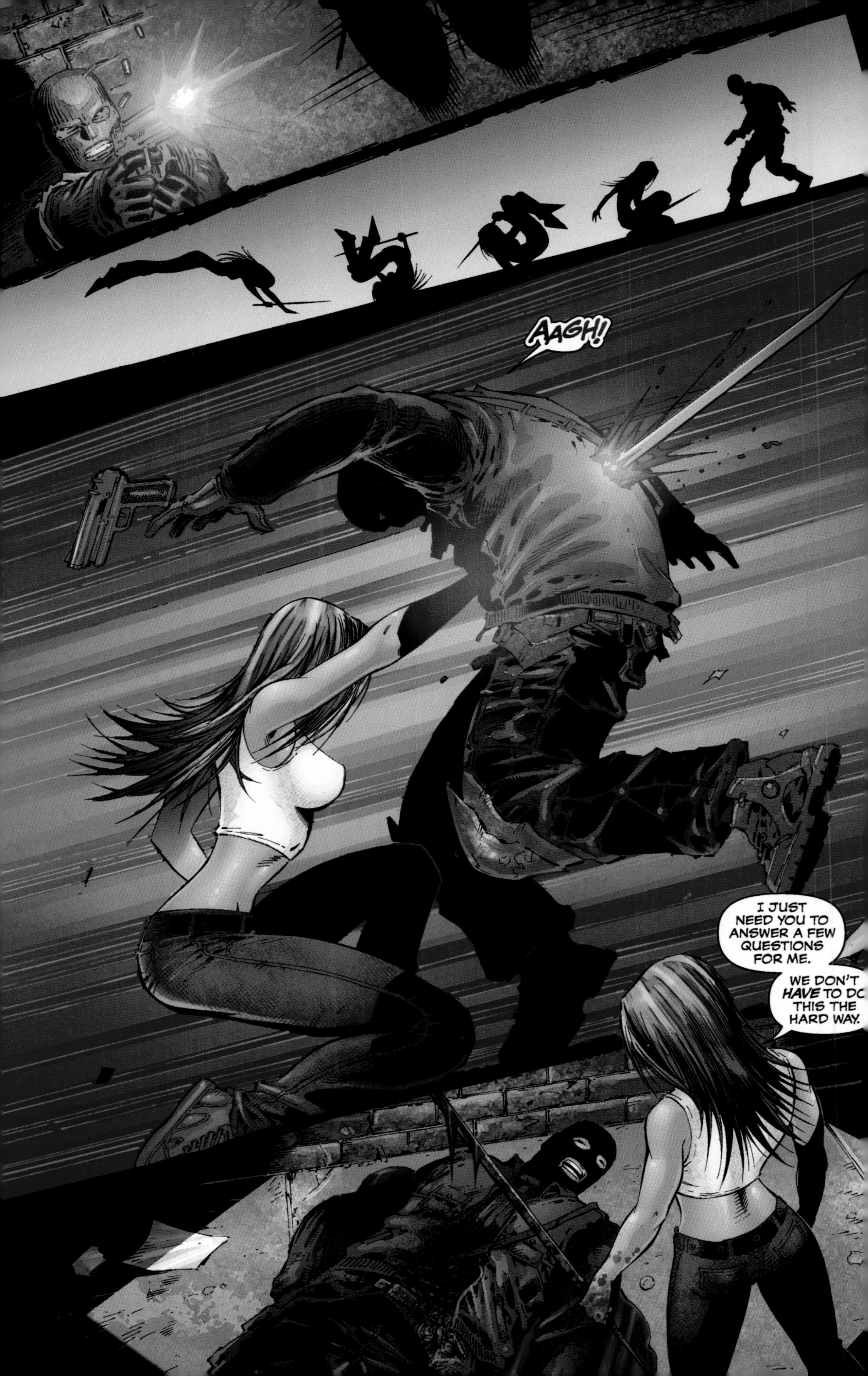
AAGH!
I JUST NEED YOU TO ANSWER A FEW QUESTIONS FOR ME.
WE DON'T *HAVE* TO DO THIS THE HARD WAY.

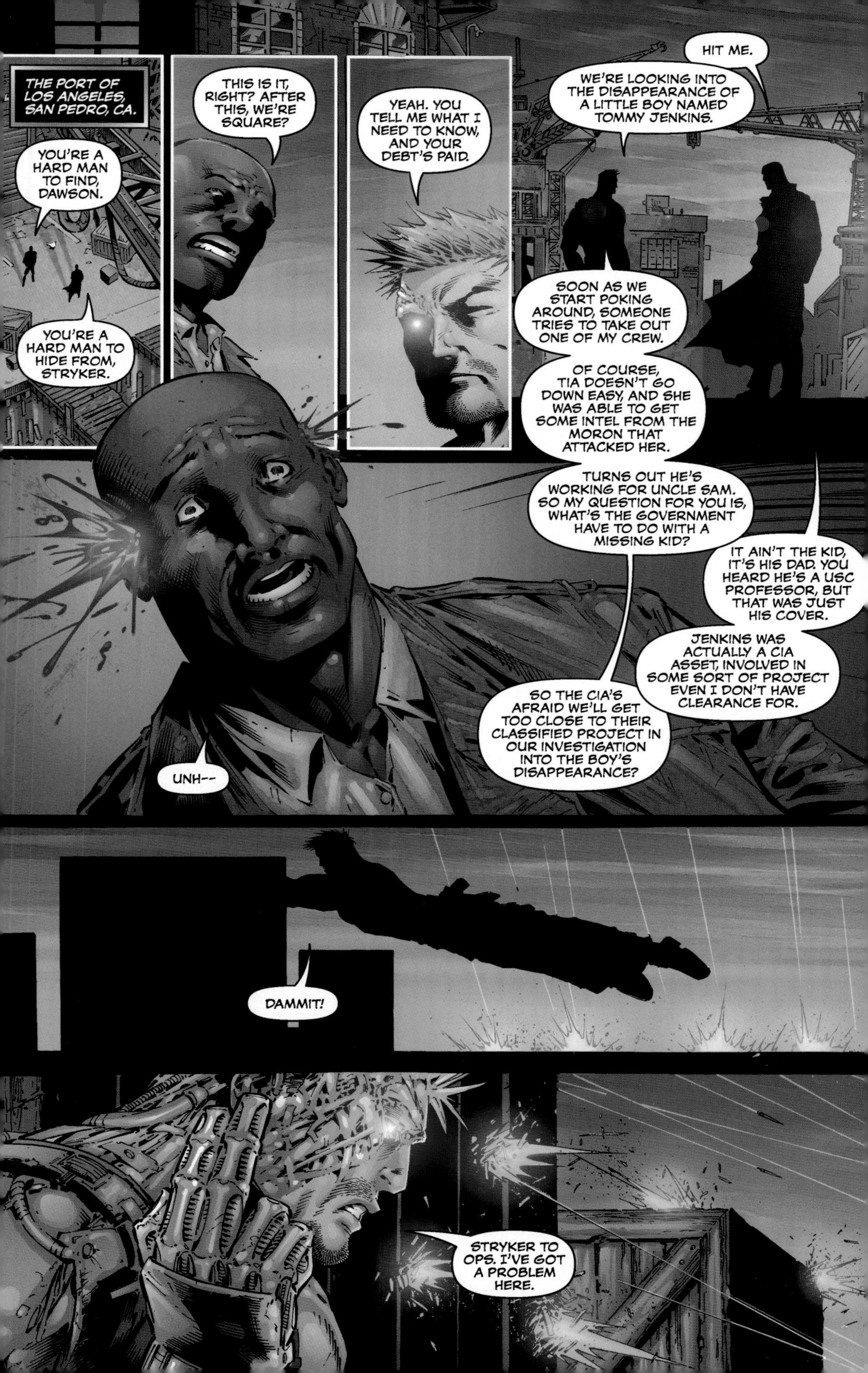
THE PORT OF LOS ANGELES, SAN PEDRO, CA.
YOU'RE A HARD MAN TO FIND, DAWSON.
YOU'RE A HARD MAN TO HIDE FROM, STRYKER.
THIS IS IT, RIGHT? AFTER THIS, WE'RE SQUARE?
YEAH. YOU TELL ME WHAT I NEED TO KNOW, AND YOUR DEBT'S PAID.
HIT ME.
WE'RE LOOKING INTO THE DISAPPEARANCE OF A LITTLE BOY NAMED TOMMY JENKINS.
SOON AS WE START POKING AROUND, SOMEONE TRIES TO TAKE OUT ONE OF MY CREW.
OF COURSE, TIA DOESN'T GO DOWN EASY, AND SHE WAS ABLE TO GET SOME INTEL FROM THE MORON THAT ATTACKED HER.
TURNS OUT HE'S WORKING FOR UNCLE SAM. SO MY QUESTION FOR YOU IS, WHAT'S THE GOVERNMENT HAVE TO DO WITH A MISSING KID?
IT AIN'T THE KID, IT'S HIS DAD. YOU HEARD HE'S A USC PROFESSOR, BUT THAT WAS JUST HIS COVER.
JENKINS WAS ACTUALLY A CIA ASSET, INVOLVED IN SOME SORT OF PROJECT EVEN I DON'T HAVE CLEARANCE FOR.
SO THE CIA'S AFRAID WE'LL GET TOO CLOSE TO THEIR CLASSIFIED PROJECT IN OUR INVESTIGATION INTO THE BOY'S DISAPPEARANCE?
UNH--
DAMMIT!
STRYKER TO OPS. I'VE GOT A PROBLEM HERE.

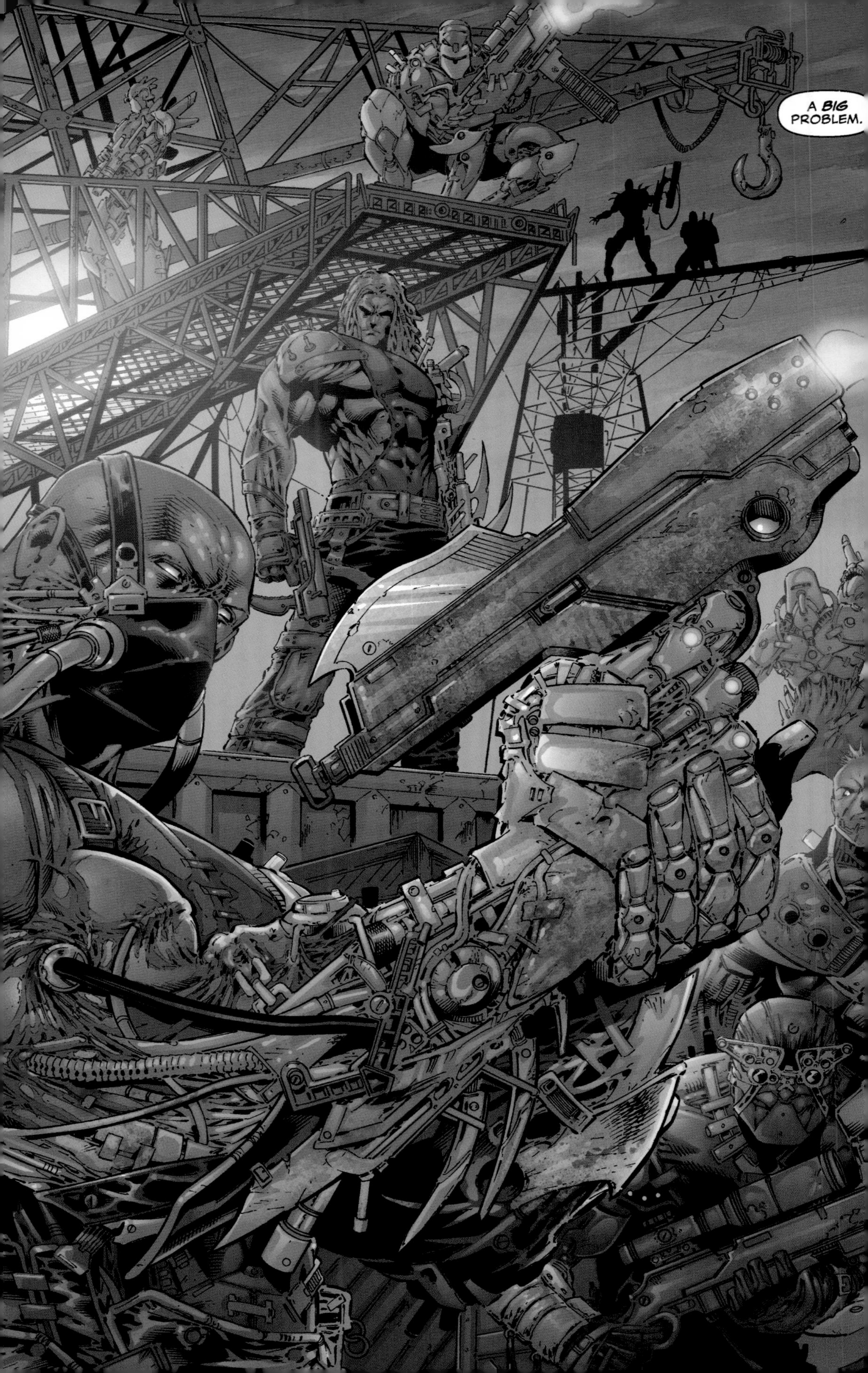
A BIG PROBLEM.

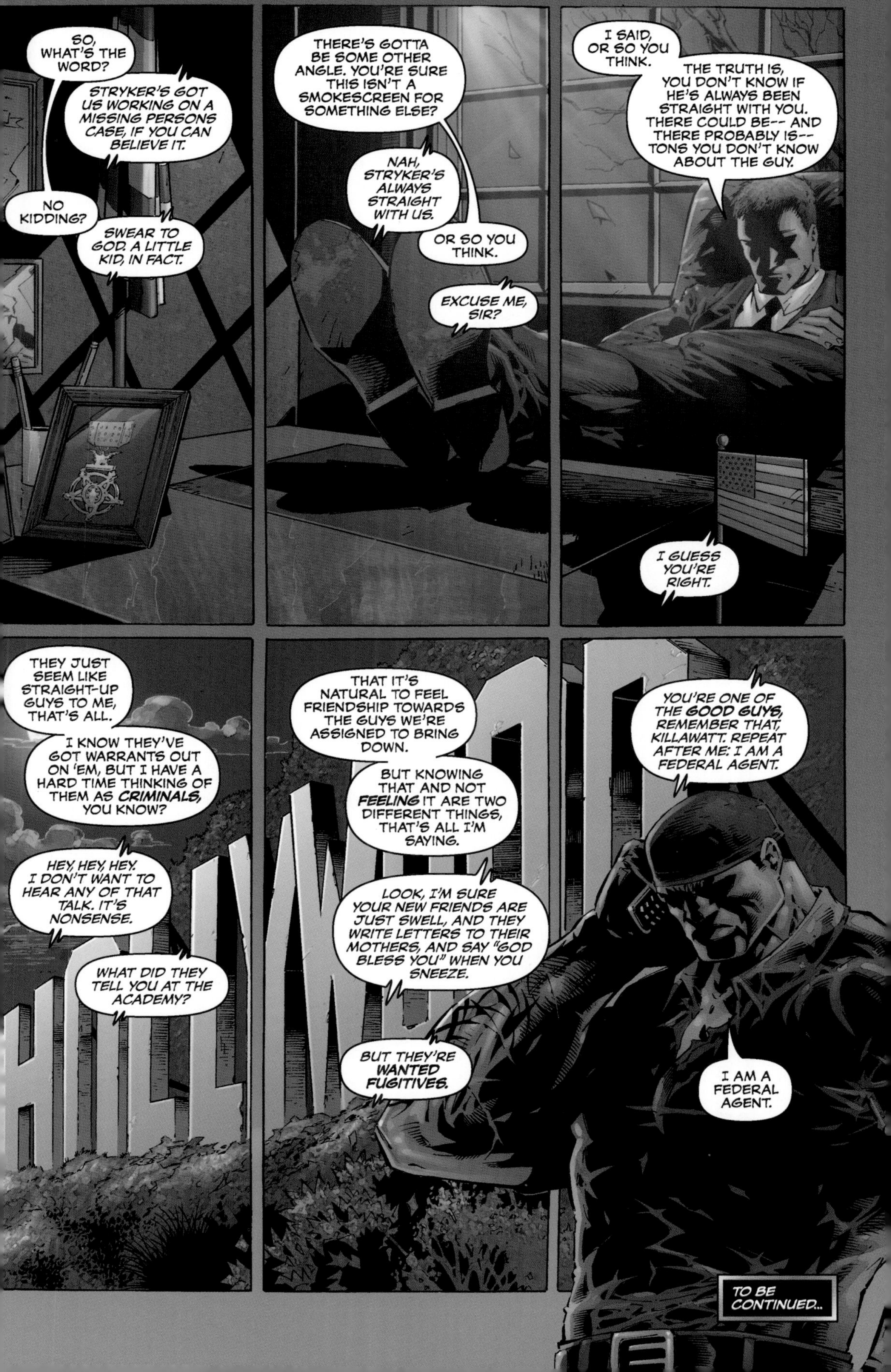
SO, WHAT'S THE WORD?
STRYKER'S GOT US WORKING ON A MISSING PERSONS CASE, IF YOU CAN BELIEVE IT.
NO KIDDING?
SWEAR TO GOD. A LITTLE KID, IN FACT.
THERE'S GOTTA BE SOME OTHER ANGLE. YOU'RE SURE THIS ISN'T A SMOKESCREEN FOR SOMETHING ELSE?
NAH, STRYKER'S ALWAYS STRAIGHT WITH US.
OR SO YOU THINK.
EXCUSE ME, SIR?
I SAID, OR SO YOU THINK.
THE TRUTH IS, YOU DON'T KNOW IF HE'S ALWAYS BEEN STRAIGHT WITH YOU. THERE COULD BE-- AND THERE PROBABLY IS-- TONS YOU DON'T KNOW ABOUT THE GUY.
I GUESS YOU'RE RIGHT.
THEY JUST SEEM LIKE STRAIGHT-UP GUYS TO ME, THAT'S ALL.
I KNOW THEY'VE GOT WARRANTS OUT ON 'EM, BUT I HAVE A HARD TIME THINKING OF THEM AS CRIMINALS, YOU KNOW?
HEY, HEY, HEY. I DON'T WANT TO HEAR ANY OF THAT TALK. IT'S NONSENSE.
WHAT DID THEY TELL YOU AT THE ACADEMY?
THAT IT'S NATURAL TO FEEL FRIENDSHIP TOWARDS THE GUYS WE'RE ASSIGNED TO BRING DOWN.
BUT KNOWING THAT AND NOT FEELING IT ARE TWO DIFFERENT THINGS, THAT'S ALL I'M SAYING.
LOOK, I'M SURE YOUR NEW FRIENDS ARE JUST SWELL, AND THEY WRITE LETTERS TO THEIR MOTHERS, AND SAY "GOD BLESS YOU" WHEN YOU SNEEZE.
BUT THEY'RE WANTED FUGITIVES.
YOU'RE ONE OF THE GOOD GUYS, REMEMBER THAT, KILLAWATT. REPEAT AFTER ME: I AM A FEDERAL AGENT.
I AM A FEDERAL AGENT.
TO BE CONTINUED...

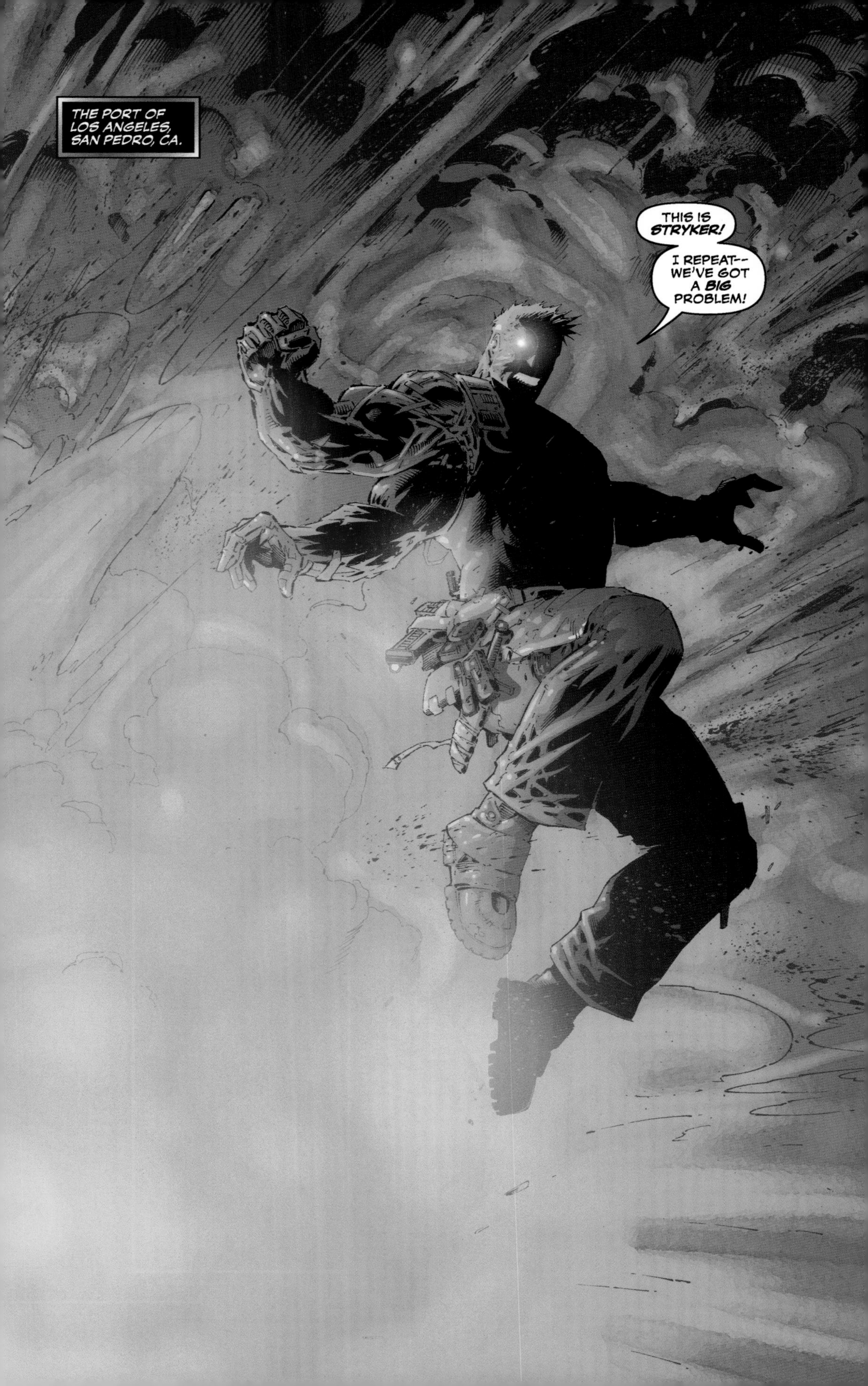
THE PORT OF LOS ANGELES, SAN PEDRO, CA.
THIS IS STRYKER!
I REPEAT-- WE'VE GOT A BIG PROBLEM!

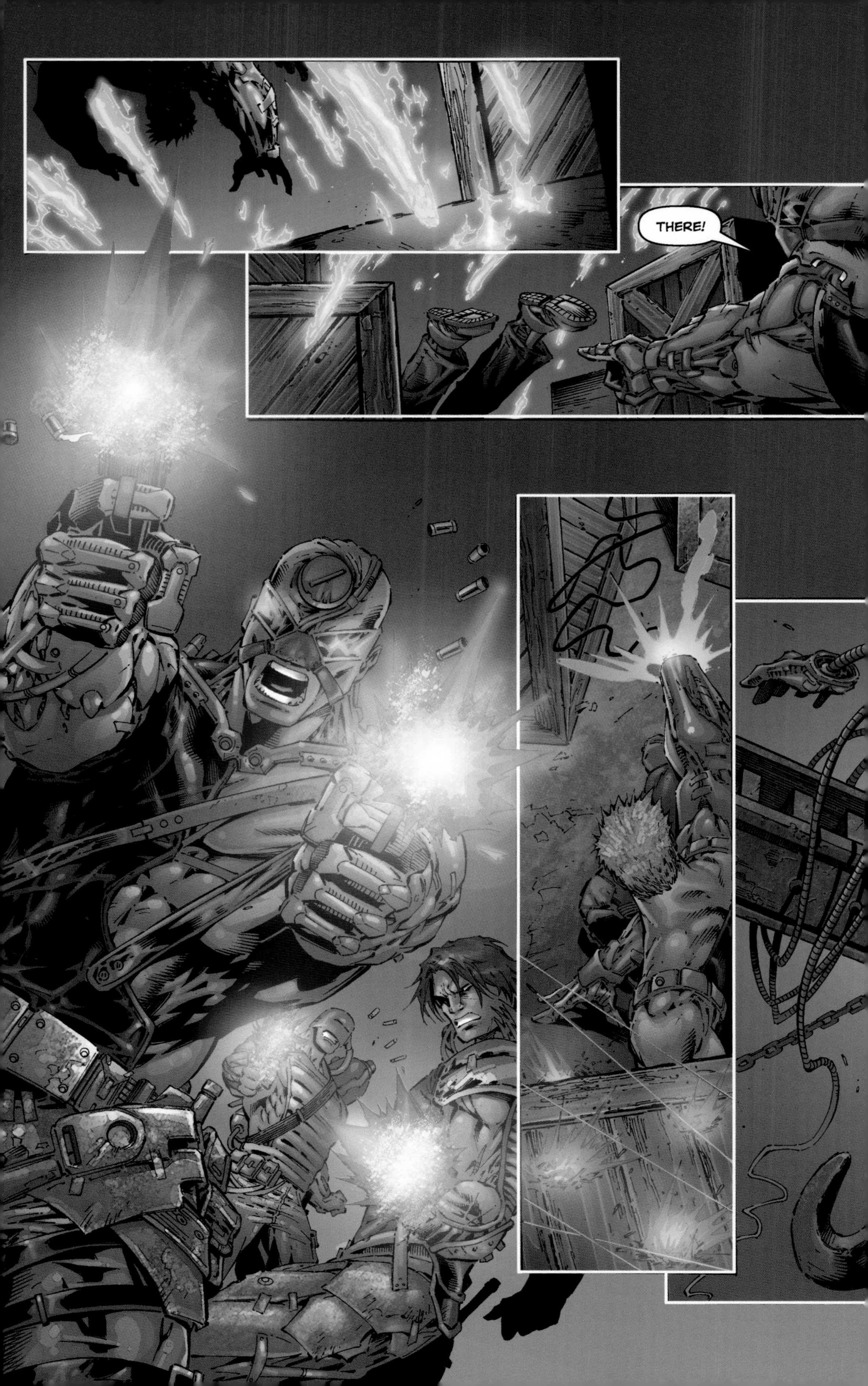
THERE!

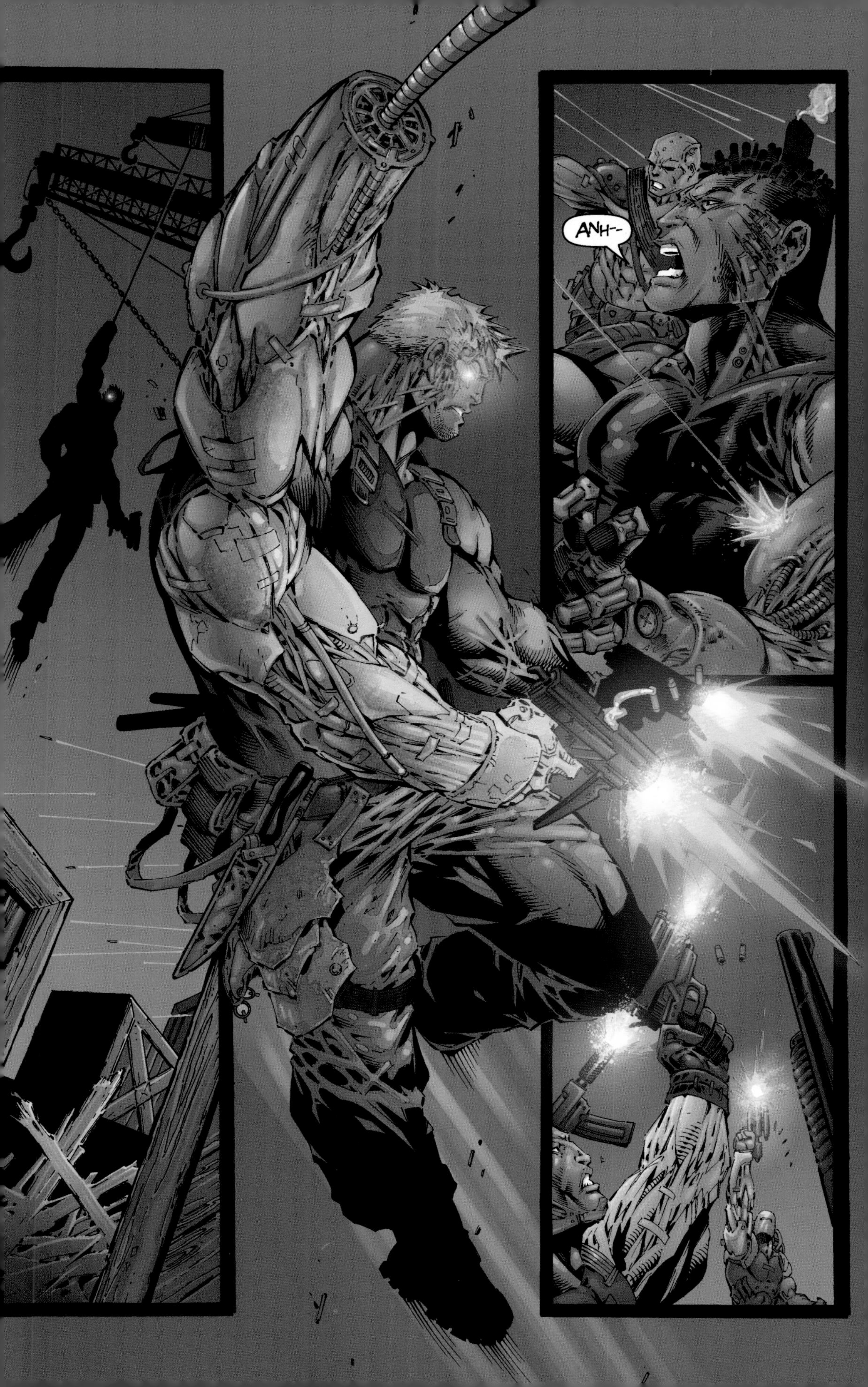
ANH--

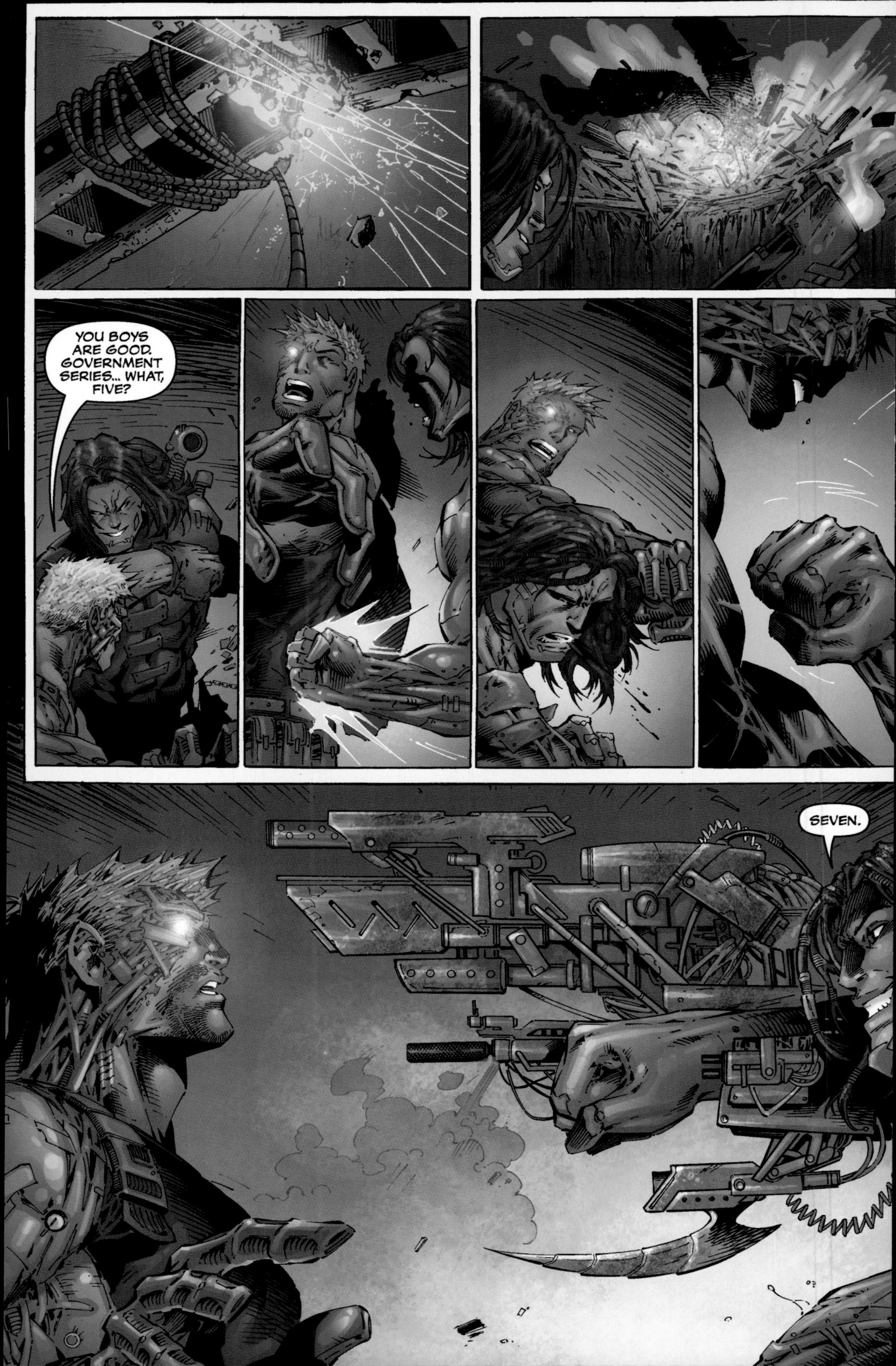
YOU BOYS ARE GOOD. GOVERNMENT SERIES... WHAT, FIVE?
SEVEN.

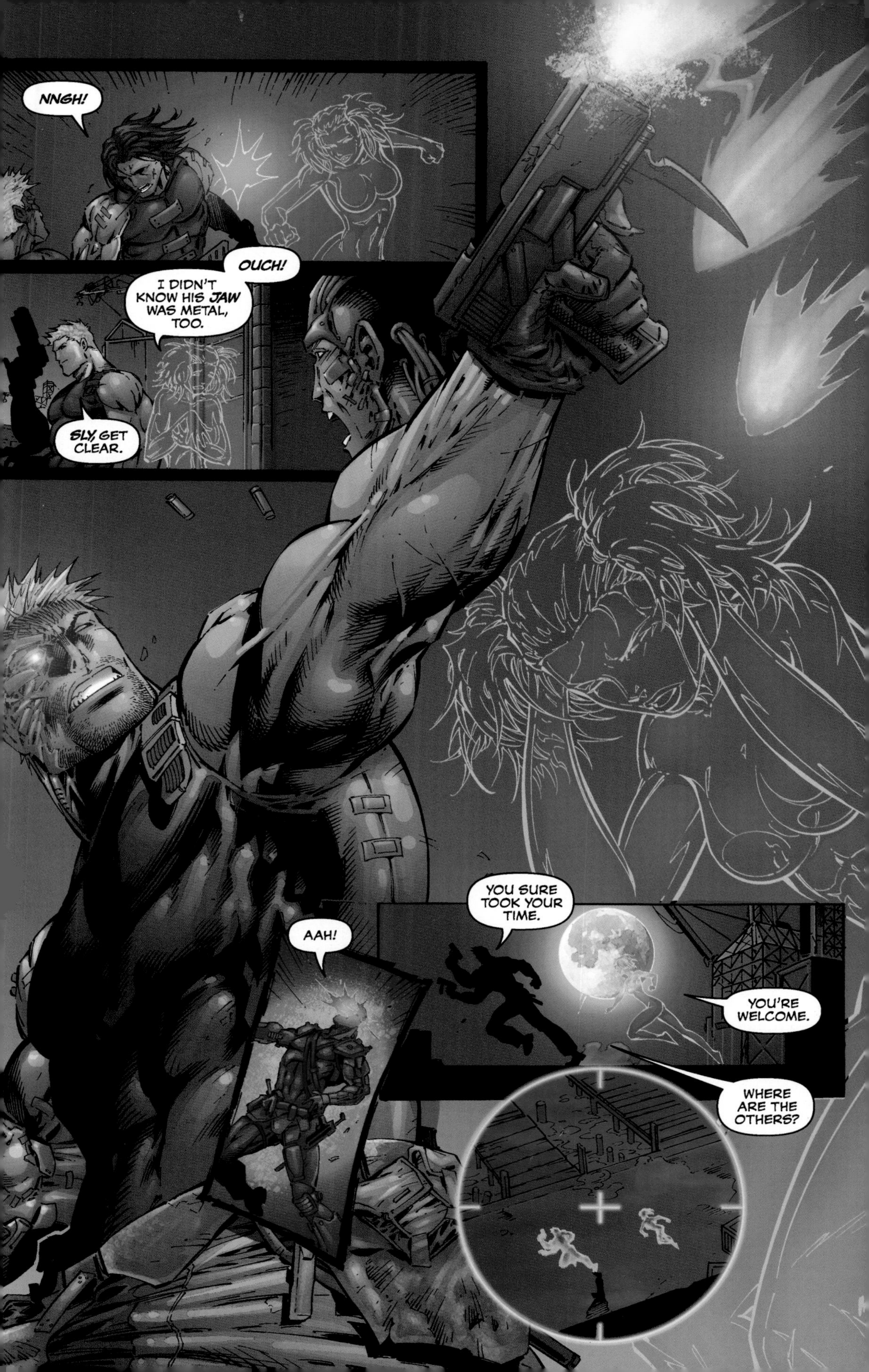
NNGH!
OUCH!
I DIDN'T KNOW HIS JAW WAS METAL, TOO.
SLY, GET CLEAR.
AAH!
YOU SURE TOOK YOUR TIME.
YOU'RE WELCOME.
WHERE ARE THE OTHERS?

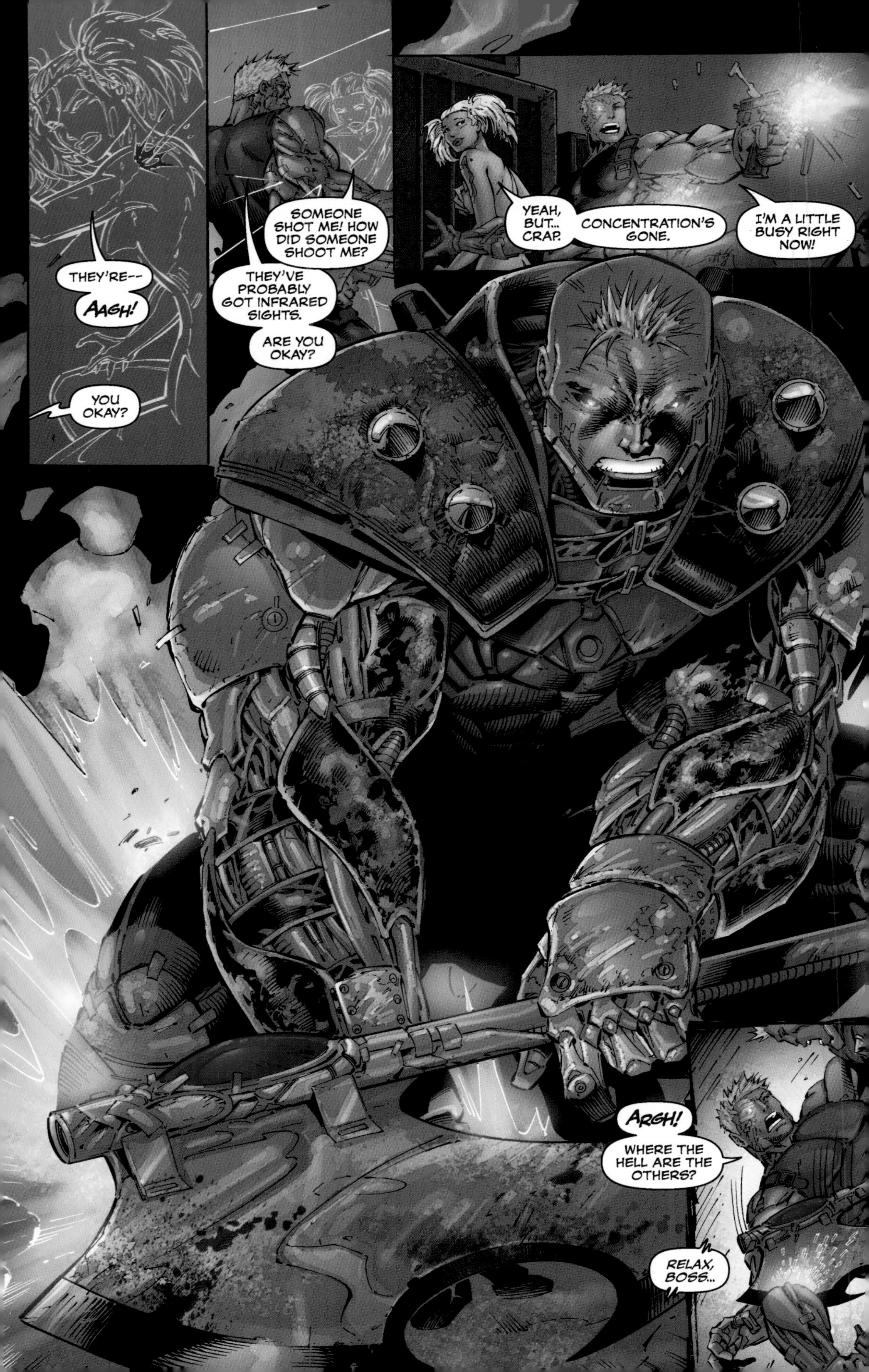
THEY'RE--
AAGH!
YOU OKAY?
SOMEONE SHOT ME! HOW DID SOMEONE SHOOT ME?
THEY'VE PROBABLY GOT INFRARED SIGHTS.
ARE YOU OKAY?
YEAH, BUT... CRAP.
CONCENTRATION'S GONE.
I'M A LITTLE BUSY RIGHT NOW!
ARGH!
WHERE THE HELL ARE THE OTHERS?
RELAX, BOSS...

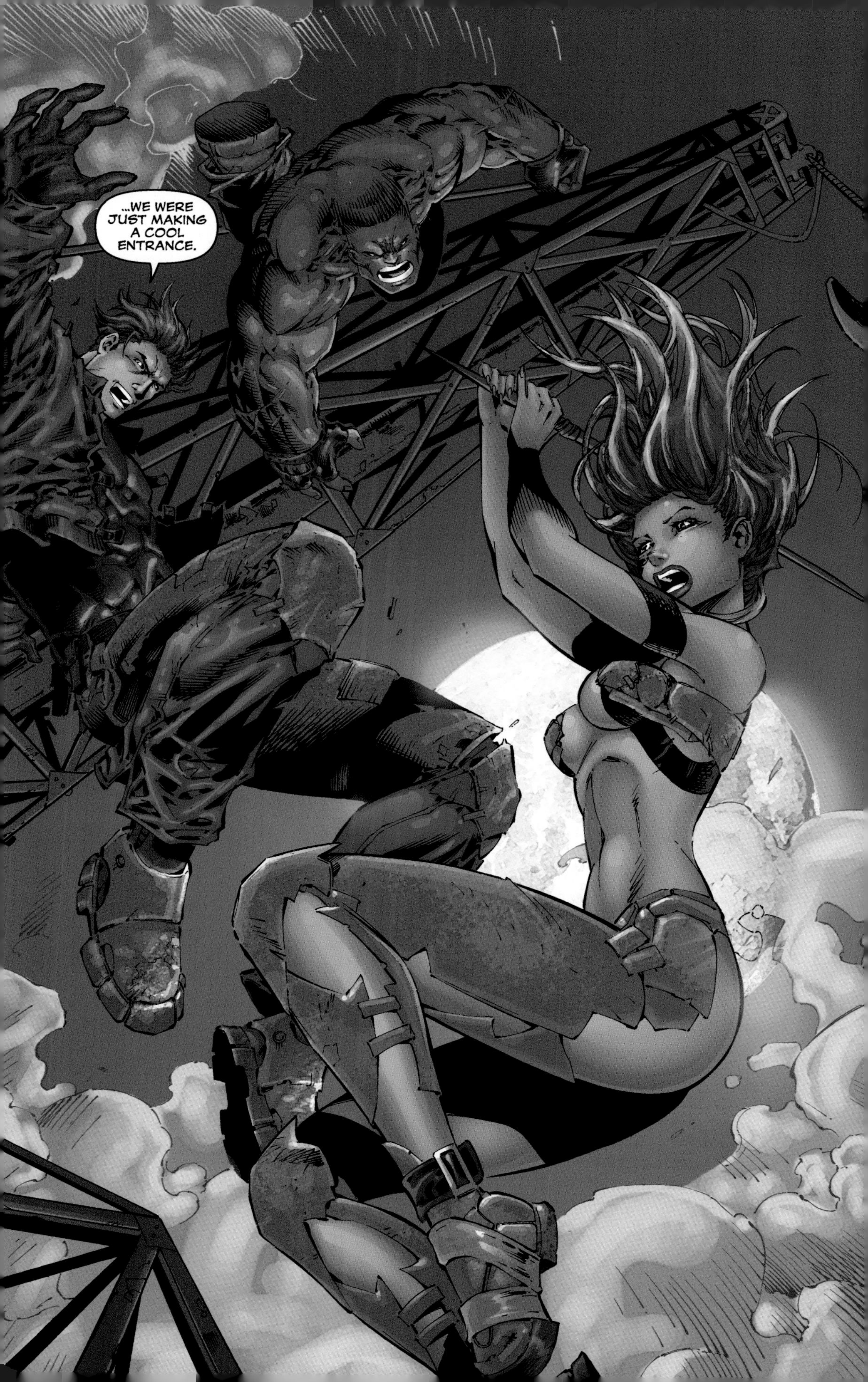
...WE WERE JUST MAKING A COOL ENTRANCE.

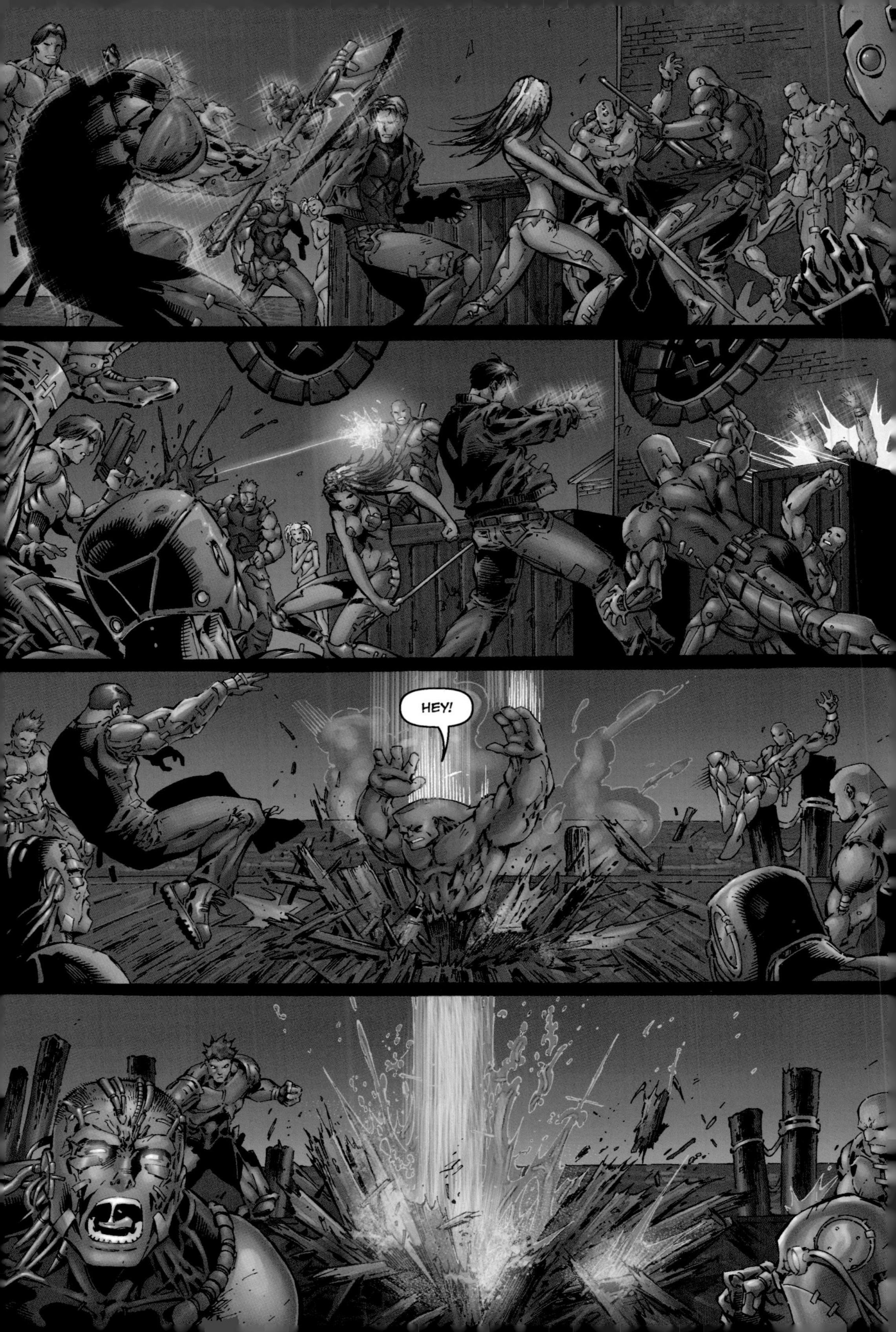
HEY!

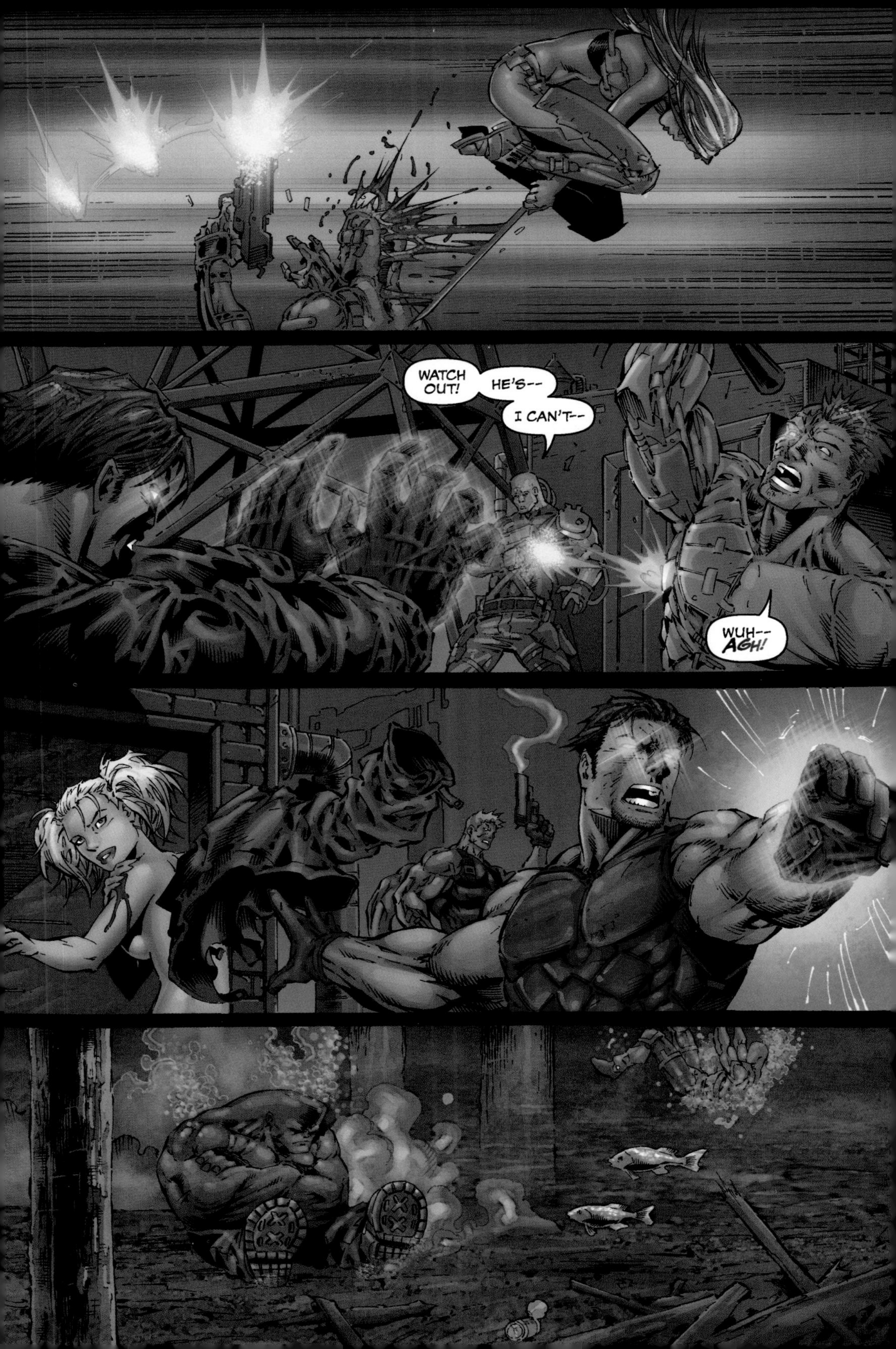
WATCH OUT!
HE'S--
I CAN'T--
WUH--AGH!

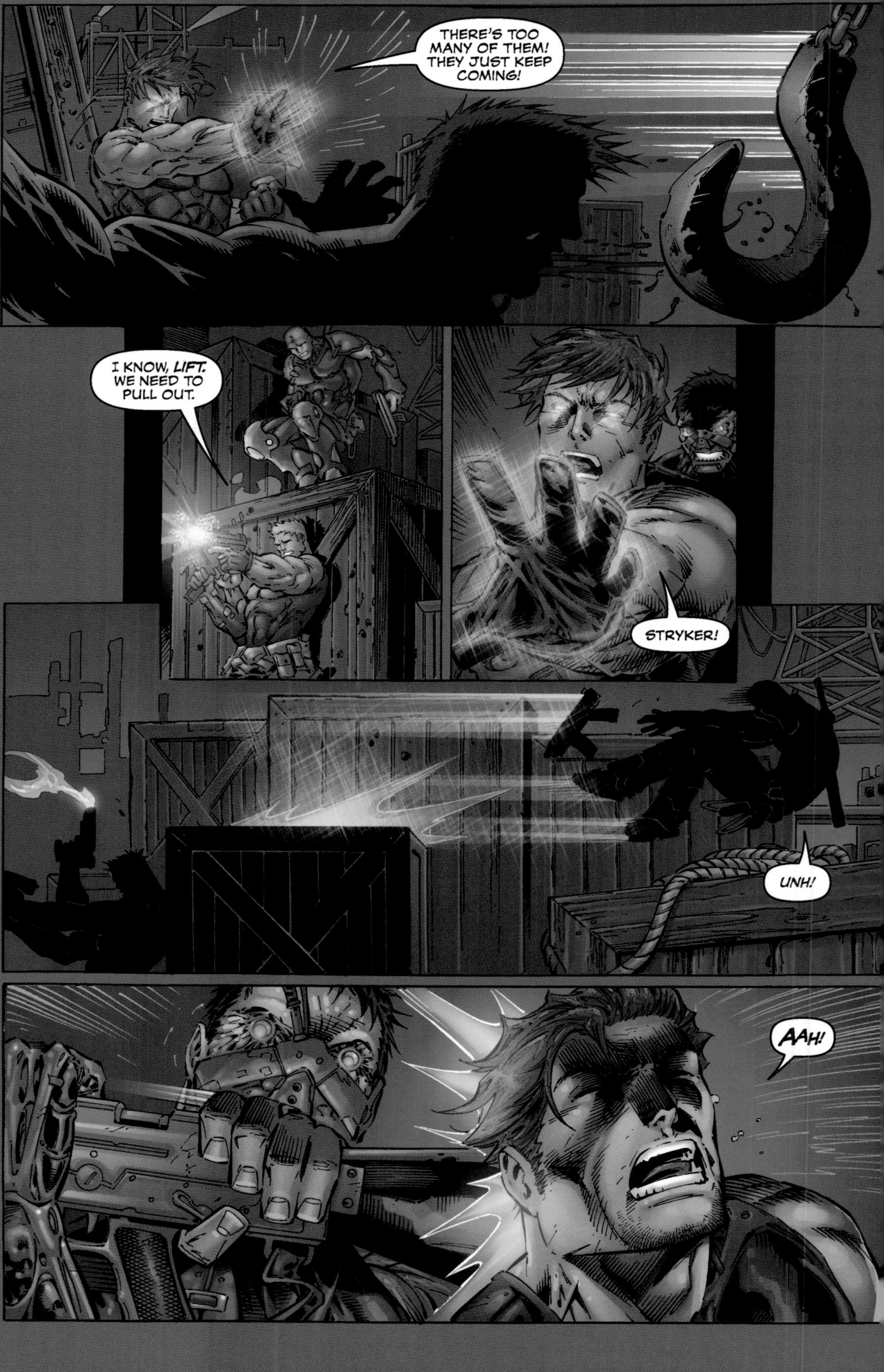
THERE'S TOO MANY OF THEM! THEY JUST KEEP COMING!
I KNOW, LIFT. WE NEED TO PULL OUT.
STRYKER!
UNH!
AAH!

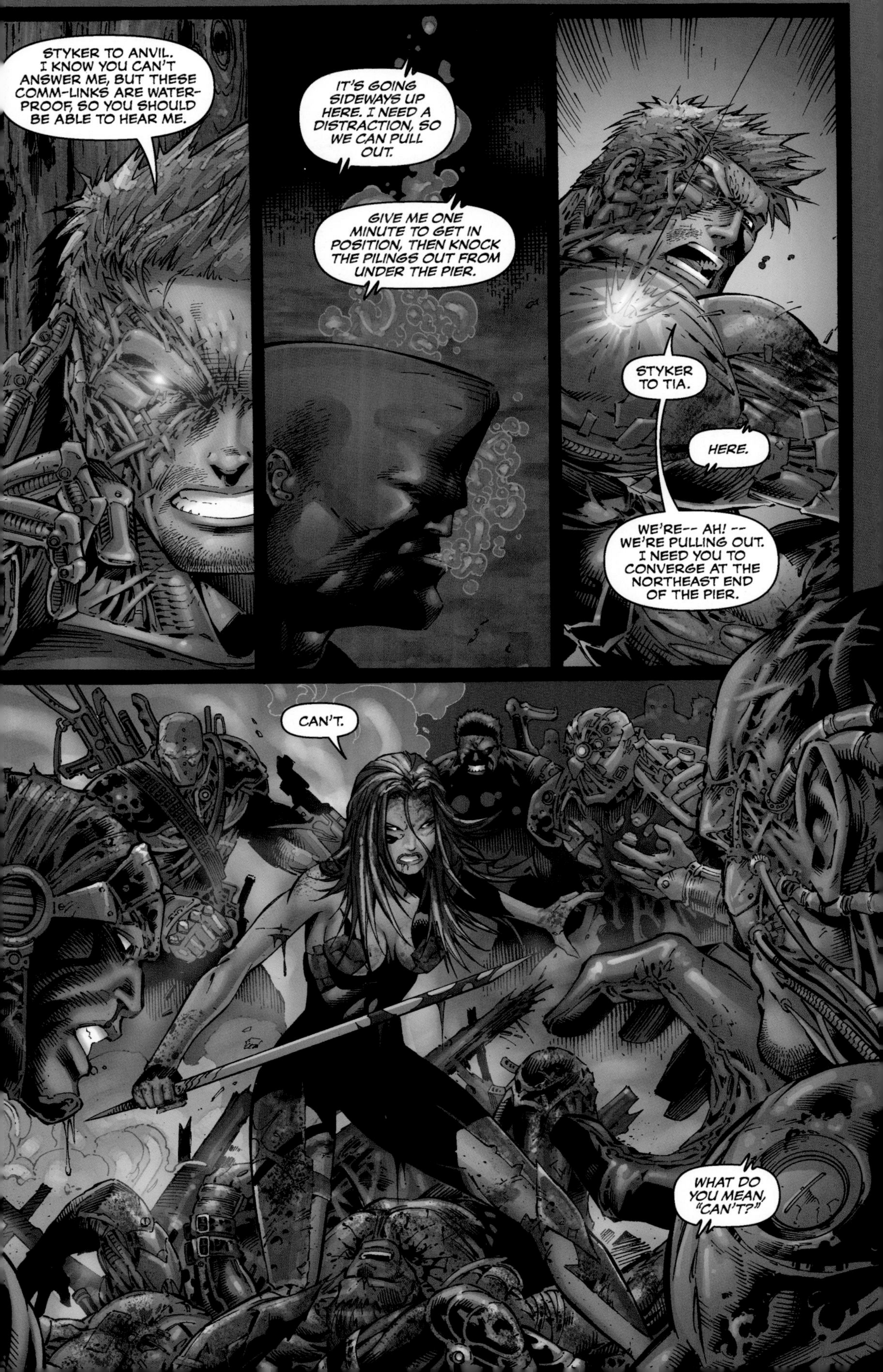
STYKER TO ANVIL. I KNOW YOU CAN'T ANSWER ME, BUT THESE COMM-LINKS ARE WATER-PROOF, SO YOU SHOULD BE ABLE TO HEAR ME.
IT'S GOING SIDEWAYS UP HERE. I NEED A DISTRACTION, SO WE CAN PULL OUT.
GIVE ME ONE MINUTE TO GET IN POSITION, THEN KNOCK THE PILINGS OUT FROM UNDER THE PIER.
STYKER TO TIA.
HERE.
WE'RE-- AH! --WE'RE PULLING OUT. I NEED YOU TO CONVERGE AT THE NORTHEAST END OF THE PIER.
CAN'T.
WHAT DO YOU MEAN, "CAN'T?"

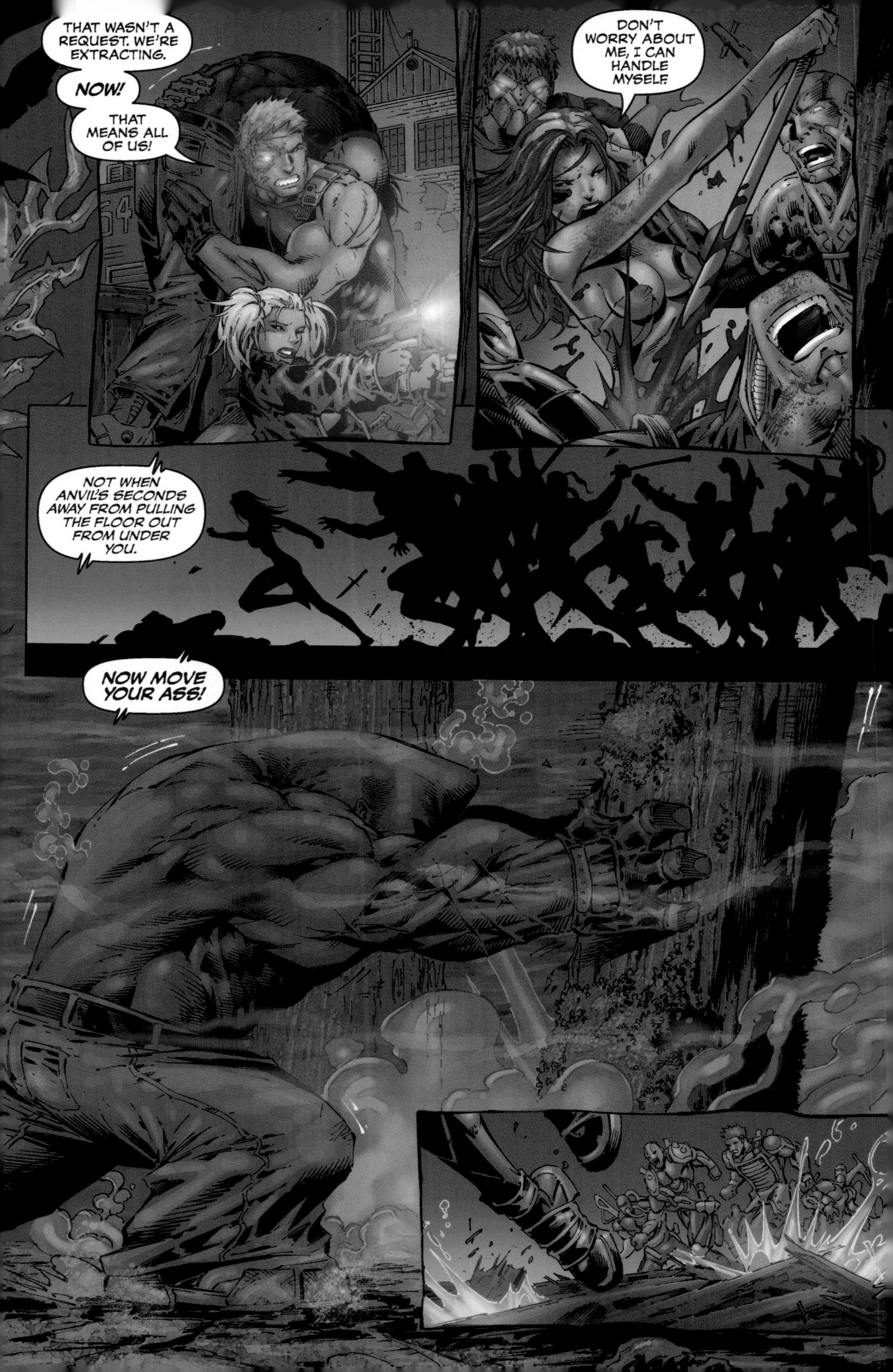
THAT WASN'T A REQUEST. WE'RE EXTRACTING.
NOW!
THAT MEANS ALL OF US!
DON'T WORRY ABOUT ME, I CAN HANDLE MYSELF.
NOT WHEN ANVIL'S SECONDS AWAY FROM PULLING THE FLOOR OUT FROM UNDER YOU.
NOW MOVE YOUR ASS!
!!

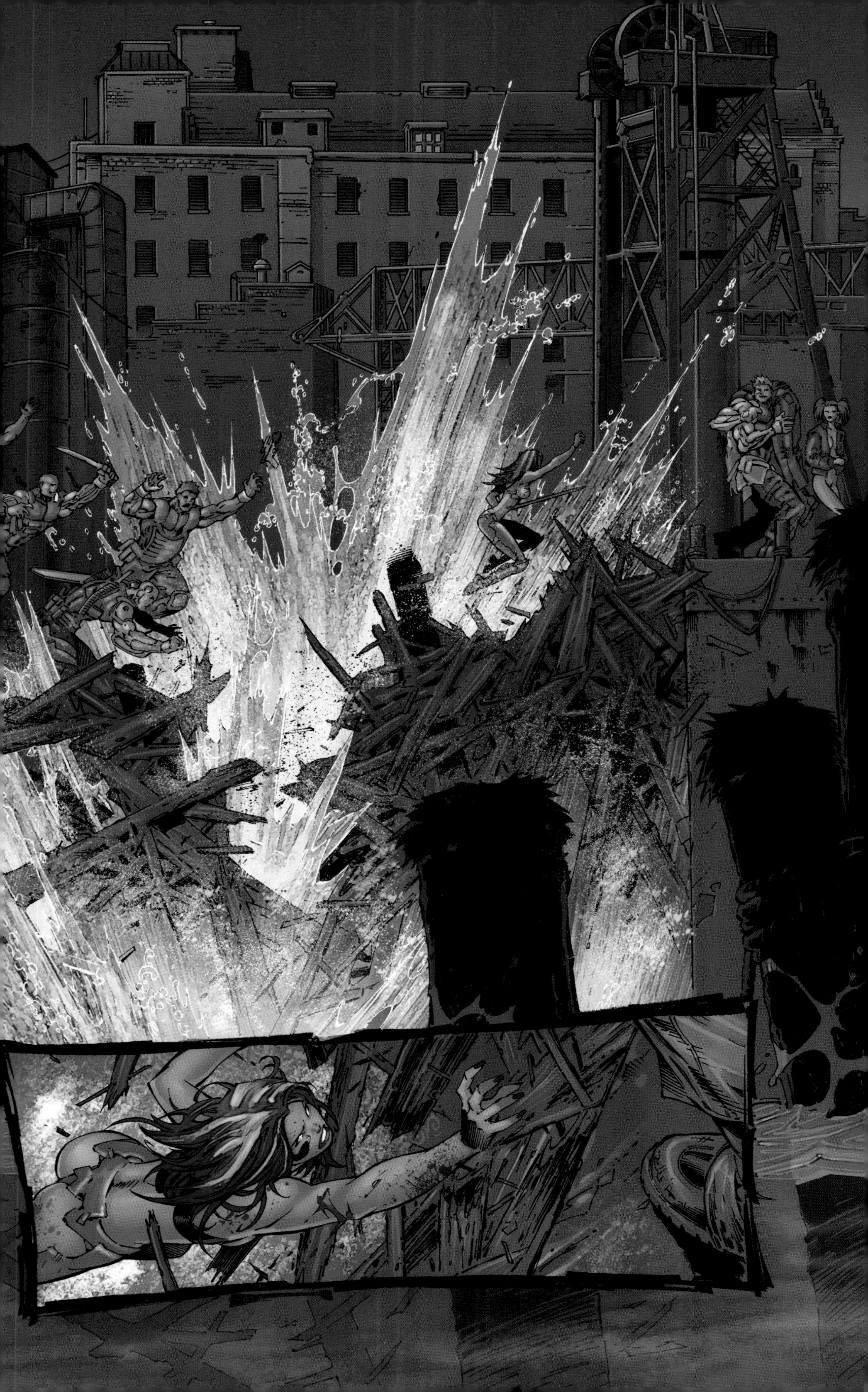

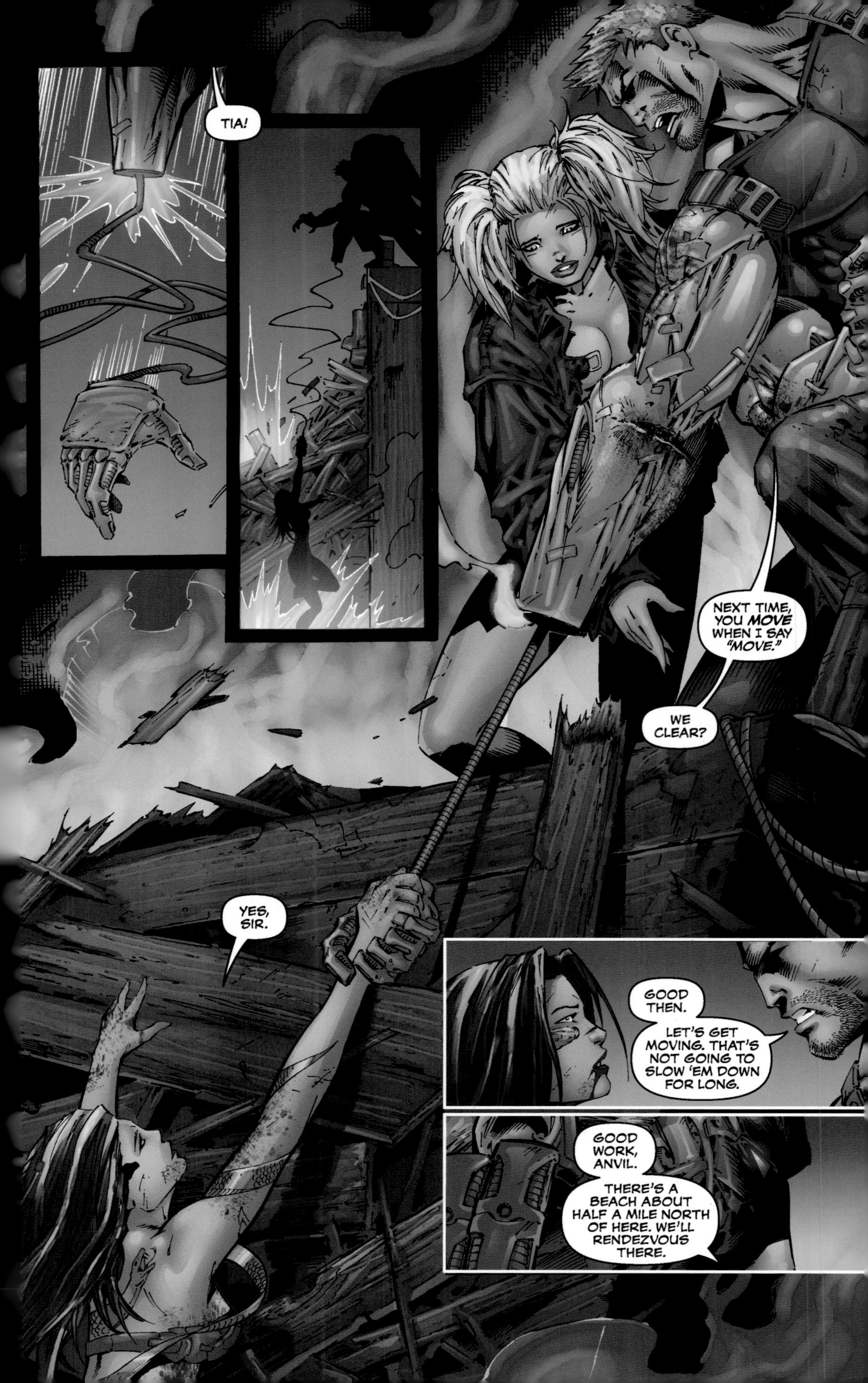
TIA!
NEXT TIME, YOU MOVE WHEN I SAY "MOVE."
WE CLEAR?
YES, SIR.
GOOD THEN.
LET'S GET MOVING. THAT'S NOT GOING TO SLOW 'EM DOWN FOR LONG.
GOOD WORK, ANVIL.
THERE'S A BEACH ABOUT HALF A MILE NORTH OF HERE. WE'LL RENDEZVOUS THERE.

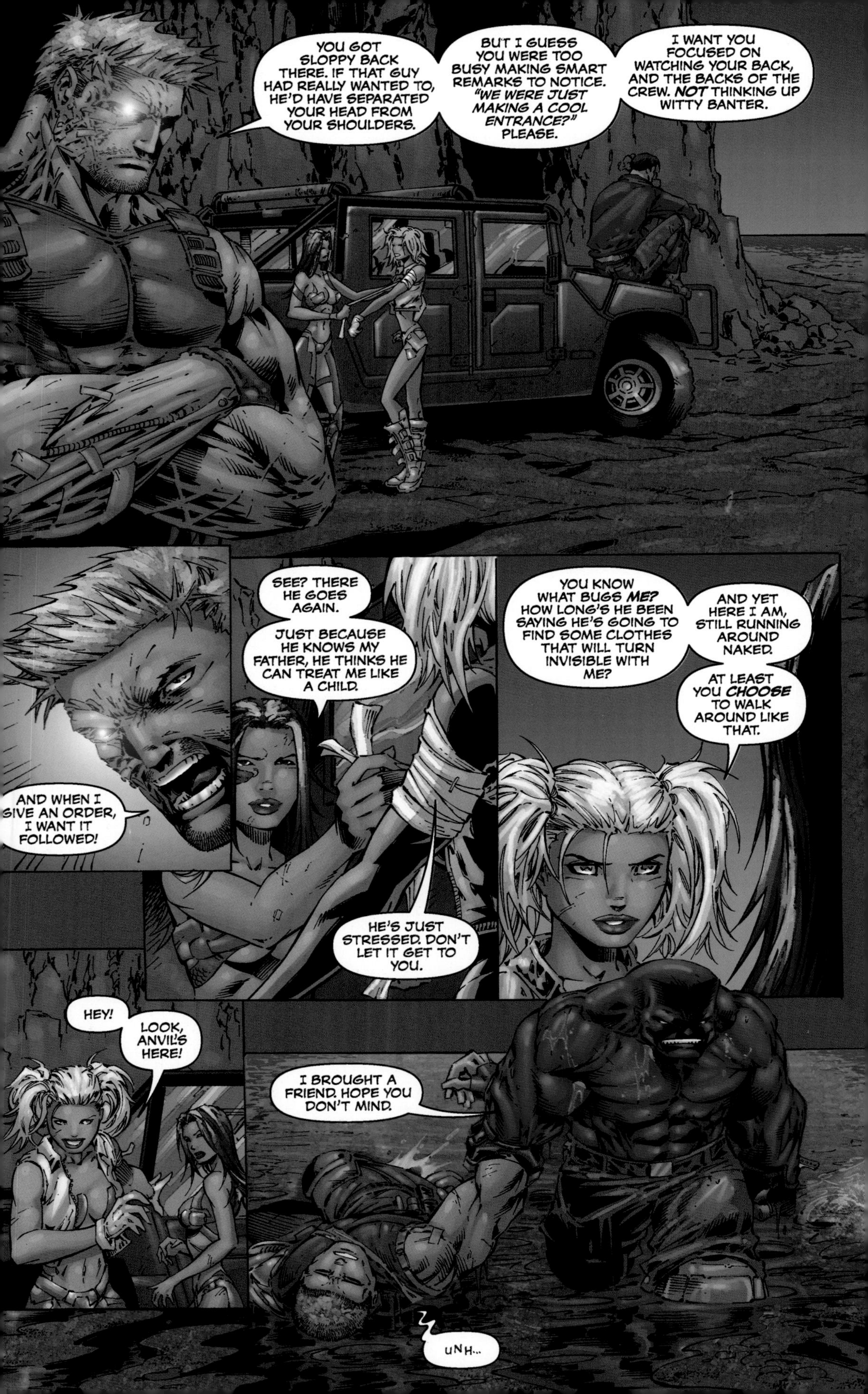
YOU GOT SLOPPY BACK THERE. IF THAT GUY HAD REALLY WANTED TO, HE'D HAVE SEPARATED YOUR HEAD FROM YOUR SHOULDERS.
BUT I GUESS YOU WERE TOO BUSY MAKING SMART REMARKS TO NOTICE. "WE WERE JUST MAKING A COOL ENTRANCE?" PLEASE.
I WANT YOU FOCUSED ON WATCHING YOUR BACK, AND THE BACKS OF THE CREW. NOT THINKING UP WITTY BANTER.
SEE? THERE HE GOES AGAIN.
JUST BECAUSE HE KNOWS MY FATHER, HE THINKS HE CAN TREAT ME LIKE A CHILD.
AND WHEN I GIVE AN ORDER, I WANT IT FOLLOWED!
HE'S JUST STRESSED. DON'T LET IT GET TO YOU.
YOU KNOW WHAT BUGS ME? HOW LONG'S HE BEEN SAYING HE'S GOING TO FIND SOME CLOTHES THAT WILL TURN INVISIBLE WITH ME?
AND YET HERE I AM, STILL RUNNING AROUND NAKED.
AT LEAST YOU CHOOSE TO WALK AROUND LIKE THAT.
HEY!
LOOK, ANVIL'S HERE!
I BROUGHT A FRIEND. HOPE YOU DON'T MIND.
UNH...

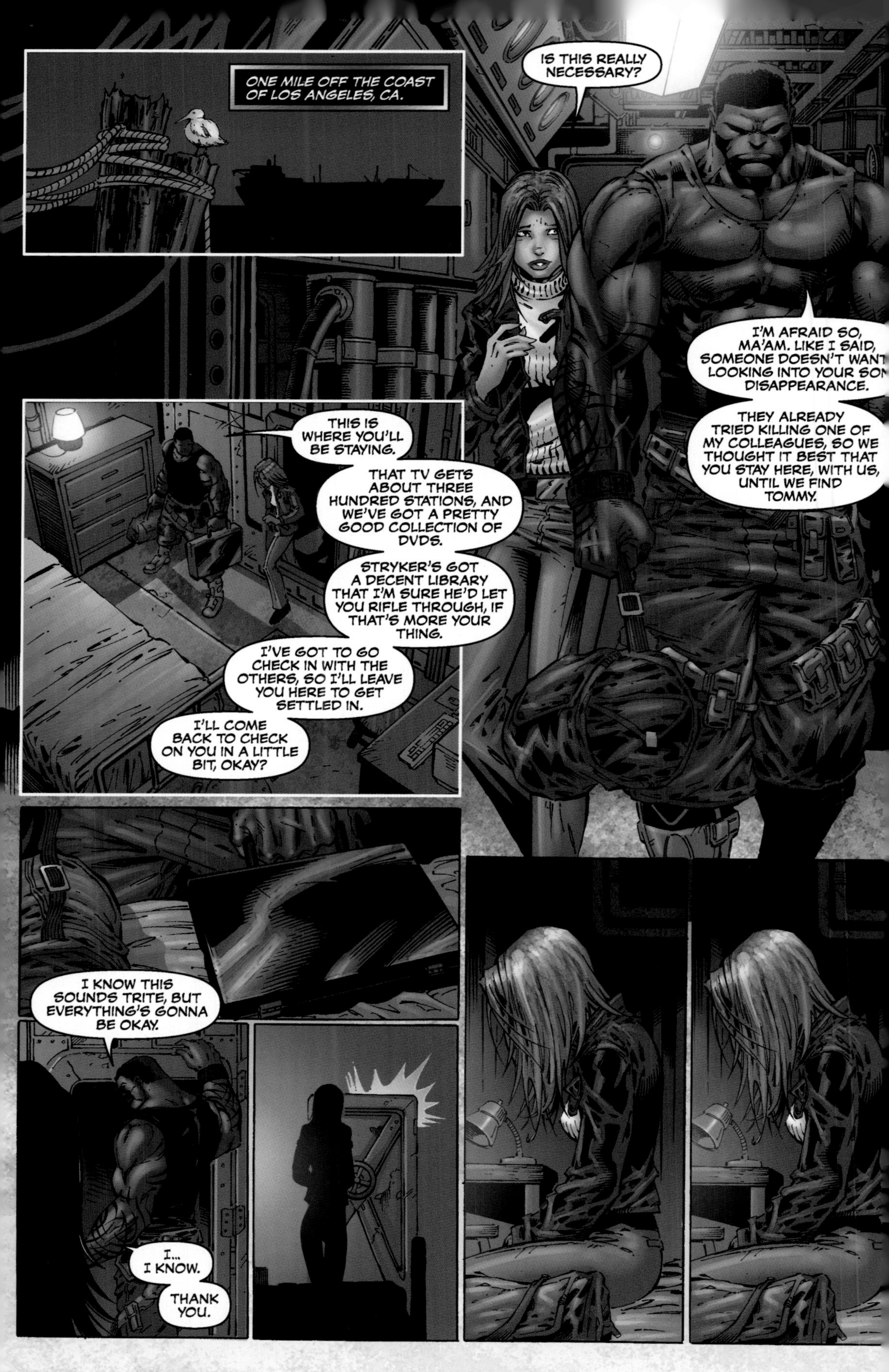
ONE MILE OFF THE COAST OF LOS ANGELES, CA.
IS THIS REALLY NECESSARY?
I'M AFRAID SO, MA'AM. LIKE I SAID, SOMEONE DOESN'T WANT LOOKING INTO YOUR SON DISAPPEARANCE.
THEY ALREADY TRIED KILLING ONE OF MY COLLEAGUES, SO WE THOUGHT IT BEST THAT YOU STAY HERE, WITH US, UNTIL WE FIND TOMMY.
THIS IS WHERE YOU'LL BE STAYING.
THAT TV GETS ABOUT THREE HUNDRED STATIONS, AND WE'VE GOT A PRETTY GOOD COLLECTION OF DVDS.
STRYKER'S GOT A DECENT LIBRARY THAT I'M SURE HE'D LET YOU RIFLE THROUGH, IF THAT'S MORE YOUR THING.
I'VE GOT TO GO CHECK IN WITH THE OTHERS, SO I'LL LEAVE YOU HERE TO GET SETTLED IN.
I'LL COME BACK TO CHECK ON YOU IN A LITTLE BIT, OKAY?
I KNOW THIS SOUNDS TRITE, BUT EVERYTHING'S GONNA BE OKAY.
I... I KNOW.
THANK YOU.

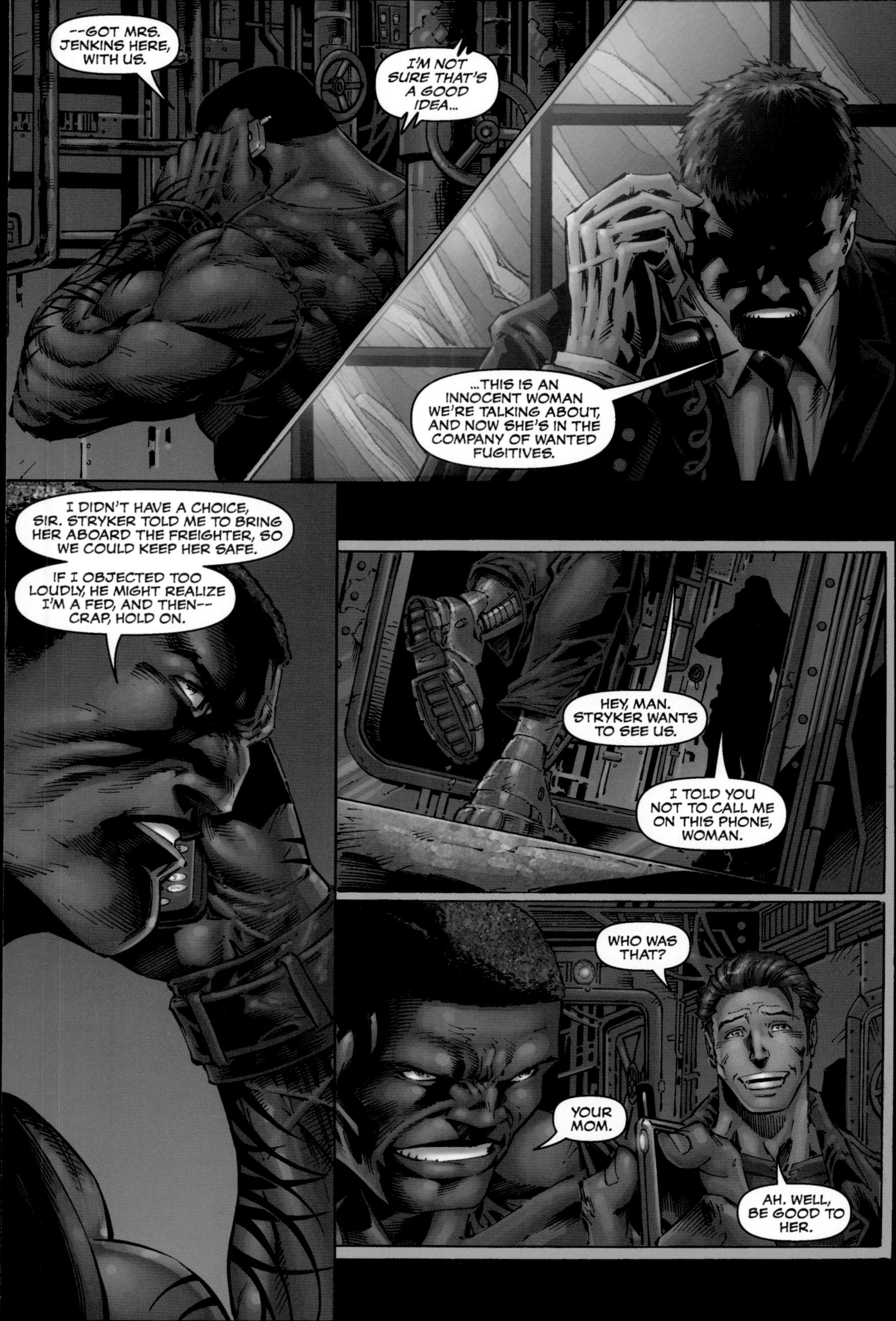
--GOT MRS. JENKINS HERE, WITH US.
I'M NOT SURE THAT'S A GOOD IDEA...
...THIS IS AN INNOCENT WOMAN WE'RE TALKING ABOUT, AND NOW SHE'S IN THE COMPANY OF WANTED FUGITIVES.
I DIDN'T HAVE A CHOICE, SIR. STRYKER TOLD ME TO BRING HER ABOARD THE FREIGHTER, SO WE COULD KEEP HER SAFE.
IF I OBJECTED TOO LOUDLY, HE MIGHT REALIZE I'M A FED, AND THEN--CRAP, HOLD ON.
HEY, MAN. STRYKER WANTS TO SEE US.
I TOLD YOU NOT TO CALL ME ON THIS PHONE, WOMAN.
WHO WAS THAT?
YOUR MOM.
AH. WELL, BE GOOD TO HER.

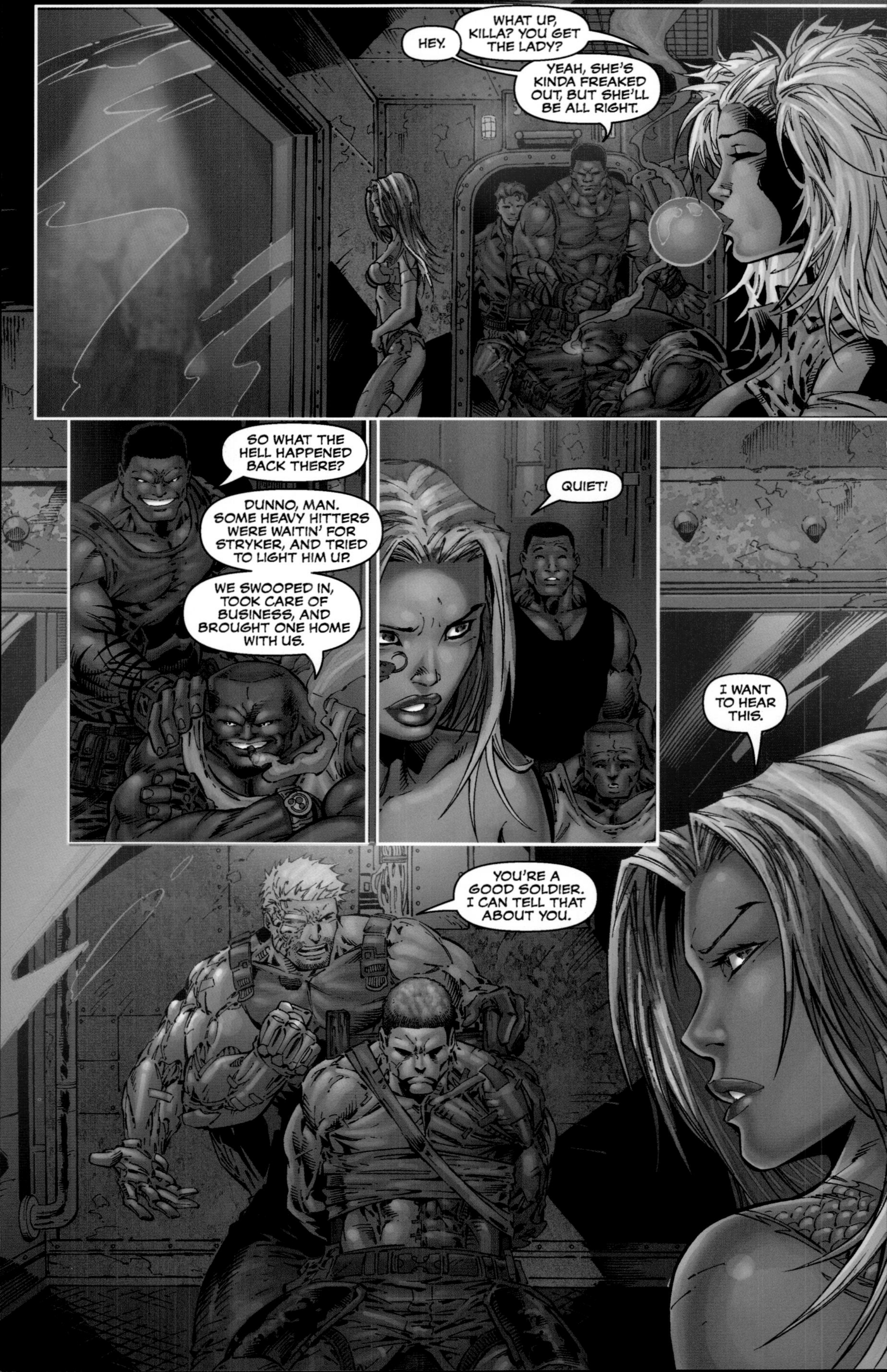

HEY.
WHAT UP, KILLA? YOU GET THE LADY?
YEAH, SHE'S KINDA FREAKED OUT, BUT SHE'LL BE ALL RIGHT.
SO WHAT THE HELL HAPPENED BACK THERE?
DUNNO, MAN. SOME HEAVY HITTERS WERE WAITIN' FOR STRYKER, AND TRIED TO LIGHT HIM UP.
WE SWOOPED IN, TOOK CARE OF BUSINESS, AND BROUGHT ONE HOME WITH US.
QUIET!
I WANT TO HEAR THIS.
YOU'RE A GOOD SOLDIER. I CAN TELL THAT ABOUT YOU.

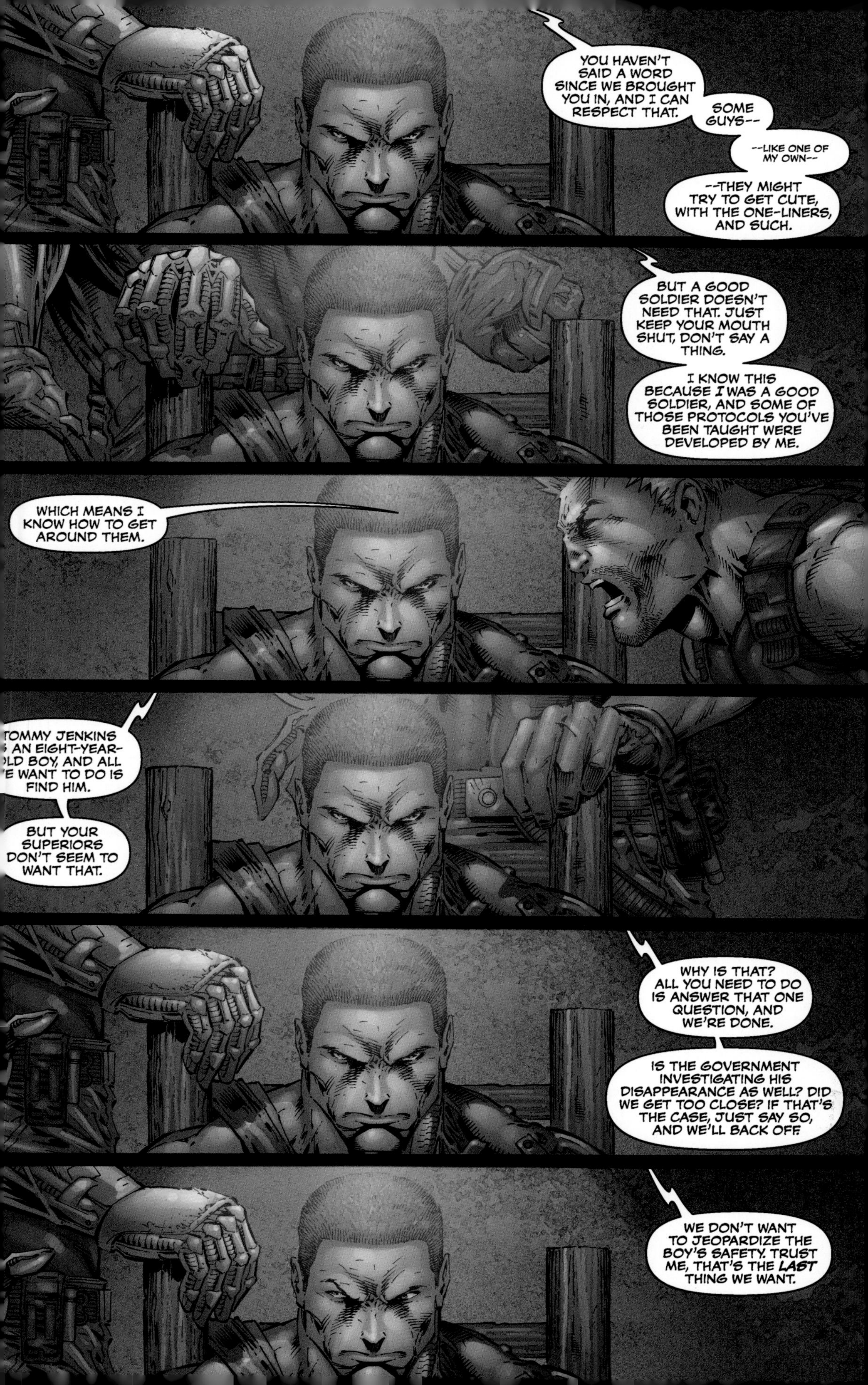
YOU HAVEN'T SAID A WORD SINCE WE BROUGHT YOU IN, AND I CAN RESPECT THAT.
SOME GUYS--
--LIKE ONE OF MY OWN--
--THEY MIGHT TRY TO GET CUTE, WITH THE ONE-LINERS, AND SUCH.
BUT A GOOD SOLDIER DOESN'T NEED THAT. JUST KEEP YOUR MOUTH SHUT, DON'T SAY A THING.
I KNOW THIS BECAUSE *I* WAS A GOOD SOLDIER, AND SOME OF THOSE PROTOCOLS YOU'VE BEEN TAUGHT WERE DEVELOPED BY ME.
WHICH MEANS I KNOW HOW TO GET AROUND THEM.
TOMMY JENKINS IS AN EIGHT-YEAR-OLD BOY, AND ALL WE WANT TO DO IS FIND HIM.
BUT YOUR SUPERIORS DON'T SEEM TO WANT THAT.
WHY IS THAT? ALL YOU NEED TO DO IS ANSWER THAT ONE QUESTION, AND WE'RE DONE.
IS THE GOVERNMENT INVESTIGATING HIS DISAPPEARANCE AS WELL? DID WE GET TOO CLOSE? IF THAT'S THE CASE, JUST SAY SO, AND WE'LL BACK OFF.
WE DON'T WANT TO JEOPARDIZE THE BOY'S SAFETY. TRUST ME, THAT'S THE *LAST* THING WE WANT.

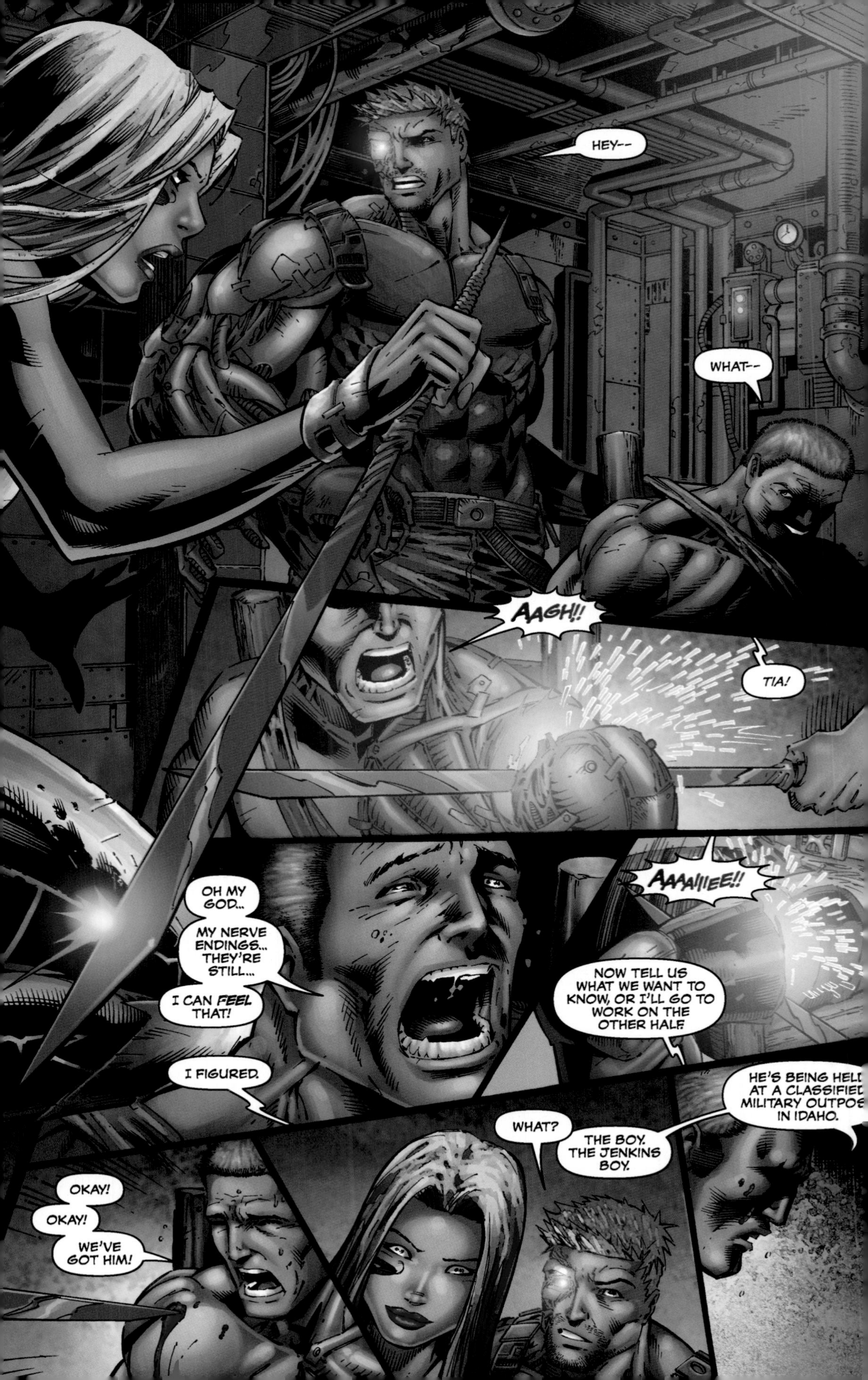
HEY--
WHAT--
AAGH!!
TIA!
OH MY GOD...
MY NERVE ENDINGS... THEY'RE STILL...
I CAN FEEL THAT!
I FIGURED.
AAAAIIIEE!!
NOW TELL US WHAT WE WANT TO KNOW, OR I'LL GO TO WORK ON THE OTHER HALF.
OKAY!
OKAY!
WE'VE GOT HIM!
WHAT?
THE BOY. THE JENKINS BOY.
HE'S BEING HELD AT A CLASSIFIED MILITARY OUTPOST IN IDAHO.

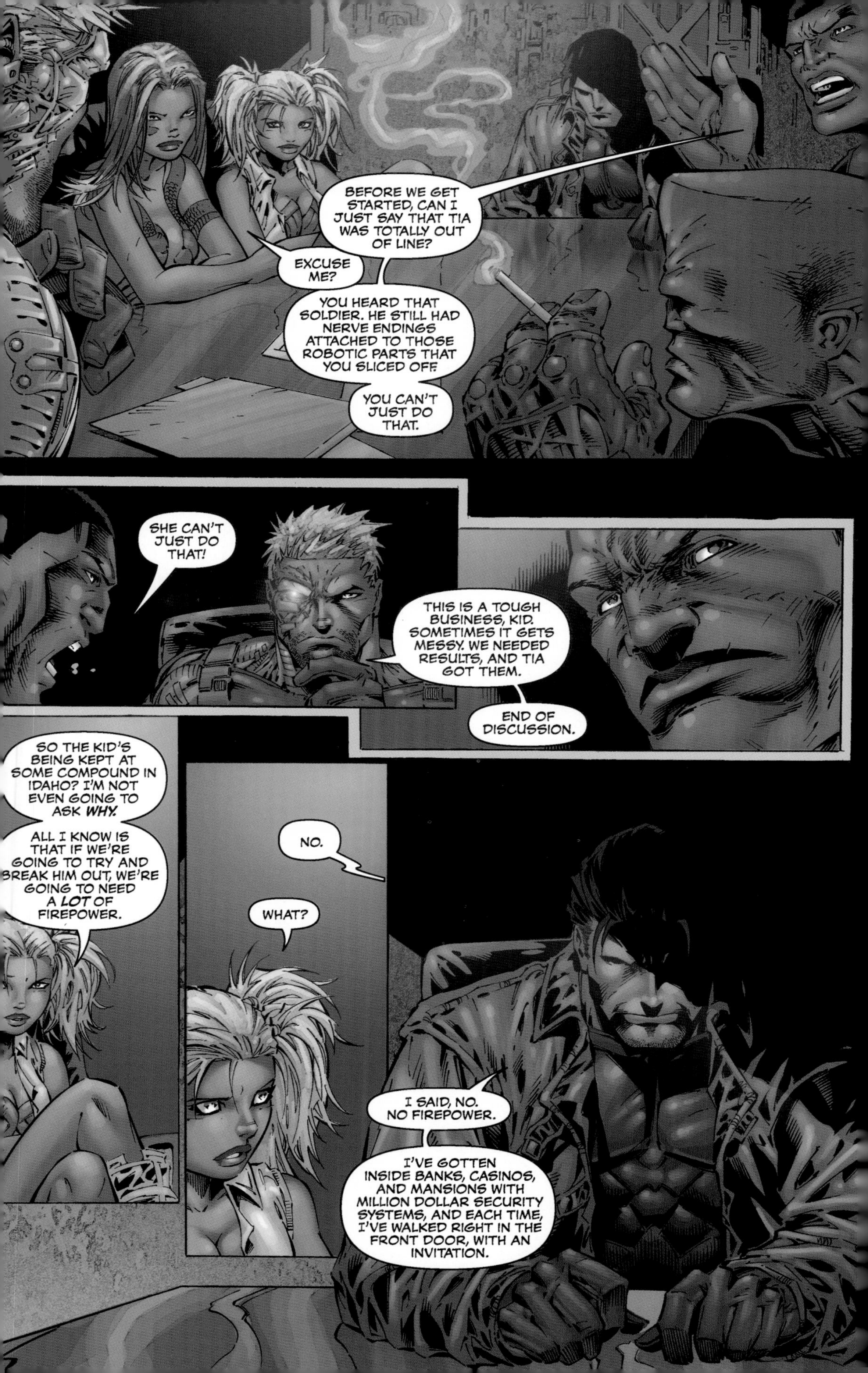
BEFORE WE GET STARTED, CAN I JUST SAY THAT TIA WAS TOTALLY OUT OF LINE?
EXCUSE ME?
YOU HEARD THAT SOLDIER. HE STILL HAD NERVE ENDINGS ATTACHED TO THOSE ROBOTIC PARTS THAT YOU SLICED OFF.
YOU CAN'T JUST DO THAT.
SHE CAN'T JUST DO THAT!
THIS IS A TOUGH BUSINESS, KID. SOMETIMES IT GETS MESSY. WE NEEDED RESULTS, AND TIA GOT THEM.
END OF DISCUSSION.
SO THE KID'S BEING KEPT AT SOME COMPOUND IN IDAHO? I'M NOT EVEN GOING TO ASK *WHY.*
ALL I KNOW IS THAT IF WE'RE GOING TO TRY AND BREAK HIM OUT, WE'RE GOING TO NEED A *LOT* OF FIREPOWER.
NO.
WHAT?
I SAID, NO. NO FIREPOWER.
I'VE GOTTEN INSIDE BANKS, CASINOS, AND MANSIONS WITH MILLION DOLLAR SECURITY SYSTEMS, AND EACH TIME, I'VE WALKED RIGHT IN THE FRONT DOOR, WITH AN INVITATION.

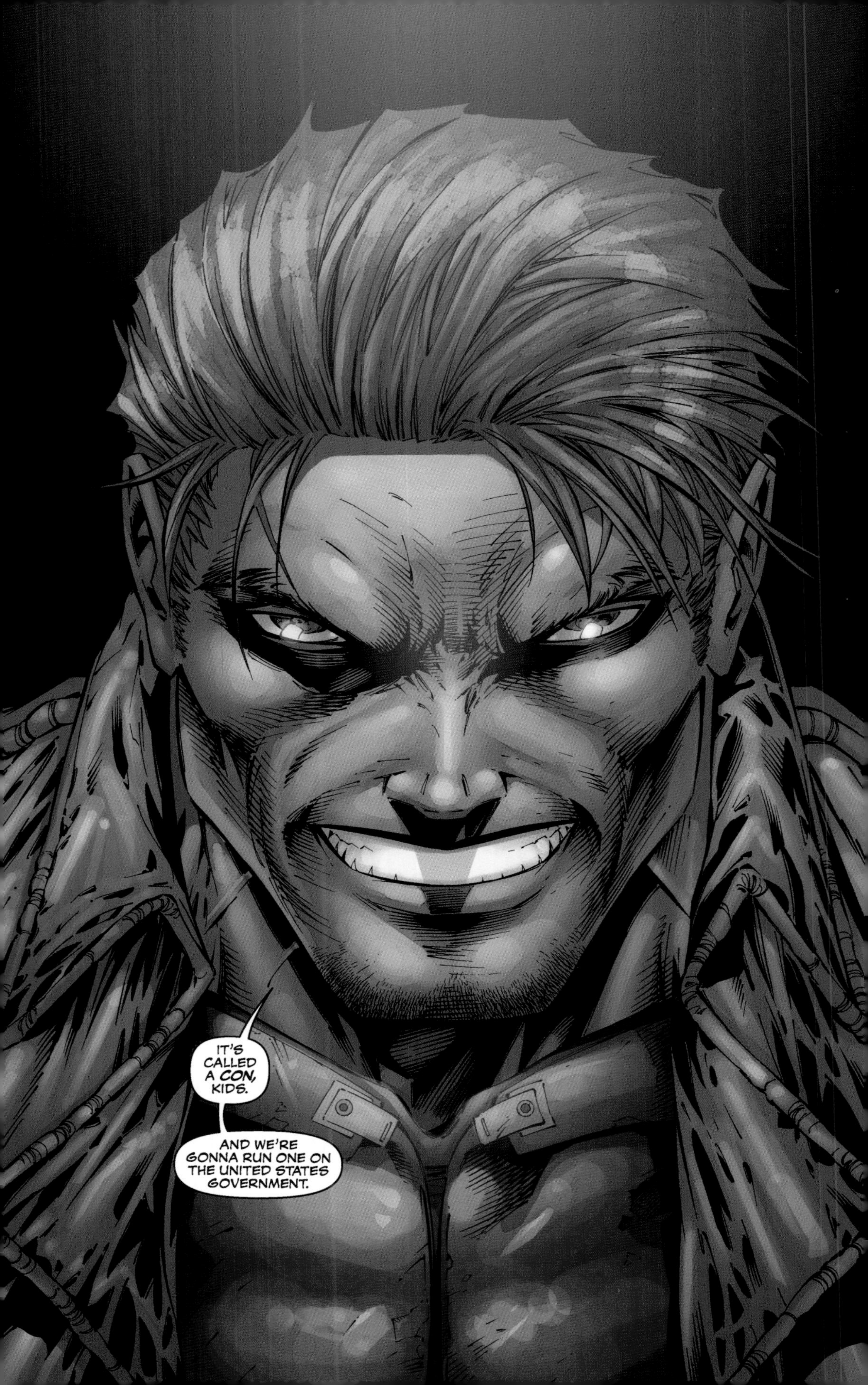
IT'S CALLED A CON, KIDS.
AND WE'RE GONNA RUN ONE ON THE UNITED STATES GOVERNMENT.

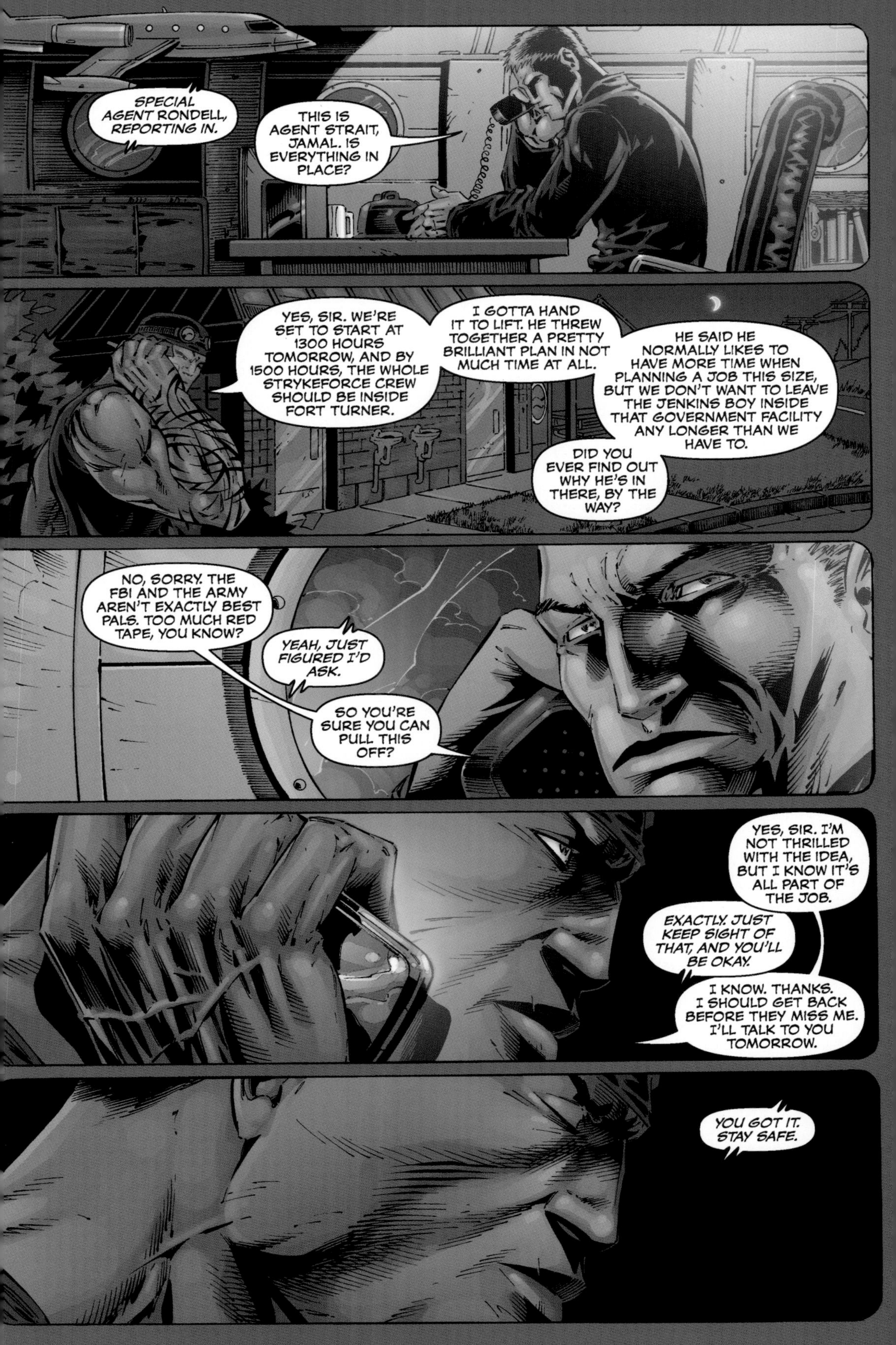
SPECIAL AGENT RONDELL, REPORTING IN.
THIS IS AGENT STRAIT, JAMAL. IS EVERYTHING IN PLACE?
YES, SIR. WE'RE SET TO START AT 1300 HOURS TOMORROW, AND BY 1500 HOURS, THE WHOLE STRYKEFORCE CREW SHOULD BE INSIDE FORT TURNER.
I GOTTA HAND IT TO LIFT. HE THREW TOGETHER A PRETTY BRILLIANT PLAN IN NOT MUCH TIME AT ALL.
HE SAID HE NORMALLY LIKES TO HAVE MORE TIME WHEN PLANNING A JOB THIS SIZE, BUT WE DON'T WANT TO LEAVE THE JENKINS BOY INSIDE THAT GOVERNMENT FACILITY ANY LONGER THAN WE HAVE TO.
DID YOU EVER FIND OUT WHY HE'S IN THERE, BY THE WAY?
NO, SORRY. THE FBI AND THE ARMY AREN'T EXACTLY BEST PALS. TOO MUCH RED TAPE, YOU KNOW?
YEAH, JUST FIGURED I'D ASK.
SO YOU'RE SURE YOU CAN PULL THIS OFF?
YES, SIR. I'M NOT THRILLED WITH THE IDEA, BUT I KNOW IT'S ALL PART OF THE JOB.
EXACTLY. JUST KEEP SIGHT OF THAT, AND YOU'LL BE OKAY.
I KNOW. THANKS. I SHOULD GET BACK BEFORE THEY MISS ME. I'LL TALK TO YOU TOMORROW.
YOU GOT IT. STAY SAFE.

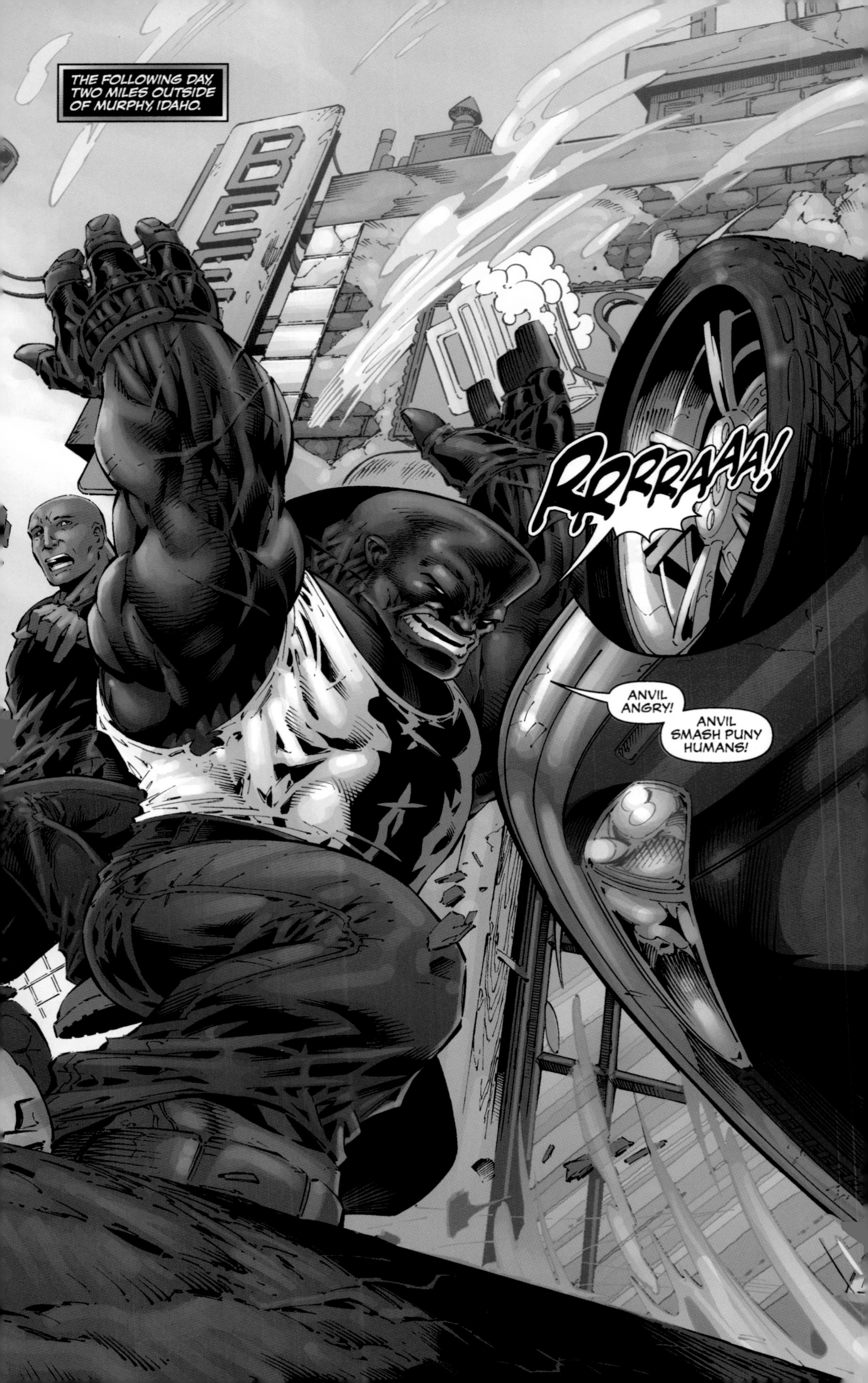
THE FOLLOWING DAY, TWO MILES OUTSIDE OF MURPHY, IDAHO.
RRRRAAA!
ANVIL ANGRY!
ANVIL SMASH PUNY HUMANS!

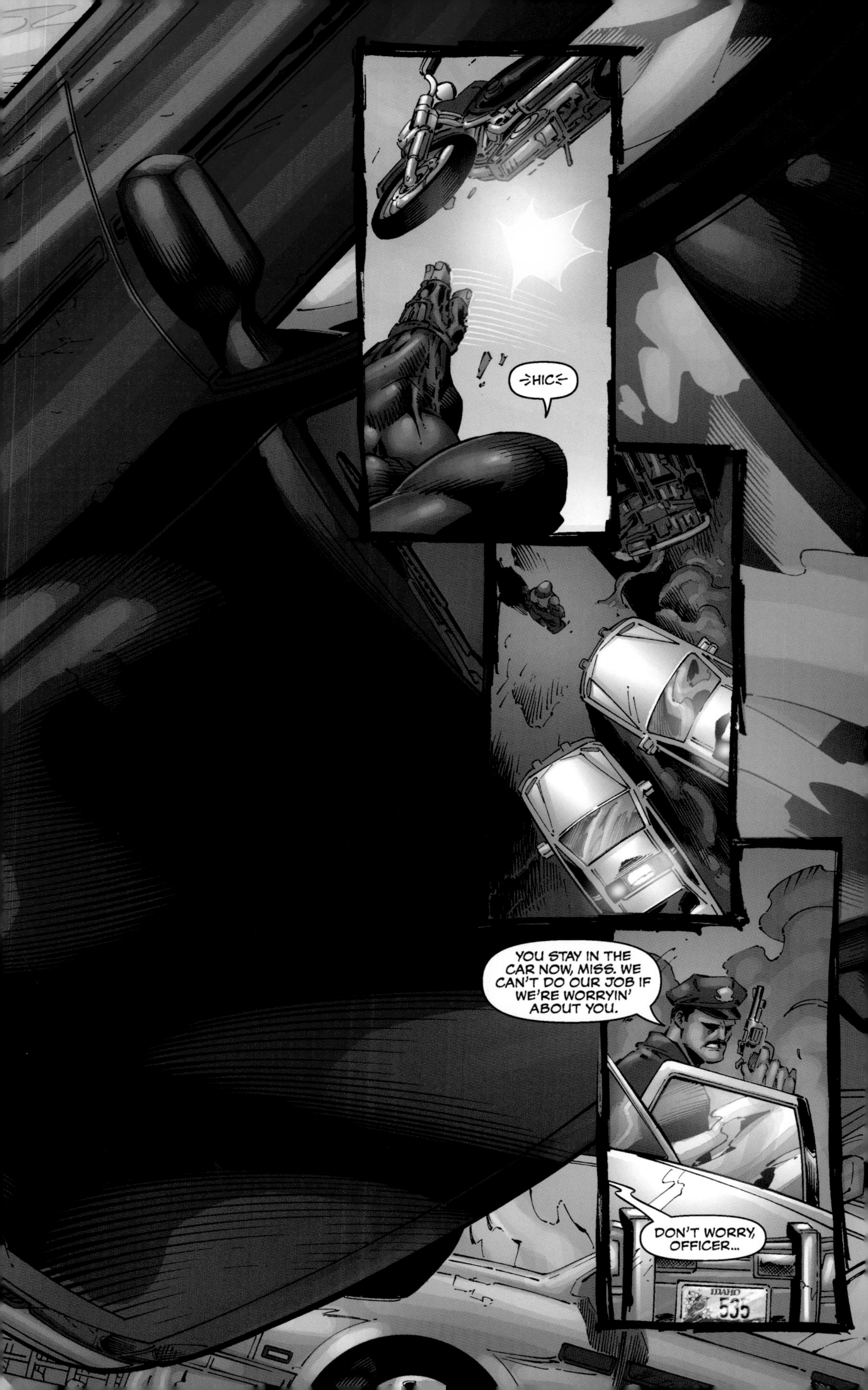
HIC
YOU STAY IN THE CAR NOW, MISS. WE CAN'T DO OUR JOB IF WE'RE WORRYIN' ABOUT YOU.
DON'T WORRY, OFFICER...

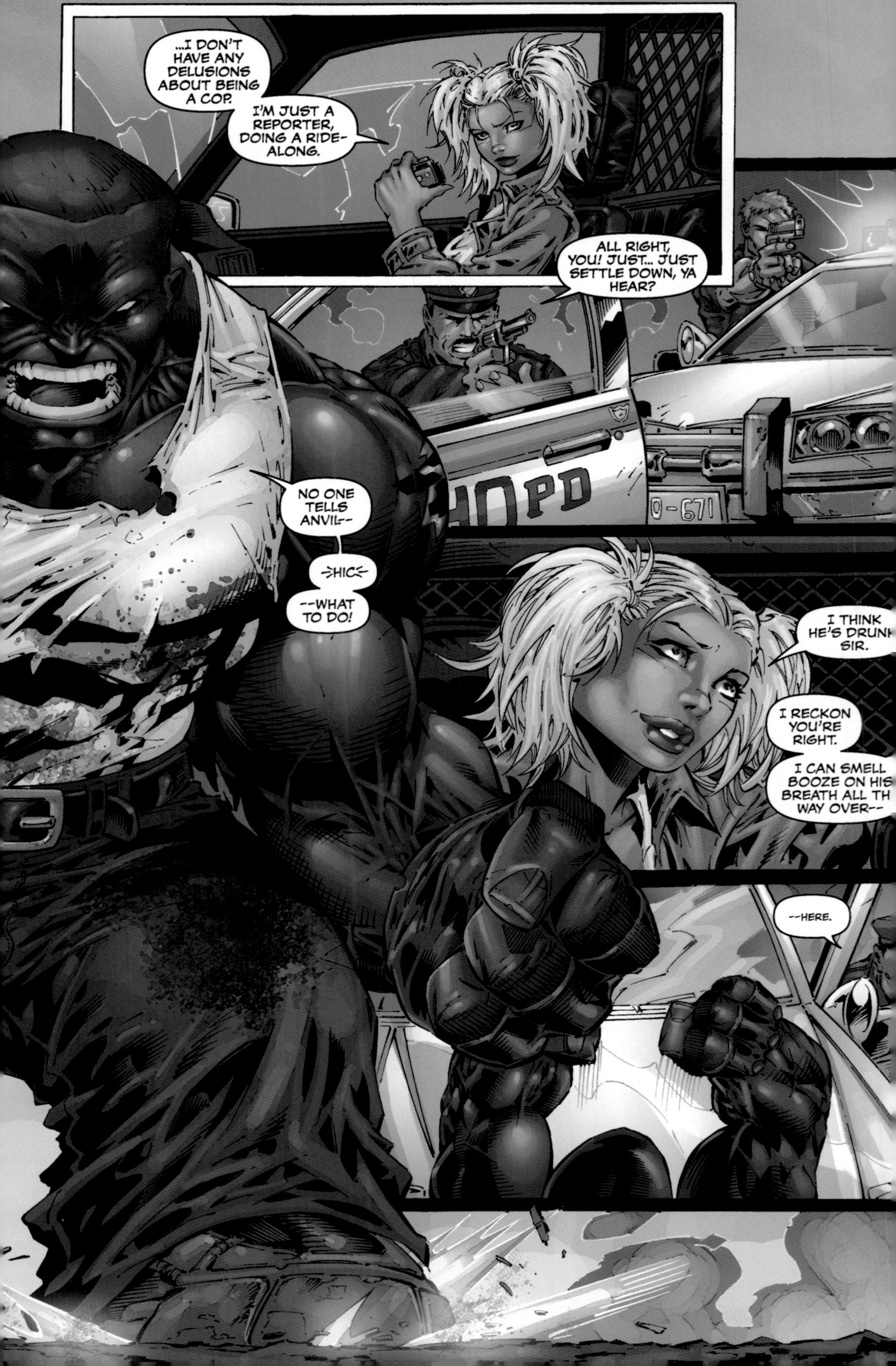

...I DON'T HAVE ANY DELUSIONS ABOUT BEING A COP.
I'M JUST A REPORTER, DOING A RIDE-ALONG.
ALL RIGHT, YOU! JUST... JUST SETTLE DOWN, YA HEAR?
NO ONE TELLS ANVIL--
HIC
--WHAT TO DO!
I THINK HE'S DRUNK SIR.
I RECKON YOU'RE RIGHT.
I CAN SMELL BOOZE ON HIS BREATH ALL TH WAY OVER--
--HERE.

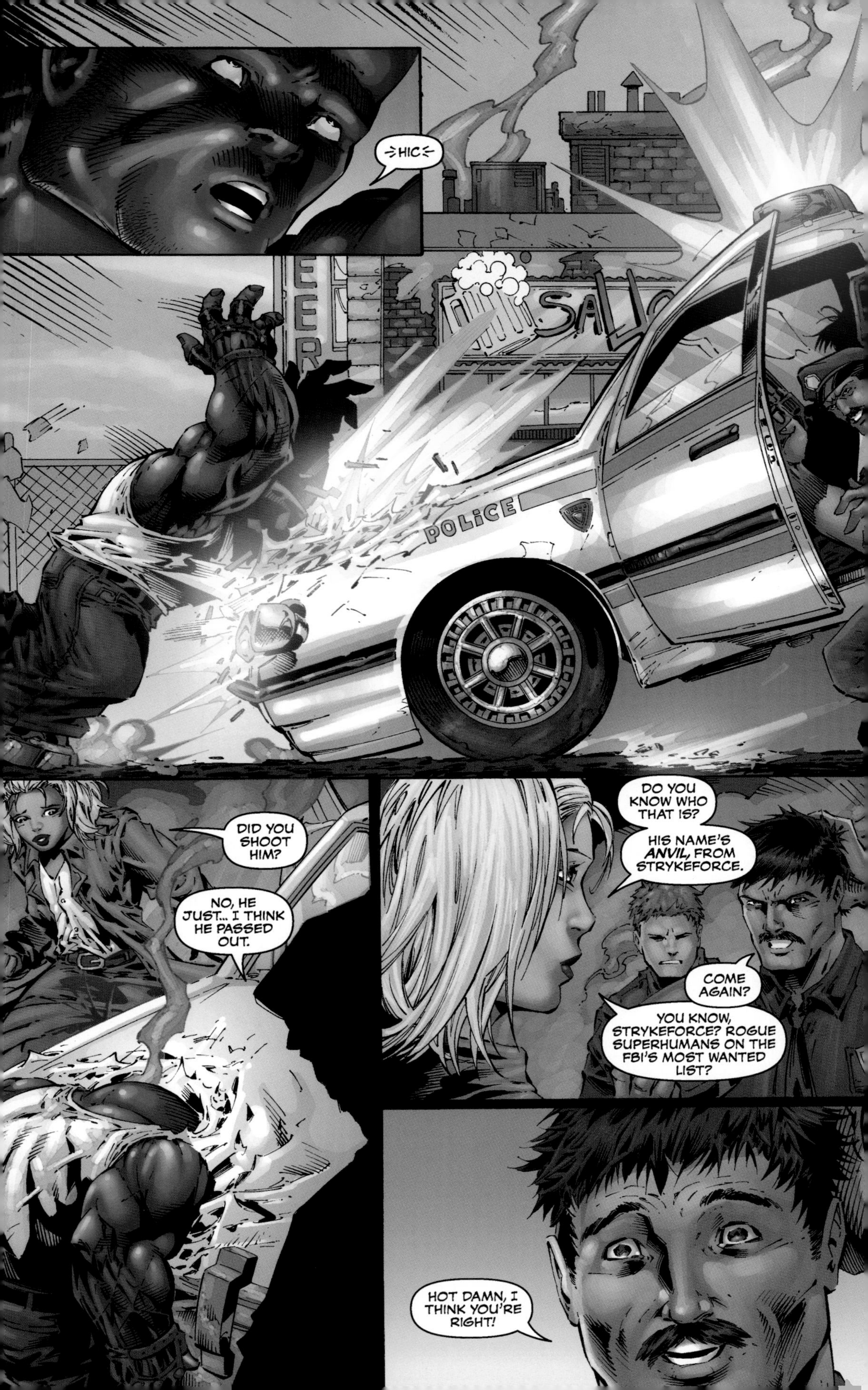

HIC
POLICE
DID YOU SHOOT HIM?
NO, HE JUST... I THINK HE PASSED OUT.
DO YOU KNOW WHO THAT IS?
HIS NAME'S *ANVIL*, FROM STRYKEFORCE.
COME AGAIN?
YOU KNOW, STRYKEFORCE? ROGUE SUPERHUMANS ON THE FBI'S MOST WANTED LIST?
HOT DAMN, I THINK YOU'RE RIGHT!

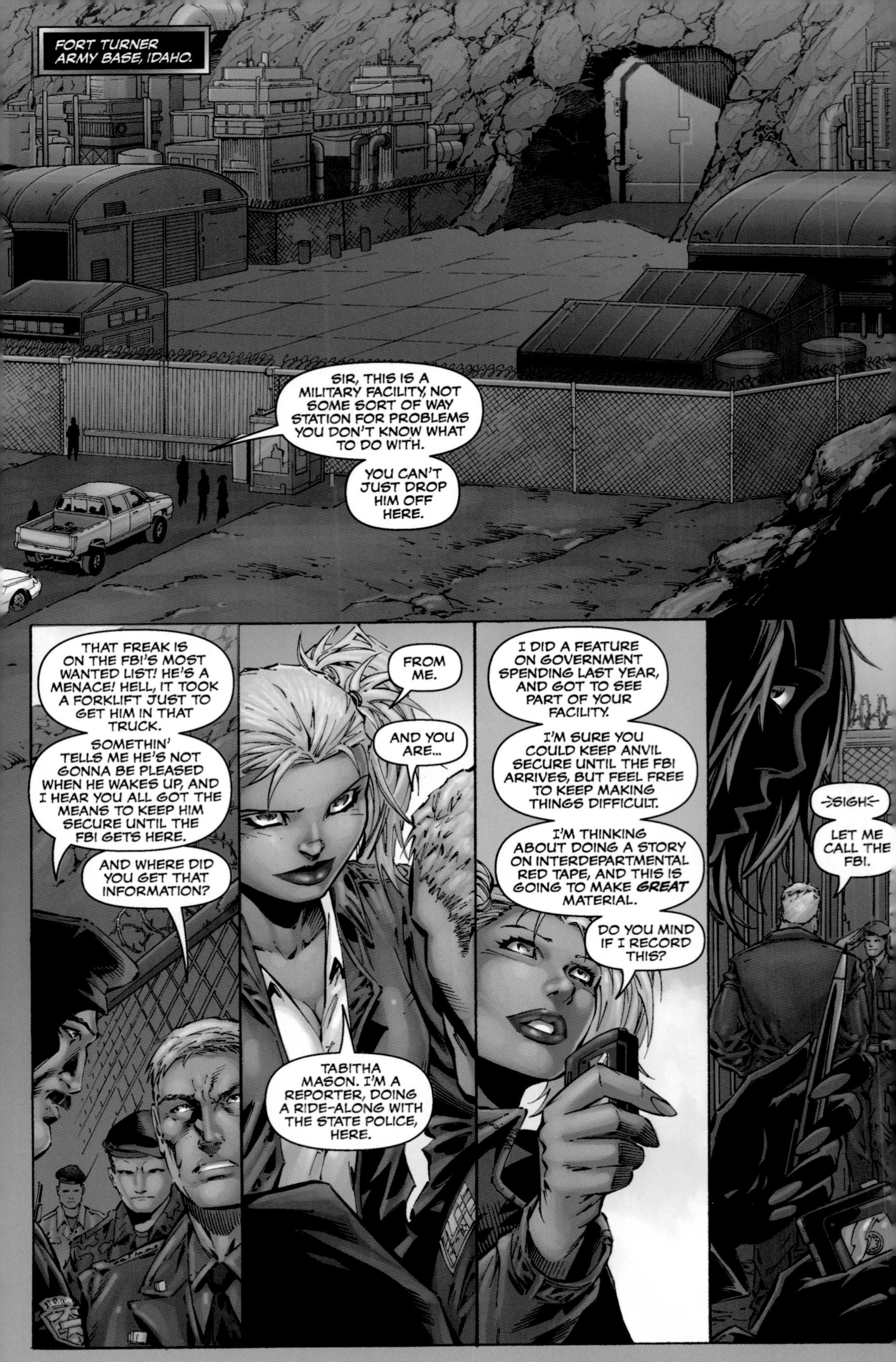
FORT TURNER ARMY BASE, IDAHO.
SIR, THIS IS A MILITARY FACILITY, NOT SOME SORT OF WAY STATION FOR PROBLEMS YOU DON'T KNOW WHAT TO DO WITH.
YOU CAN'T JUST DROP HIM OFF HERE.
THAT FREAK IS ON THE FBI'S MOST WANTED LIST! HE'S A MENACE! HELL, IT TOOK A FORKLIFT JUST TO GET HIM IN THAT TRUCK.
SOMETHIN' TELLS ME HE'S NOT GONNA BE PLEASED WHEN HE WAKES UP, AND I HEAR YOU ALL GOT THE MEANS TO KEEP HIM SECURE UNTIL THE FBI GETS HERE.
AND WHERE DID YOU GET THAT INFORMATION?
FROM ME.
AND YOU ARE...
TABITHA MASON. I'M A REPORTER, DOING A RIDE-ALONG WITH THE STATE POLICE, HERE.
I DID A FEATURE ON GOVERNMENT SPENDING LAST YEAR, AND GOT TO SEE PART OF YOUR FACILITY.
I'M SURE YOU COULD KEEP ANVIL SECURE UNTIL THE FBI ARRIVES, BUT FEEL FREE TO KEEP MAKING THINGS DIFFICULT.
I'M THINKING ABOUT DOING A STORY ON INTERDEPARTMENTAL RED TAPE, AND THIS IS GOING TO MAKE GREAT MATERIAL.
DO YOU MIND IF I RECORD THIS?
SIGH
LET ME CALL THE FBI.

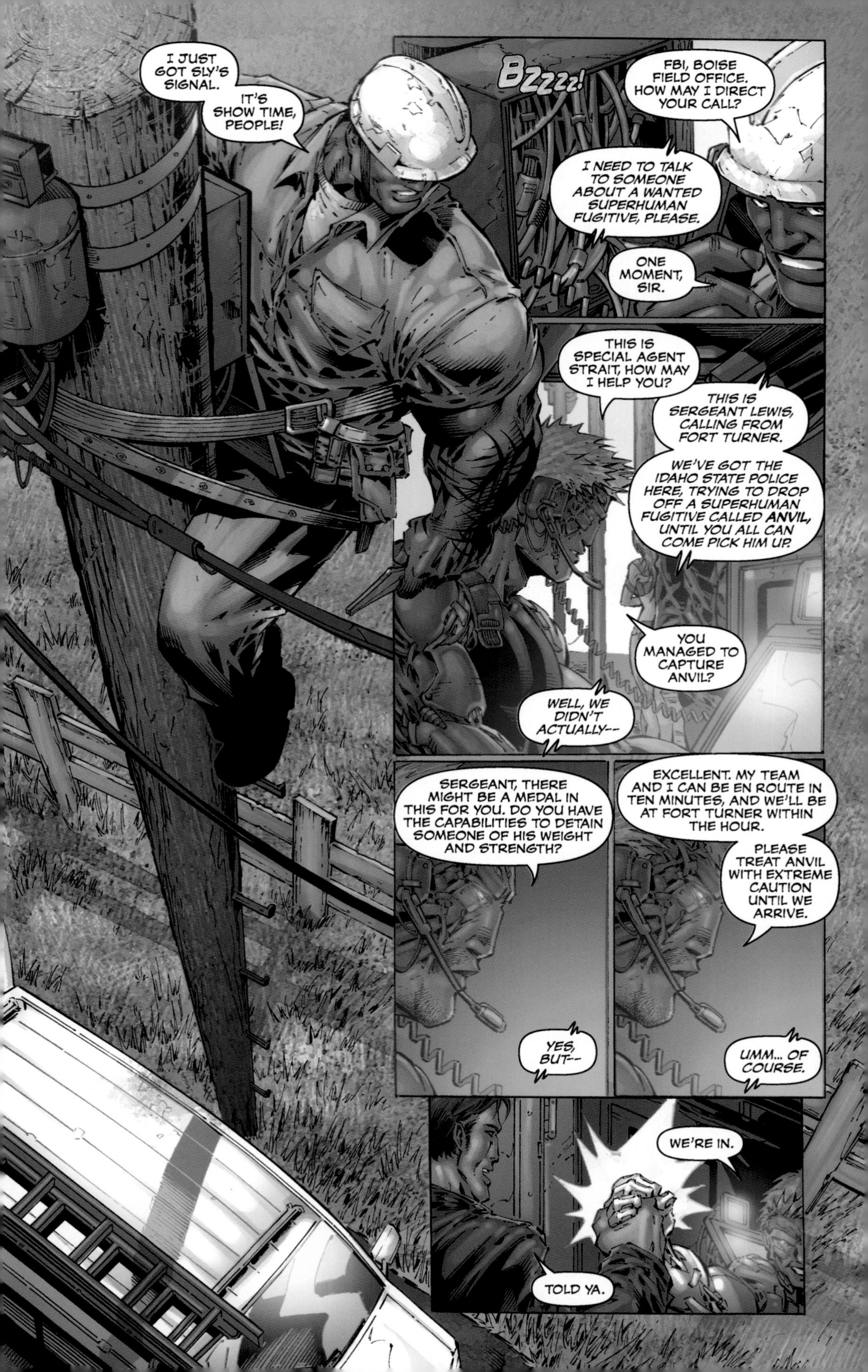
I JUST GOT SLY'S SIGNAL.
IT'S SHOW TIME, PEOPLE!
BZZZZ!
FBI, BOISE FIELD OFFICE. HOW MAY I DIRECT YOUR CALL?
I NEED TO TALK TO SOMEONE ABOUT A WANTED SUPERHUMAN FUGITIVE, PLEASE.
ONE MOMENT, SIR.
THIS IS SPECIAL AGENT STRAIT, HOW MAY I HELP YOU?
THIS IS SERGEANT LEWIS, CALLING FROM FORT TURNER.
WE'VE GOT THE IDAHO STATE POLICE HERE, TRYING TO DROP OFF A SUPERHUMAN FUGITIVE CALLED ANVIL, UNTIL YOU ALL CAN COME PICK HIM UP.
YOU MANAGED TO CAPTURE ANVIL?
WELL, WE DIDN'T ACTUALLY--
SERGEANT, THERE MIGHT BE A MEDAL IN THIS FOR YOU. DO YOU HAVE THE CAPABILITIES TO DETAIN SOMEONE OF HIS WEIGHT AND STRENGTH?
YES, BUT--
EXCELLENT. MY TEAM AND I CAN BE EN ROUTE IN TEN MINUTES, AND WE'LL BE AT FORT TURNER WITHIN THE HOUR.
PLEASE TREAT ANVIL WITH EXTREME CAUTION UNTIL WE ARRIVE.
UMM... OF COURSE.
WE'RE IN.
TOLD YA.

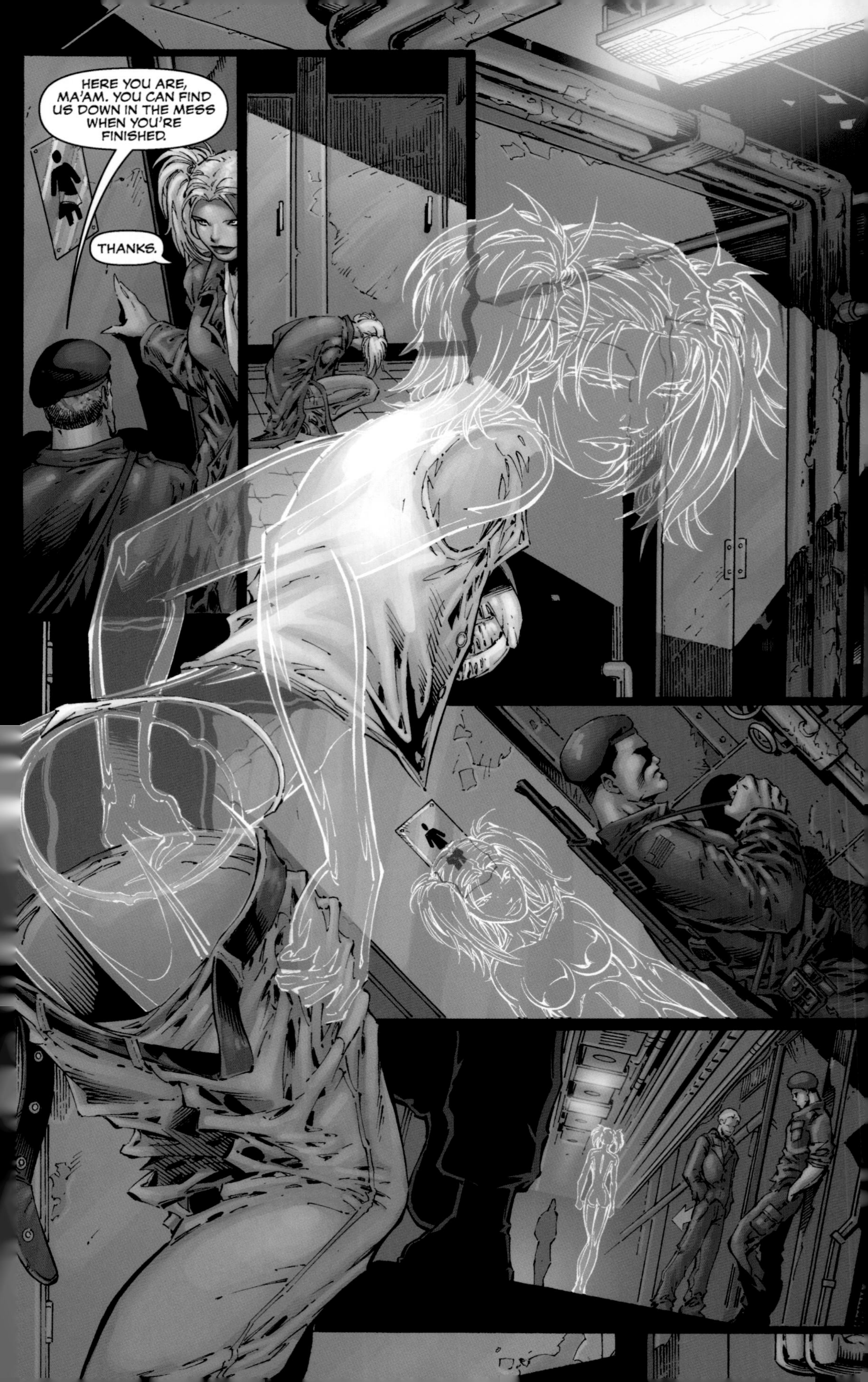
HERE YOU ARE, MA'AM. YOU CAN FIND US DOWN IN THE MESS WHEN YOU'RE FINISHED.
THANKS.

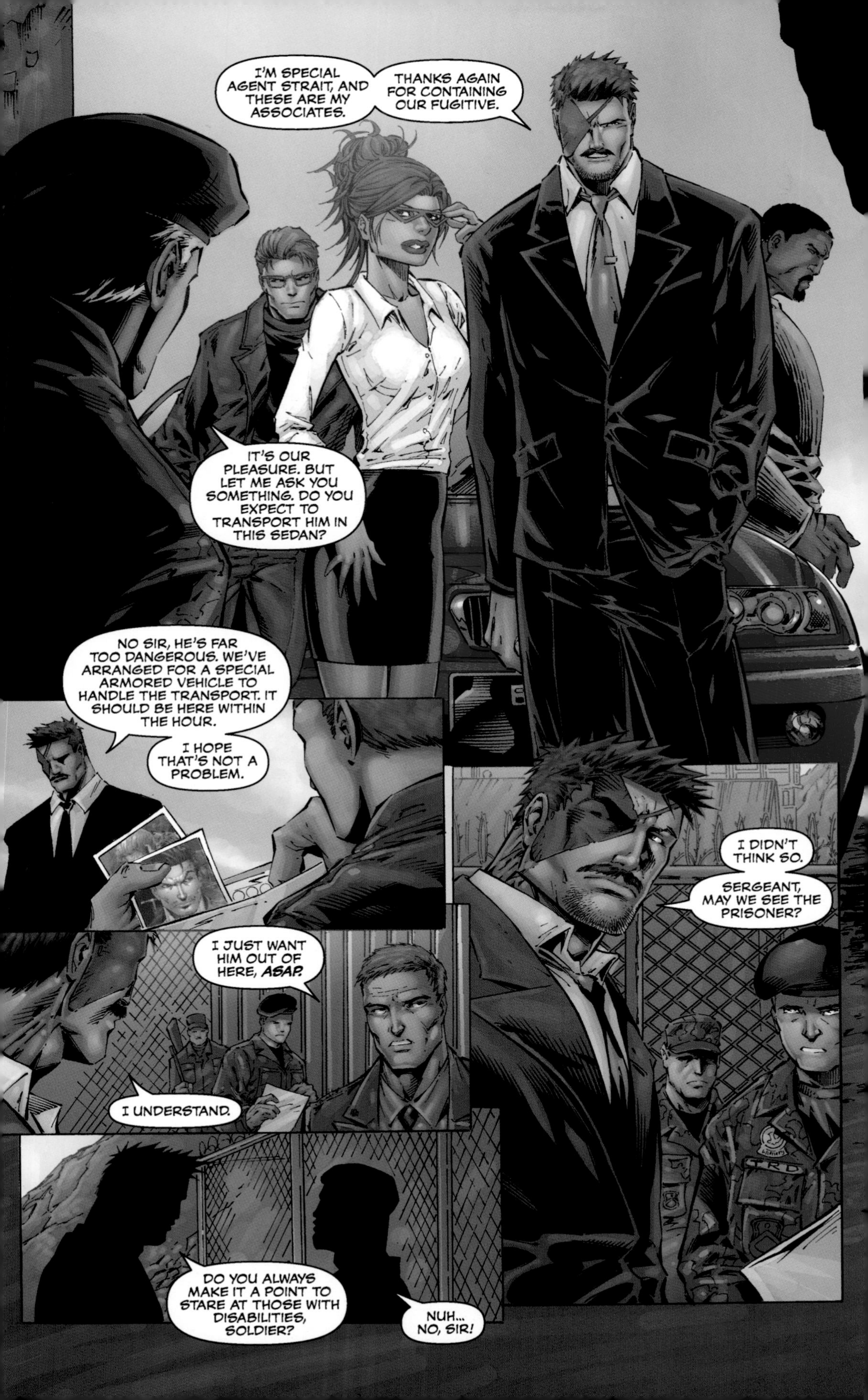
I'M SPECIAL AGENT STRAIT, AND THESE ARE MY ASSOCIATES.
THANKS AGAIN FOR CONTAINING OUR FUGITIVE.
IT'S OUR PLEASURE. BUT LET ME ASK YOU SOMETHING. DO YOU EXPECT TO TRANSPORT HIM IN THIS SEDAN?
NO SIR, HE'S FAR TOO DANGEROUS. WE'VE ARRANGED FOR A SPECIAL ARMORED VEHICLE TO HANDLE THE TRANSPORT. IT SHOULD BE HERE WITHIN THE HOUR.
I HOPE THAT'S NOT A PROBLEM.
I DIDN'T THINK SO.
SERGEANT, MAY WE SEE THE PRISONER?
I JUST WANT HIM OUT OF HERE, ASAP.
I UNDERSTAND.
DO YOU ALWAYS MAKE IT A POINT TO STARE AT THOSE WITH DISABILITIES, SOLDIER?
NUH... NO, SIR!

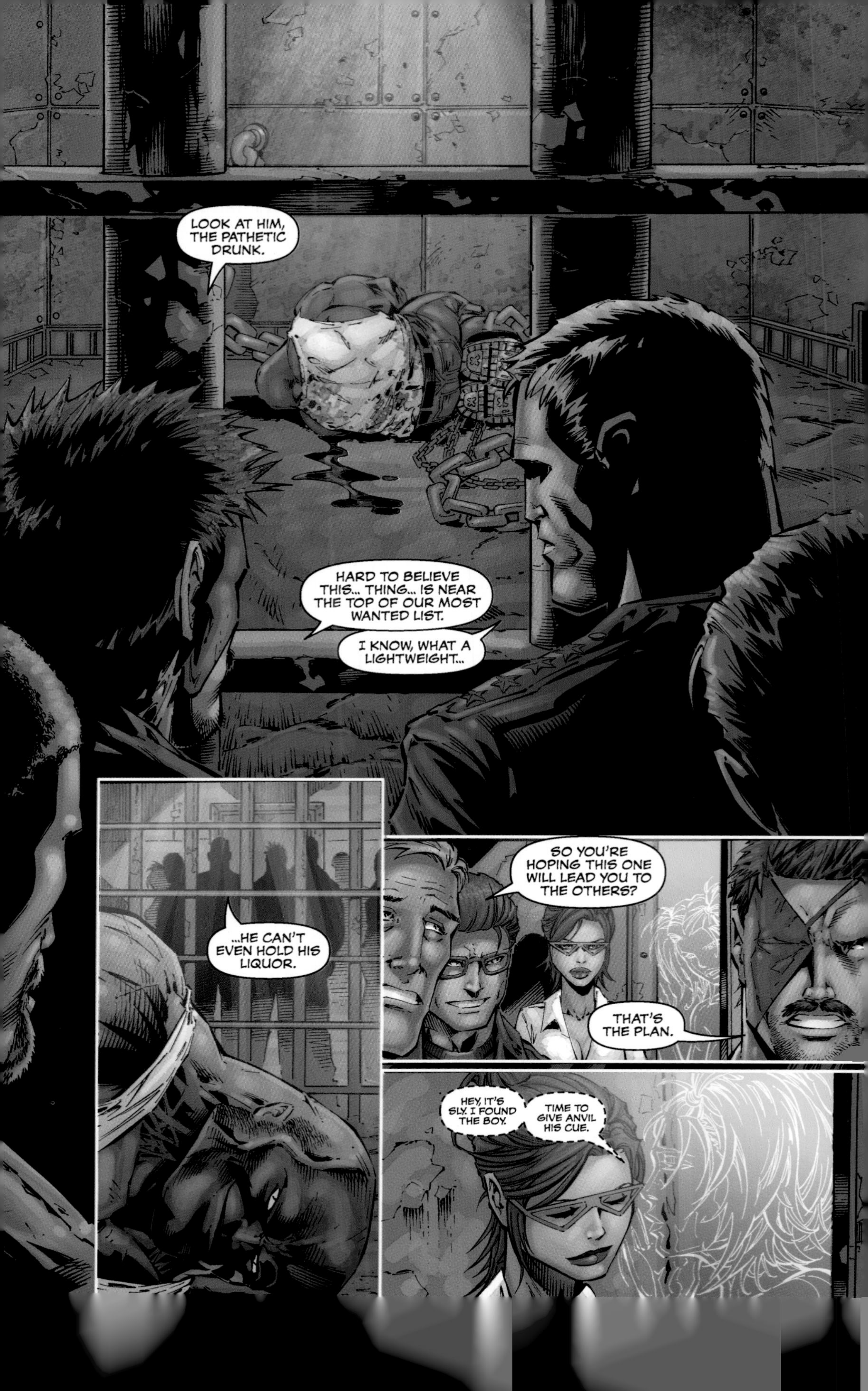
LOOK AT HIM, THE PATHETIC DRUNK.
HARD TO BELIEVE THIS... THING... IS NEAR THE TOP OF OUR MOST WANTED LIST.
I KNOW, WHAT A LIGHTWEIGHT...
...HE CAN'T EVEN HOLD HIS LIQUOR.
SO YOU'RE HOPING THIS ONE WILL LEAD YOU TO THE OTHERS?
THAT'S THE PLAN.
HEY, IT'S SLY. I FOUND THE BOY.
TIME TO GIVE ANVIL HIS CUE.

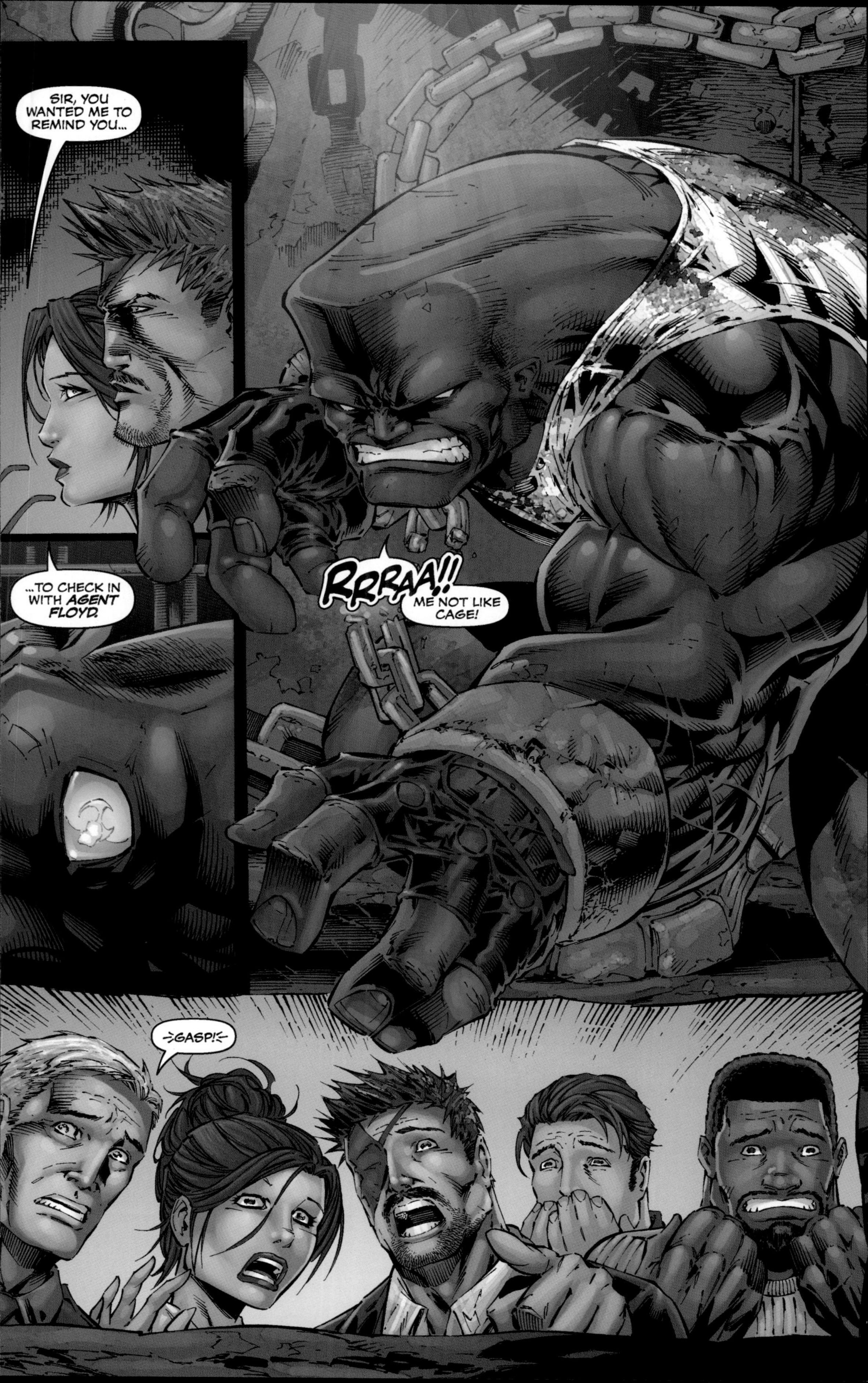
SIR, YOU WANTED ME TO REMIND YOU...
...TO CHECK IN WITH AGENT FLOYD.
RRRAA!!
ME NOT LIKE CAGE!
GASP!

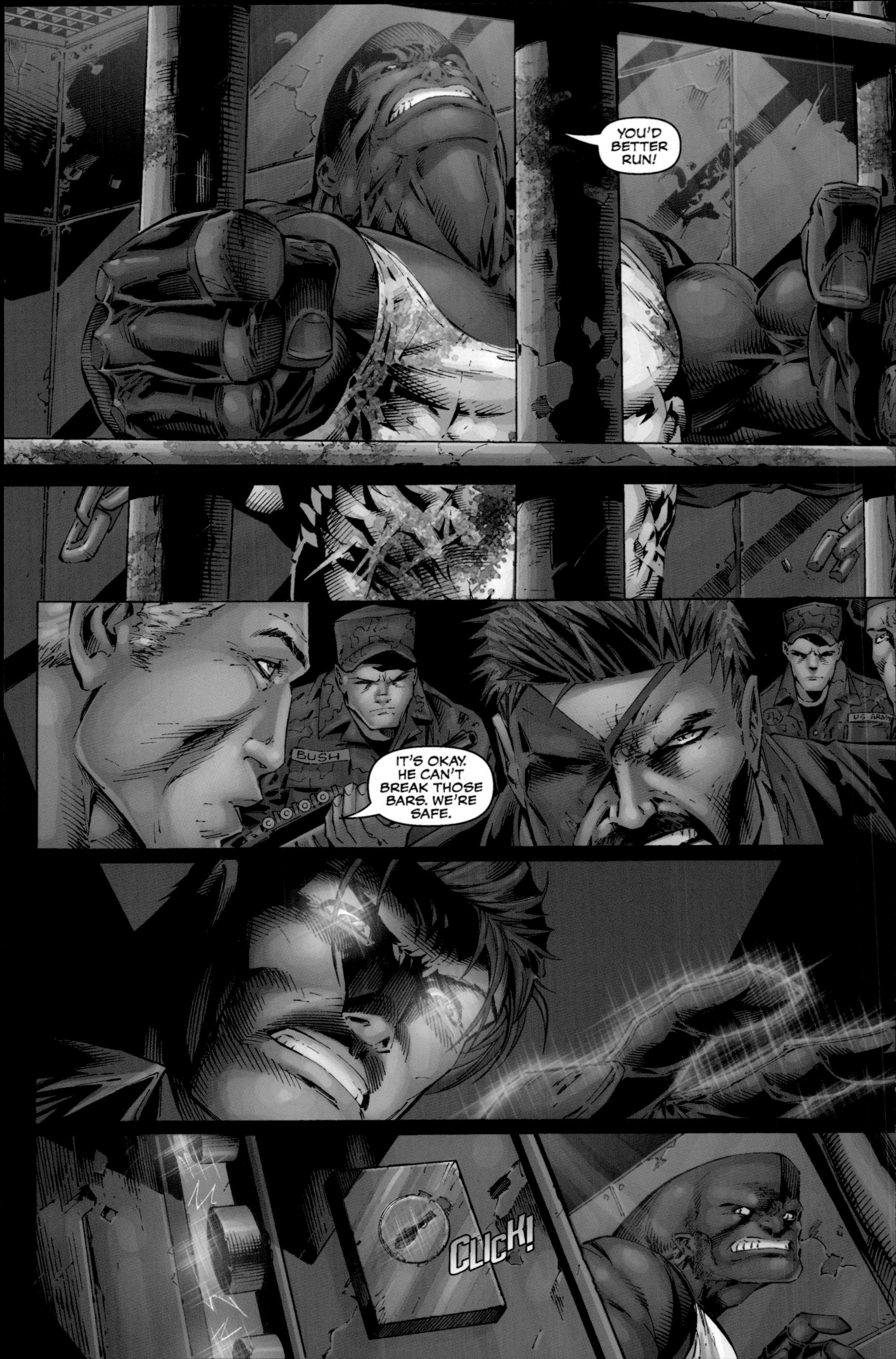
YOU'D BETTER RUN!
BUSH
US ARMY
IT'S OKAY. HE CAN'T BREAK THOSE BARS. WE'RE SAFE.
CLICK!

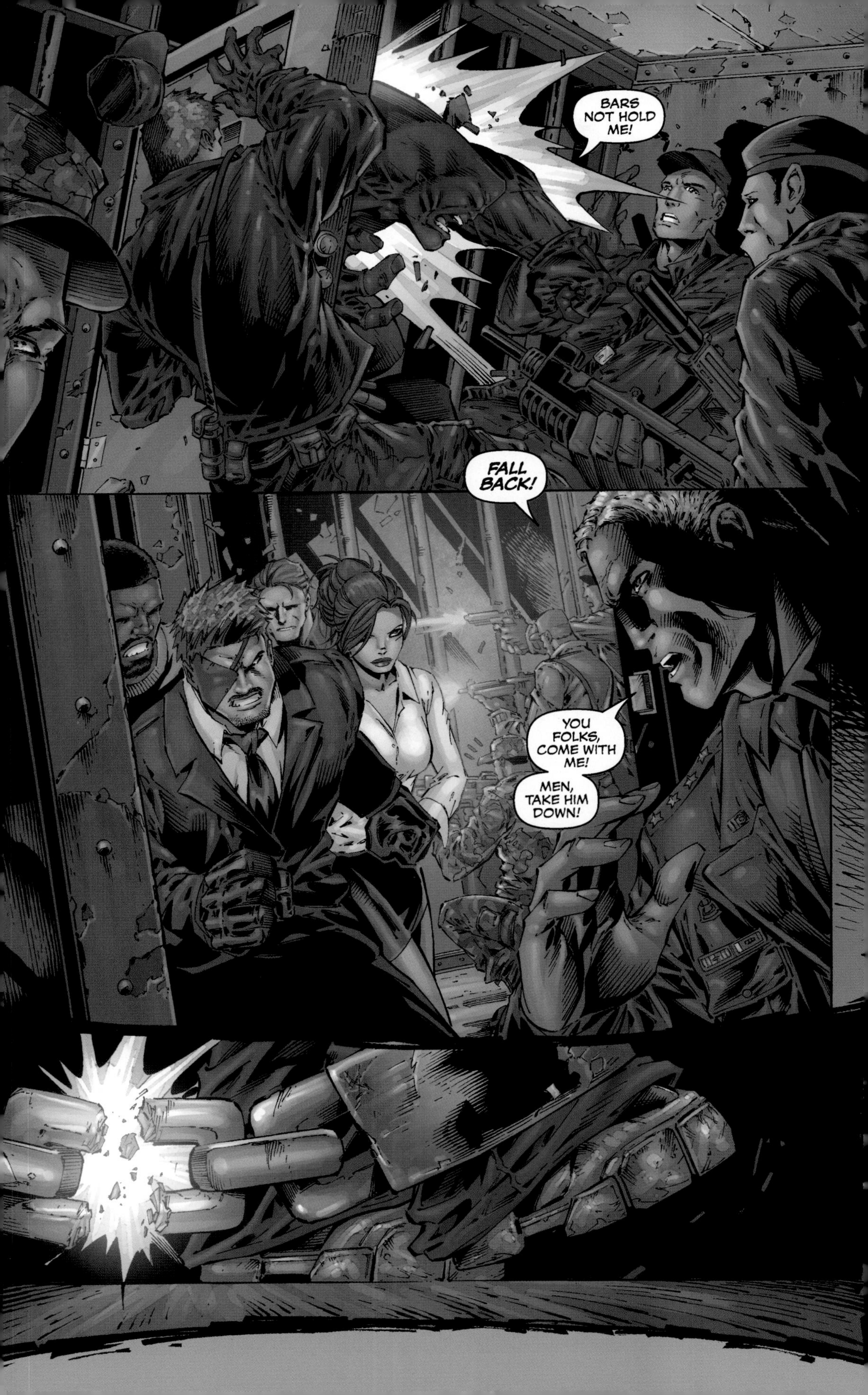
BARS NOT HOLD ME!
FALL BACK!
YOU FOLKS, COME WITH ME!
MEN, TAKE HIM DOWN!

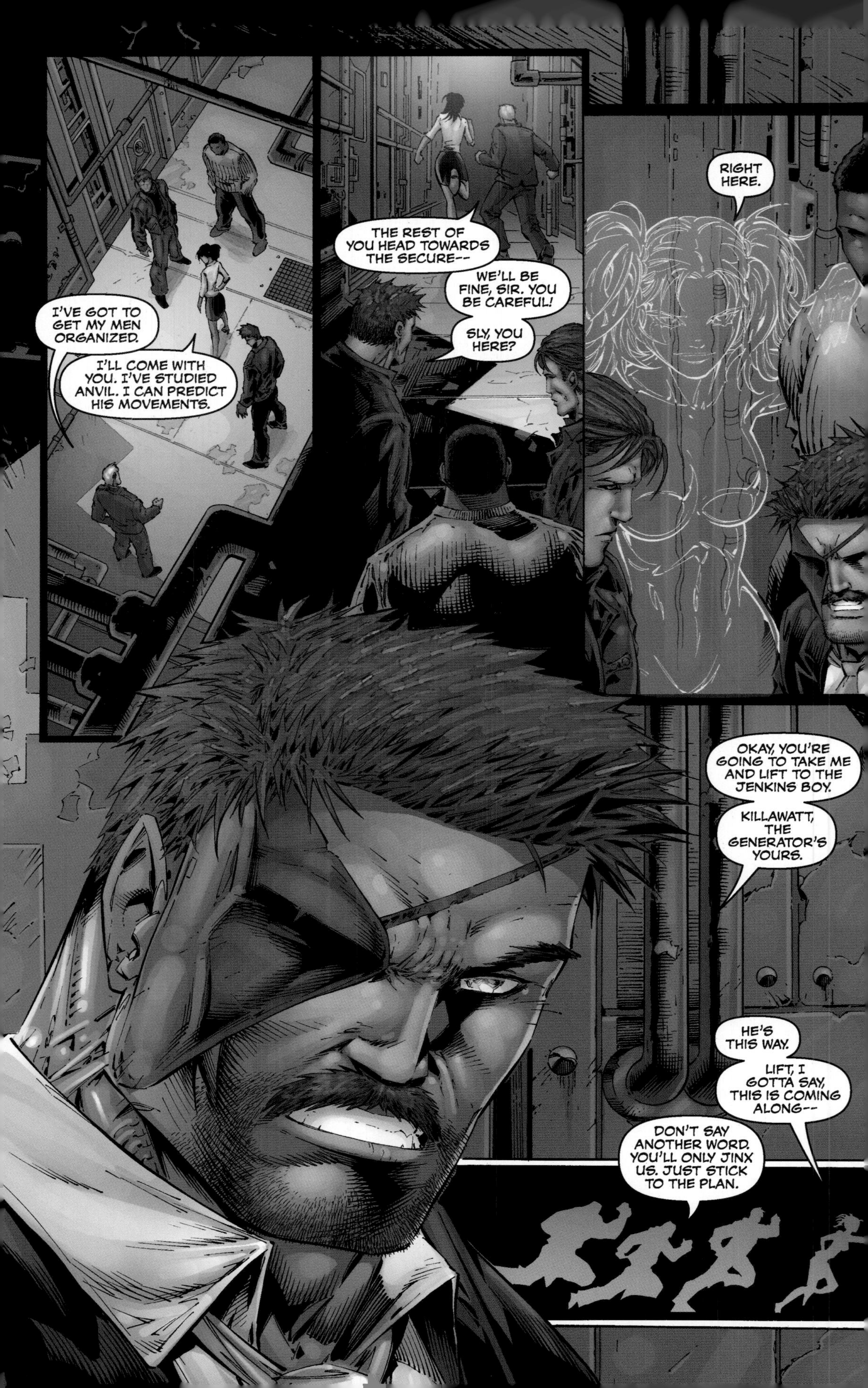
I'VE GOT TO GET MY MEN ORGANIZED.
I'LL COME WITH YOU. I'VE STUDIED ANVIL. I CAN PREDICT HIS MOVEMENTS.
THE REST OF YOU HEAD TOWARDS THE SECURE--
WE'LL BE FINE, SIR. YOU BE CAREFUL!
SLY, YOU HERE?
RIGHT HERE.
OKAY, YOU'RE GOING TO TAKE ME AND LIFT TO THE JENKINS BOY.
KILLAWATT, THE GENERATOR'S YOURS.
HE'S THIS WAY.
LIFT, I GOTTA SAY, THIS IS COMING ALONG--
DON'T SAY ANOTHER WORD. YOU'LL ONLY JINX US. JUST STICK TO THE PLAN.

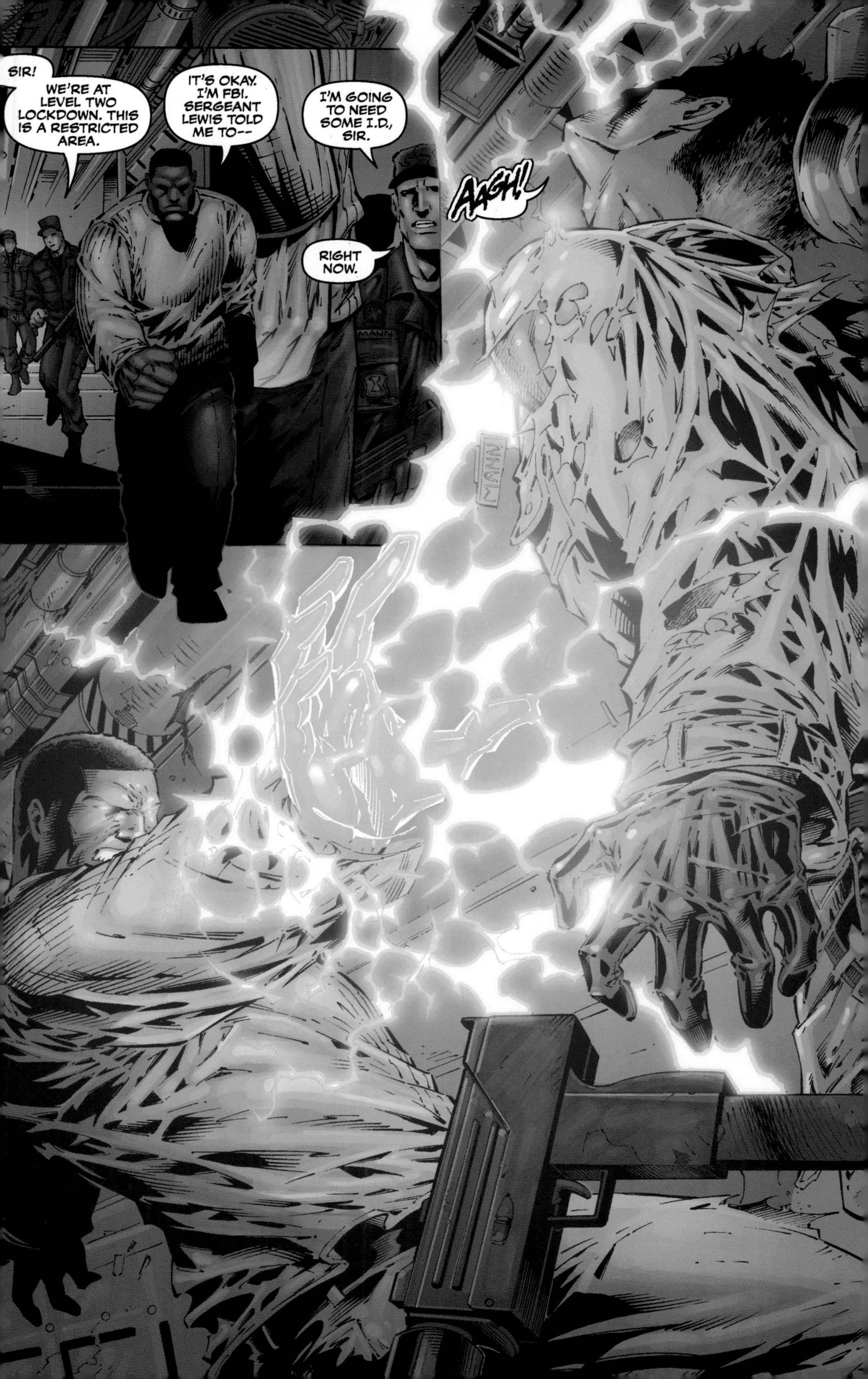

SIR!
WE'RE AT LEVEL TWO LOCKDOWN. THIS IS A RESTRICTED AREA.
IT'S OKAY. I'M FBI. SERGEANT LEWIS TOLD ME TO--
I'M GOING TO NEED SOME I.D., SIR.
RIGHT NOW.
AAGH!

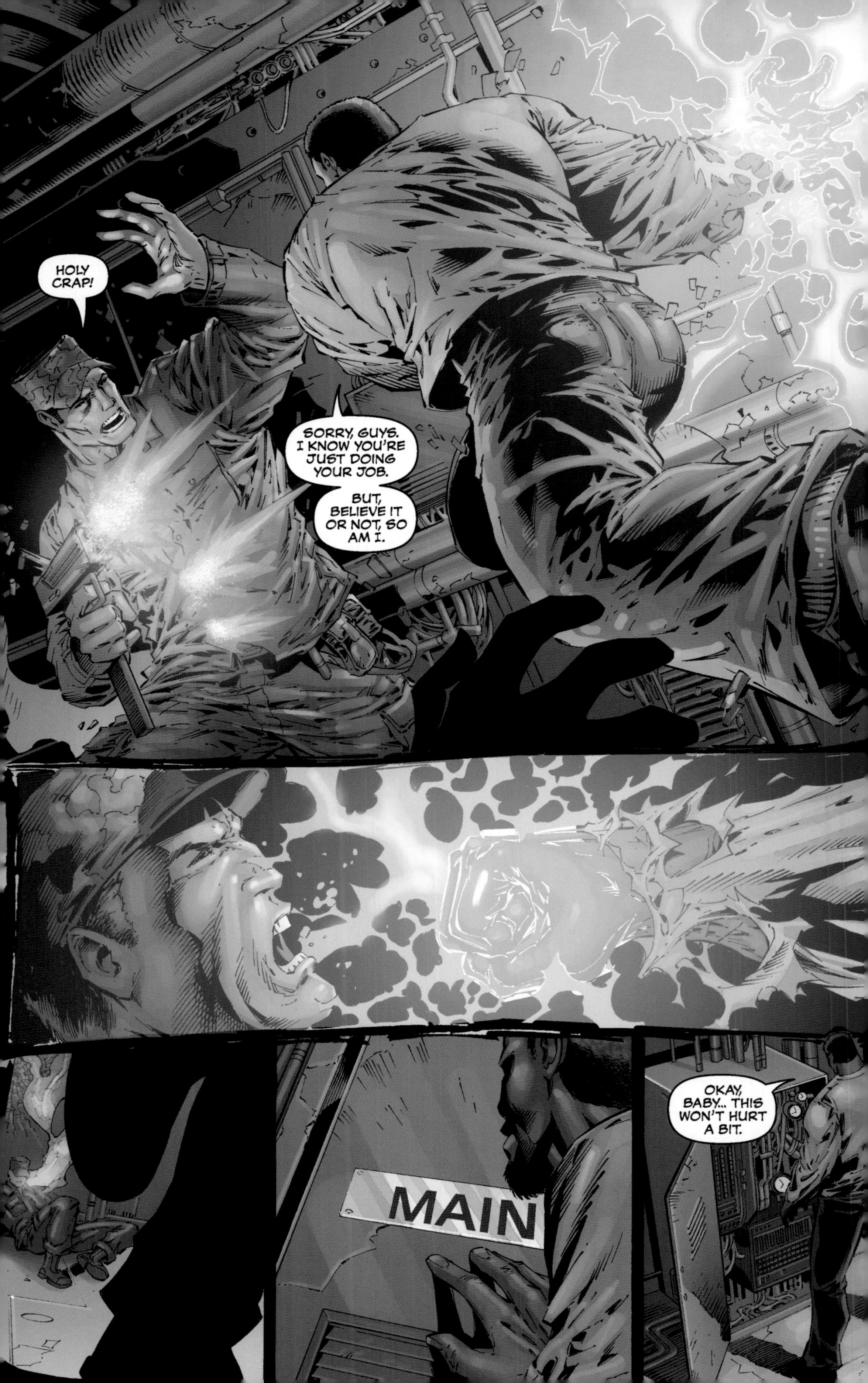
HOLY CRAP!
SORRY, GUYS. I KNOW YOU'RE JUST DOING YOUR JOB.
BUT, BELIEVE IT OR NOT, SO AM I.
MAIN
OKAY, BABY... THIS WON'T HURT A BIT.

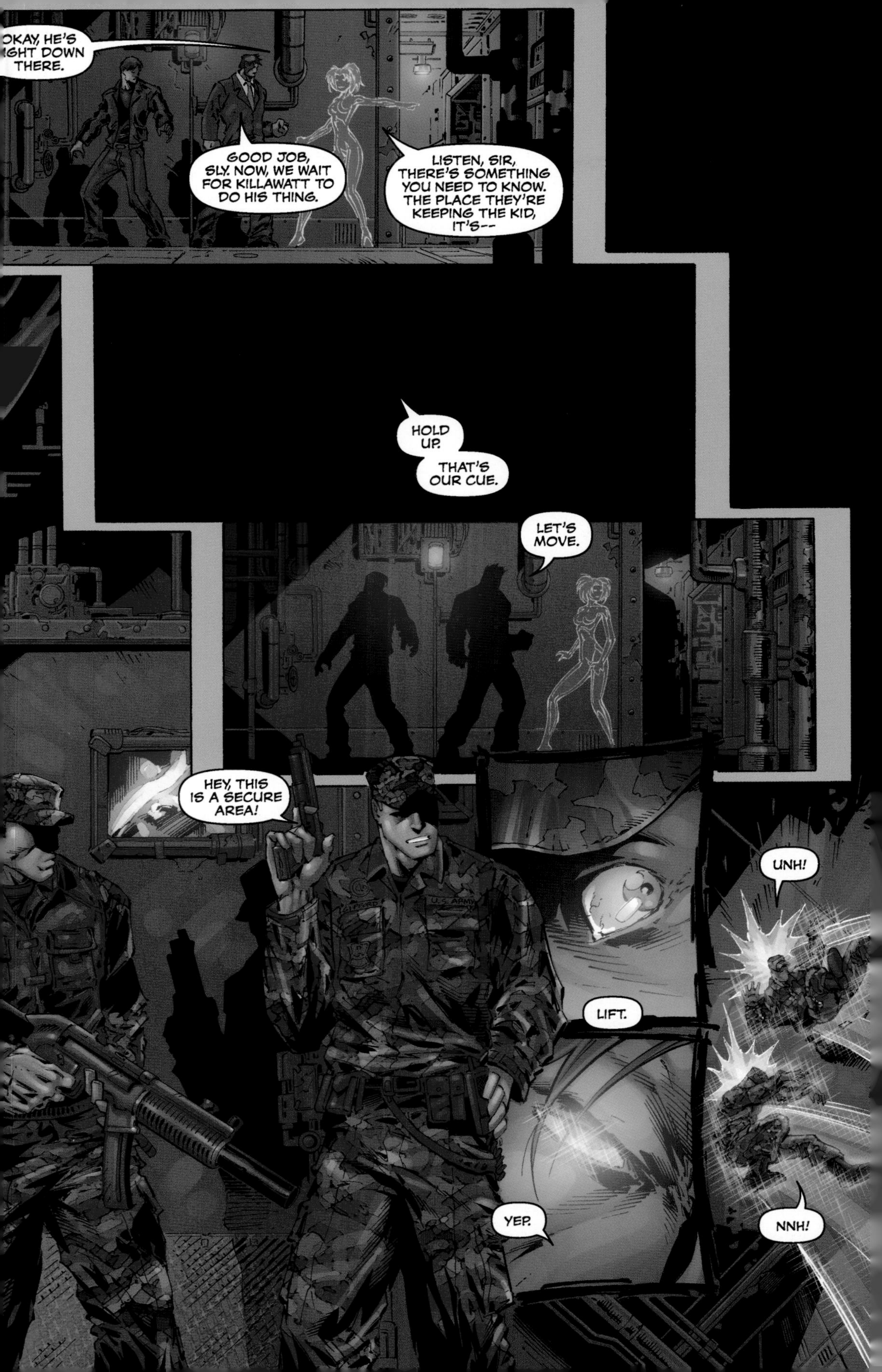
OKAY, HE'S
GHT DOWN
THERE.
GOOD JOB, SLY. NOW, WE WAIT FOR KILLAWATT TO DO HIS THING.
LISTEN, SIR, THERE'S SOMETHING YOU NEED TO KNOW. THE PLACE THEY'RE KEEPING THE KID, IT'S--
HOLD UP.
THAT'S OUR CUE.
LET'S MOVE.
HEY, THIS IS A SECURE AREA!
LIFT.
YEP.
UNH!
NNH!

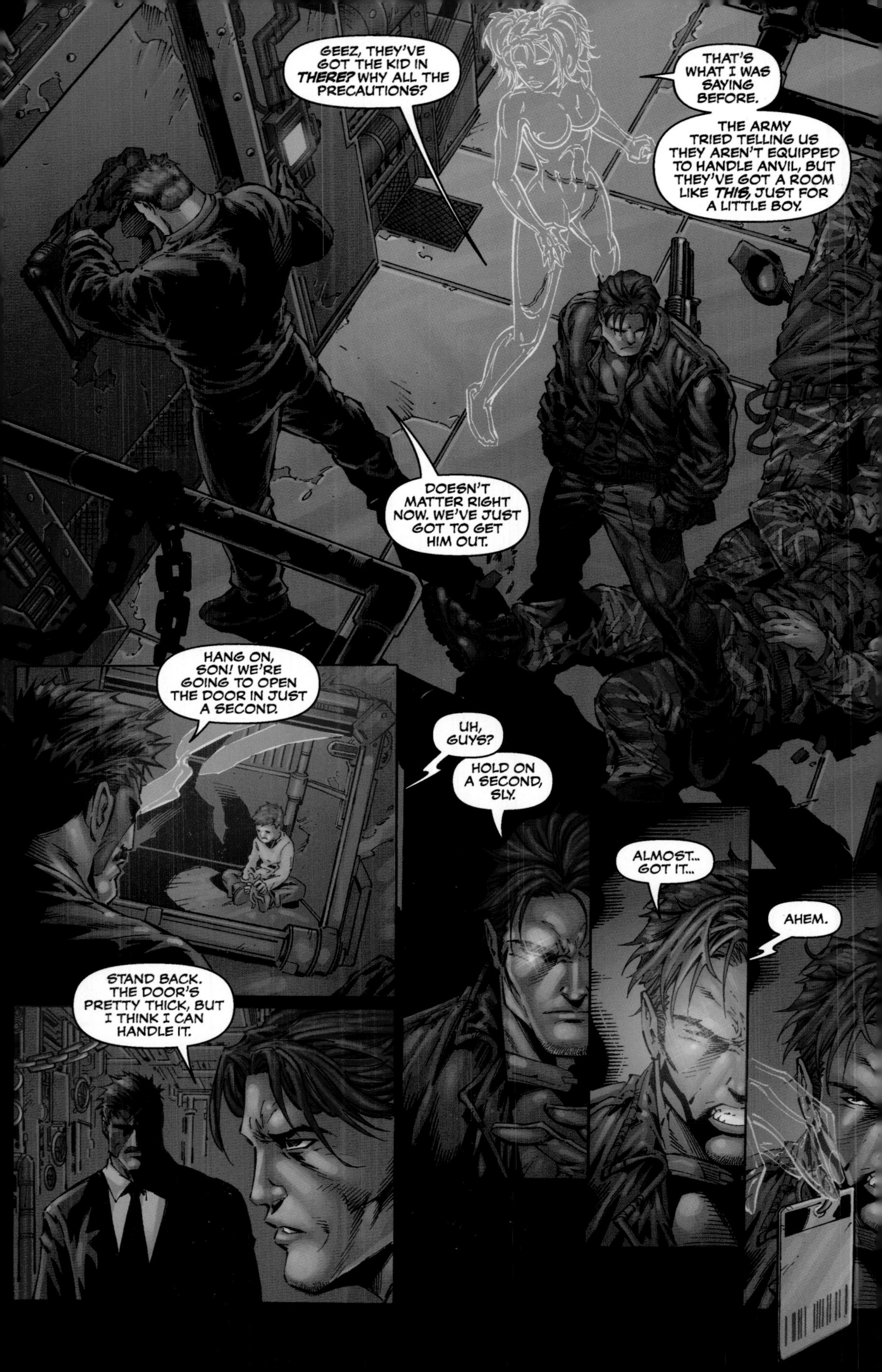
GEEZ, THEY'VE GOT THE KID IN *THERE?* WHY ALL THE PRECAUTIONS?
THAT'S WHAT I WAS SAYING BEFORE.
THE ARMY TRIED TELLING US THEY AREN'T EQUIPPED TO HANDLE ANVIL, BUT THEY'VE GOT A ROOM LIKE *THIS*, JUST FOR A LITTLE BOY.
DOESN'T MATTER RIGHT NOW. WE'VE JUST GOT TO GET HIM OUT.
HANG ON, SON! WE'RE GOING TO OPEN THE DOOR IN JUST A SECOND.
UH, GUYS?
HOLD ON A SECOND, SLY.
STAND BACK. THE DOOR'S PRETTY THICK, BUT I THINK I CAN HANDLE IT.
ALMOST... GOT IT...
AHEM.

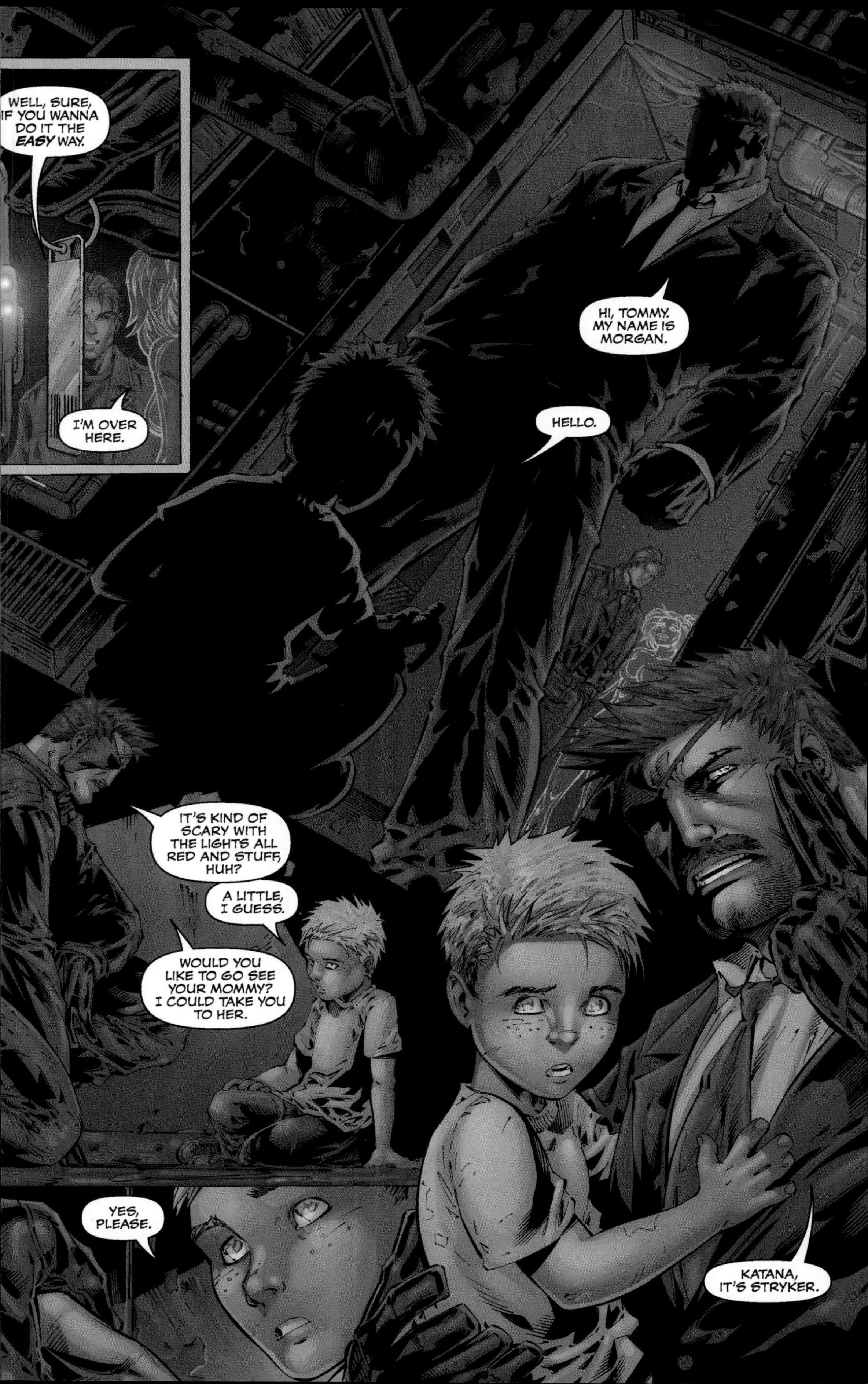
WELL, SURE, IF YOU WANNA DO IT THE EASY WAY.
I'M OVER HERE.
HI, TOMMY. MY NAME IS MORGAN.
HELLO.
IT'S KIND OF SCARY WITH THE LIGHTS ALL RED AND STUFF, HUH?
A LITTLE, I GUESS.
WOULD YOU LIKE TO GO SEE YOUR MOMMY? I COULD TAKE YOU TO HER.
YES, PLEASE.
KATANA, IT'S STRYKER.

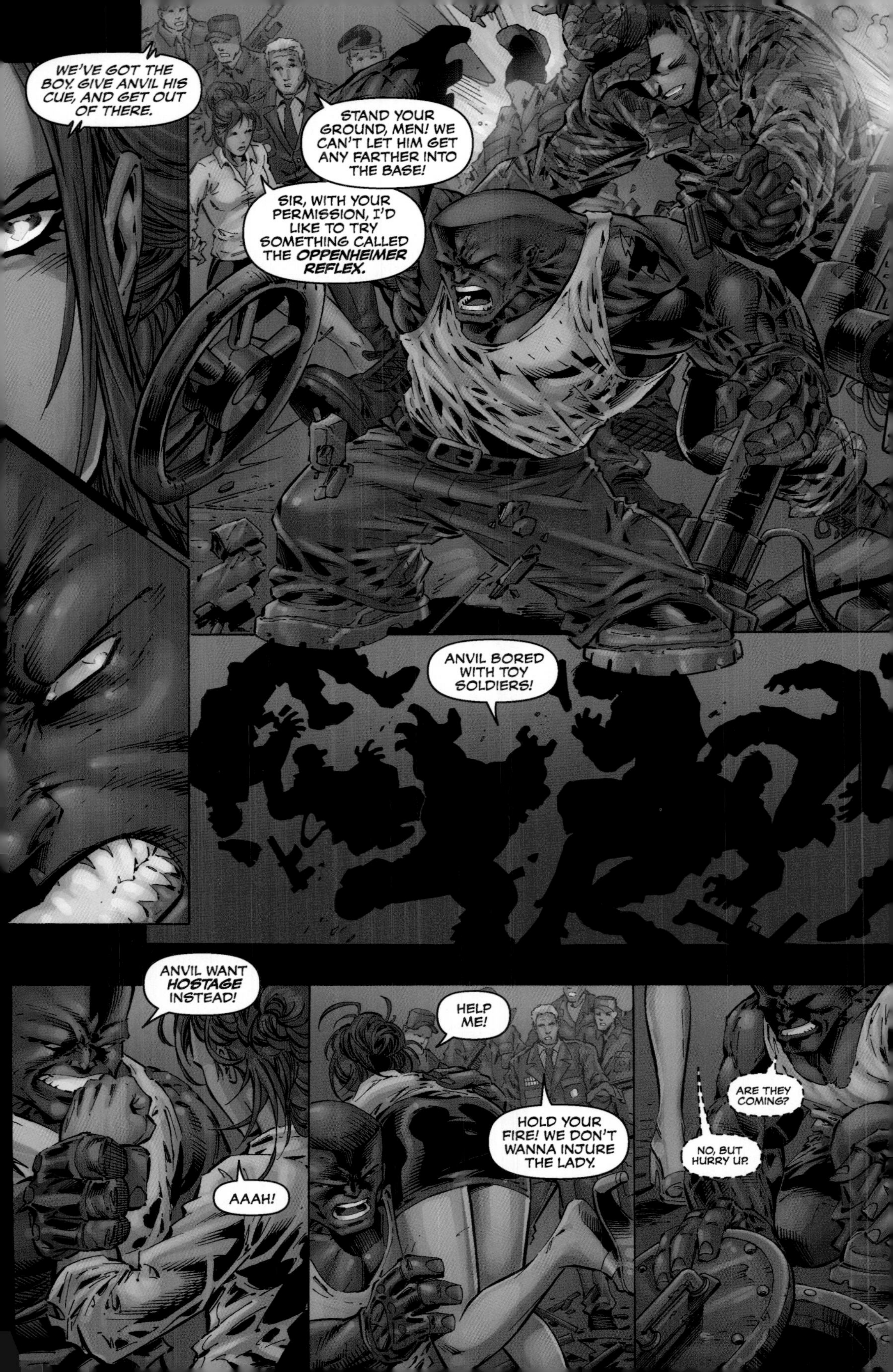
WE'VE GOT THE BOY. GIVE ANVIL HIS CUE, AND GET OUT OF THERE.
STAND YOUR GROUND, MEN! WE CAN'T LET HIM GET ANY FARTHER INTO THE BASE!
SIR, WITH YOUR PERMISSION, I'D LIKE TO TRY SOMETHING CALLED THE OPPENHEIMER REFLEX.
ANVIL BORED WITH TOY SOLDIERS!
ANVIL WANT HOSTAGE INSTEAD!
AAAH!
HELP ME!
HOLD YOUR FIRE! WE DON'T WANNA INJURE THE LADY.
ARE THEY COMING?
NO, BUT HURRY UP.

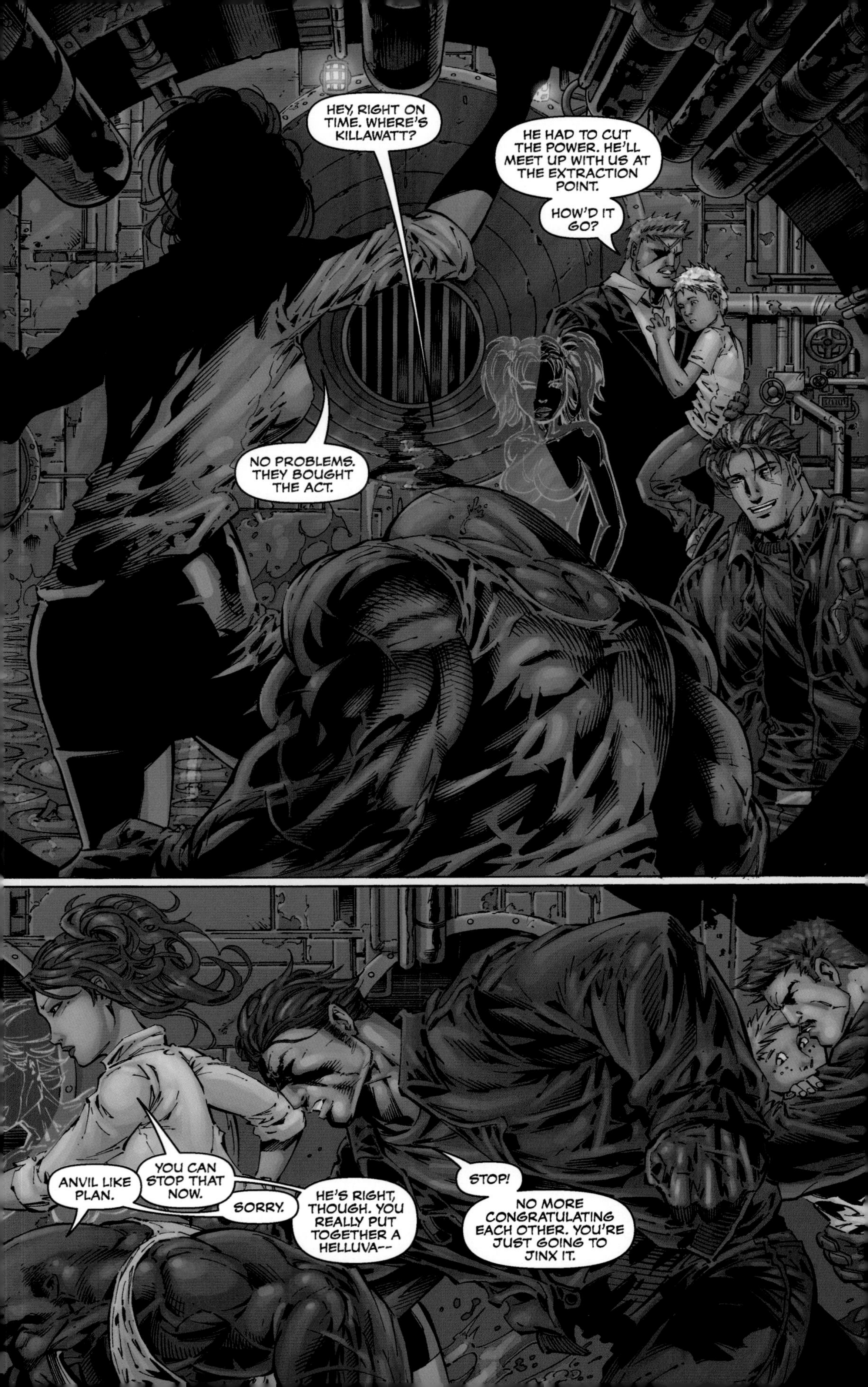
HEY, RIGHT ON TIME. WHERE'S KILLAWATT?
HE HAD TO CUT THE POWER. HE'LL MEET UP WITH US AT THE EXTRACTION POINT.
HOW'D IT GO?
NO PROBLEMS. THEY BOUGHT THE ACT.
ANVIL LIKE PLAN.
YOU CAN STOP THAT NOW.
SORRY.
HE'S RIGHT, THOUGH. YOU REALLY PUT TOGETHER A HELLUVA--
STOP!
NO MORE CONGRATULATING EACH OTHER. YOU'RE JUST GOING TO JINX IT.

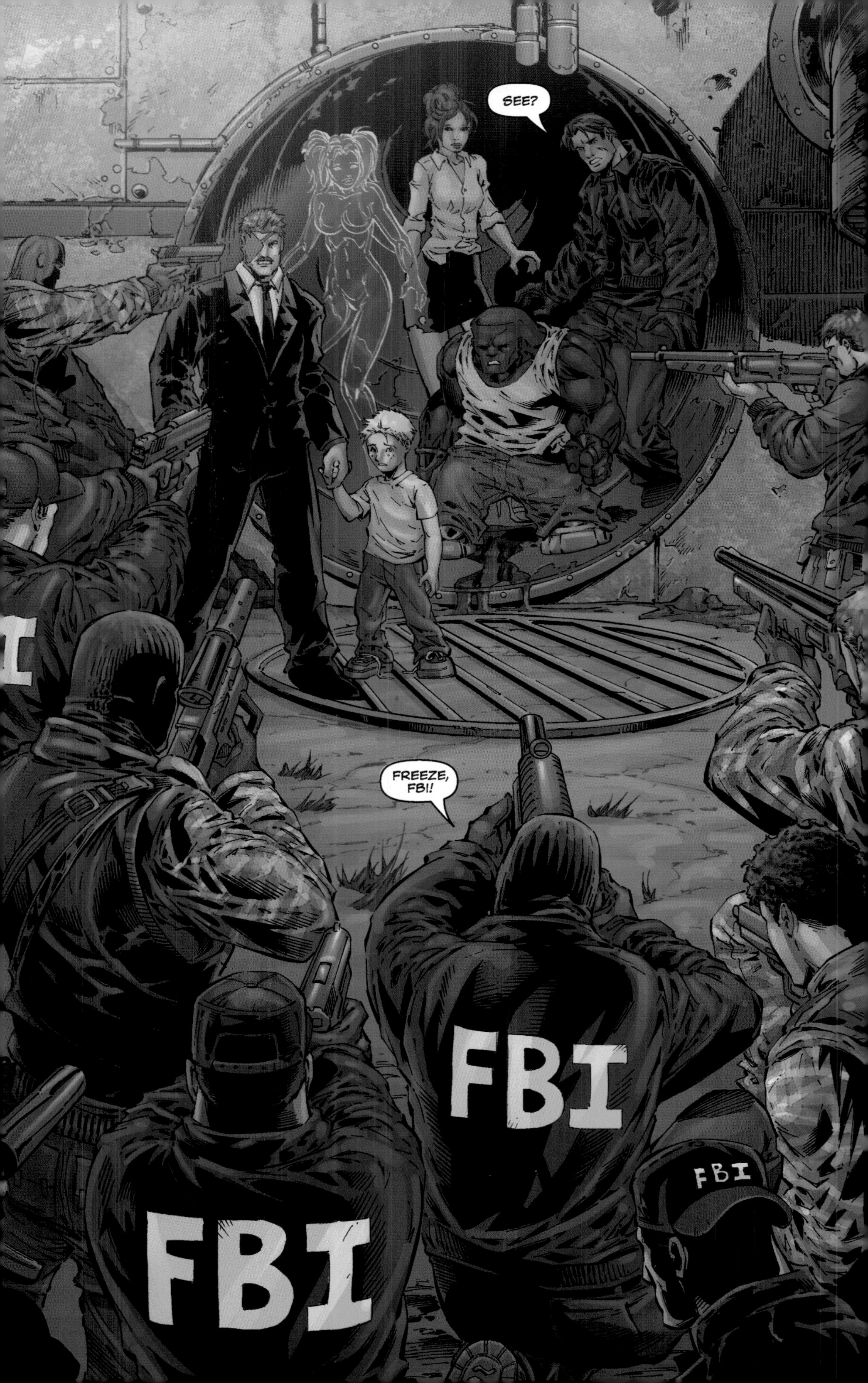
SEE?
FREEZE, FBI!
FBI
FBI
FBI

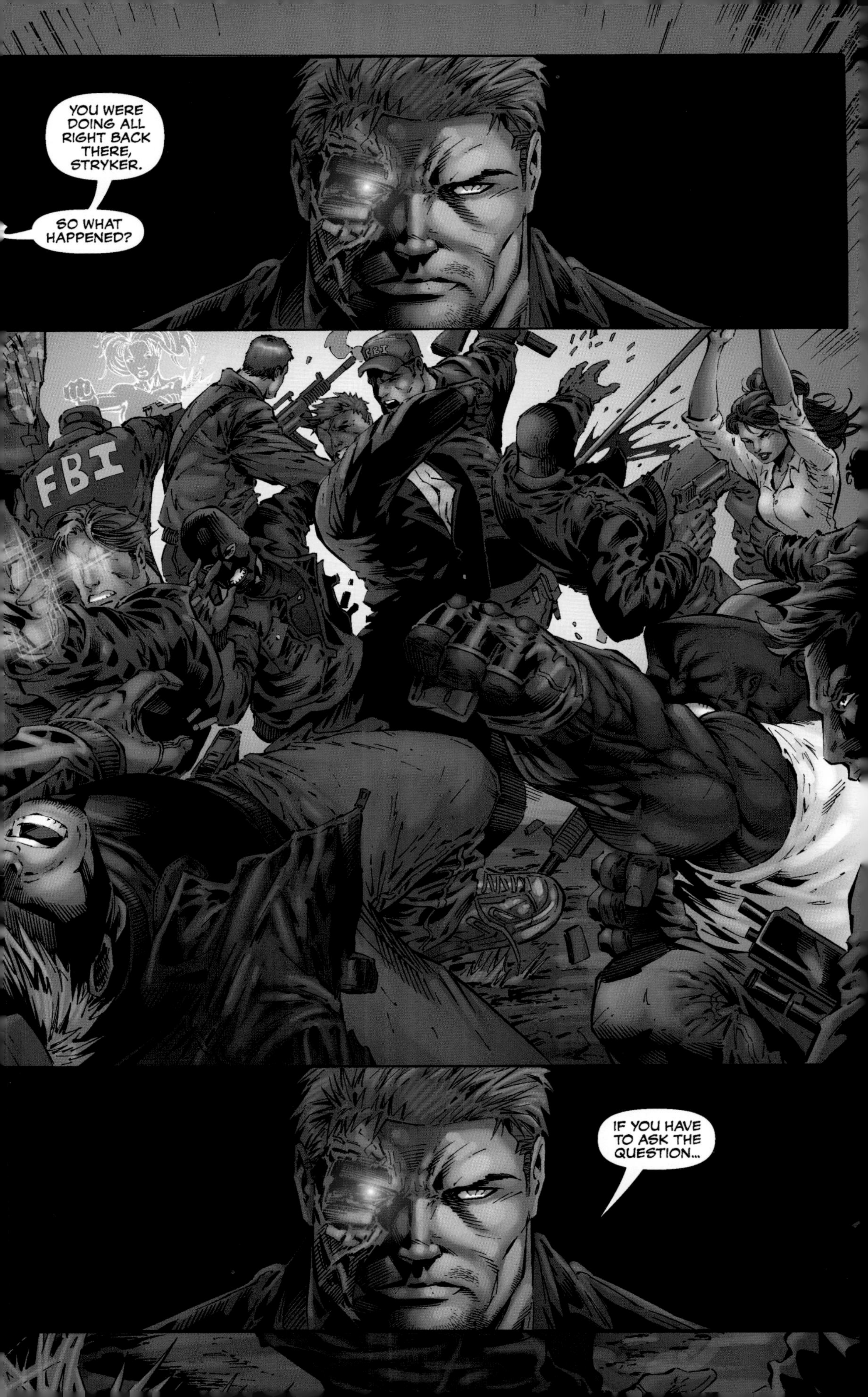
YOU WERE DOING ALL RIGHT BACK THERE, STRYKER.
SO WHAT HAPPENED?
FBI
FBI
FBI
IF YOU HAVE TO ASK THE QUESTION...

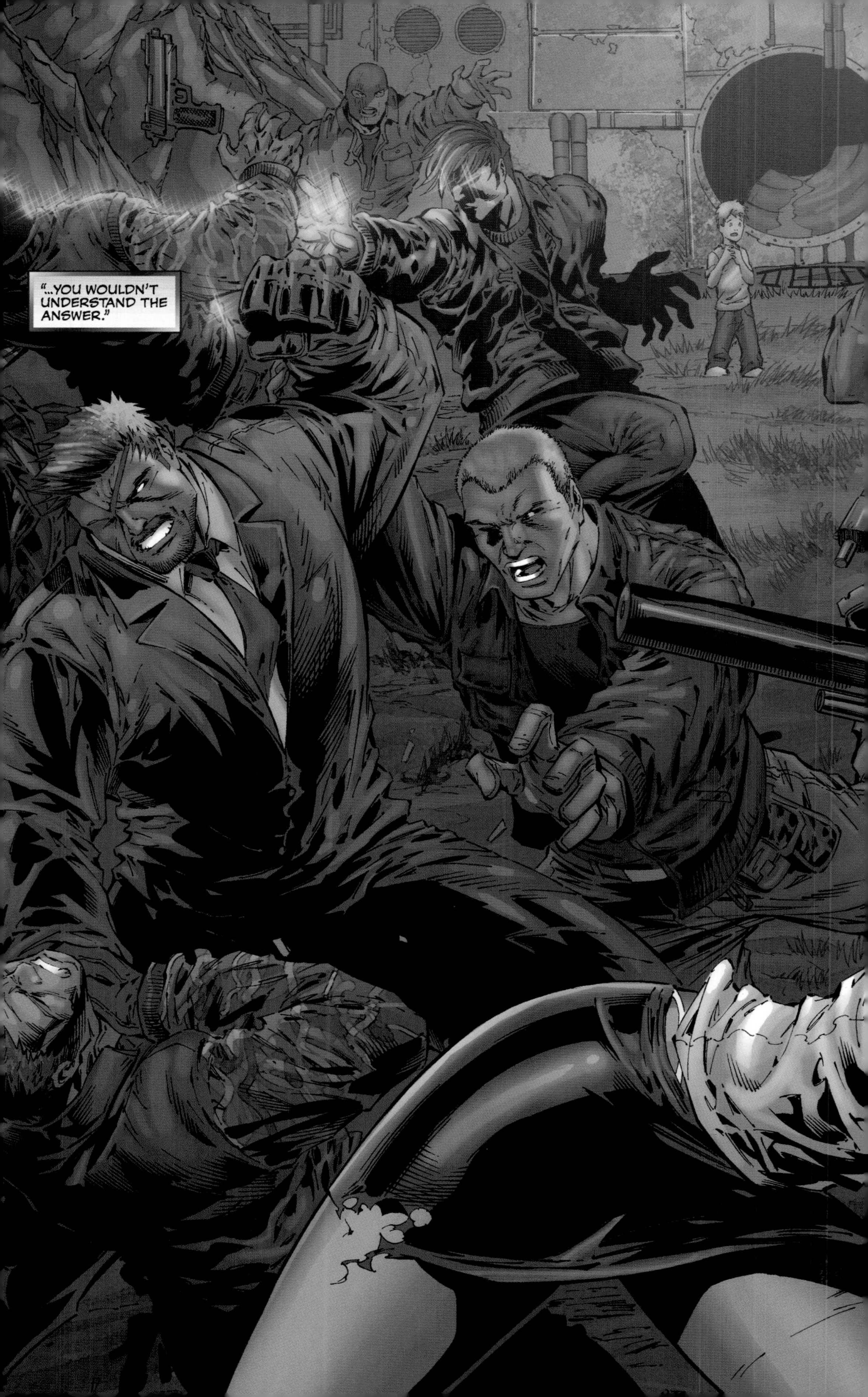
"...YOU WOULDN'T UNDERSTAND THE ANSWER."

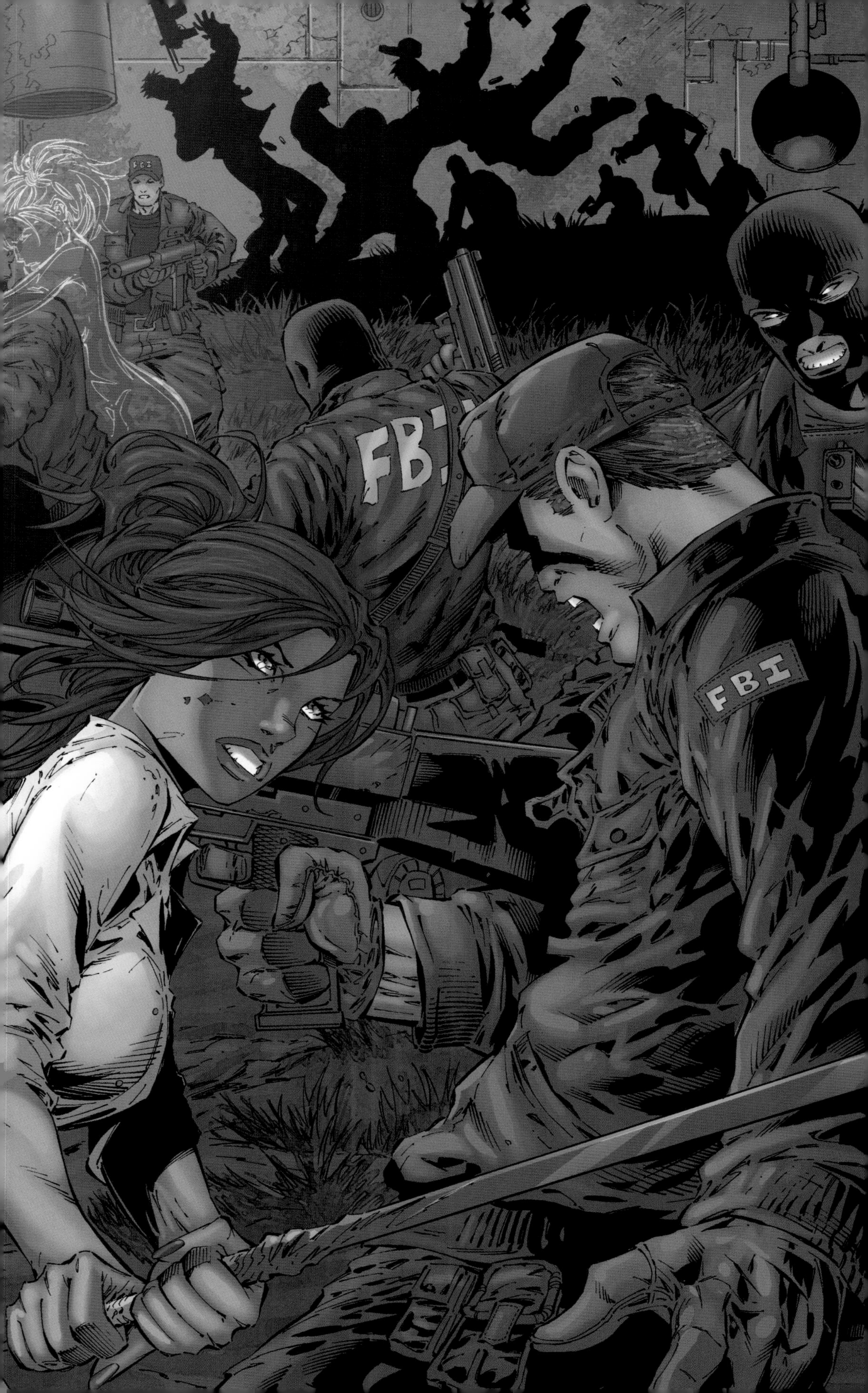
FBI
FBI

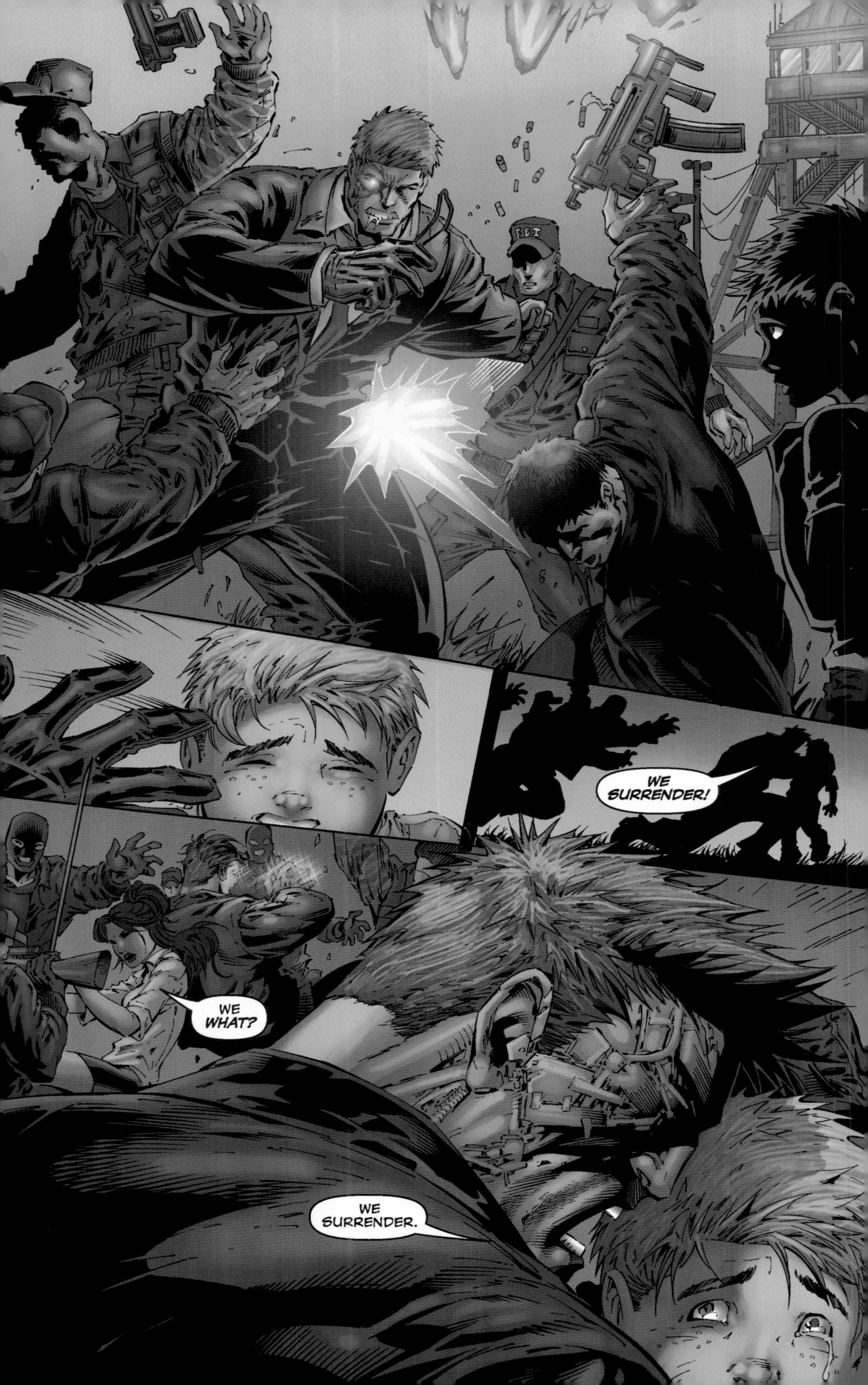
WE SURRENDER!
WE WHAT?
WE SURRENDER.

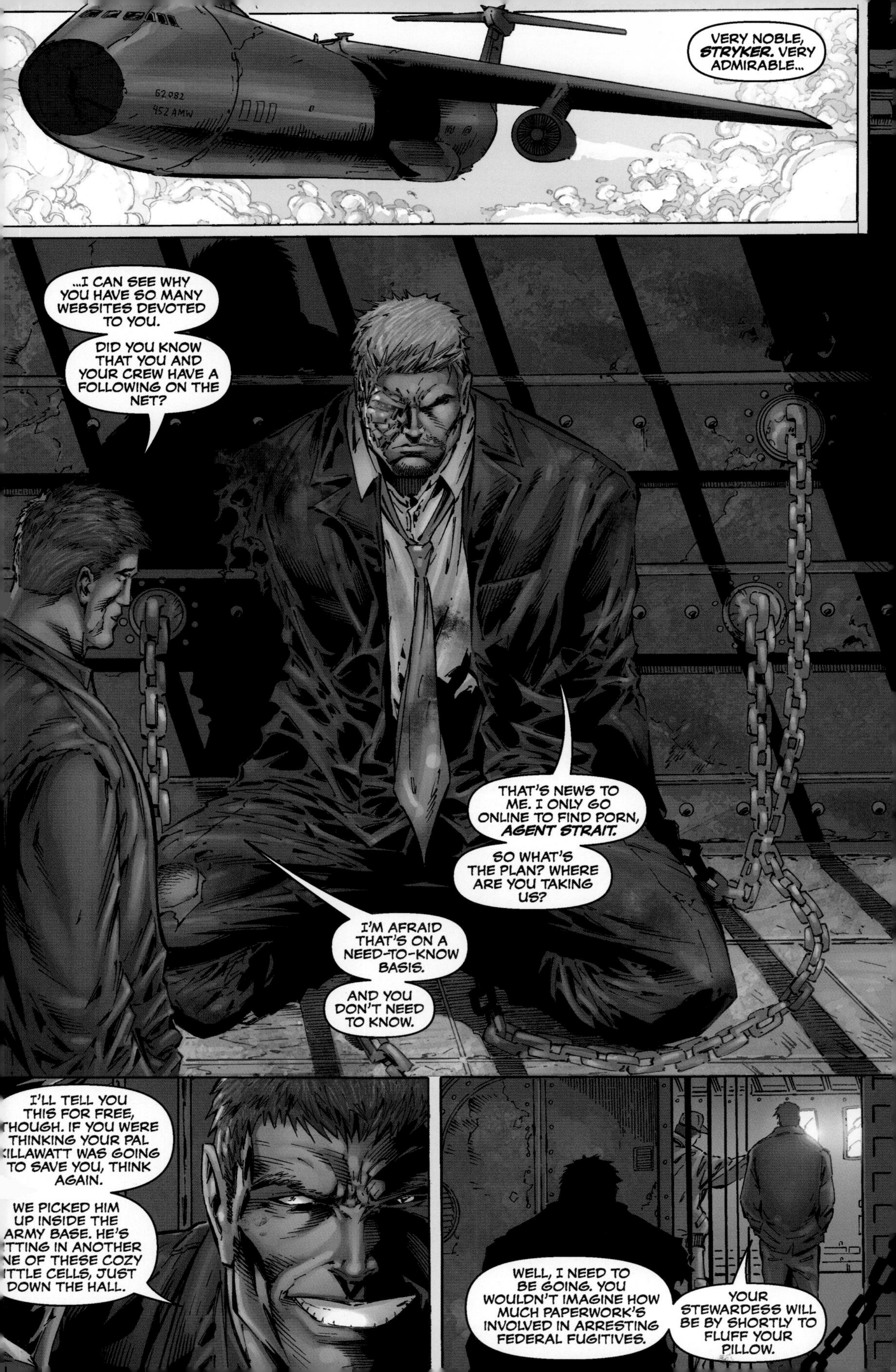
VERY NOBLE, STRYKER. VERY ADMIRABLE...
...I CAN SEE WHY YOU HAVE SO MANY WEBSITES DEVOTED TO YOU.
DID YOU KNOW THAT YOU AND YOUR CREW HAVE A FOLLOWING ON THE NET?
THAT'S NEWS TO ME. I ONLY GO ONLINE TO FIND PORN, AGENT STRAIT.
SO WHAT'S THE PLAN? WHERE ARE YOU TAKING US?
I'M AFRAID THAT'S ON A NEED-TO-KNOW BASIS.
AND YOU DON'T NEED TO KNOW.
I'LL TELL YOU THIS FOR FREE, THOUGH. IF YOU WERE THINKING YOUR PAL KILLAWATT WAS GOING TO SAVE YOU, THINK AGAIN.
WE PICKED HIM UP INSIDE THE ARMY BASE. HE'S SITTING IN ANOTHER ONE OF THESE COZY LITTLE CELLS, JUST DOWN THE HALL.
WELL, I NEED TO BE GOING. YOU WOULDN'T IMAGINE HOW MUCH PAPERWORK'S INVOLVED IN ARRESTING FEDERAL FUGITIVES.
YOUR STEWARDESS WILL BE BY SHORTLY TO FLUFF YOUR PILLOW.

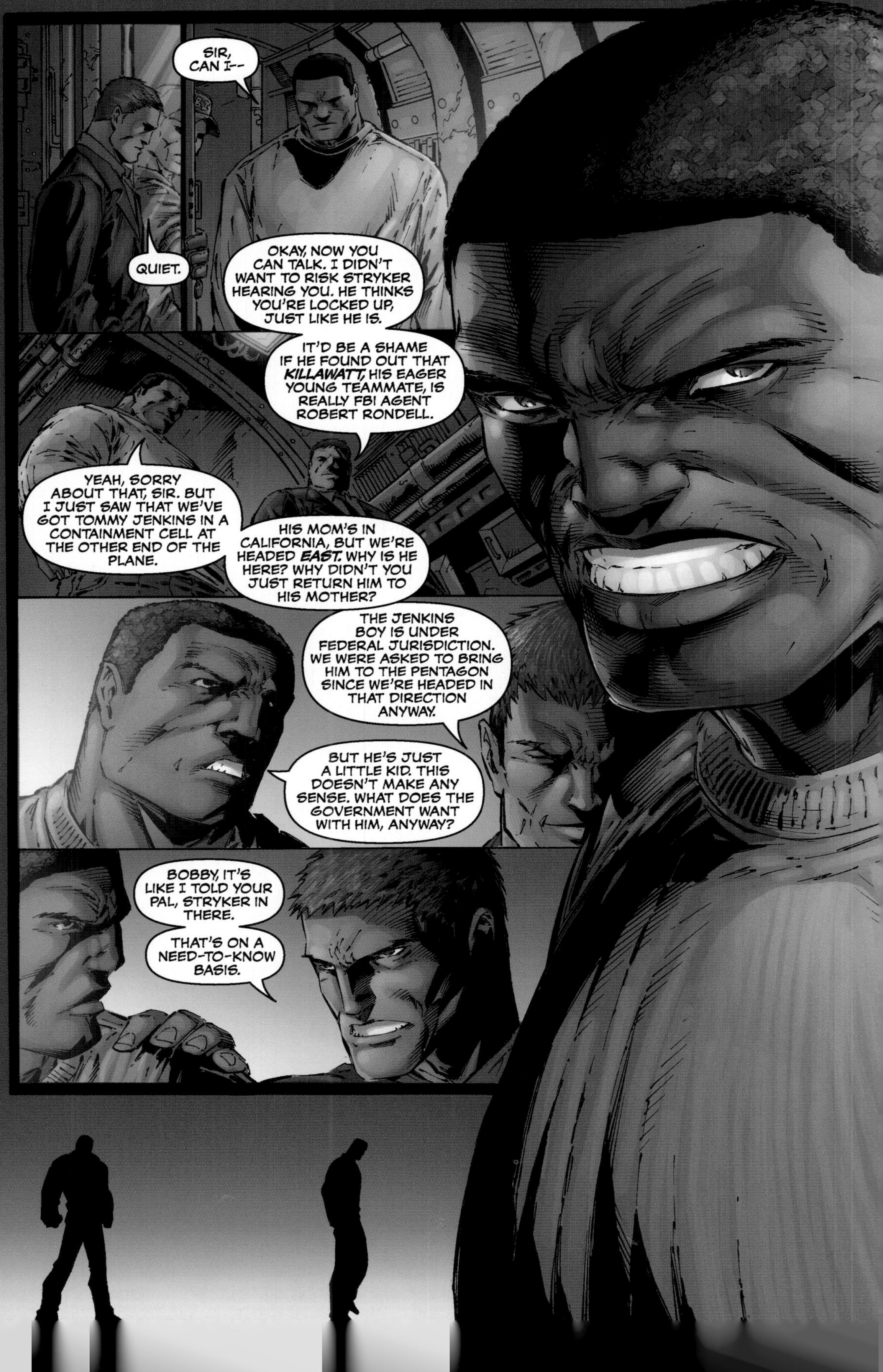
SIR, CAN I--
QUIET.
OKAY, NOW YOU CAN TALK. I DIDN'T WANT TO RISK STRYKER HEARING YOU. HE THINKS YOU'RE LOCKED UP, JUST LIKE HE IS.
IT'D BE A SHAME IF HE FOUND OUT THAT KILLAWATT, HIS EAGER YOUNG TEAMMATE, IS REALLY FBI AGENT ROBERT RONDELL.
YEAH, SORRY ABOUT THAT, SIR. BUT I JUST SAW THAT WE'VE GOT TOMMY JENKINS IN A CONTAINMENT CELL AT THE OTHER END OF THE PLANE.
HIS MOM'S IN CALIFORNIA, BUT WE'RE HEADED EAST. WHY IS HE HERE? WHY DIDN'T YOU JUST RETURN HIM TO HIS MOTHER?
THE JENKINS BOY IS UNDER FEDERAL JURISDICTION. WE WERE ASKED TO BRING HIM TO THE PENTAGON SINCE WE'RE HEADED IN THAT DIRECTION ANYWAY.
BUT HE'S JUST A LITTLE KID. THIS DOESN'T MAKE ANY SENSE. WHAT DOES THE GOVERNMENT WANT WITH HIM, ANYWAY?
BOBBY, IT'S LIKE I TOLD YOUR PAL, STRYKER IN THERE.
THAT'S ON A NEED-TO-KNOW BASIS.

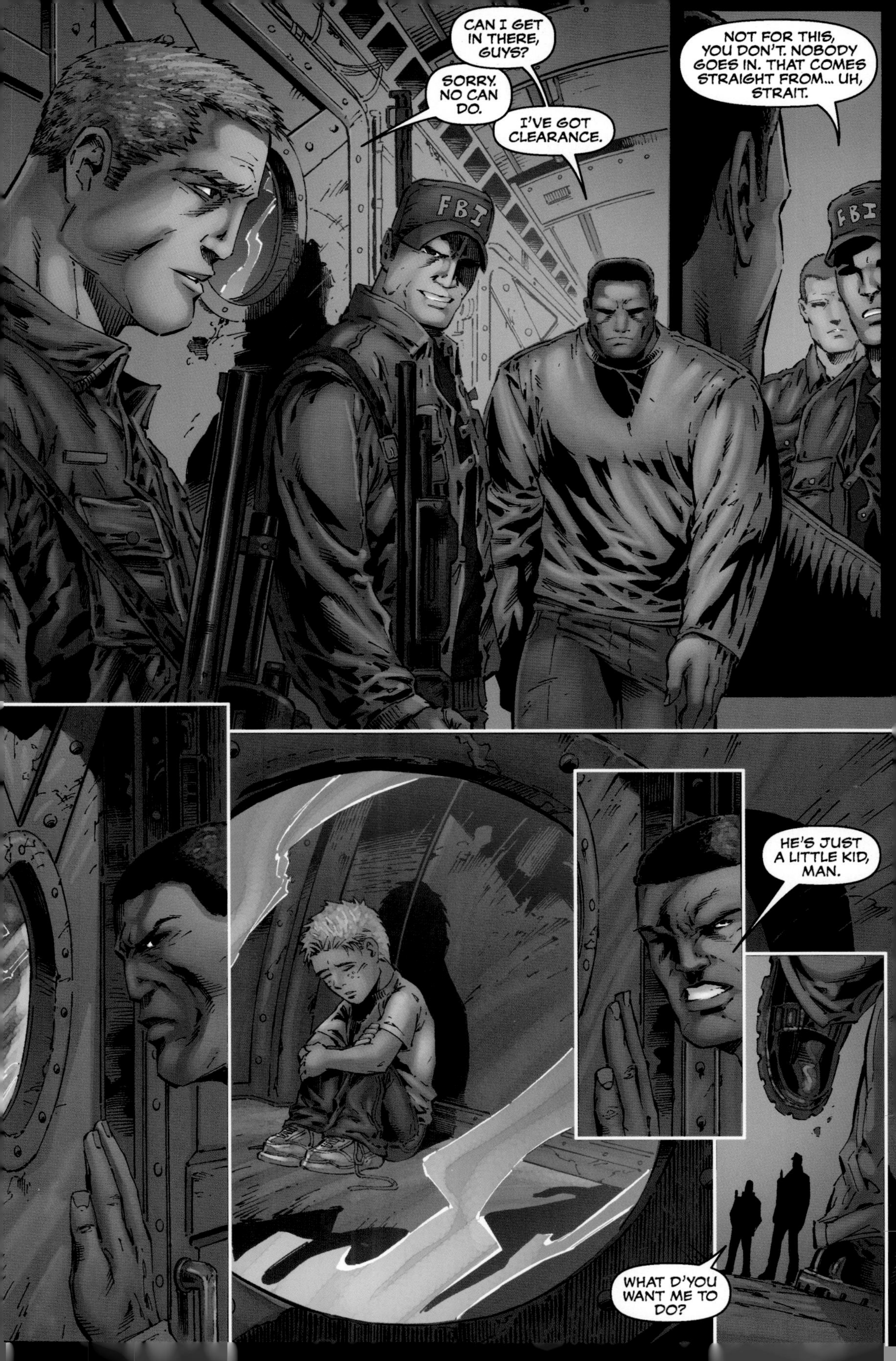
CAN I GET IN THERE, GUYS?
SORRY. NO CAN DO.
I'VE GOT CLEARANCE.
NOT FOR THIS, YOU DON'T. NOBODY GOES IN. THAT COMES STRAIGHT FROM... UH, STRAIT.
HE'S JUST A LITTLE KID, MAN.
WHAT D'YOU WANT ME TO DO?

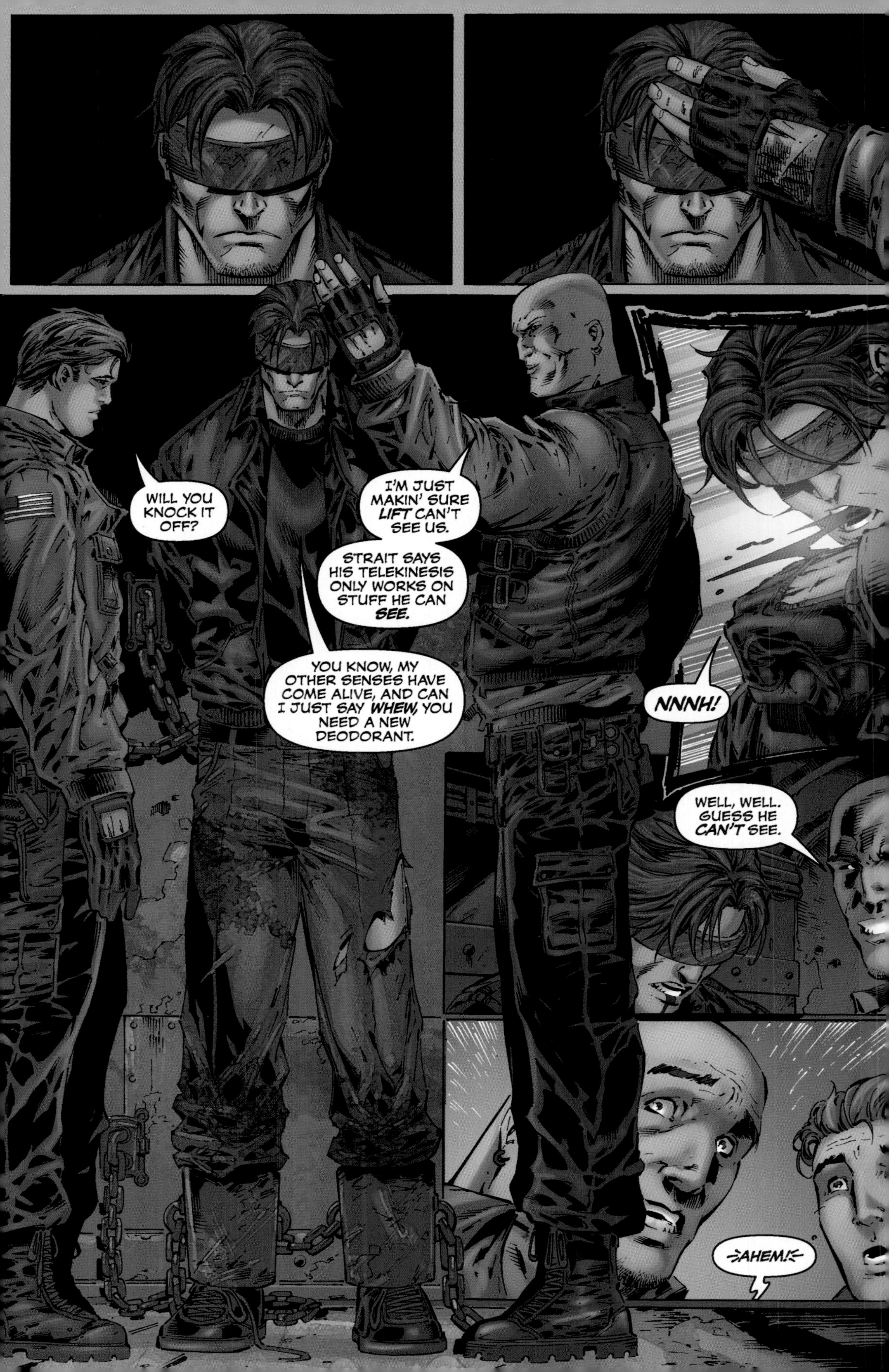
WILL YOU KNOCK IT OFF?
I'M JUST MAKIN' SURE LIFT CAN'T SEE US.
STRAIT SAYS HIS TELEKINESIS ONLY WORKS ON STUFF HE CAN SEE.
YOU KNOW, MY OTHER SENSES HAVE COME ALIVE, AND CAN I JUST SAY WHEW, YOU NEED A NEW DEODORANT.
NNNH!
WELL, WELL. GUESS HE CAN'T SEE.
AHEM!

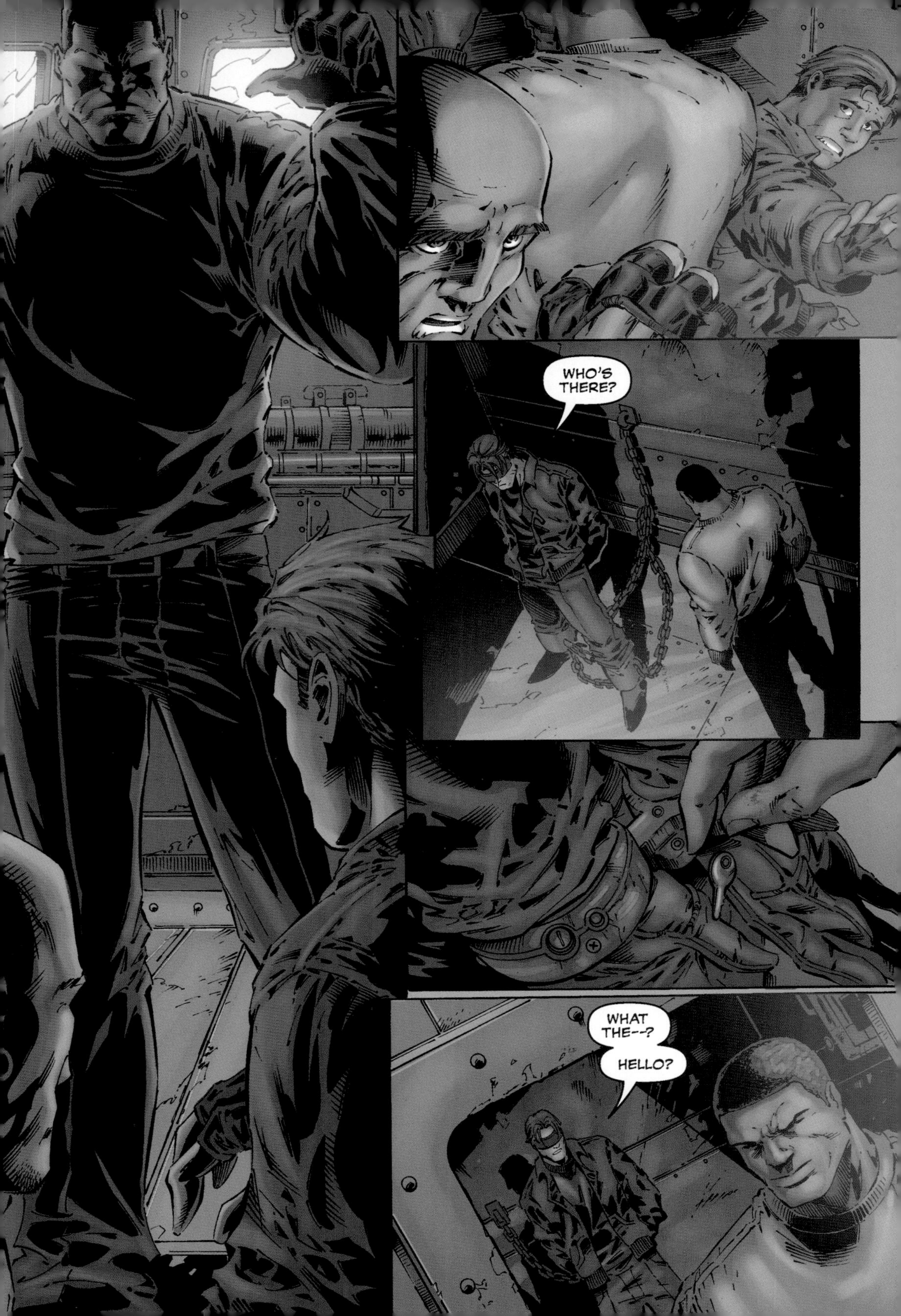
WHO'S THERE?
WHAT THE--?
HELLO?

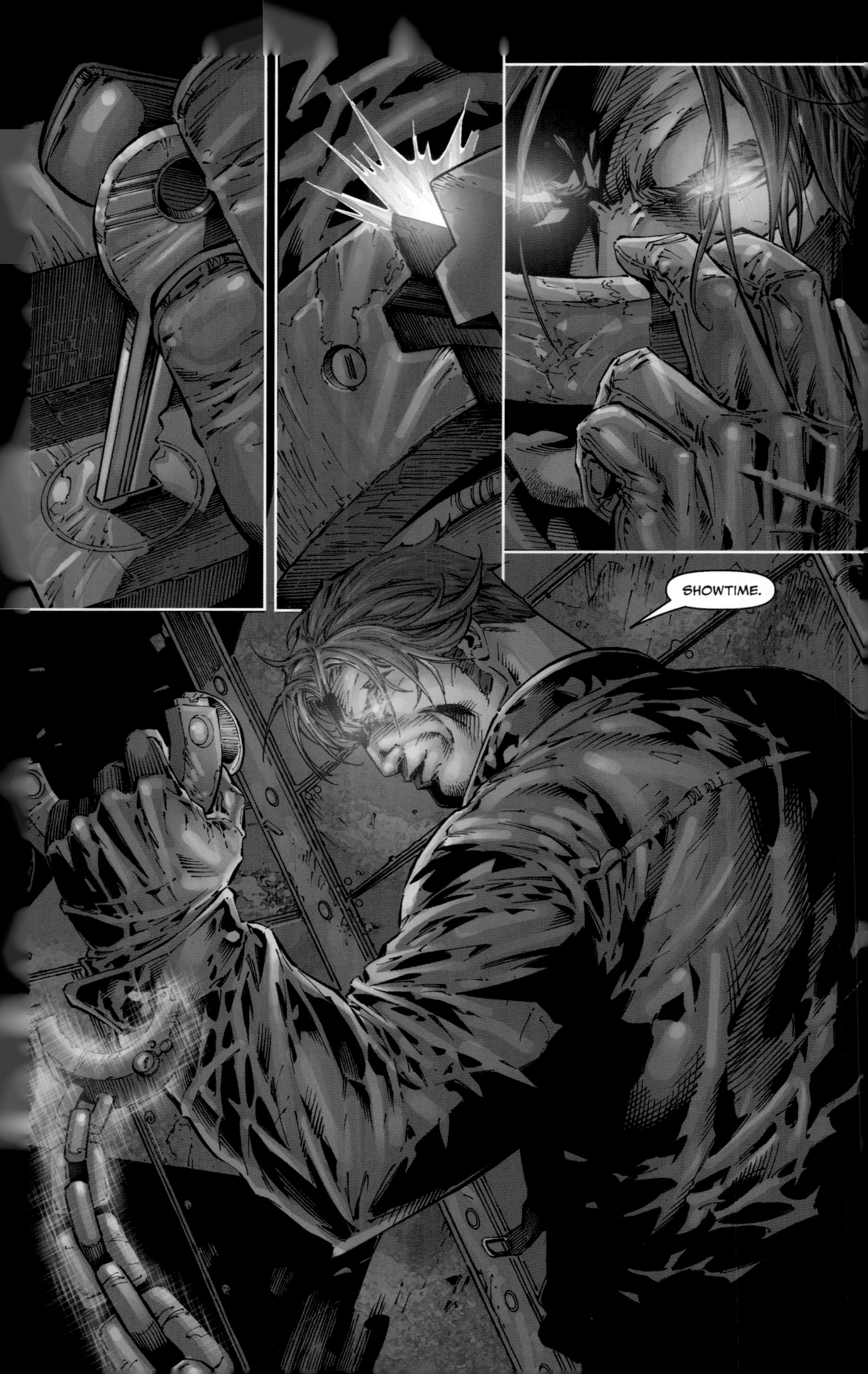
SHOWTIME.

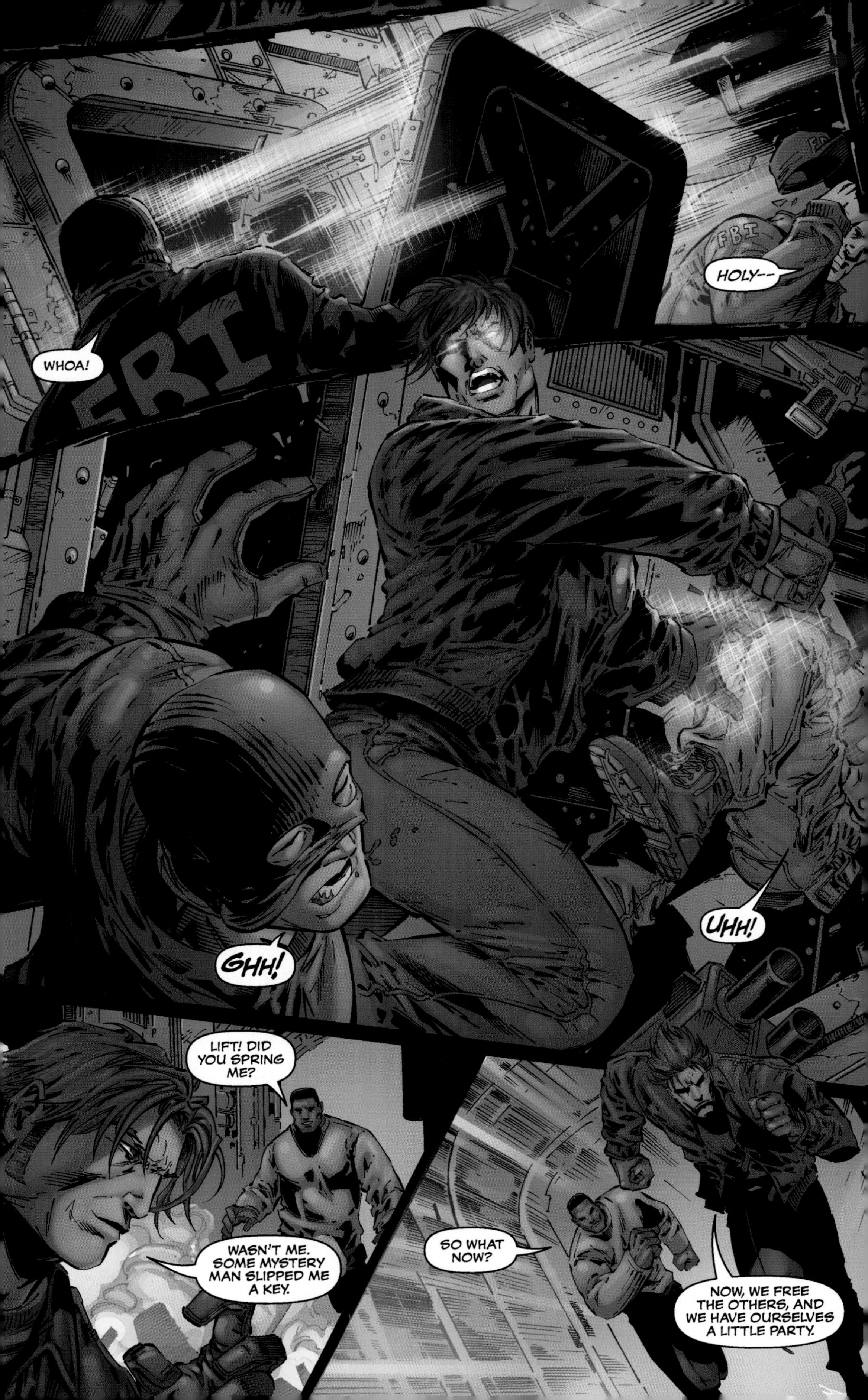
HOLY--
WHOA!
GHH!
UHH!
LIFT! DID YOU SPRING ME?
WASN'T ME. SOME MYSTERY MAN SLIPPED ME A KEY.
SO WHAT NOW?
NOW, WE FREE THE OTHERS, AND WE HAVE OURSELVES A LITTLE PARTY.

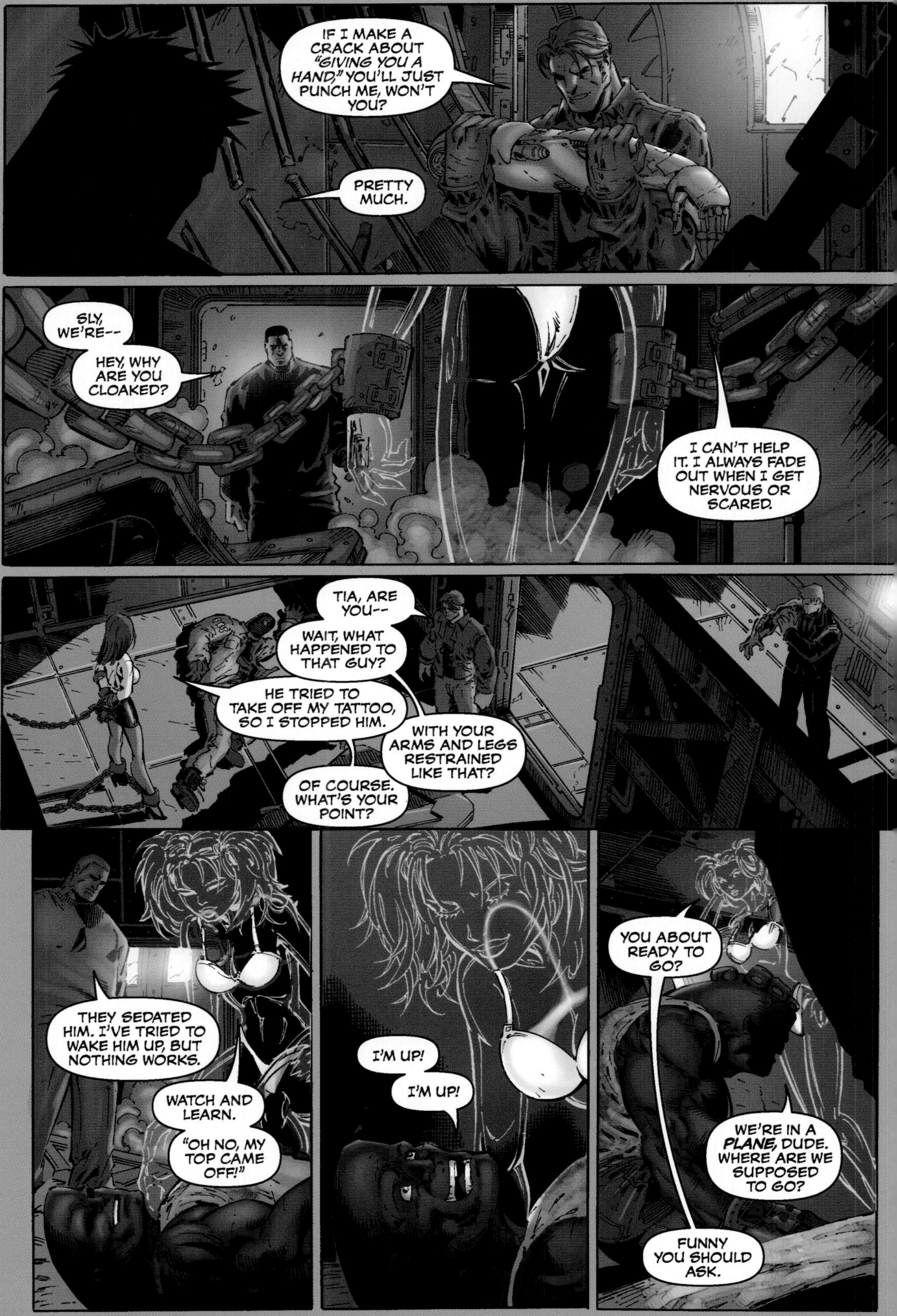

IF I MAKE A CRACK ABOUT "GIVING YOU A HAND," YOU'LL JUST PUNCH ME, WON'T YOU?
PRETTY MUCH.
SLY, WE'RE--
HEY, WHY ARE YOU CLOAKED?
I CAN'T HELP IT. I ALWAYS FADE OUT WHEN I GET NERVOUS OR SCARED.
TIA, ARE YOU--
WAIT, WHAT HAPPENED TO THAT GUY?
HE TRIED TO TAKE OFF MY TATTOO, SO I STOPPED HIM.
WITH YOUR ARMS AND LEGS RESTRAINED LIKE THAT?
OF COURSE. WHAT'S YOUR POINT?
THEY SEDATED HIM. I'VE TRIED TO WAKE HIM UP, BUT NOTHING WORKS.
WATCH AND LEARN.
"OH NO, MY TOP CAME OFF!"
I'M UP!
I'M UP!
YOU ABOUT READY TO GO?
WE'RE IN A PLANE, DUDE. WHERE ARE WE SUPPOSED TO GO?
FUNNY YOU SHOULD ASK.

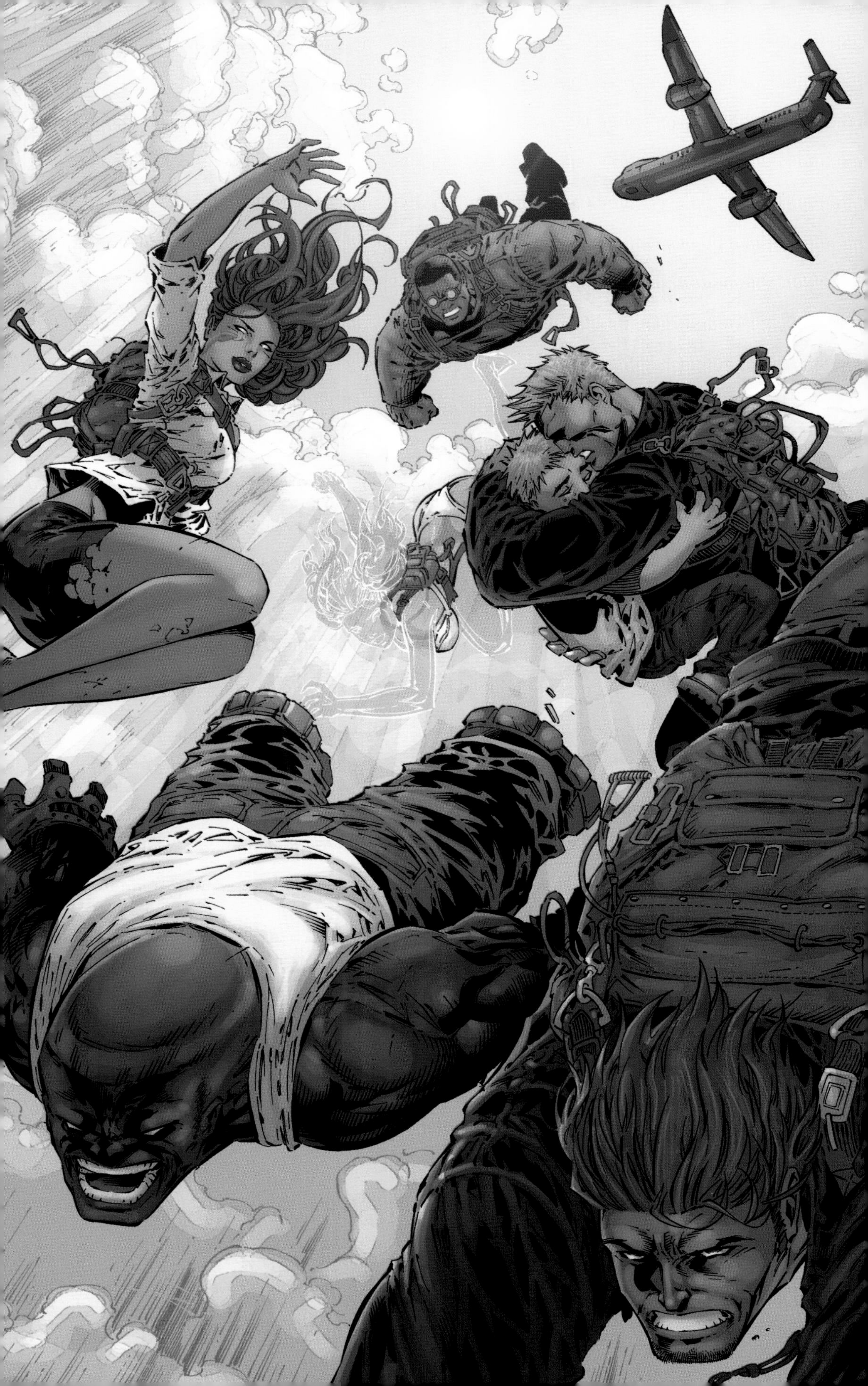

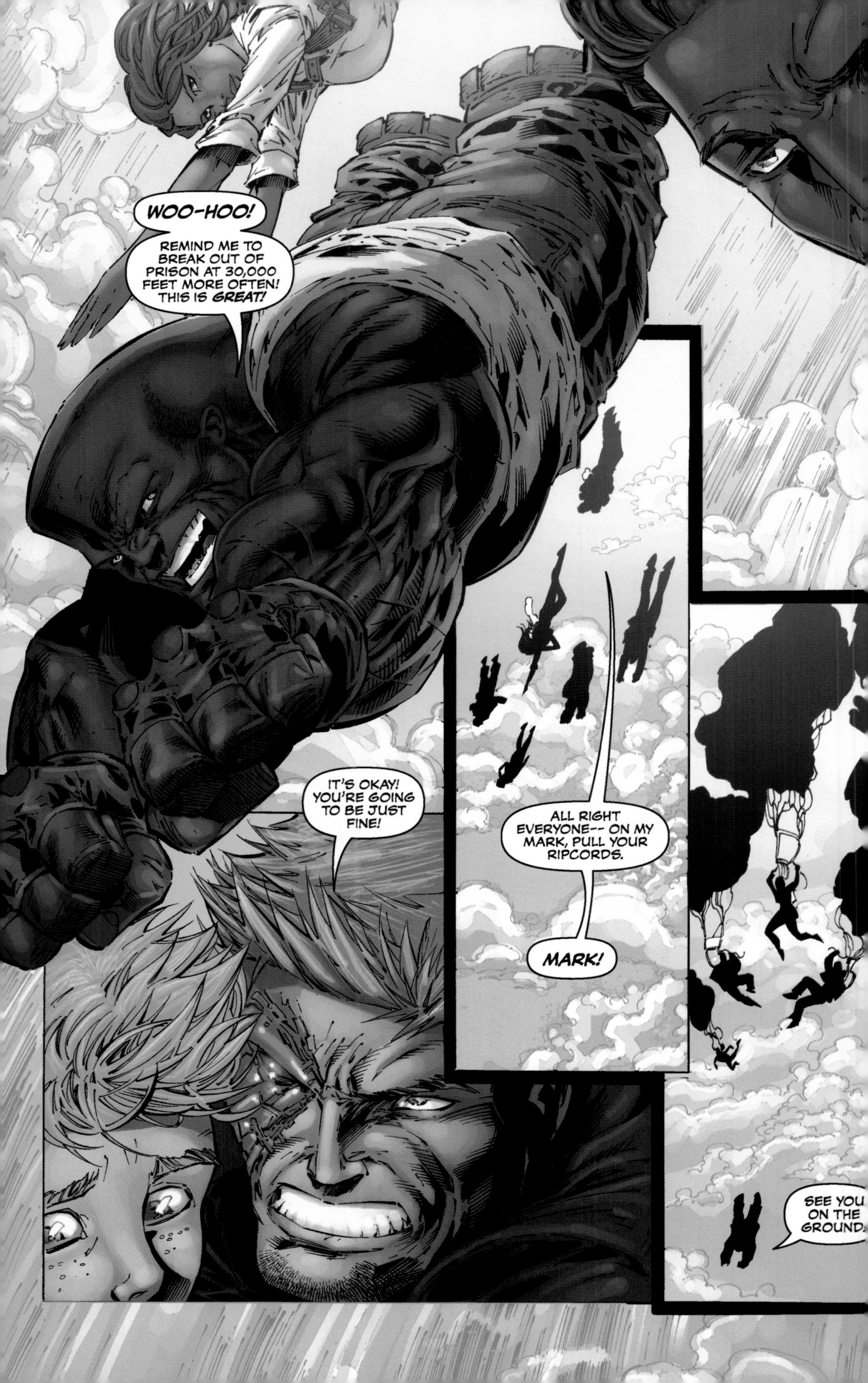
WOO-HOO!
REMIND ME TO BREAK OUT OF PRISON AT 30,000 FEET MORE OFTEN! THIS IS GREAT!
IT'S OKAY! YOU'RE GOING TO BE JUST FINE!
ALL RIGHT EVERYONE-- ON MY MARK, PULL YOUR RIPCORDS.
MARK!
SEE YOU ON THE GROUND.

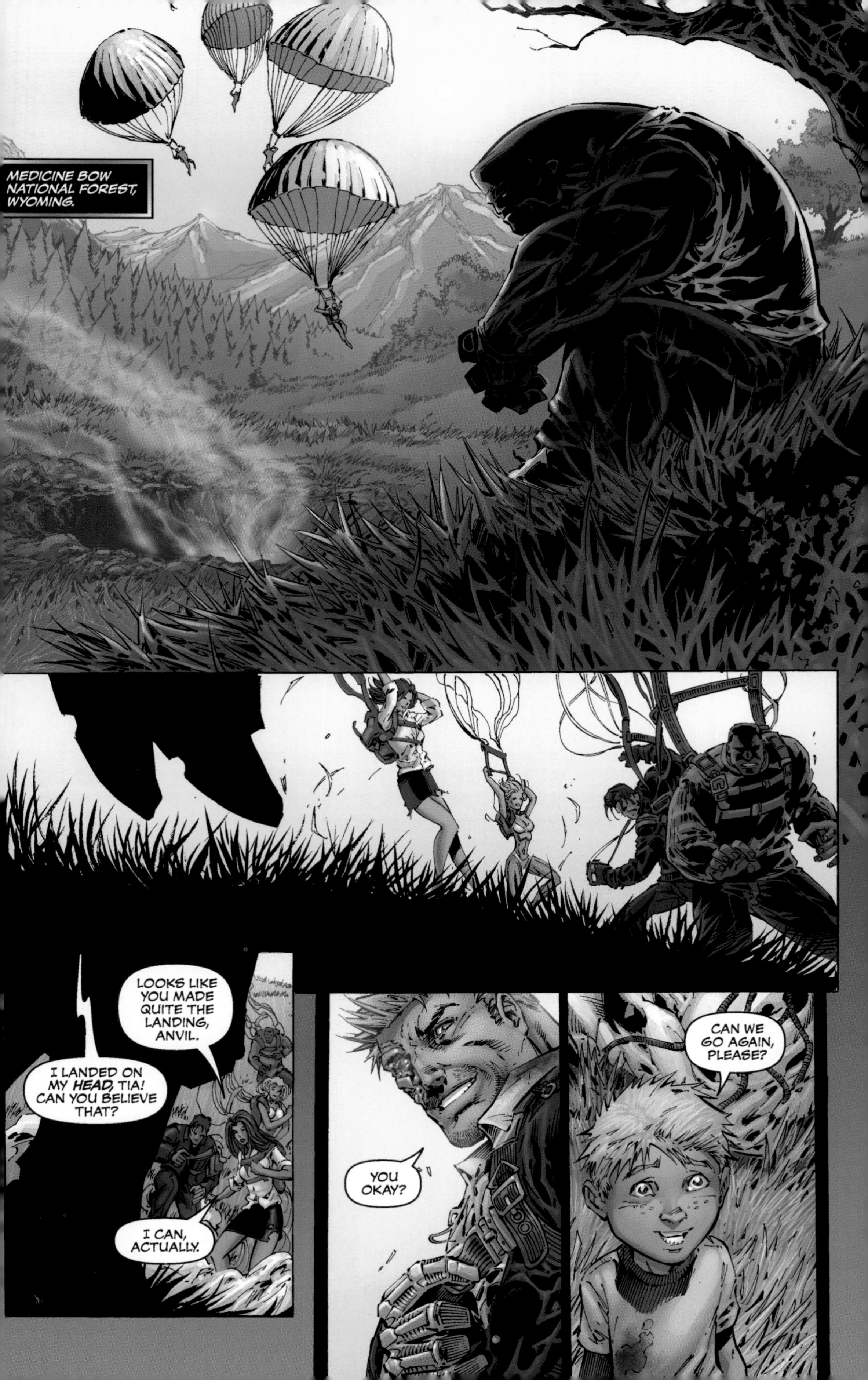
MEDICINE BOW NATIONAL FOREST, WYOMING.
LOOKS LIKE YOU MADE QUITE THE LANDING, ANVIL.
I LANDED ON MY *HEAD,* TIA! CAN YOU BELIEVE THAT?
I CAN, ACTUALLY.
YOU OKAY?
CAN WE GO AGAIN, PLEASE?

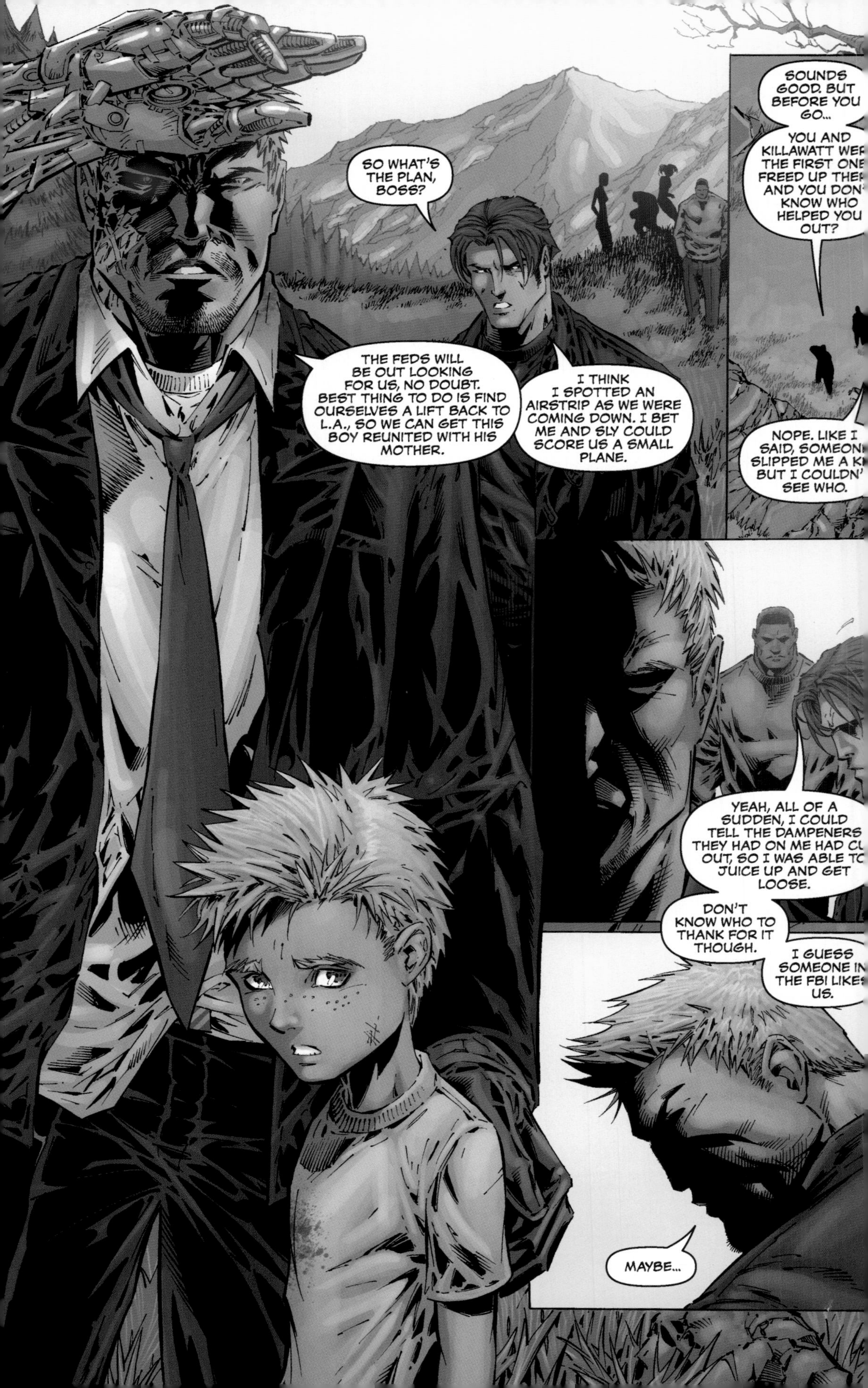
SO WHAT'S THE PLAN, BOSS?
THE FEDS WILL BE OUT LOOKING FOR US, NO DOUBT. BEST THING TO DO IS FIND OURSELVES A LIFT BACK TO L.A., SO WE CAN GET THIS BOY REUNITED WITH HIS MOTHER.
I THINK I SPOTTED AN AIRSTRIP AS WE WERE COMING DOWN. I BET ME AND SLY COULD SCORE US A SMALL PLANE.
SOUNDS GOOD. BUT BEFORE YOU GO...
YOU AND KILLAWATT WER THE FIRST ONE FREED UP THER AND YOU DON' KNOW WHO HELPED YOU OUT?
NOPE. LIKE I SAID, SOMEON SLIPPED ME A K BUT I COULDN' SEE WHO.
YEAH, ALL OF A SUDDEN, I COULD TELL THE DAMPENERS THEY HAD ON ME HAD C OUT, SO I WAS ABLE T JUICE UP AND GET LOOSE.
DON'T KNOW WHO TO THANK FOR IT THOUGH.
I GUESS SOMEONE IN THE FBI LIKE US.
MAYBE...

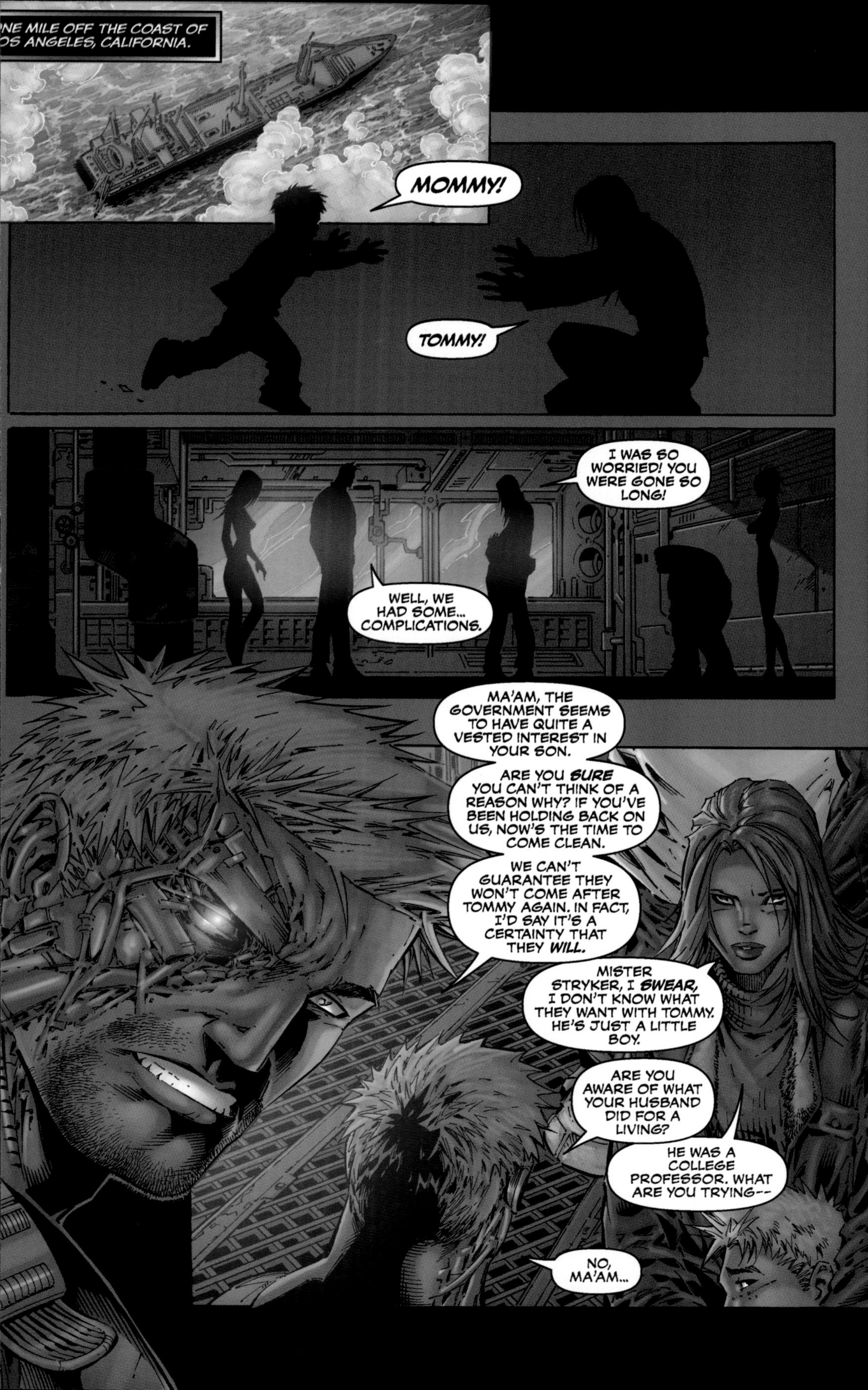
ONE MILE OFF THE COAST OF LOS ANGELES, CALIFORNIA.
MOMMY!
TOMMY!
I WAS SO WORRIED! YOU WERE GONE SO LONG!
WELL, WE HAD SOME... COMPLICATIONS.
MA'AM, THE GOVERNMENT SEEMS TO HAVE QUITE A VESTED INTEREST IN YOUR SON.
ARE YOU SURE YOU CAN'T THINK OF A REASON WHY? IF YOU'VE BEEN HOLDING BACK ON US, NOW'S THE TIME TO COME CLEAN.
WE CAN'T GUARANTEE THEY WON'T COME AFTER TOMMY AGAIN. IN FACT, I'D SAY IT'S A CERTAINTY THAT THEY WILL.
MISTER STRYKER, I SWEAR, I DON'T KNOW WHAT THEY WANT WITH TOMMY. HE'S JUST A LITTLE BOY.
ARE YOU AWARE OF WHAT YOUR HUSBAND DID FOR A LIVING?
HE WAS A COLLEGE PROFESSOR. WHAT ARE YOU TRYING--
NO, MA'AM...

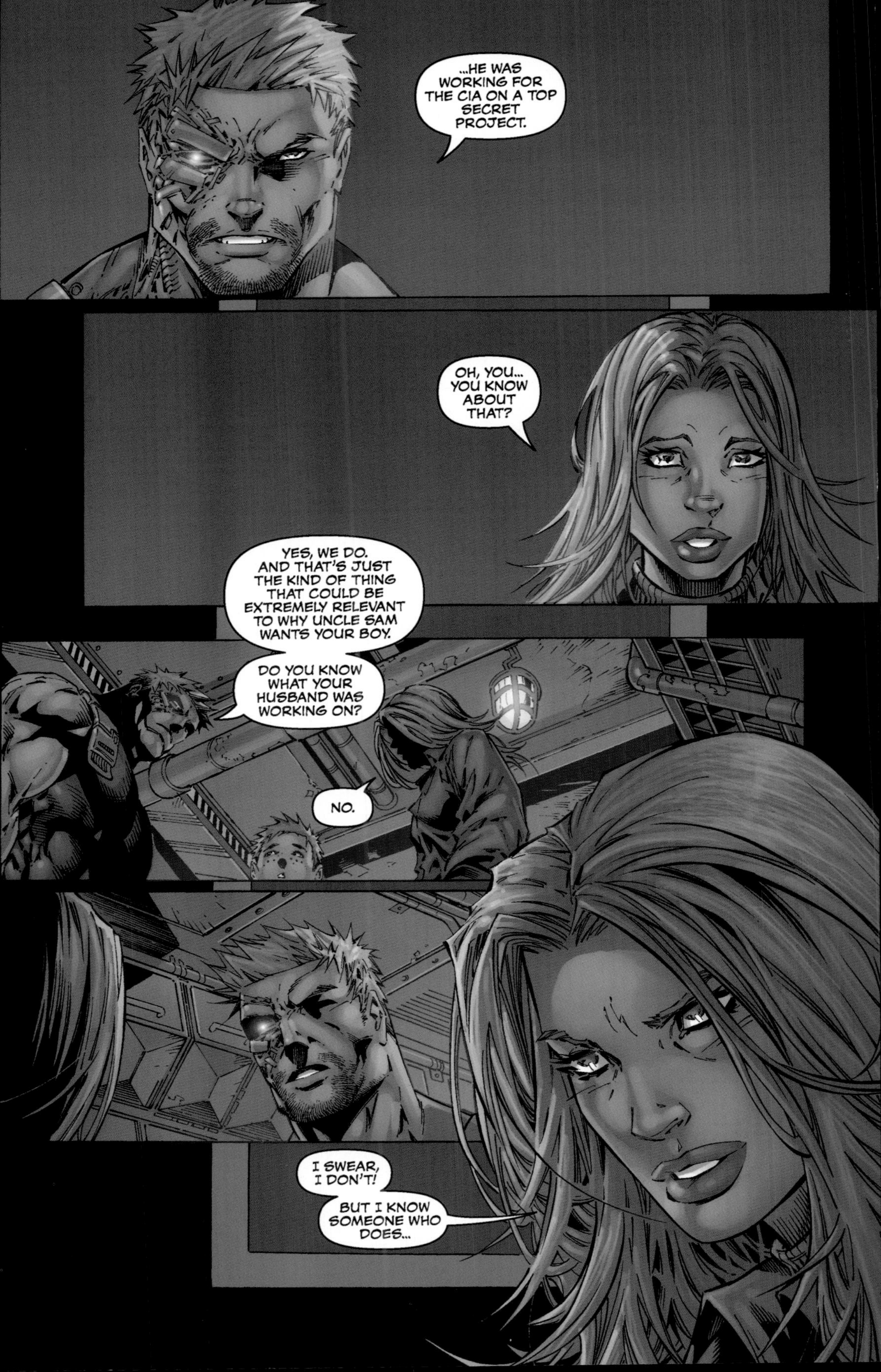
...HE WAS WORKING FOR THE CIA ON A TOP SECRET PROJECT.
OH, YOU... YOU KNOW ABOUT THAT?
YES, WE DO. AND THAT'S JUST THE KIND OF THING THAT COULD BE EXTREMELY RELEVANT TO WHY UNCLE SAM WANTS YOUR BOY.
DO YOU KNOW WHAT YOUR HUSBAND WAS WORKING ON?
NO.
I SWEAR, I DON'T!
BUT I KNOW SOMEONE WHO DOES...

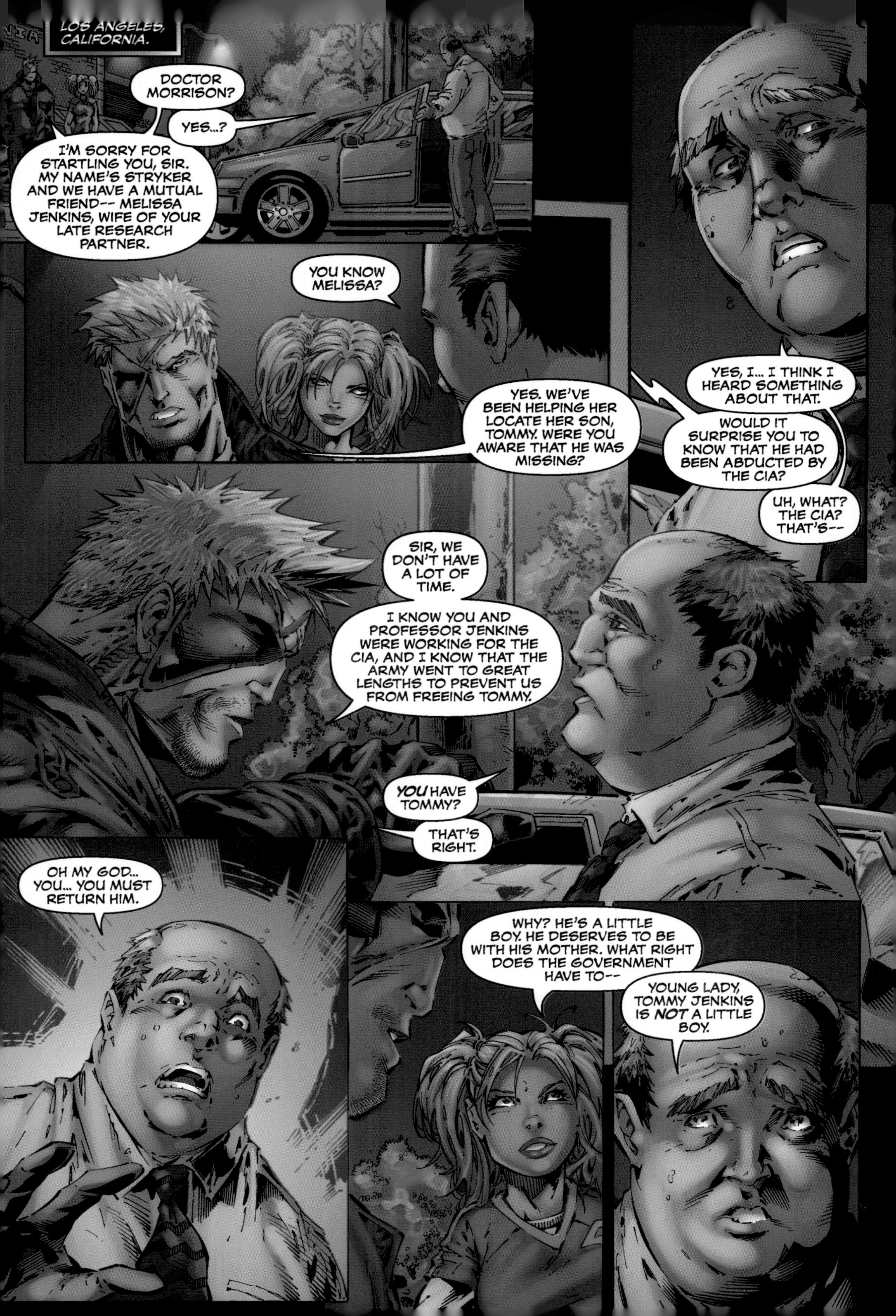
LOS ANGELES, CALIFORNIA.
DOCTOR MORRISON?
YES...?
I'M SORRY FOR STARTLING YOU, SIR. MY NAME'S STRYKER AND WE HAVE A MUTUAL FRIEND-- MELISSA JENKINS, WIFE OF YOUR LATE RESEARCH PARTNER.
YOU KNOW MELISSA?
YES. WE'VE BEEN HELPING HER LOCATE HER SON, TOMMY. WERE YOU AWARE THAT HE WAS MISSING?
YES, I... I THINK I HEARD SOMETHING ABOUT THAT.
WOULD IT SURPRISE YOU TO KNOW THAT HE HAD BEEN ABDUCTED BY THE CIA?
UH, WHAT? THE CIA? THAT'S--
SIR, WE DON'T HAVE A LOT OF TIME.
I KNOW YOU AND PROFESSOR JENKINS WERE WORKING FOR THE CIA, AND I KNOW THAT THE ARMY WENT TO GREAT LENGTHS TO PREVENT US FROM FREEING TOMMY.
YOU HAVE TOMMY?
THAT'S RIGHT.
OH MY GOD... YOU... YOU MUST RETURN HIM.
WHY? HE'S A LITTLE BOY. HE DESERVES TO BE WITH HIS MOTHER. WHAT RIGHT DOES THE GOVERNMENT HAVE TO--
YOUNG LADY, TOMMY JENKINS IS *NOT* A LITTLE BOY.

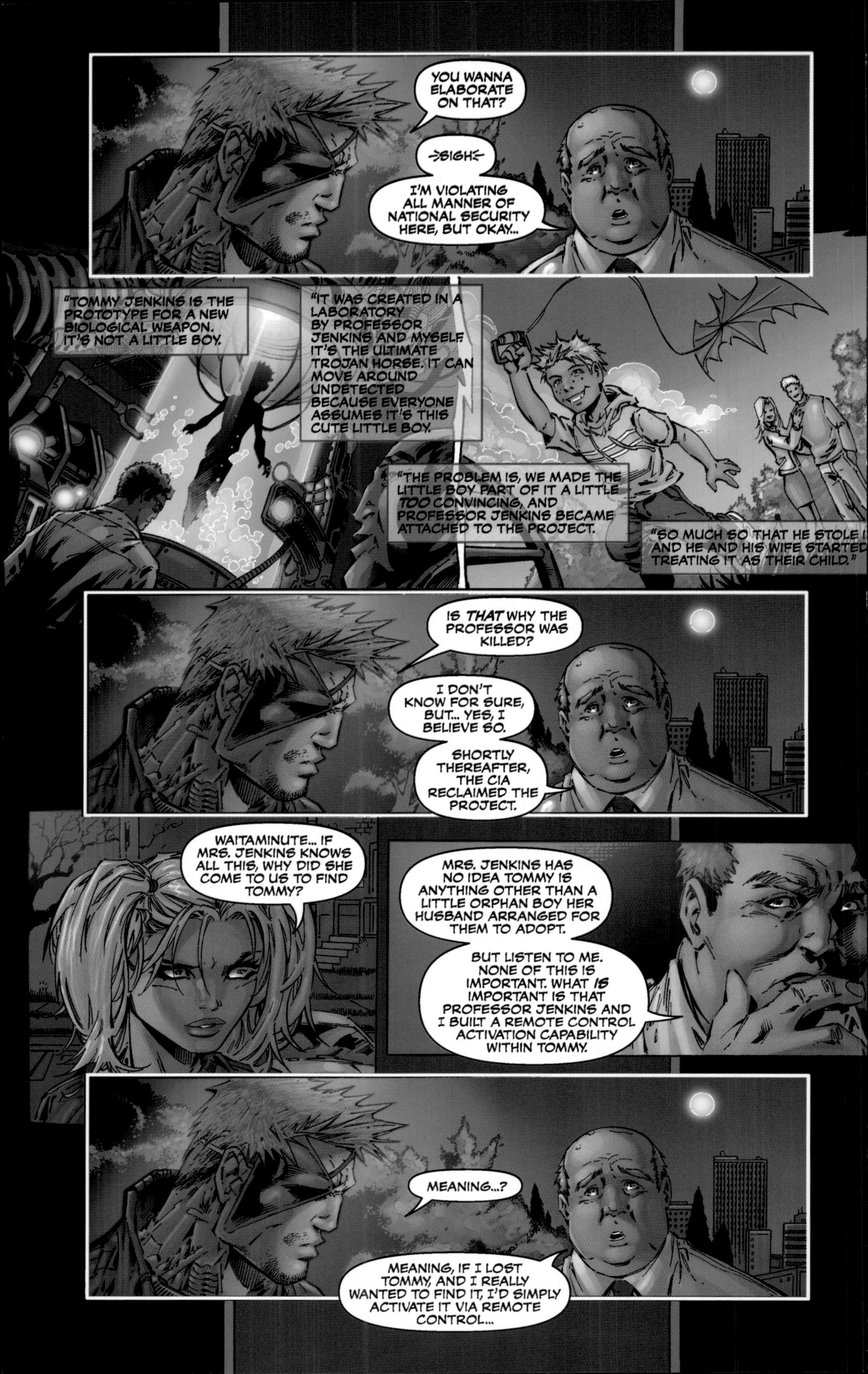
YOU WANNA ELABORATE ON THAT?
-SIGH-
I'M VIOLATING ALL MANNER OF NATIONAL SECURITY HERE, BUT OKAY...
"TOMMY JENKINS IS THE PROTOTYPE FOR A NEW BIOLOGICAL WEAPON. IT'S NOT A LITTLE BOY.
"IT WAS CREATED IN A LABORATORY BY PROFESSOR JENKINS AND MYSELF. IT'S THE ULTIMATE TROJAN HORSE. IT CAN MOVE AROUND UNDETECTED BECAUSE EVERYONE ASSUMES IT'S THIS CUTE LITTLE BOY.
"THE PROBLEM IS, WE MADE THE LITTLE BOY PART OF IT A LITTLE TOO CONVINCING, AND PROFESSOR JENKINS BECAME ATTACHED TO THE PROJECT.
"SO MUCH SO THAT HE STOLE I AND HE AND HIS WIFE STARTED TREATING IT AS THEIR CHILD."
IS THAT WHY THE PROFESSOR WAS KILLED?
I DON'T KNOW FOR SURE, BUT... YES, I BELIEVE SO.
SHORTLY THEREAFTER, THE CIA RECLAIMED THE PROJECT.
WAITAMINUTE... IF MRS. JENKINS KNOWS ALL THIS, WHY DID SHE COME TO US TO FIND TOMMY?
MRS. JENKINS HAS NO IDEA TOMMY IS ANYTHING OTHER THAN A LITTLE ORPHAN BOY HER HUSBAND ARRANGED FOR THEM TO ADOPT.
BUT LISTEN TO ME. NONE OF THIS IS IMPORTANT. WHAT IS IMPORTANT IS THAT PROFESSOR JENKINS AND I BUILT A REMOTE CONTROL ACTIVATION CAPABILITY WITHIN TOMMY.
MEANING...?
MEANING, IF I LOST TOMMY, AND I REALLY WANTED TO FIND IT, I'D SIMPLY ACTIVATE IT VIA REMOTE CONTROL...

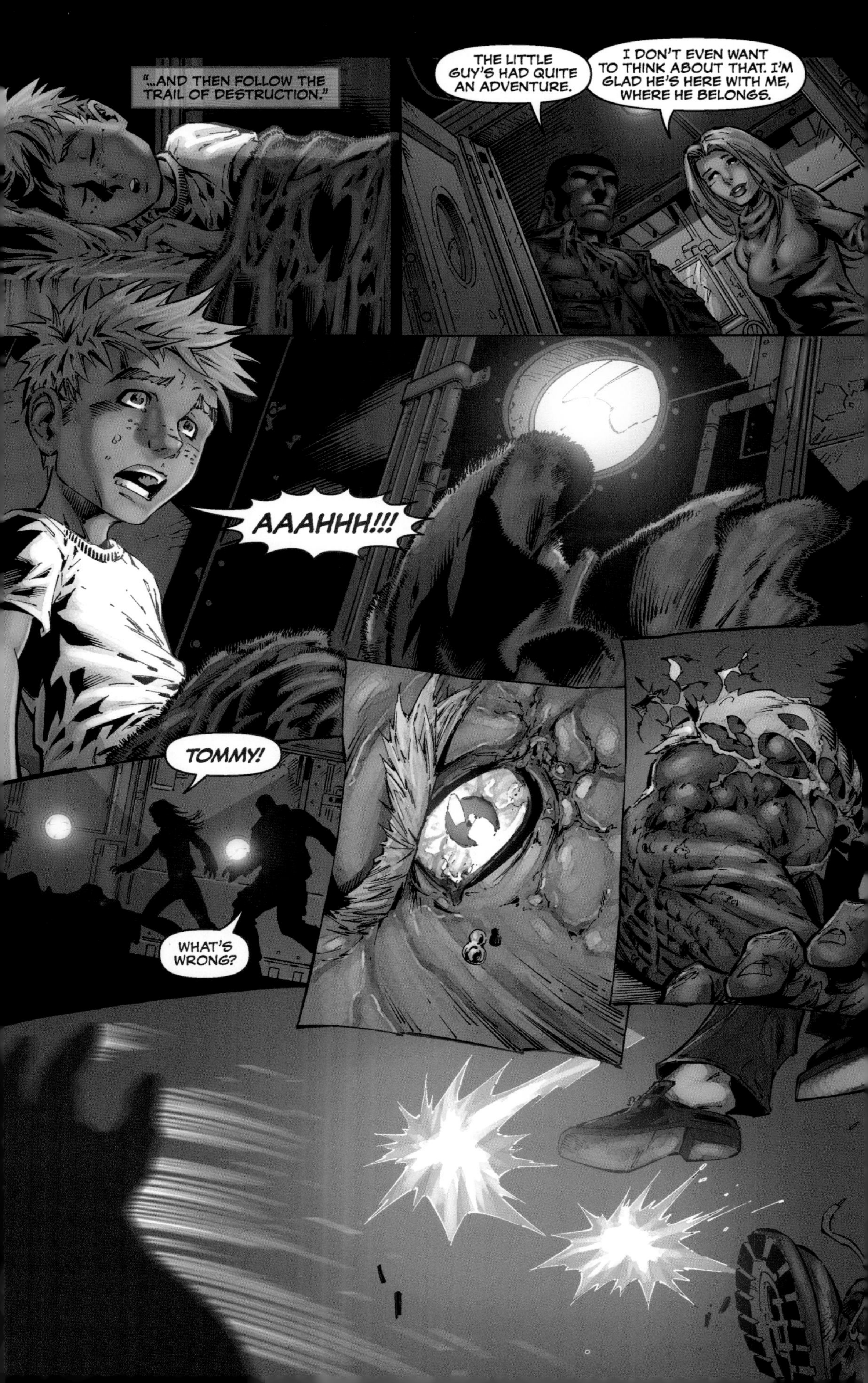
"...AND THEN FOLLOW THE TRAIL OF DESTRUCTION."
THE LITTLE GUY'S HAD QUITE AN ADVENTURE.
I DON'T EVEN WANT TO THINK ABOUT THAT. I'M GLAD HE'S HERE WITH ME, WHERE HE BELONGS.
AAAHHH!!!
TOMMY!
WHAT'S WRONG?

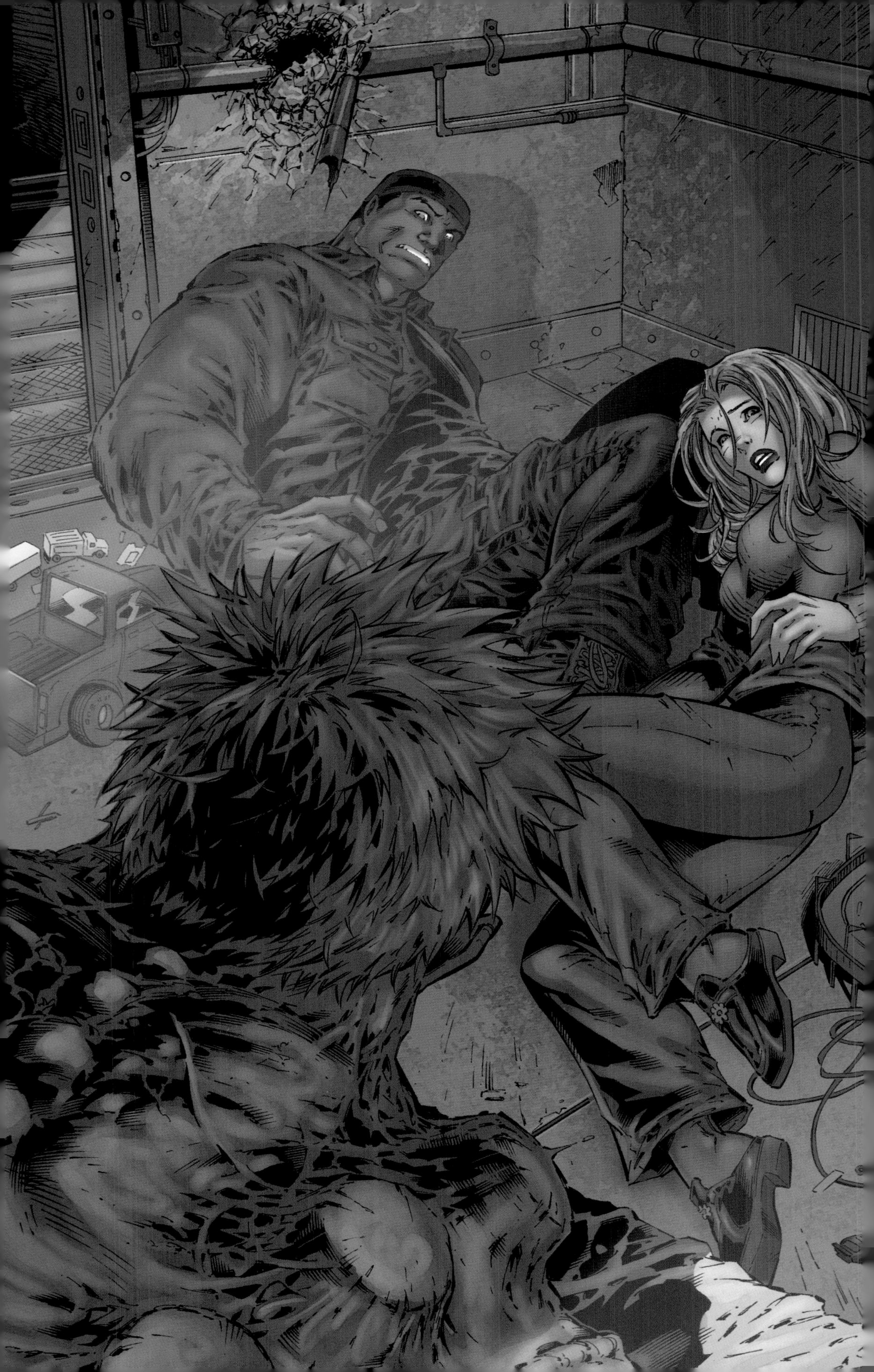

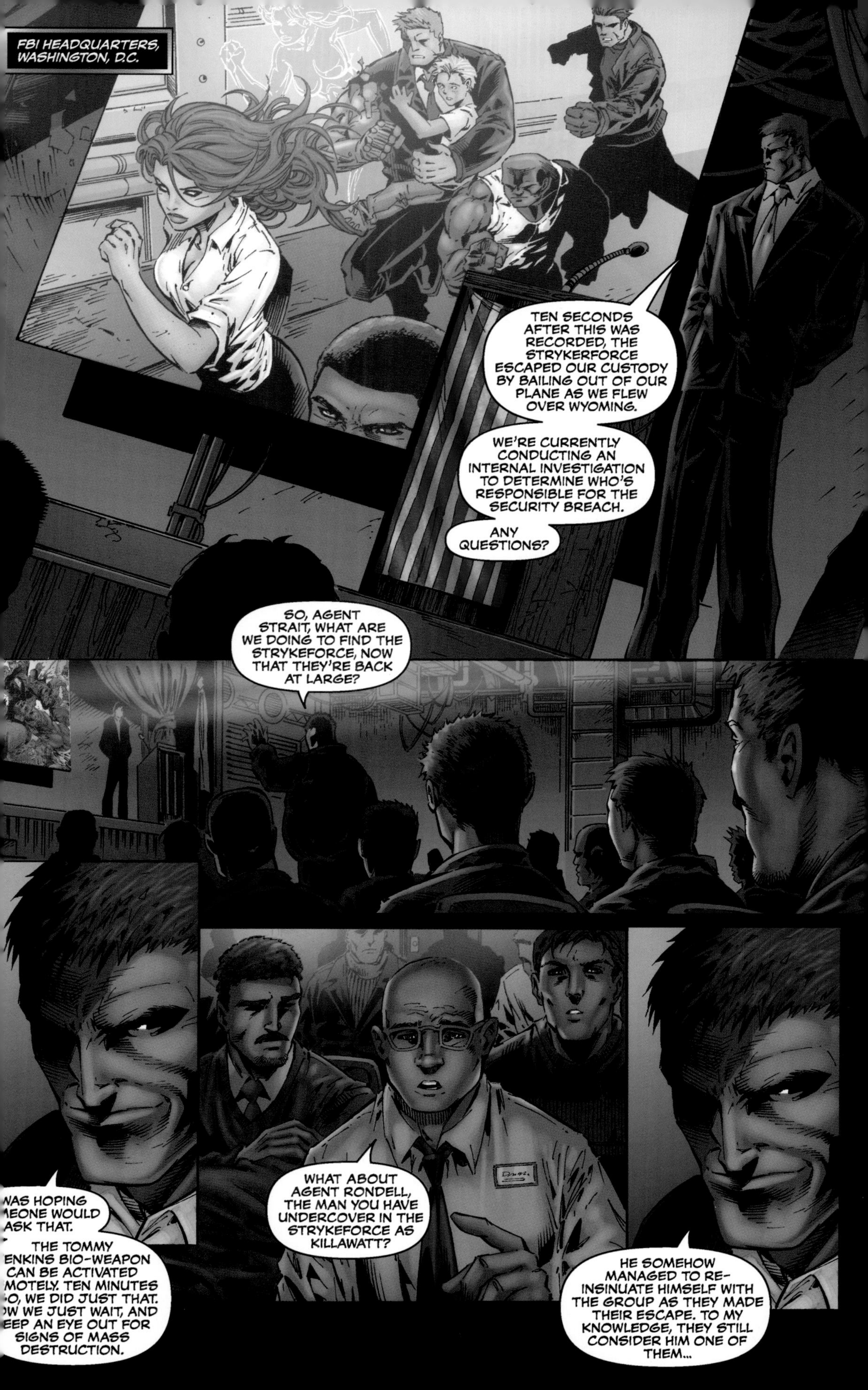
FBI HEADQUARTERS, WASHINGTON, D.C.
TEN SECONDS AFTER THIS WAS RECORDED, THE STRYKERFORCE ESCAPED OUR CUSTODY BY BAILING OUT OF OUR PLANE AS WE FLEW OVER WYOMING.
WE'RE CURRENTLY CONDUCTING AN INTERNAL INVESTIGATION TO DETERMINE WHO'S RESPONSIBLE FOR THE SECURITY BREACH.
ANY QUESTIONS?
SO, AGENT STRAIT, WHAT ARE WE DOING TO FIND THE STRYKEFORCE, NOW THAT THEY'RE BACK AT LARGE?
WAS HOPING MEONE WOULD ASK THAT.
THE TOMMY ENKINS BIO-WEAPON CAN BE ACTIVATED MOTELY. TEN MINUTES O, WE DID JUST THAT. W WE JUST WAIT, AND EEP AN EYE OUT FOR SIGNS OF MASS DESTRUCTION.
WHAT ABOUT AGENT RONDELL, THE MAN YOU HAVE UNDERCOVER IN THE STRYKEFORCE AS KILLAWATT?
HE SOMEHOW MANAGED TO RE-INSINUATE HIMSELF WITH THE GROUP AS THEY MADE THEIR ESCAPE. TO MY KNOWLEDGE, THEY STILL CONSIDER HIM ONE OF THEM...

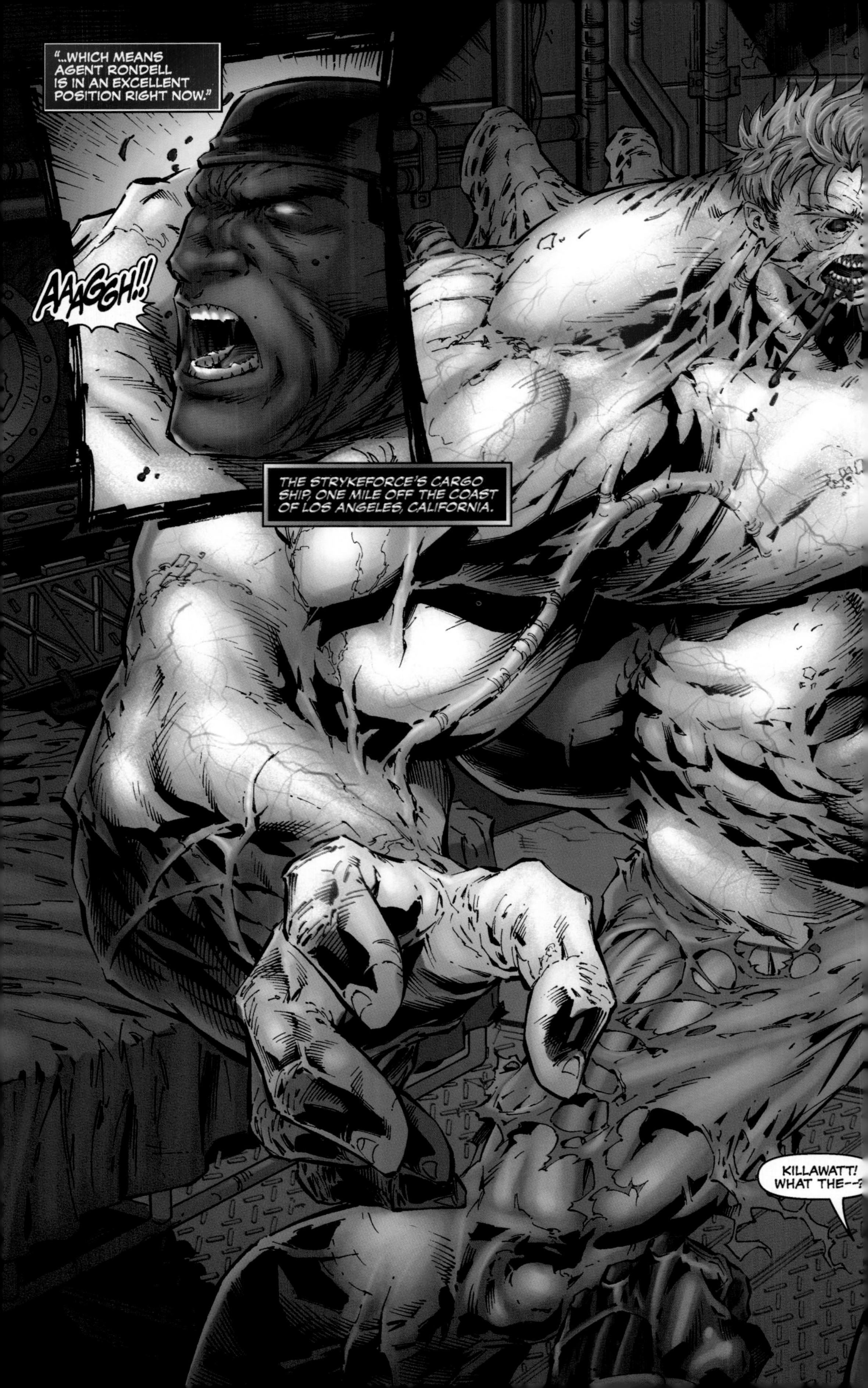
"...WHICH MEANS AGENT RONDELL IS IN AN EXCELLENT POSITION RIGHT NOW."
AAAGGH!!
THE STRYKEFORCE'S CARGO SHIP, ONE MILE OFF THE COAST OF LOS ANGELES, CALIFORNIA.
KILLAWATT! WHAT THE--?

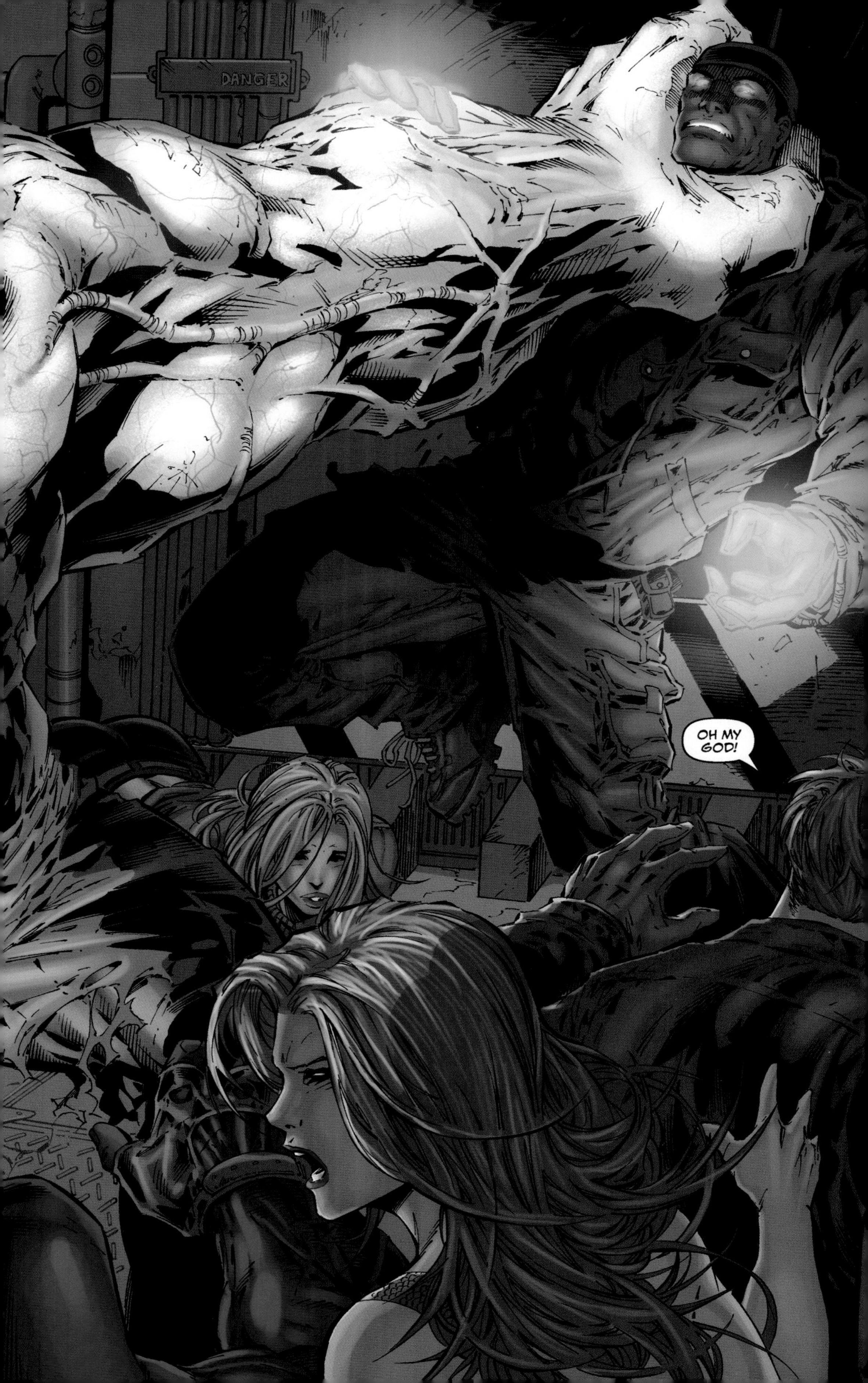
DANGER
OH MY GOD!

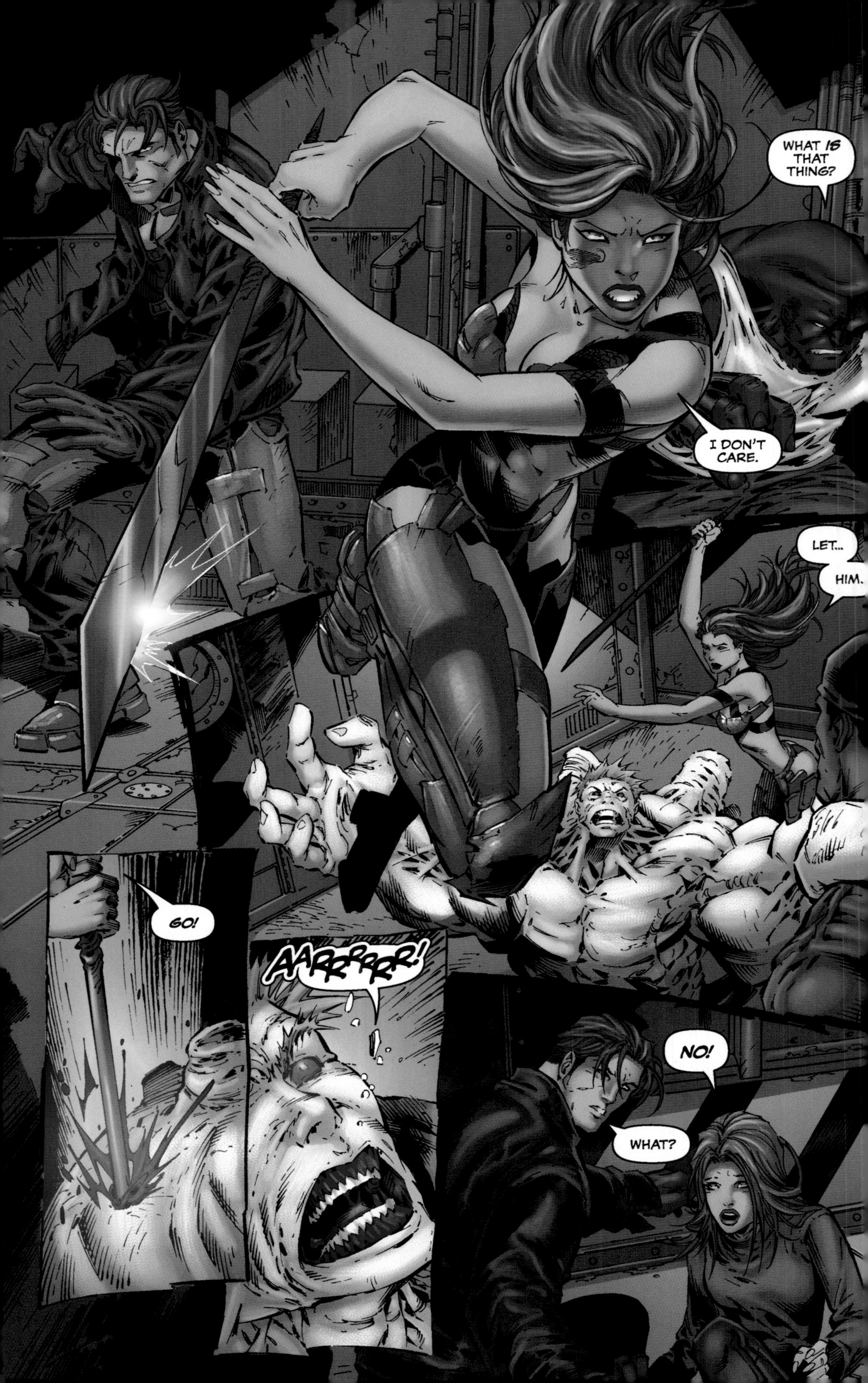
WHAT *IS* THAT THING?
I DON'T CARE.
LET...
HIM.
GO!
AARRRRRR!
NO!
WHAT?

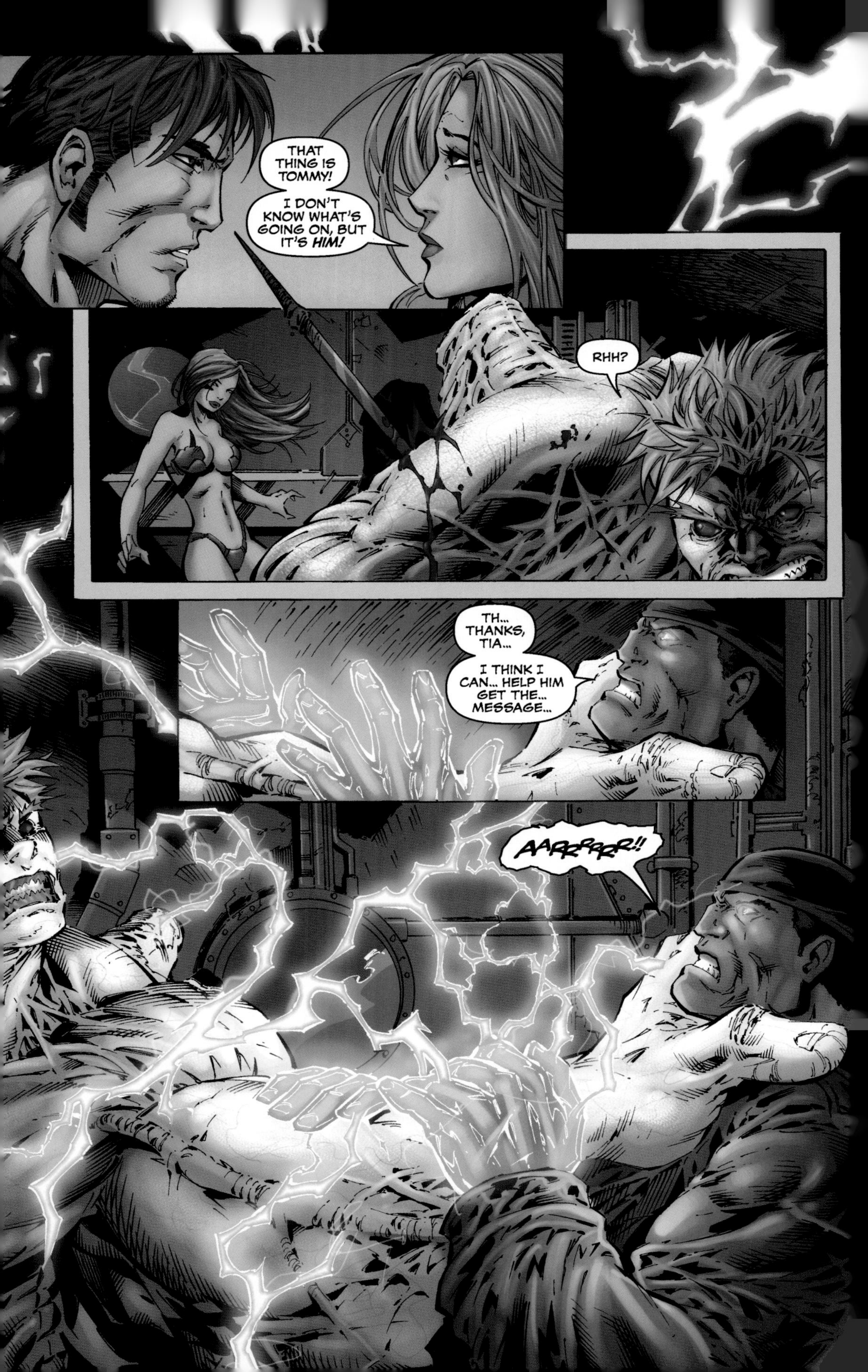
THAT THING IS TOMMY!
I DON'T KNOW WHAT'S GOING ON, BUT IT'S HIM!
RHH?
TH... THANKS, TIA...
I THINK I CAN... HELP HIM GET THE... MESSAGE...
AARRRRRR!!

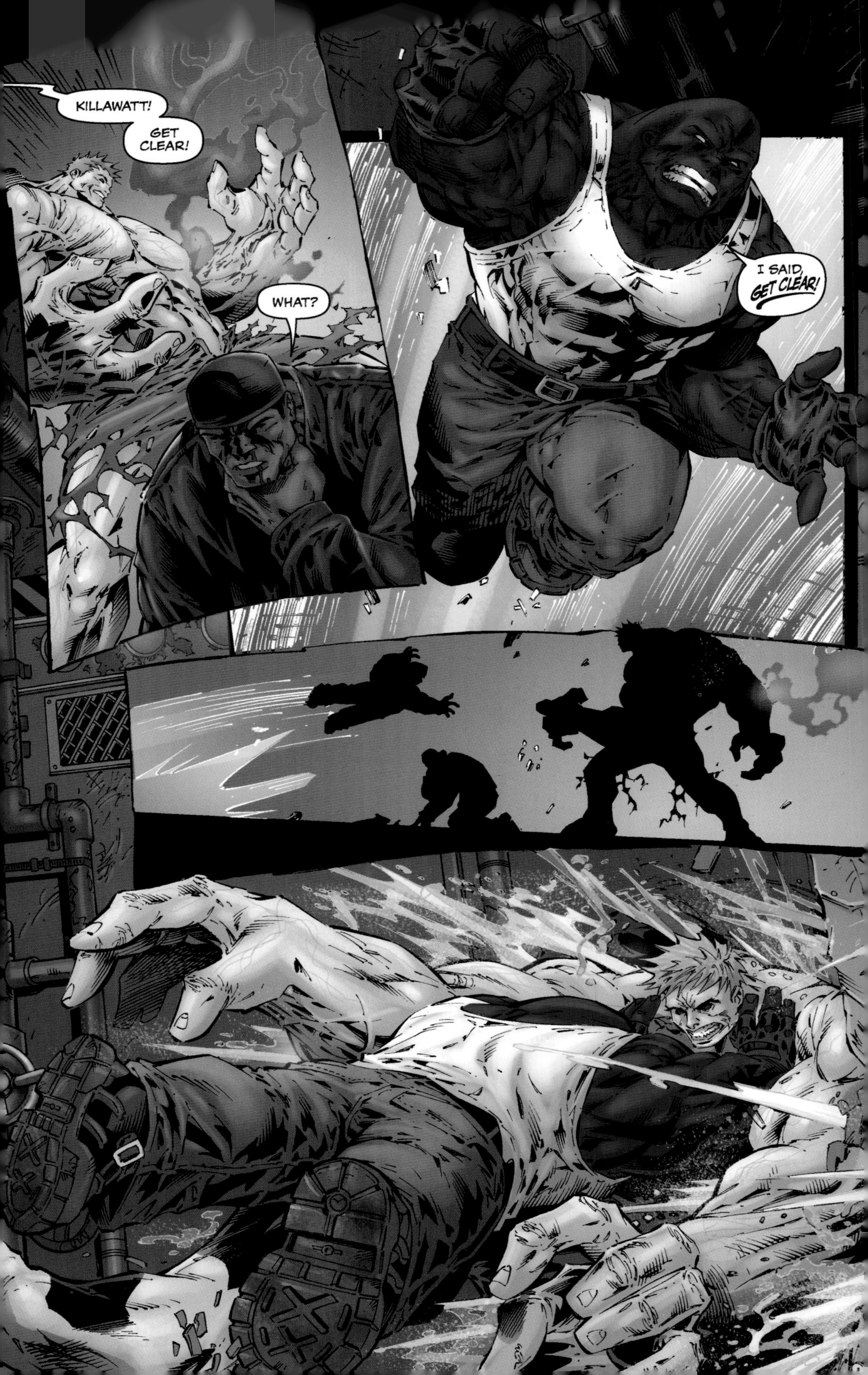
KILLAWATT!
GET CLEAR!
WHAT?
I SAID, GET CLEAR!

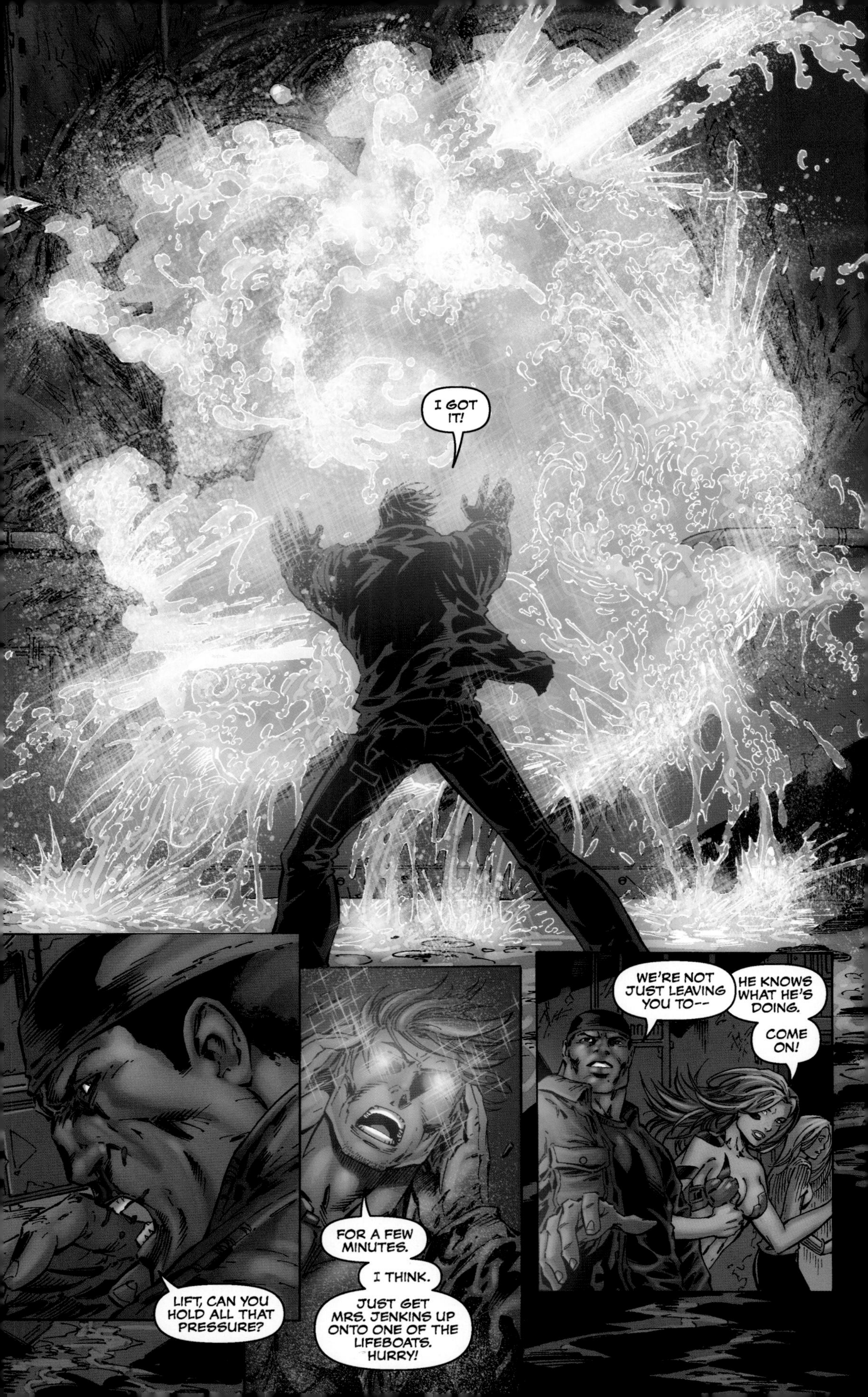
I GOT IT!
LIFT, CAN YOU HOLD ALL THAT PRESSURE?
FOR A FEW MINUTES.
I THINK.
JUST GET MRS. JENKINS UP ONTO ONE OF THE LIFEBOATS. HURRY!
WE'RE NOT JUST LEAVING YOU TO--
HE KNOWS WHAT HE'S DOING.
COME ON!

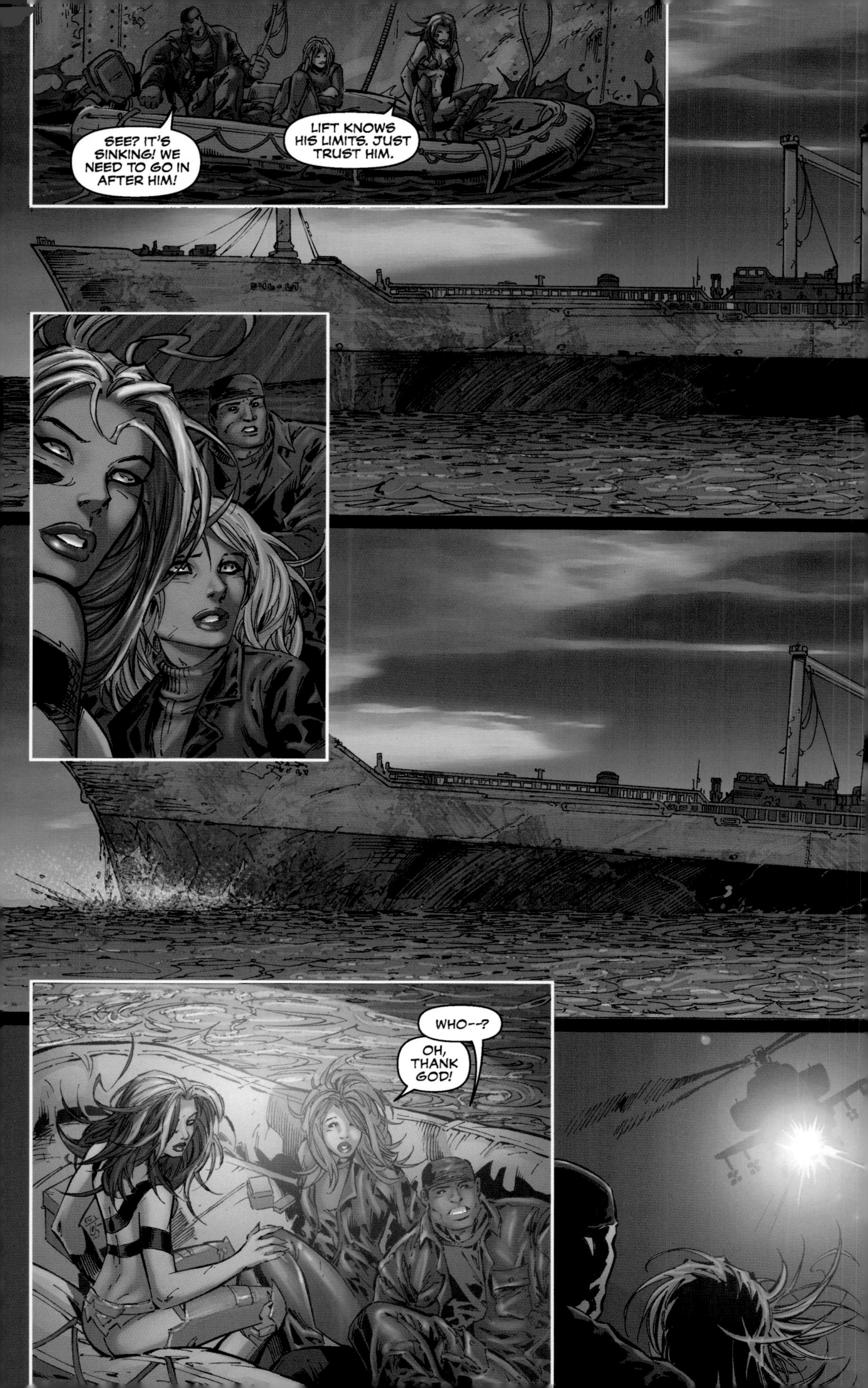

SEE? IT'S SINKING! WE NEED TO GO IN AFTER HIM!
LIFT KNOWS HIS LIMITS. JUST TRUST HIM.
WHO--?
OH, THANK GOD!

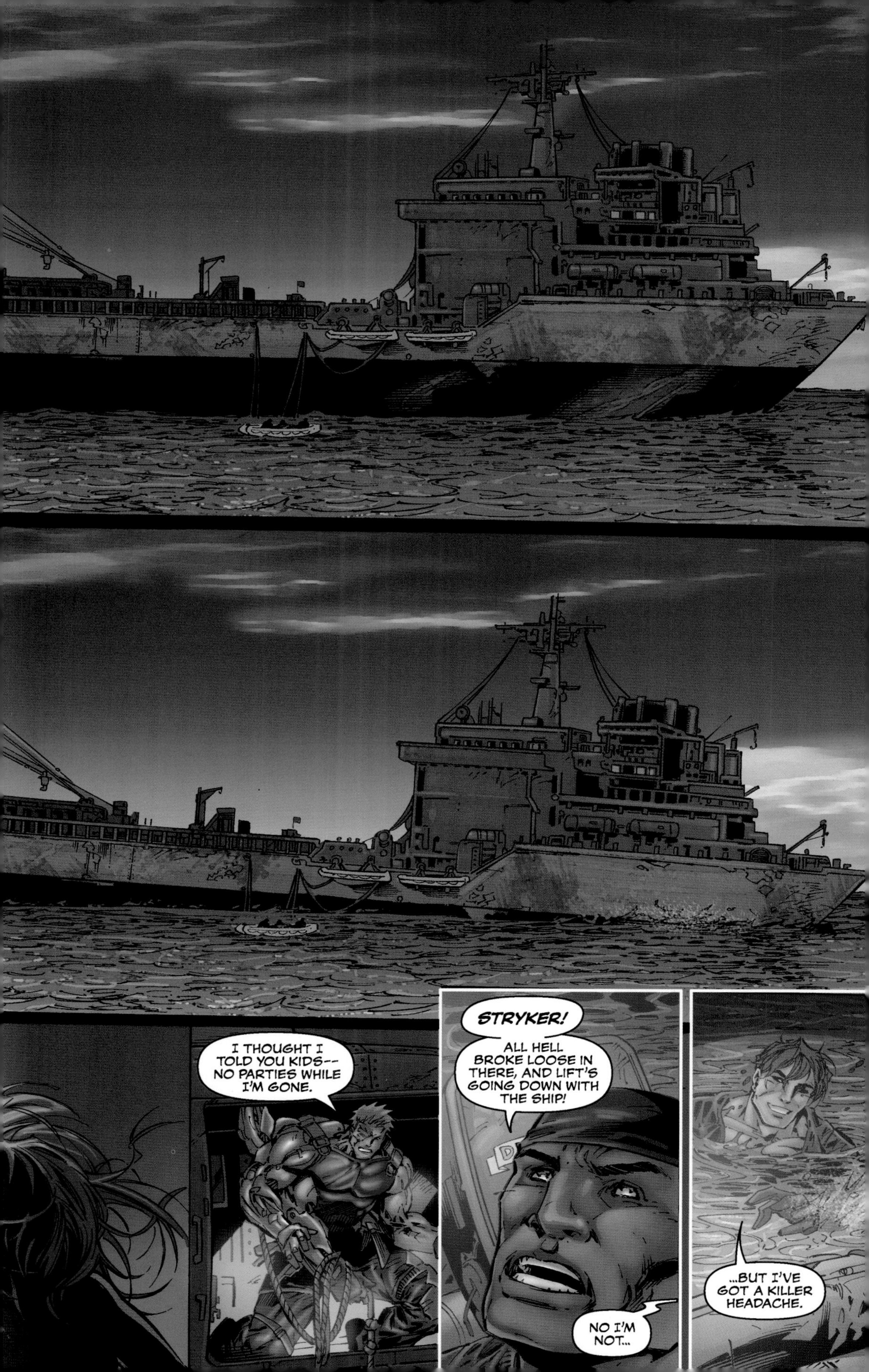
I THOUGHT I TOLD YOU KIDS-- NO PARTIES WHILE I'M GONE.
STRYKER!
ALL HELL BROKE LOOSE IN THERE, AND LIFT'S GOING DOWN WITH THE SHIP!
NO I'M NOT...
...BUT I'VE GOT A KILLER HEADACHE.

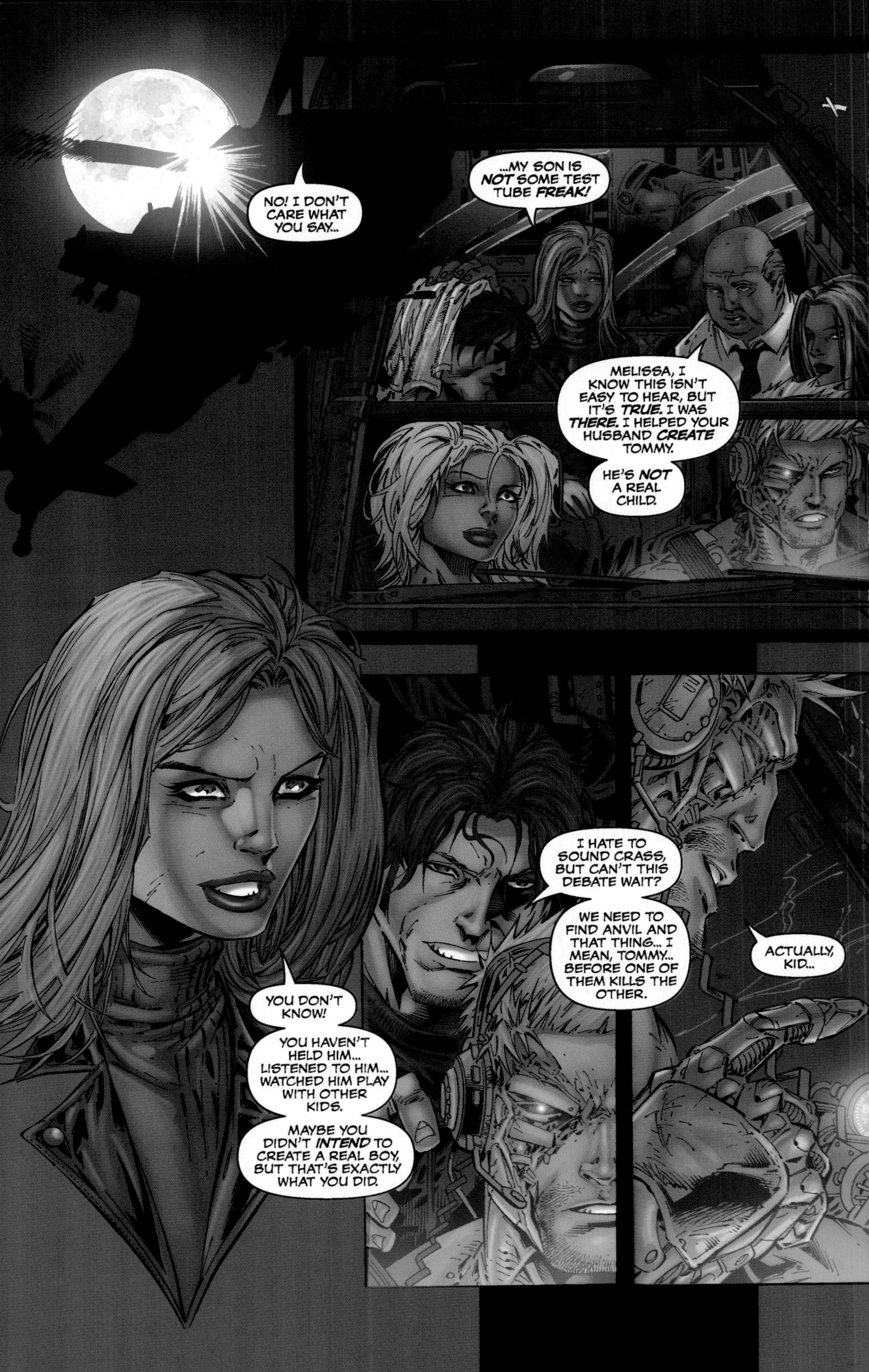
NO! I DON'T CARE WHAT YOU SAY...
...MY SON IS NOT SOME TEST TUBE FREAK!
MELISSA, I KNOW THIS ISN'T EASY TO HEAR, BUT IT'S TRUE. I WAS THERE. I HELPED YOUR HUSBAND CREATE TOMMY.
HE'S NOT A REAL CHILD.
YOU DON'T KNOW!
YOU HAVEN'T HELD HIM... LISTENED TO HIM... WATCHED HIM PLAY WITH OTHER KIDS.
MAYBE YOU DIDN'T INTEND TO CREATE A REAL BOY, BUT THAT'S EXACTLY WHAT YOU DID.
I HATE TO SOUND CRASS, BUT CAN'T THIS DEBATE WAIT?
WE NEED TO FIND ANVIL AND THAT THING... I MEAN, TOMMY... BEFORE ONE OF THEM KILLS THE OTHER.
ACTUALLY, KID...

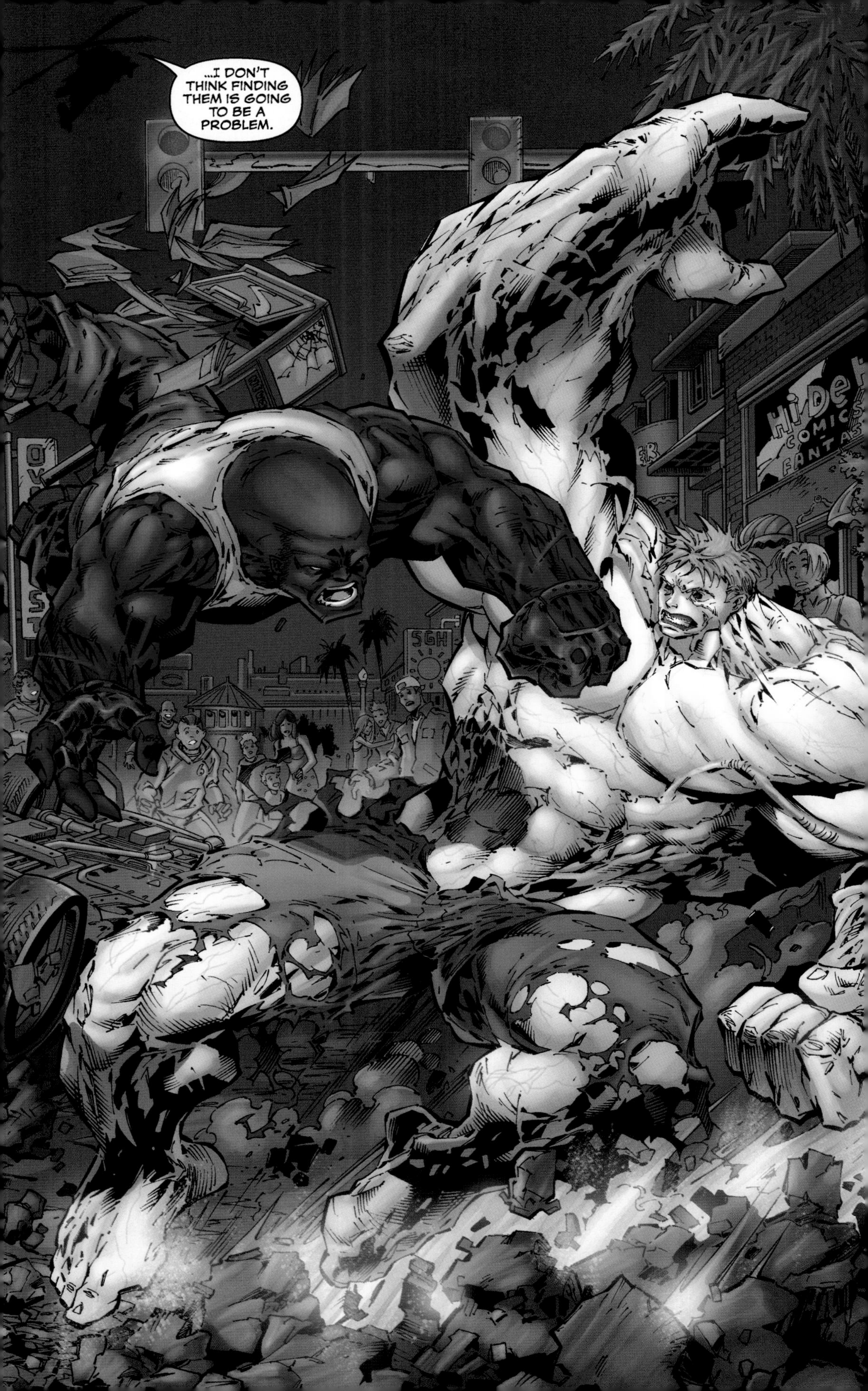
...I DON'T THINK FINDING THEM IS GOING TO BE A PROBLEM.

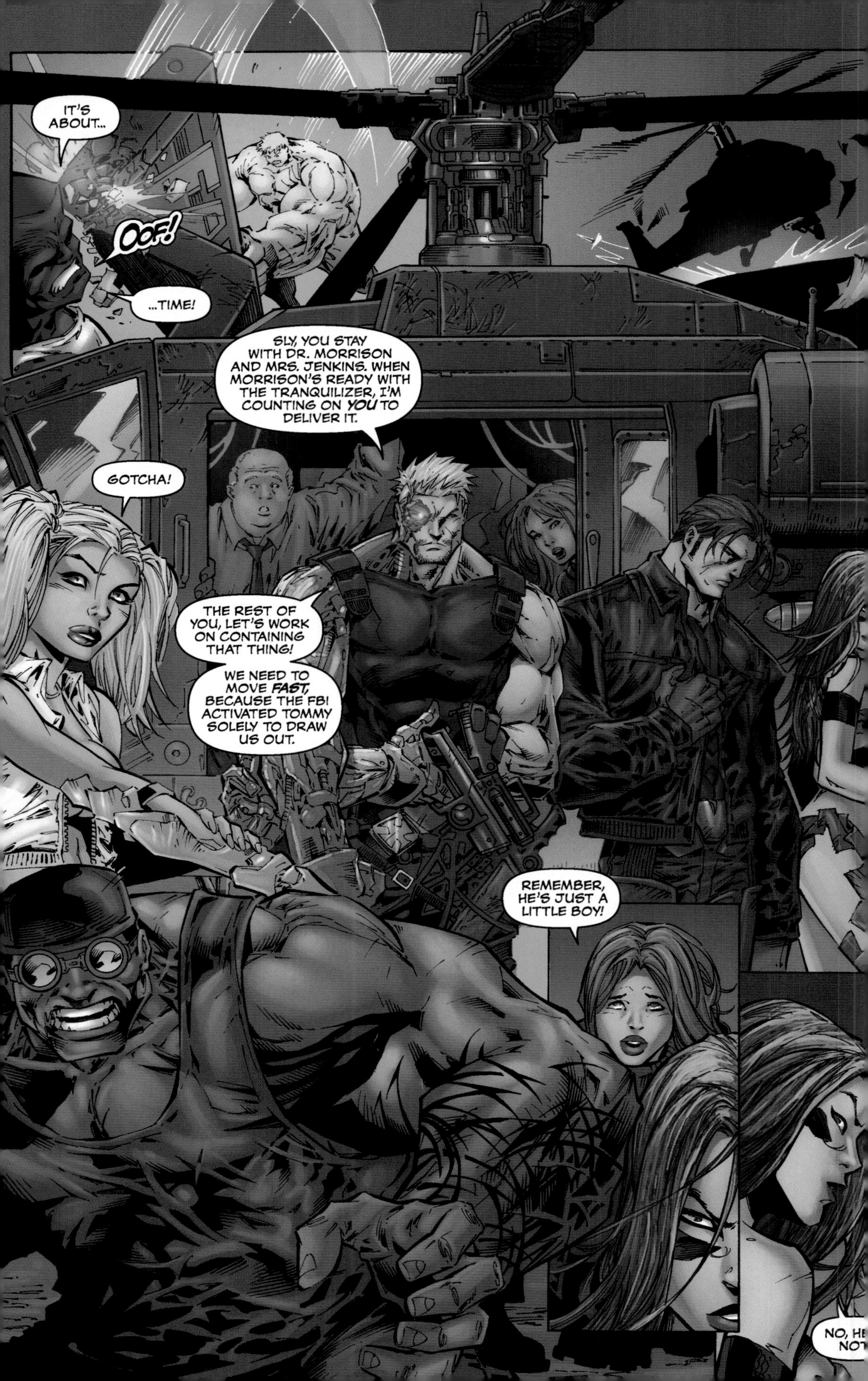

IT'S ABOUT...
OOF!
...TIME!
SLY, YOU STAY WITH DR. MORRISON AND MRS. JENKINS. WHEN MORRISON'S READY WITH THE TRANQUILIZER, I'M COUNTING ON YOU TO DELIVER IT.
GOTCHA!
THE REST OF YOU, LET'S WORK ON CONTAINING THAT THING!
WE NEED TO MOVE FAST, BECAUSE THE FBI ACTIVATED TOMMY SOLELY TO DRAW US OUT.
REMEMBER, HE'S JUST A LITTLE BOY!

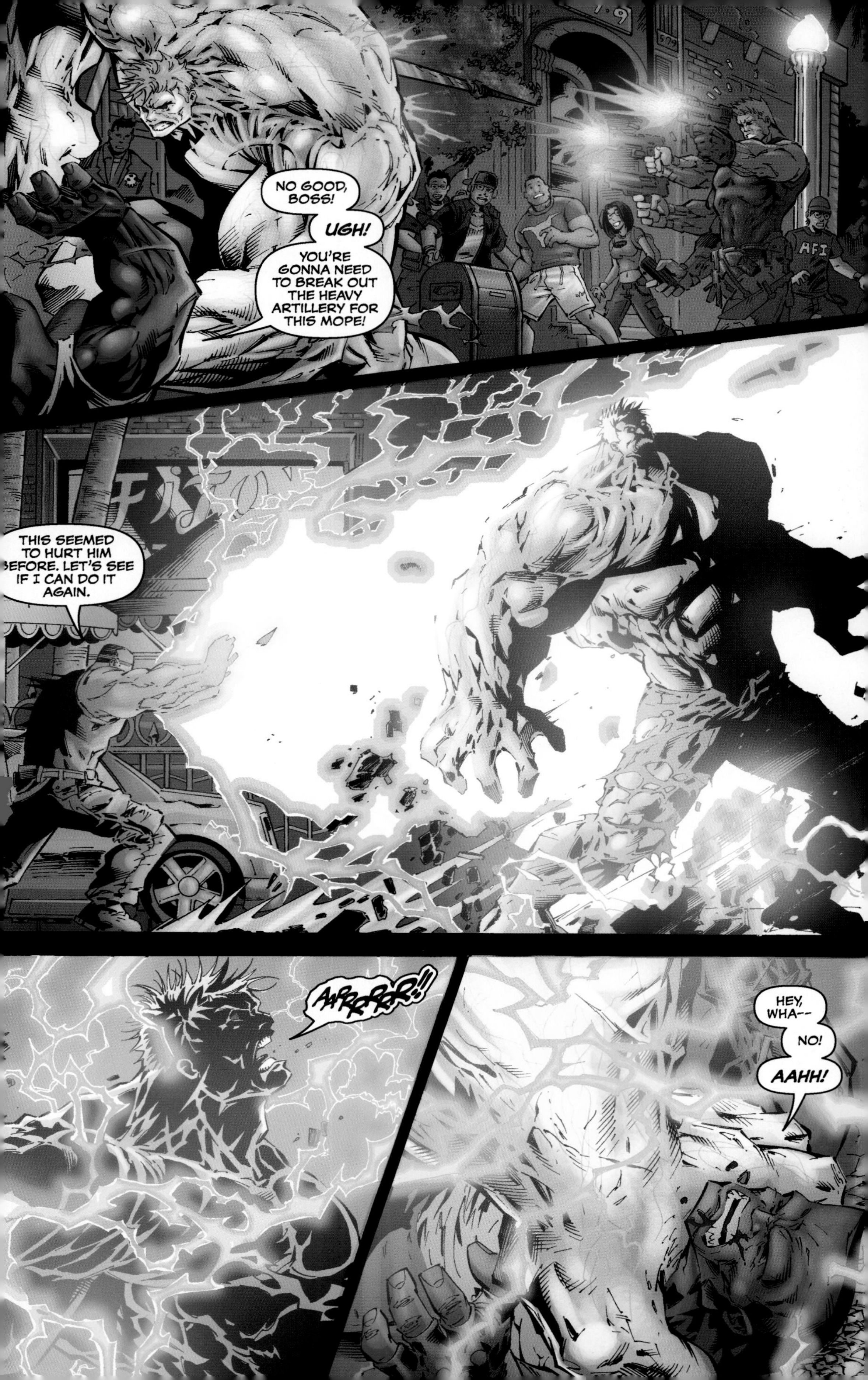
NO GOOD, BOSS!
UGH!
YOU'RE GONNA NEED TO BREAK OUT THE HEAVY ARTILLERY FOR THIS MOPE!
THIS SEEMED TO HURT HIM BEFORE. LET'S SEE IF I CAN DO IT AGAIN.
AARRRRRR!!
HEY, WHA--
NO!
AAHH!

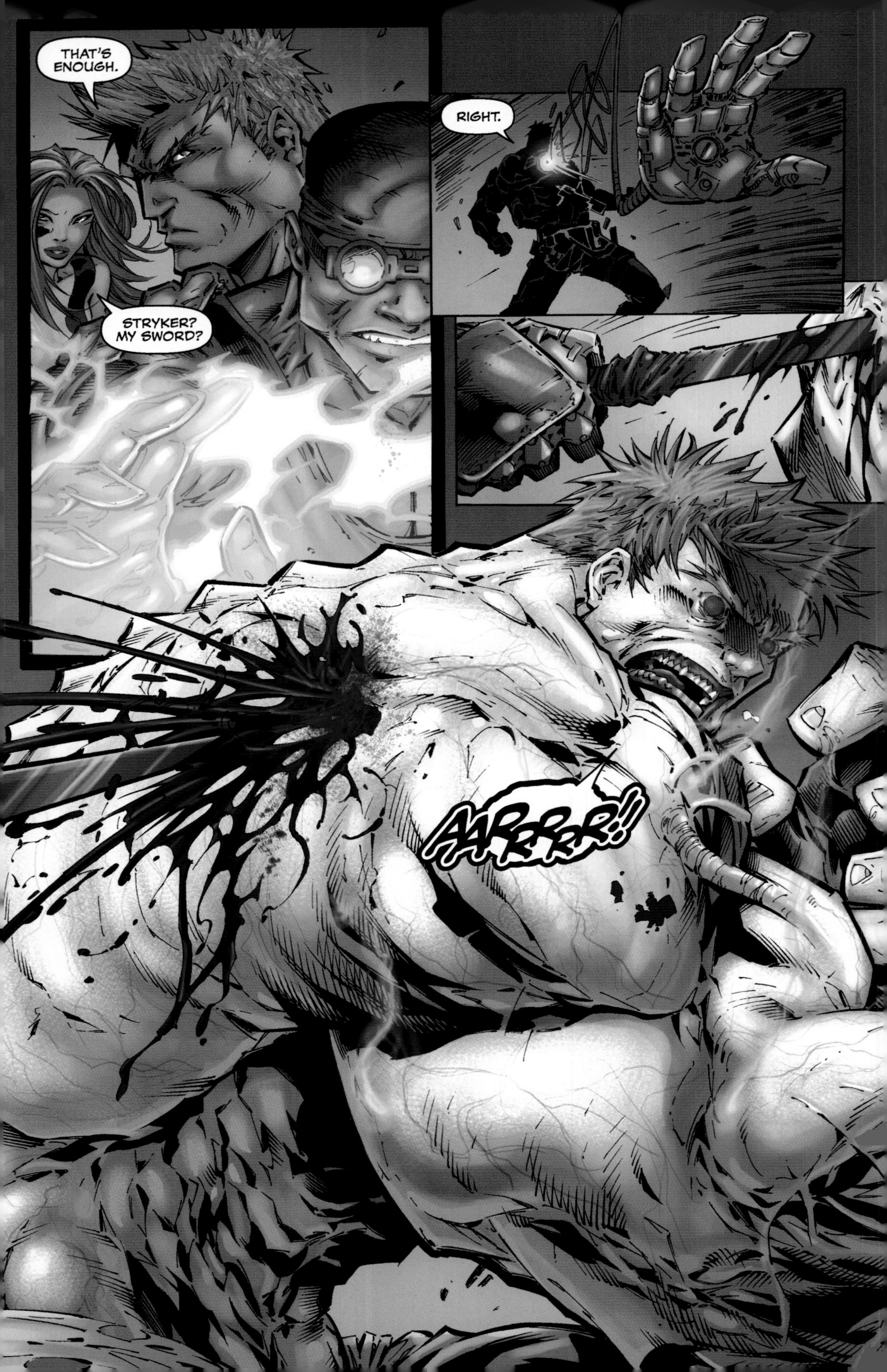
THAT'S ENOUGH.
STRYKER? MY SWORD?
RIGHT.
AARRRRR!!

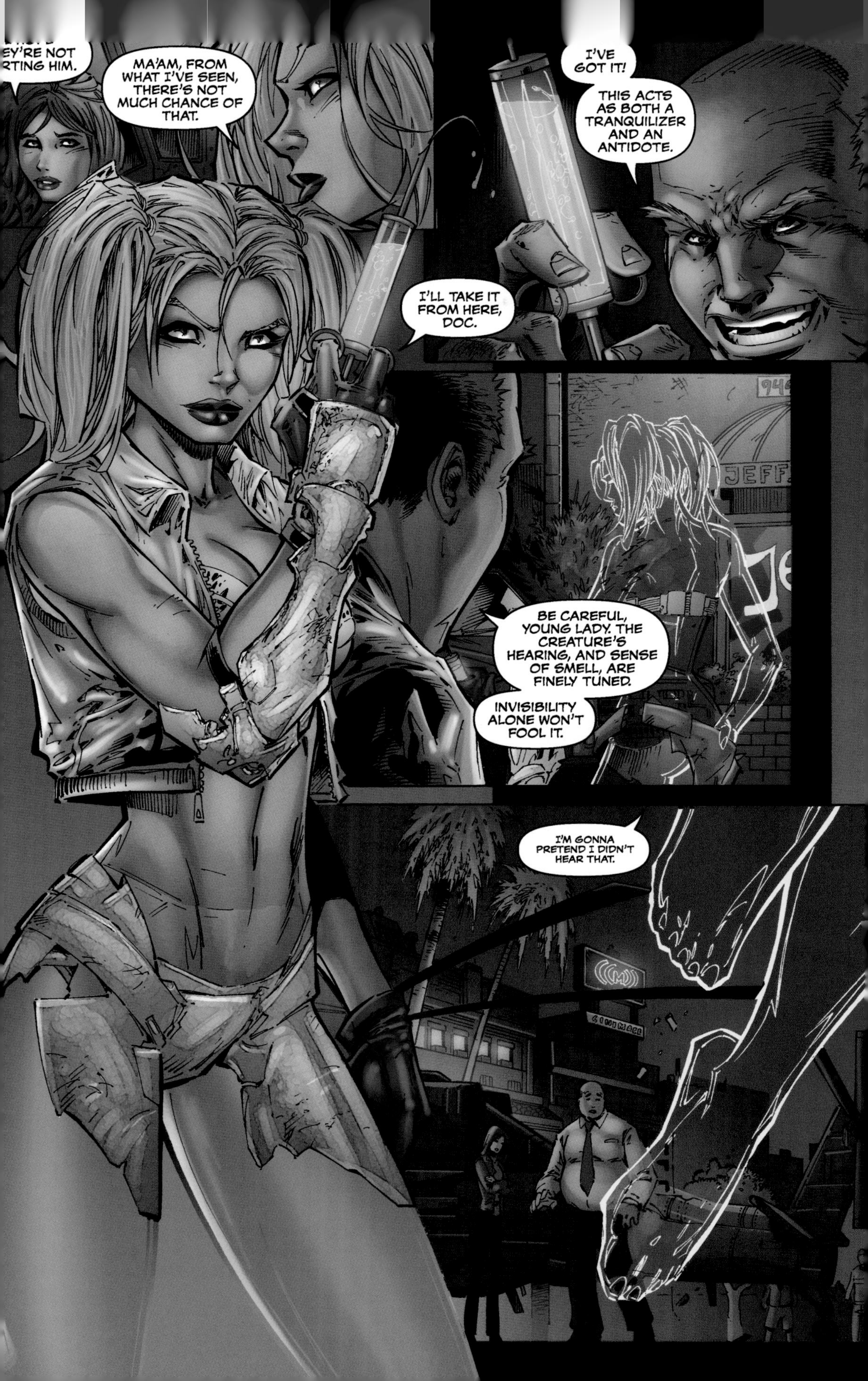
EY'RE NOT
RTING HIM.
MA'AM, FROM WHAT I'VE SEEN, THERE'S NOT MUCH CHANCE OF THAT.
I'VE GOT IT!
THIS ACTS AS BOTH A TRANQUILIZER AND AN ANTIDOTE.
I'LL TAKE IT FROM HERE, DOC.
JEFF
BE CAREFUL, YOUNG LADY. THE CREATURE'S HEARING, AND SENSE OF SMELL, ARE FINELY TUNED.
INVISIBILITY ALONE WON'T FOOL IT.
I'M GONNA PRETEND I DIDN'T HEAR THAT.

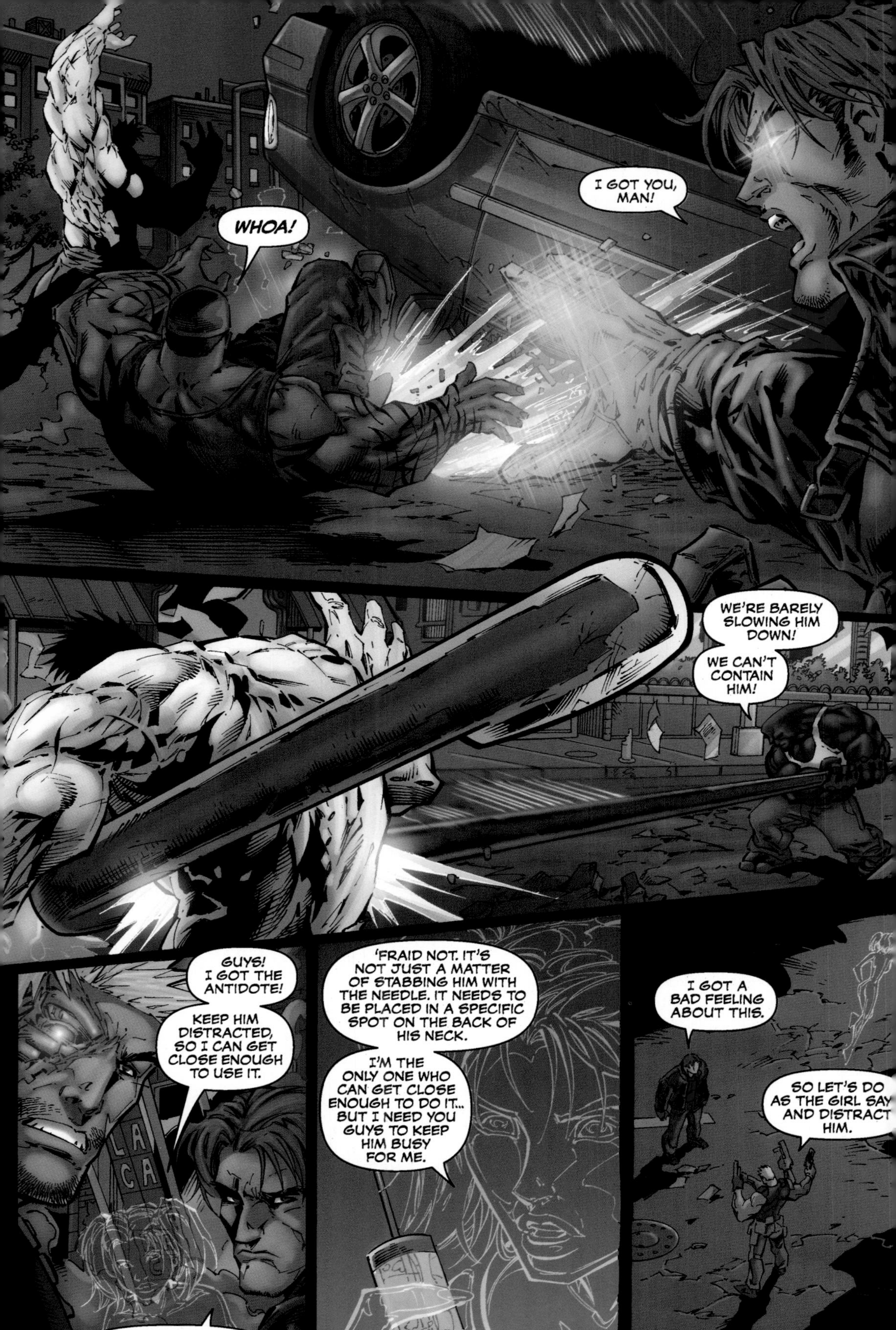

I GOT YOU, MAN!
WHOA!
WE'RE BARELY SLOWING HIM DOWN!
WE CAN'T CONTAIN HIM!
GUYS! I GOT THE ANTIDOTE!
KEEP HIM DISTRACTED, SO I CAN GET CLOSE ENOUGH TO USE IT.
'FRAID NOT. IT'S NOT JUST A MATTER OF STABBING HIM WITH THE NEEDLE. IT NEEDS TO BE PLACED IN A SPECIFIC SPOT ON THE BACK OF HIS NECK.
I'M THE ONLY ONE WHO CAN GET CLOSE ENOUGH TO DO IT... BUT I NEED YOU GUYS TO KEEP HIM BUSY FOR ME.
SCREW THAT. I
I GOT A BAD FEELING ABOUT THIS.
SO LET'S DO AS THE GIRL SAY AND DISTRACT HIM.

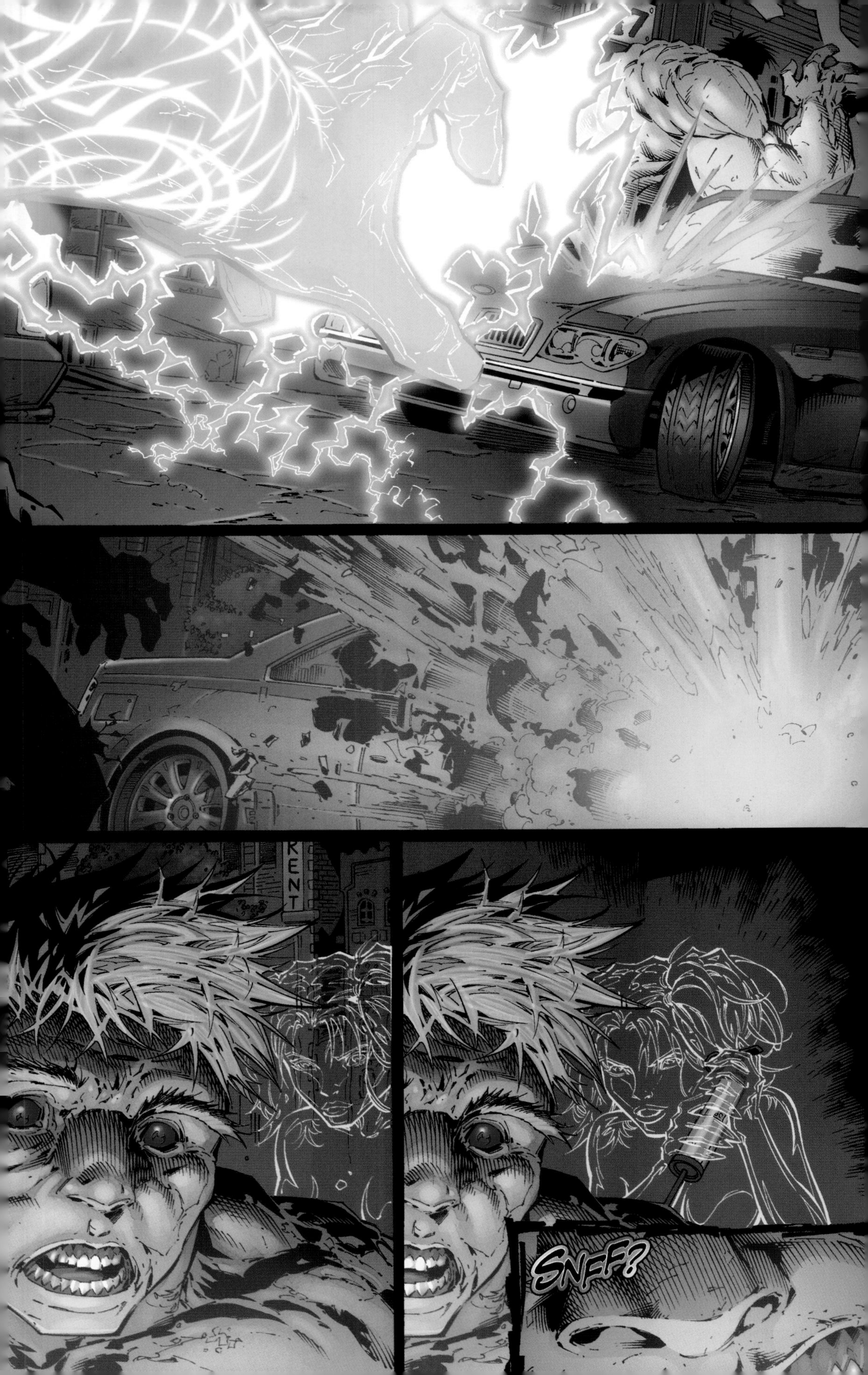
RENT
SNFF?

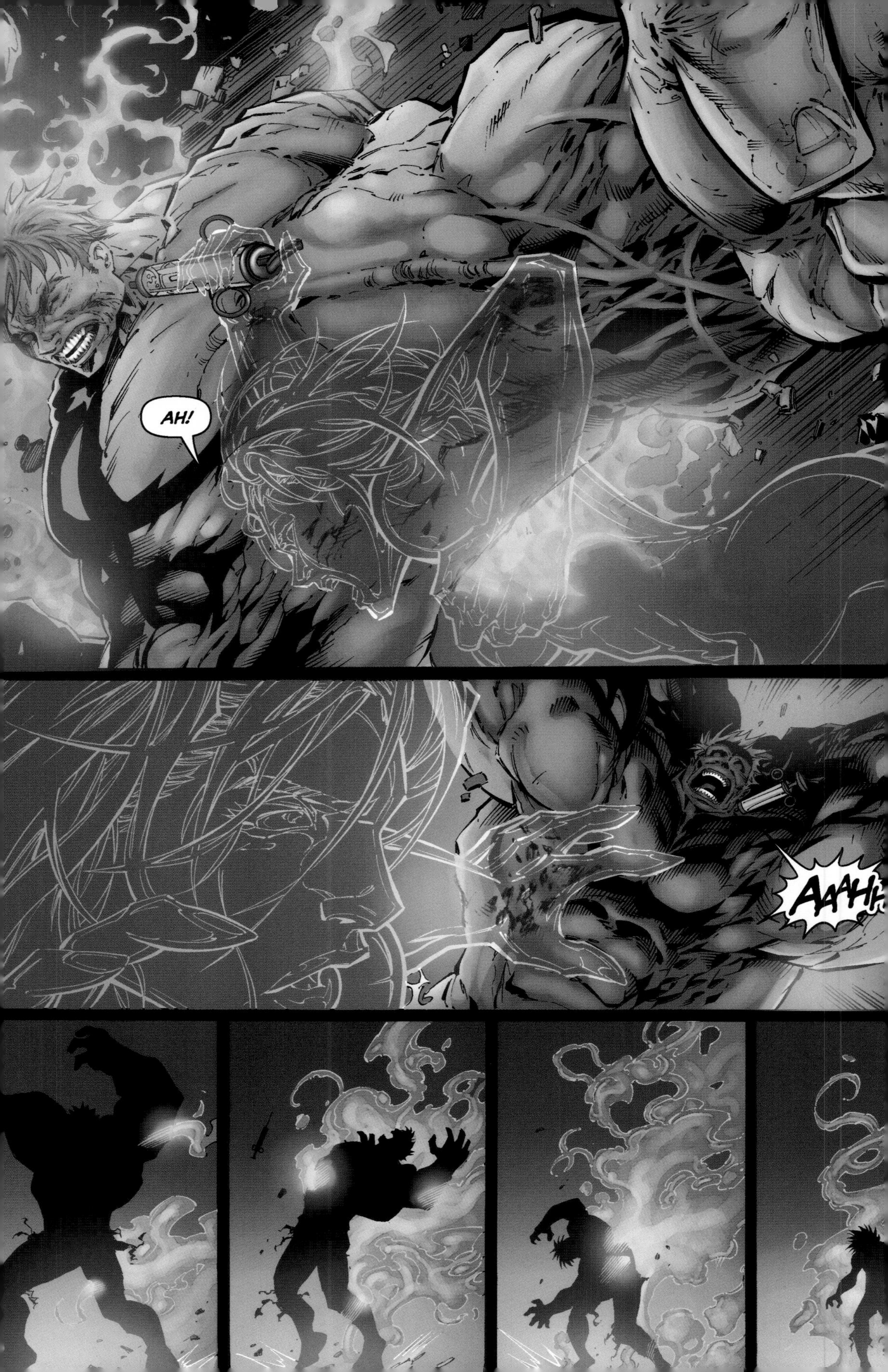
AH!
AAAHH

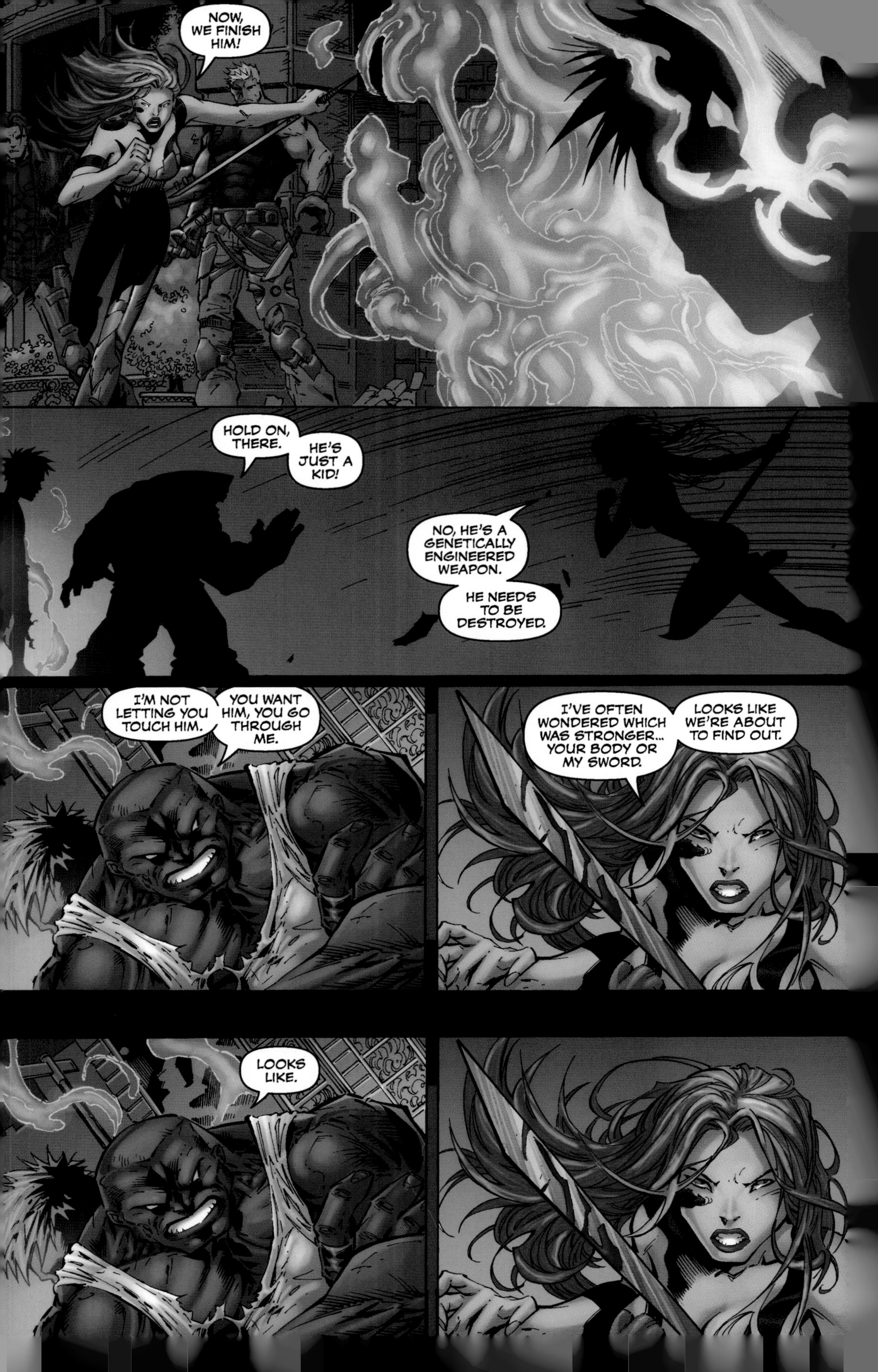
NOW, WE FINISH HIM!
HOLD ON, THERE.
HE'S JUST A KID!
NO, HE'S A GENETICALLY ENGINEERED WEAPON.
HE NEEDS TO BE DESTROYED.
I'M NOT LETTING YOU TOUCH HIM.
YOU WANT HIM, YOU GO THROUGH ME.
I'VE OFTEN WONDERED WHICH WAS STRONGER... YOUR BODY OR MY SWORD.
LOOKS LIKE WE'RE ABOUT TO FIND OUT.
LOOKS LIKE.

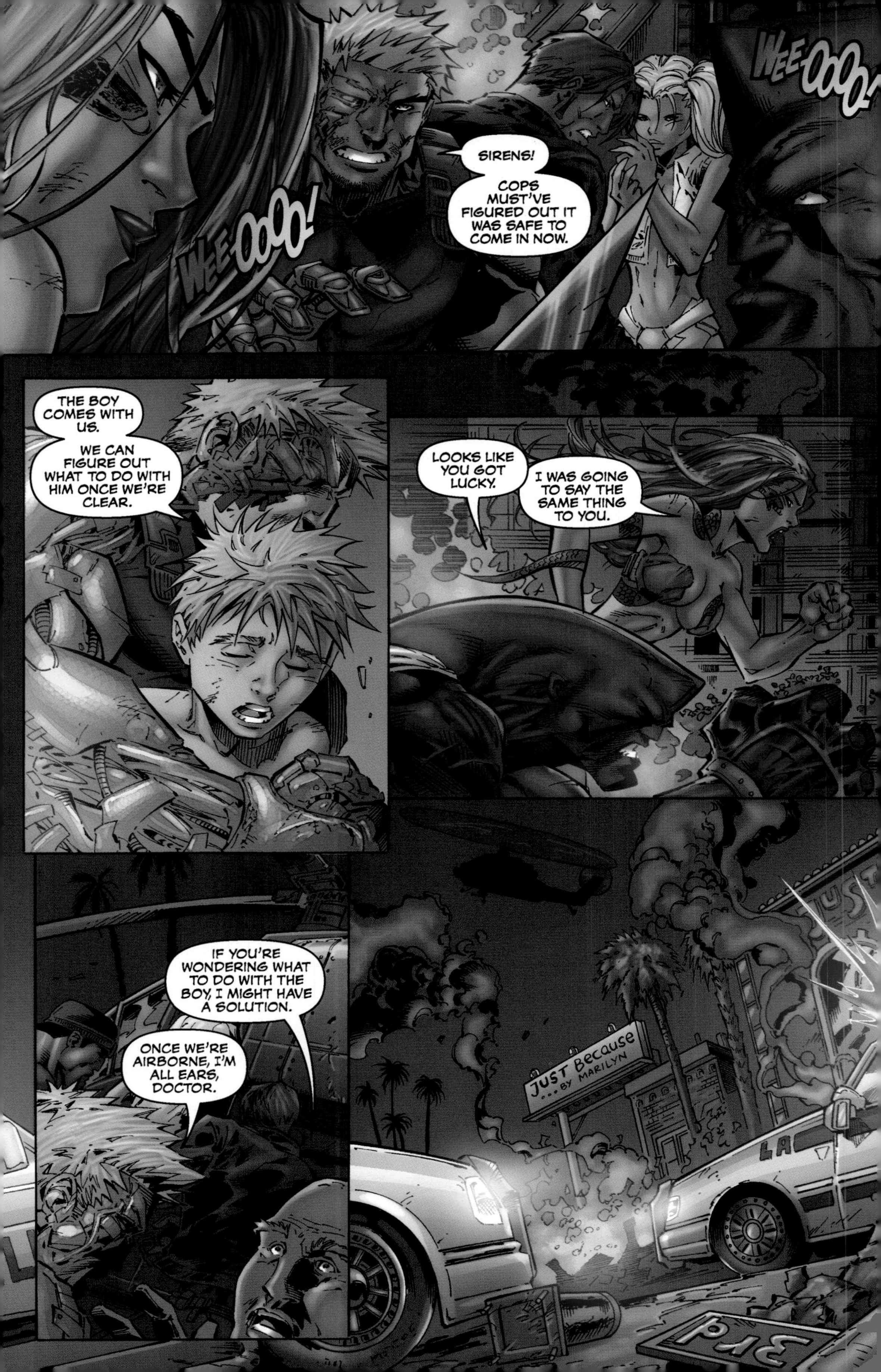
WEE-OOOO!
SIRENS!
COPS MUST'VE FIGURED OUT IT WAS SAFE TO COME IN NOW.
WEE-OOOO!
THE BOY COMES WITH US.
WE CAN FIGURE OUT WHAT TO DO WITH HIM ONCE WE'RE CLEAR.
LOOKS LIKE YOU GOT LUCKY.
I WAS GOING TO SAY THE SAME THING TO YOU.
IF YOU'RE WONDERING WHAT TO DO WITH THE BOY, I MIGHT HAVE A SOLUTION.
ONCE WE'RE AIRBORNE, I'M ALL EARS, DOCTOR.
JUST Because
... BY MARILYN
LA
3rd

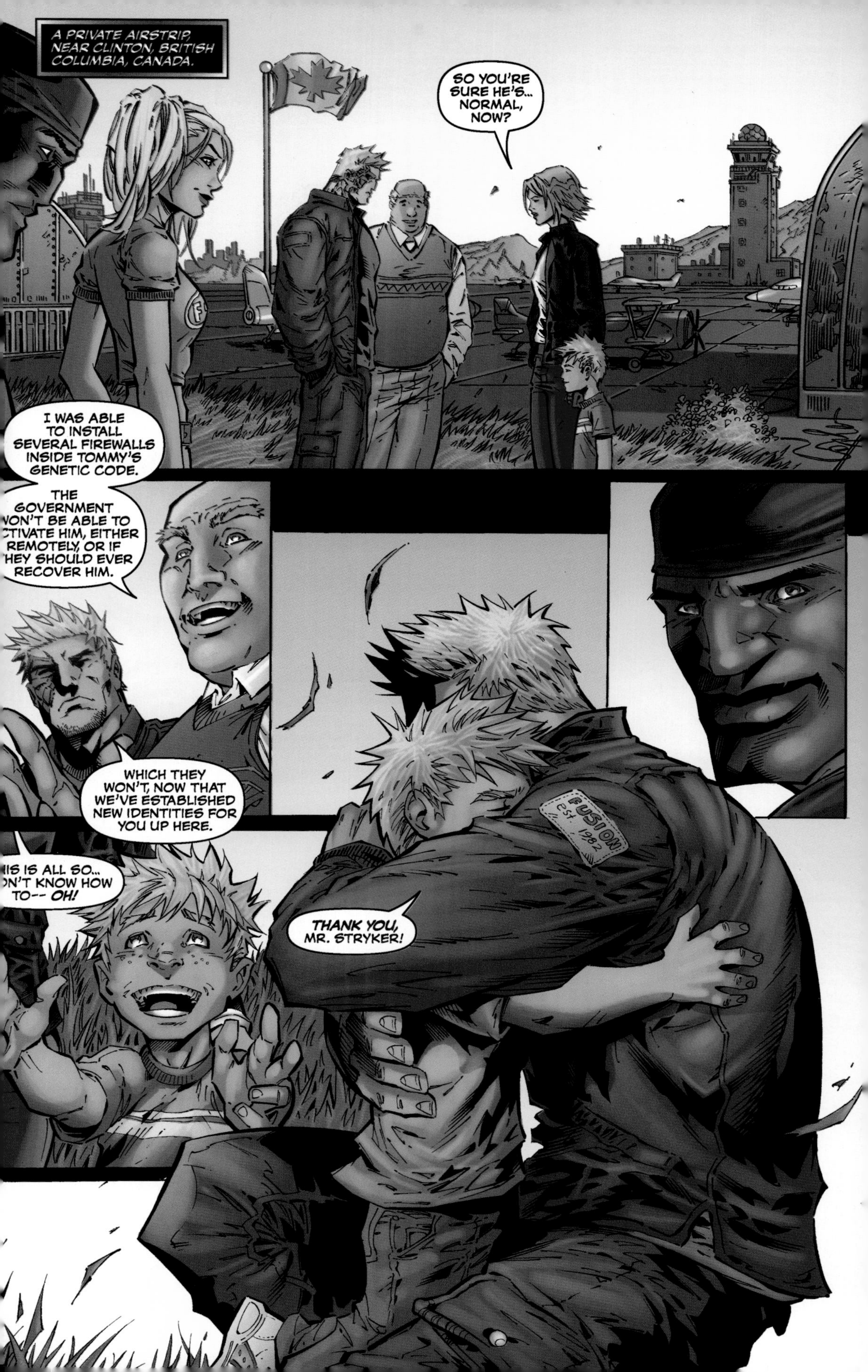
A PRIVATE AIRSTRIP, NEAR CLINTON, BRITISH COLUMBIA, CANADA.
SO YOU'RE SURE HE'S... NORMAL, NOW?
I WAS ABLE TO INSTALL SEVERAL FIREWALLS INSIDE TOMMY'S GENETIC CODE.
THE GOVERNMENT WON'T BE ABLE TO ACTIVATE HIM, EITHER REMOTELY, OR IF THEY SHOULD EVER RECOVER HIM.
WHICH THEY WON'T, NOW THAT WE'VE ESTABLISHED NEW IDENTITIES FOR YOU UP HERE.
THIS IS ALL SO... I DON'T KNOW HOW TO-- OH!
THANK YOU, MR. STRYKER!
FUSION est. 1982

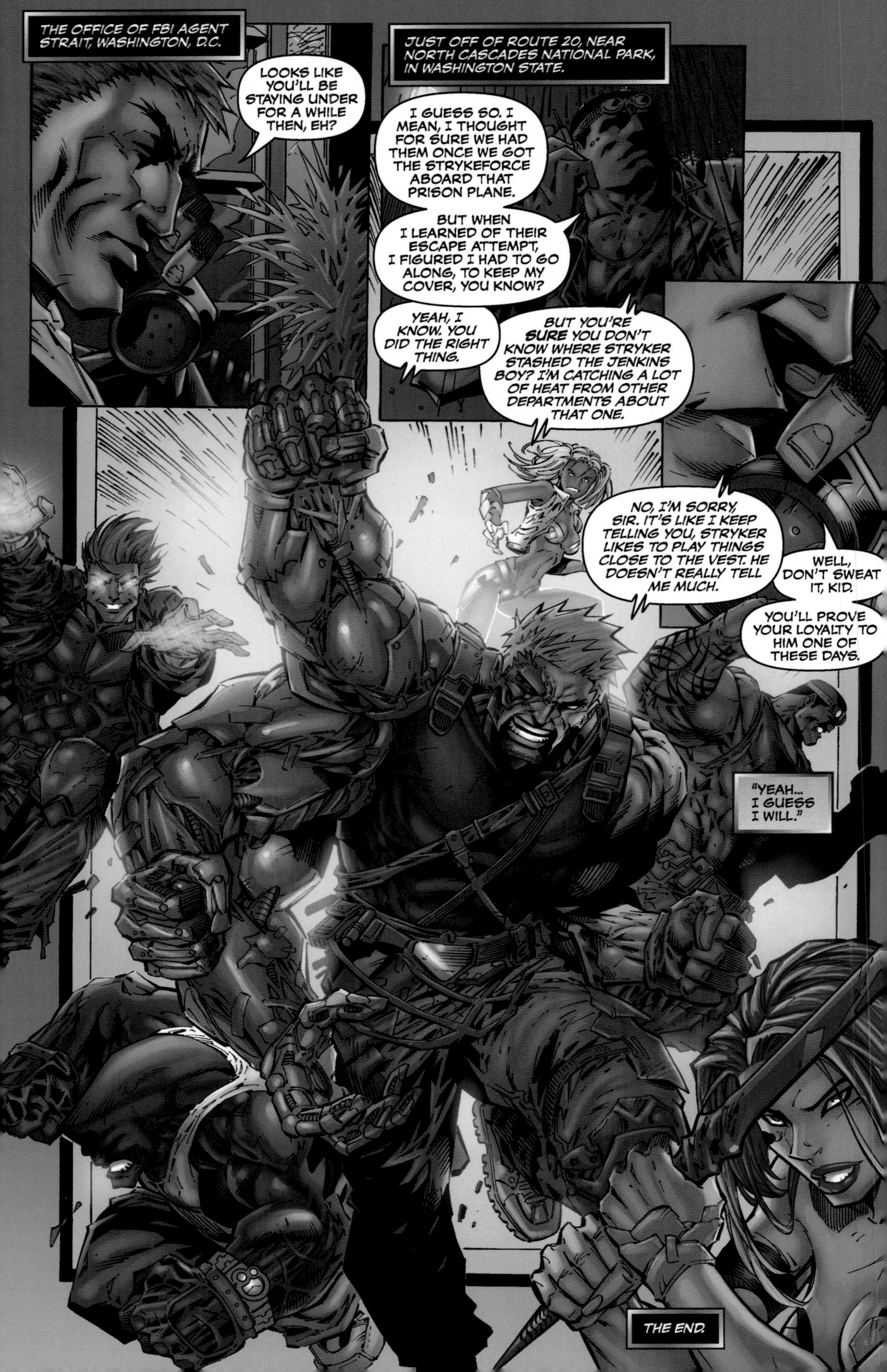
THE OFFICE OF FBI AGENT STRAIT, WASHINGTON, D.C.
JUST OFF OF ROUTE 20, NEAR NORTH CASCADES NATIONAL PARK, IN WASHINGTON STATE.
LOOKS LIKE YOU'LL BE STAYING UNDER FOR A WHILE THEN, EH?
I GUESS SO. I MEAN, I THOUGHT FOR SURE WE HAD THEM ONCE WE GOT THE STRYKEFORCE ABOARD THAT PRISON PLANE.
BUT WHEN I LEARNED OF THEIR ESCAPE ATTEMPT, I FIGURED I HAD TO GO ALONG, TO KEEP MY COVER, YOU KNOW?
YEAH, I KNOW. YOU DID THE RIGHT THING.
BUT YOU'RE SURE YOU DON'T KNOW WHERE STRYKER STASHED THE JENKINS BOY? I'M CATCHING A LOT OF HEAT FROM OTHER DEPARTMENTS ABOUT THAT ONE.
NO, I'M SORRY, SIR. IT'S LIKE I KEEP TELLING YOU, STRYKER LIKES TO PLAY THINGS CLOSE TO THE VEST. HE DOESN'T REALLY TELL ME MUCH.
WELL, DON'T SWEAT IT, KID.
YOU'LL PROVE YOUR LOYALTY TO HIM ONE OF THESE DAYS.
"YEAH... I GUESS I WILL."
THE END.

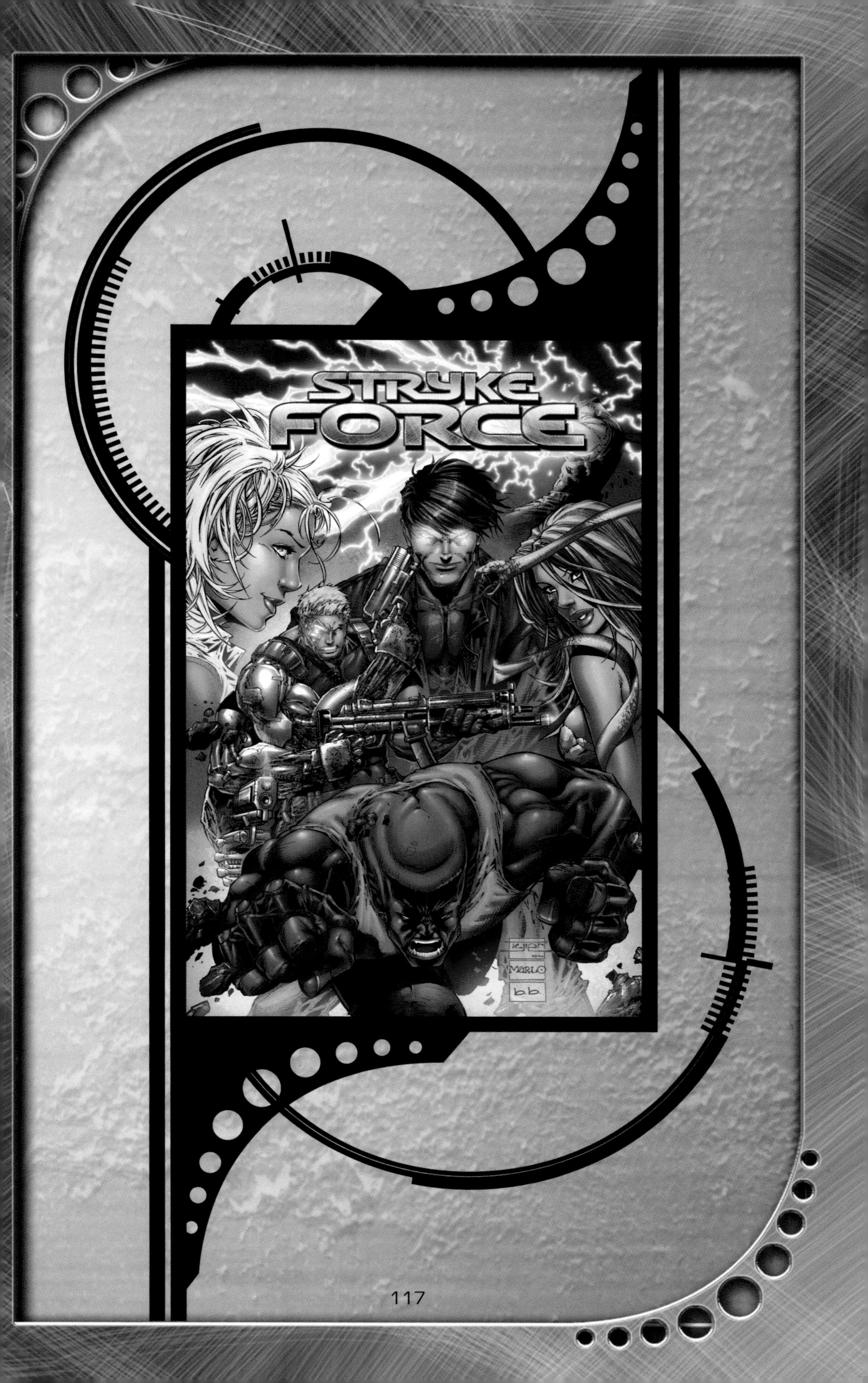
STRYKE
FORCE

CODENAME:

STRYKE
FORCE

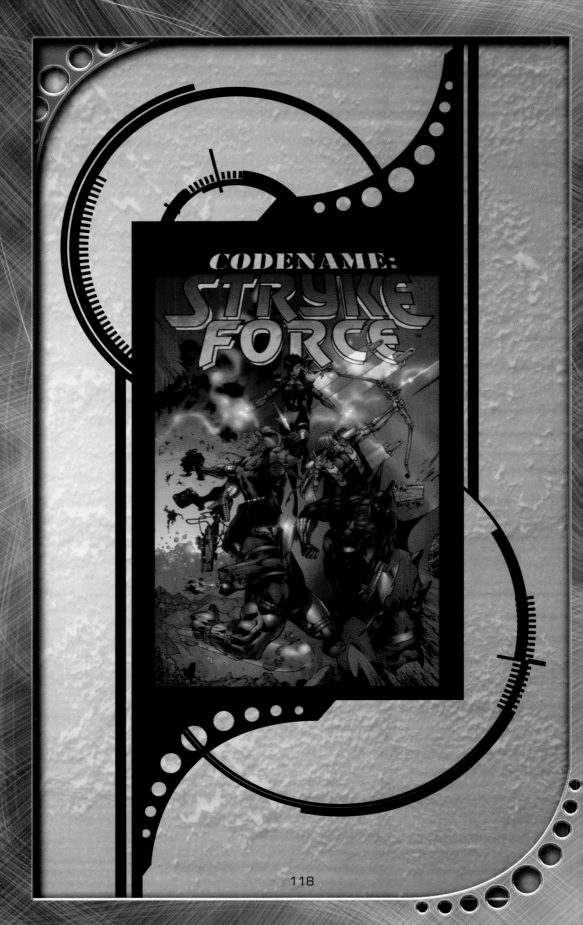

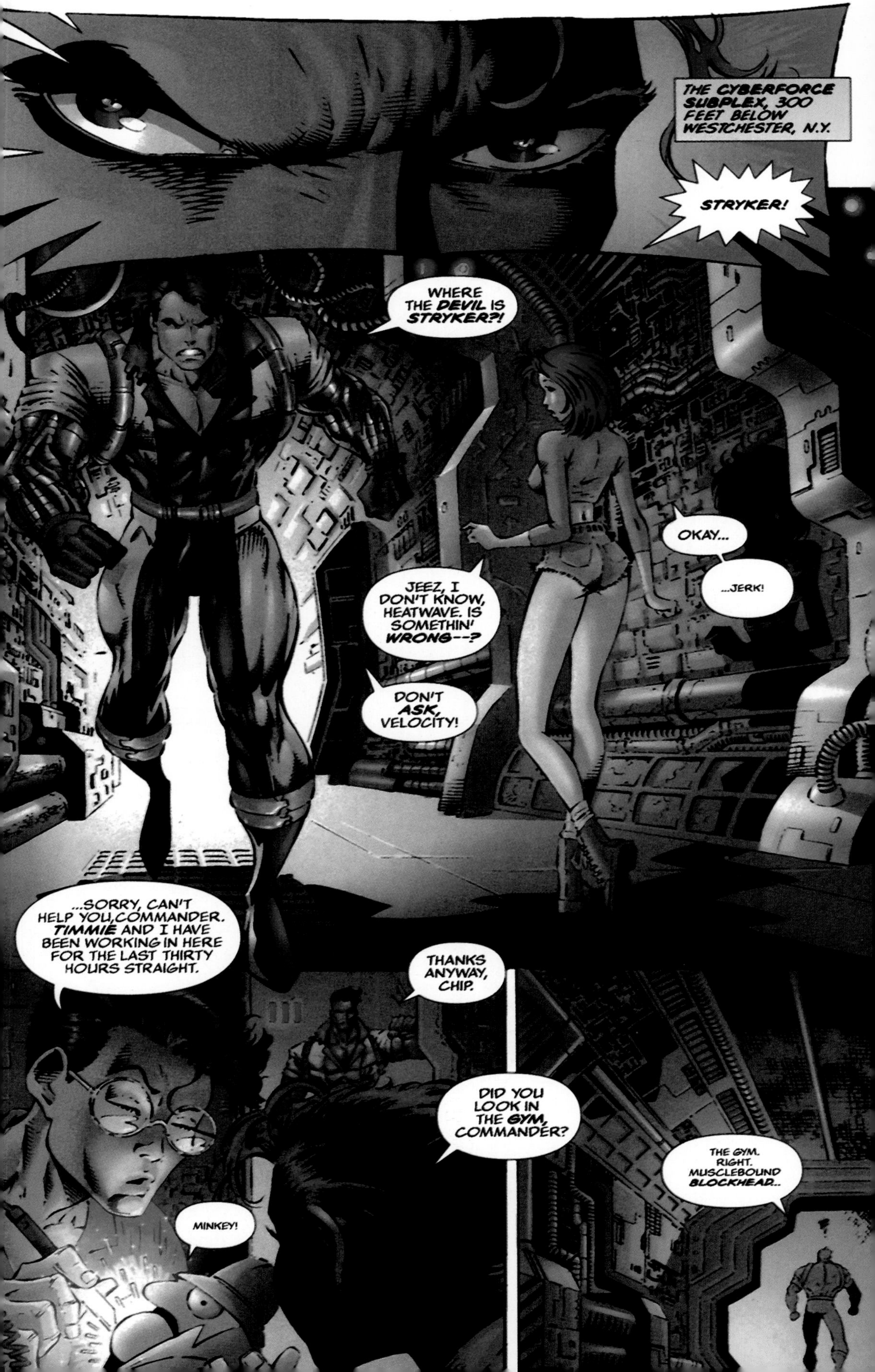
THE CYBERFORCE SUBPLEX, 300 FEET BELOW WESTCHESTER, N.Y.
STRYKER!
WHERE THE DEVIL IS STRYKER?!
JEEZ, I DON'T KNOW, HEATWAVE. IS SOMETHIN' WRONG--?
DON'T ASK, VELOCITY!
OKAY...
...JERK!
...SORRY, CAN'T HELP YOU,COMMANDER. TIMMIE AND I HAVE BEEN WORKING IN HERE FOR THE LAST THIRTY HOURS STRAIGHT.
THANKS ANYWAY, CHIP.
DID YOU LOOK IN THE GYM, COMMANDER?
MINKEY!
THE GYM. RIGHT. MUSCLEBOUND BLOCKHEAD...

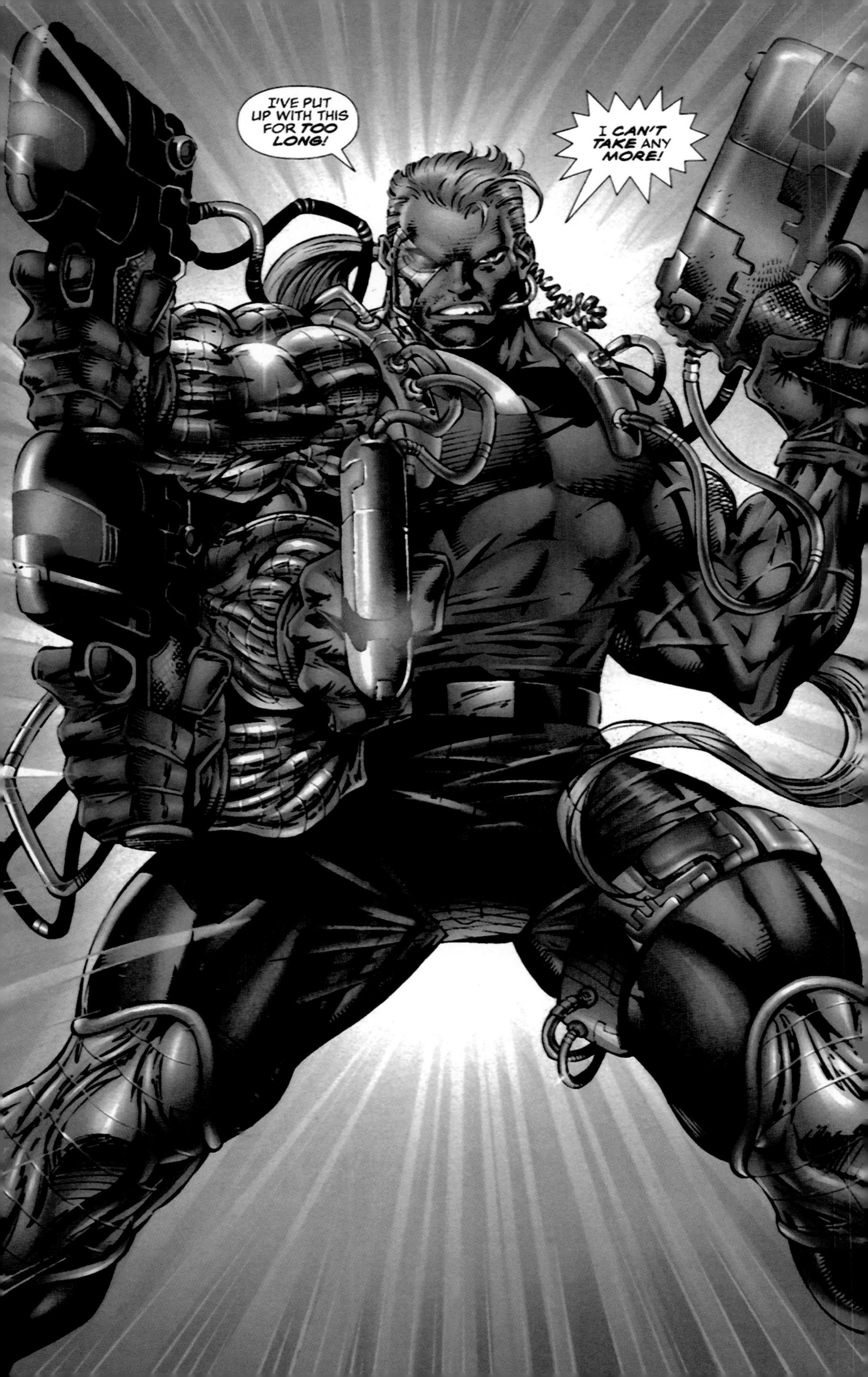
I'VE PUT UP WITH THIS FOR *TOO LONG!*
I *CAN'T TAKE* ANY *MORE!*

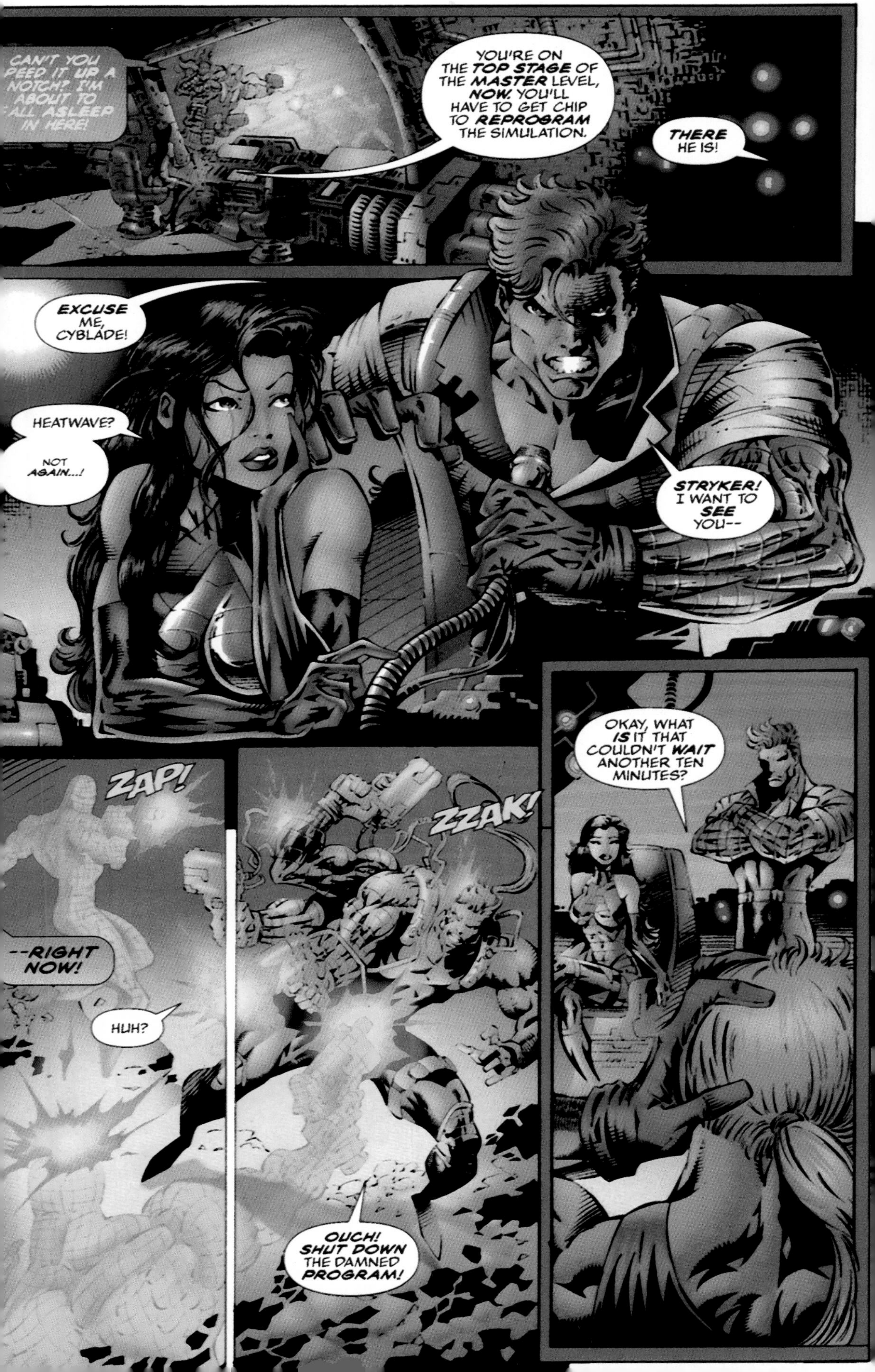
CAN'T YOU SPEED IT UP A NOTCH? I'M ABOUT TO FALL ASLEEP IN HERE!
YOU'RE ON THE TOP STAGE OF THE MASTER LEVEL, NOW. YOU'LL HAVE TO GET CHIP TO REPROGRAM THE SIMULATION.
THERE HE IS!
EXCUSE ME, CYBLADE!
HEATWAVE?
NOT AGAIN...!
STRYKER! I WANT TO SEE YOU--
ZAP!
--RIGHT NOW!
HUH?
ZZAK!
OUCH! SHUT DOWN THE DAMNED PROGRAM!
OKAY, WHAT IS IT THAT COULDN'T WAIT ANOTHER TEN MINUTES?

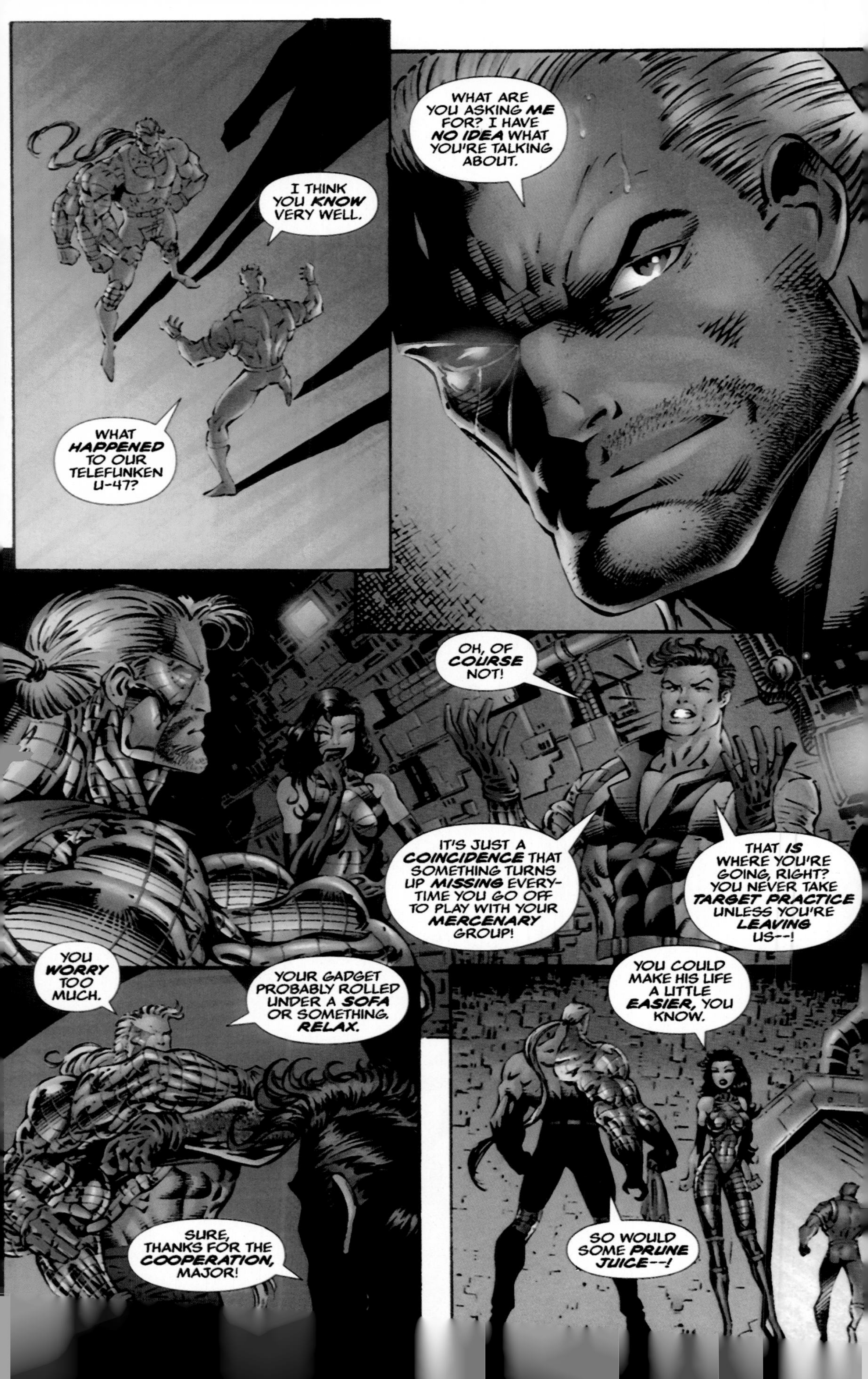

WHAT HAPPENED TO OUR TELEFUNKEN U-47?
I THINK YOU KNOW VERY WELL.
WHAT ARE YOU ASKING ME FOR? I HAVE NO IDEA WHAT YOU'RE TALKING ABOUT.
OH, OF COURSE NOT!
IT'S JUST A COINCIDENCE THAT SOMETHING TURNS UP MISSING EVERY-TIME YOU GO OFF TO PLAY WITH YOUR MERCENARY GROUP!
THAT IS WHERE YOU'RE GOING, RIGHT? YOU NEVER TAKE TARGET PRACTICE UNLESS YOU'RE LEAVING US--!
YOU WORRY TOO MUCH.
YOUR GADGET PROBABLY ROLLED UNDER A SOFA OR SOMETHING. RELAX.
SURE, THANKS FOR THE COOPERATION, MAJOR!
YOU COULD MAKE HIS LIFE A LITTLE EASIER, YOU KNOW.
SO WOULD SOME PRUNE JUICE--!

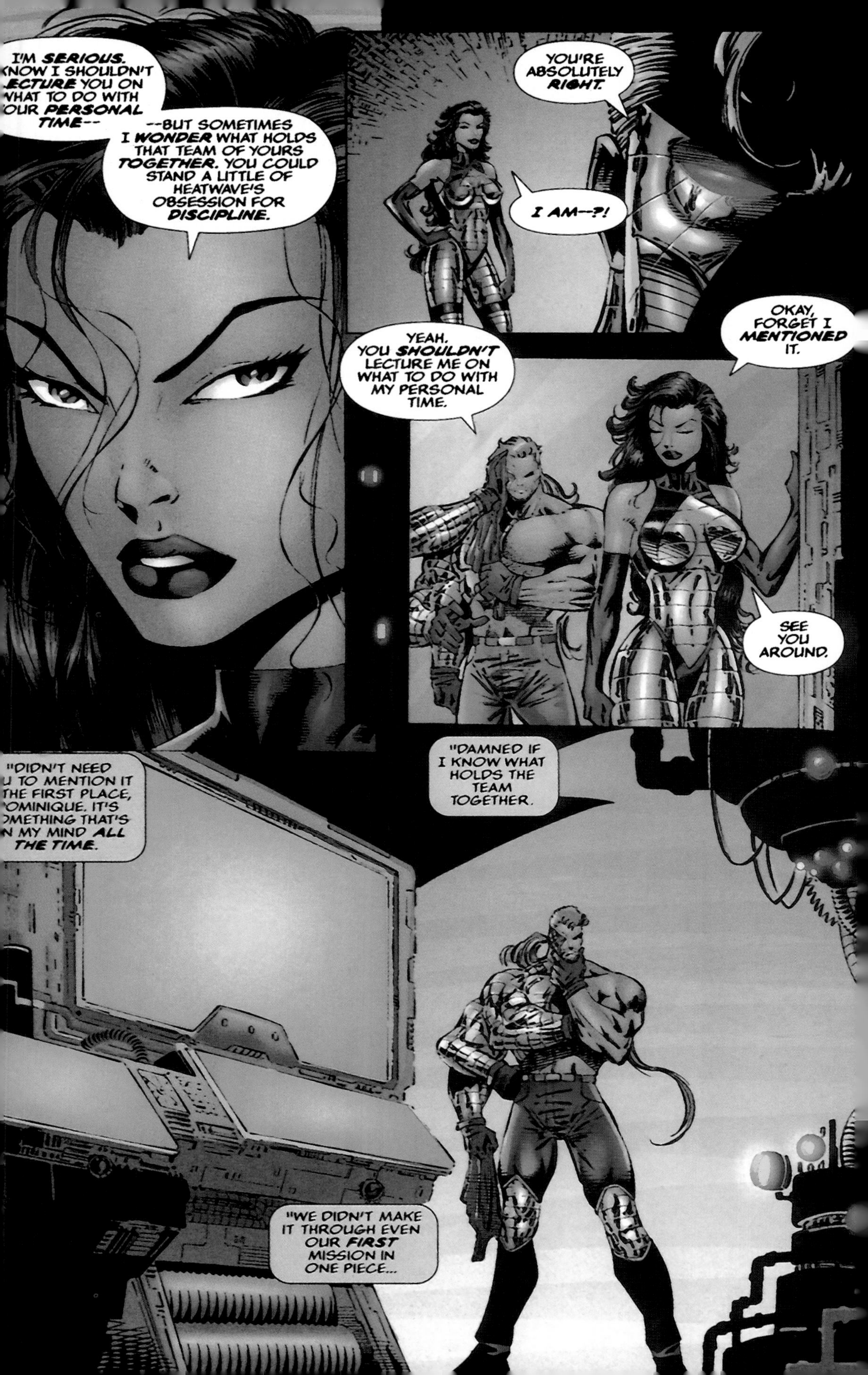

I'M SERIOUS. KNOW I SHOULDN'T LECTURE YOU ON WHAT TO DO WITH YOUR PERSONAL TIME--
--BUT SOMETIMES I WONDER WHAT HOLDS THAT TEAM OF YOURS TOGETHER. YOU COULD STAND A LITTLE OF HEATWAVE'S OBSESSION FOR DISCIPLINE.
YOU'RE ABSOLUTELY RIGHT.
I AM--?!
YEAH. YOU SHOULDN'T LECTURE ME ON WHAT TO DO WITH MY PERSONAL TIME.
OKAY, FORGET I MENTIONED IT.
SEE YOU AROUND.
"DIDN'T NEED U TO MENTION IT THE FIRST PLACE, DOMINIQUE. IT'S SOMETHING THAT'S N MY MIND ALL THE TIME.
"DAMNED IF I KNOW WHAT HOLDS THE TEAM TOGETHER.
"WE DIDN'T MAKE IT THROUGH EVEN OUR FIRST MISSION IN ONE PIECE...

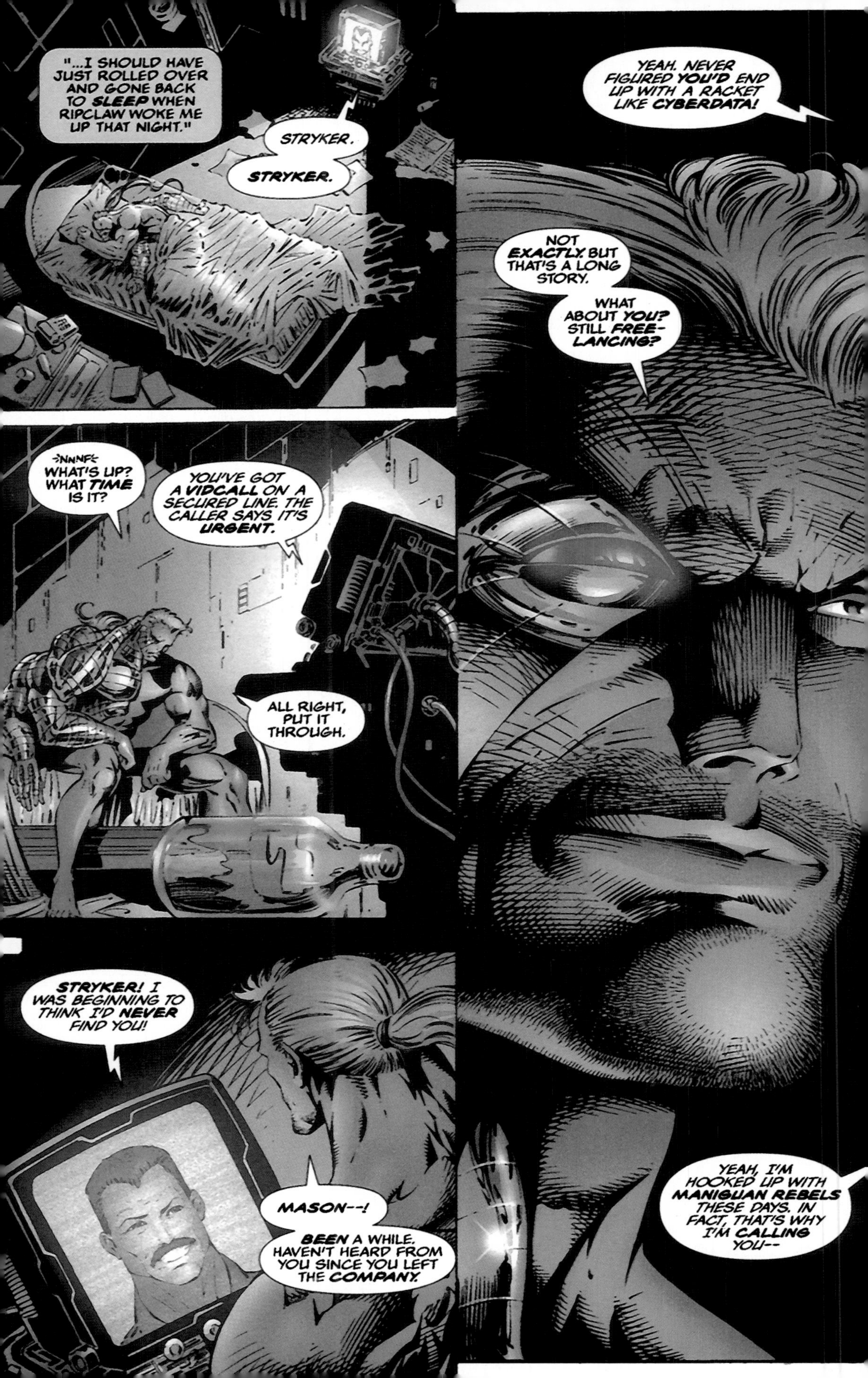
"...I SHOULD HAVE JUST ROLLED OVER AND GONE BACK TO SLEEP WHEN RIPCLAW WOKE ME UP THAT NIGHT."
STRYKER.
STRYKER.
NNNF WHAT'S UP? WHAT TIME IS IT?
YOU'VE GOT A VIDCALL ON A SECURED LINE. THE CALLER SAYS IT'S URGENT.
ALL RIGHT, PUT IT THROUGH.
STRYKER! I WAS BEGINNING TO THINK I'D NEVER FIND YOU!
MASON--!
BEEN A WHILE. HAVEN'T HEARD FROM YOU SINCE YOU LEFT THE COMPANY.
YEAH. NEVER FIGURED YOU'D END UP WITH A RACKET LIKE CYBERDATA!
NOT EXACTLY. BUT THAT'S A LONG STORY.
WHAT ABOUT YOU? STILL FREE-LANCING?
YEAH, I'M HOOKED UP WITH MANIGUAN REBELS THESE DAYS. IN FACT, THAT'S WHY I'M CALLING YOU--

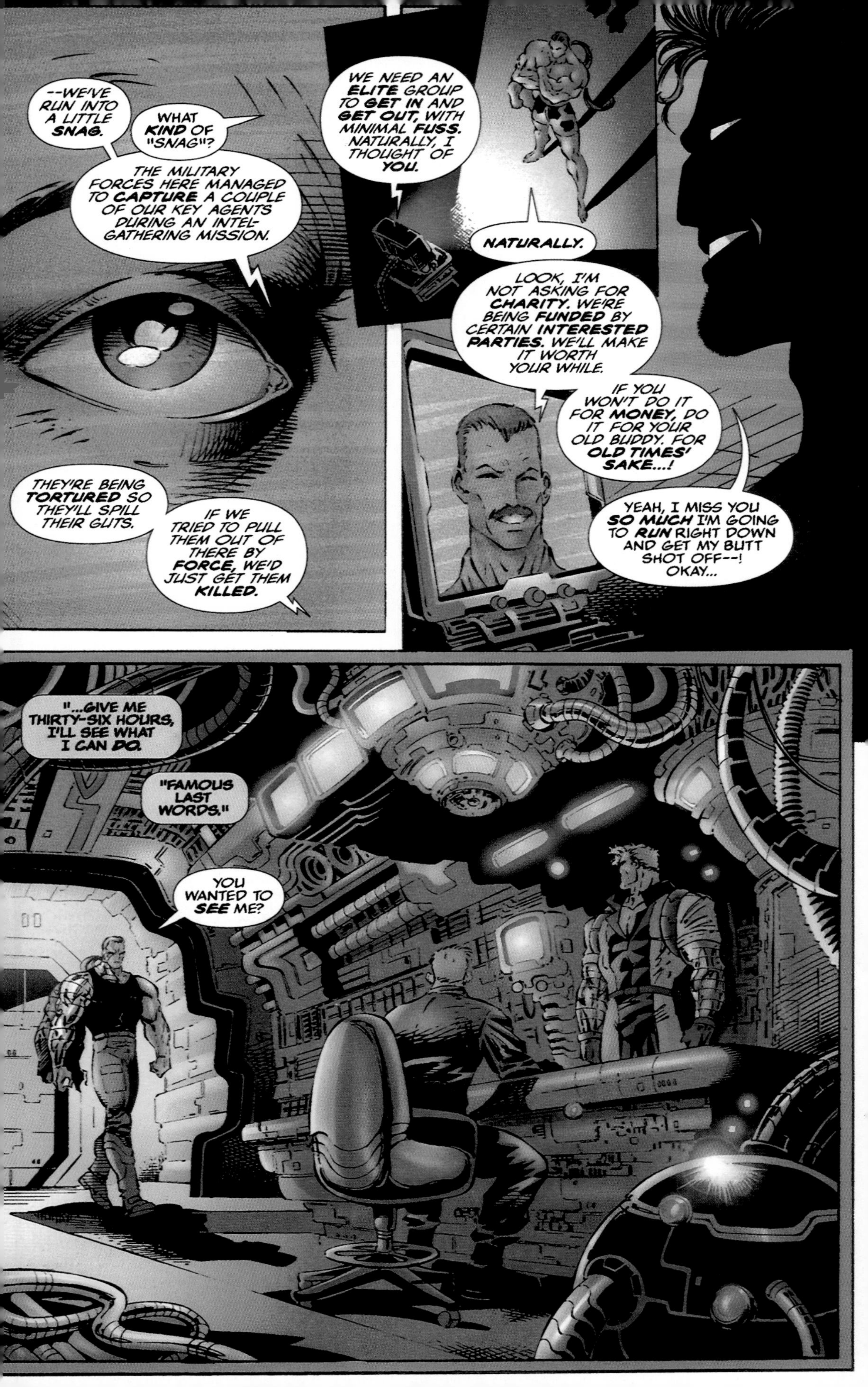
--WE'VE RUN INTO A LITTLE SNAG.
WHAT KIND OF "SNAG"?
THE MILITARY FORCES HERE MANAGED TO CAPTURE A COUPLE OF OUR KEY AGENTS DURING AN INTEL-GATHERING MISSION.
THEY'RE BEING TORTURED SO THEY'LL SPILL THEIR GUTS.
IF WE TRIED TO PULL THEM OUT OF THERE BY FORCE, WE'D JUST GET THEM KILLED.
WE NEED AN ELITE GROUP TO GET IN AND GET OUT, WITH MINIMAL FUSS. NATURALLY, I THOUGHT OF YOU.
NATURALLY.
LOOK, I'M NOT ASKING FOR CHARITY. WE'RE BEING FUNDED BY CERTAIN INTERESTED PARTIES. WE'LL MAKE IT WORTH YOUR WHILE.
IF YOU WON'T DO IT FOR MONEY, DO IT FOR YOUR OLD BUDDY. FOR OLD TIMES' SAKE...!
YEAH, I MISS YOU SO MUCH I'M GOING TO RUN RIGHT DOWN AND GET MY BUTT SHOT OFF--! OKAY...
"...GIVE ME THIRTY-SIX HOURS, I'LL SEE WHAT I CAN DO.
"FAMOUS LAST WORDS."
YOU WANTED TO SEE ME?

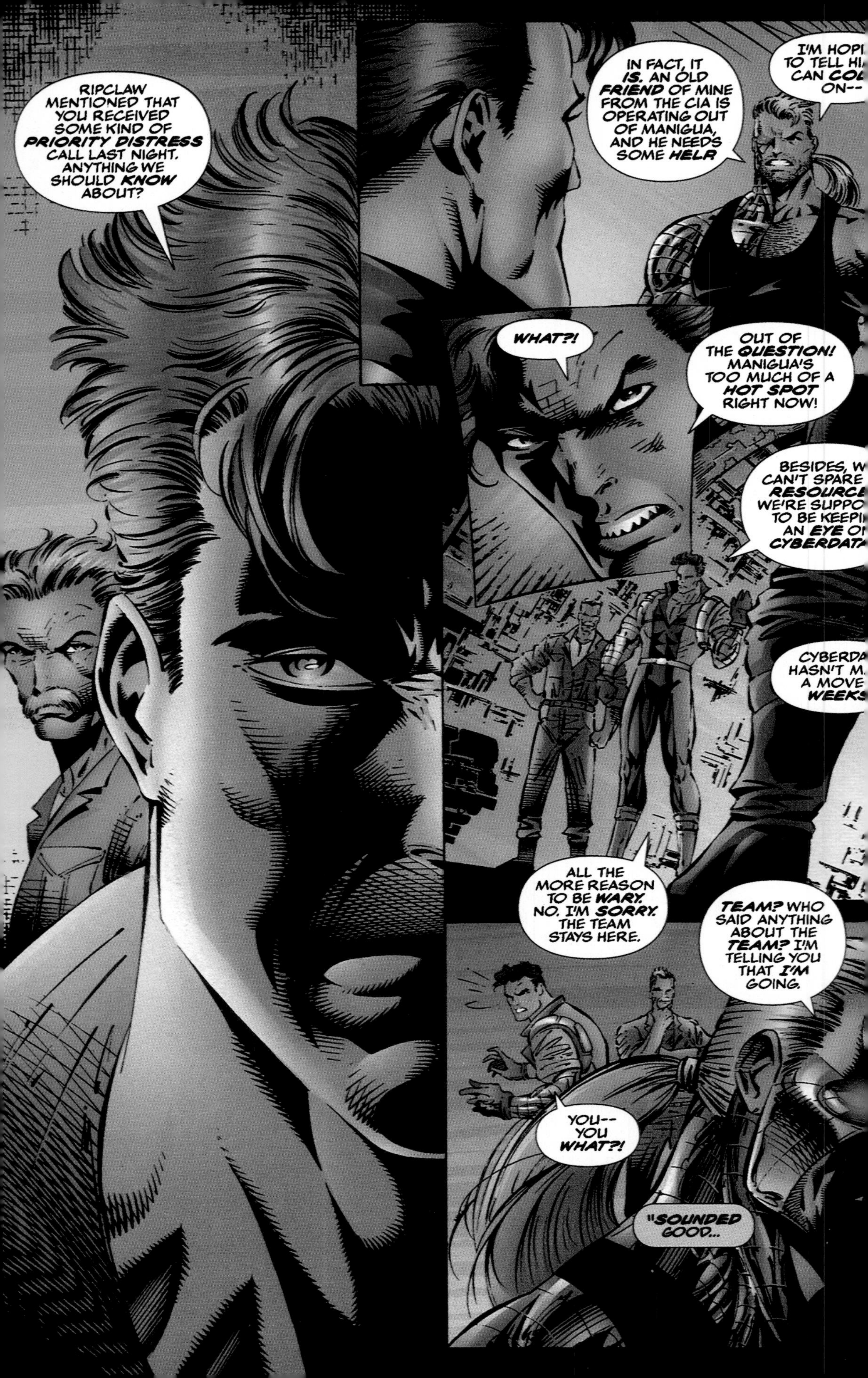

RIPCLAW MENTIONED THAT YOU RECEIVED SOME KIND OF PRIORITY DISTRESS CALL LAST NIGHT. ANYTHING WE SHOULD KNOW ABOUT?
IN FACT, IT IS. AN OLD FRIEND OF MINE FROM THE CIA IS OPERATING OUT OF MANIGUA, AND HE NEEDS SOME HELP.
WHAT?!
OUT OF THE QUESTION! MANIGUA'S TOO MUCH OF A HOT SPOT RIGHT NOW!
ALL THE MORE REASON TO BE WARY. NO. I'M SORRY. THE TEAM STAYS HERE.
TEAM? WHO SAID ANYTHING ABOUT THE TEAM? I'M TELLING YOU THAT I'M GOING.
YOU-- YOU WHAT?!
"SOUNDED GOOD...

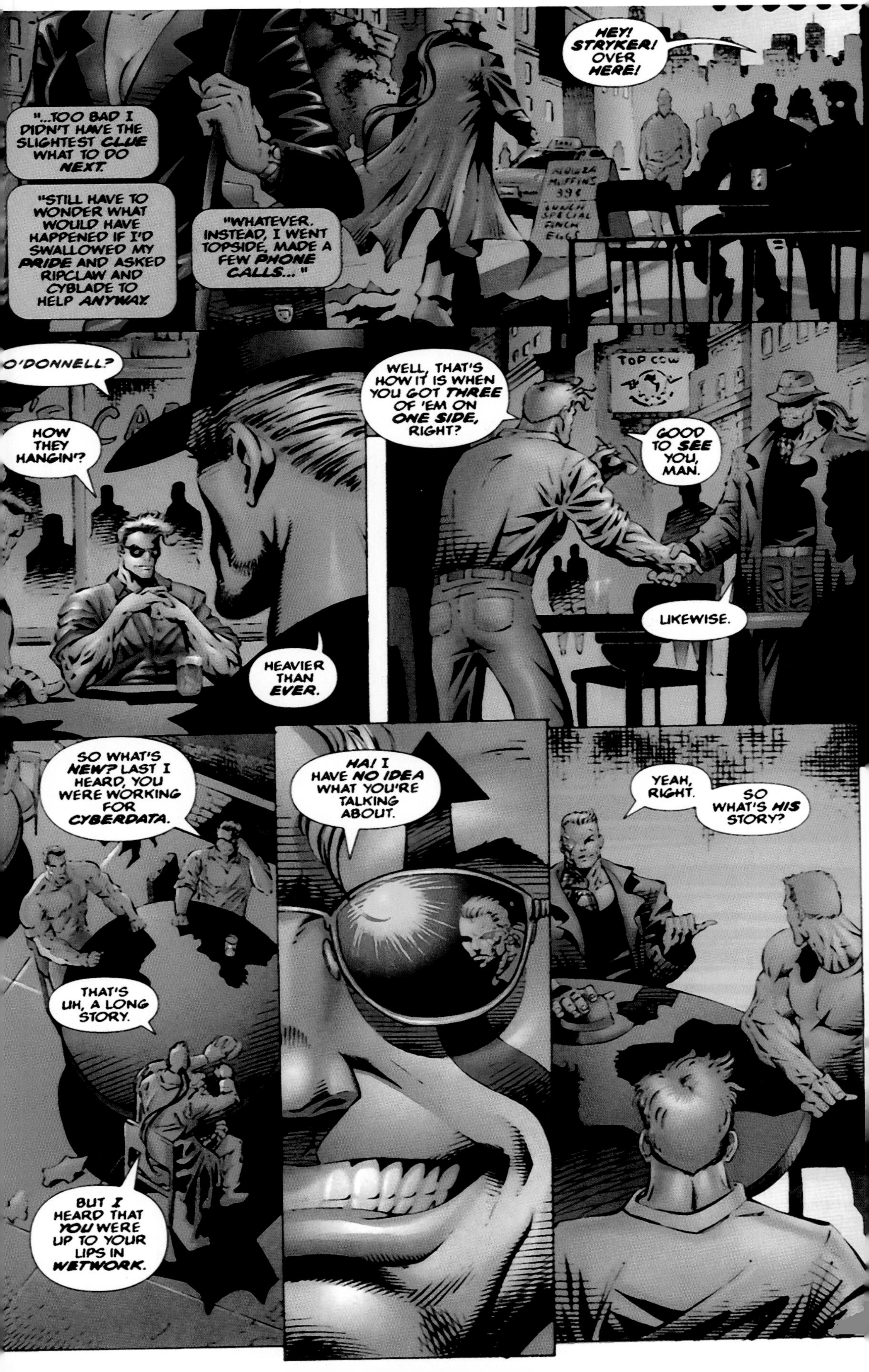
"...TOO BAD I DIDN'T HAVE THE SLIGHTEST CLUE WHAT TO DO NEXT.
"STILL HAVE TO WONDER WHAT WOULD HAVE HAPPENED IF I'D SWALLOWED MY PRIDE AND ASKED RIPCLAW AND CYBLADE TO HELP ANYWAY.
"WHATEVER. INSTEAD, I WENT TOPSIDE, MADE A FEW PHONE CALLS..."
HEY! STRYKER! OVER HERE!
O'DONNELL?
HOW THEY HANGIN'?
HEAVIER THAN EVER.
WELL, THAT'S HOW IT IS WHEN YOU GOT THREE OF 'EM ON ONE SIDE, RIGHT?
TOP COW
GOOD TO SEE YOU, MAN.
LIKEWISE.
SO WHAT'S NEW? LAST I HEARD, YOU WERE WORKING FOR CYBERDATA.
THAT'S UH, A LONG STORY.
BUT I HEARD THAT YOU WERE UP TO YOUR LIPS IN WETWORK.
HA! I HAVE NO IDEA WHAT YOU'RE TALKING ABOUT.
YEAH, RIGHT.
SO WHAT'S HIS STORY?

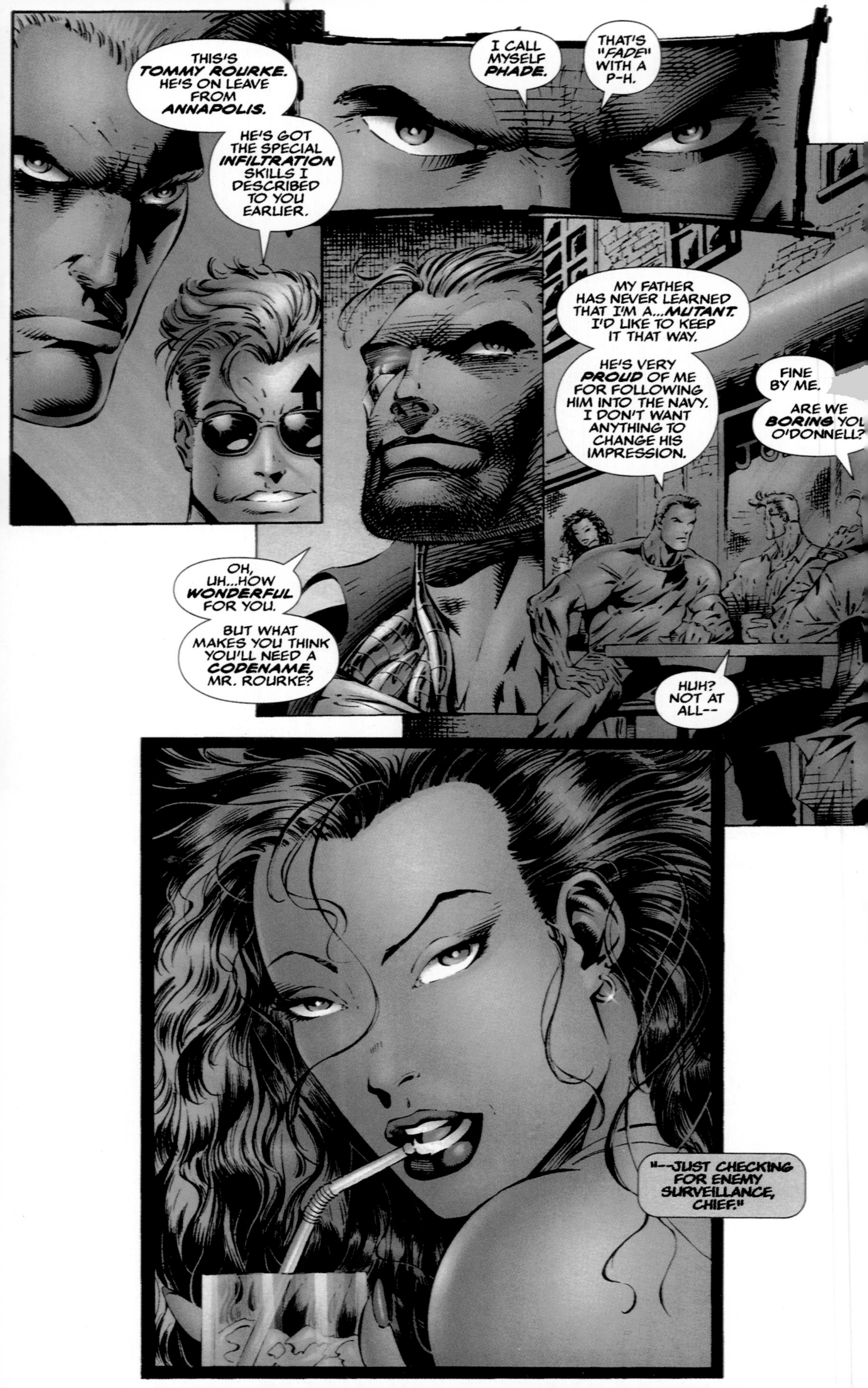
THIS'S TOMMY ROURKE. HE'S ON LEAVE FROM ANNAPOLIS.
HE'S GOT THE SPECIAL INFILTRATION SKILLS I DESCRIBED TO YOU EARLIER.
I CALL MYSELF PHADE.
THAT'S "FADE" WITH A P-H.
OH, UH...HOW WONDERFUL FOR YOU.
BUT WHAT MAKES YOU THINK YOU'LL NEED A CODENAME, MR. ROURKE?
MY FATHER HAS NEVER LEARNED THAT I'M A...MUTANT. I'D LIKE TO KEEP IT THAT WAY.
HE'S VERY PROUD OF ME FOR FOLLOWING HIM INTO THE NAVY. I DON'T WANT ANYTHING TO CHANGE HIS IMPRESSION.
FINE BY ME.
ARE WE BORING YOU O'DONNELL?
HUH? NOT AT ALL--
"--JUST CHECKING FOR ENEMY SURVEILLANCE, CHIEF."

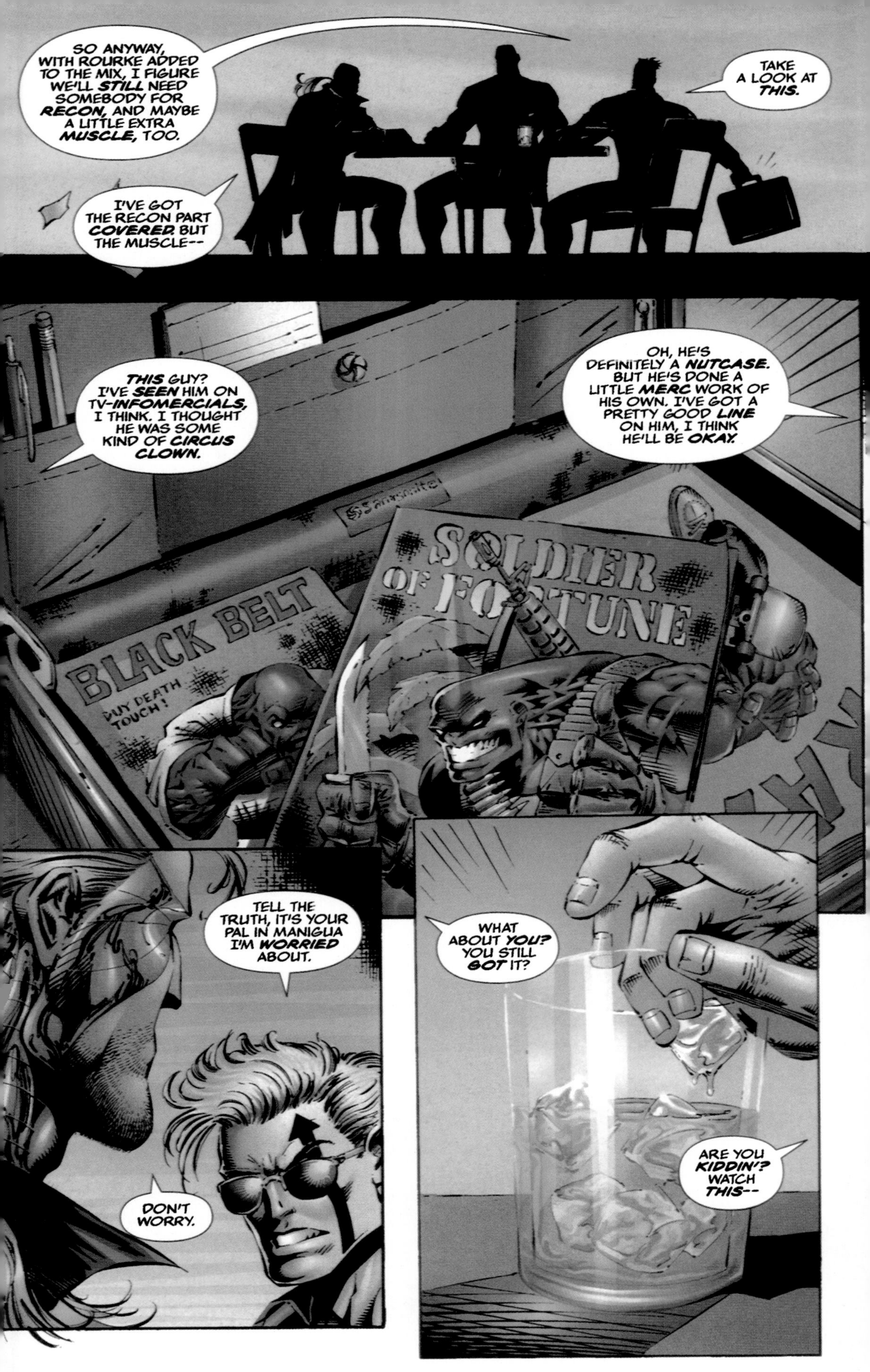
SO ANYWAY, WITH ROURKE ADDED TO THE MIX, I FIGURE WE'LL STILL NEED SOMEBODY FOR RECON, AND MAYBE A LITTLE EXTRA MUSCLE, TOO.
TAKE A LOOK AT THIS.
I'VE GOT THE RECON PART COVERED, BUT THE MUSCLE--
THIS GUY? I'VE SEEN HIM ON TV-INFOMERCIALS, I THINK. I THOUGHT HE WAS SOME KIND OF CIRCUS CLOWN.
OH, HE'S DEFINITELY A NUTCASE. BUT HE'S DONE A LITTLE MERC WORK OF HIS OWN. I'VE GOT A PRETTY GOOD LINE ON HIM, I THINK HE'LL BE OKAY.
SOLDIER OF FORTUNE
BLACK BELT
DIM DEATH TOUCH!
TELL THE TRUTH, IT'S YOUR PAL IN MANIGUA I'M WORRIED ABOUT.
DON'T WORRY.
WHAT ABOUT YOU? YOU STILL GOT IT?
ARE YOU KIDDIN'? WATCH THIS--

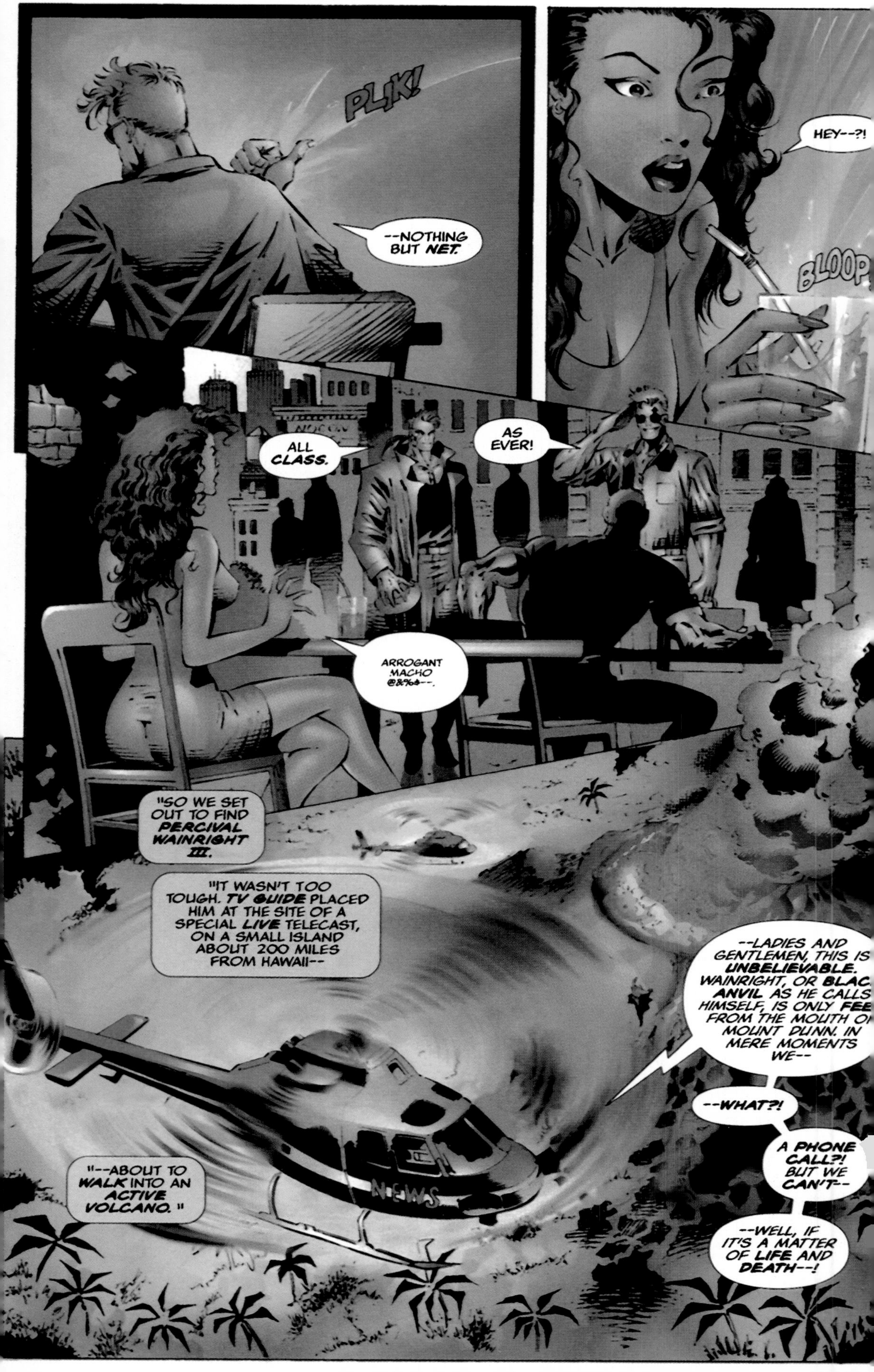
PLIK!
--NOTHING BUT NET.
HEY--?!
BLOOP!
ALL CLASS.
AS EVER!
ARROGANT MACHO @&%#--.
"SO WE SET OUT TO FIND PERCIVAL WAINRIGHT III.
"IT WASN'T TOO TOUGH. TV GUIDE PLACED HIM AT THE SITE OF A SPECIAL LIVE TELECAST, ON A SMALL ISLAND ABOUT 200 MILES FROM HAWAII--
--LADIES AND GENTLEMEN, THIS IS UNBELIEVABLE. WAINRIGHT, OR BLACK ANVIL AS HE CALLS HIMSELF, IS ONLY FEET FROM THE MOUTH OF MOUNT DUNN. IN MERE MOMENTS WE--
--WHAT?!
A PHONE CALL?! BUT WE CAN'T--
--WELL, IF IT'S A MATTER OF LIFE AND DEATH--!
"--ABOUT TO WALK INTO AN ACTIVE VOLCANO."
NEWS

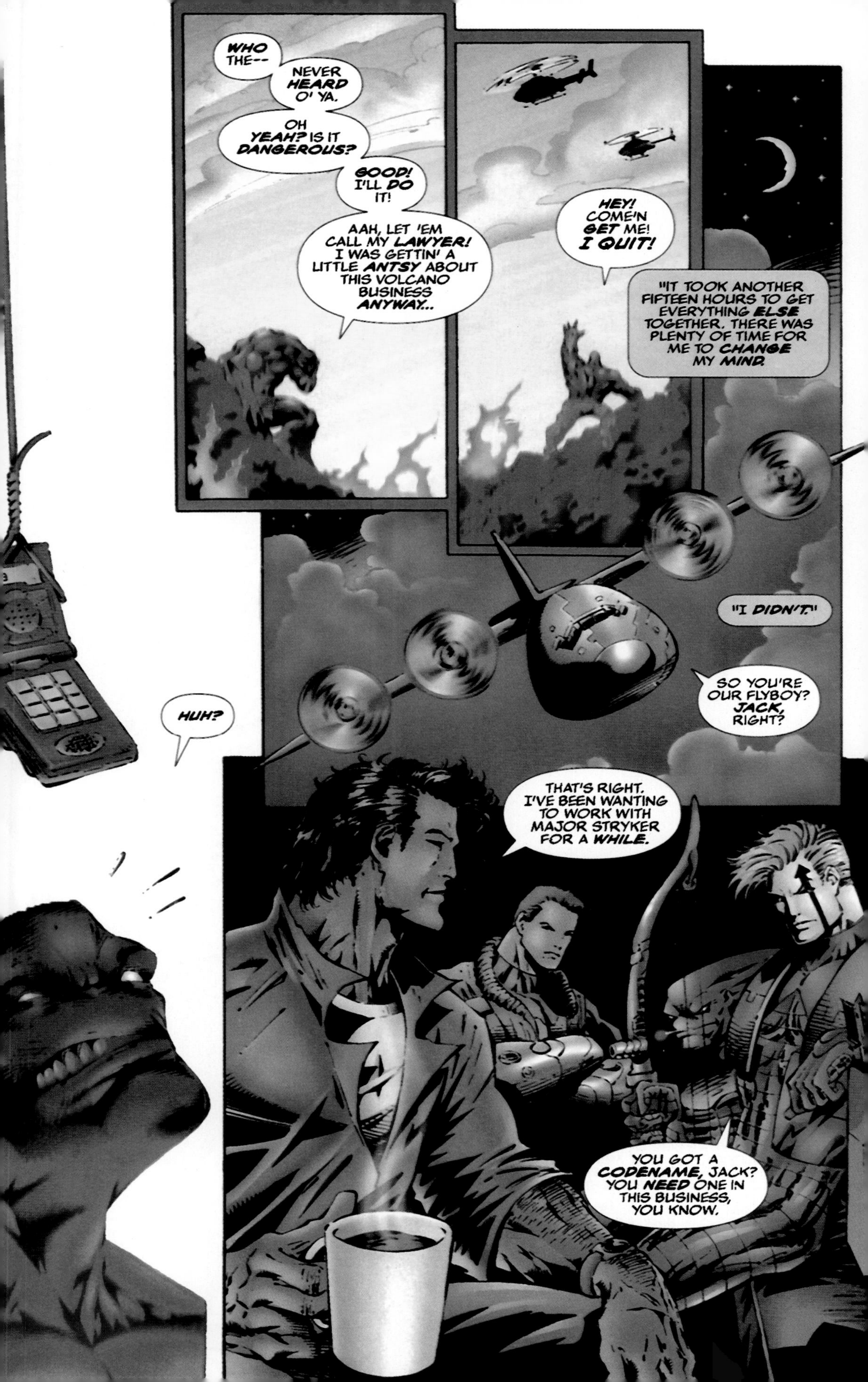
WHO THE--
NEVER HEARD O' YA.
OH YEAH? IS IT DANGEROUS?
GOOD! I'LL DO IT!
AAH, LET 'EM CALL MY LAWYER! I WAS GETTIN' A LITTLE ANTSY ABOUT THIS VOLCANO BUSINESS ANYWAY...
HEY! COME'N GET ME! I QUIT!
HUH?
"IT TOOK ANOTHER FIFTEEN HOURS TO GET EVERYTHING ELSE TOGETHER. THERE WAS PLENTY OF TIME FOR ME TO CHANGE MY MIND.
"I DIDN'T."
SO YOU'RE OUR FLYBOY? JACK, RIGHT?
THAT'S RIGHT. I'VE BEEN WANTING TO WORK WITH MAJOR STRYKER FOR A WHILE.
YOU GOT A CODENAME, JACK? YOU NEED ONE IN THIS BUSINESS, YOU KNOW.

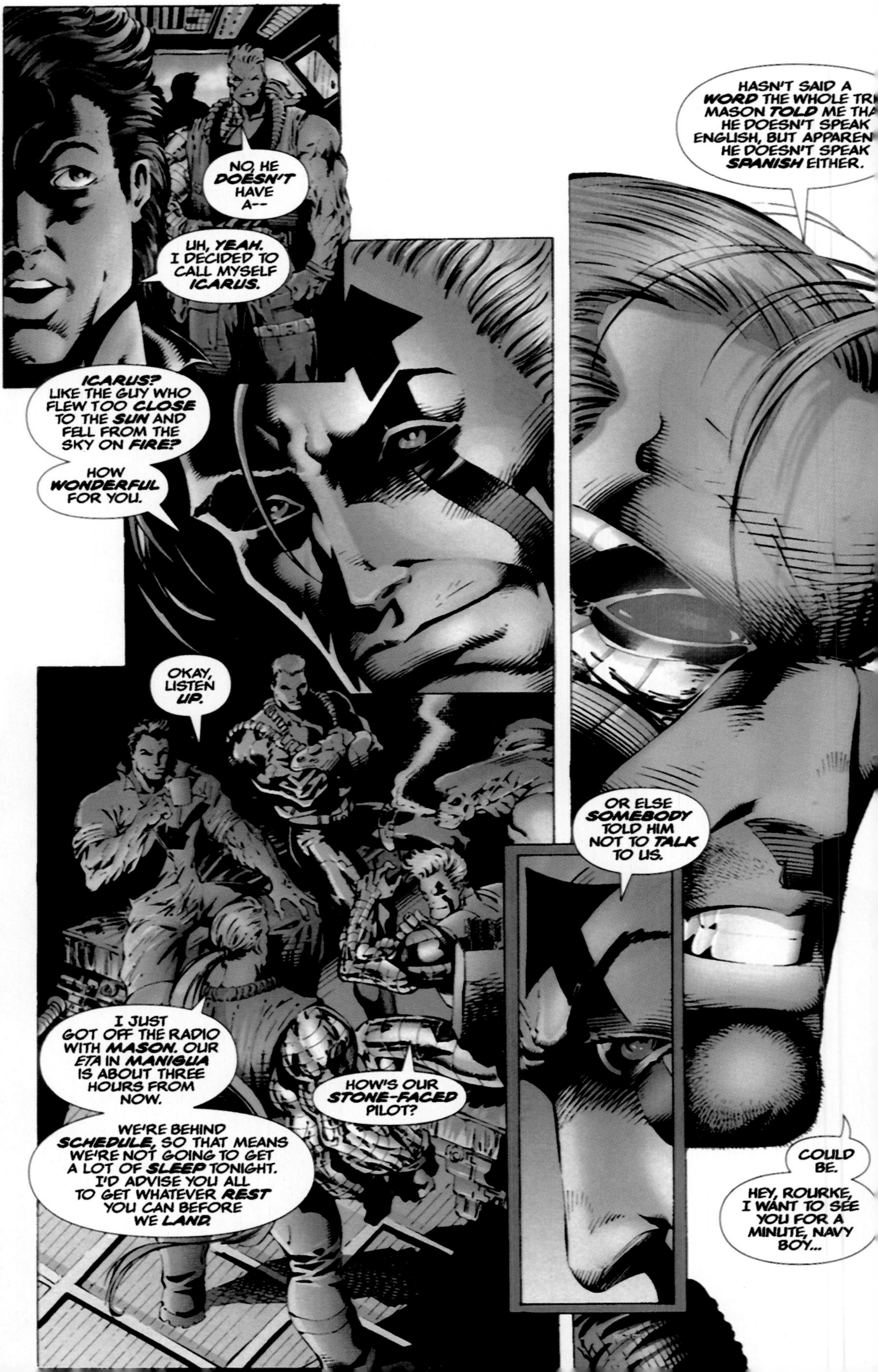
NO, HE DOESN'T HAVE A--
UH, YEAH. I DECIDED TO CALL MYSELF ICARUS.
ICARUS? LIKE THE GUY WHO FLEW TOO CLOSE TO THE SUN AND FELL FROM THE SKY ON FIRE?
HOW WONDERFUL FOR YOU.
HASN'T SAID A WORD THE WHOLE TR MASON TOLD ME THA HE DOESN'T SPEAK ENGLISH, BUT APPAREN HE DOESN'T SPEAK SPANISH EITHER.
OKAY, LISTEN UP.
I JUST GOT OFF THE RADIO WITH MASON. OUR ETA IN MANIGUA IS ABOUT THREE HOURS FROM NOW.
WE'RE BEHIND SCHEDULE, SO THAT MEANS WE'RE NOT GOING TO GET A LOT OF SLEEP TONIGHT. I'D ADVISE YOU ALL TO GET WHATEVER REST YOU CAN BEFORE WE LAND.
HOW'S OUR STONE-FACED PILOT?
OR ELSE SOMEBODY TOLD HIM NOT TO TALK TO US.
COULD BE.
HEY, ROURKE, I WANT TO SEE YOU FOR A MINUTE, NAVY BOY...

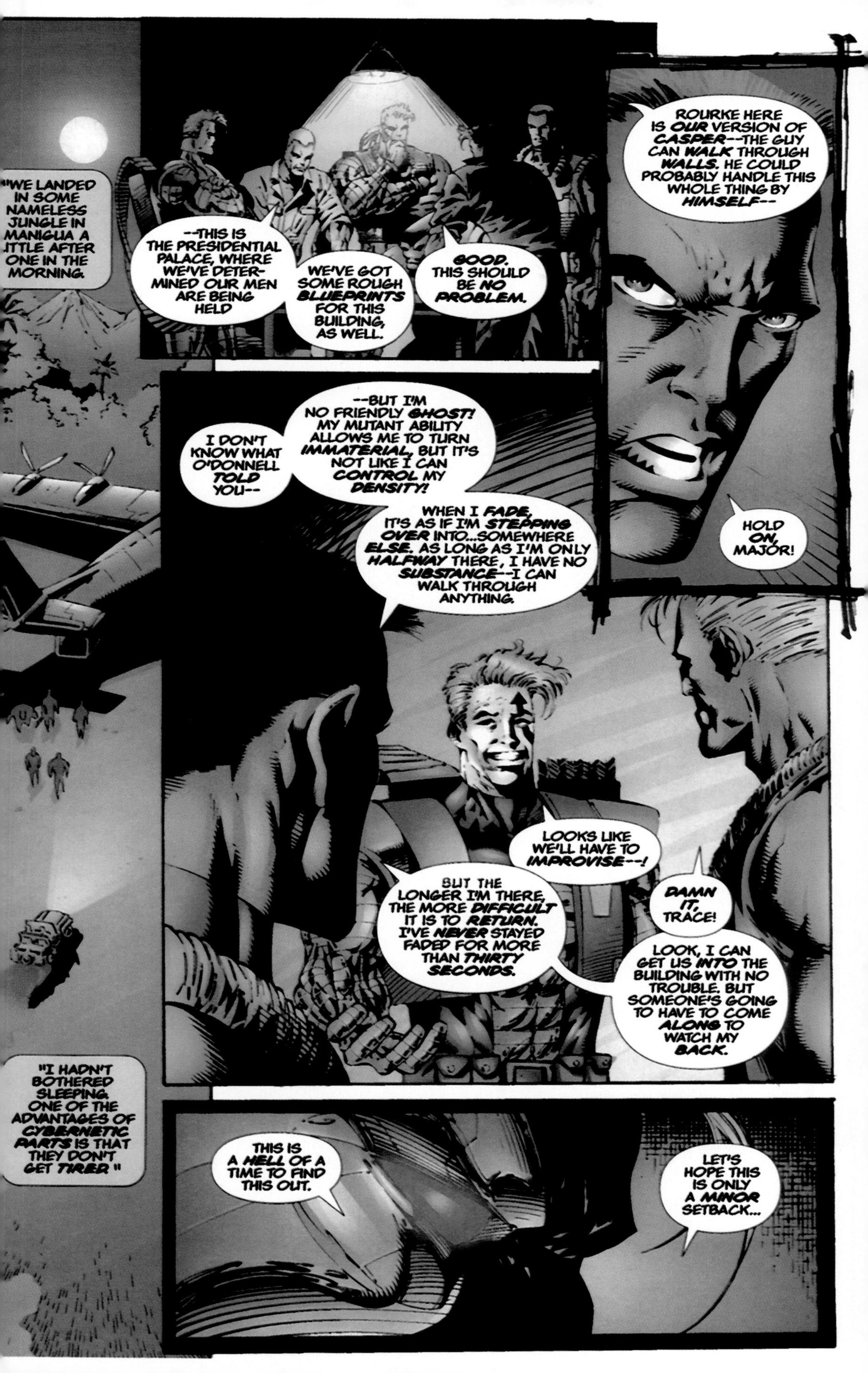
"WE LANDED IN SOME NAMELESS JUNGLE IN MANIGUA A LITTLE AFTER ONE IN THE MORNING.
--THIS IS THE PRESIDENTIAL PALACE, WHERE WE'VE DETERMINED OUR MEN ARE BEING HELD
WE'VE GOT SOME ROUGH BLUEPRINTS FOR THIS BUILDING, AS WELL.
GOOD. THIS SHOULD BE NO PROBLEM.
ROURKE HERE IS OUR VERSION OF CASPER--THE GUY CAN WALK THROUGH WALLS. HE COULD PROBABLY HANDLE THIS WHOLE THING BY HIMSELF--
HOLD ON, MAJOR!
I DON'T KNOW WHAT O'DONNELL TOLD YOU--
--BUT I'M NO FRIENDLY GHOST! MY MUTANT ABILITY ALLOWS ME TO TURN IMMATERIAL, BUT IT'S NOT LIKE I CAN CONTROL MY DENSITY!
WHEN I FADE, IT'S AS IF I'M STEPPING OVER INTO...SOMEWHERE ELSE. AS LONG AS I'M ONLY HALFWAY THERE, I HAVE NO SUBSTANCE--I CAN WALK THROUGH ANYTHING.
BUT THE LONGER I'M THERE, THE MORE DIFFICULT IT IS TO RETURN. I'VE NEVER STAYED FADED FOR MORE THAN THIRTY SECONDS.
LOOKS LIKE WE'LL HAVE TO IMPROVISE--!
DAMN IT, TRACE!
LOOK, I CAN GET US INTO THE BUILDING WITH NO TROUBLE. BUT SOMEONE'S GOING TO HAVE TO COME ALONG TO WATCH MY BACK.
"I HADN'T BOTHERED SLEEPING. ONE OF THE ADVANTAGES OF CYBERNETIC PARTS IS THAT THEY DON'T GET TIRED."
THIS IS A HELL OF A TIME TO FIND THIS OUT.
LET'S HOPE THIS IS ONLY A MINOR SETBACK...

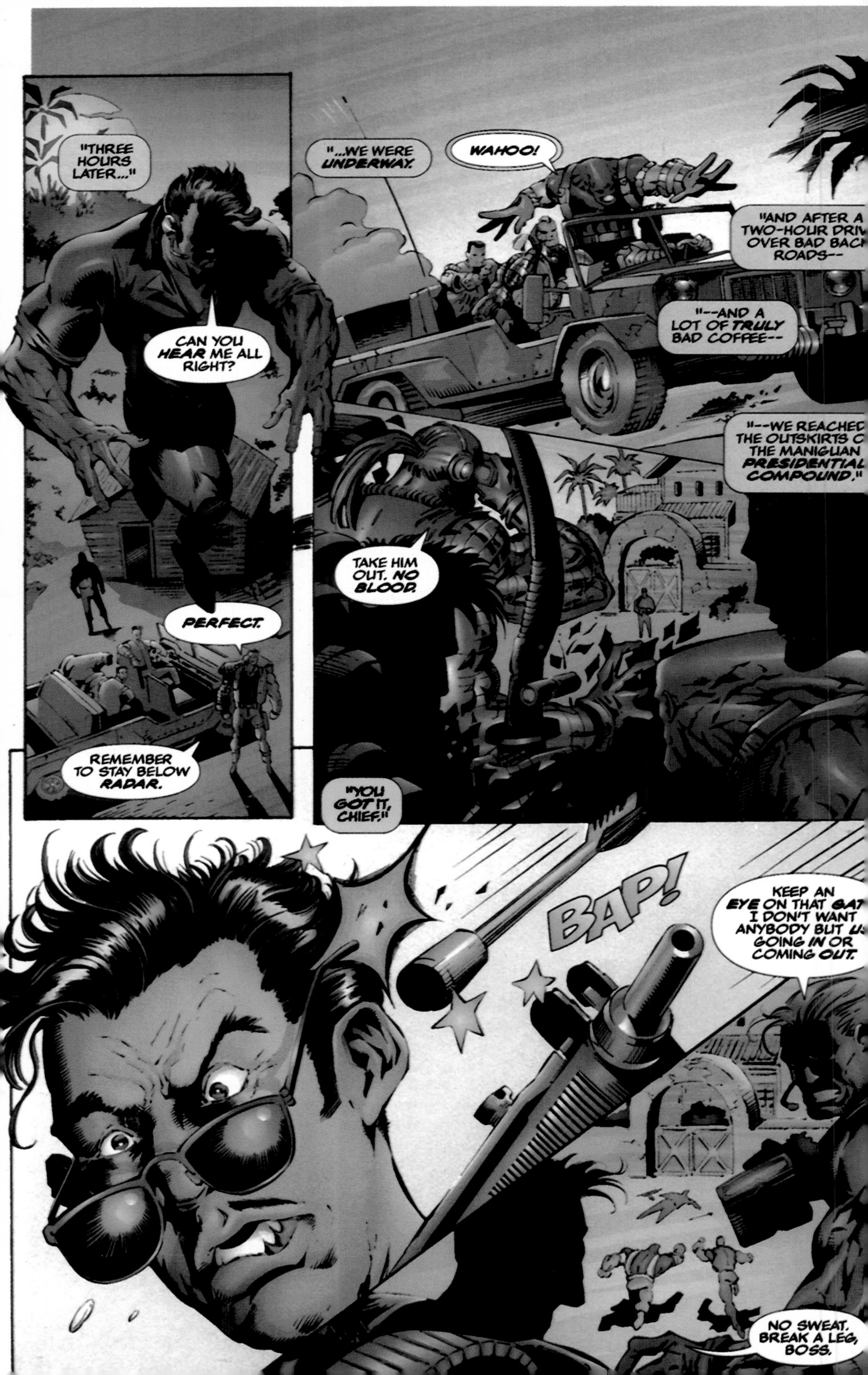
"THREE HOURS LATER..."
CAN YOU HEAR ME ALL RIGHT?
PERFECT.
REMEMBER TO STAY BELOW RADAR.
"...WE WERE UNDERWAY.
WAHOO!
"AND AFTER A TWO-HOUR DRIV OVER BAD BACK ROADS--
"--AND A LOT OF TRULY BAD COFFEE--
"--WE REACHED THE OUTSKIRTS O THE MANIGUAN PRESIDENTIAL COMPOUND."
TAKE HIM OUT. NO BLOOD.
"YOU GOT IT, CHIEF."
BAP!
KEEP AN EYE ON THAT GAT I DON'T WANT ANYBODY BUT US GOING IN OR COMING OUT.
NO SWEAT. BREAK A LEG, BOSS.

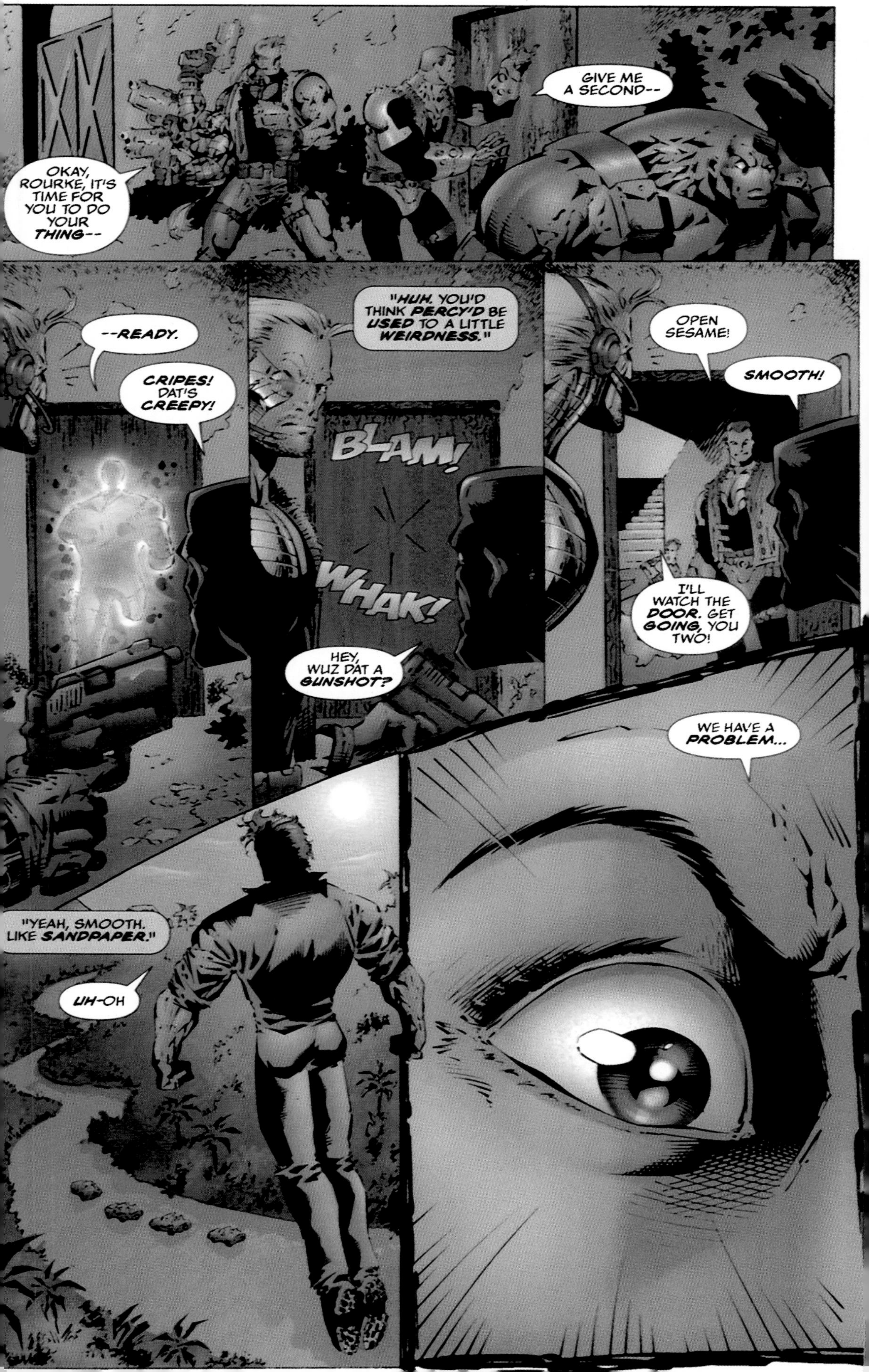

OKAY, ROURKE, IT'S TIME FOR YOU TO DO YOUR THING--
GIVE ME A SECOND--
--READY.
CRIPES! DAT'S CREEPY!
"HUH. YOU'D THINK PERCY'D BE USED TO A LITTLE WEIRDNESS."
BLAM!
WHAK!
HEY, WUZ DAT A GUNSHOT?
OPEN SESAME!
SMOOTH!
I'LL WATCH THE DOOR. GET GOING, YOU TWO!
"YEAH, SMOOTH. LIKE SANDPAPER."
UH-OH
WE HAVE A PROBLEM...

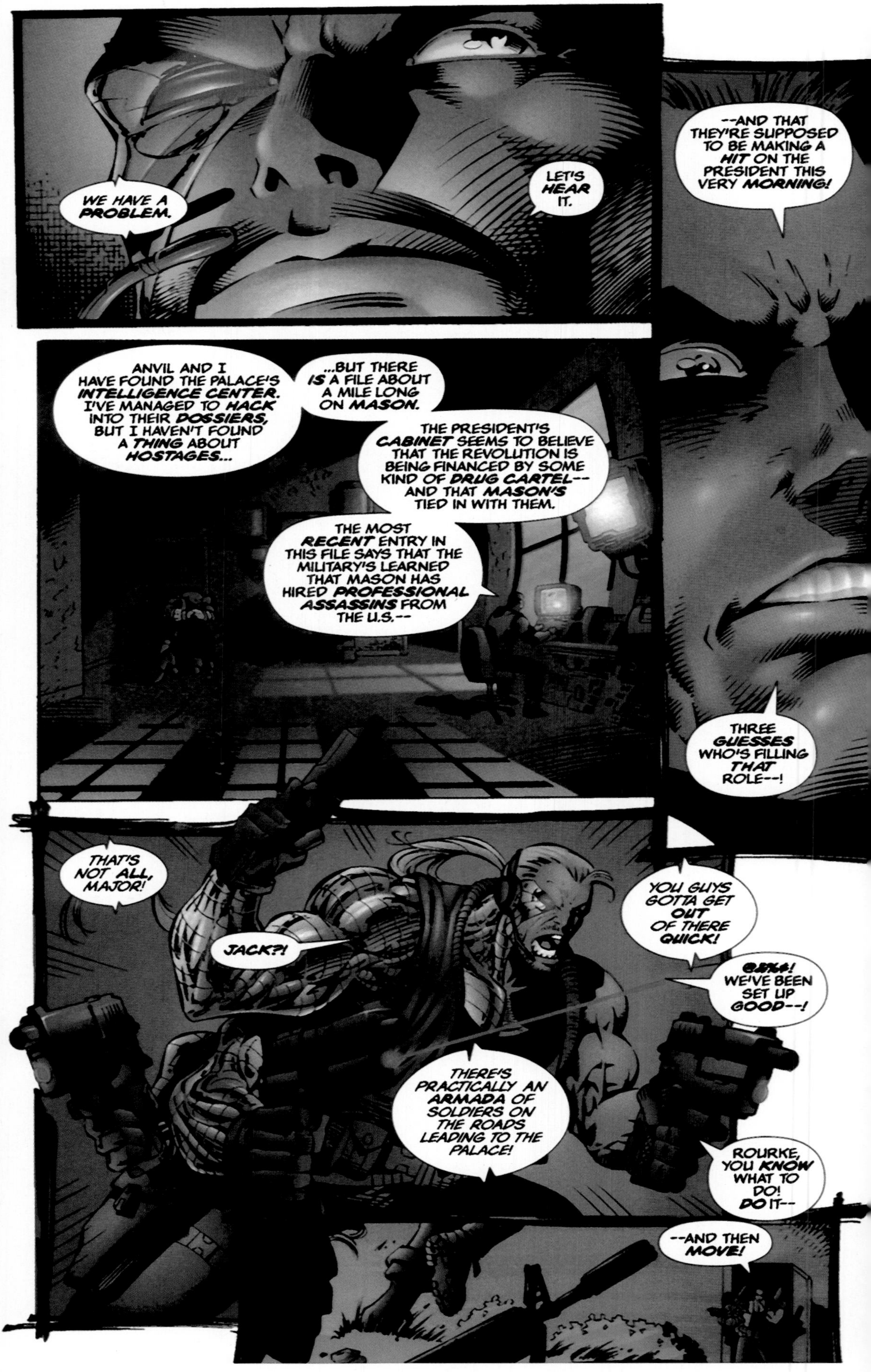
WE HAVE A PROBLEM.
LET'S HEAR IT.
--AND THAT THEY'RE SUPPOSED TO BE MAKING A HIT ON THE PRESIDENT THIS VERY MORNING!
ANVIL AND I HAVE FOUND THE PALACE'S INTELLIGENCE CENTER. I'VE MANAGED TO HACK INTO THEIR DOSSIERS, BUT I HAVEN'T FOUND A THING ABOUT HOSTAGES...
...BUT THERE IS A FILE ABOUT A MILE LONG ON MASON.
THE PRESIDENT'S CABINET SEEMS TO BELIEVE THAT THE REVOLUTION IS BEING FINANCED BY SOME KIND OF DRUG CARTEL-- AND THAT MASON'S TIED IN WITH THEM.
THE MOST RECENT ENTRY IN THIS FILE SAYS THAT THE MILITARY'S LEARNED THAT MASON HAS HIRED PROFESSIONAL ASSASSINS FROM THE U.S.--
THREE GUESSES WHO'S FILLING THAT ROLE--!
THAT'S NOT ALL, MAJOR!
JACK?!
YOU GUYS GOTTA GET OUT OF THERE QUICK!
@&%$! WE'VE BEEN SET UP GOOD--!
THERE'S PRACTICALLY AN ARMADA OF SOLDIERS ON THE ROADS LEADING TO THE PALACE!
ROURKE, YOU KNOW WHAT TO DO! DO IT--
--AND THEN MOVE!

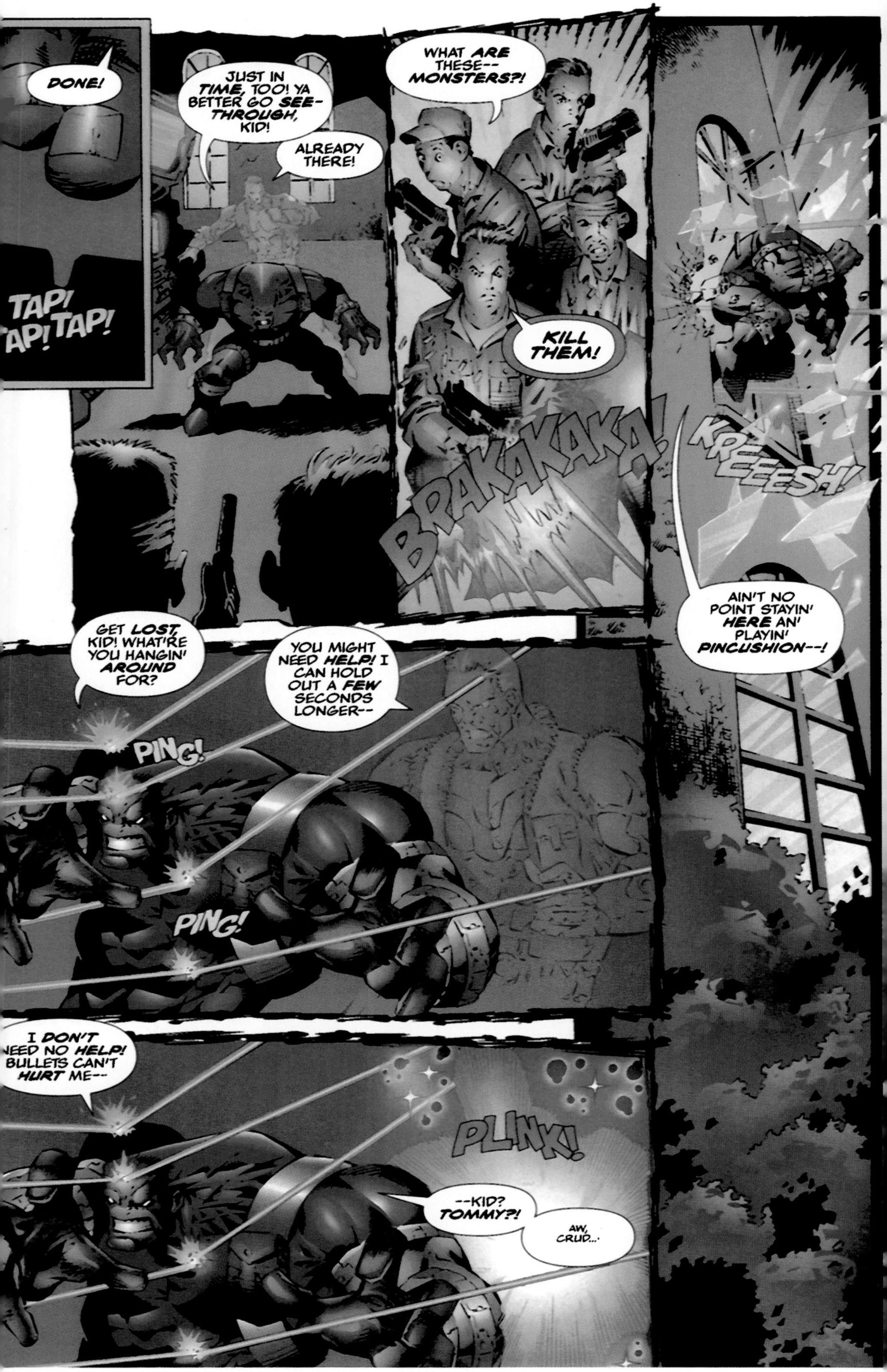
DONE!
TAP! TAP! TAP!
JUST IN TIME, TOO! YA BETTER GO SEE-THROUGH, KID!
ALREADY THERE!
WHAT ARE THESE-- MONSTERS?!
KILL THEM!
BRAKAKAKA!
KREEESH!
AIN'T NO POINT STAYIN' HERE AN' PLAYIN' PINCUSHION--!
GET LOST, KID! WHAT'RE YOU HANGIN' AROUND FOR?
YOU MIGHT NEED HELP! I CAN HOLD OUT A FEW SECONDS LONGER--
PING!
PING!
I DON'T NEED NO HELP! BULLETS CAN'T HURT ME--
PLINK!
--KID? TOMMY?!
AW, CRUD...

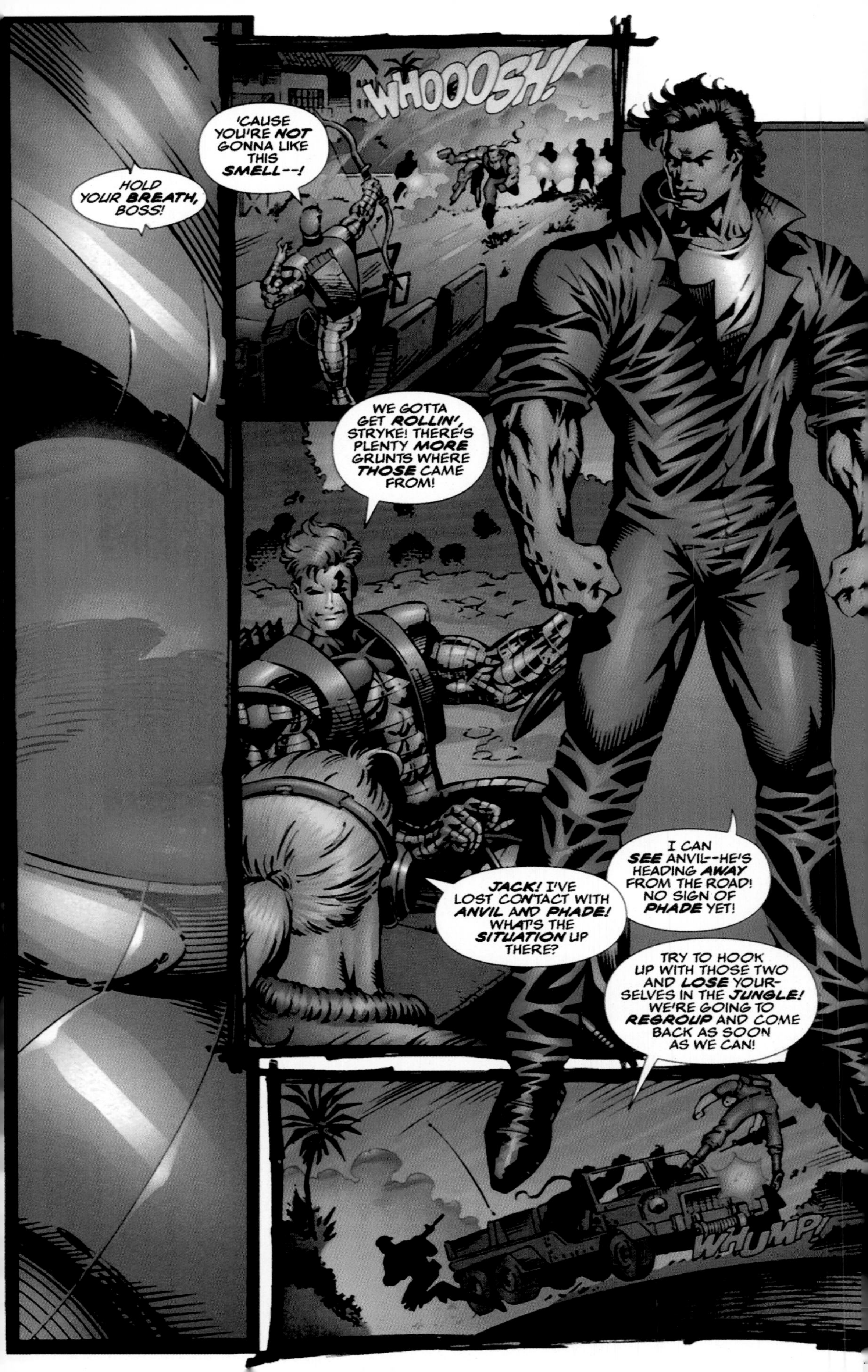

WHOOOSH!
HOLD YOUR BREATH, BOSS!
'CAUSE YOU'RE NOT GONNA LIKE THIS SMELL--!
WE GOTTA GET ROLLIN', STRYKE! THERE'S PLENTY MORE GRUNTS WHERE THOSE CAME FROM!
JACK! I'VE LOST CONTACT WITH ANVIL AND PHADE! WHAT'S THE SITUATION UP THERE?
I CAN SEE ANVIL--HE'S HEADING AWAY FROM THE ROAD! NO SIGN OF PHADE YET!
TRY TO HOOK UP WITH THOSE TWO AND LOSE YOUR-SELVES IN THE JUNGLE! WE'RE GOING TO REGROUP AND COME BACK AS SOON AS WE CAN!
WHUMP!

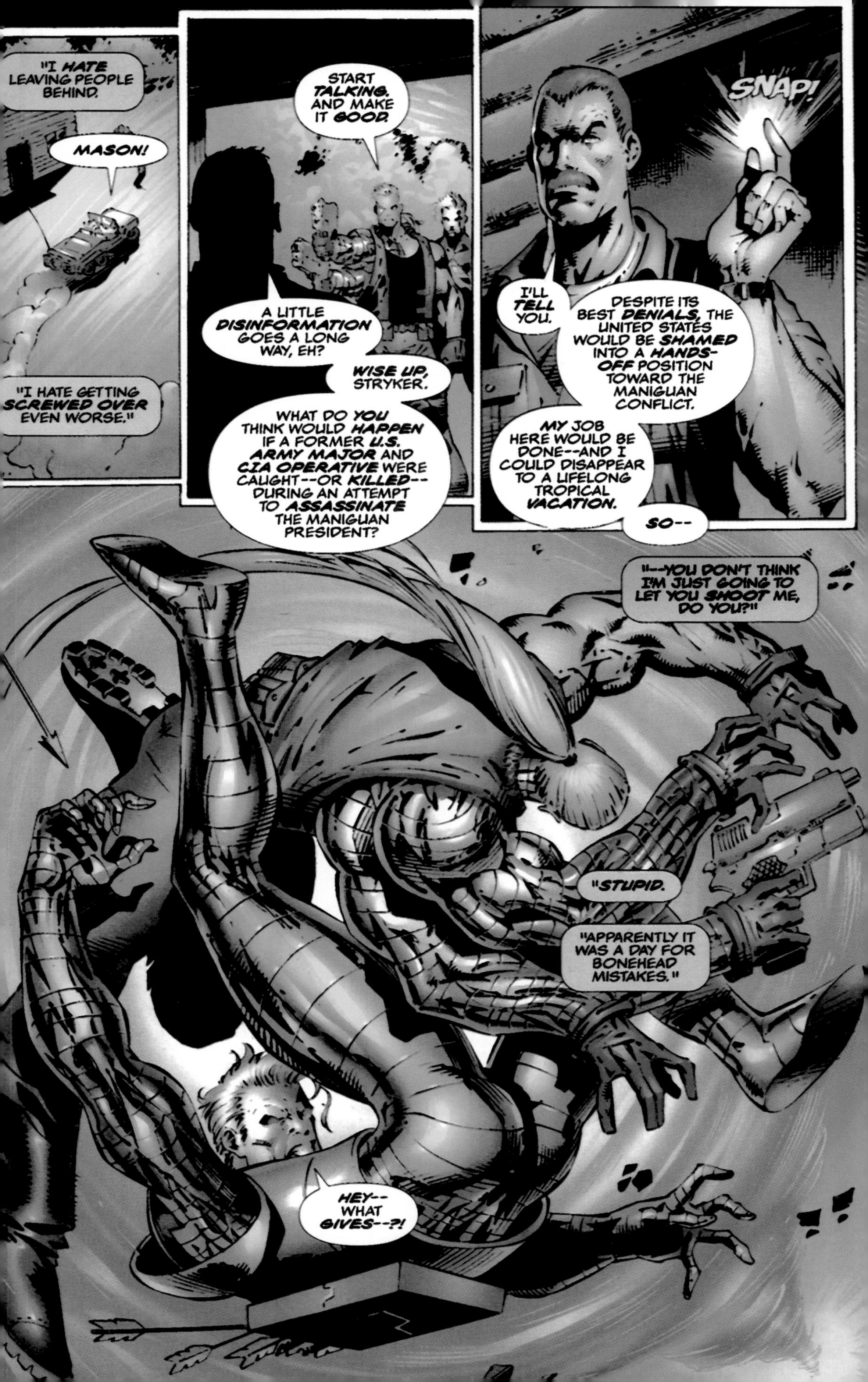
"I HATE LEAVING PEOPLE BEHIND.
MASON!
"I HATE GETTING SCREWED OVER EVEN WORSE."
START TALKING. AND MAKE IT GOOD.
A LITTLE DISINFORMATION GOES A LONG WAY, EH?
WISE UP, STRYKER.
WHAT DO YOU THINK WOULD HAPPEN IF A FORMER U.S. ARMY MAJOR AND CIA OPERATIVE WERE CAUGHT--OR KILLED--DURING AN ATTEMPT TO ASSASSINATE THE MANIGUAN PRESIDENT?
SNAP!
I'LL TELL YOU.
DESPITE ITS BEST DENIALS, THE UNITED STATES WOULD BE SHAMED INTO A HANDS-OFF POSITION TOWARD THE MANIGUAN CONFLICT.
MY JOB HERE WOULD BE DONE--AND I COULD DISAPPEAR TO A LIFELONG TROPICAL VACATION.
SO--
"--YOU DON'T THINK I'M JUST GOING TO LET YOU SHOOT ME, DO YOU?"
"STUPID.
"APPARENTLY IT WAS A DAY FOR BONEHEAD MISTAKES."
HEY-- WHAT GIVES--?!

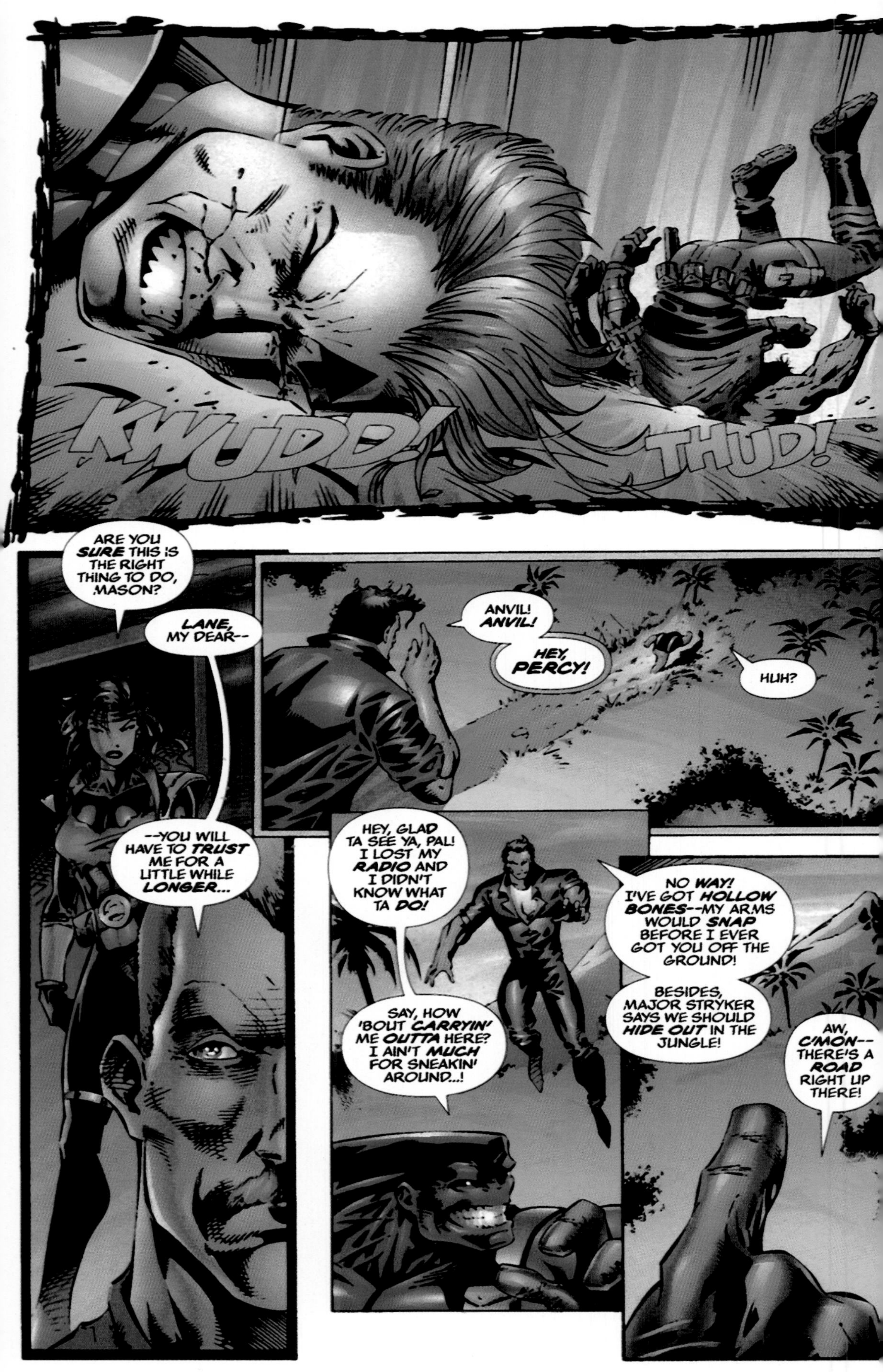
KWUDD!
THUD!
ARE YOU SURE THIS IS THE RIGHT THING TO DO, MASON?
LANE, MY DEAR--
--YOU WILL HAVE TO TRUST ME FOR A LITTLE WHILE LONGER...
ANVIL! ANVIL!
HEY, PERCY!
HUH?
HEY, GLAD TA SEE YA, PAL! I LOST MY RADIO AND I DIDN'T KNOW WHAT TA DO!
SAY, HOW 'BOUT CARRYIN' ME OUTTA HERE? I AIN'T MUCH FOR SNEAKIN' AROUND...!
NO WAY! I'VE GOT HOLLOW BONES--MY ARMS WOULD SNAP BEFORE I EVER GOT YOU OFF THE GROUND!
BESIDES, MAJOR STRYKER SAYS WE SHOULD HIDE OUT IN THE JUNGLE!
AW, C'MON-- THERE'S A ROAD RIGHT UP THERE!

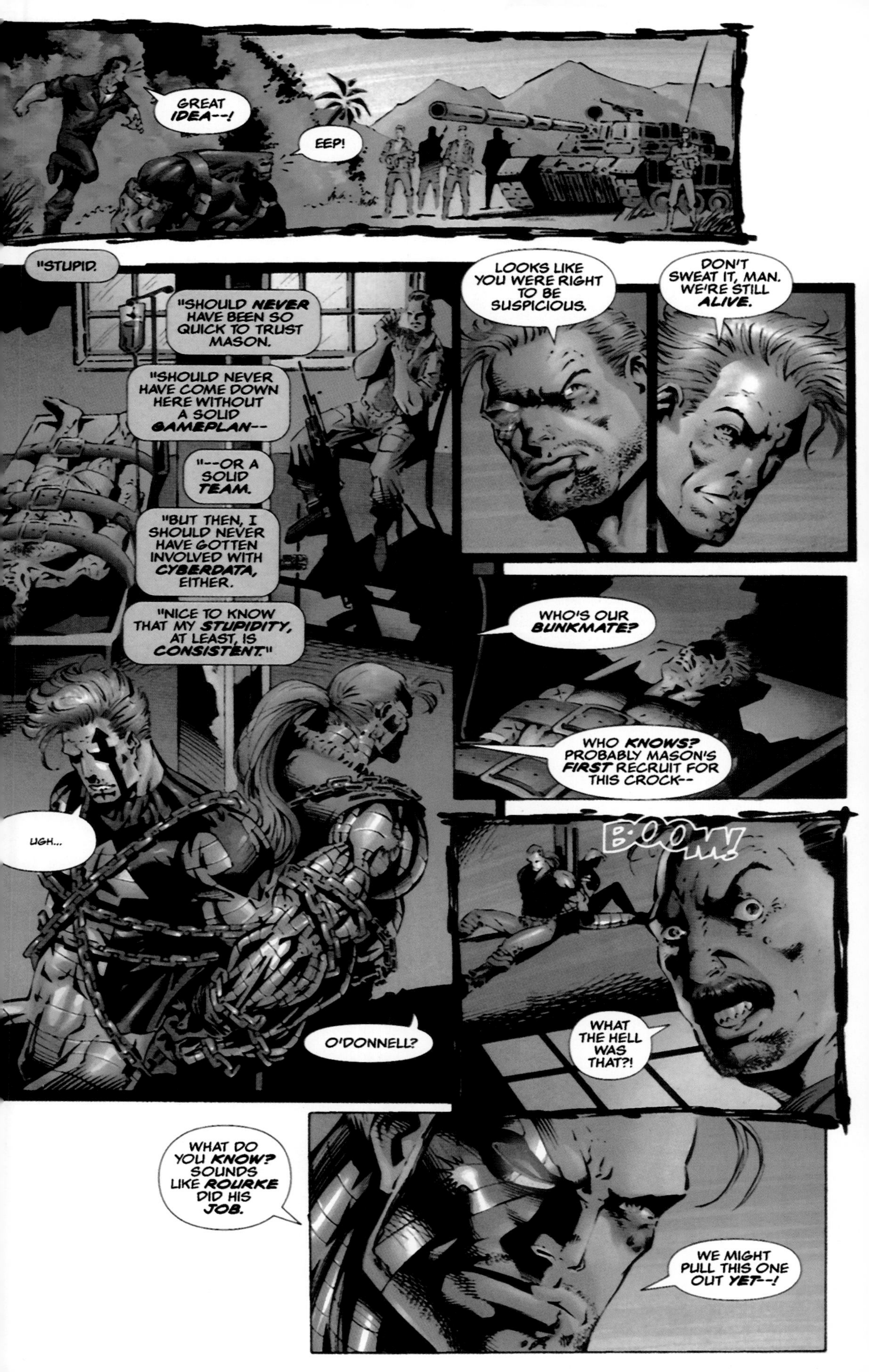

GREAT IDEA--!
EEP!
"STUPID.
"SHOULD NEVER HAVE BEEN SO QUICK TO TRUST MASON.
"SHOULD NEVER HAVE COME DOWN HERE WITHOUT A SOLID GAMEPLAN--
"--OR A SOLID TEAM.
"BUT THEN, I SHOULD NEVER HAVE GOTTEN INVOLVED WITH CYBERDATA, EITHER.
"NICE TO KNOW THAT MY STUPIDITY, AT LEAST, IS CONSISTENT."
UGH...
O'DONNELL?
LOOKS LIKE YOU WERE RIGHT TO BE SUSPICIOUS.
DON'T SWEAT IT, MAN. WE'RE STILL ALIVE.
WHO'S OUR BUNKMATE?
WHO KNOWS? PROBABLY MASON'S FIRST RECRUIT FOR THIS CROCK--
BOOM!
WHAT THE HELL WAS THAT?!
WHAT DO YOU KNOW? SOUNDS LIKE ROURKE DID HIS JOB.
WE MIGHT PULL THIS ONE OUT YET--!

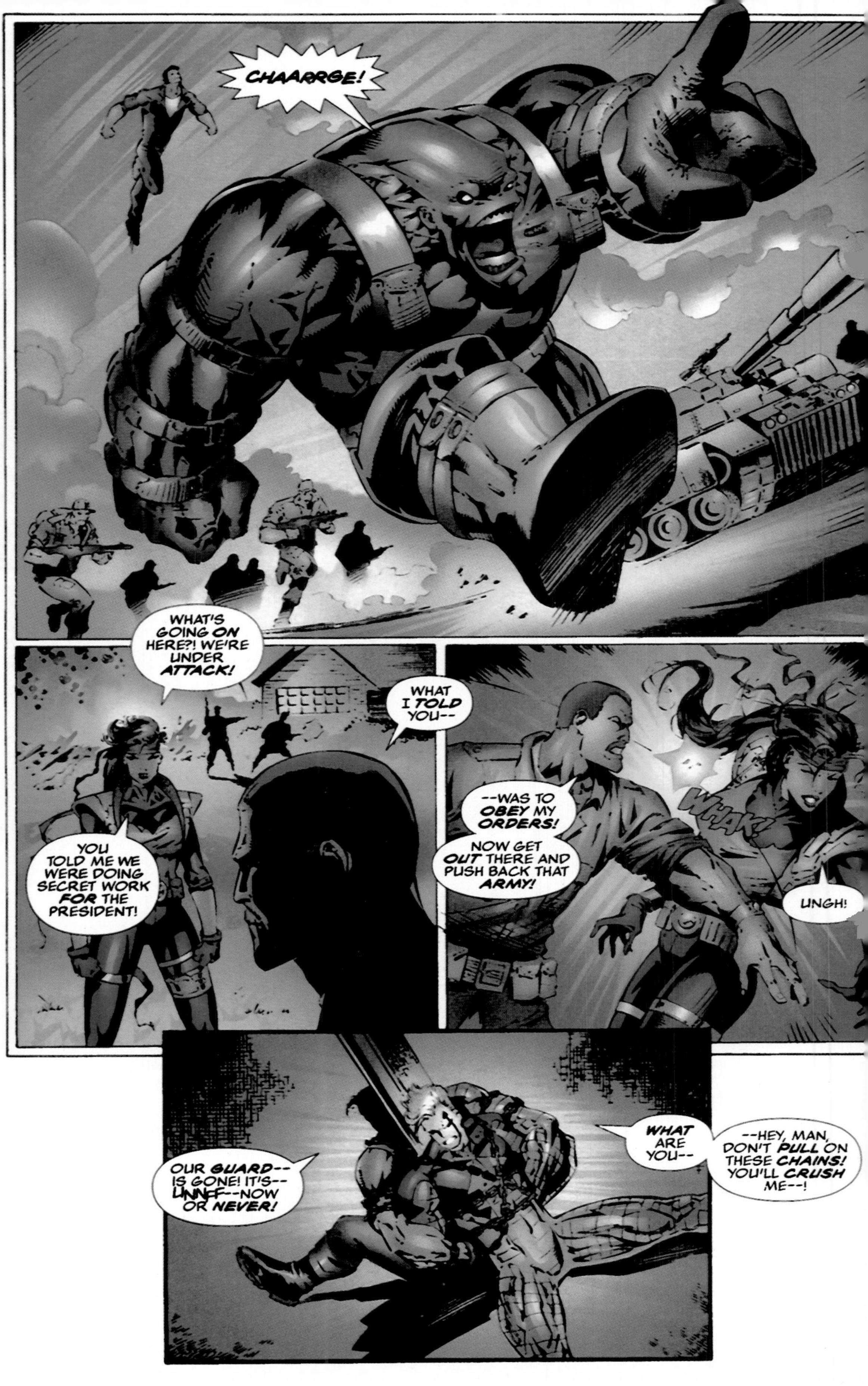
CHAARRGE!
WHAT'S GOING ON HERE?! WE'RE UNDER ATTACK!
WHAT I TOLD YOU--
YOU TOLD ME WE WERE DOING SECRET WORK FOR THE PRESIDENT!
--WAS TO OBEY MY ORDERS!
NOW GET OUT THERE AND PUSH BACK THAT ARMY!
WHAK!
UNGH!
OUR GUARD-- IS GONE! IT'S-- UNNFF--NOW OR NEVER!
WHAT ARE YOU--
--HEY, MAN, DON'T PULL ON THESE CHAINS! YOU'LL CRUSH ME--!

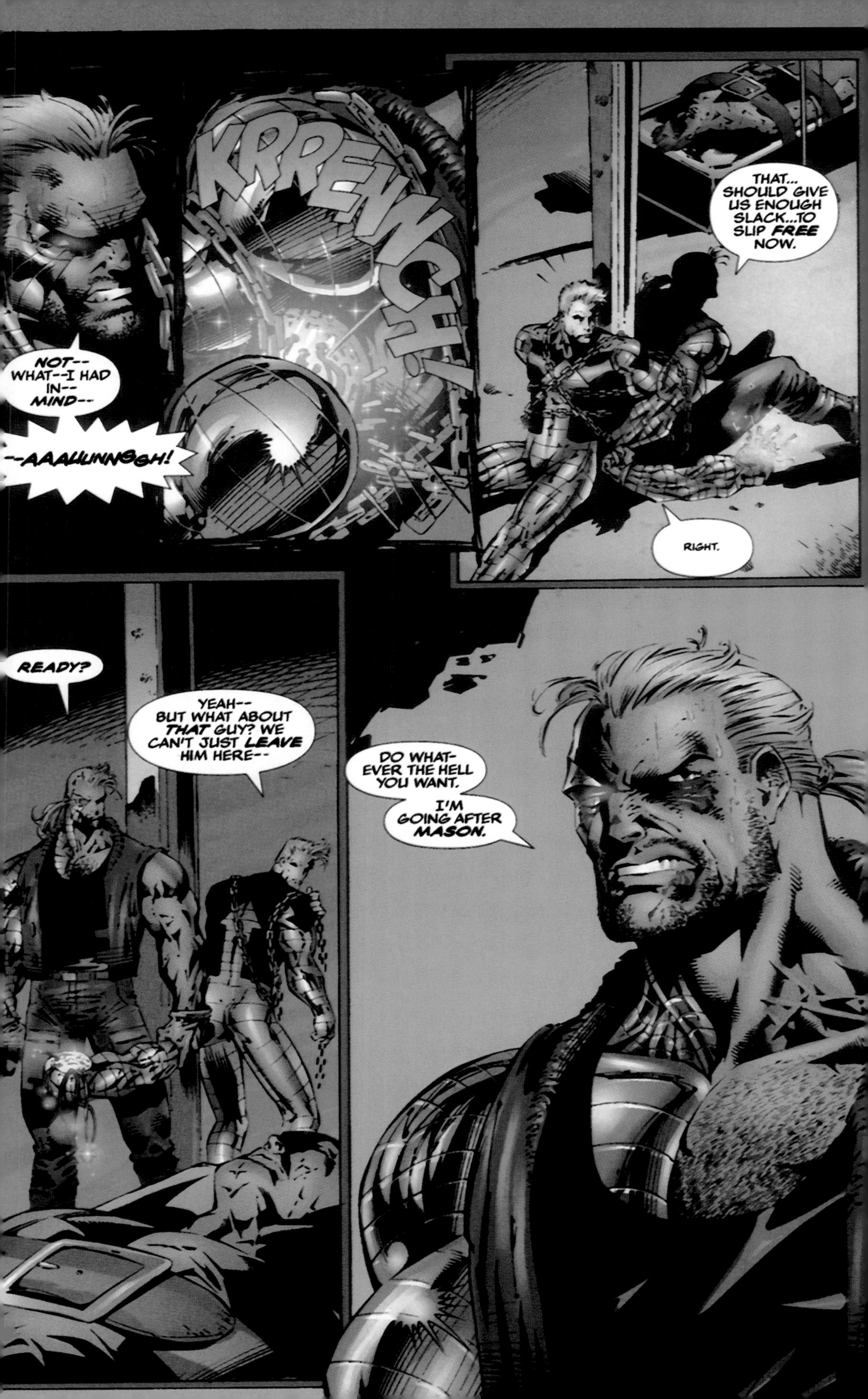
NOT--
WHAT--I HAD IN--
MIND--
--AAAUUNNGGH!
KRRENNCH!
THAT... SHOULD GIVE US ENOUGH SLACK...TO SLIP FREE NOW.
RIGHT.
READY?
YEAH-- BUT WHAT ABOUT THAT GUY? WE CAN'T JUST LEAVE HIM HERE--
DO WHAT-EVER THE HELL YOU WANT.
I'M GOING AFTER MASON.

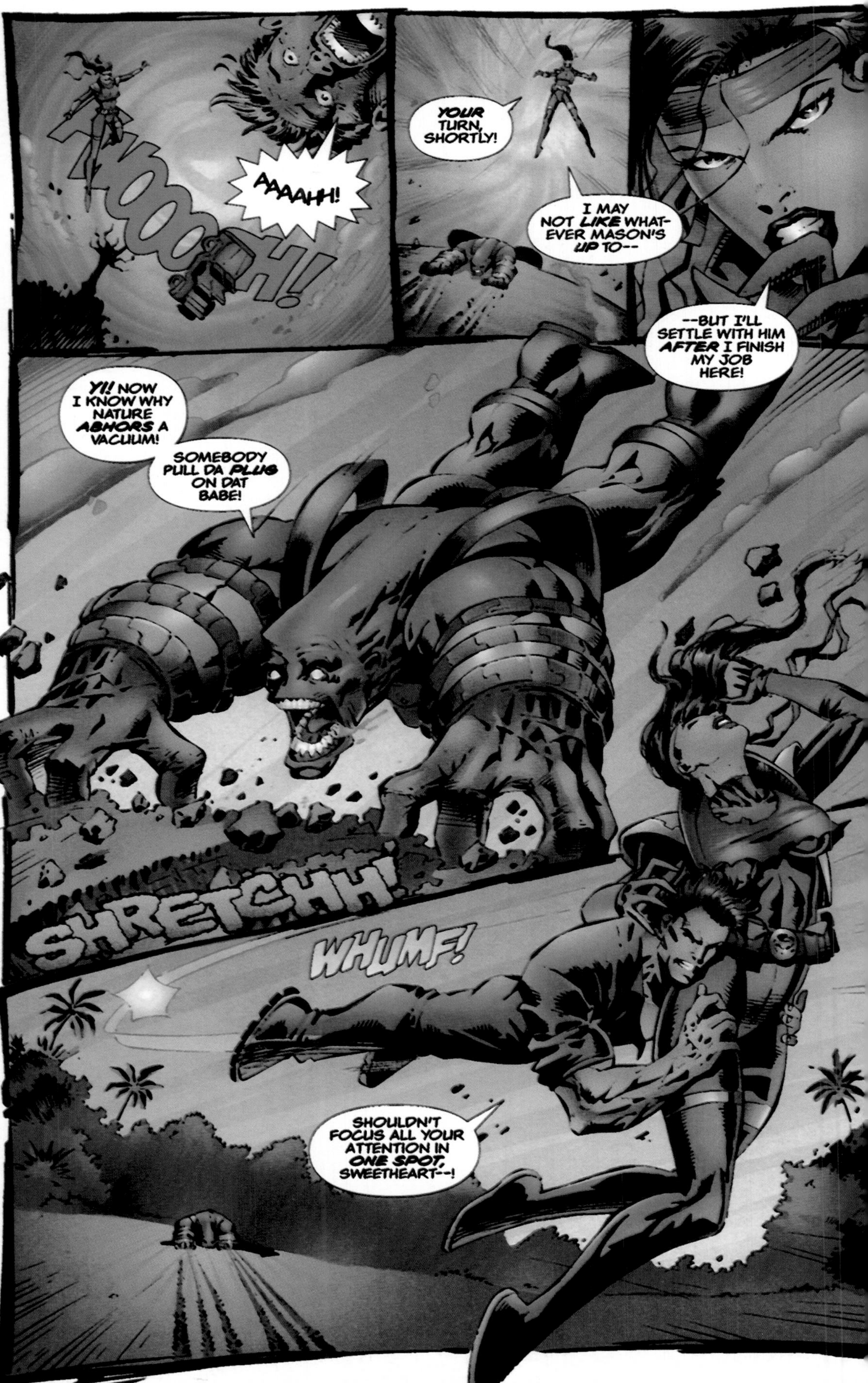
WHOOOSH!
AAAAHH!
YOUR TURN, SHORTLY!
I MAY NOT LIKE WHAT-EVER MASON'S UP TO--
--BUT I'LL SETTLE WITH HIM AFTER I FINISH MY JOB HERE!
YI! NOW I KNOW WHY NATURE ABHORS A VACUUM!
SOMEBODY PULL DA PLUG ON DAT BABE!
SHRETCHH!
WHUMF!
SHOULDN'T FOCUS ALL YOUR ATTENTION IN ONE SPOT, SWEETHEART--!

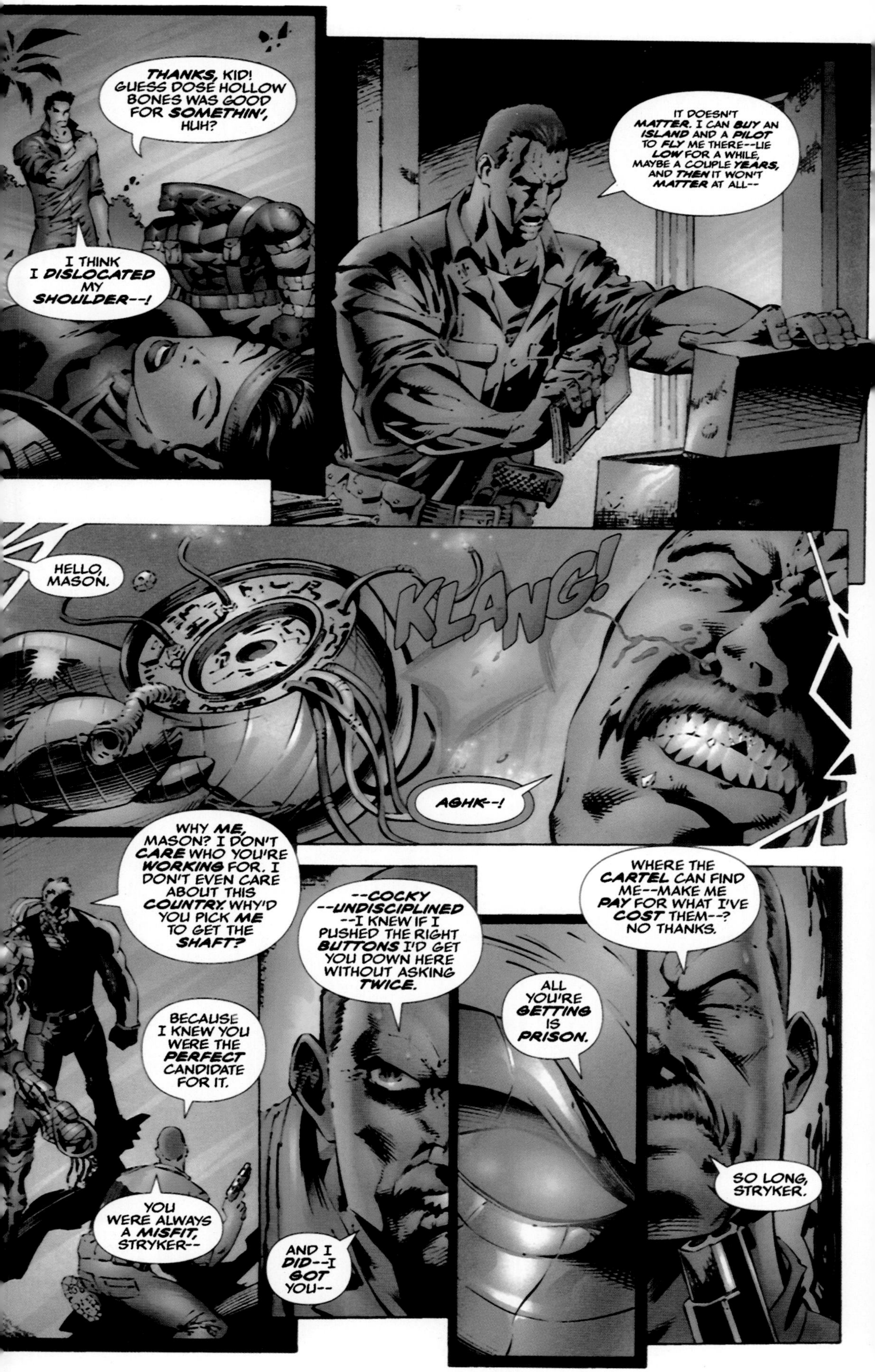
THANKS, KID! GUESS DOSE HOLLOW BONES WAS GOOD FOR SOMETHIN', HUH?
I THINK I DISLOCATED MY SHOULDER--!
IT DOESN'T MATTER. I CAN BUY AN ISLAND AND A PILOT TO FLY ME THERE--LIE LOW FOR A WHILE, MAYBE A COUPLE YEARS, AND THEN IT WON'T MATTER AT ALL--
HELLO, MASON.
KLANG!
AGHK--!
WHY ME, MASON? I DON'T CARE WHO YOU'RE WORKING FOR. I DON'T EVEN CARE ABOUT THIS COUNTRY. WHY'D YOU PICK ME TO GET THE SHAFT?
BECAUSE I KNEW YOU WERE THE PERFECT CANDIDATE FOR IT.
YOU WERE ALWAYS A MISFIT, STRYKER--
--COCKY --UNDISCIPLINED --I KNEW IF I PUSHED THE RIGHT BUTTONS I'D GET YOU DOWN HERE WITHOUT ASKING TWICE.
AND I DID--I GOT YOU--
ALL YOU'RE GETTING IS PRISON.
WHERE THE CARTEL CAN FIND ME--MAKE ME PAY FOR WHAT I'VE COST THEM--? NO THANKS.
SO LONG, STRYKER.

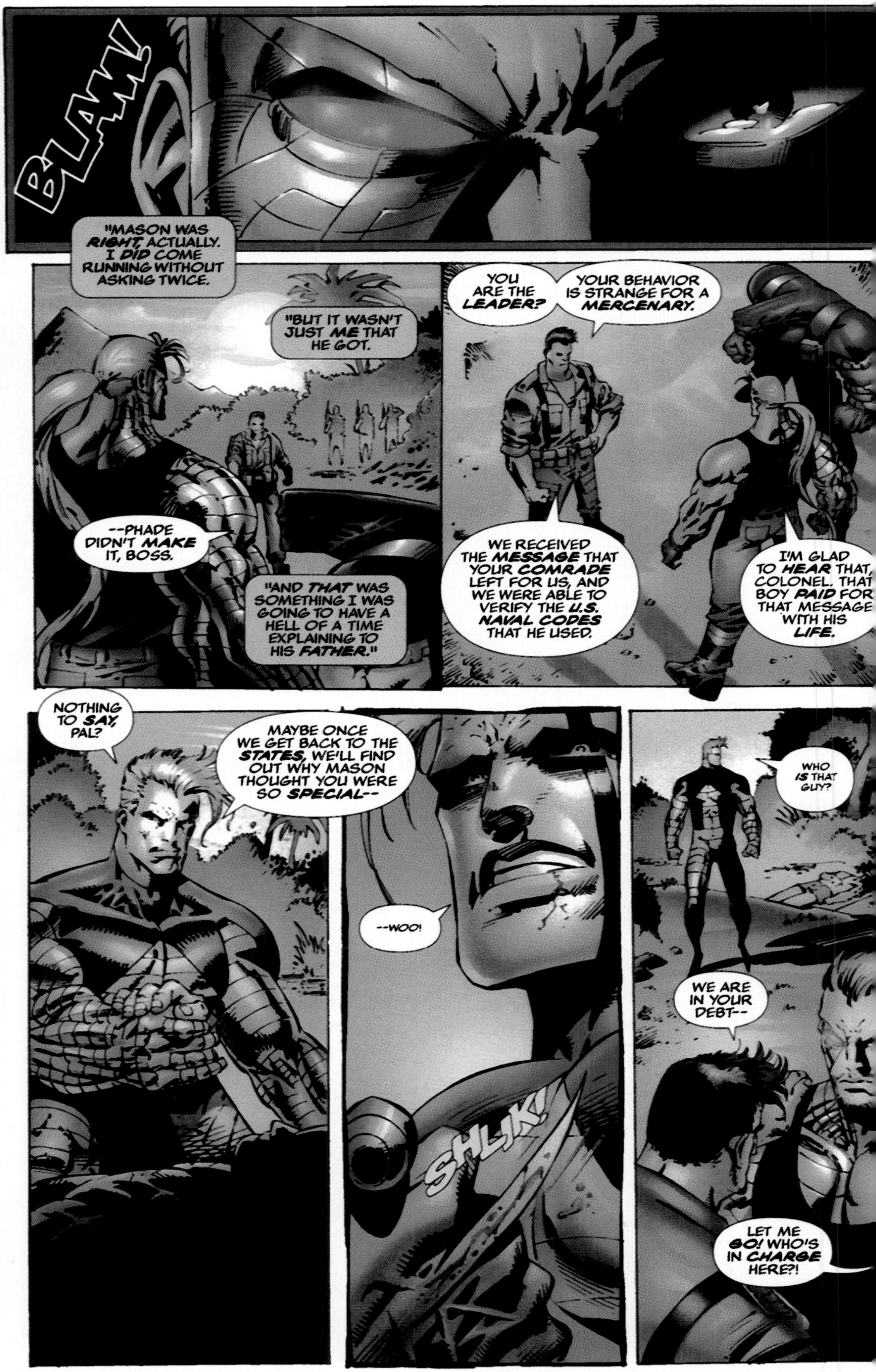
BLAM!
"MASON WAS RIGHT, ACTUALLY. I DID COME RUNNING WITHOUT ASKING TWICE.
"BUT IT WASN'T JUST ME THAT HE GOT.
--PHADE DIDN'T MAKE IT, BOSS.
"AND THAT WAS SOMETHING I WAS GOING TO HAVE A HELL OF A TIME EXPLAINING TO HIS FATHER."
YOU ARE THE LEADER?
YOUR BEHAVIOR IS STRANGE FOR A MERCENARY.
WE RECEIVED THE MESSAGE THAT YOUR COMRADE LEFT FOR US, AND WE WERE ABLE TO VERIFY THE U.S. NAVAL CODES THAT HE USED.
I'M GLAD TO HEAR THAT, COLONEL. THAT BOY PAID FOR THAT MESSAGE WITH HIS LIFE.
NOTHING TO SAY, PAL?
MAYBE ONCE WE GET BACK TO THE STATES, WE'LL FIND OUT WHY MASON THOUGHT YOU WERE SO SPECIAL--
--WOO!
SHLIK!
WHO IS THAT GUY?
WE ARE IN YOUR DEBT--
LET ME GO! WHO'S IN CHARGE HERE?!

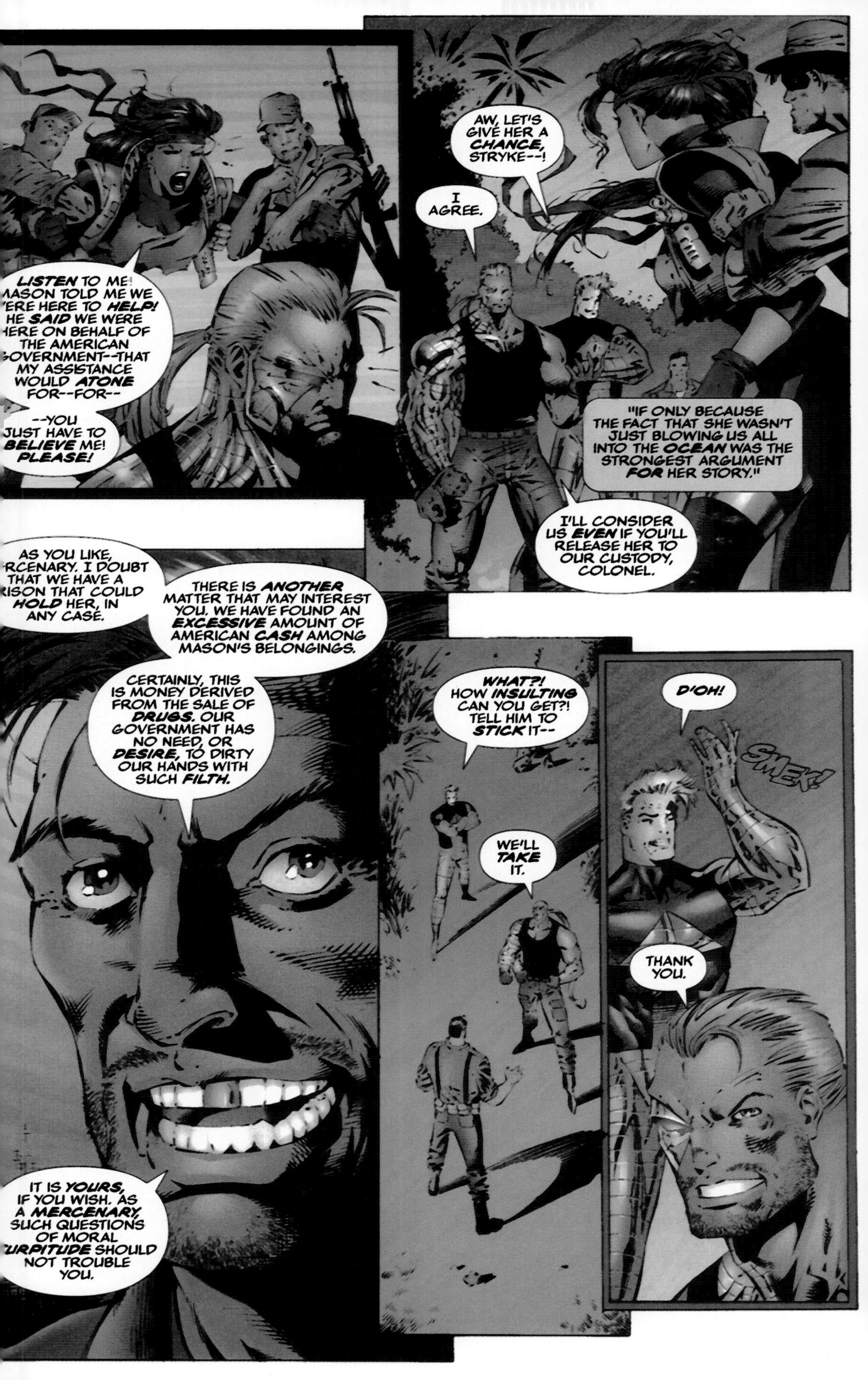
LISTEN TO ME! MASON TOLD ME WE WERE HERE TO HELP! HE SAID WE WERE HERE ON BEHALF OF THE AMERICAN GOVERNMENT--THAT MY ASSISTANCE WOULD ATONE FOR--FOR--
--YOU JUST HAVE TO BELIEVE ME! PLEASE!
AW, LET'S GIVE HER A CHANCE, STRYKE--!
I AGREE.
"IF ONLY BECAUSE THE FACT THAT SHE WASN'T JUST BLOWING US ALL INTO THE OCEAN WAS THE STRONGEST ARGUMENT FOR HER STORY."
I'LL CONSIDER US EVEN IF YOU'LL RELEASE HER TO OUR CUSTODY, COLONEL.
AS YOU LIKE, RCENARY. I DOUBT THAT WE HAVE A RISON THAT COULD HOLD HER, IN ANY CASE.
THERE IS ANOTHER MATTER THAT MAY INTEREST YOU. WE HAVE FOUND AN EXCESSIVE AMOUNT OF AMERICAN CASH AMONG MASON'S BELONGINGS.
CERTAINLY, THIS IS MONEY DERIVED FROM THE SALE OF DRUGS. OUR GOVERNMENT HAS NO NEED, OR DESIRE, TO DIRTY OUR HANDS WITH SUCH FILTH.
IT IS YOURS, IF YOU WISH. AS A MERCENARY, SUCH QUESTIONS OF MORAL TURPITUDE SHOULD NOT TROUBLE YOU.
WHAT?! HOW INSULTING CAN YOU GET?! TELL HIM TO STICK IT--
WE'LL TAKE IT.
D'OH!
SMEK!
THANK YOU.

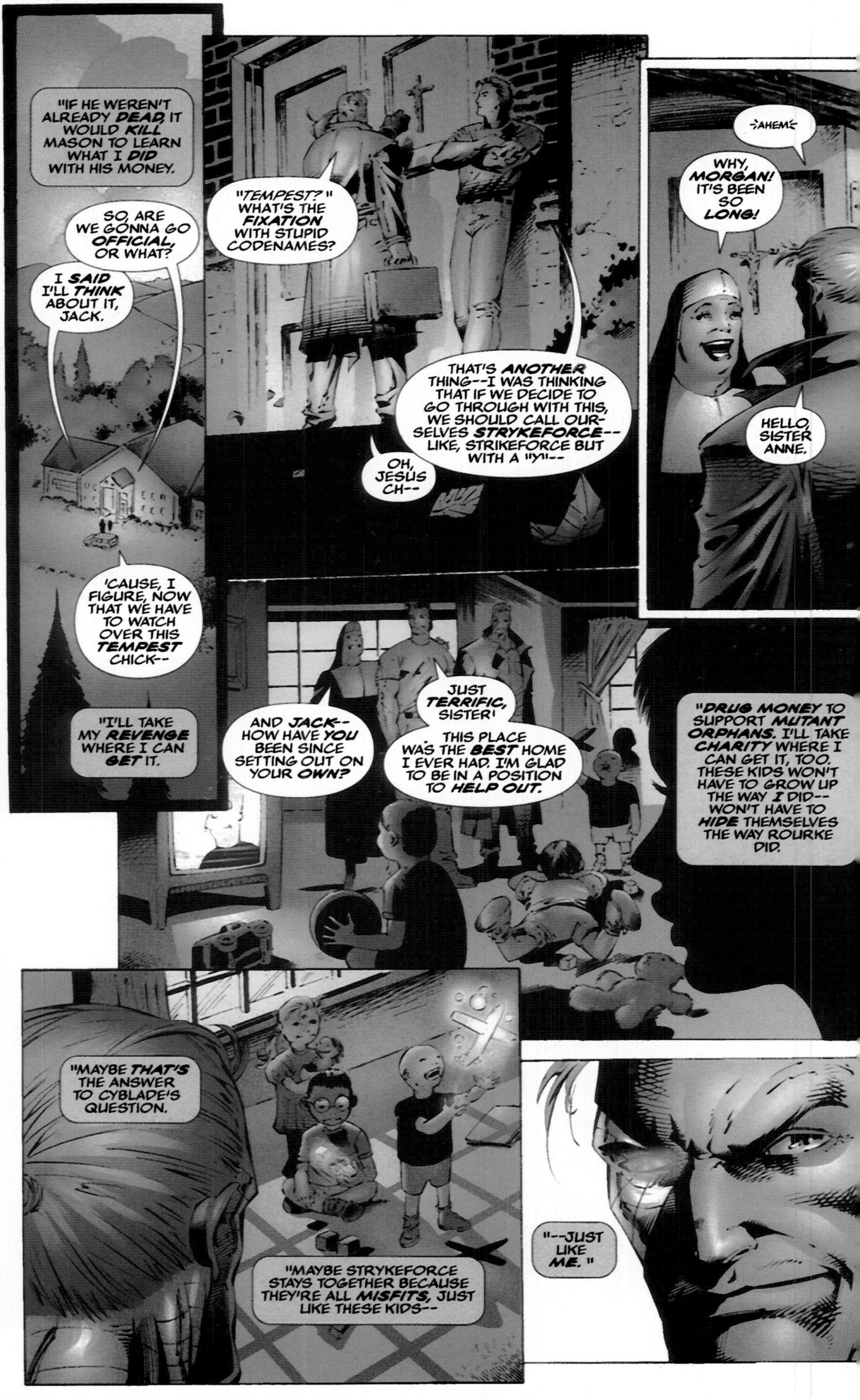

"IF HE WEREN'T ALREADY DEAD, IT WOULD KILL MASON TO LEARN WHAT I DID WITH HIS MONEY.
SO, ARE WE GONNA GO OFFICIAL, OR WHAT?
I SAID I'LL THINK ABOUT IT, JACK.
'CAUSE, I FIGURE, NOW THAT WE HAVE TO WATCH OVER THIS TEMPEST CHICK--
"I'LL TAKE MY REVENGE WHERE I CAN GET IT.
"TEMPEST?" WHAT'S THE FIXATION WITH STUPID CODENAMES?
THAT'S ANOTHER THING--I WAS THINKING THAT IF WE DECIDE TO GO THROUGH WITH THIS, WE SHOULD CALL OURSELVES STRYKEFORCE--LIKE, STRIKEFORCE BUT WITH A "Y"--
OH, JESUS CH--
AHEM
WHY, MORGAN! IT'S BEEN SO LONG!
HELLO, SISTER ANNE.
AND JACK--HOW HAVE YOU BEEN SINCE SETTING OUT ON YOUR OWN?
JUST TERRIFIC, SISTER!
THIS PLACE WAS THE BEST HOME I EVER HAD. I'M GLAD TO BE IN A POSITION TO HELP OUT.
"DRUG MONEY TO SUPPORT MUTANT ORPHANS. I'LL TAKE CHARITY WHERE I CAN GET IT, TOO. THESE KIDS WON'T HAVE TO GROW UP THE WAY I DID--WON'T HAVE TO HIDE THEMSELVES THE WAY ROURKE DID.
"MAYBE THAT'S THE ANSWER TO CYBLADE'S QUESTION.
"MAYBE STRYKEFORCE STAYS TOGETHER BECAUSE THEY'RE ALL MISFITS, JUST LIKE THESE KIDS--
"--JUST LIKE ME."

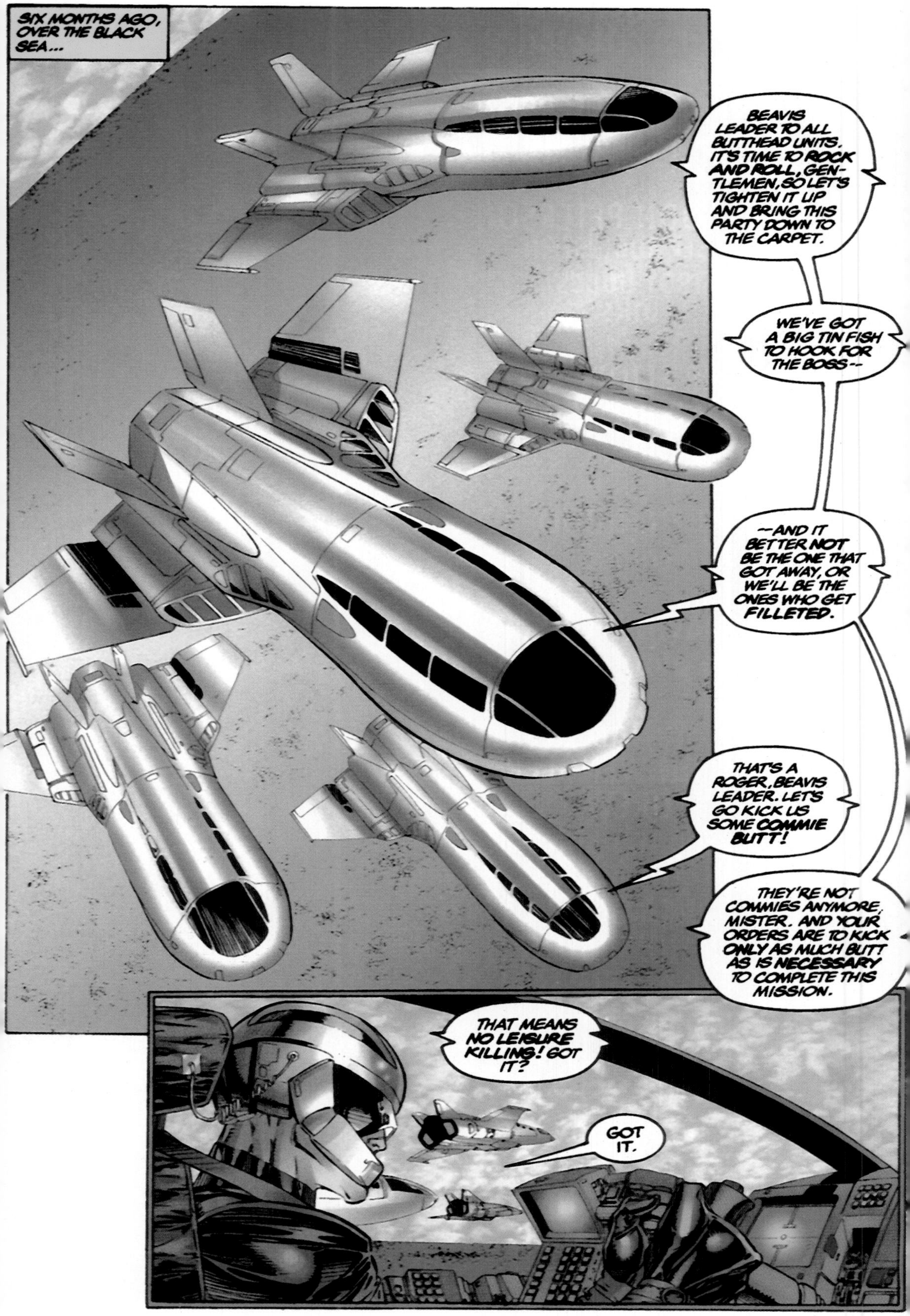
SIX MONTHS AGO, OVER THE BLACK SEA...
BEAVIS LEADER TO ALL BUTTHEAD UNITS. IT'S TIME TO ROCK AND ROLL, GENTLEMEN, SO LET'S TIGHTEN IT UP AND BRING THIS PARTY DOWN TO THE CARPET.
WE'VE GOT A BIG TIN FISH TO HOOK FOR THE BOSS--
--AND IT BETTER NOT BE THE ONE THAT GOT AWAY, OR WE'LL BE THE ONES WHO GET FILLETED.
THAT'S A ROGER, BEAVIS LEADER. LET'S GO KICK US SOME COMMIE BUTT!
THEY'RE NOT COMMIES ANYMORE, MISTER. AND YOUR ORDERS ARE TO KICK ONLY AS MUCH BUTT AS IS NECESSARY TO COMPLETE THIS MISSION.
THAT MEANS NO LEISURE KILLING! GOT IT?
GOT IT.

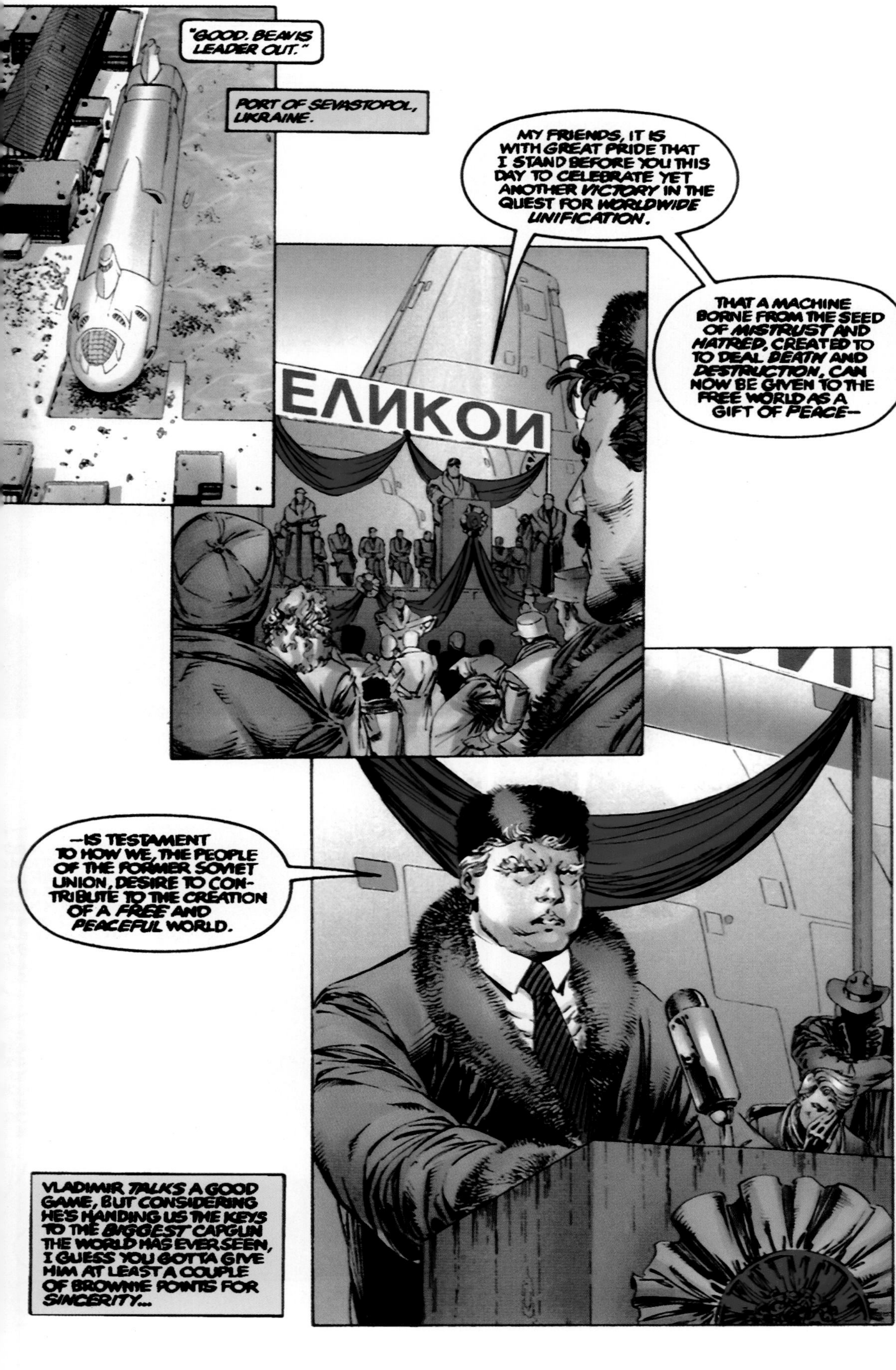
"GOOD. BEAVIS LEADER OUT."
PORT OF SEVASTOPOL, UKRAINE.
MY FRIENDS, IT IS WITH GREAT PRIDE THAT I STAND BEFORE YOU THIS DAY TO CELEBRATE YET ANOTHER VICTORY IN THE QUEST FOR WORLDWIDE UNIFICATION.
THAT A MACHINE BORNE FROM THE SEED OF MISTRUST AND HATRED, CREATED TO TO DEAL DEATH AND DESTRUCTION, CAN NOW BE GIVEN TO THE FREE WORLD AS A GIFT OF PEACE--
ЕЛNКОИ
--IS TESTAMENT TO HOW WE, THE PEOPLE OF THE FORMER SOVIET UNION, DESIRE TO CONTRIBUTE TO THE CREATION OF A FREE AND PEACEFUL WORLD.
VLADIMIR TALKS A GOOD GAME, BUT CONSIDERING HE'S HANDING US THE KEYS TO THE BIGGEST CAPGUN THE WORLD HAS EVER SEEN, I GUESS YOU GOTTA GIVE HIM AT LEAST A COUPLE OF BROWNIE POINTS FOR SINCERITY...

...BUT I'M NOT BEIN' PAID TO PONDER POLITICAL TRUTHS. I'M PAID TO BE A *WATCHDOG*.

YOU SEEM A LITTLE *TENSE*, MR. STRYKER. IS THERE ANYTHING WRONG?

NO SIR, MR. PRESIDENT. EVERYTHING IS JUST FINE.

LET'S NOT BE SO FORMAL. YOU CAN CALL ME *BILL*.

OKAY BILL, YOU CAN CALL ME *MR. STRYKER*.

ER... YES... WELL, I'M STILL NOT CONVINCED THAT YOUR SERVICES ARE *NEEDED* HERE. WHAT WITH ALL THE EXTRA SECURITY BEING SUPPLIED TO MYSELF AND ALL THE OTHER FOREIGN DIPLOMATS.

AND, I'M AFRAID MY SECRET SERVICE AGENTS DON'T MUCH *LIKE YOU.*

REMIND ME TO CRY.

THERE'S ALSO THE QUESTION OF YOUR *FEE.* ALTHOUGH THE MISSUS INSISTED YOU BE HIRED, I DON'T KNOW IF WE CAN AFFORD A *TEN MILLION DOLLAR* BODYGUARD.

THAT'S OKAY, BILL. THE FIRST LADY ASSURED ME THAT YOU COULD WORK OUT A LITTLE *TAX CUT* DEAL FOR ME WITH THE IRS.

HEH HEH. YEAH, RIGHT.

HE THINKS I'M KIDDING.

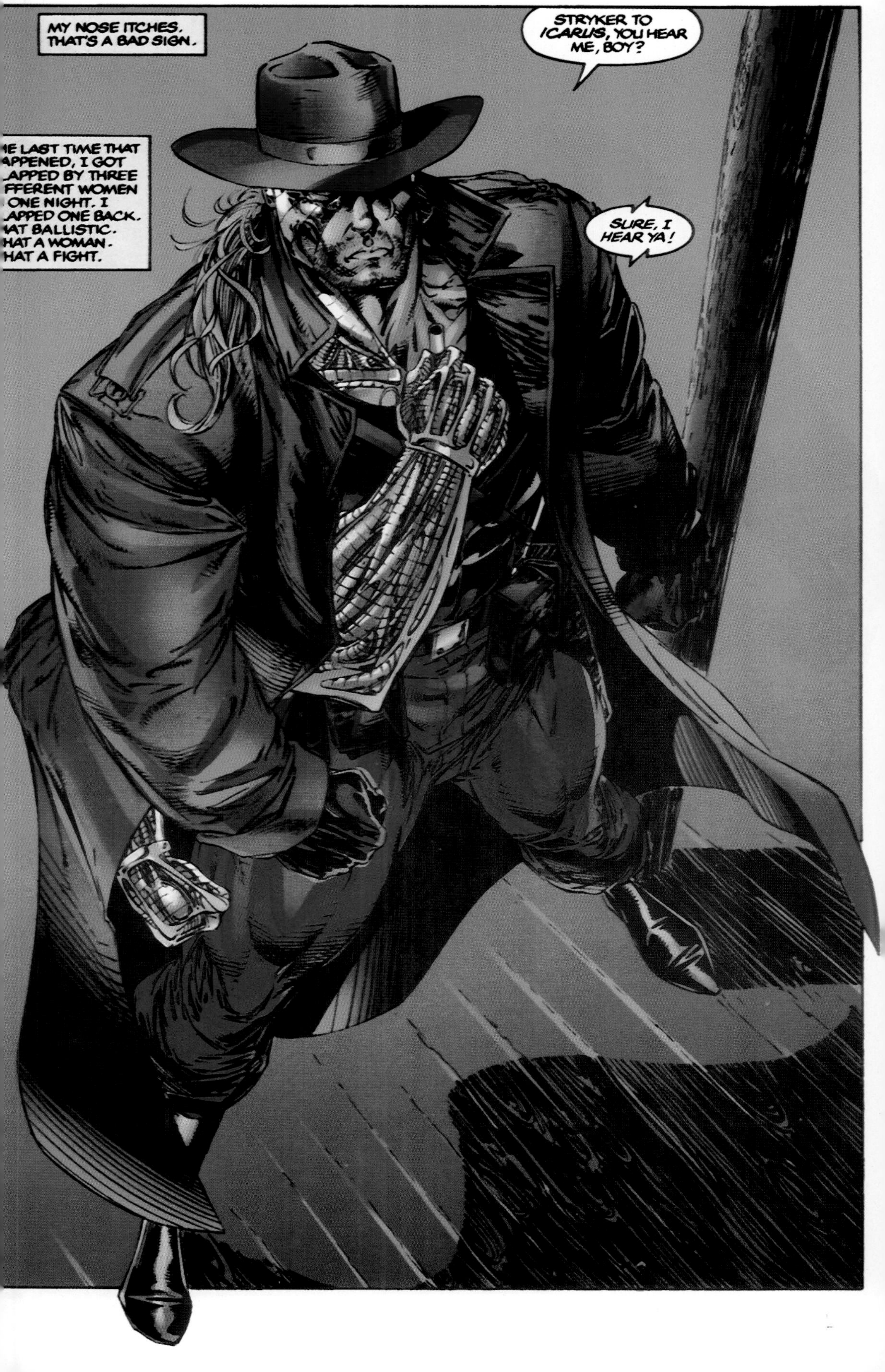
MY NOSE ITCHES. THAT'S A BAD SIGN.
STRYKER TO ICARUS, YOU HEAR ME, BOY?
HE LAST TIME THAT APPENED, I GOT LAPPED BY THREE FFERENT WOMEN ONE NIGHT. I LAPPED ONE BACK. HAT BALLISTIC. HAT A WOMAN. HAT A FIGHT.
SURE, I HEAR YA!

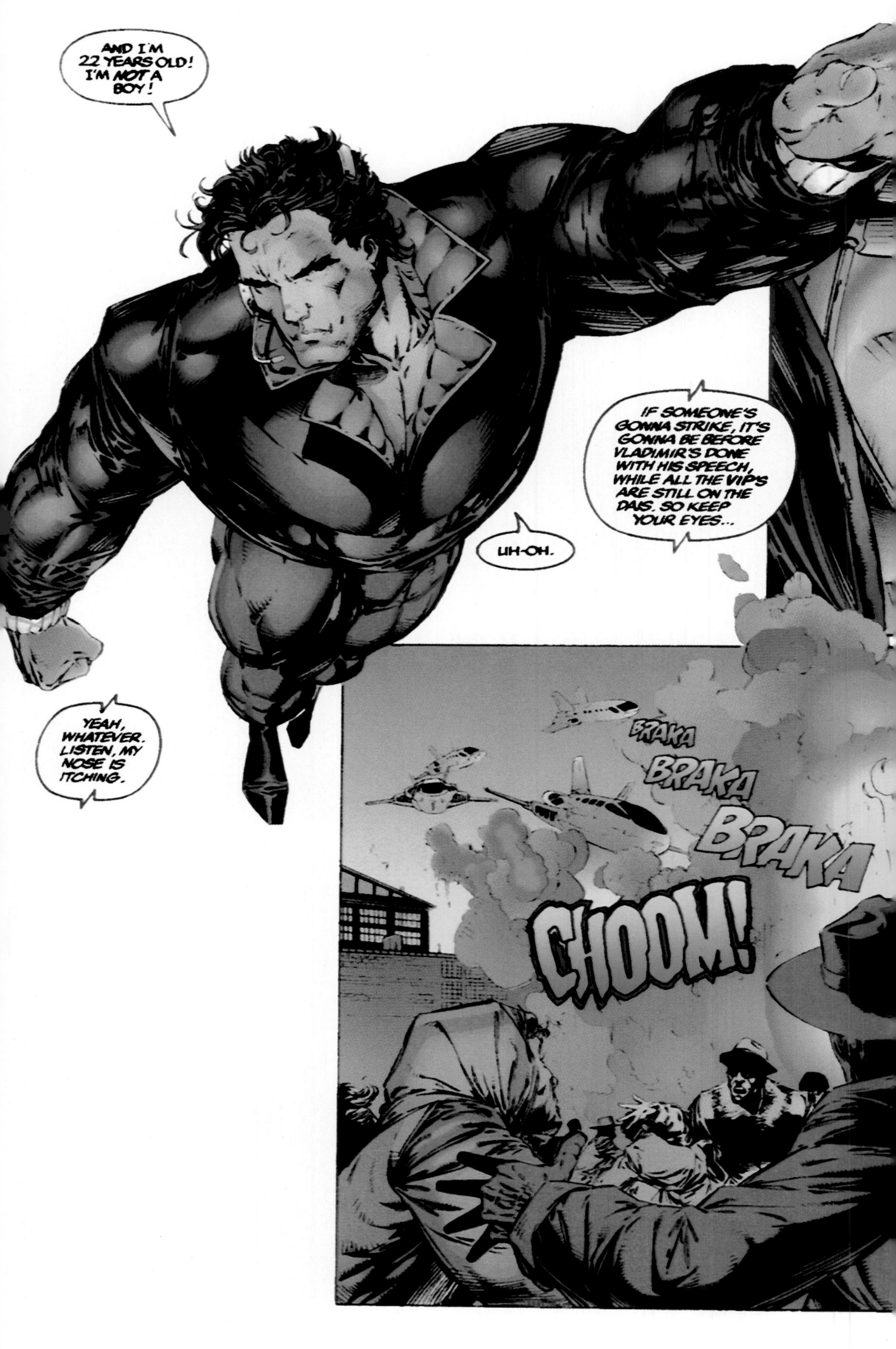
AND I'M 22 YEARS OLD! I'M NOT A BOY!
YEAH, WHATEVER. LISTEN, MY NOSE IS ITCHING.
IF SOMEONE'S GONNA STRIKE, IT'S GONNA BE BEFORE VLADIMIR'S DONE WITH HIS SPEECH, WHILE ALL THE VIP'S ARE STILL ON THE DAIS. SO KEEP YOUR EYES...
UH-OH.
BRAKA
BRAKA
BRAKA
CHOOM!

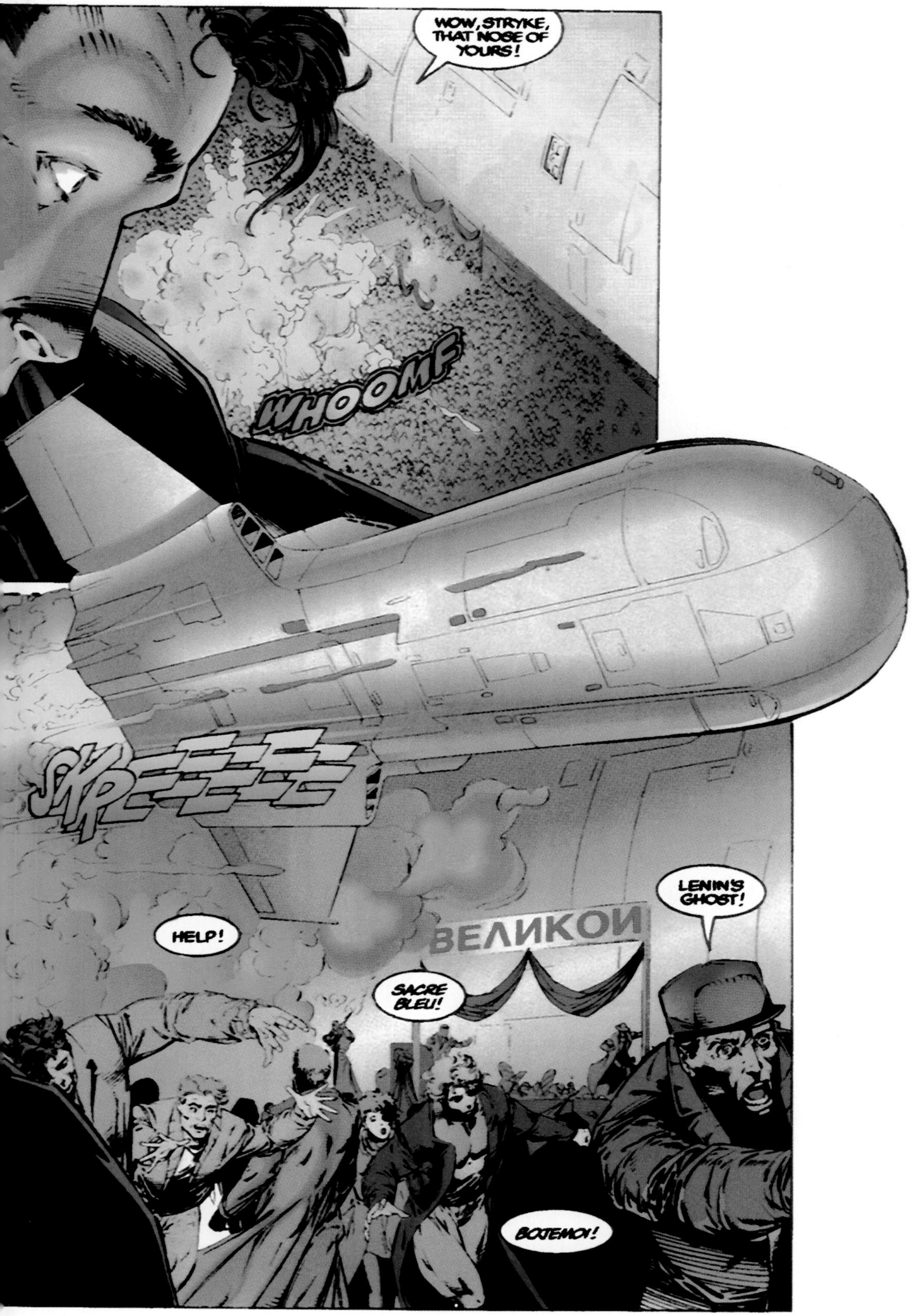
WOW, STRYKE, THAT NOSE OF YOURS!
WHOOMF
SKREEEEE
LENIN'S GHOST!
HELP!
ВЕЛИКОИ
SACRE BLEU!
BOJEMOI!

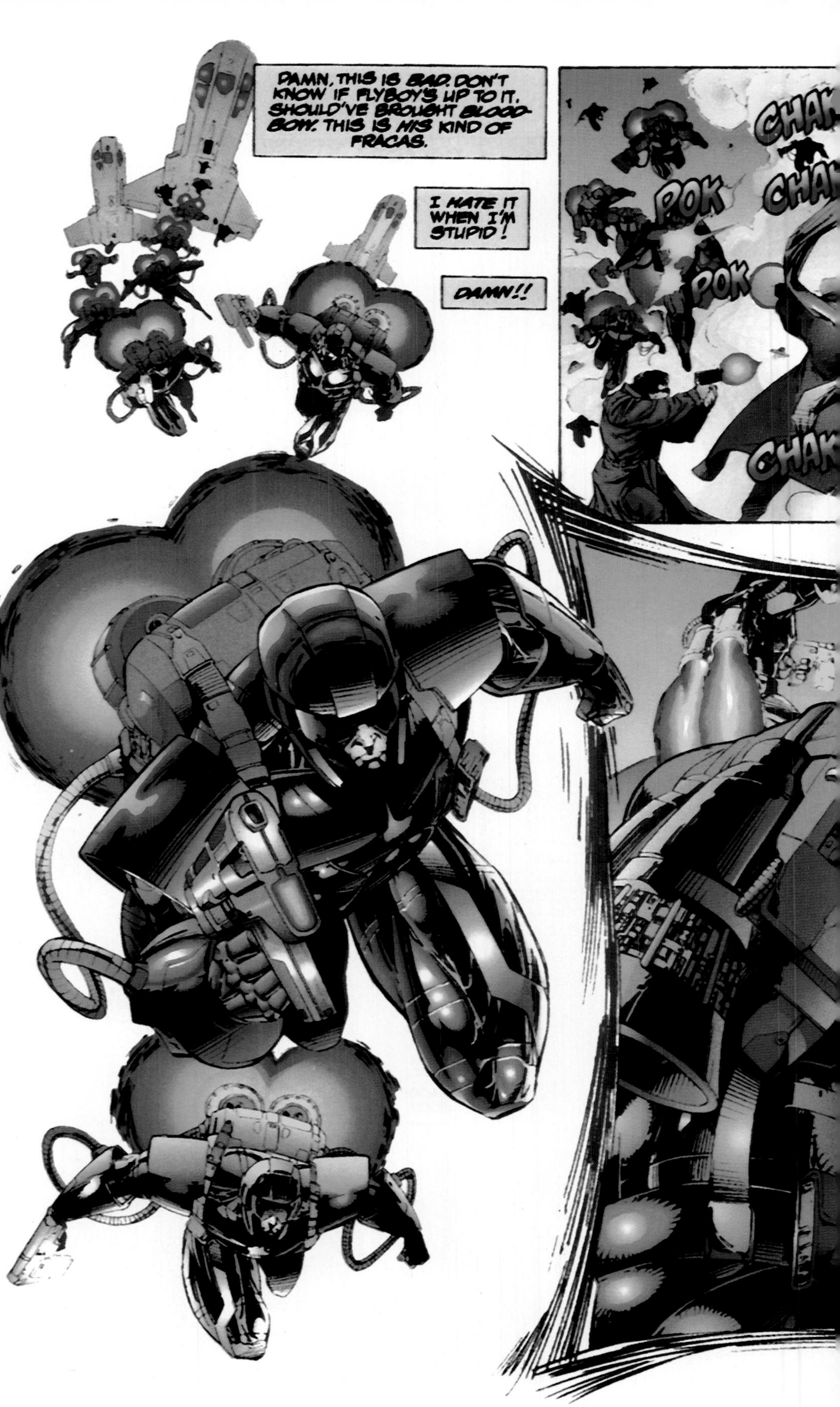
DAMN, THIS IS BAD. DON'T KNOW IF FLYBOY'S UP TO IT. SHOULD'VE BROUGHT BLOODBOW. THIS IS HIS KIND OF FRACAS.
I HATE IT WHEN I'M STUPID!
DAMN!!
POK
POK

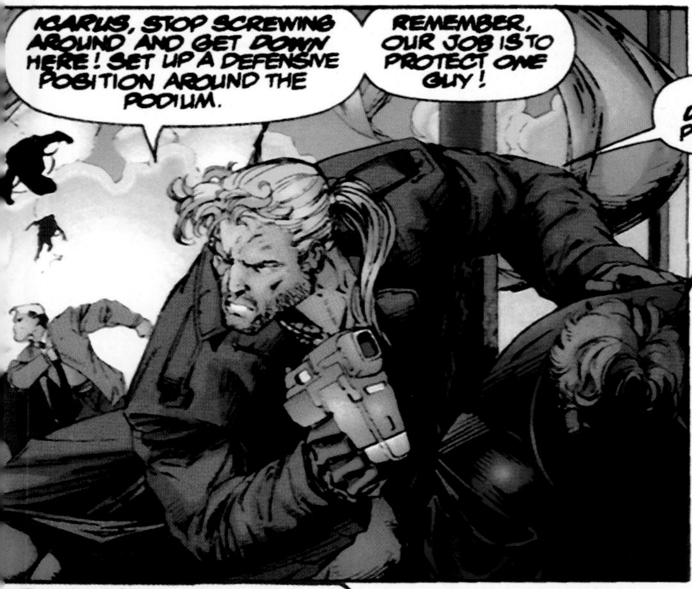
ICARUS, STOP SCREWING AROUND AND GET DOWN HERE! SET UP A DEFENSIVE POSITION AROUND THE PODIUM.
REMEMBER, OUR JOB IS TO PROTECT ONE GUY!
STAY DOWN, MR. PRESIDENT!!
BILL...
I'LL BILL YOU LATER. RIGHT NOW I HAVE TO SAVE YOUR LIFE, SO STAY DOWN!!

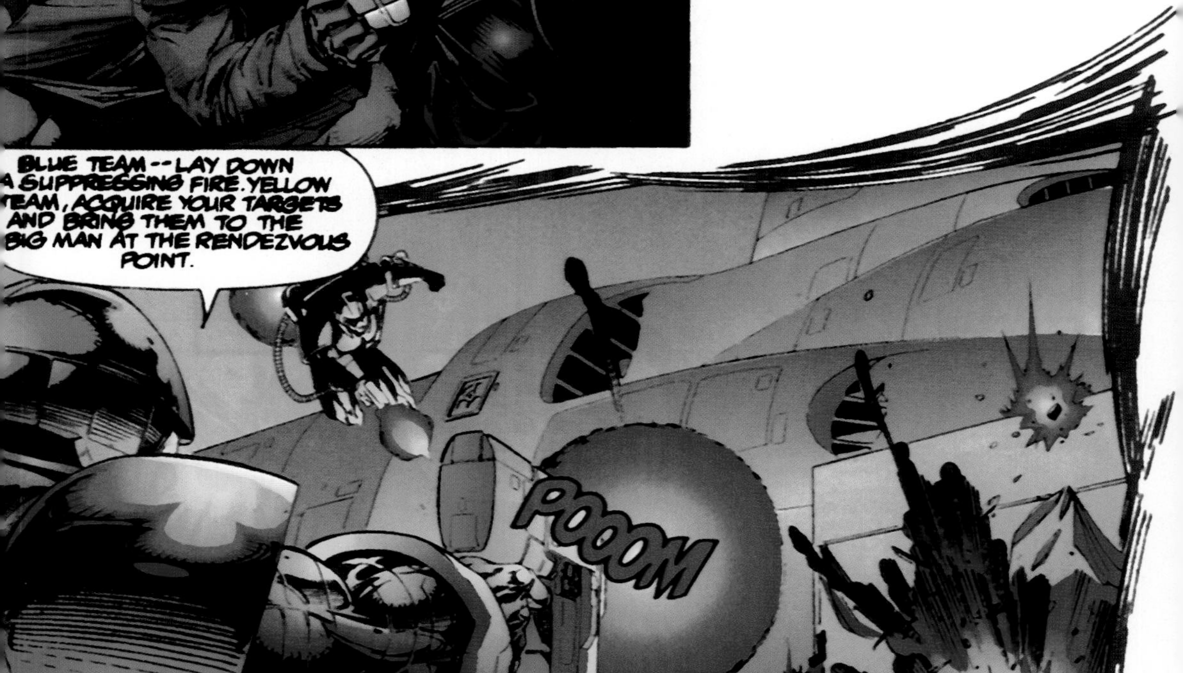
BLUE TEAM--LAY DOWN A SUPPRESSING FIRE. YELLOW TEAM, ACQUIRE YOUR TARGETS AND BRING THEM TO THE BIG MAN AT THE RENDEZVOUS POINT.
POOOM
POOM
POOM
AAAIII!
WHUMPH!

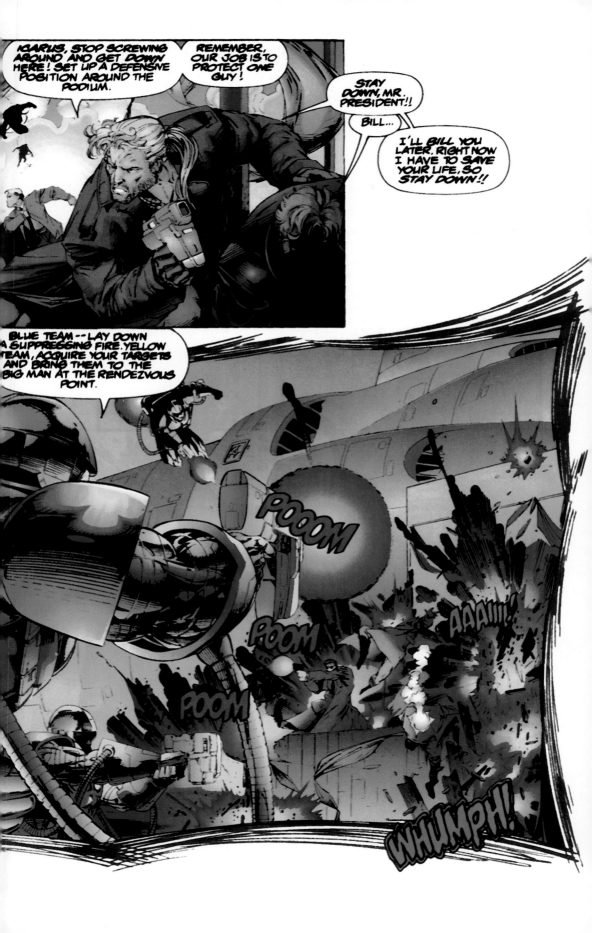

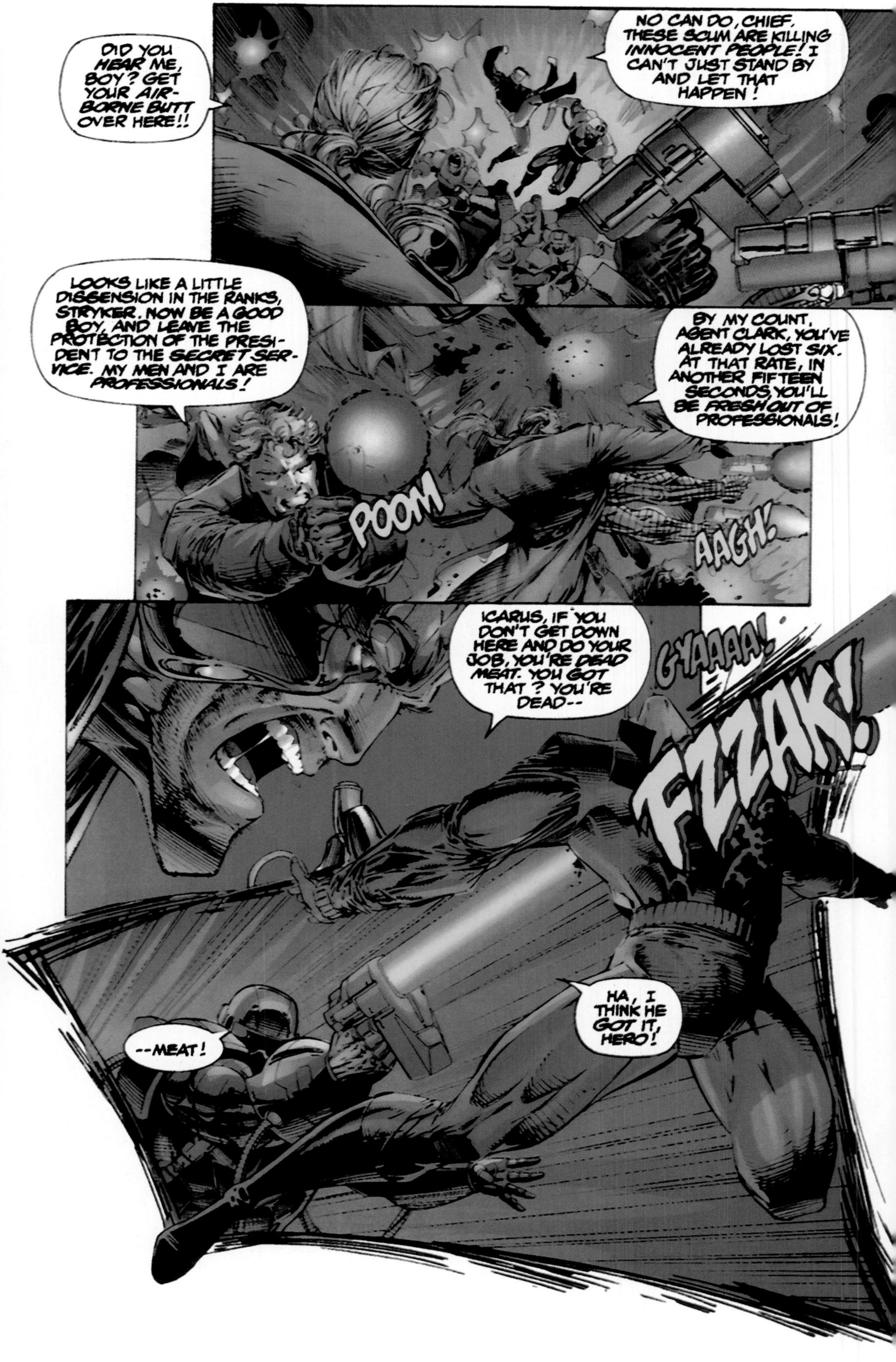
DID YOU HEAR ME, BOY? GET YOUR AIR-BORNE BUTT OVER HERE!!
NO CAN DO, CHIEF. THESE SCUM ARE KILLING INNOCENT PEOPLE! I CAN'T JUST STAND BY AND LET THAT HAPPEN!
LOOKS LIKE A LITTLE DISSENSION IN THE RANKS, STRYKER. NOW BE A GOOD BOY, AND LEAVE THE PROTECTION OF THE PRESIDENT TO THE SECRET SERVICE. MY MEN AND I ARE PROFESSIONALS!
BY MY COUNT, AGENT CLARK, YOU'VE ALREADY LOST SIX. AT THAT RATE, IN ANOTHER FIFTEEN SECONDS, YOU'LL BE FRESH OUT OF PROFESSIONALS!
POOM
AAGH!
ICARUS, IF YOU DON'T GET DOWN HERE AND DO YOUR JOB, YOU'RE DEAD MEAT. YOU GOT THAT? YOU'RE DEAD--
GYAAAA!
FZZAK!
--MEAT!
HA, I THINK HE GOT IT, HERO!

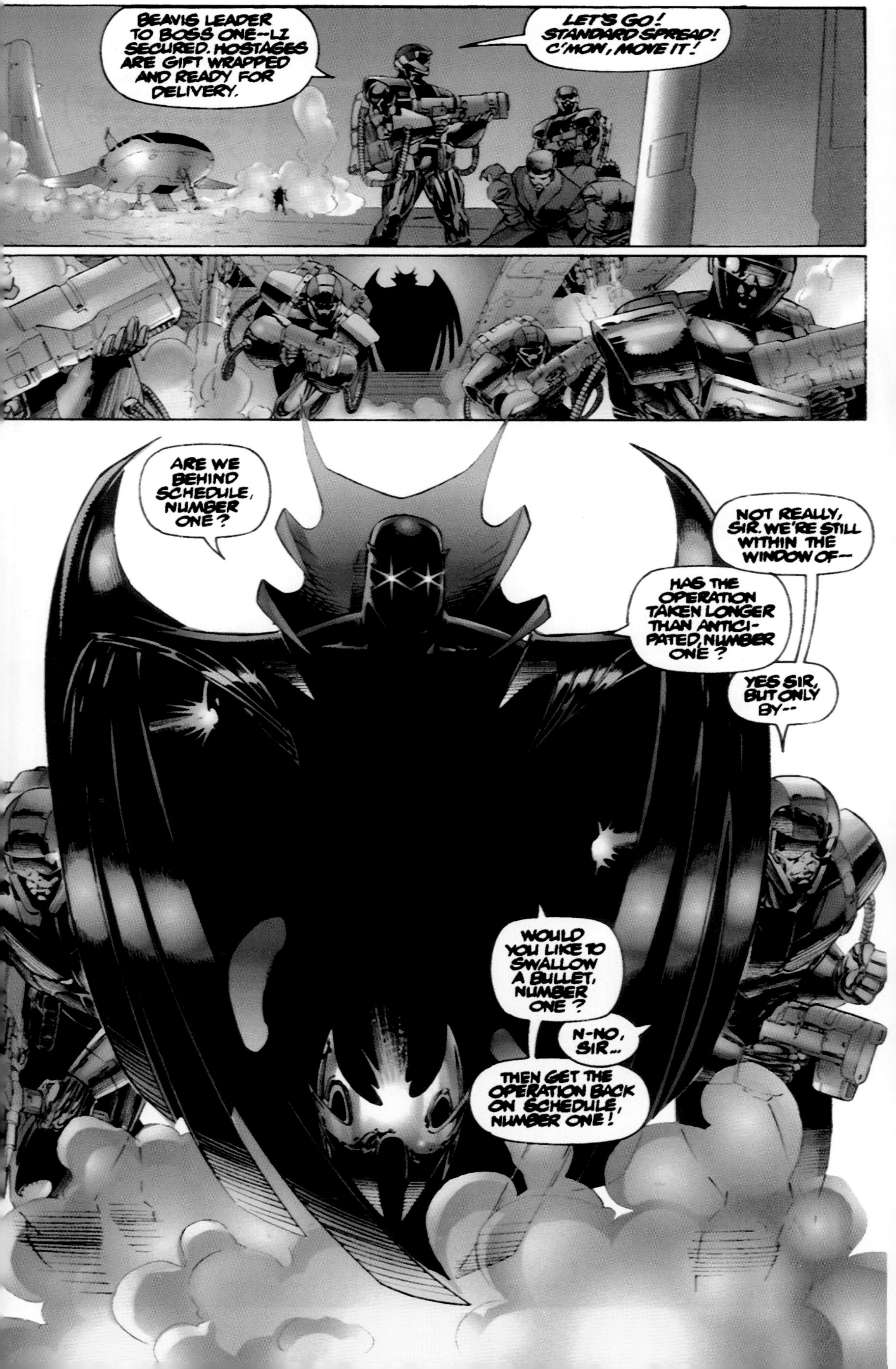
BEAVIS LEADER TO BOSS ONE--LZ SECURED. HOSTAGES ARE GIFT WRAPPED AND READY FOR DELIVERY.
LET'S GO! STANDARD SPREAD! C'MON, MOVE IT!
ARE WE BEHIND SCHEDULE, NUMBER ONE?
NOT REALLY, SIR. WE'RE STILL WITHIN THE WINDOW OF--
HAS THE OPERATION TAKEN LONGER THAN ANTICIPATED, NUMBER ONE?
YES SIR, BUT ONLY BY--
WOULD YOU LIKE TO SWALLOW A BULLET, NUMBER ONE?
N-NO, SIR...
THEN GET THE OPERATION BACK ON SCHEDULE, NUMBER ONE!

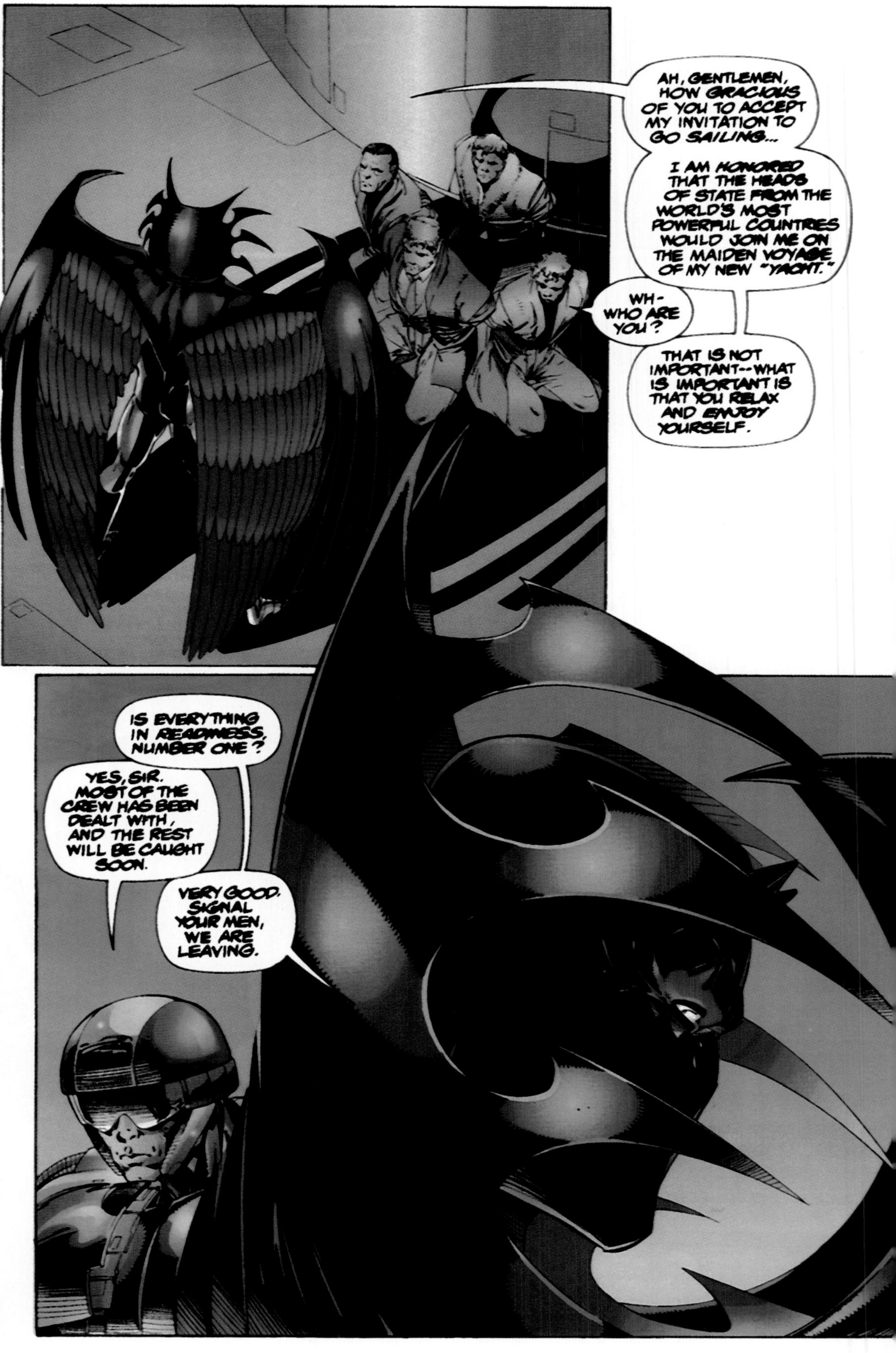
AH, GENTLEMEN, HOW GRACIOUS OF YOU TO ACCEPT MY INVITATION TO GO SAILING...
I AM HONORED THAT THE HEADS OF STATE FROM THE WORLD'S MOST POWERFUL COUNTRIES WOULD JOIN ME ON THE MAIDEN VOYAGE OF MY NEW "YACHT."
WH- WHO ARE YOU?
THAT IS NOT IMPORTANT--WHAT IS IMPORTANT IS THAT YOU RELAX AND ENJOY YOURSELF.
IS EVERYTHING IN READINESS, NUMBER ONE?
YES, SIR. MOST OF THE CREW HAS BEEN DEALT WITH, AND THE REST WILL BE CAUGHT SOON.
VERY GOOD. SIGNAL YOUR MEN, WE ARE LEAVING.

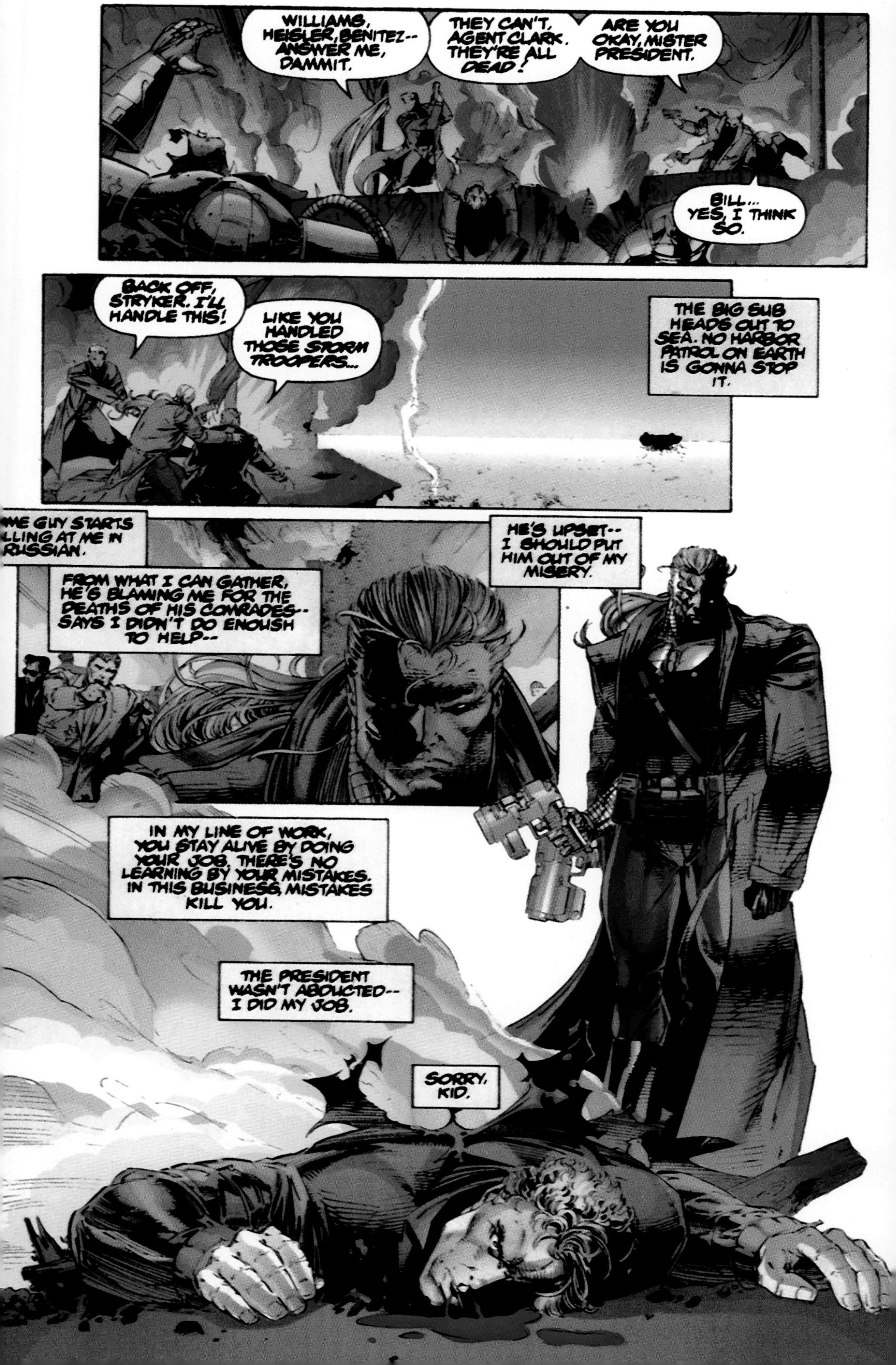
WILLIAMS, HEISLER, BENITEZ-- ANSWER ME, DAMMIT.
THEY CAN'T, AGENT CLARK. THEY'RE ALL DEAD!
ARE YOU OKAY, MISTER PRESIDENT.
BILL... YES, I THINK SO.
BACK OFF, STRYKER. I'LL HANDLE THIS!
LIKE YOU HANDLED THOSE STORM TROOPERS...
THE BIG SUB HEADS OUT TO SEA. NO HARBOR PATROL ON EARTH IS GONNA STOP IT.
ME GUY STARTS LLING AT ME IN RUSSIAN.
FROM WHAT I CAN GATHER, HE'S BLAMING ME FOR THE DEATHS OF HIS COMRADES-- SAYS I DIDN'T DO ENOUGH TO HELP--
HE'S UPSET-- I SHOULD PUT HIM OUT OF MY MISERY.
IN MY LINE OF WORK, YOU STAY ALIVE BY DOING YOUR JOB. THERE'S NO LEARNING BY YOUR MISTAKES. IN THIS BUSINESS, MISTAKES KILL YOU.
THE PRESIDENT WASN'T ABDUCTED-- I DID MY JOB.
SORRY, KID.

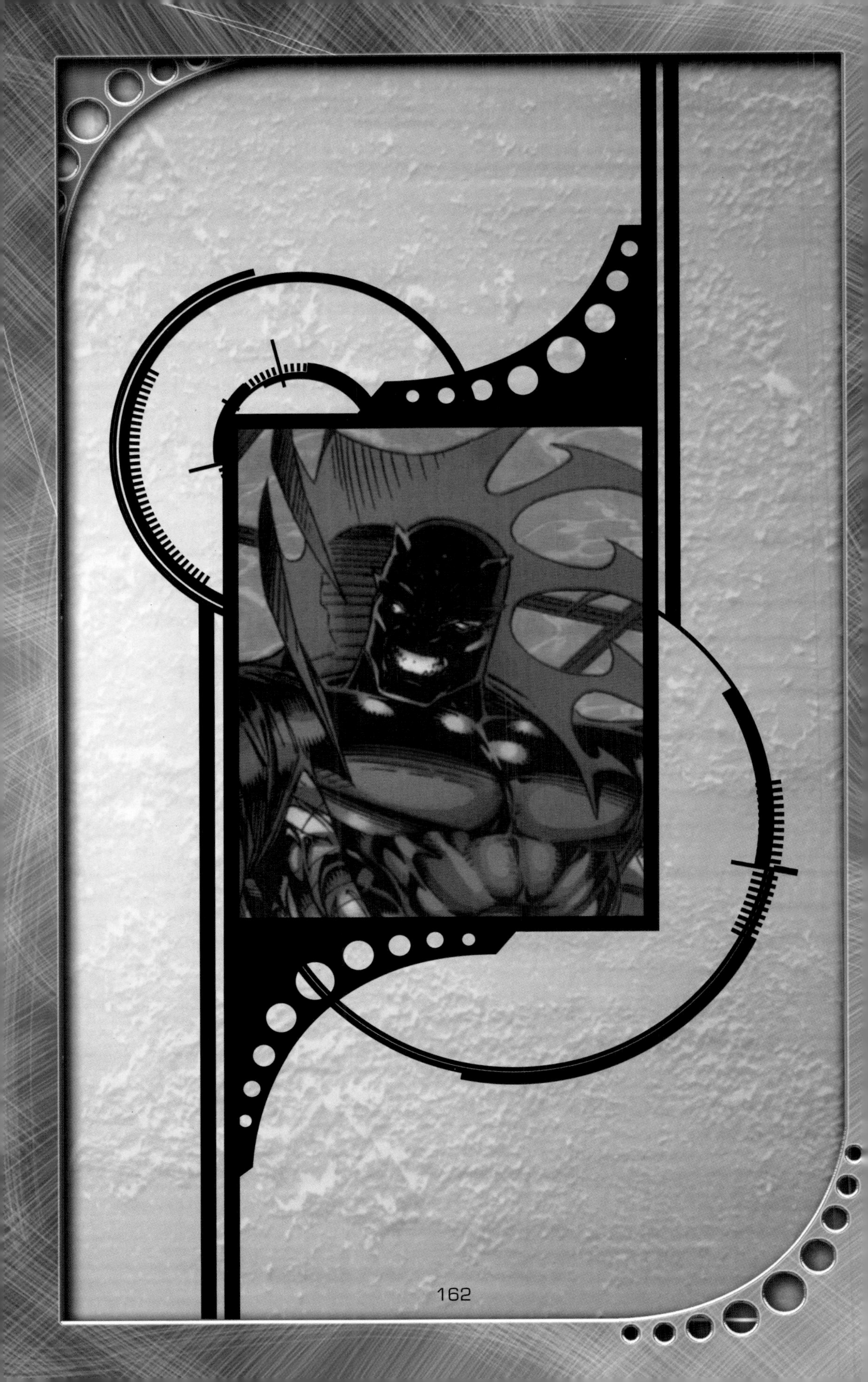

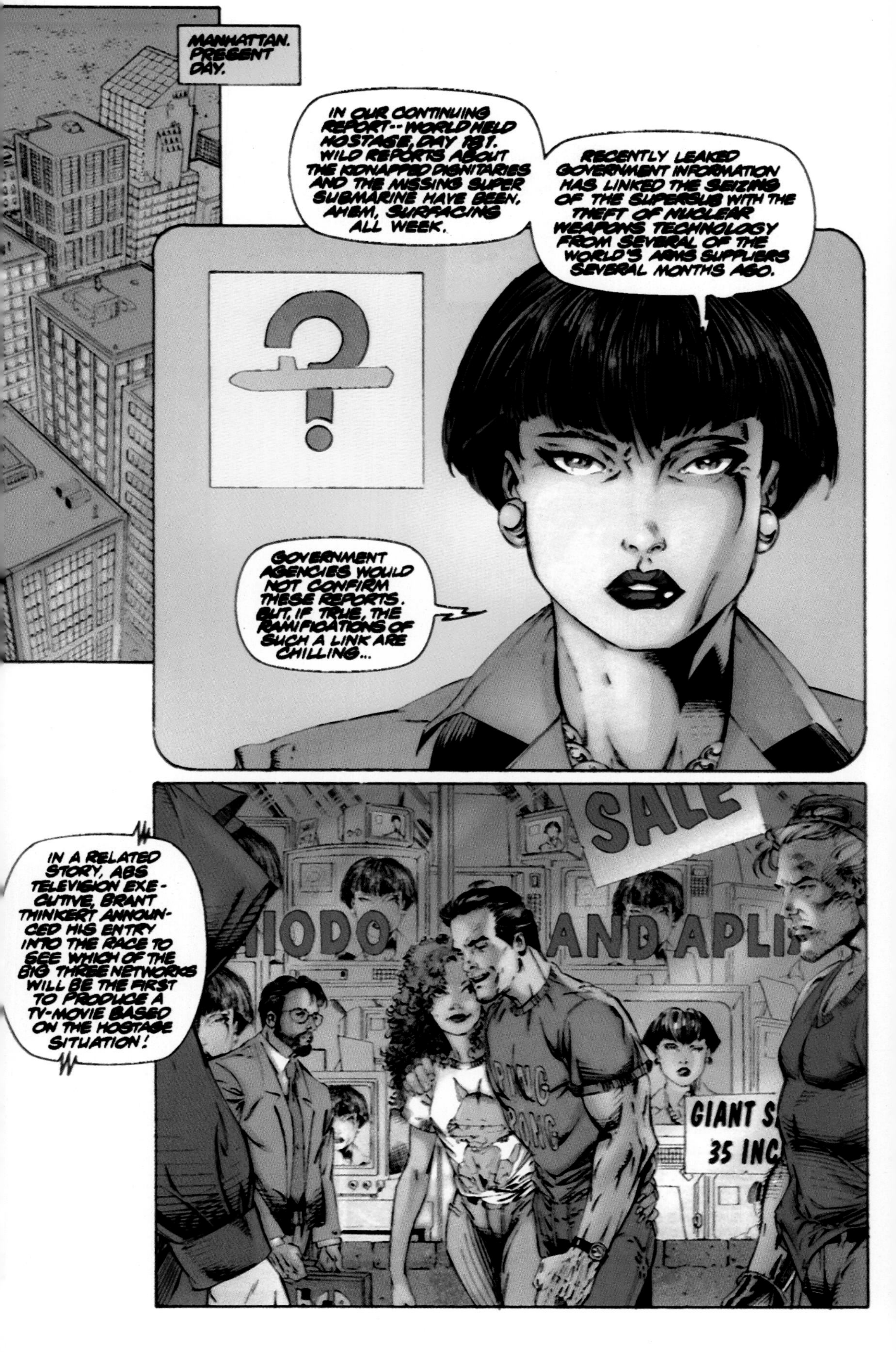
MANHATTAN. PRESENT DAY.
IN OUR CONTINUING REPORT-- WORLD HELD HOSTAGE, DAY 181. WILD REPORTS ABOUT THE KIDNAPPED DIGNITARIES AND THE MISSING SUPER SUBMARINE HAVE BEEN, AHEM, SURFACING ALL WEEK.
RECENTLY LEAKED GOVERNMENT INFORMATION HAS LINKED THE SEIZING OF THE SUPERSUB WITH THE THEFT OF NUCLEAR WEAPONS TECHNOLOGY FROM SEVERAL OF THE WORLD'S ARMS SUPPLIERS SEVERAL MONTHS AGO.
GOVERNMENT AGENCIES WOULD NOT CONFIRM THESE REPORTS. BUT, IF TRUE, THE RAMIFICATIONS OF SUCH A LINK ARE CHILLING...
SALE
IN A RELATED STORY, ABS TELEVISION EXE-CUTIVE, BRANT THINKERT ANNOUN-CED HIS ENTRY INTO THE RACE TO SEE WHICH OF THE BIG THREE NETWORKS WILL BE THE FIRST TO PRODUCE A TV-MOVIE BASED ON THE HOSTAGE SITUATION!
AND APLI
GIANT S
35 INC

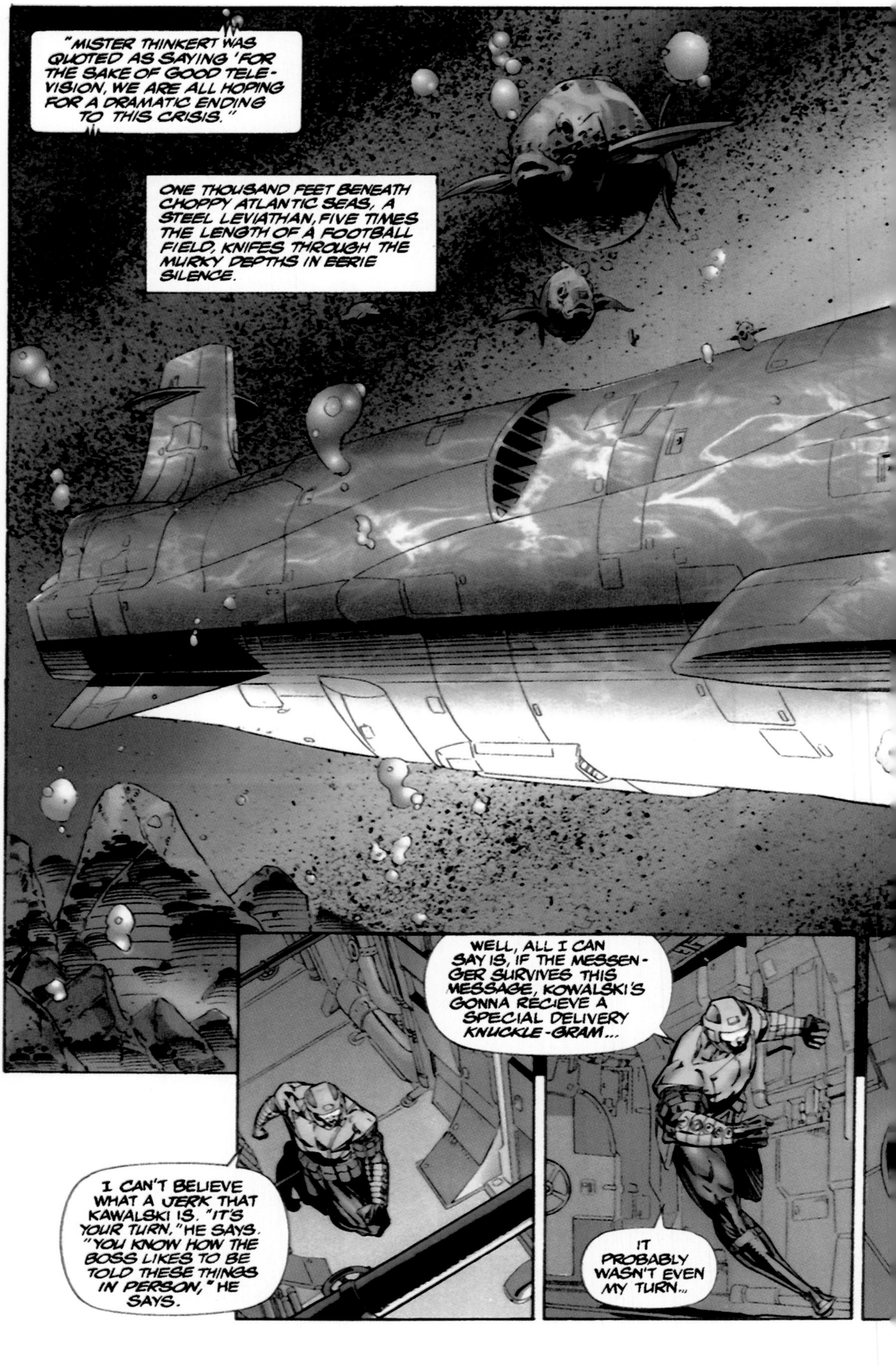
"MISTER THINKERT WAS QUOTED AS SAYING 'FOR THE SAKE OF GOOD TELE-VISION, WE ARE ALL HOPING FOR A DRAMATIC ENDING TO THIS CRISIS.'"
ONE THOUSAND FEET BENEATH CHOPPY ATLANTIC SEAS, A STEEL LEVIATHAN, FIVE TIMES THE LENGTH OF A FOOTBALL FIELD, KNIFES THROUGH THE MURKY DEPTHS IN EERIE SILENCE.
WELL, ALL I CAN SAY IS, IF THE MESSEN-GER SURVIVES THIS MESSAGE, KOWALSKI'S GONNA RECIEVE A SPECIAL DELIVERY KNUCKLE-GRAM...
I CAN'T BELIEVE WHAT A JERK THAT KAWALSKI IS. "IT'S YOUR TURN," HE SAYS. "YOU KNOW HOW THE BOSS LIKES TO BE TOLD THESE THINGS IN PERSON," HE SAYS.
IT PROBABLY WASN'T EVEN MY TURN...

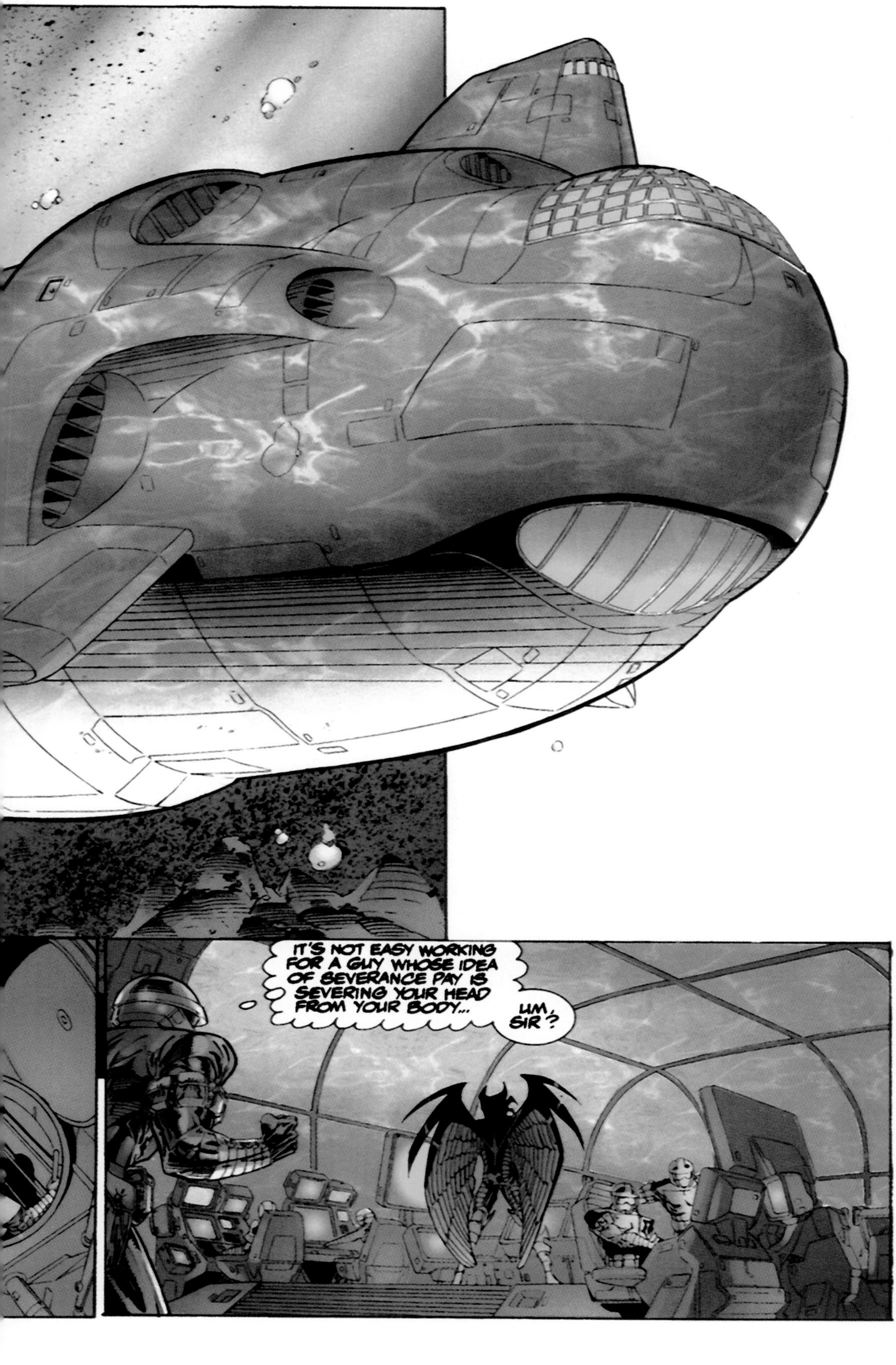
IT'S NOT EASY WORKING FOR A GUY WHOSE IDEA OF SEVERANCE PAY IS SEVERING YOUR HEAD FROM YOUR BODY...
UM, SIR?

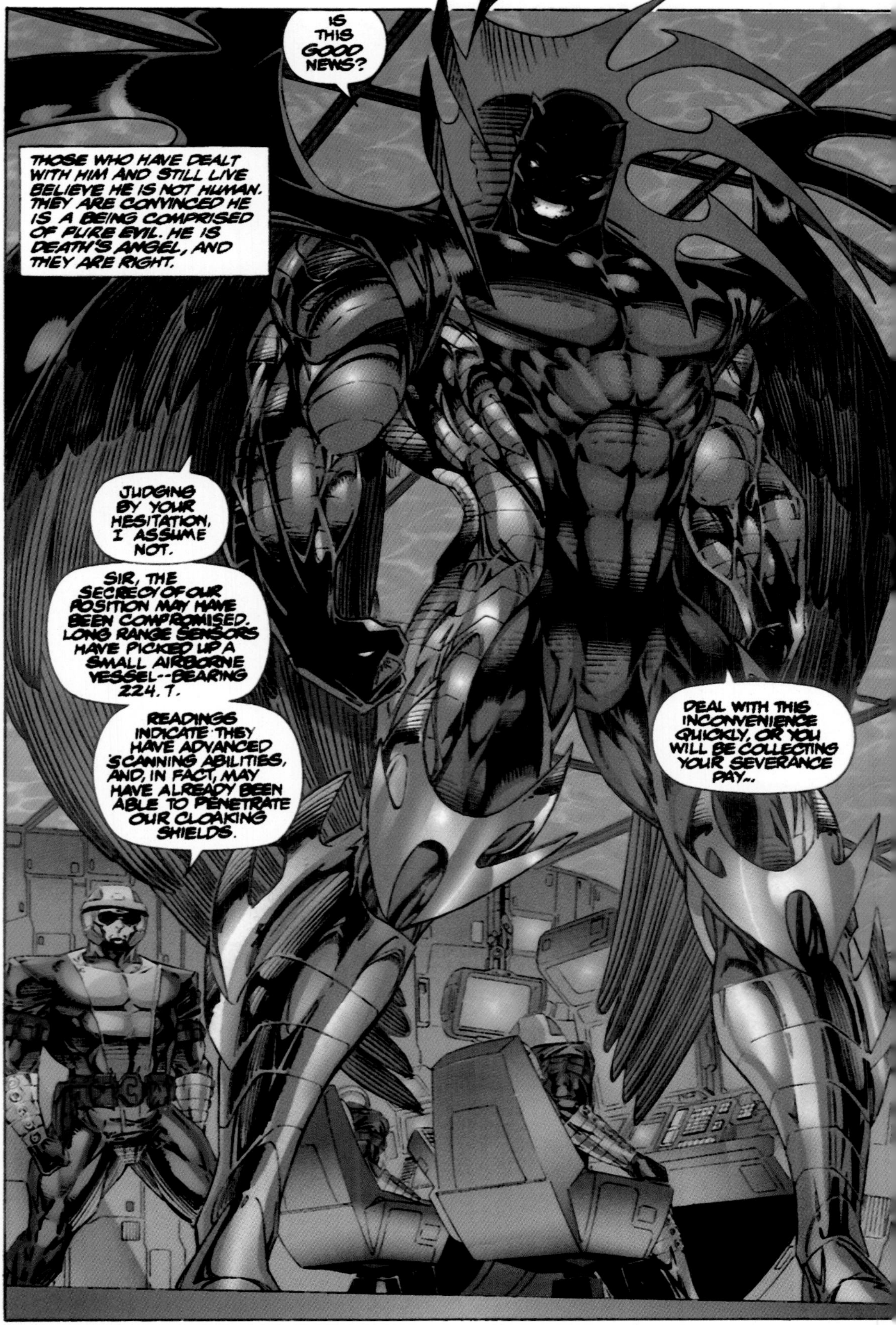
IS THIS GOOD NEWS?
THOSE WHO HAVE DEALT WITH HIM AND STILL LIVE BELIEVE HE IS NOT HUMAN. THEY ARE CONVINCED HE IS A BEING COMPRISED OF PURE EVIL. HE IS DEATH'S ANGEL, AND THEY ARE RIGHT.
JUDGING BY YOUR HESITATION, I ASSUME NOT.
SIR, THE SECRECY OF OUR POSITION MAY HAVE BEEN COMPROMISED. LONG RANGE SENSORS HAVE PICKED UP A SMALL AIRBORNE VESSEL--BEARING 224.7.
READINGS INDICATE THEY HAVE ADVANCED SCANNING ABILITIES, AND, IN FACT, MAY HAVE ALREADY BEEN ABLE TO PENETRATE OUR CLOAKING SHIELDS.
DEAL WITH THIS INCONVENIENCE QUICKLY, OR YOU WILL BE COLLECTING YOUR SEVERANCE PAY...

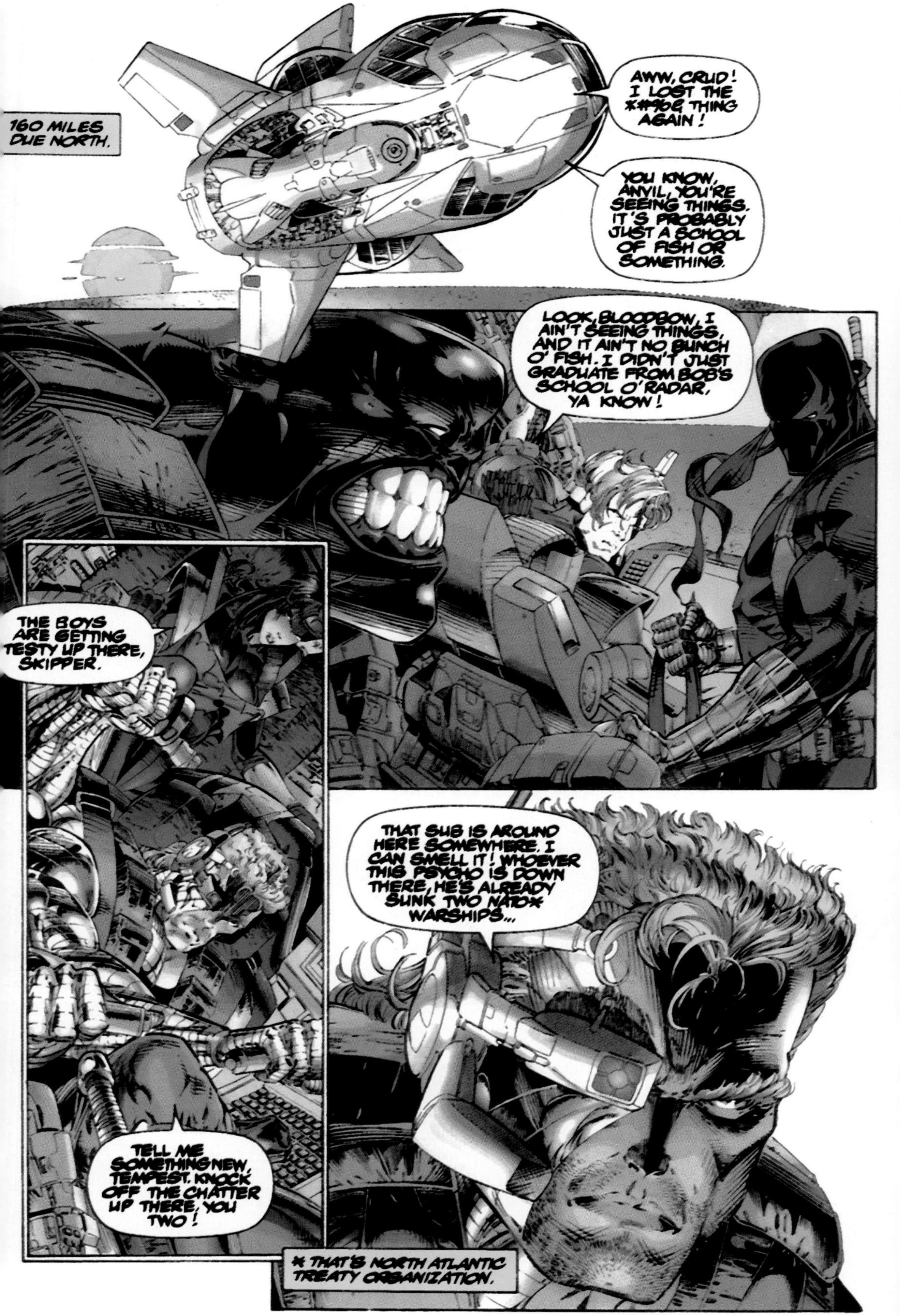
160 MILES DUE NORTH.
AWW, CRUD! I LOST THE *#%@ THING AGAIN!
YOU KNOW, ANVIL, YOU'RE SEEING THINGS. IT'S PROBABLY JUST A SCHOOL OF FISH OR SOMETHING.
LOOK, BLOODBOW, I AIN'T SEEING THINGS, AND IT AIN'T NO BUNCH O' FISH. I DIDN'T JUST GRADUATE FROM BOB'S SCHOOL O' RADAR, YA KNOW!
THE BOYS ARE GETTING TESTY UP THERE, SKIPPER.
THAT SUB IS AROUND HERE SOMEWHERE. I CAN SMELL IT! WHOEVER THIS PSYCHO IS DOWN THERE, HE'S ALREADY SUNK TWO NATO* WARSHIPS...
TELL ME SOMETHING NEW, TEMPEST. KNOCK OFF THE CHATTER UP THERE, YOU TWO!
* THAT'S NORTH ATLANTIC TREATY ORGANIZATION.

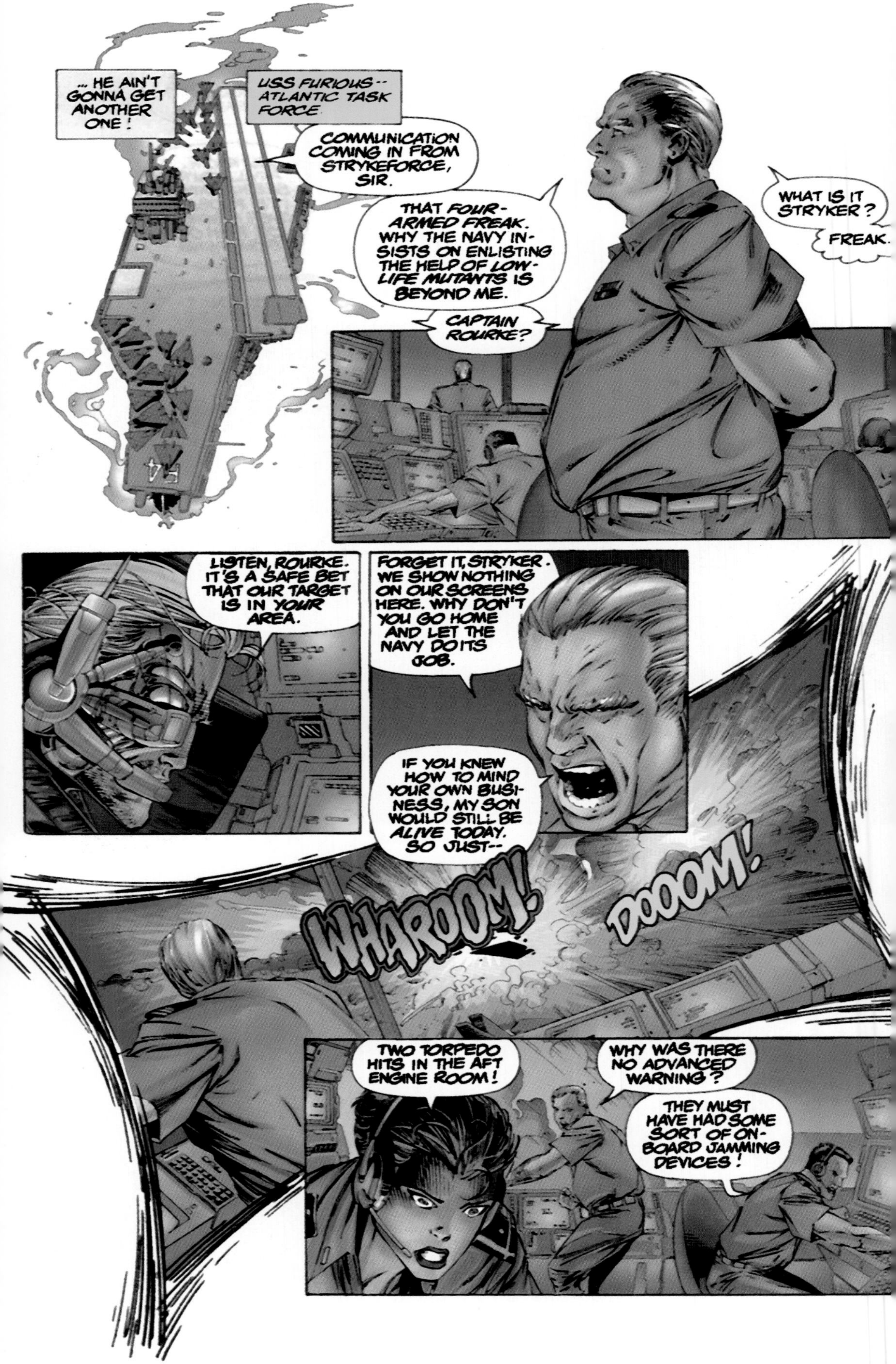
... HE AIN'T GONNA GET ANOTHER ONE!
USS FURIOUS -- ATLANTIC TASK FORCE
COMMUNICATION COMING IN FROM STRYKEFORCE, SIR.
THAT FOUR-ARMED FREAK. WHY THE NAVY INSISTS ON ENLISTING THE HELP OF LOW-LIFE MUTANTS IS BEYOND ME.
CAPTAIN ROURKE?
WHAT IS IT STRYKER?
FREAK.
LISTEN, ROURKE. IT'S A SAFE BET THAT OUR TARGET IS IN YOUR AREA.
FORGET IT, STRYKER. WE SHOW NOTHING ON OUR SCREENS HERE. WHY DON'T YOU GO HOME AND LET THE NAVY DO ITS JOB.
IF YOU KNEW HOW TO MIND YOUR OWN BUSINESS, MY SON WOULD STILL BE ALIVE TODAY. SO JUST--
WHAROOM!
DOOOM!
TWO TORPEDO HITS IN THE AFT ENGINE ROOM!
WHY WAS THERE NO ADVANCED WARNING?
THEY MUST HAVE HAD SOME SORT OF ON-BOARD JAMMING DEVICES!

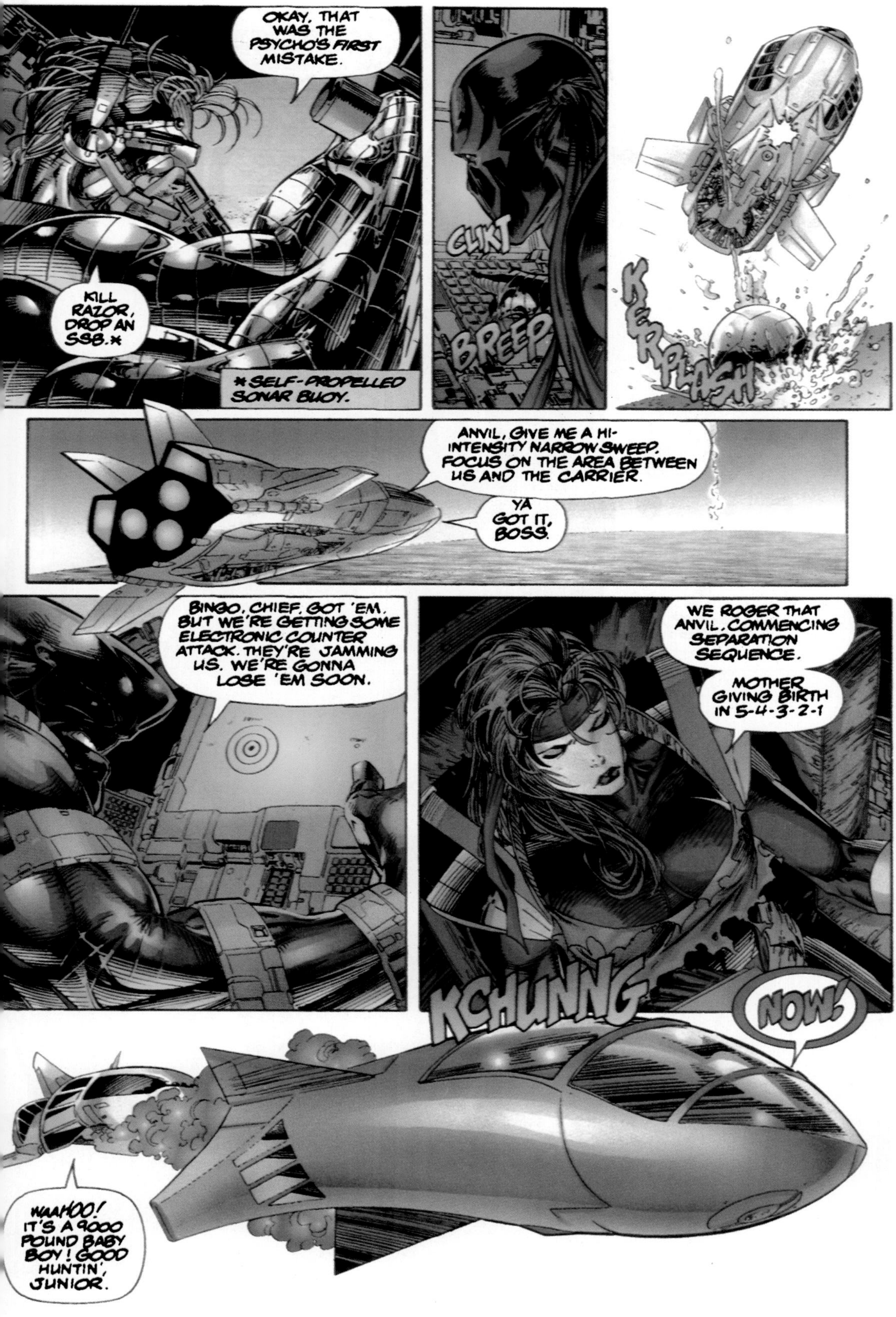
OKAY, THAT WAS THE PSYCHO'S FIRST MISTAKE.
KILL RAZOR, DROP AN SSB.*
*SELF-PROPELLED SONAR BUOY.
CLIKT
BREEP
KERPLASH
ANVIL, GIVE ME A HI-INTENSITY NARROW SWEEP. FOCUS ON THE AREA BETWEEN US AND THE CARRIER.
YA GOT IT, BOSS.
BINGO, CHIEF, GOT 'EM. BUT WE'RE GETTING SOME ELECTRONIC COUNTER ATTACK. THEY'RE JAMMING US. WE'RE GONNA LOSE 'EM SOON.
WE ROGER THAT ANVIL. COMMENCING SEPARATION SEQUENCE.
MOTHER GIVING BIRTH IN 5-4-3-2-1
KCHUNNG
NOW!
WAAHOO! IT'S A 9000 POUND BABY BOY! GOOD HUNTIN', JUNIOR.

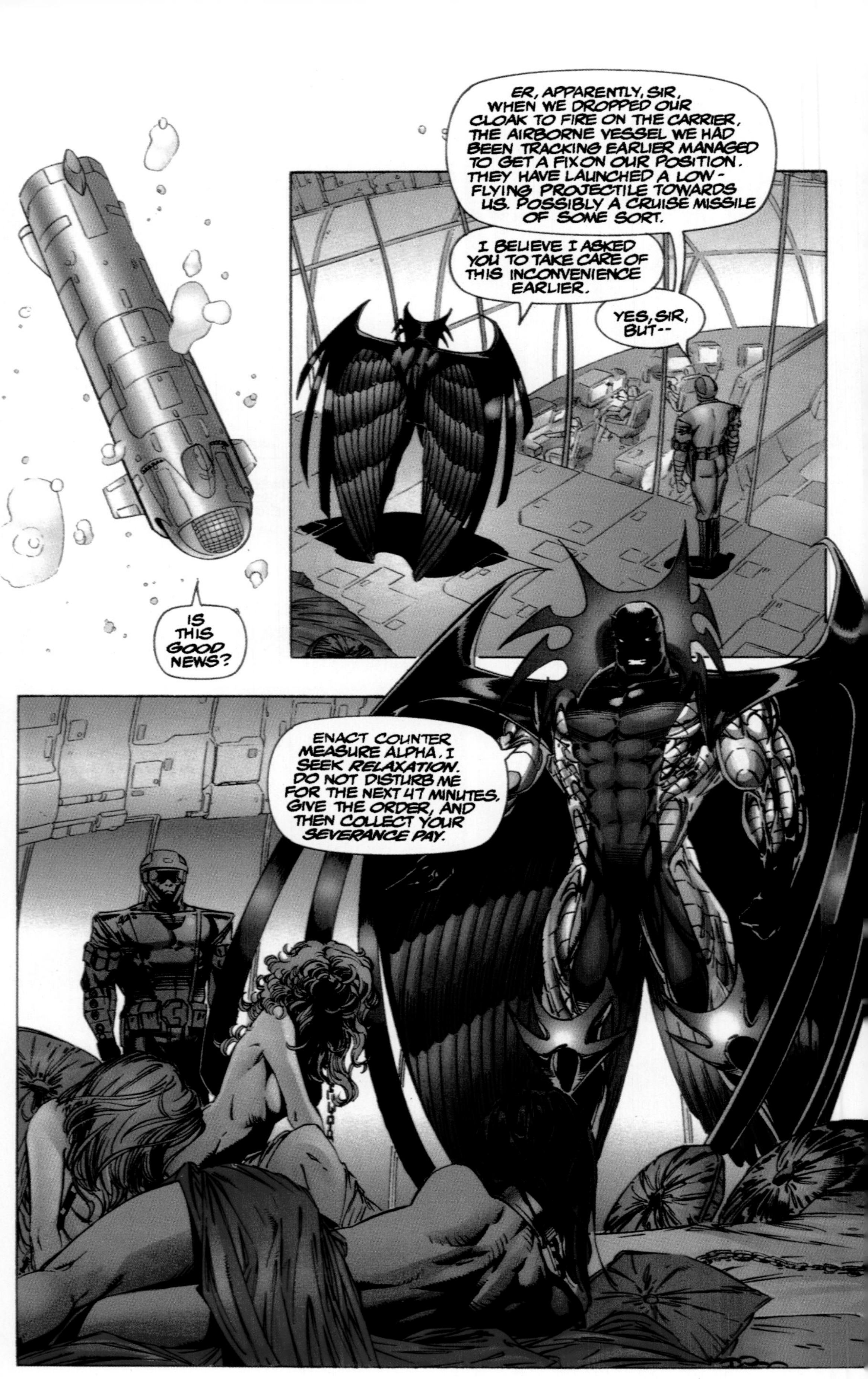
ER, APPARENTLY, SIR, WHEN WE DROPPED OUR CLOAK TO FIRE ON THE CARRIER, THE AIRBORNE VESSEL WE HAD BEEN TRACKING EARLIER MANAGED TO GET A FIX ON OUR POSITION. THEY HAVE LAUNCHED A LOW-FLYING PROJECTILE TOWARDS US. POSSIBLY A CRUISE MISSILE OF SOME SORT.
I BELIEVE I ASKED YOU TO TAKE CARE OF THIS INCONVENIENCE EARLIER.
YES, SIR, BUT--
IS THIS GOOD NEWS?
ENACT COUNTER MEASURE ALPHA. I SEEK RELAXATION. DO NOT DISTURB ME FOR THE NEXT 47 MINUTES. GIVE THE ORDER, AND THEN COLLECT YOUR SEVERANCE PAY.

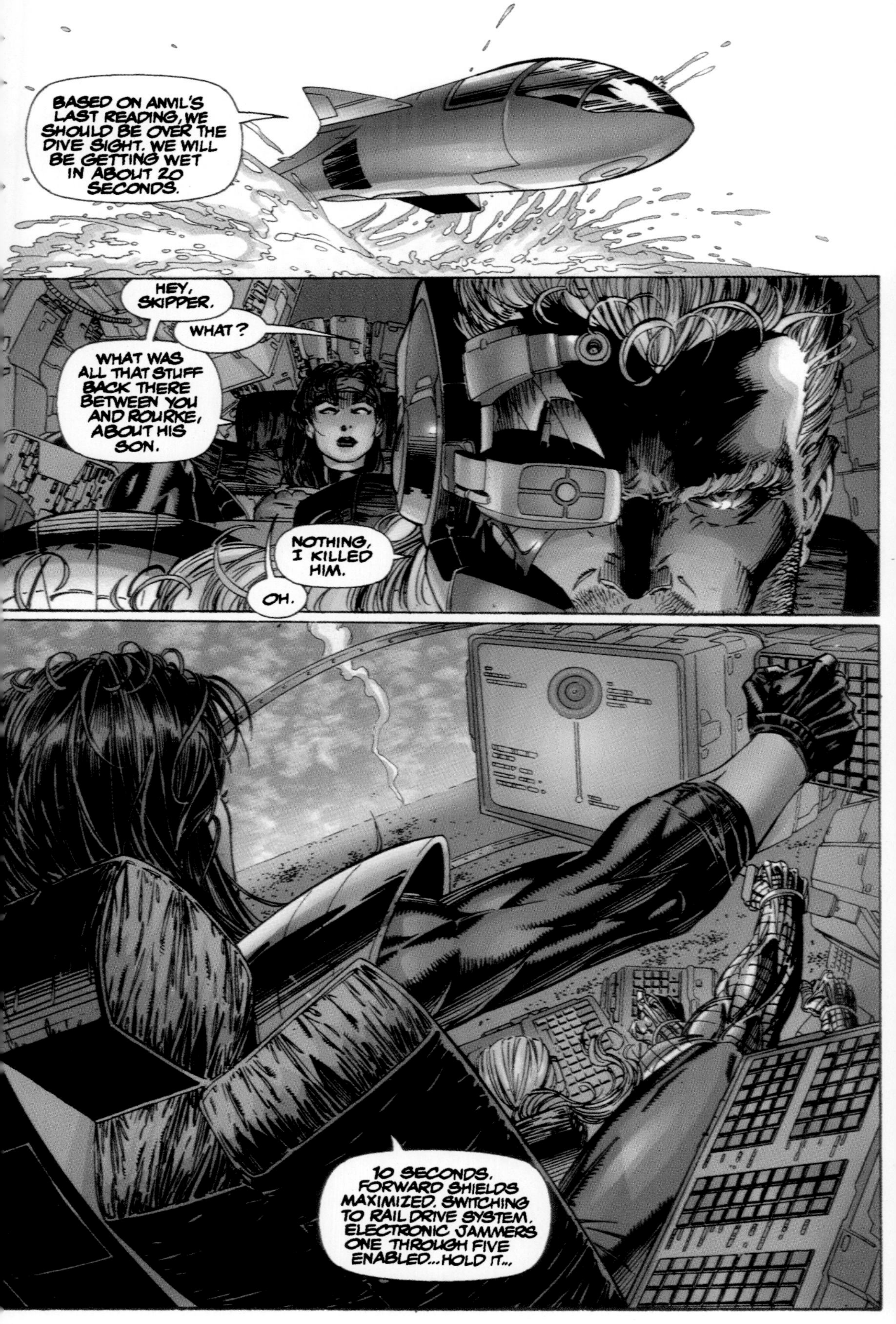
BASED ON ANVIL'S LAST READING, WE SHOULD BE OVER THE DIVE SIGHT. WE WILL BE GETTING WET IN ABOUT 20 SECONDS.
HEY, SKIPPER.
WHAT?
WHAT WAS ALL THAT STUFF BACK THERE BETWEEN YOU AND ROURKE, ABOUT HIS SON.
NOTHING, I KILLED HIM.
OH.
10 SECONDS. FORWARD SHIELDS MAXIMIZED. SWITCHING TO RAIL DRIVE SYSTEM. ELECTRONIC JAMMERS ONE THROUGH FIVE ENABLED... HOLD IT...

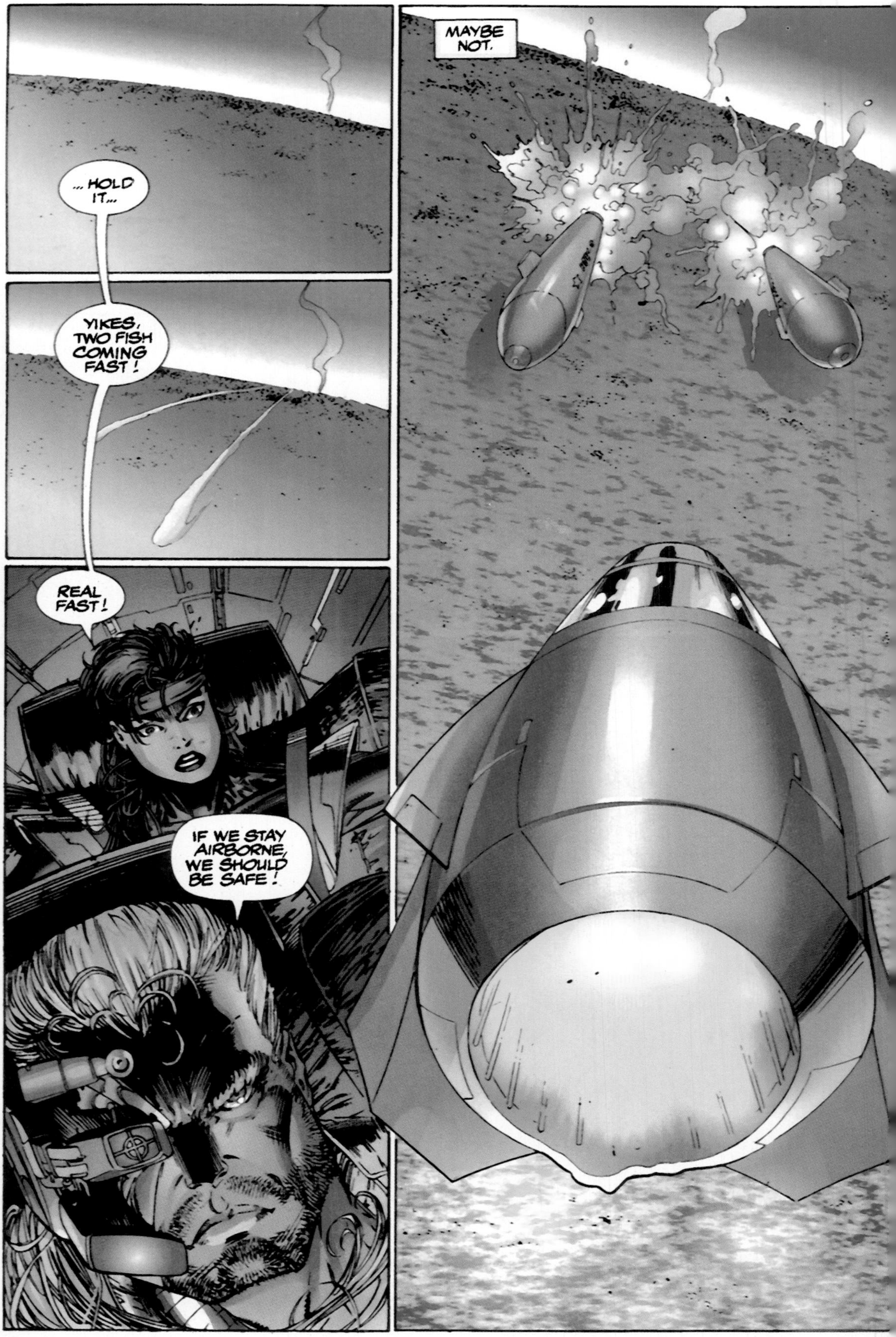
...HOLD IT...
YIKES, TWO FISH COMING FAST!
REAL FAST!
IF WE STAY AIRBORNE, WE SHOULD BE SAFE!
MAYBE NOT.

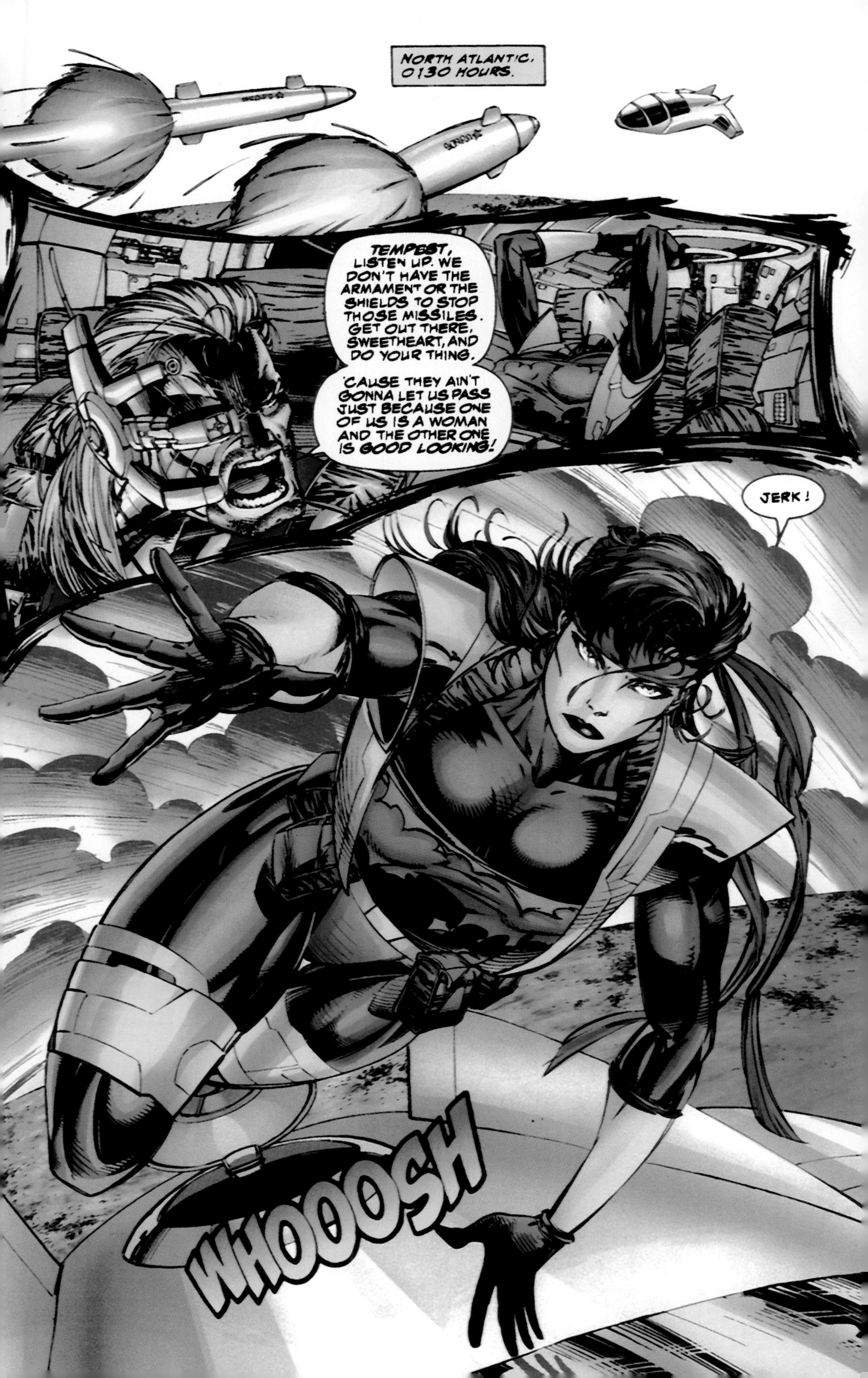
NORTH ATLANTIC, 0130 HOURS.
TEMPEST, LISTEN UP. WE DON'T HAVE THE ARMAMENT OR THE SHIELDS TO STOP THOSE MISSILES. GET OUT THERE, SWEETHEART, AND DO YOUR THING.
'CAUSE THEY AIN'T GONNA LET US PASS JUST BECAUSE ONE OF US IS A WOMAN AND THE OTHER ONE IS GOOD LOOKING!
JERK!
WHOOOSH

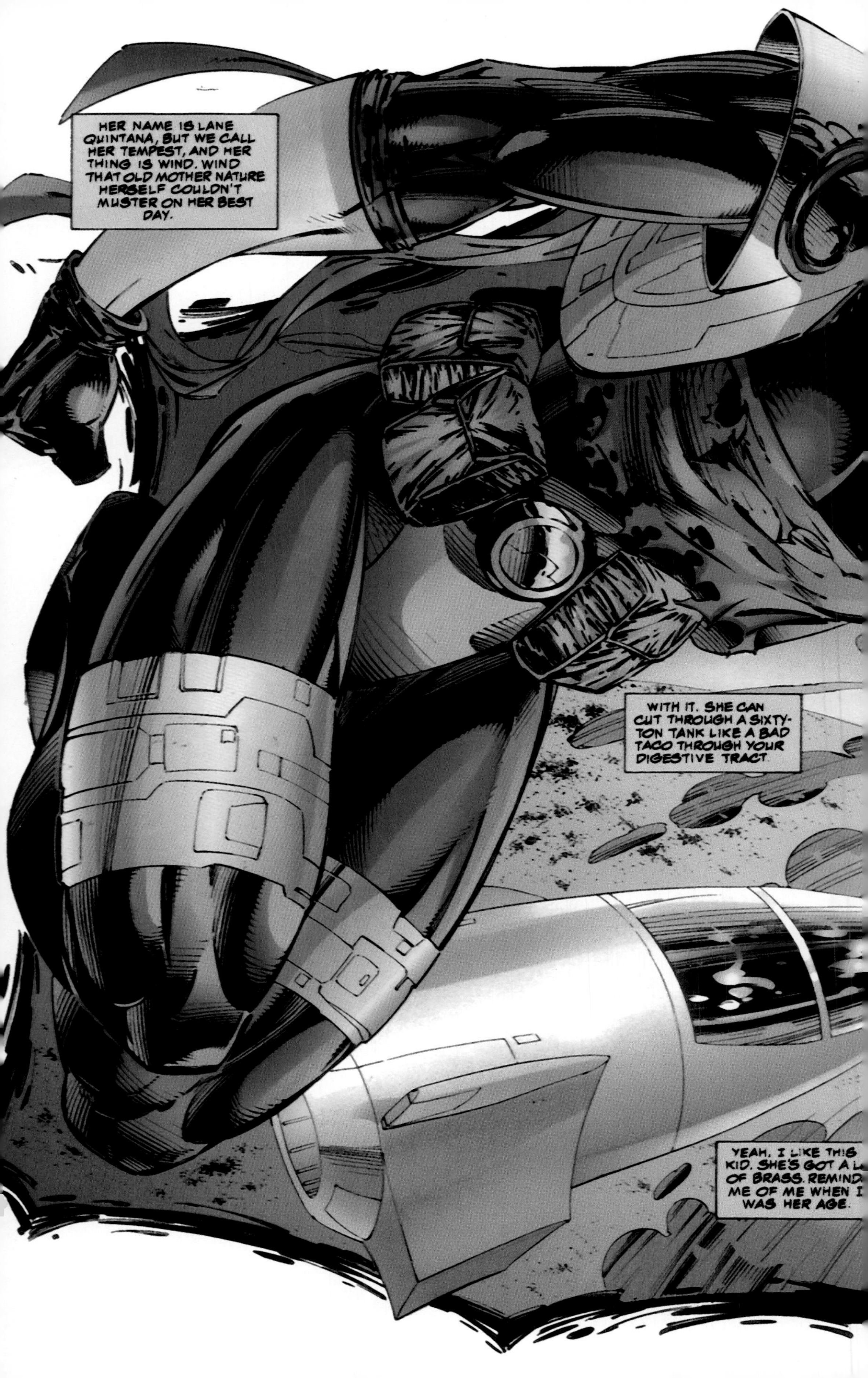
HER NAME IS LANE QUINTANA, BUT WE CALL HER TEMPEST, AND HER THING IS WIND. WIND THAT OLD MOTHER NATURE HERSELF COULDN'T MUSTER ON HER BEST DAY.
WITH IT, SHE CAN CUT THROUGH A SIXTY-TON TANK LIKE A BAD TACO THROUGH YOUR DIGESTIVE TRACT.
YEAH, I LIKE THIS KID. SHE'S GOT A L OF BRASS. REMIND ME OF ME WHEN I WAS HER AGE.

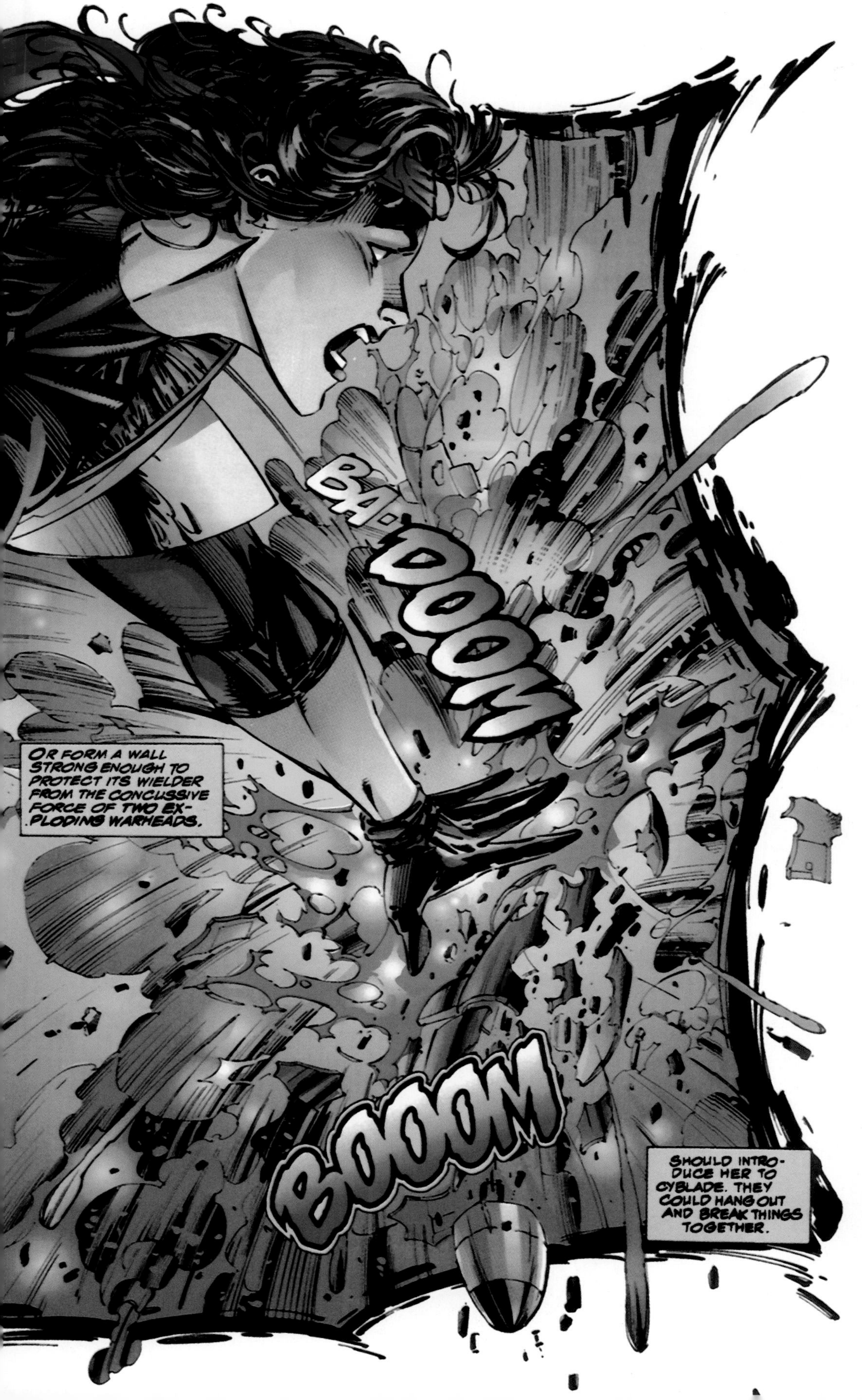
BA-DOOM
OR FORM A WALL STRONG ENOUGH TO PROTECT ITS WIELDER FROM THE CONCUSSIVE FORCE OF TWO EX-PLODING WARHEADS.
BOOOM
SHOULD INTRO-DUCE HER TO CYBLADE. THEY COULD HANG OUT AND BREAK THINGS TOGETHER.

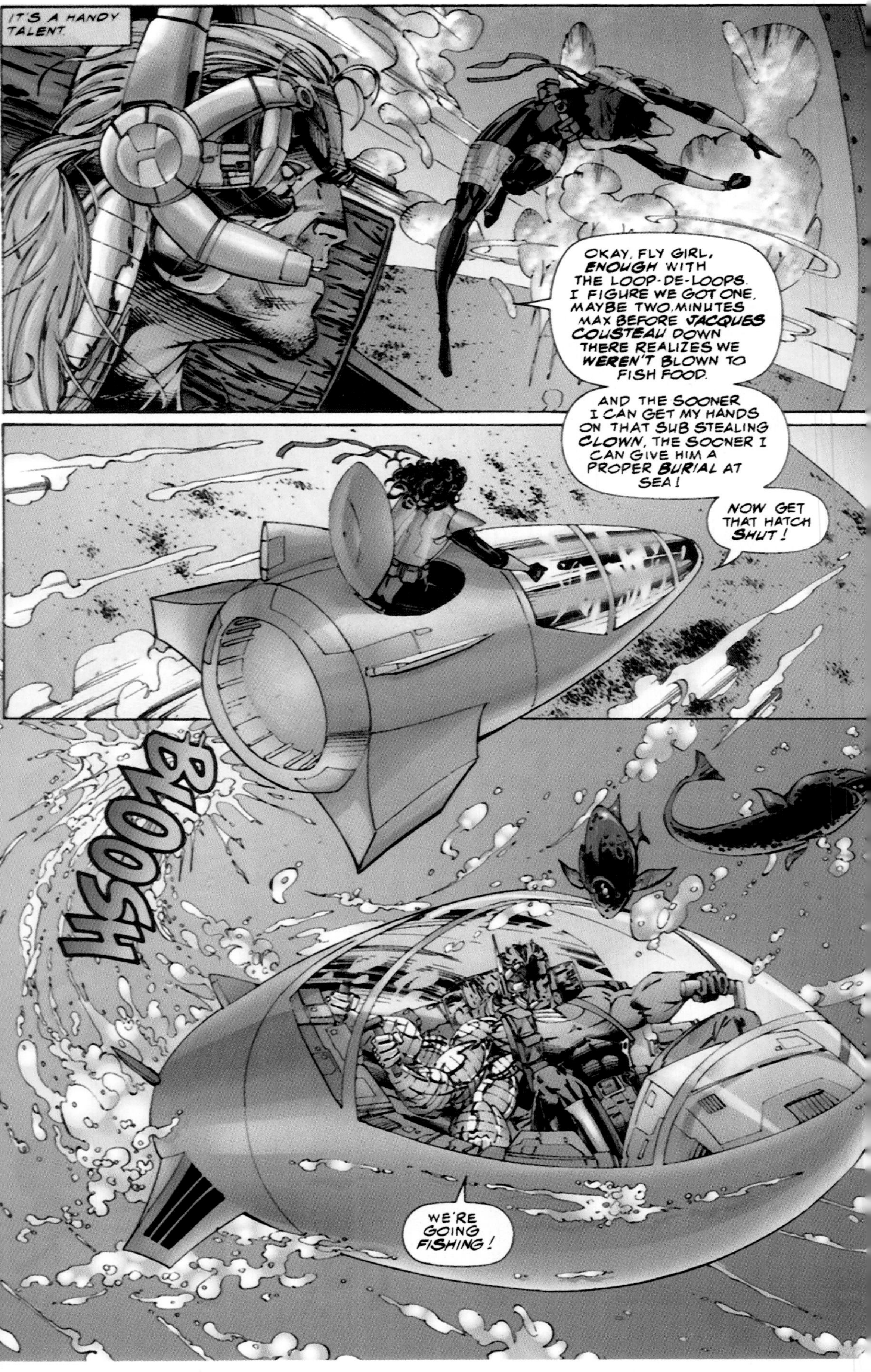
IT'S A HANDY TALENT.
OKAY, FLY GIRL, ENOUGH WITH THE LOOP-DE-LOOPS. I FIGURE WE GOT ONE, MAYBE TWO, MINUTES MAX BEFORE JACQUES COUSTEAU DOWN THERE REALIZES WE WEREN'T BLOWN TO FISH FOOD.
AND THE SOONER I CAN GET MY HANDS ON THAT SUB STEALING CLOWN, THE SOONER I CAN GIVE HIM A PROPER BURIAL AT SEA!
NOW GET THAT HATCH SHUT!
BLOOSH
WE'RE GOING FISHING!

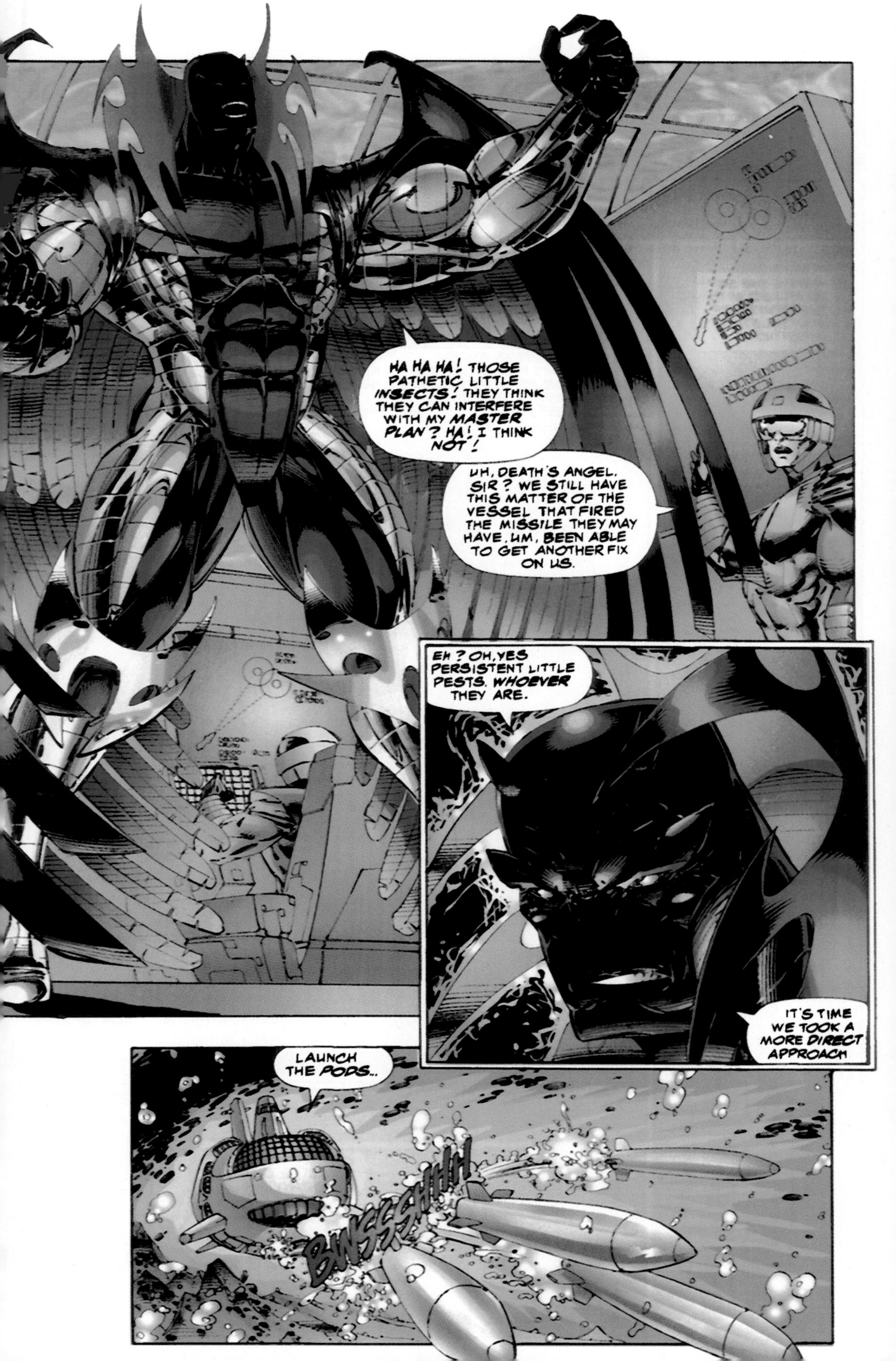
HA HA HA! THOSE PATHETIC LITTLE INSECTS! THEY THINK THEY CAN INTERFERE WITH MY MASTER PLAN? HA! I THINK NOT!
UH, DEATH'S ANGEL, SIR? WE STILL HAVE THIS MATTER OF THE VESSEL THAT FIRED THE MISSILE THEY MAY HAVE, UM, BEEN ABLE TO GET ANOTHER FIX ON US.
EH? OH, YES PERSISTENT LITTLE PESTS. WHOEVER THEY ARE.
IT'S TIME WE TOOK A MORE DIRECT APPROACH
LAUNCH THE PODS..
BWSSSHHH

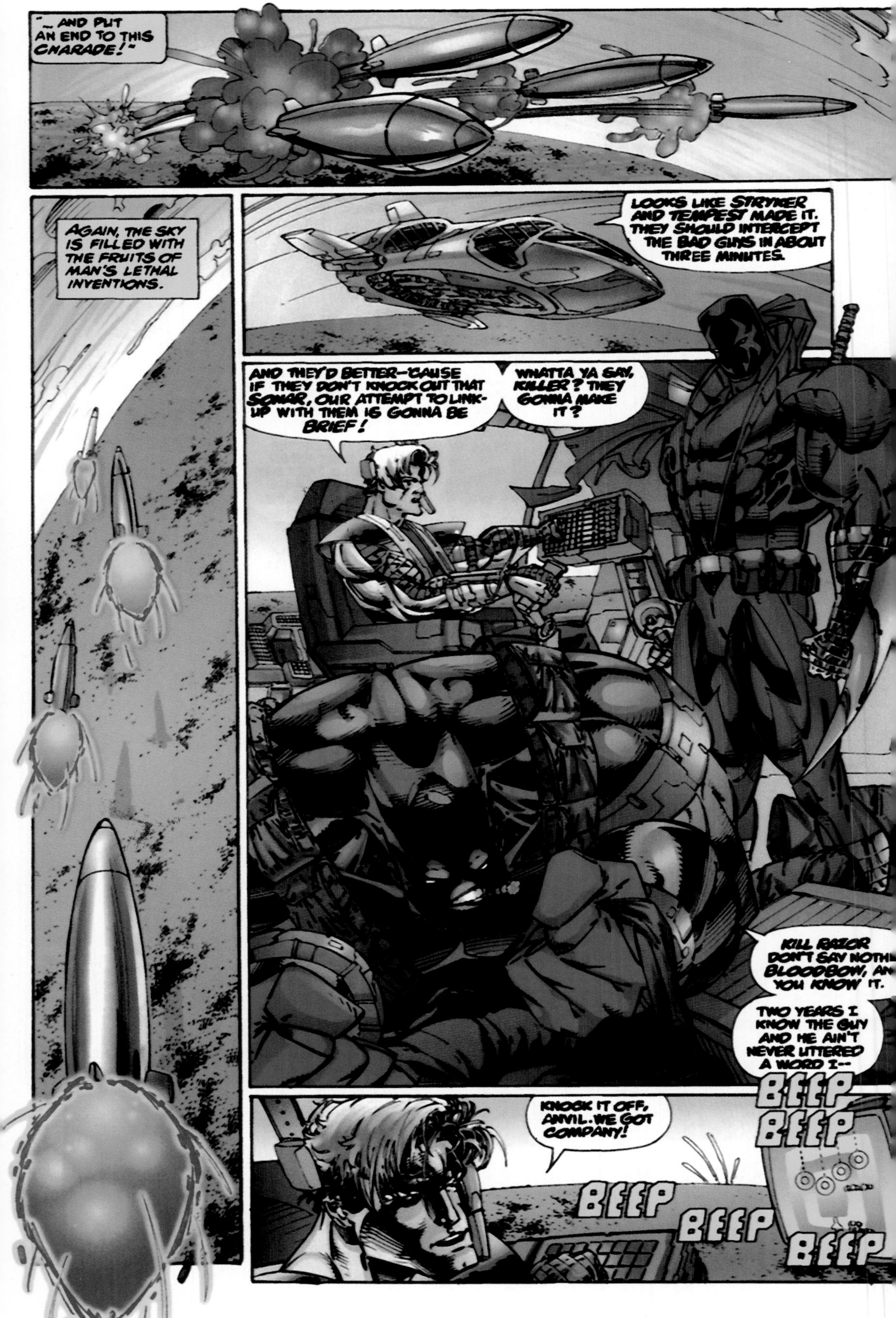
"...AND PUT AN END TO THIS CHARADE!"
AGAIN, THE SKY IS FILLED WITH THE FRUITS OF MAN'S LETHAL INVENTIONS.
LOOKS LIKE STRYKER AND TEMPEST MADE IT. THEY SHOULD INTERCEPT THE BAD GUYS IN ABOUT THREE MINUTES.
AND THEY'D BETTER--'CAUSE IF THEY DON'T KNOCK OUT THAT SONAR, OUR ATTEMPT TO LINK-UP WITH THEM IS GONNA BE BRIEF!
WHATTA YA SAY, KILLER? THEY GONNA MAKE IT?
TWO YEARS I KNOW THE GUY AND HE AIN'T NEVER UTTERED A WORD I--
BEEP
BEEP
KNOCK IT OFF, ANVIL. WE GOT COMPANY!
BEEP
BEEP
BEEP

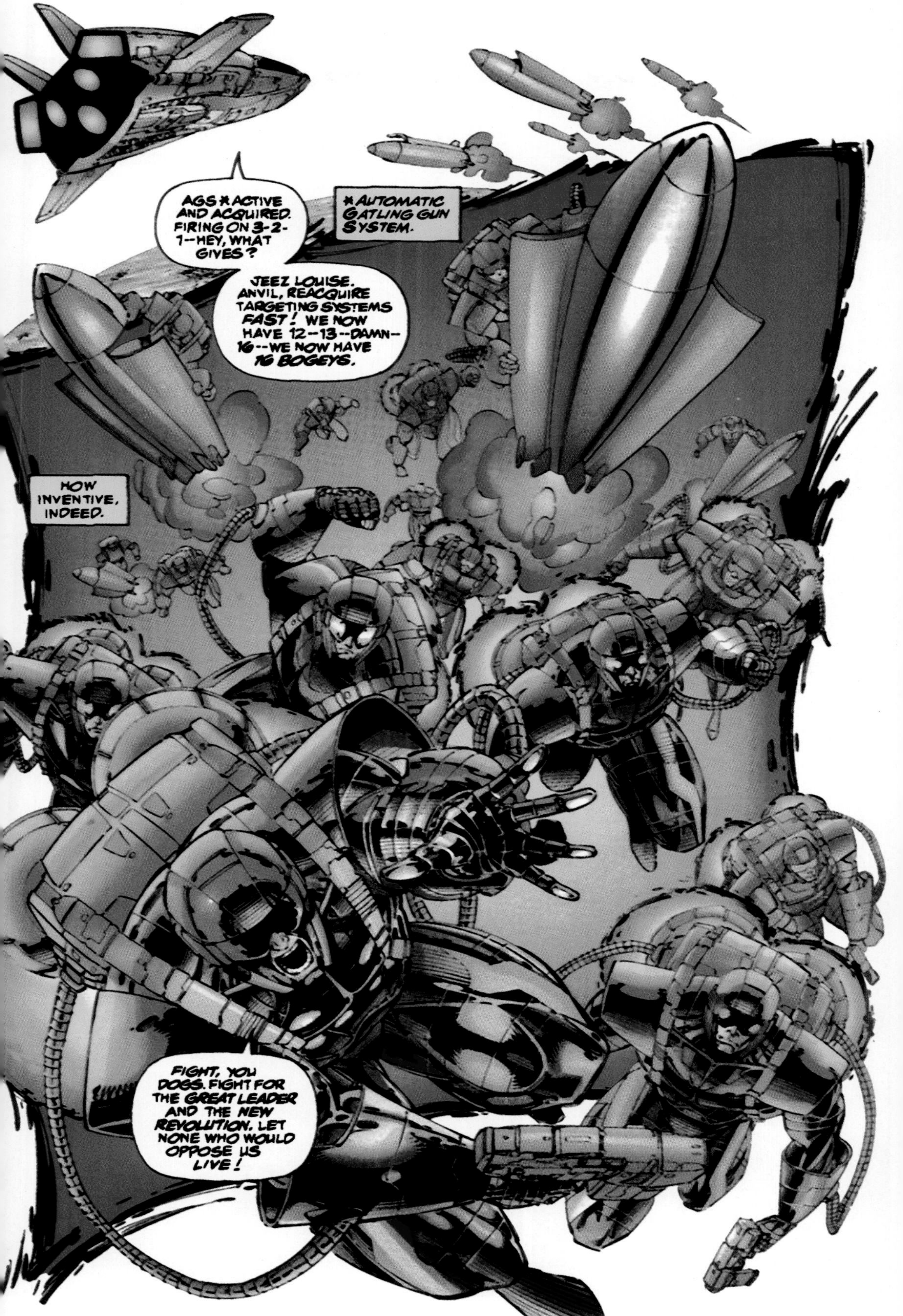
AGS* ACTIVE AND ACQUIRED. FIRING ON 3-2-1--HEY, WHAT GIVES?
*AUTOMATIC GATLING GUN SYSTEM.
JEEZ LOUISE. ANVIL, REACQUIRE TARGETING SYSTEMS FAST! WE NOW HAVE 12--13--DAMN--16--WE NOW HAVE 16 BOGEYS.
HOW INVENTIVE, INDEED.
FIGHT, YOU DOGS. FIGHT FOR THE GREAT LEADER AND THE NEW REVOLUTION. LET NONE WHO WOULD OPPOSE US LIVE!

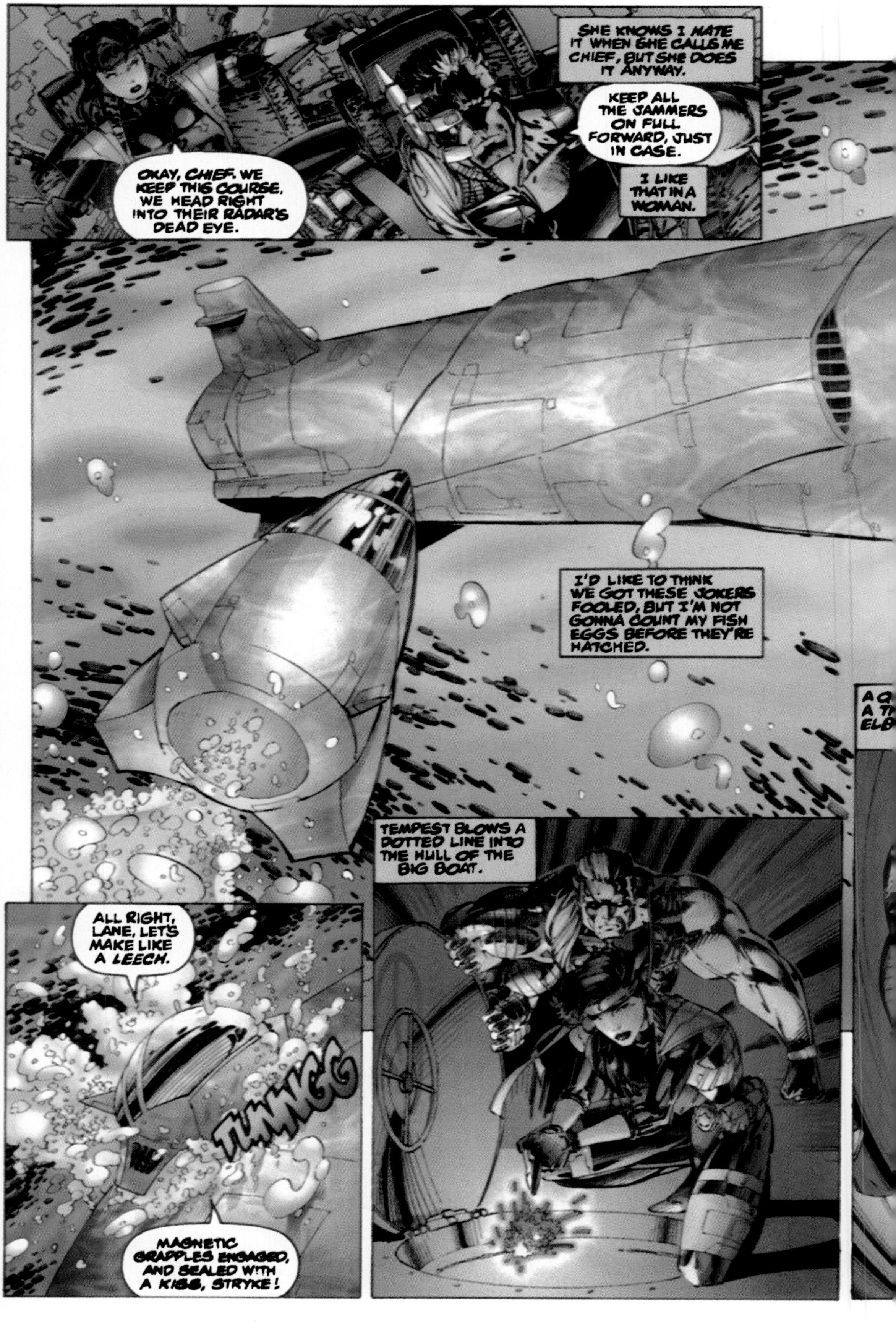
OKAY, CHIEF. WE KEEP THIS COURSE, WE HEAD RIGHT INTO THEIR RADAR'S DEAD EYE.
SHE KNOWS I HATE IT WHEN SHE CALLS ME CHIEF, BUT SHE DOES IT ANYWAY.
KEEP ALL THE JAMMERS ON FULL FORWARD, JUST IN CASE.
I LIKE THAT IN A WOMAN.
I'D LIKE TO THINK WE GOT THESE JOKERS FOOLED, BUT I'M NOT GONNA COUNT MY FISH EGGS BEFORE THEY'RE HATCHED.
ALL RIGHT, LANE, LET'S MAKE LIKE A LEECH.
TUNNGG
MAGNETIC GRAPPLES ENGAGED, AND SEALED WITH A KISS, STRYKE!
TEMPEST BLOWS A DOTTED LINE INTO THE HULL OF THE BIG BOAT.

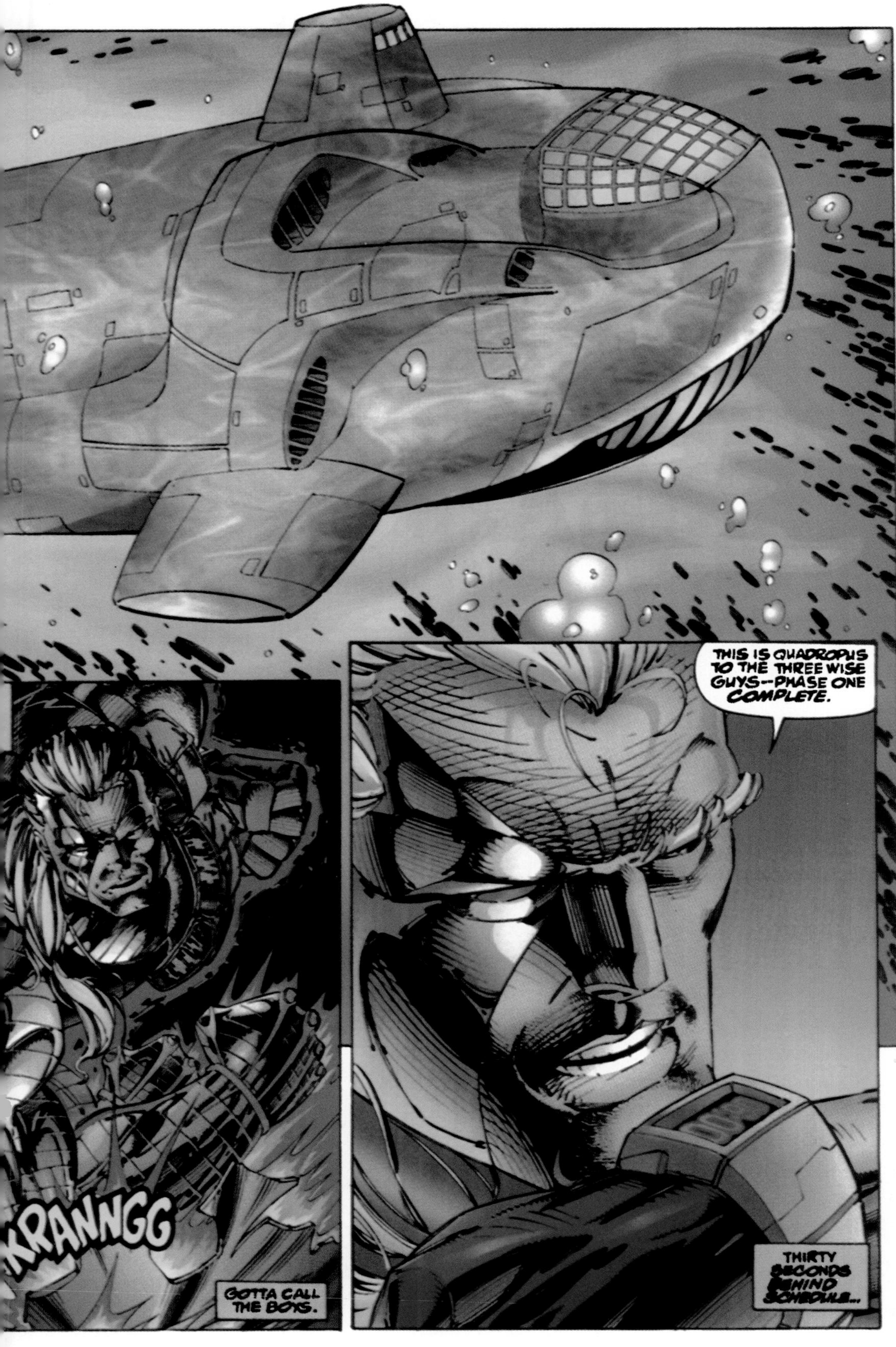
KRANNGG
GOTTA CALL THE BOYS.
THIS IS QUADROPUS TO THE THREE WISE GUYS--PHASE ONE COMPLETE.
THIRTY SECONDS BEHIND SCHEDULE...

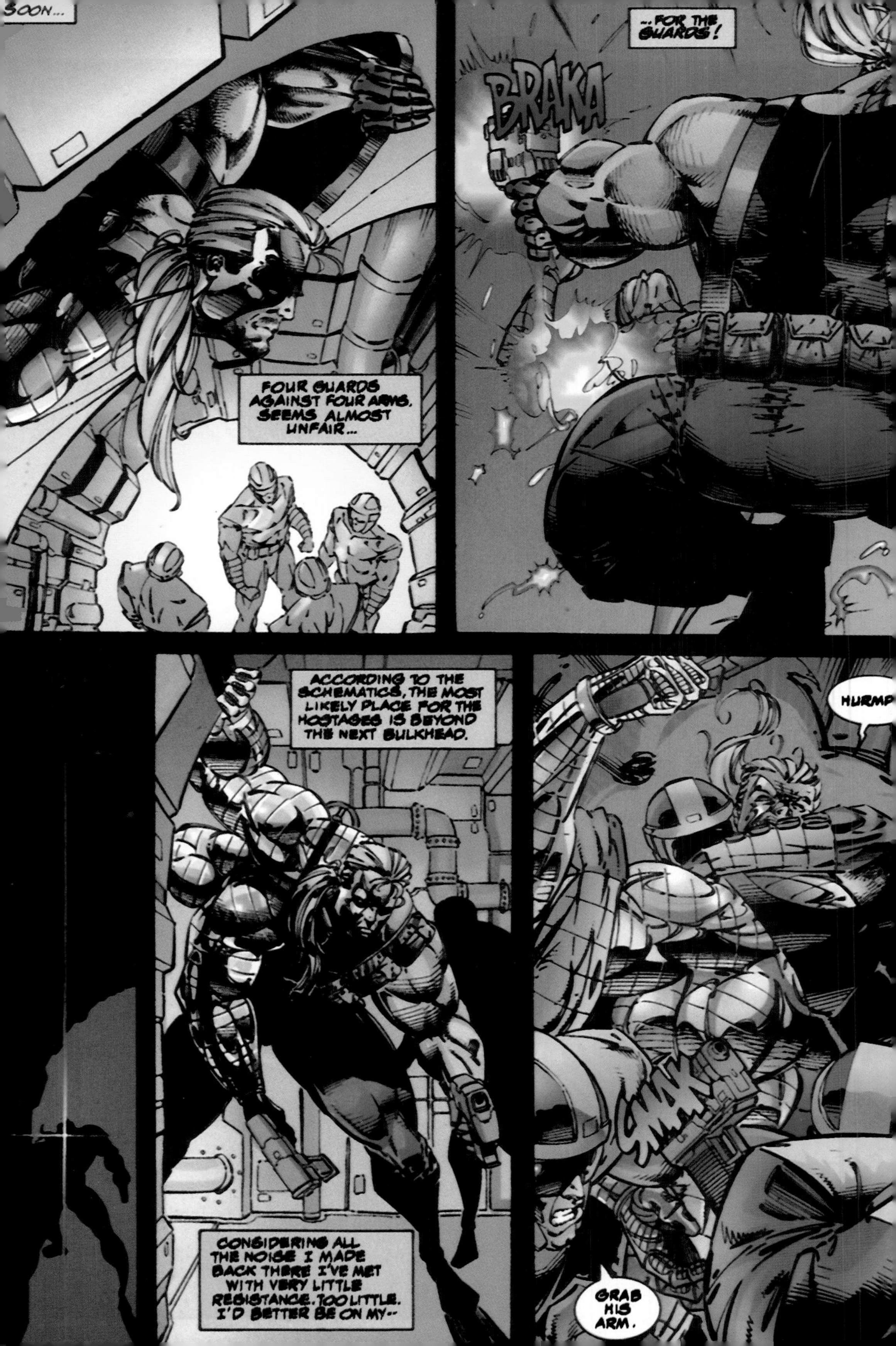
SOON...
FOUR GUARDS AGAINST FOUR ARMS. SEEMS ALMOST UNFAIR...
...FOR THE GUARDS!
BRAKA
ACCORDING TO THE SCHEMATICS, THE MOST LIKELY PLACE FOR THE HOSTAGES IS BEYOND THE NEXT BULKHEAD.
CONSIDERING ALL THE NOISE I MADE BACK THERE I'VE MET WITH VERY LITTLE RESISTANCE. TOO LITTLE. I'D BETTER BE ON MY--
HURMP
GRAB HIS ARM.

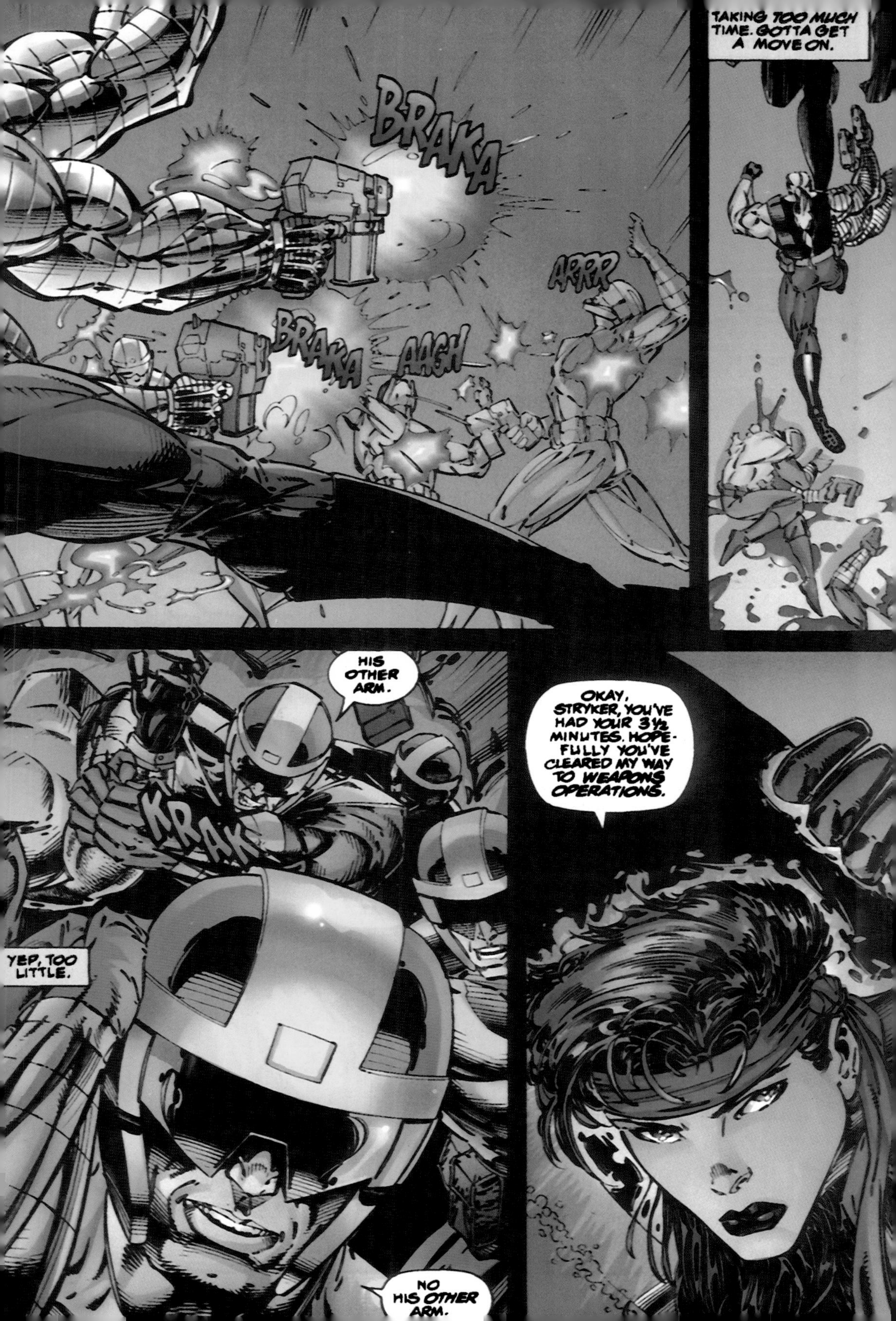
BRAKA
TAKING TOO MUCH TIME. GOTTA GET A MOVE ON.
ARRR
BRAKA
AAGH
HIS OTHER ARM.
KRAK
YEP, TOO LITTLE.
NO HIS OTHER ARM.
OKAY, STRYKER, YOU'VE HAD YOUR 3½ MINUTES. HOPE-FULLY YOU'VE CLEARED MY WAY TO WEAPONS OPERATIONS.

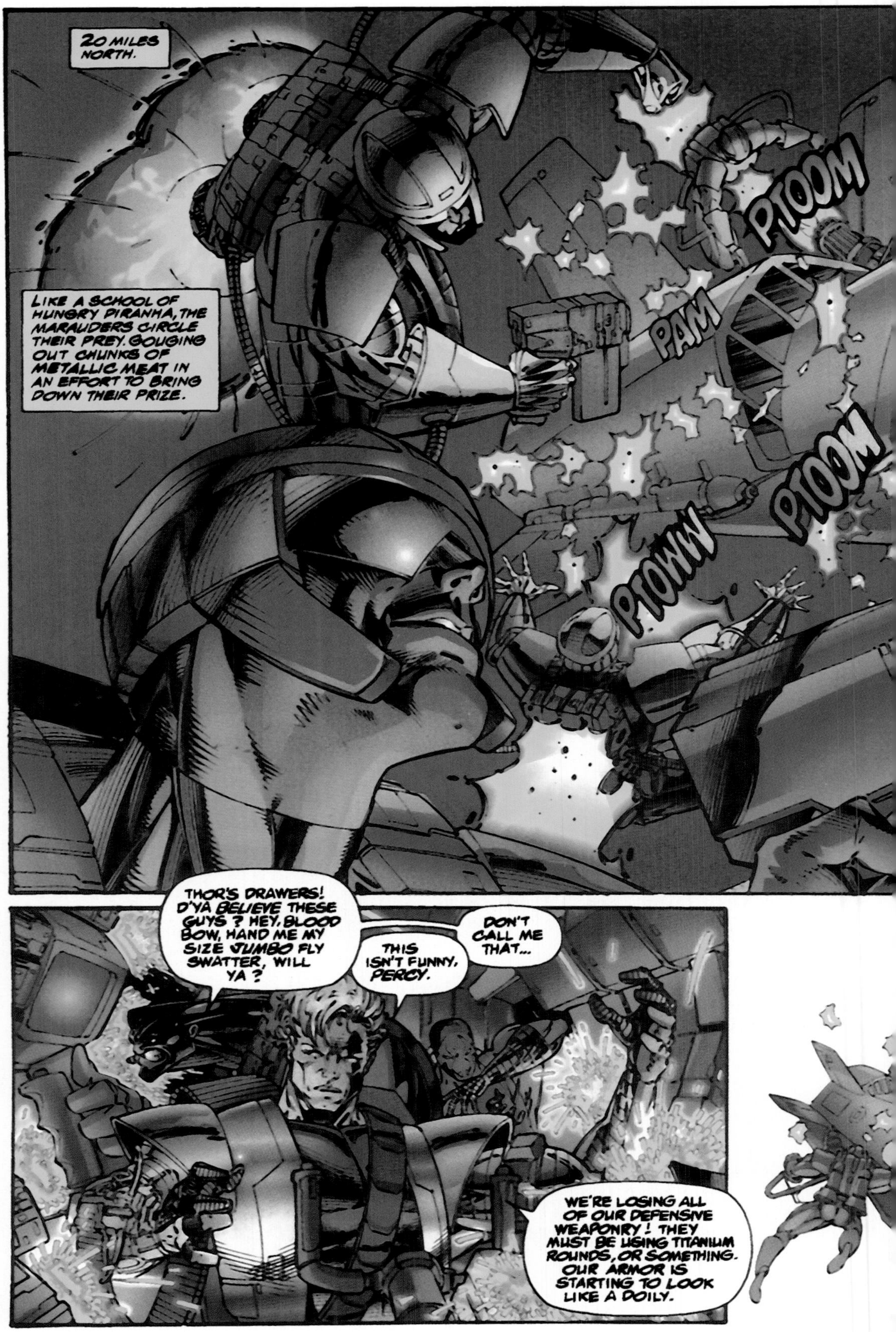
20 MILES NORTH.
LIKE A SCHOOL OF HUNGRY PIRANHA, THE MARAUDERS CIRCLE THEIR PREY. GOUGING OUT CHUNKS OF METALLIC MEAT IN AN EFFORT TO BRING DOWN THEIR PRIZE.
PTOOM
PAM
PTOOM
PTOWW
THOR'S DRAWERS! D'YA BELIEVE THESE GUYS? HEY, BLOOD BOW, HAND ME MY SIZE JUMBO FLY SWATTER, WILL YA?
THIS ISN'T FUNNY, PERCY.
DON'T CALL ME THAT...
WE'RE LOSING ALL OF OUR DEFENSIVE WEAPONRY! THEY MUST BE USING TITANIUM ROUNDS, OR SOMETHING. OUR ARMOR IS STARTING TO LOOK LIKE A DOILY.

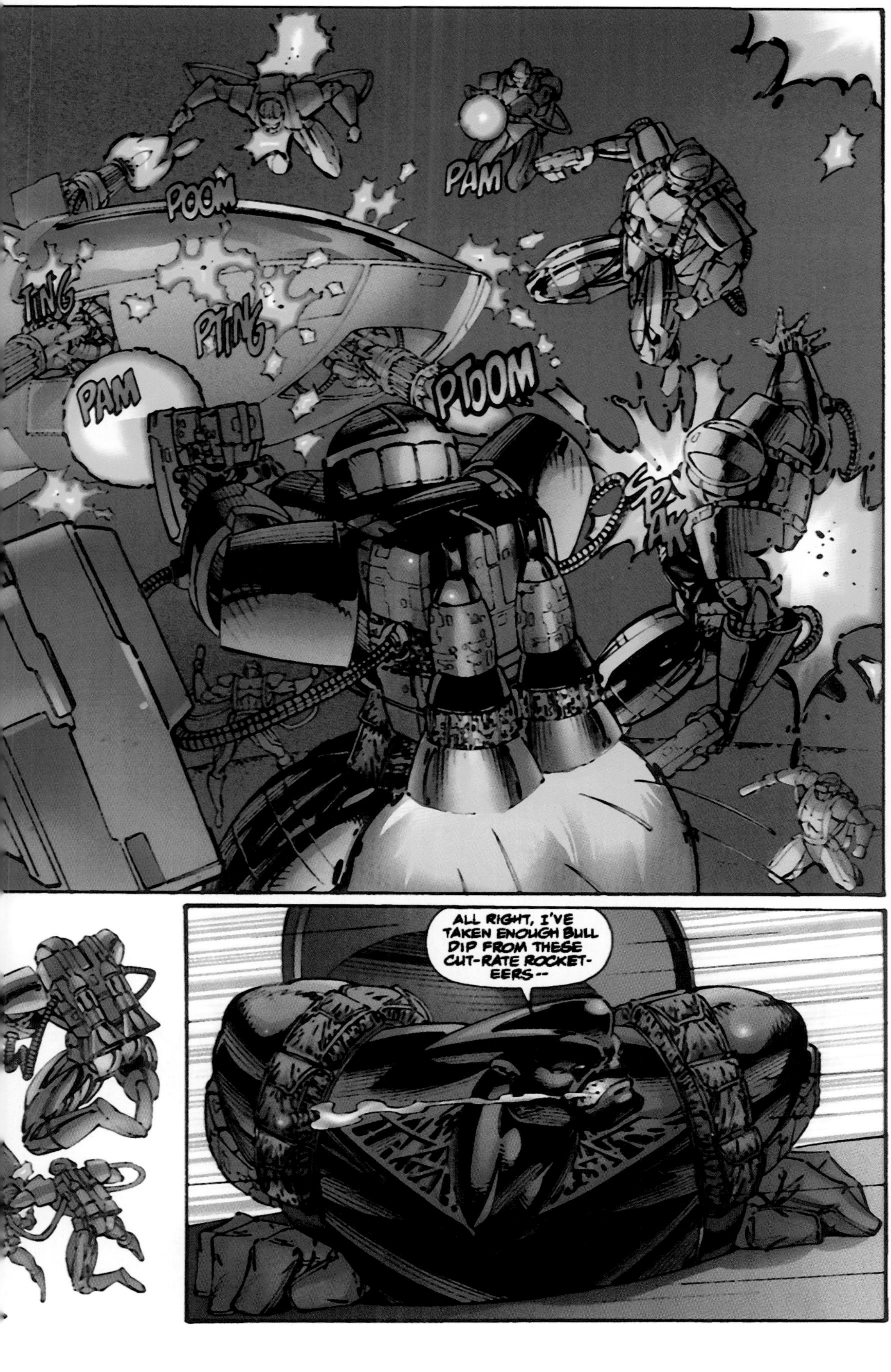
PAM
POOM
TING
PTING
PAM
PTOOM
SPAK
ALL RIGHT, I'VE TAKEN ENOUGH BULL DIP FROM THESE CUT-RATE ROCKETEERS--

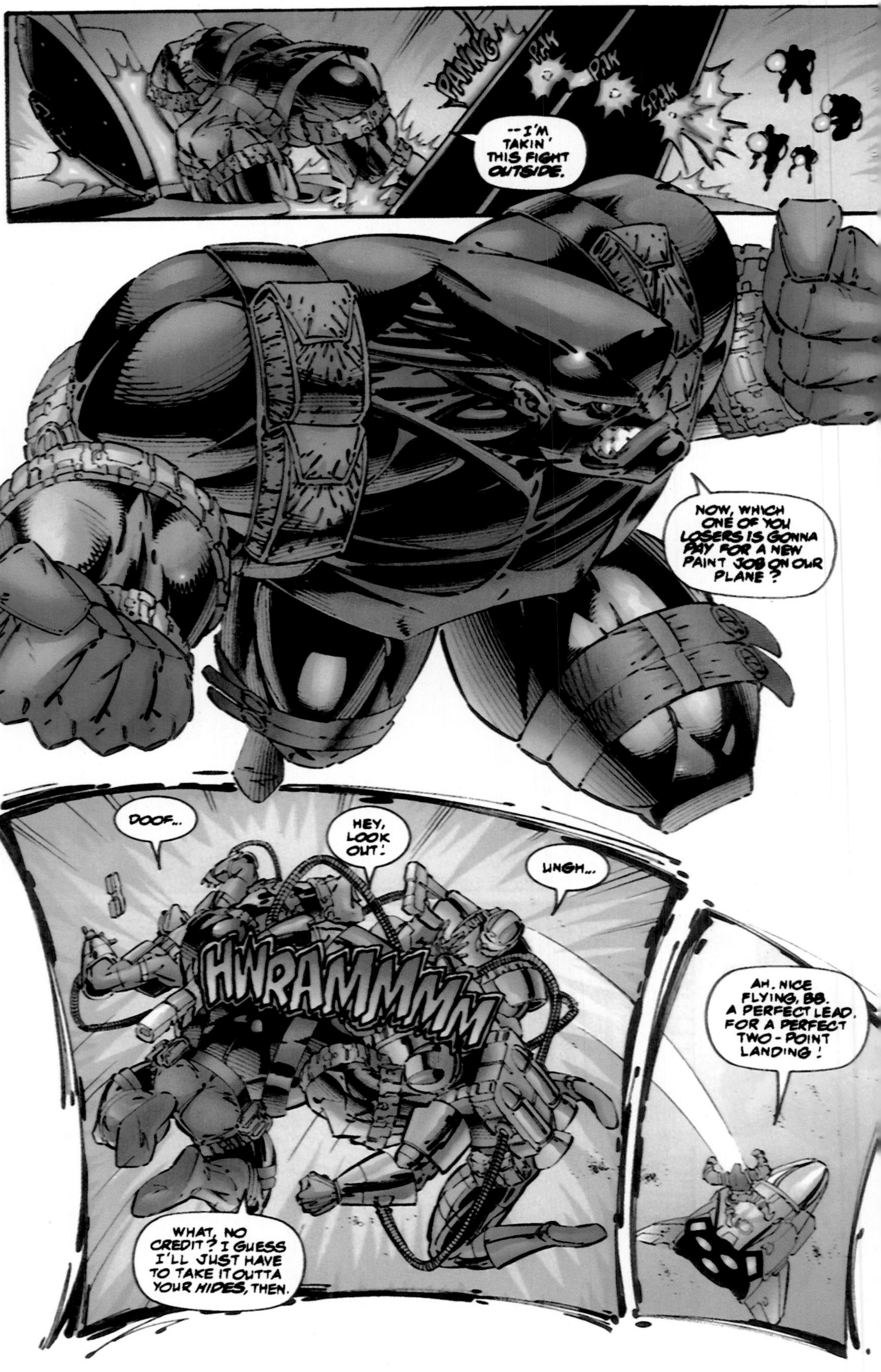
PANNG
PAK
PAK
SPAK
--I'M TAKIN' THIS FIGHT OUTSIDE.
NOW, WHICH ONE OF YOU LOSERS IS GONNA PAY FOR A NEW PAINT JOB ON OUR PLANE?
DOOF..
HEY, LOOK OUT!
UNGH...
HWRAMMMMM
WHAT, NO CREDIT? I GUESS I'LL JUST HAVE TO TAKE IT OUTTA YOUR HIDES, THEN.
AH. NICE FLYING, BB. A PERFECT LEAD FOR A PERFECT TWO-POINT LANDING!

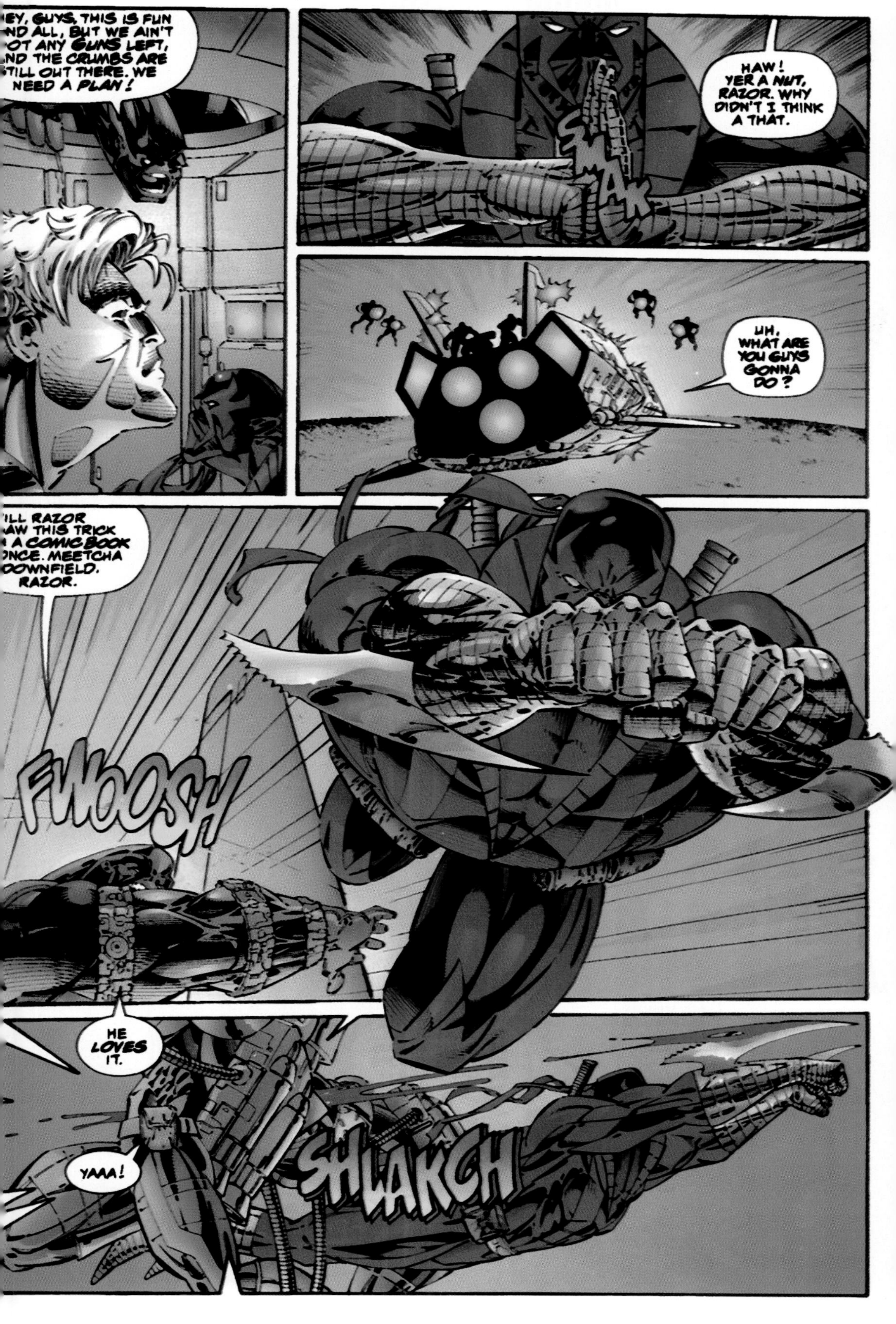
HEY, GUYS, THIS IS FUN AND ALL, BUT WE AIN'T GOT ANY GUNS LEFT, AND THE CRUMBS ARE STILL OUT THERE. WE NEED A PLAN!
HAW! YER A NUT, RAZOR. WHY DIDN'T I THINK A THAT.
SMAK
UH, WHAT ARE YOU GUYS GONNA DO?
WILL RAZOR SAW THIS TRICK IN A COMIC BOOK ONCE. MEETCHA DOWNFIELD. RAZOR.
FWOOSH
HE LOVES IT.
YAAA!
SHLAKCH

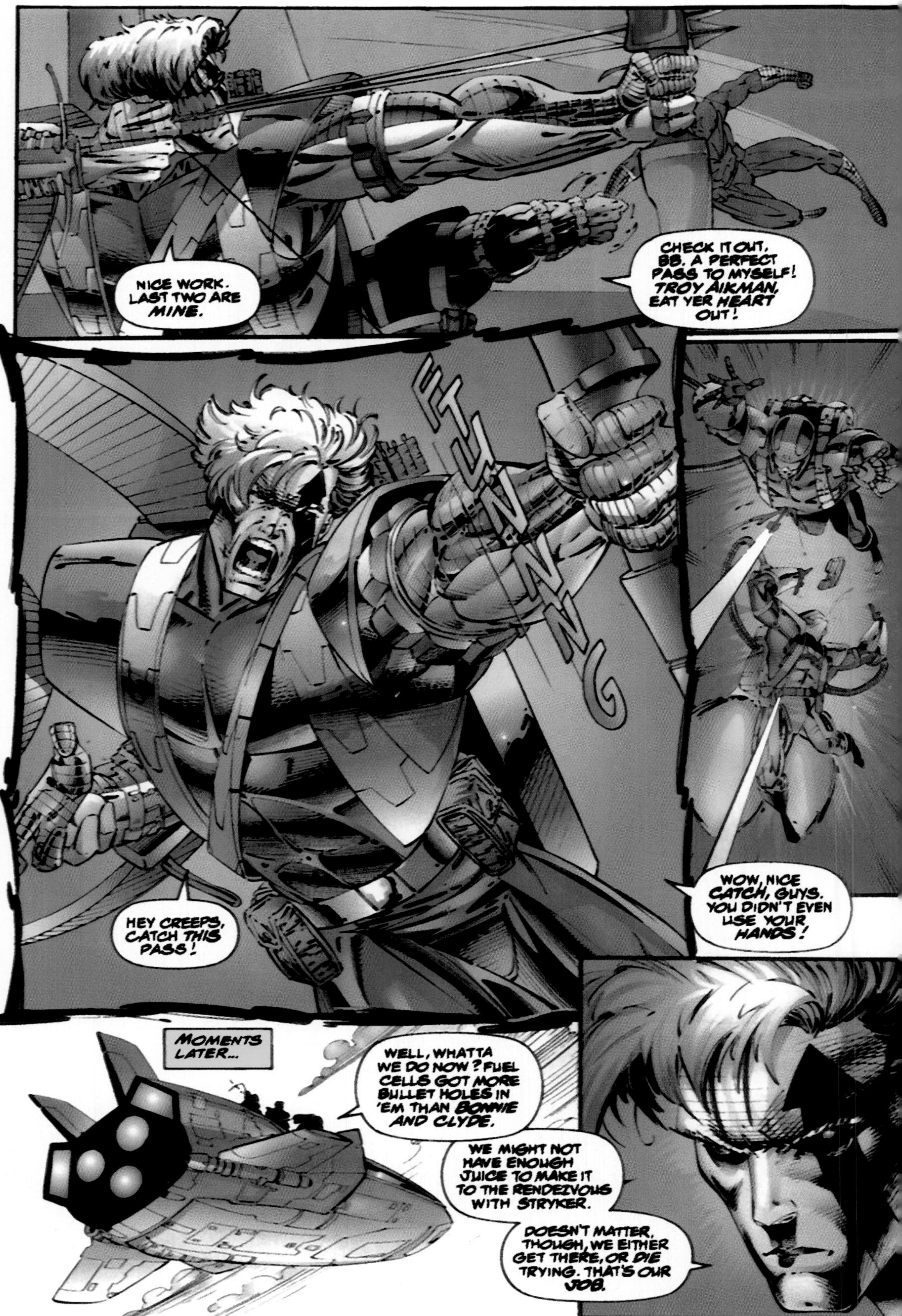
NICE WORK. LAST TWO ARE MINE.
CHECK IT OUT, BB. A PERFECT PASS TO MYSELF! TROY AIKMAN, EAT YER HEART OUT!
TSUNNNG
HEY CREEPS, CATCH THIS PASS!
WOW, NICE CATCH, GUYS. YOU DIDN'T EVEN USE YOUR HANDS!
MOMENTS LATER...
WELL, WHATTA WE DO NOW? FUEL CELLS GOT MORE BULLET HOLES IN 'EM THAN BONNIE AND CLYDE.
WE MIGHT NOT HAVE ENOUGH JUICE TO MAKE IT TO THE RENDEZVOUS WITH STRYKER.
DOESN'T MATTER, THOUGH. WE EITHER GET THERE, OR DIE TRYING. THAT'S OUR JOB.

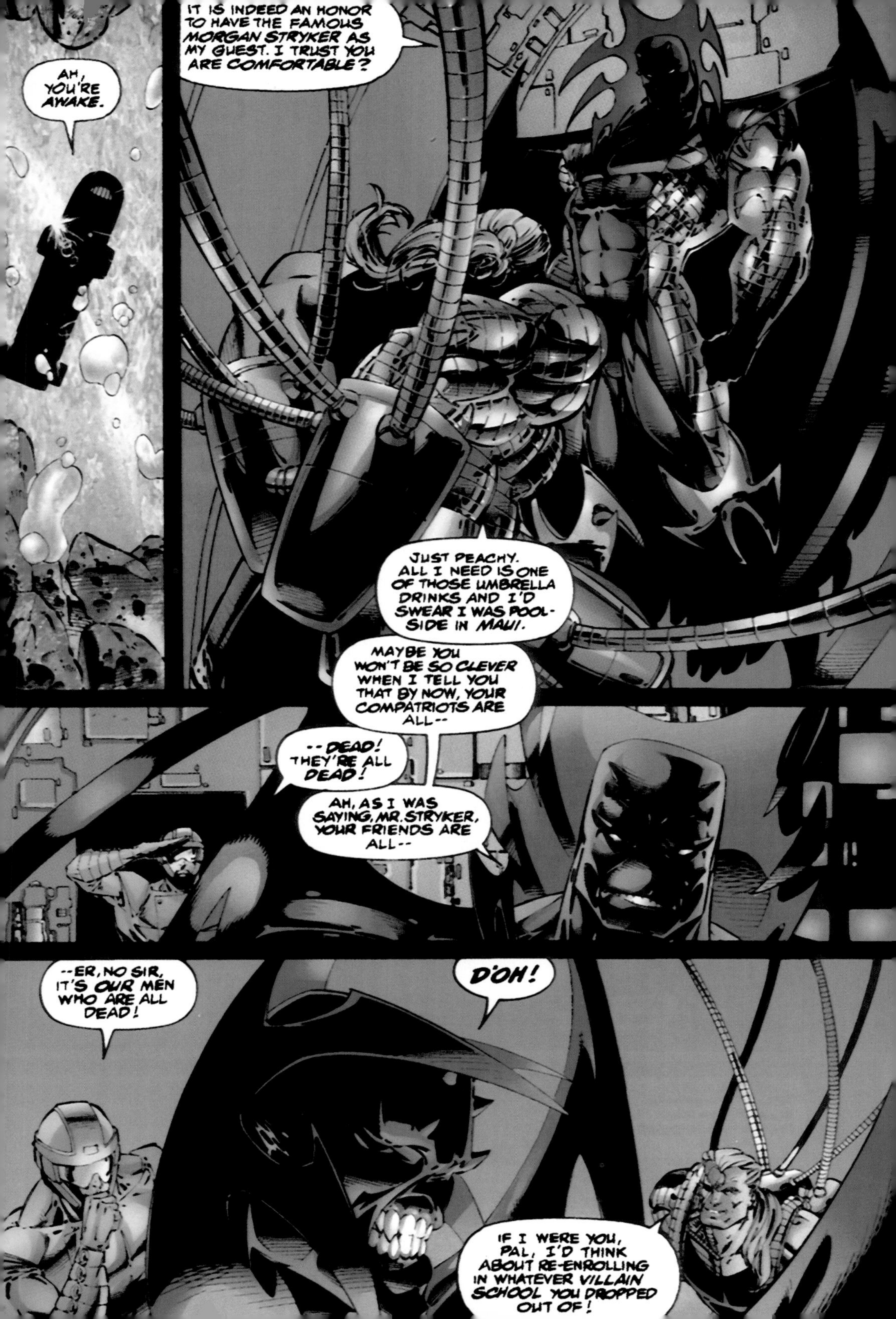
AH, YOU'RE AWAKE.
IT IS INDEED AN HONOR TO HAVE THE FAMOUS MORGAN STRYKER AS MY GUEST. I TRUST YOU ARE COMFORTABLE?
JUST PEACHY. ALL I NEED IS ONE OF THOSE UMBRELLA DRINKS AND I'D SWEAR I WAS POOL-SIDE IN MAUI.
MAYBE YOU WON'T BE SO CLEVER WHEN I TELL YOU THAT BY NOW, YOUR COMPATRIOTS ARE ALL--
--DEAD! THEY'RE ALL DEAD!
AH, AS I WAS SAYING, MR. STRYKER, YOUR FRIENDS ARE ALL--
--ER, NO SIR, IT'S OUR MEN WHO ARE ALL DEAD!
D'OH!
IF I WERE YOU, PAL, I'D THINK ABOUT RE-ENROLLING IN WHATEVER VILLAIN SCHOOL YOU DROPPED OUT OF!

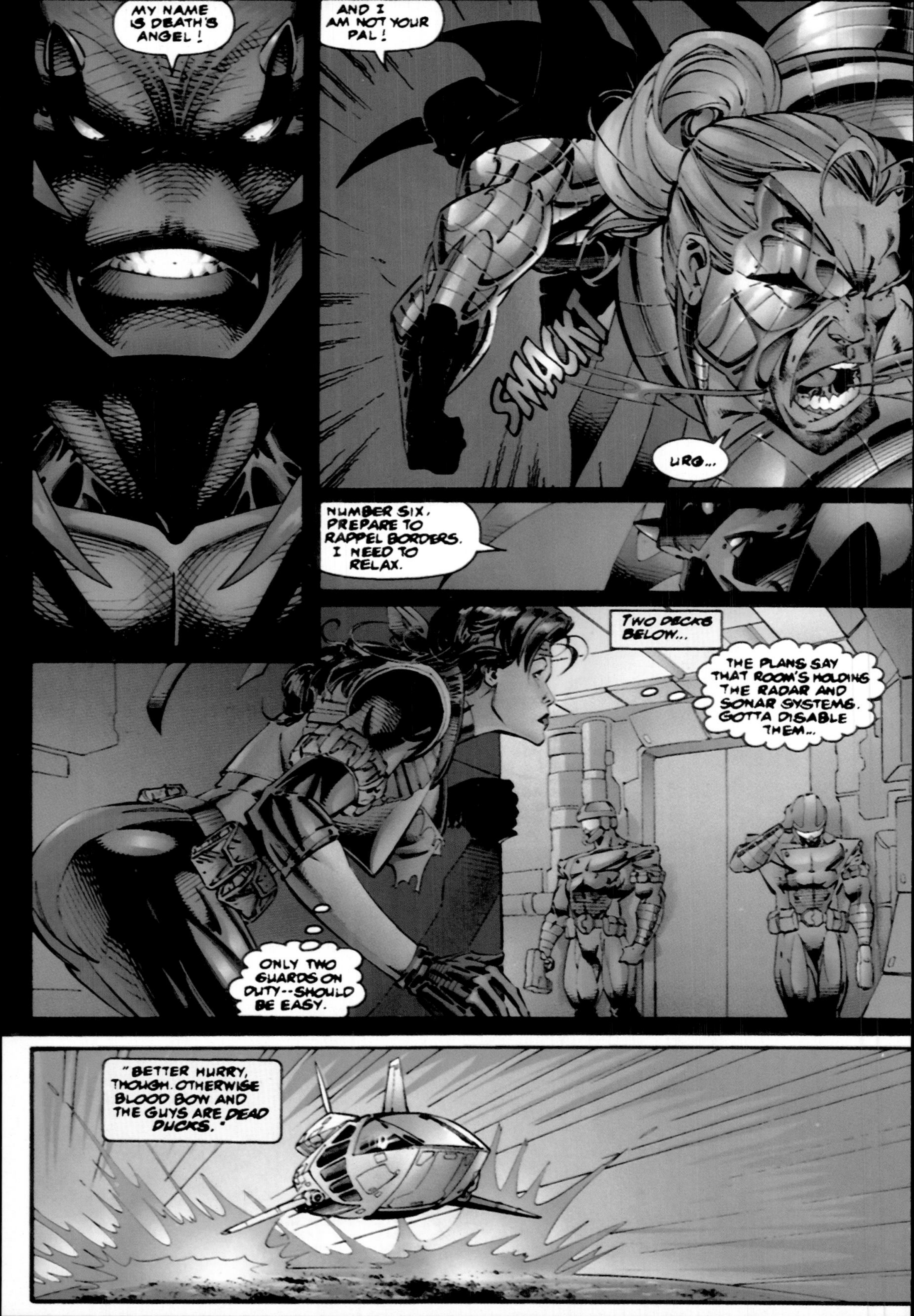

MY NAME IS DEATH'S ANGEL!
AND I AM NOT YOUR PAL!
SMACK!
URG...
NUMBER SIX, PREPARE TO RAPPEL BORDERS. I NEED TO RELAX.
TWO DECKS BELOW...
THE PLANS SAY THAT ROOM'S HOLDING THE RADAR AND SONAR SYSTEMS. GOTTA DISABLE THEM...
ONLY TWO GUARDS ON DUTY--SHOULD BE EASY.
"BETTER HURRY, THOUGH. OTHERWISE BLOOD BOW AND THE GUYS ARE DEAD DUCKS."

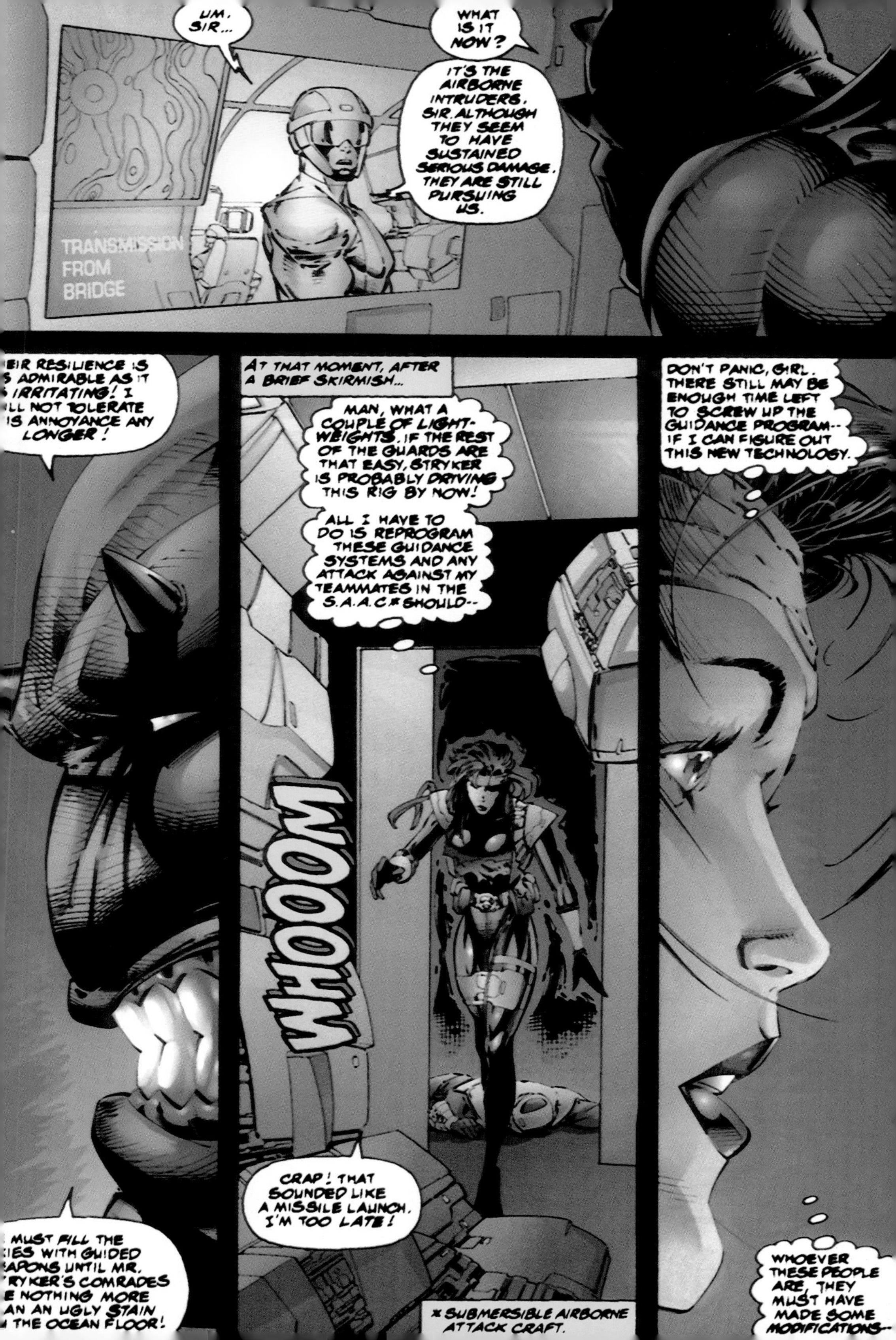
UM, SIR...
WHAT IS IT NOW?
IT'S THE AIRBORNE INTRUDERS, SIR. ALTHOUGH THEY SEEM TO HAVE SUSTAINED SERIOUS DAMAGE, THEY ARE STILL PURSUING US.
TRANSMISSION FROM BRIDGE
EIR RESILIENCE IS S ADMIRABLE AS IT S IRRITATING! I ILL NOT TOLERATE IS ANNOYANCE ANY LONGER!
AT THAT MOMENT, AFTER A BRIEF SKIRMISH...
MAN, WHAT A COUPLE OF LIGHT-WEIGHTS. IF THE REST OF THE GUARDS ARE THAT EASY, STRYKER IS PROBABLY DRIVING THIS RIG BY NOW!
ALL I HAVE TO DO IS REPROGRAM THESE GUIDANCE SYSTEMS AND ANY ATTACK AGAINST MY TEAMMATES IN THE S.A.A.C.* SHOULD--
WHOOOM
DON'T PANIC, GIRL. THERE STILL MAY BE ENOUGH TIME LEFT TO SCREW UP THE GUIDANCE PROGRAM-- IF I CAN FIGURE OUT THIS NEW TECHNOLOGY.
CRAP! THAT SOUNDED LIKE A MISSILE LAUNCH. I'M TOO LATE!
E MUST FILL THE KIES WITH GUIDED EAPONS UNTIL MR. TRYKER'S COMRADES E NOTHING MORE AN AN UGLY STAIN N THE OCEAN FLOOR!
WHOEVER THESE PEOPLE ARE, THEY MUST HAVE MADE SOME MODIFICATIONS--
* SUBMERSIBLE AIRBORNE ATTACK CRAFT.

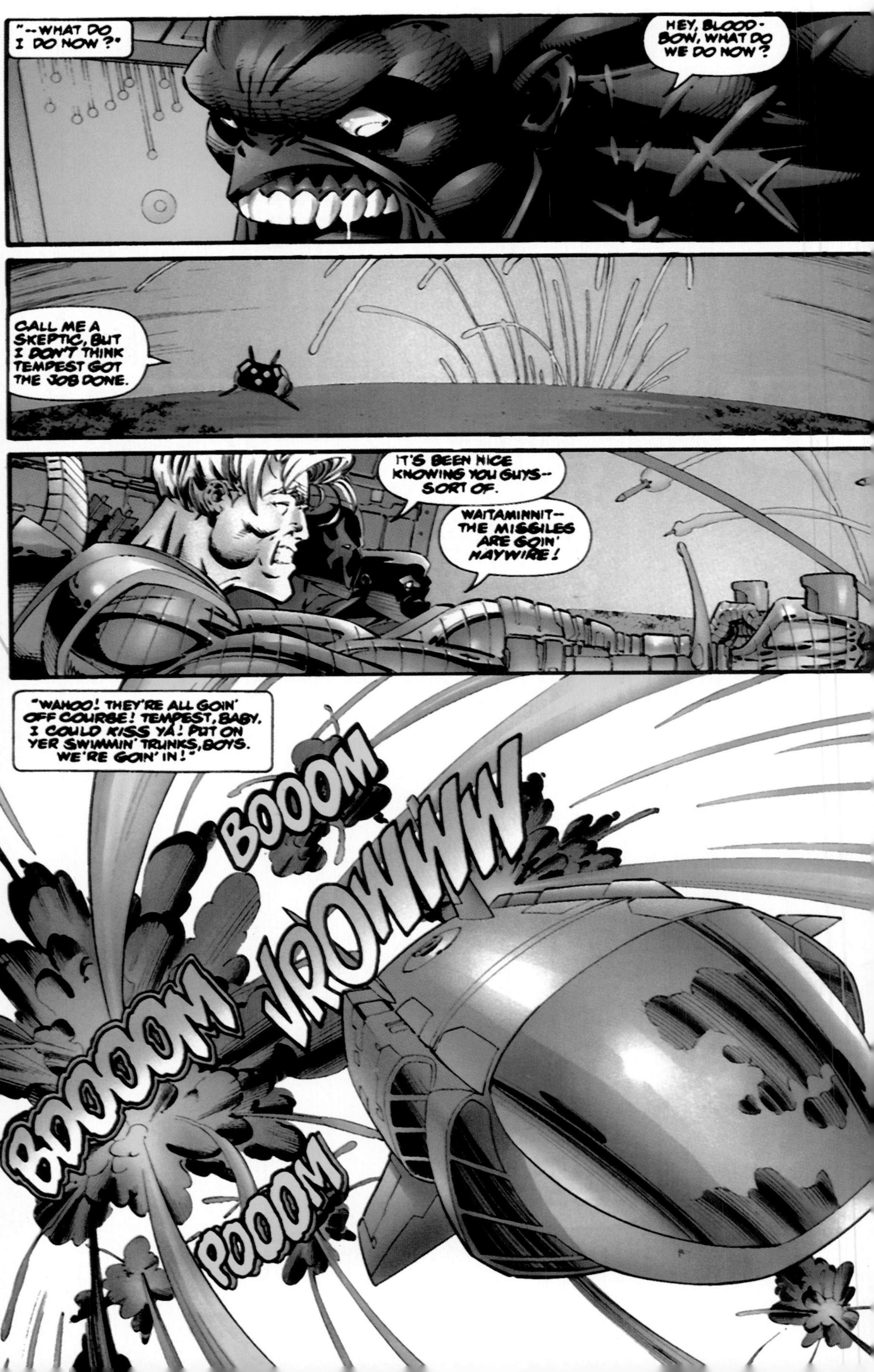
"--WHAT DO I DO NOW?"
HEY, BLOOD-BOW, WHAT DO WE DO NOW?
CALL ME A SKEPTIC, BUT I DON'T THINK TEMPEST GOT THE JOB DONE.
IT'S BEEN NICE KNOWING YOU GUYS-- SORT OF.
WAITAMINNIT-- THE MISSILES ARE GOIN' HAYWIRE!
"WAHOO! THEY'RE ALL GOIN' OFF COURSE! TEMPEST, BABY, I COULD KISS YA! PUT ON YER SWIMMIN' TRUNKS, BOYS. WE'RE GOIN' IN!"
BOOOM
VROWWW
BOOOOM
POOOM

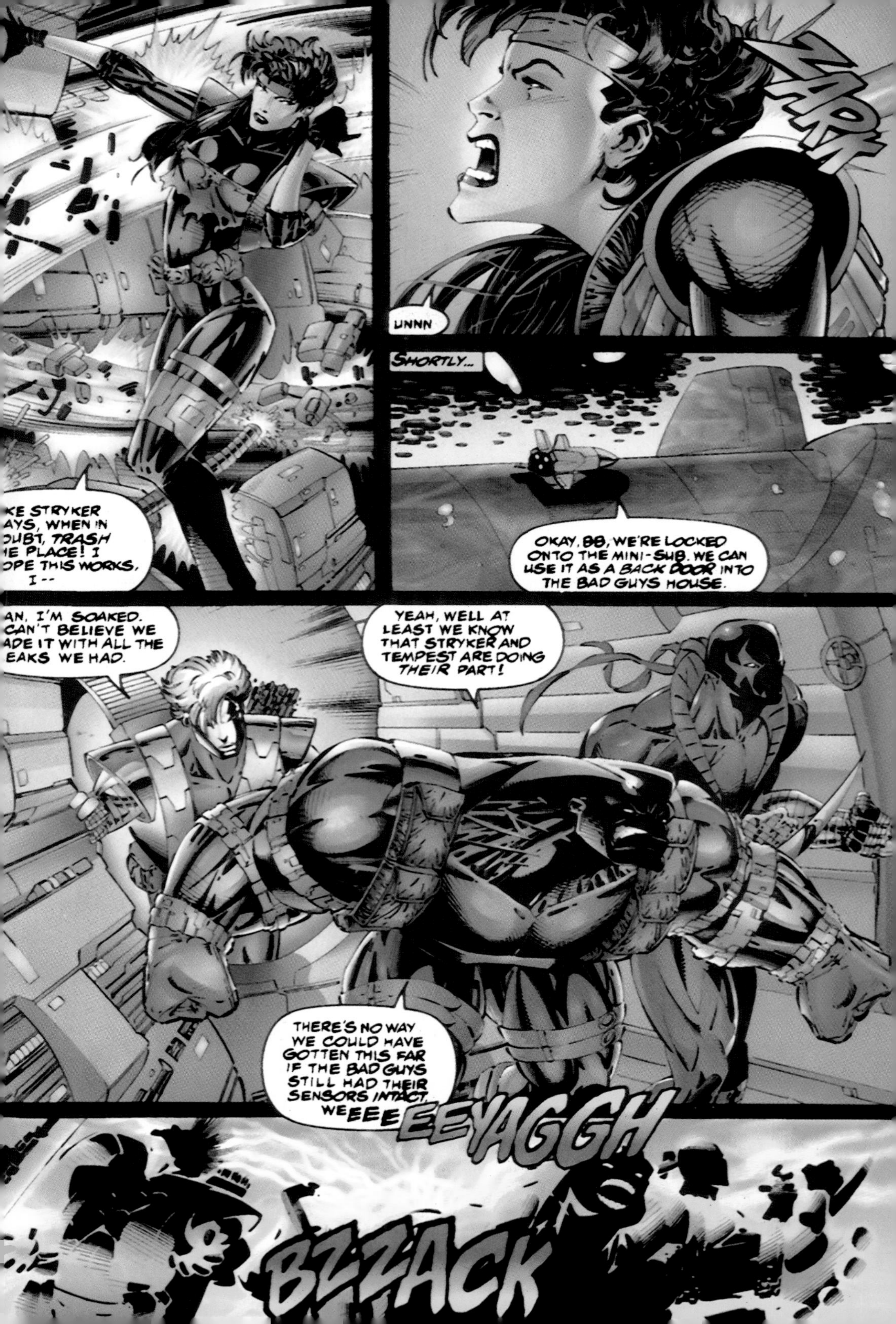

KE STRYKER
AYS, WHEN IN
OUBT, TRASH
HE PLACE! I
OPE THIS WORKS,
I --
ZAPK
UNNN
SHORTLY...
OKAY, BB, WE'RE LOCKED ONTO THE MINI-SUB. WE CAN USE IT AS A BACK DOOR INTO THE BAD GUYS HOUSE.
AN, I'M SOAKED. CAN'T BELIEVE WE ADE IT WITH ALL THE EAKS WE HAD.
YEAH, WELL AT LEAST WE KNOW THAT STRYKER AND TEMPEST ARE DOING THEIR PART!
THERE'S NO WAY WE COULD HAVE GOTTEN THIS FAR IF THE BAD GUYS STILL HAD THEIR SENSORS INTACT. WEEEEEYAGGH
BZZACK

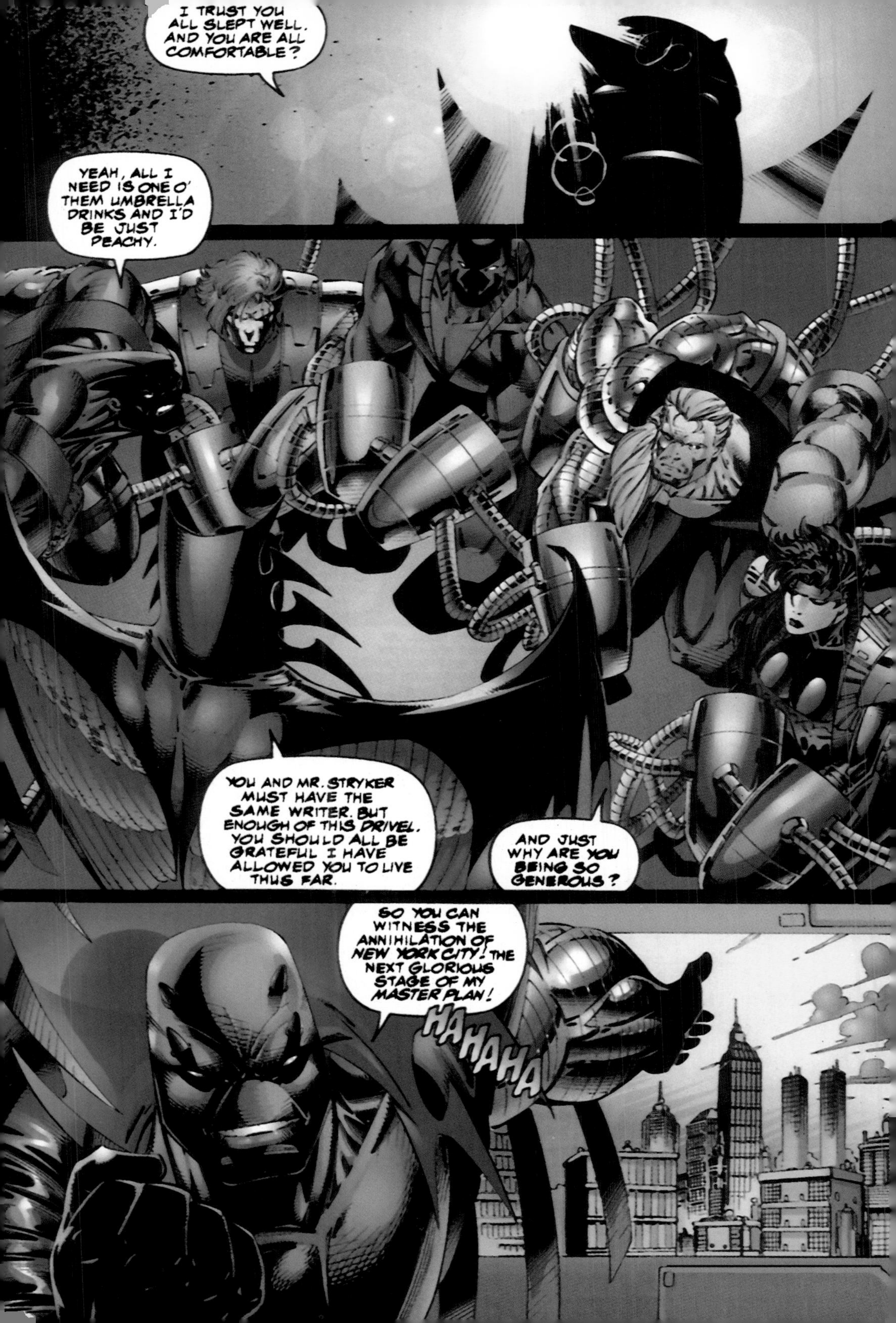

I TRUST YOU ALL SLEPT WELL. AND YOU ARE ALL COMFORTABLE?
YEAH, ALL I NEED IS ONE O' THEM UMBRELLA DRINKS AND I'D BE JUST PEACHY.
YOU AND MR. STRYKER MUST HAVE THE SAME WRITER. BUT ENOUGH OF THIS DRIVEL. YOU SHOULD ALL BE GRATEFUL I HAVE ALLOWED YOU TO LIVE THUS FAR.
AND JUST WHY ARE YOU BEING SO GENEROUS?
SO YOU CAN WITNESS THE ANNIHILATION OF NEW YORK CITY! THE NEXT GLORIOUS STAGE OF MY MASTER PLAN!
HAHAHA

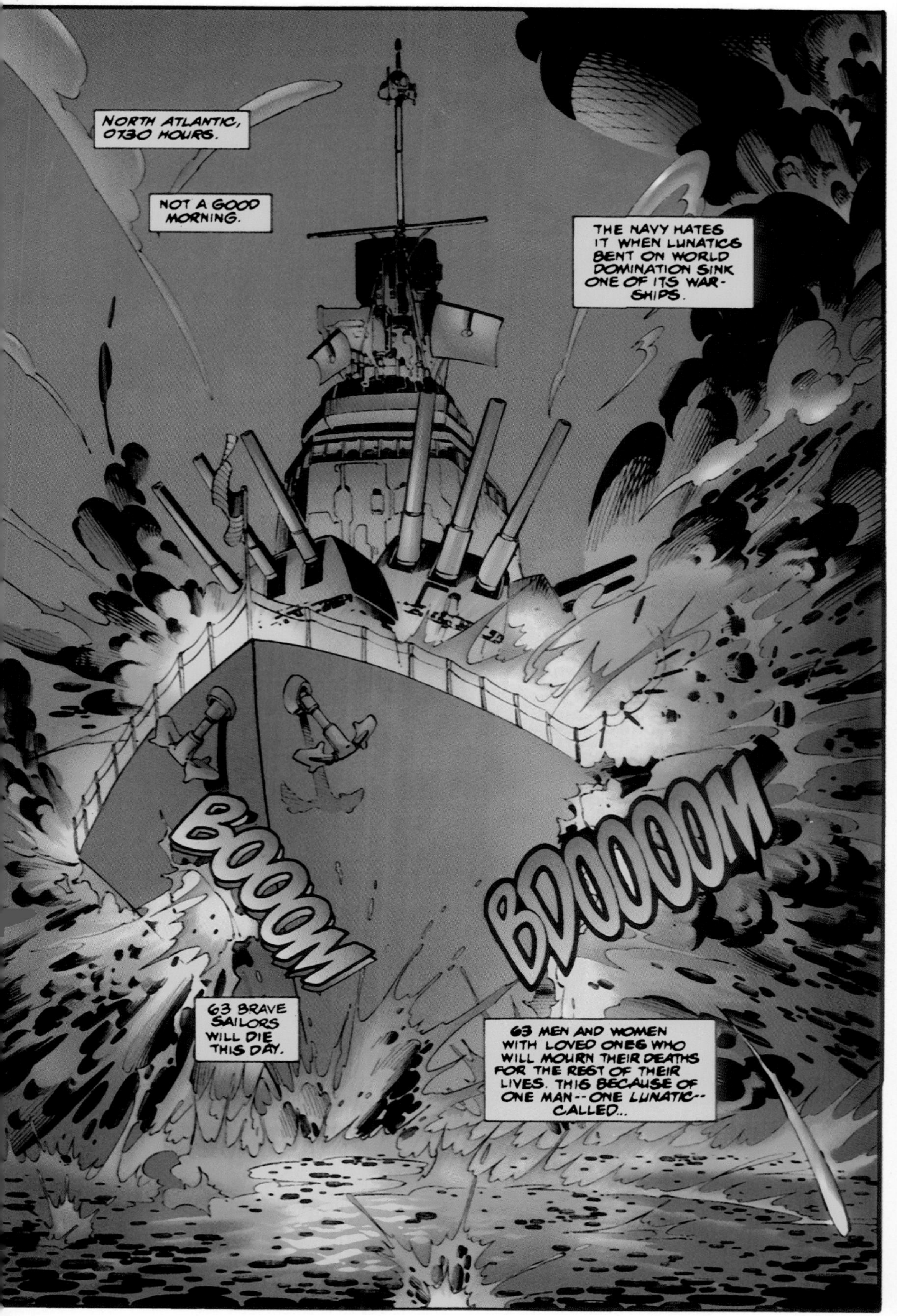
NORTH ATLANTIC, 0730 HOURS.
NOT A GOOD MORNING.
THE NAVY HATES IT WHEN LUNATICS BENT ON WORLD DOMINATION SINK ONE OF ITS WAR-SHIPS.
BOOOM
BDOOOOM
63 BRAVE SAILORS WILL DIE THIS DAY.
63 MEN AND WOMEN WITH LOVED ONES WHO WILL MOURN THEIR DEATHS FOR THE REST OF THEIR LIVES. THIS BECAUSE OF ONE MAN--ONE LUNATIC--CALLED...

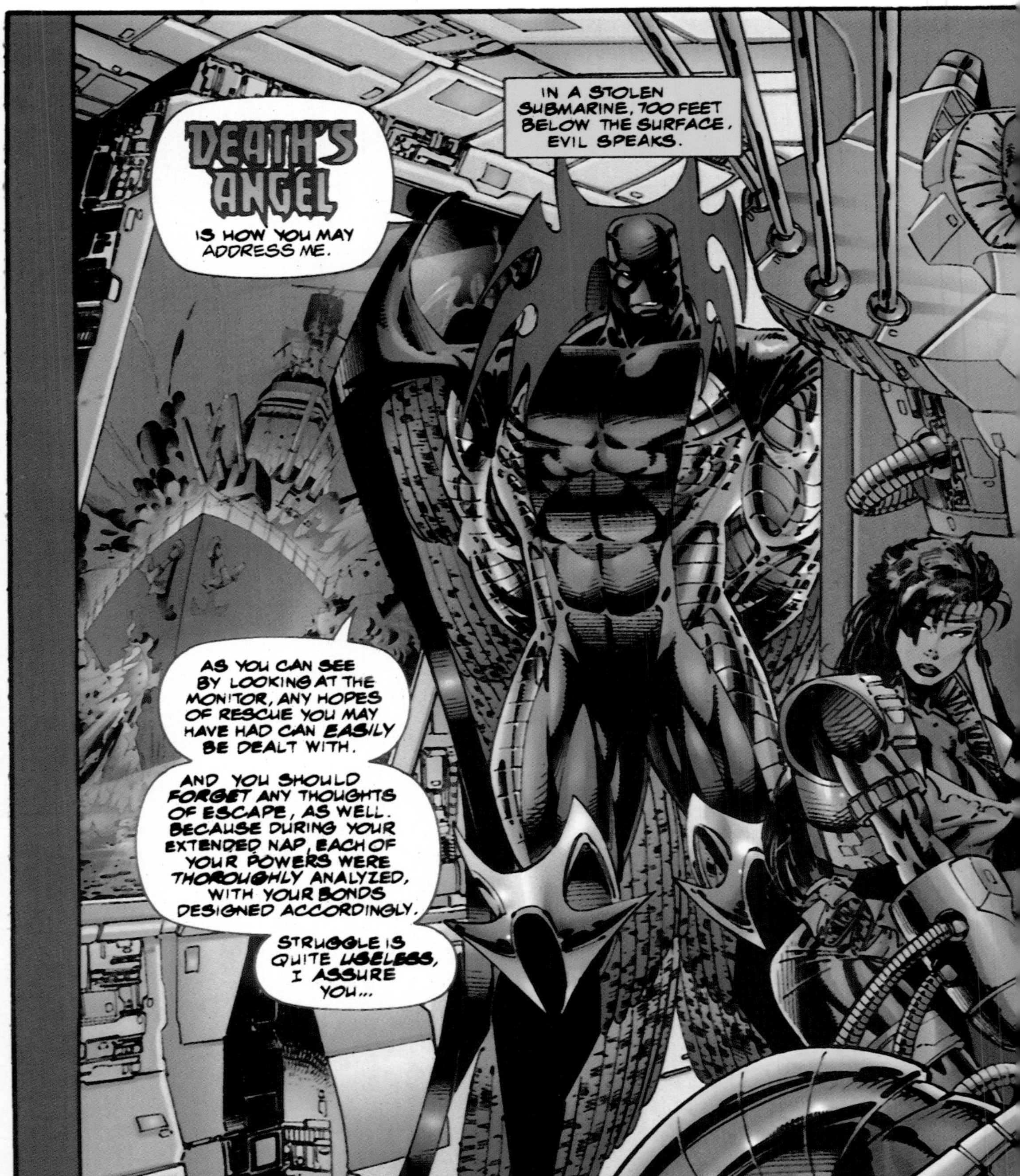
IN A STOLEN SUBMARINE, 700 FEET BELOW THE SURFACE, EVIL SPEAKS.
DEATH'S ANGEL IS HOW YOU MAY ADDRESS ME.
AS YOU CAN SEE BY LOOKING AT THE MONITOR, ANY HOPES OF RESCUE YOU MAY HAVE HAD CAN EASILY BE DEALT WITH.
AND YOU SHOULD FORGET ANY THOUGHTS OF ESCAPE, AS WELL. BECAUSE DURING YOUR EXTENDED NAP, EACH OF YOUR POWERS WERE THOROUGHLY ANALYZED, WITH YOUR BONDS DESIGNED ACCORDINGLY.
STRUGGLE IS QUITE USELESS, I ASSURE YOU...

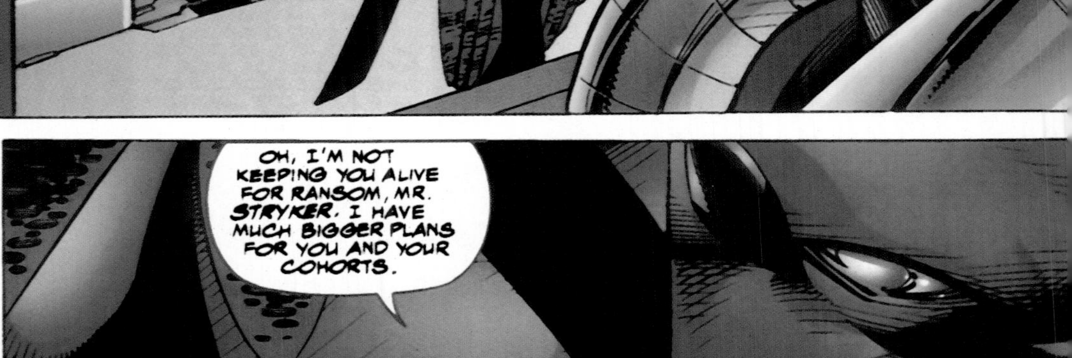
OH, I'M NOT KEEPING YOU ALIVE FOR RANSOM, MR. STRYKER. I HAVE MUCH BIGGER PLANS FOR YOU AND YOUR COHORTS.

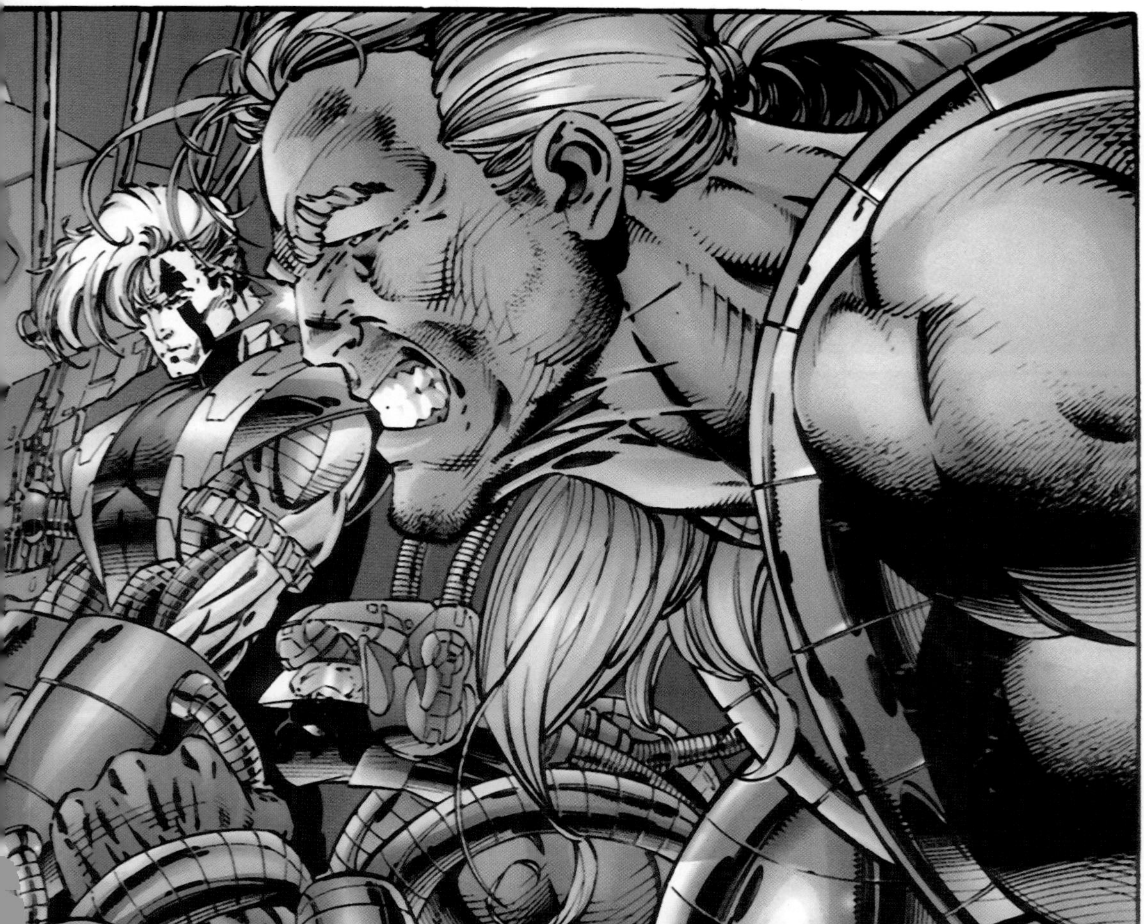
LOOK, PAL, I'M SURE WE'RE ALL VERY IMPRES-SED WITH THESE SWELL LITTLE SETS OF HAND-CUFFS, BUT WHY GO THROUGH ALL THE TROUBLE OF KEEPING US ALIVE WHEN YOU COULD JUST FEED US TO THE SHRIMPS AND BE DONE WITH IT?
THERE'S NOBODY OUT THERE WHO'D PAY MONEY TO GET US BACK.

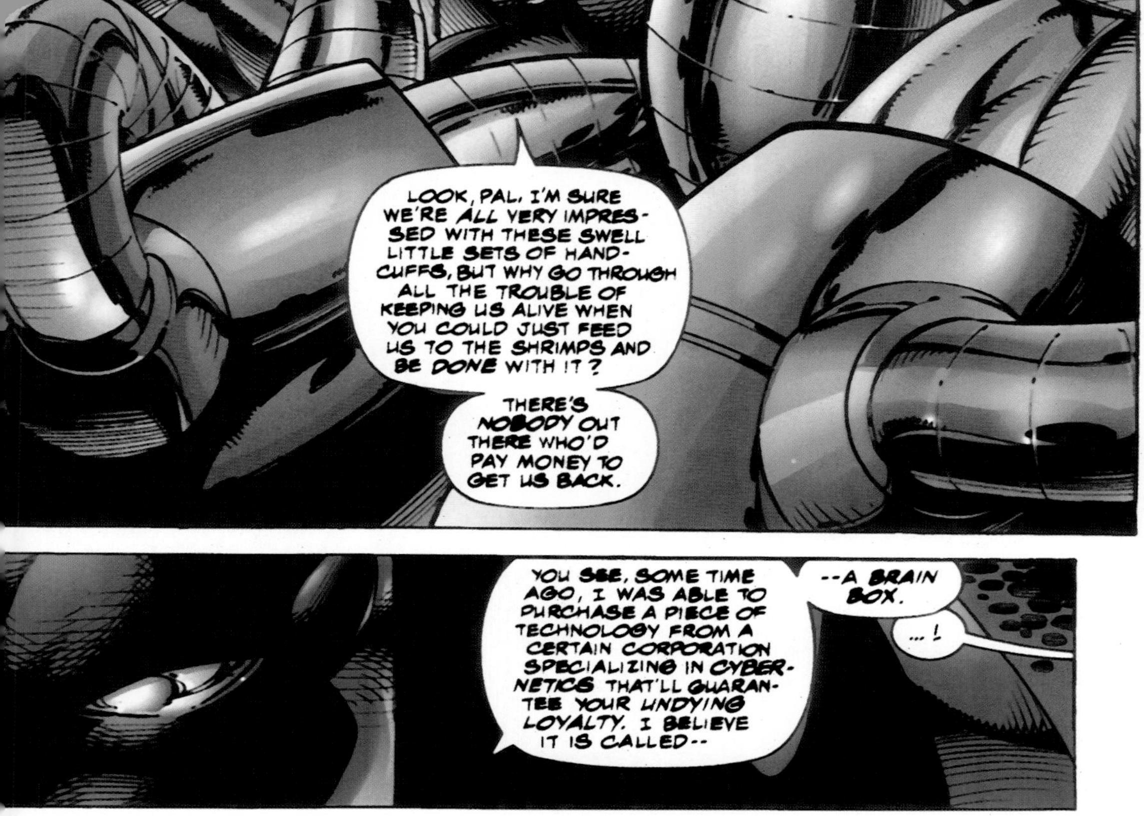
YOU SEE, SOME TIME AGO, I WAS ABLE TO PURCHASE A PIECE OF TECHNOLOGY FROM A CERTAIN CORPORATION SPECIALIZING IN CYBER-NETICS THAT'LL GUARAN-TEE YOUR UNDYING LOYALTY. I BELIEVE IT IS CALLED--
--A BRAIN BOX.
...!

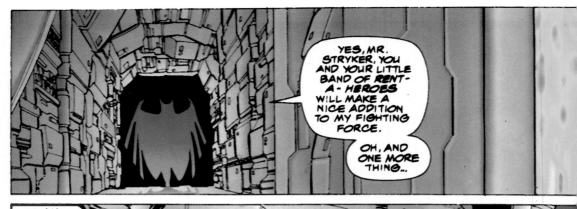

YES, MR. STRYKER, YOU AND YOUR LITTLE BAND OF *RENT-A-HEROES* WILL MAKE A NICE ADDITION TO MY FIGHTING FORCE.

OH, AND ONE MORE THING...

..., I AM *NOT* YOUR PAL.

I GUESS THAT MEANS DINNER AND A MOVIE ARE *OUT!*

OKAY, EVERYBODY, LET'S DO IT!

GOTTA HAND IT TO THOSE GUYS AT CYBER-DATA. THEY MAY HAVE SCREWED WITH MY HEAD AND MADE ME DO THINGS I DIDN'T WANT TO DO...*

*SEE CYBERFORCE #0 FOR DETAILS.

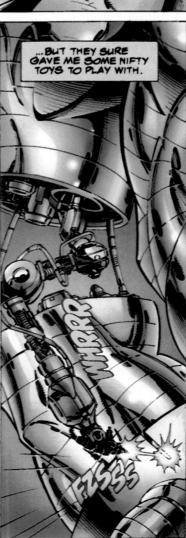

...BUT THEY SURE GAVE ME SOME NIFTY TOYS TO PLAY WITH.

I'LL HAVE YOU GUYS OUT IN A MINUTE.

I REALLY DO LOVE BEING CAPTURED.

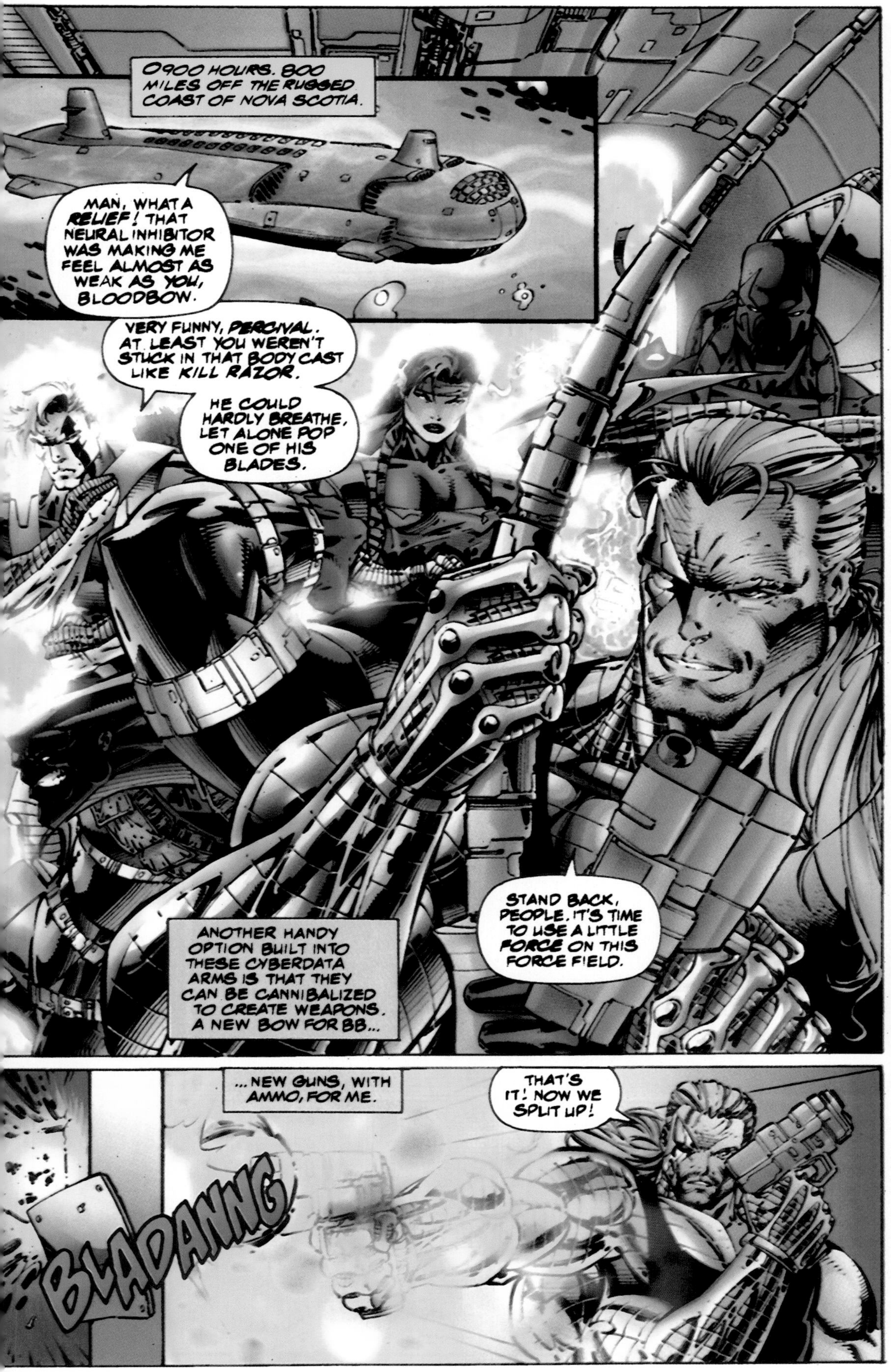
0900 HOURS. 800 MILES OFF THE RUGGED COAST OF NOVA SCOTIA.
MAN, WHAT A RELIEF! THAT NEURAL INHIBITOR WAS MAKING ME FEEL ALMOST AS WEAK AS YOU, BLOODBOW.
VERY FUNNY, PERCIVAL. AT LEAST YOU WEREN'T STUCK IN THAT BODY CAST LIKE KILL RAZOR.
HE COULD HARDLY BREATHE, LET ALONE POP ONE OF HIS BLADES.
ANOTHER HANDY OPTION BUILT INTO THESE CYBERDATA ARMS IS THAT THEY CAN BE CANNIBALIZED TO CREATE WEAPONS. A NEW BOW FOR BB...
STAND BACK, PEOPLE. IT'S TIME TO USE A LITTLE FORCE ON THIS FORCE FIELD.
...NEW GUNS, WITH AMMO, FOR ME.
THAT'S IT! NOW WE SPLIT UP!
BLADANNG

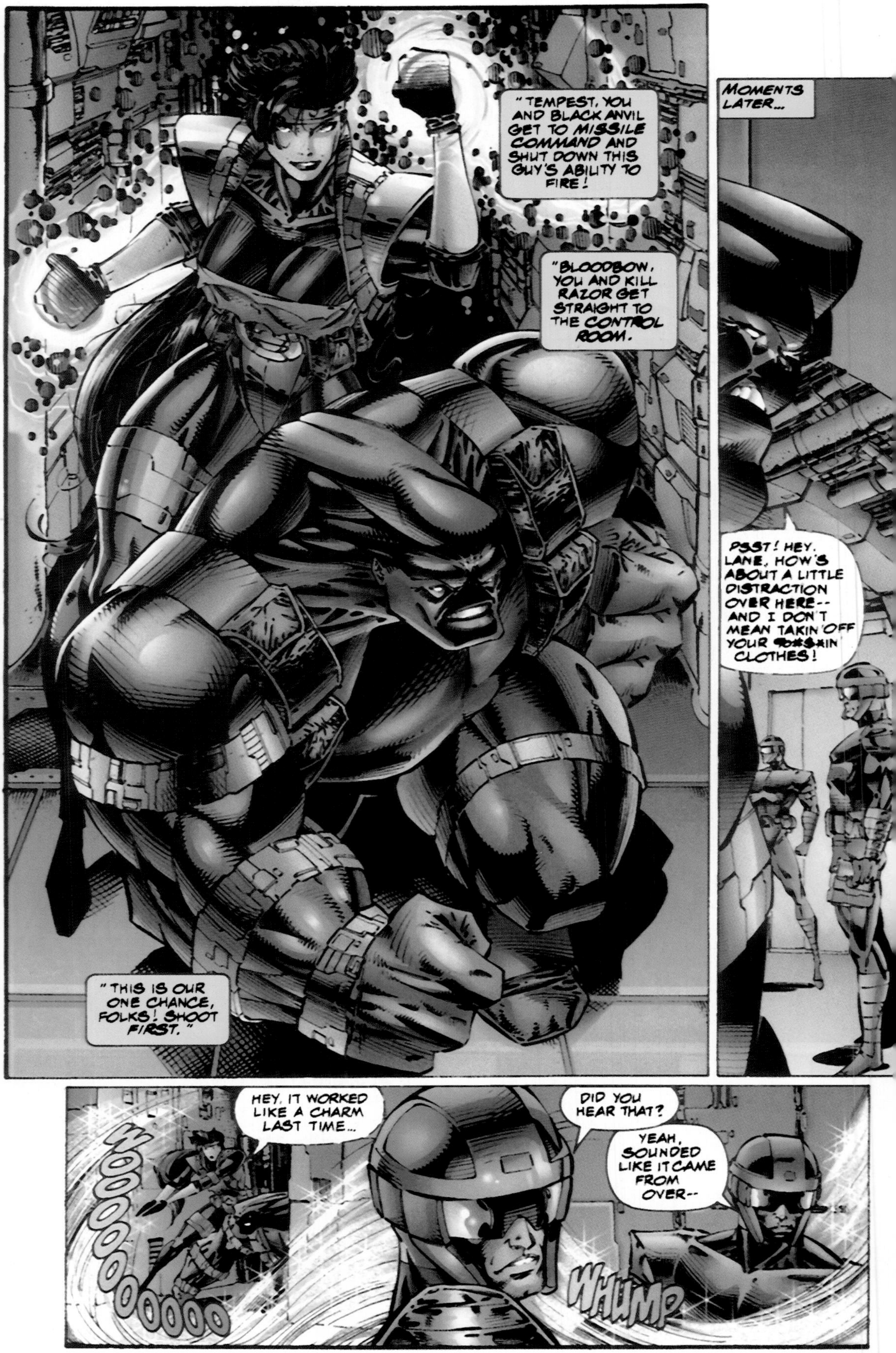

"TEMPEST, YOU AND BLACK ANVIL GET TO MISSILE COMMAND AND SHUT DOWN THIS GUY'S ABILITY TO FIRE!
"BLOODBOW, YOU AND KILL RAZOR GET STRAIGHT TO THE CONTROL ROOM.
"THIS IS OUR ONE CHANCE, FOLKS! SHOOT FIRST."
MOMENTS LATER...
PSST! HEY, LANE, HOW'S ABOUT A LITTLE DISTRACTION OVER HERE-- AND I DON'T MEAN TAKIN' OFF YOUR %#$*IN' CLOTHES!
HEY, IT WORKED LIKE A CHARM LAST TIME...
DID YOU HEAR THAT?
YEAH, SOUNDED LIKE IT CAME FROM OVER--
WOOOOOOOOOOO
WHUMP

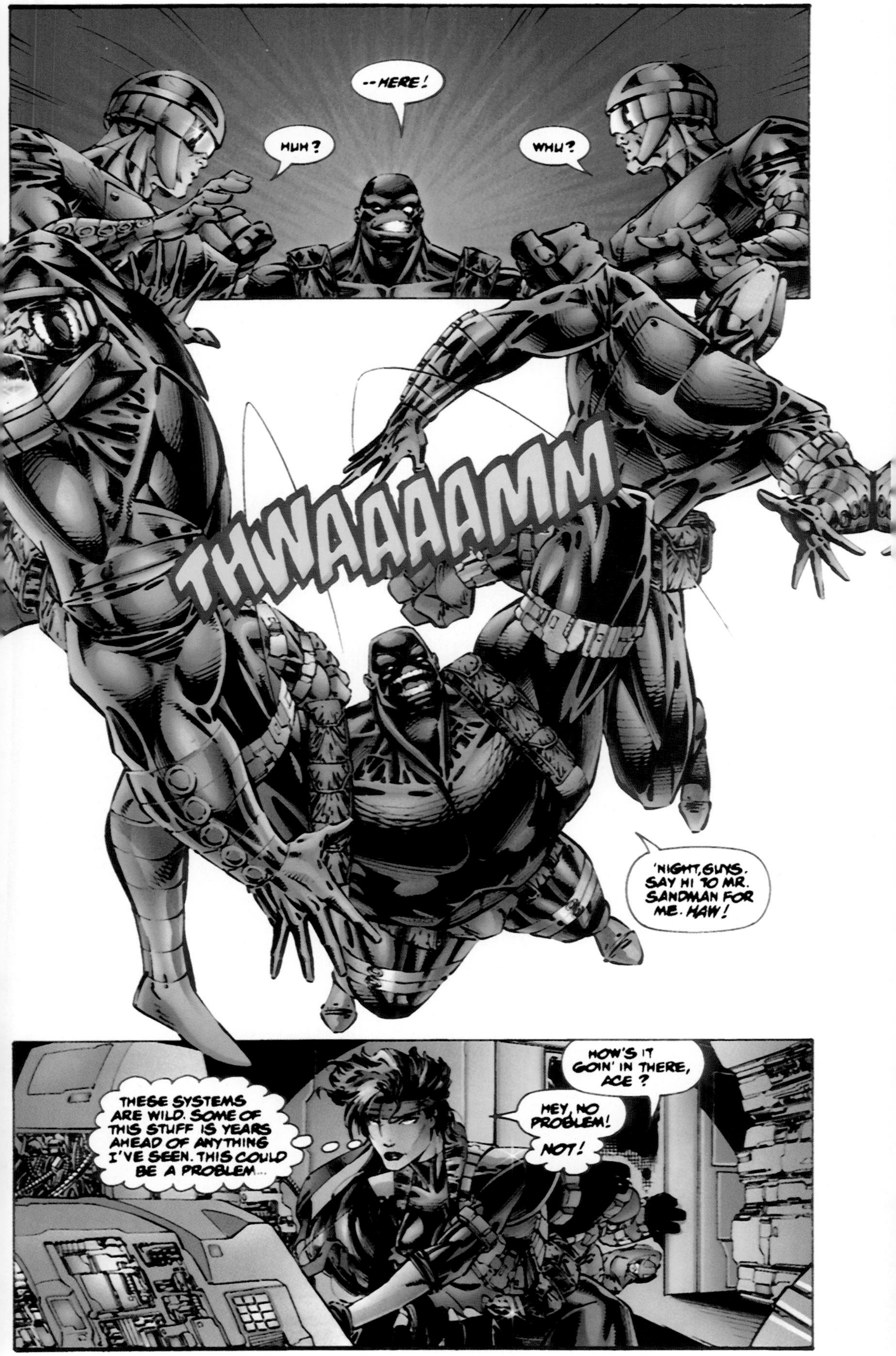
--HERE!
HUH?
WHU?
THWAAAAMM
'NIGHT, GUYS. SAY HI TO MR. SANDMAN FOR ME. HAW!
THESE SYSTEMS ARE WILD. SOME OF THIS STUFF IS YEARS AHEAD OF ANYTHING I'VE SEEN. THIS COULD BE A PROBLEM...
HOW'S IT GOIN' IN THERE, ACE?
HEY, NO PROBLEM!
NOT!

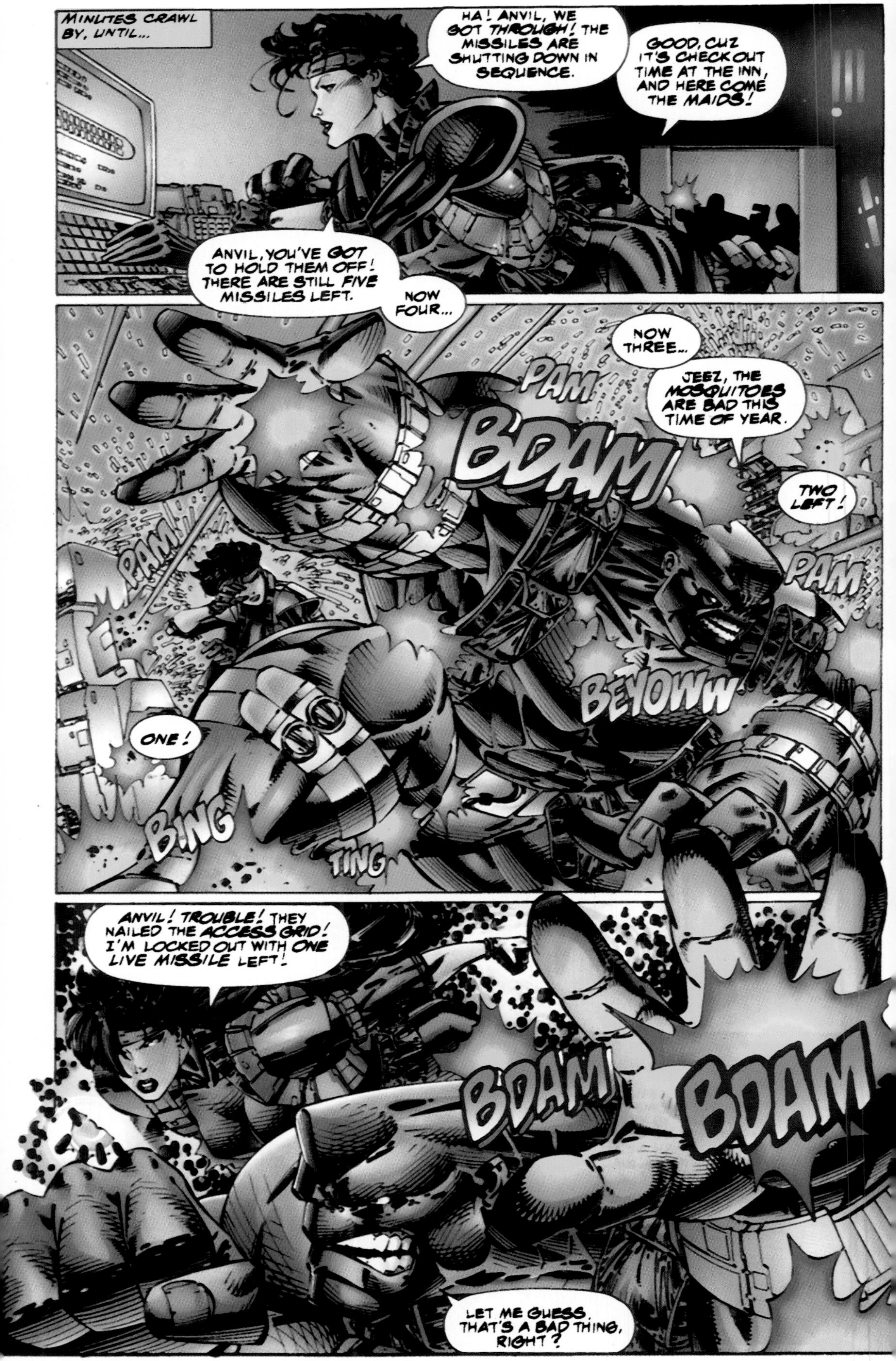
MINUTES CRAWL BY, UNTIL...
HA! ANVIL, WE GOT THROUGH! THE MISSILES ARE SHUTTING DOWN IN SEQUENCE.
GOOD, CUZ IT'S CHECKOUT TIME AT THE INN, AND HERE COME THE MAIDS!
ANVIL, YOU'VE GOT TO HOLD THEM OFF! THERE ARE STILL FIVE MISSILES LEFT.
NOW FOUR...
NOW THREE...
PAM
BDAM
JEEZ, THE MOSQUITOES ARE BAD THIS TIME OF YEAR.
TWO LEFT!
PAM
PAM
BEYOWW
ONE!
BING
TING
ANVIL! TROUBLE! THEY NAILED THE ACCESS GRID! I'M LOCKED OUT WITH ONE LIVE MISSILE LEFT!
BDAM
BDAM
LET ME GUESS. THAT'S A BAD THING, RIGHT?

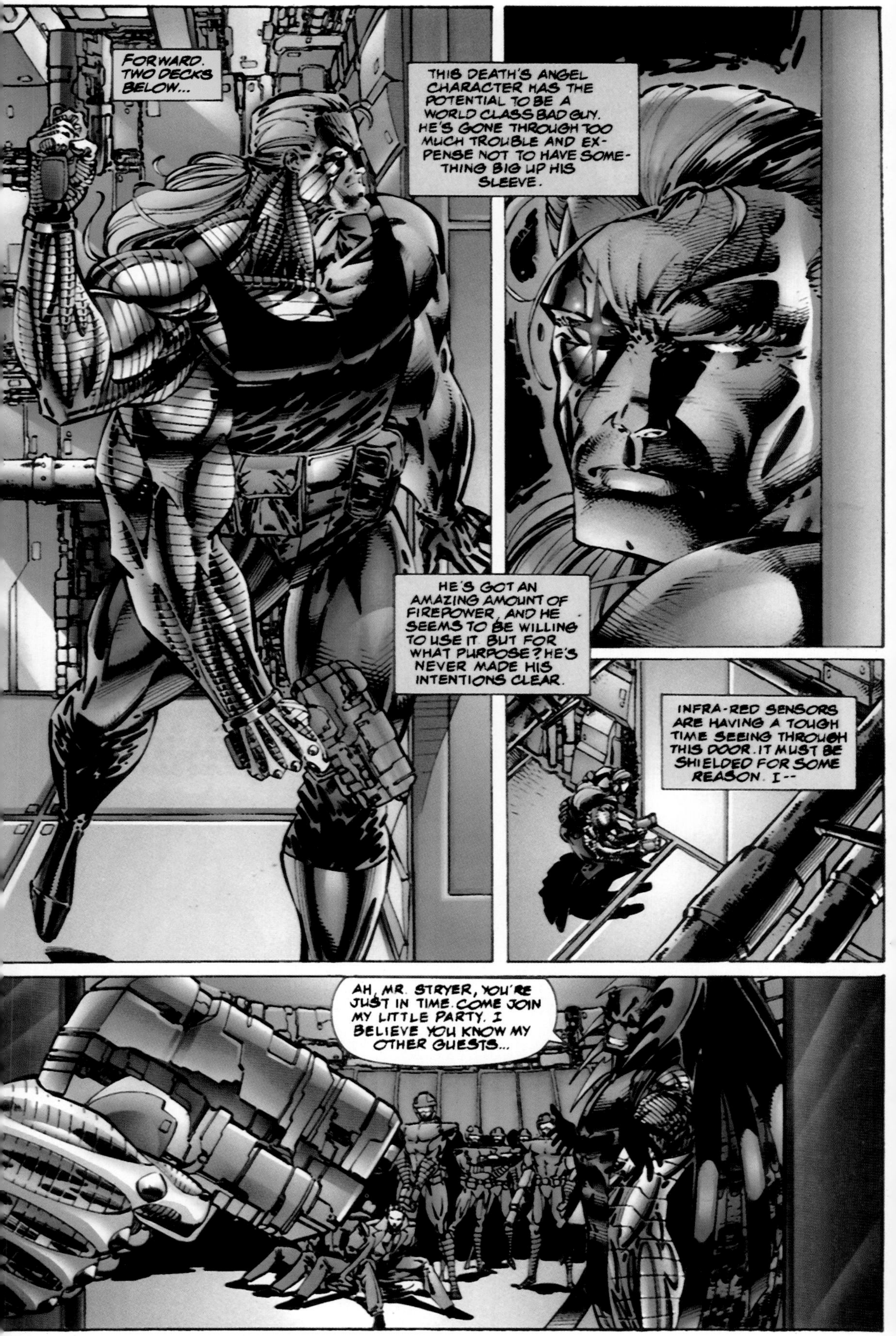
FORWARD. TWO DECKS BELOW...
THIS DEATH'S ANGEL CHARACTER HAS THE POTENTIAL TO BE A WORLD CLASS BAD GUY. HE'S GONE THROUGH TOO MUCH TROUBLE AND EXPENSE NOT TO HAVE SOMETHING BIG UP HIS SLEEVE.
HE'S GOT AN AMAZING AMOUNT OF FIREPOWER, AND HE SEEMS TO BE WILLING TO USE IT. BUT FOR WHAT PURPOSE? HE'S NEVER MADE HIS INTENTIONS CLEAR.
INFRA-RED SENSORS ARE HAVING A TOUGH TIME SEEING THROUGH THIS DOOR. IT MUST BE SHIELDED FOR SOME REASON. I--
AH, MR. STRYER, YOU'RE JUST IN TIME. COME JOIN MY LITTLE PARTY. I BELIEVE YOU KNOW MY OTHER GUESTS...

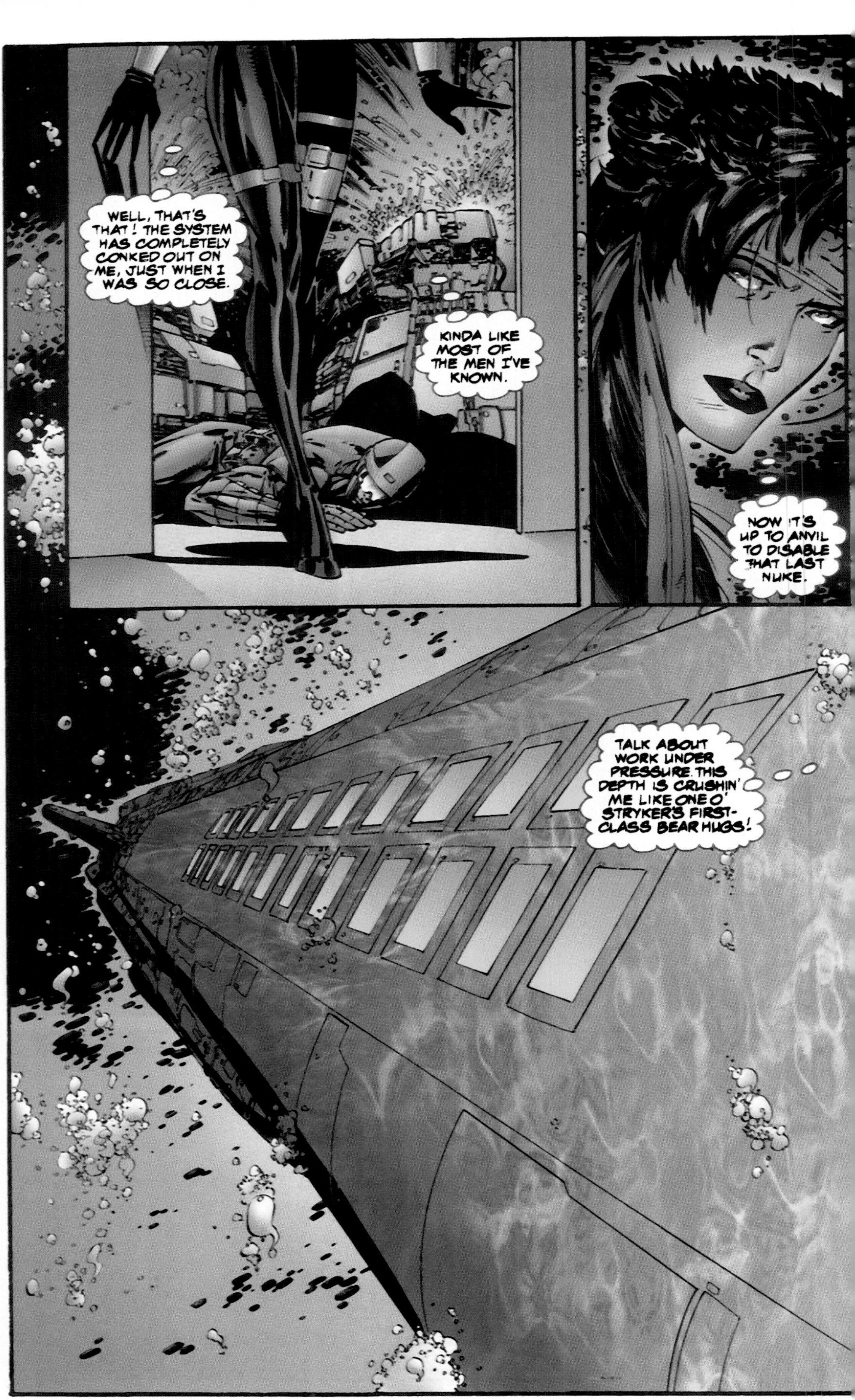
WELL, THAT'S THAT! THE SYSTEM HAS COMPLETELY CONKED OUT ON ME, JUST WHEN I WAS SO CLOSE.
KINDA LIKE MOST OF THE MEN I'VE KNOWN.
NOW IT'S UP TO ANVIL TO DISABLE THAT LAST NUKE.
TALK ABOUT WORK UNDER PRESSURE. THIS DEPTH IS CRUSHIN' ME LIKE ONE O' STRYKER'S FIRST-CLASS BEAR HUGS!

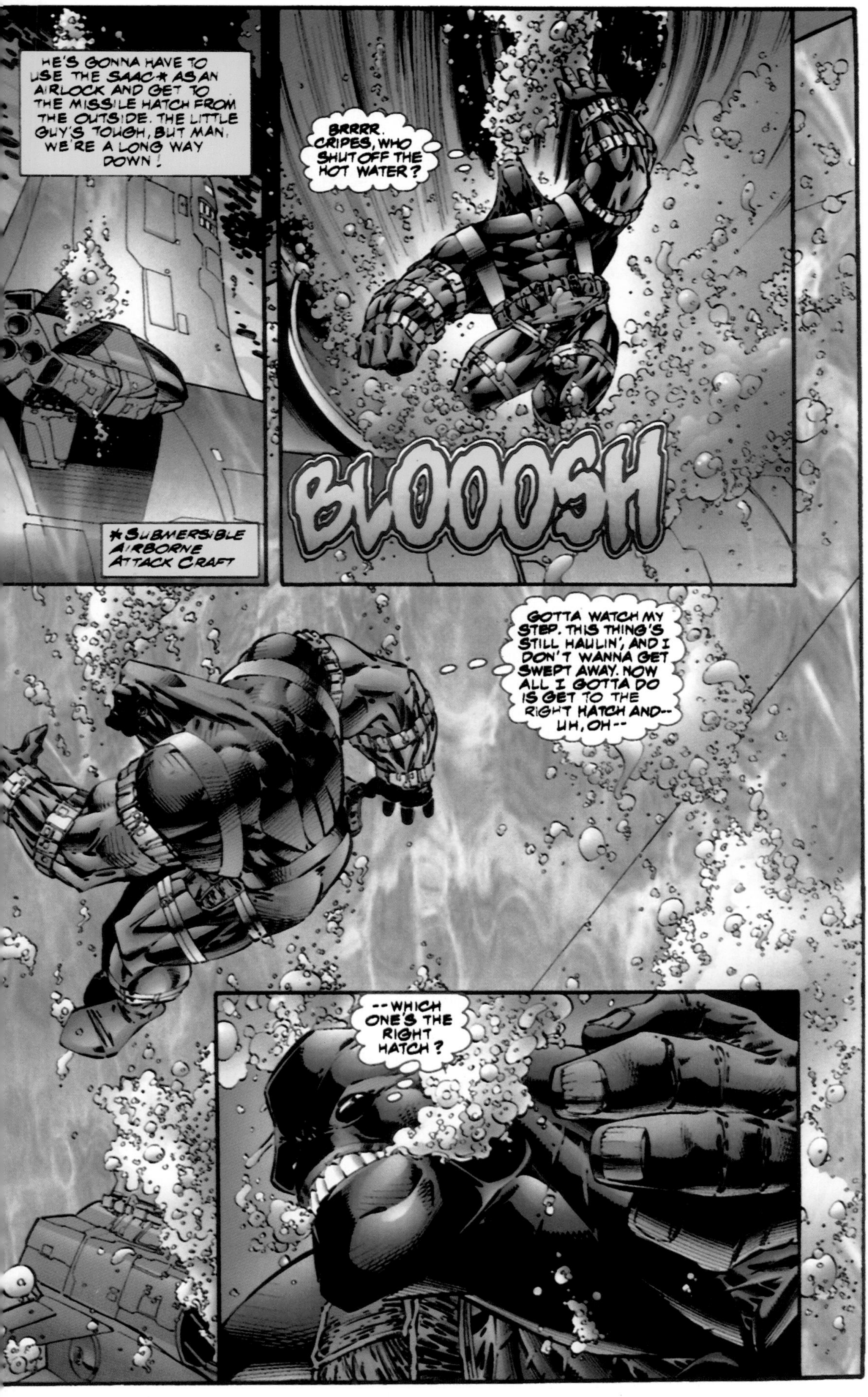
HE'S GONNA HAVE TO USE THE SAAC* AS AN AIRLOCK AND GET TO THE MISSILE HATCH FROM THE OUTSIDE. THE LITTLE GUY'S TOUGH, BUT MAN, WE'RE A LONG WAY DOWN!
*SUBMERSIBLE AIRBORNE ATTACK CRAFT
BRRRR. CRIPES, WHO SHUT OFF THE HOT WATER?
BLOOOSH
GOTTA WATCH MY STEP. THIS THING'S STILL HAULIN', AND I DON'T WANNA GET SWEPT AWAY. NOW ALL I GOTTA DO IS GET TO THE RIGHT HATCH AND-- UH, OH--
--WHICH ONE'S THE RIGHT HATCH?

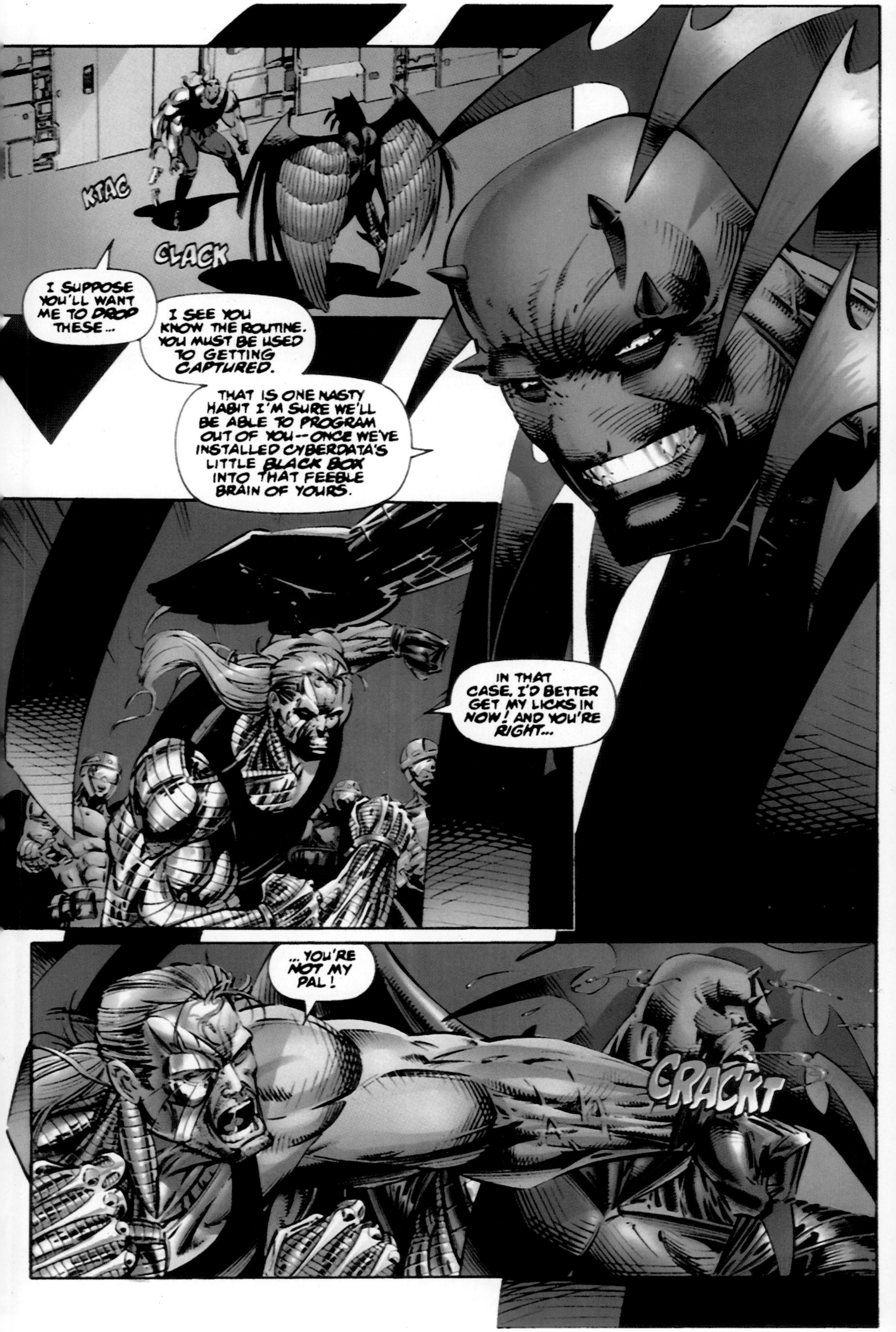
KTAC
CLACK
I SUPPOSE YOU'LL WANT ME TO DROP THESE...
I SEE YOU KNOW THE ROUTINE. YOU MUST BE USED TO GETTING CAPTURED.
THAT IS ONE NASTY HABIT I'M SURE WE'LL BE ABLE TO PROGRAM OUT OF YOU--ONCE WE'VE INSTALLED CYBERDATA'S LITTLE BLACK BOX INTO THAT FEEBLE BRAIN OF YOURS.
IN THAT CASE, I'D BETTER GET MY LICKS IN NOW! AND YOU'RE RIGHT...
...YOU'RE NOT MY PAL!
CRACKT

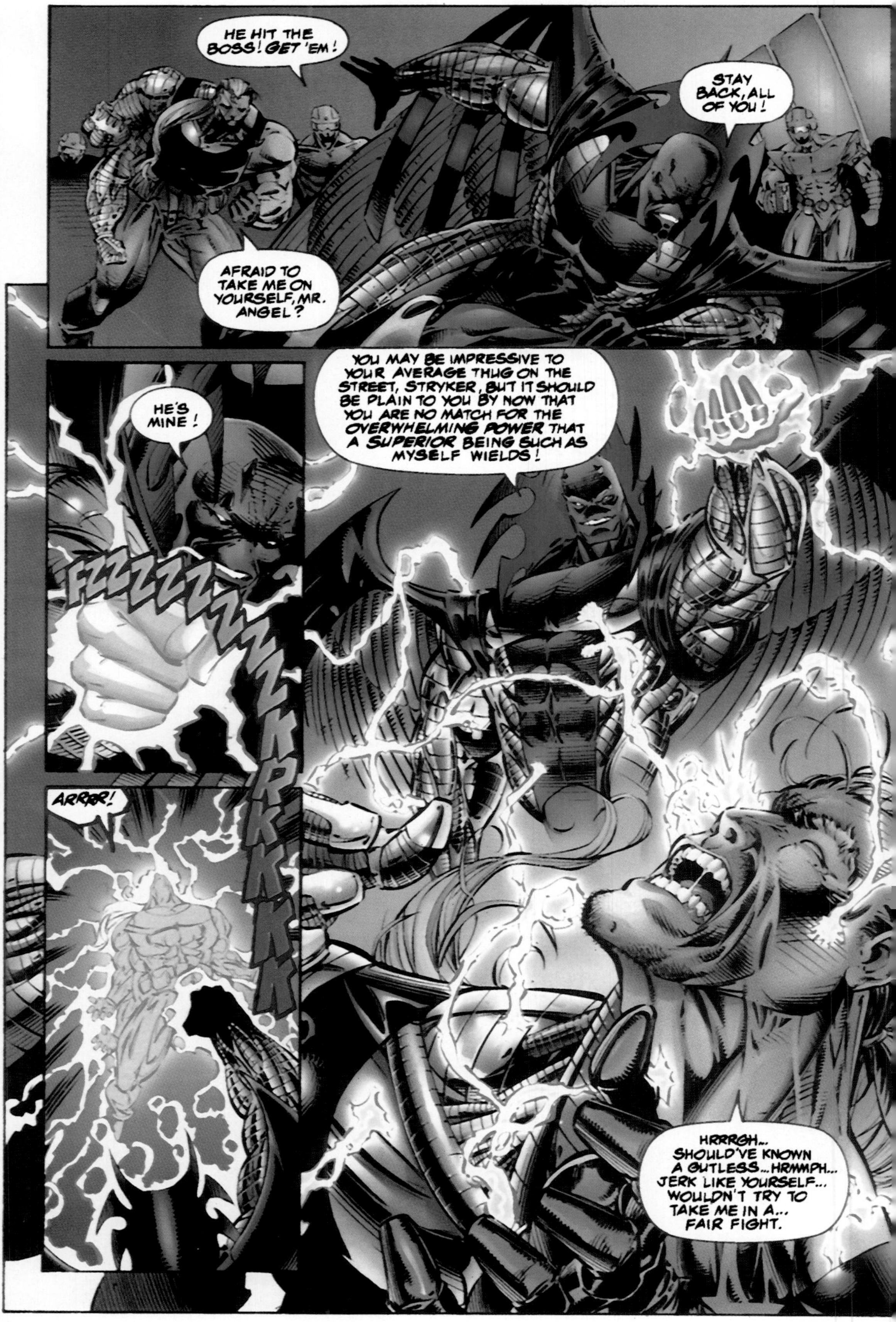
HE HIT THE BOSS! GET 'EM!
STAY BACK, ALL OF YOU!
AFRAID TO TAKE ME ON YOURSELF, MR. ANGEL?
HE'S MINE!
YOU MAY BE IMPRESSIVE TO YOUR AVERAGE THUG ON THE STREET, STRYKER, BUT IT SHOULD BE PLAIN TO YOU BY NOW THAT YOU ARE NO MATCH FOR THE OVERWHELMING POWER THAT A SUPERIOR BEING SUCH AS MYSELF WIELDS!
FZZZZZZZZZZZZZKRRKKKK
ARRRR!
HRRRGH... SHOULD'VE KNOWN A GUTLESS...HRMMPH... JERK LIKE YOURSELF... WOULDN'T TRY TO TAKE ME IN A... FAIR FIGHT.

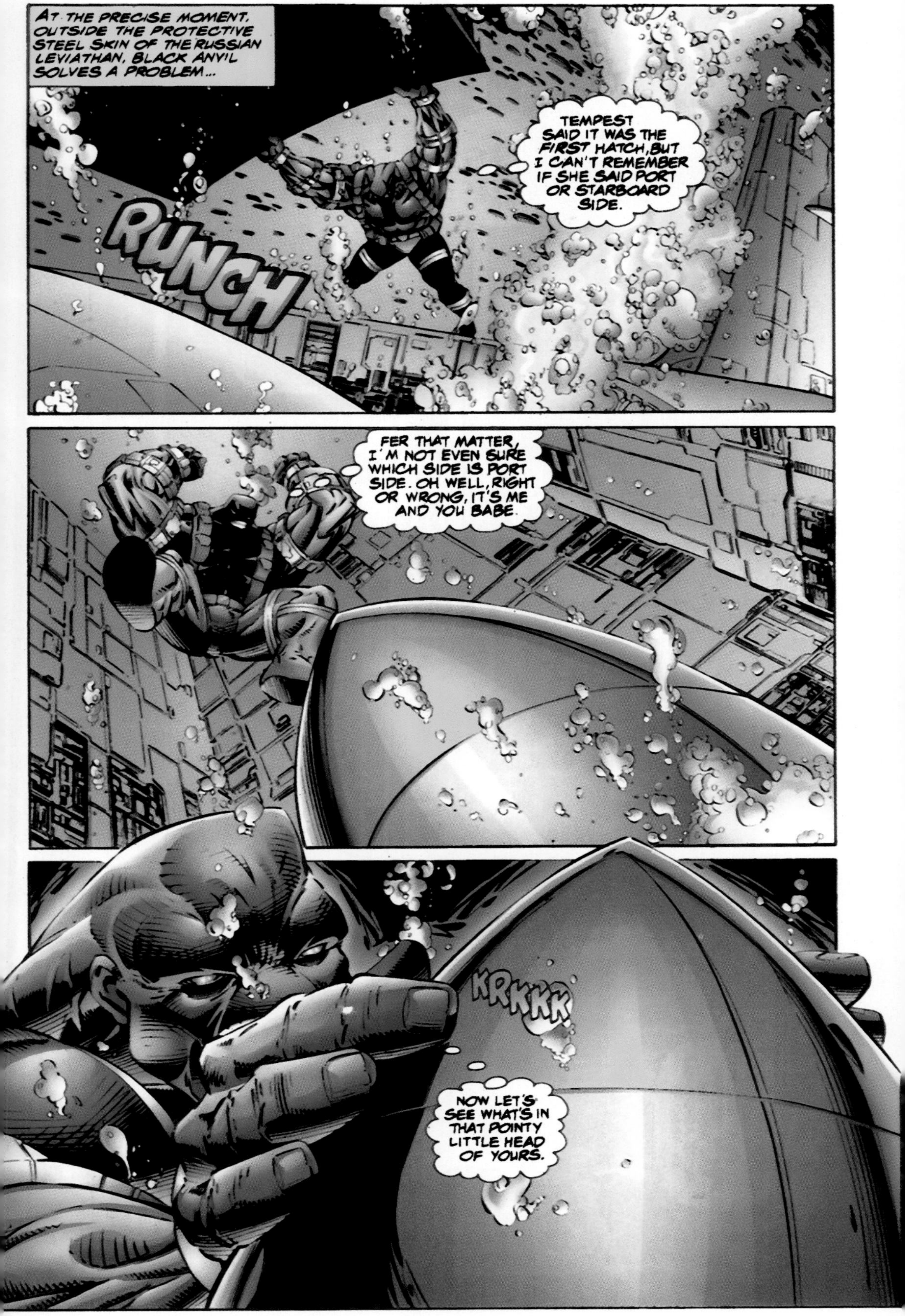
AT THE PRECISE MOMENT, OUTSIDE THE PROTECTIVE STEEL SKIN OF THE RUSSIAN LEVIATHAN, BLACK ANVIL SOLVES A PROBLEM...
TEMPEST SAID IT WAS THE FIRST HATCH, BUT I CAN'T REMEMBER IF SHE SAID PORT OR STARBOARD SIDE.
RUNCH
FER THAT MATTER, I'M NOT EVEN SURE WHICH SIDE IS PORT SIDE. OH WELL, RIGHT OR WRONG, IT'S ME AND YOU BABE.
KRKKK
NOW LET'S SEE WHAT'S IN THAT POINTY LITTLE HEAD OF YOURS.

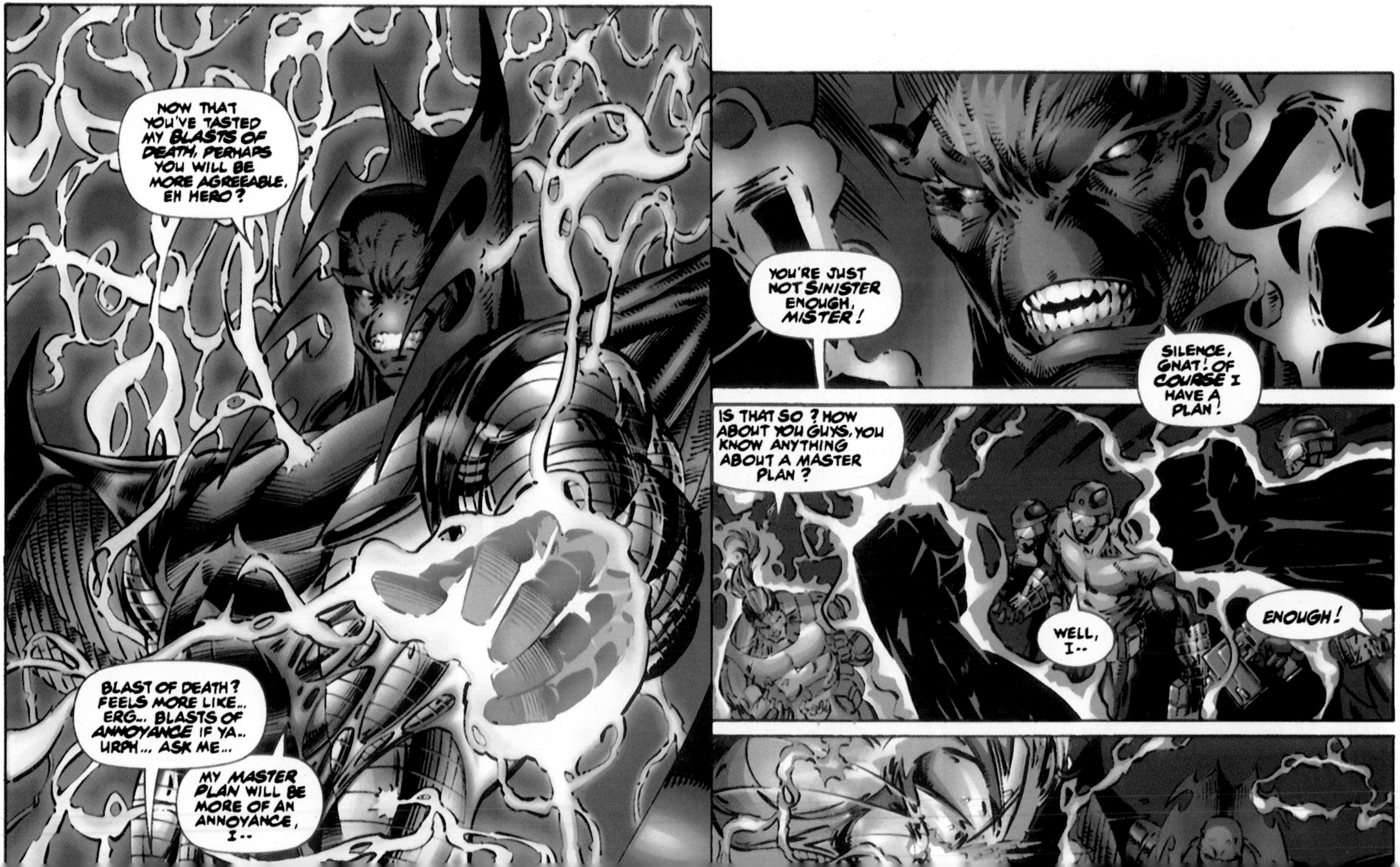
NOW THAT YOU'VE TASTED MY BLASTS OF DEATH, PERHAPS YOU WILL BE MORE AGREEABLE, EH HERO?
BLAST OF DEATH? FEELS MORE LIKE... ERG... BLASTS OF ANNOYANCE IF YA... URPH... ASK ME...
MY MASTER PLAN WILL BE MORE OF AN ANNOYANCE, I--
YOU'RE JUST NOT SINISTER ENOUGH, MISTER!
SILENCE, GNAT! OF COURSE I HAVE A PLAN!
IS THAT SO? HOW ABOUT YOU GUYS, YOU KNOW ANYTHING ABOUT A MASTER PLAN?
WELL, I--
ENOUGH!

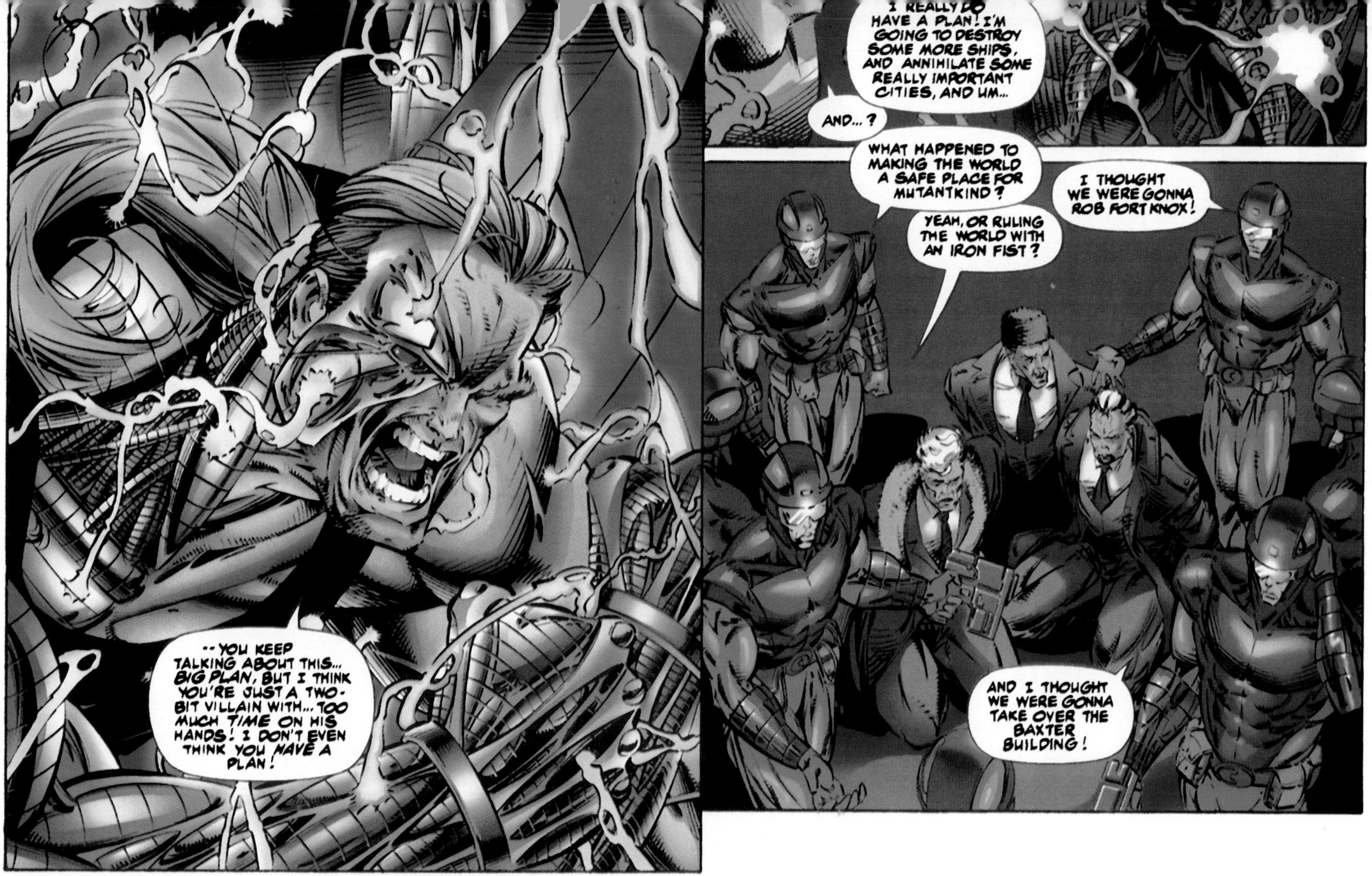

--YOU KEEP TALKING ABOUT THIS... BIG PLAN, BUT I THINK YOU'RE JUST A TWO-BIT VILLAIN WITH... TOO MUCH TIME ON HIS HANDS! I DON'T EVEN THINK YOU HAVE A PLAN!
I REALLY DO HAVE A PLAN! I'M GOING TO DESTROY SOME MORE SHIPS, AND ANNIHILATE SOME REALLY IMPORTANT CITIES, AND UM...
AND...?
WHAT HAPPENED TO MAKING THE WORLD A SAFE PLACE FOR MUTANTKIND?
YEAH, OR RULING THE WORLD WITH AN IRON FIST?
I THOUGHT WE WERE GONNA ROB FORT KNOX!
AND I THOUGHT WE WERE GONNA TAKE OVER THE BAXTER BUILDING!

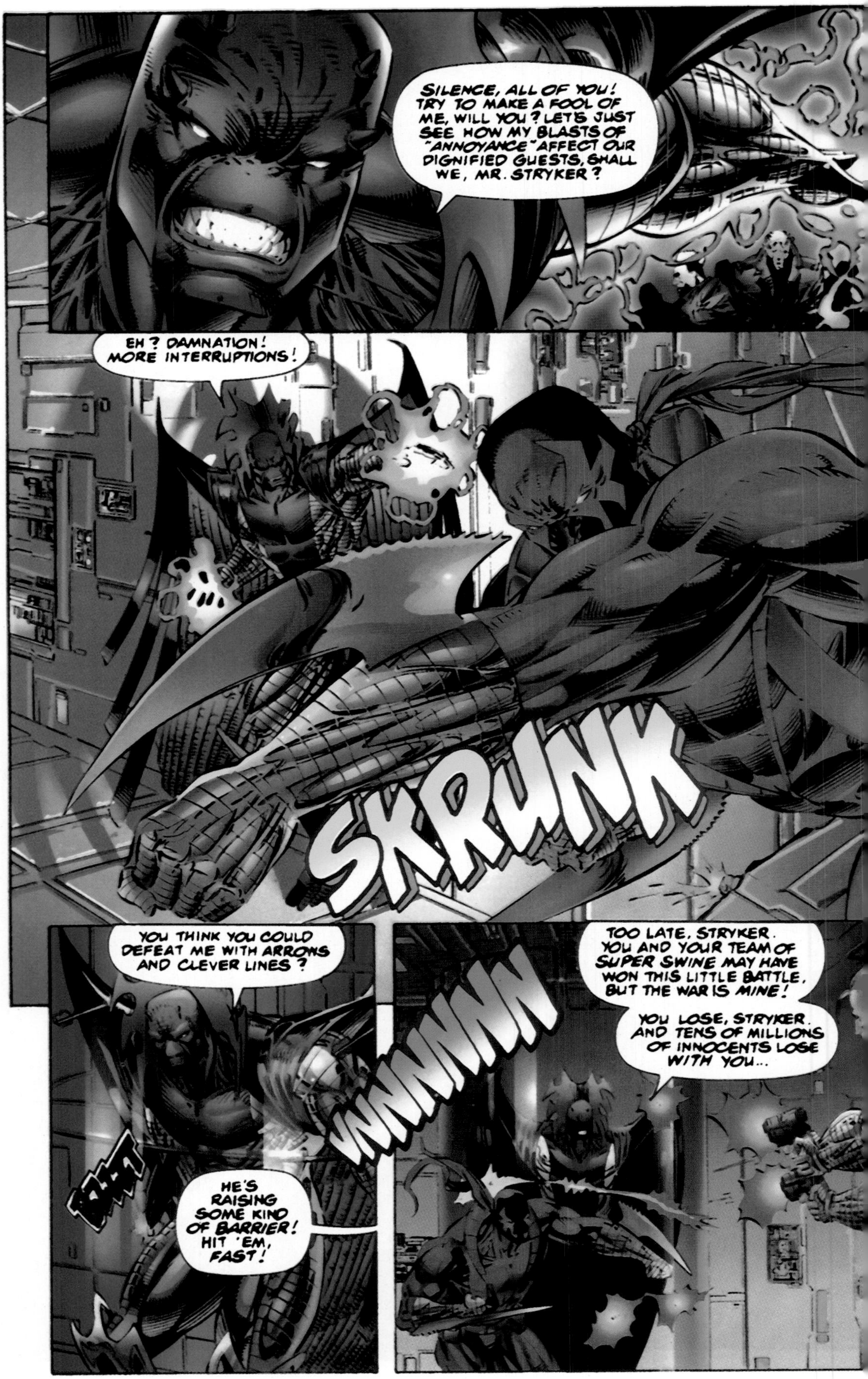
SILENCE, ALL OF YOU! TRY TO MAKE A FOOL OF ME, WILL YOU? LET'S JUST SEE HOW MY BLASTS OF "ANNOYANCE" AFFECT OUR DIGNIFIED GUESTS, SHALL WE, MR. STRYKER?
EH? DAMNATION! MORE INTERRUPTIONS!
SKRUNK
YOU THINK YOU COULD DEFEAT ME WITH ARROWS AND CLEVER LINES?
VNNNNNNN
HE'S RAISING SOME KIND OF BARRIER! HIT 'EM, FAST!
TOO LATE, STRYKER. YOU AND YOUR TEAM OF SUPER SWINE MAY HAVE WON THIS LITTLE BATTLE, BUT THE WAR IS MINE!
YOU LOSE, STRYKER. AND TENS OF MILLIONS OF INNOCENTS LOSE WITH YOU...

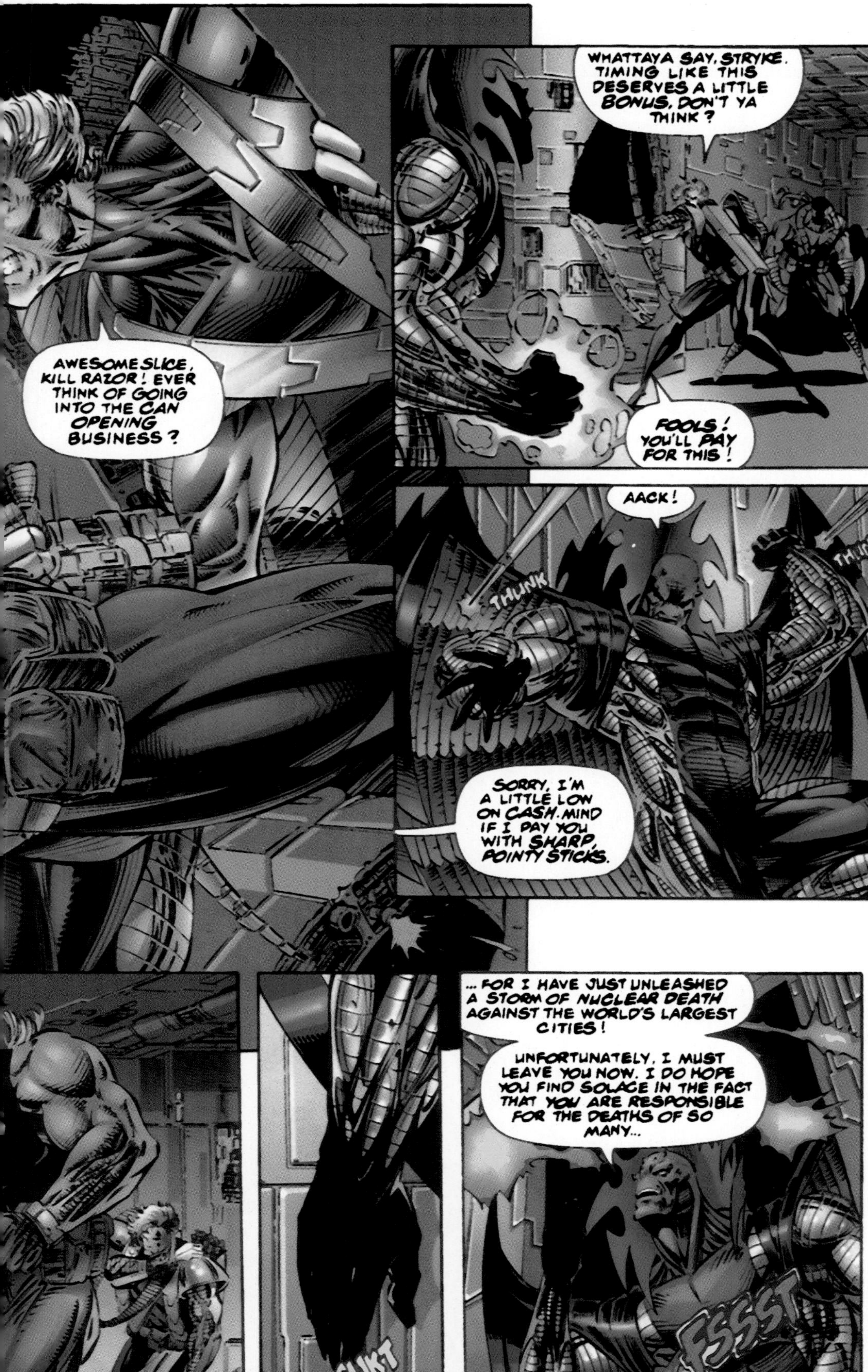
AWESOME SLICE, KILL RAZOR! EVER THINK OF GOING INTO THE CAN OPENING BUSINESS?
WHATTAYA SAY, STRYKE. TIMING LIKE THIS DESERVES A LITTLE BONUS, DON'T YA THINK?
FOOLS! YOU'LL PAY FOR THIS!
AACK!
THUNK
THUNK
SORRY, I'M A LITTLE LOW ON CASH. MIND IF I PAY YOU WITH SHARP, POINTY STICKS.
CLIKT
...FOR I HAVE JUST UNLEASHED A STORM OF NUCLEAR DEATH AGAINST THE WORLD'S LARGEST CITIES!
UNFORTUNATELY, I MUST LEAVE YOU NOW. I DO HOPE YOU FIND SOLACE IN THE FACT THAT YOU ARE RESPONSIBLE FOR THE DEATHS OF SO MANY...
FSSST

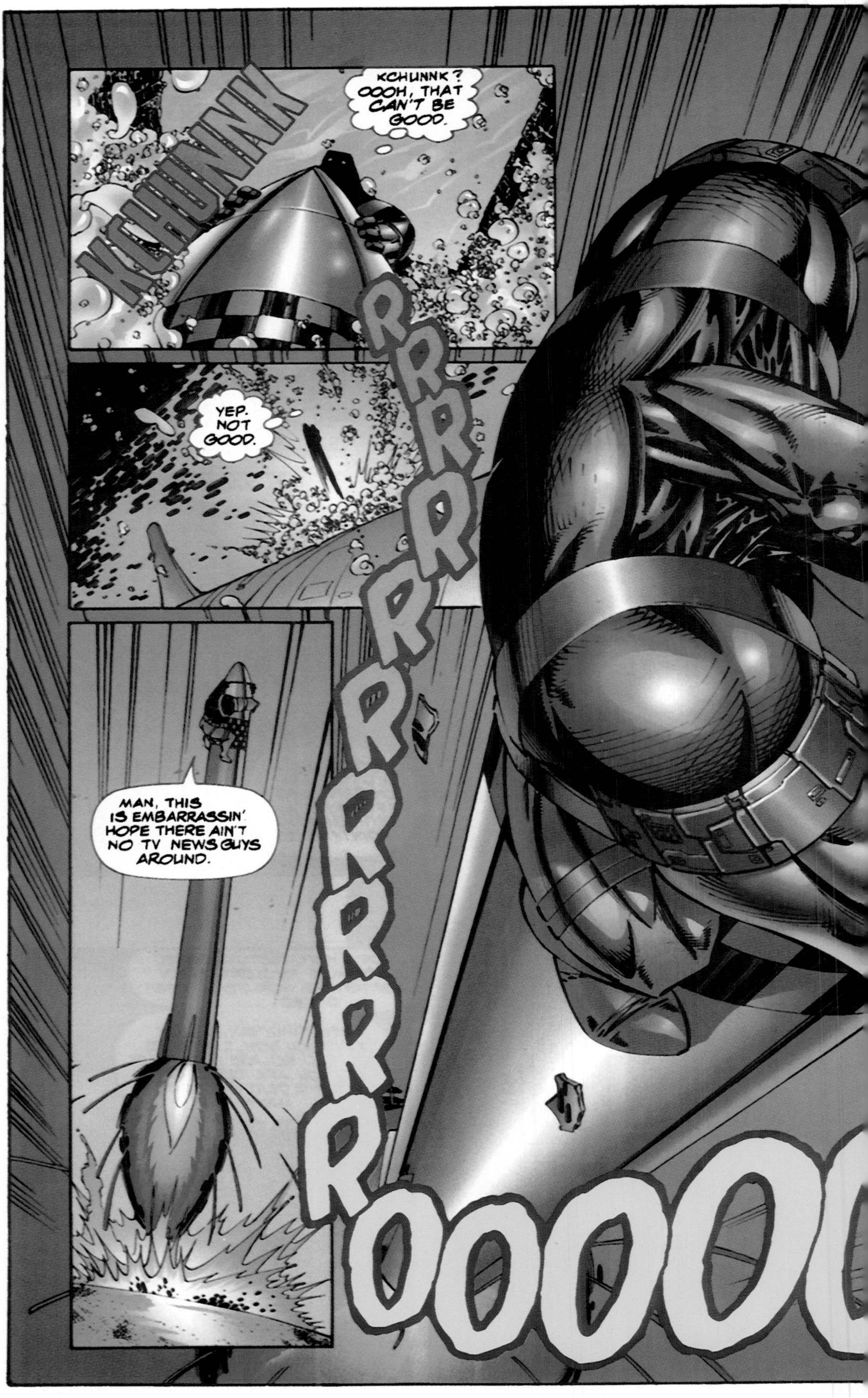
KCHUNNK
KCHUNNK? OOOH, THAT CAN'T BE GOOD.
YEP. NOT GOOD.
MAN, THIS IS EMBARRASSIN'. HOPE THERE AIN'T NO TV NEWS GUYS AROUND.
RRRRRRRRRRRROOOOO

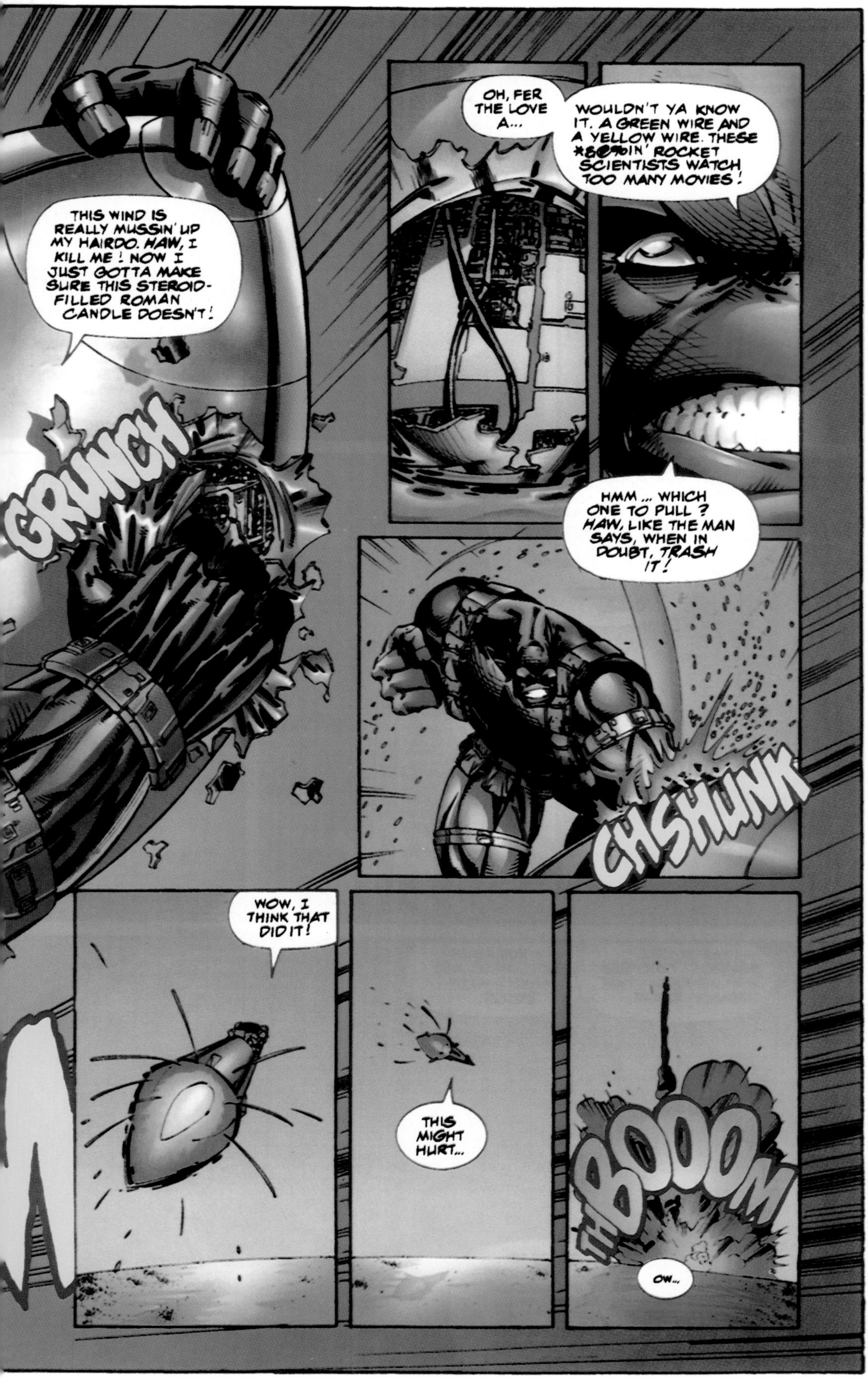

THIS WIND IS REALLY MUSSIN' UP MY HAIRDO. HAW, I KILL ME! NOW I JUST GOTTA MAKE SURE THIS STEROID-FILLED ROMAN CANDLE DOESN'T!
GRUNCH
OH, FER THE LOVE A...
WOULDN'T YA KNOW IT. A GREEN WIRE AND A YELLOW WIRE. THESE *&@%IN' ROCKET SCIENTISTS WATCH TOO MANY MOVIES!
HMM ... WHICH ONE TO PULL? HAW, LIKE THE MAN SAYS, WHEN IN DOUBT, TRASH IT!
CHSHUNK
WOW, I THINK THAT DID IT!
THIS MIGHT HURT...
THBOOOM
OW...

AS THE SHOCK WAVE FROM THE NON-NUCLEAR EXPLOSION ROCKS THE SUBMARINE, A VILLAIN MAKES GOOD HIS ESCAPE...

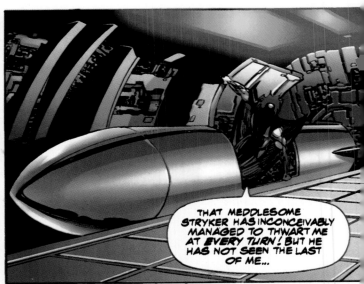

CURSES!

THAT MEDDLESOME STRYKER HAS INCONCEIVABLY MANAGED TO THWART ME AT EVERY TURN! BUT HE HAS NOT SEEN THE LAST OF ME...

NO MATTER WHAT THE COST, REVENGE WILL BE MINE! SO SWEARS **DEATH'S AN—**

WHA? I'VE LOST CONTROL OF THE VECTORING THRUSTERS! I'M GOING DOWN! I'LL CRACK LIKE AN EGG! SOMEBODY HELP MEEE

KREEEEEK

THANK YOU, TEMPEST, FOR FREE-ING US FROM THAT DEMON SCUM.

MY PLEASURE! YOU GIRLS ARE HANDY WITH TOOLS...

YES, IT IS AMAZING HOW A FEW LOOSE SCREWS WILL AFFECT THE PERFORMANCE OF AN ESCAPE POD...

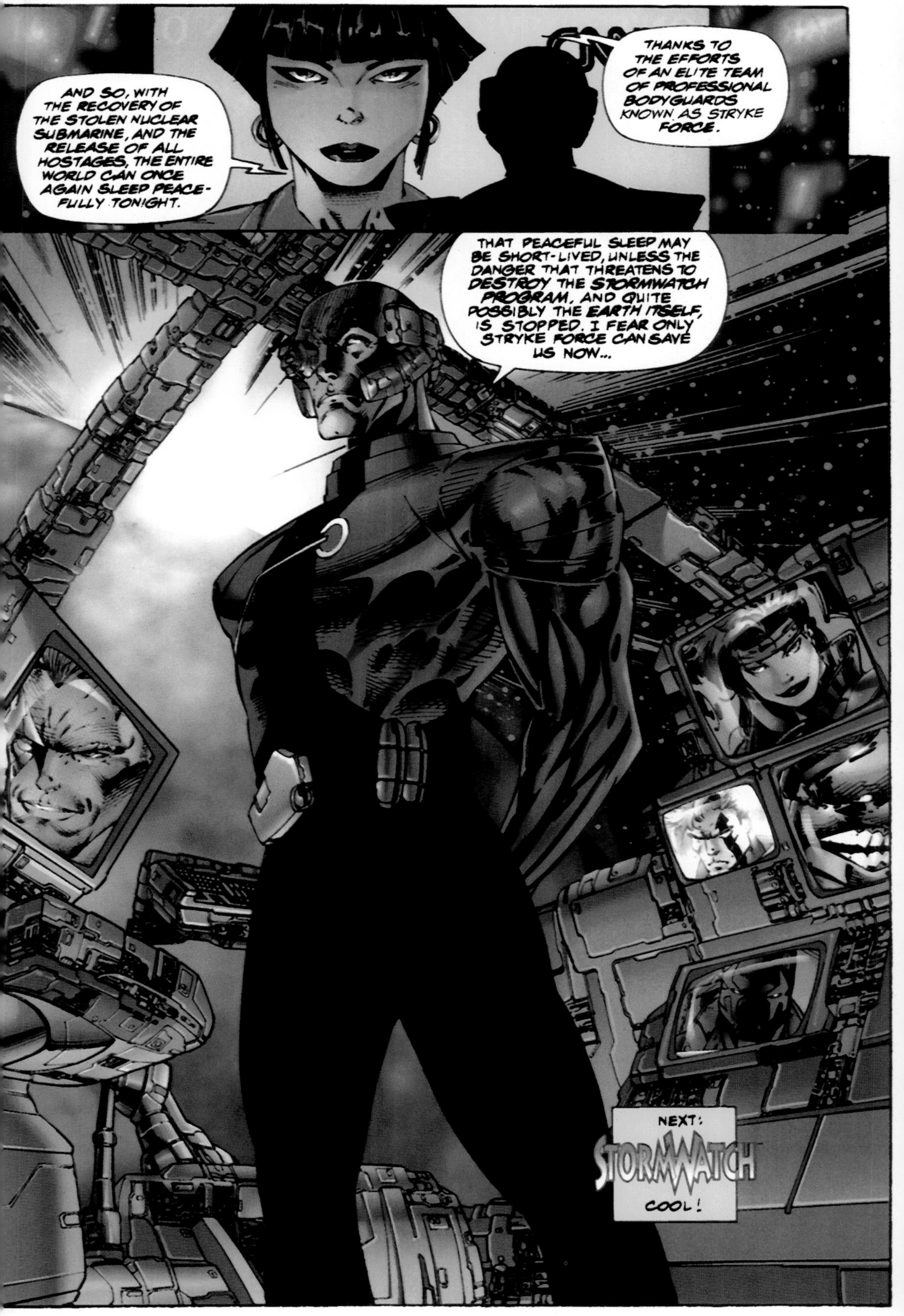
AND SO, WITH THE RECOVERY OF THE STOLEN NUCLEAR SUBMARINE, AND THE RELEASE OF ALL HOSTAGES, THE ENTIRE WORLD CAN ONCE AGAIN SLEEP PEACE-FULLY TONIGHT.
THANKS TO THE EFFORTS OF AN ELITE TEAM OF PROFESSIONAL BODYGUARDS KNOWN AS STRYKE FORCE.
THAT PEACEFUL SLEEP MAY BE SHORT-LIVED, UNLESS THE DANGER THAT THREATENS TO DESTROY THE STORMWATCH PROGRAM, AND QUITE POSSIBLY THE EARTH ITSELF, IS STOPPED. I FEAR ONLY STRYKE FORCE CAN SAVE US NOW...
NEXT:
STORMWATCH
COOL!

Art by: Marc Silvestri and Todd McWeeney

FIN.

COVER GALLERY

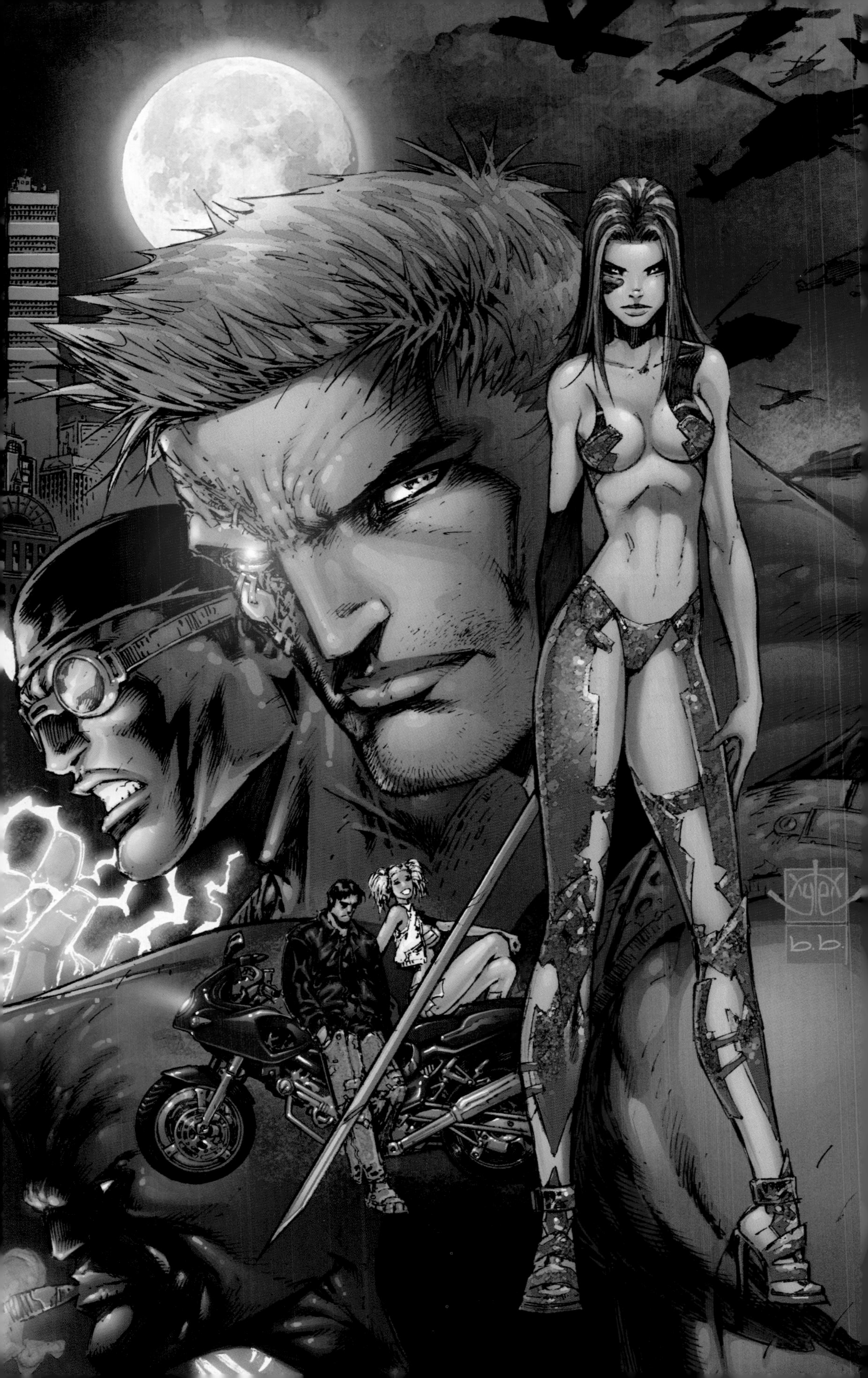

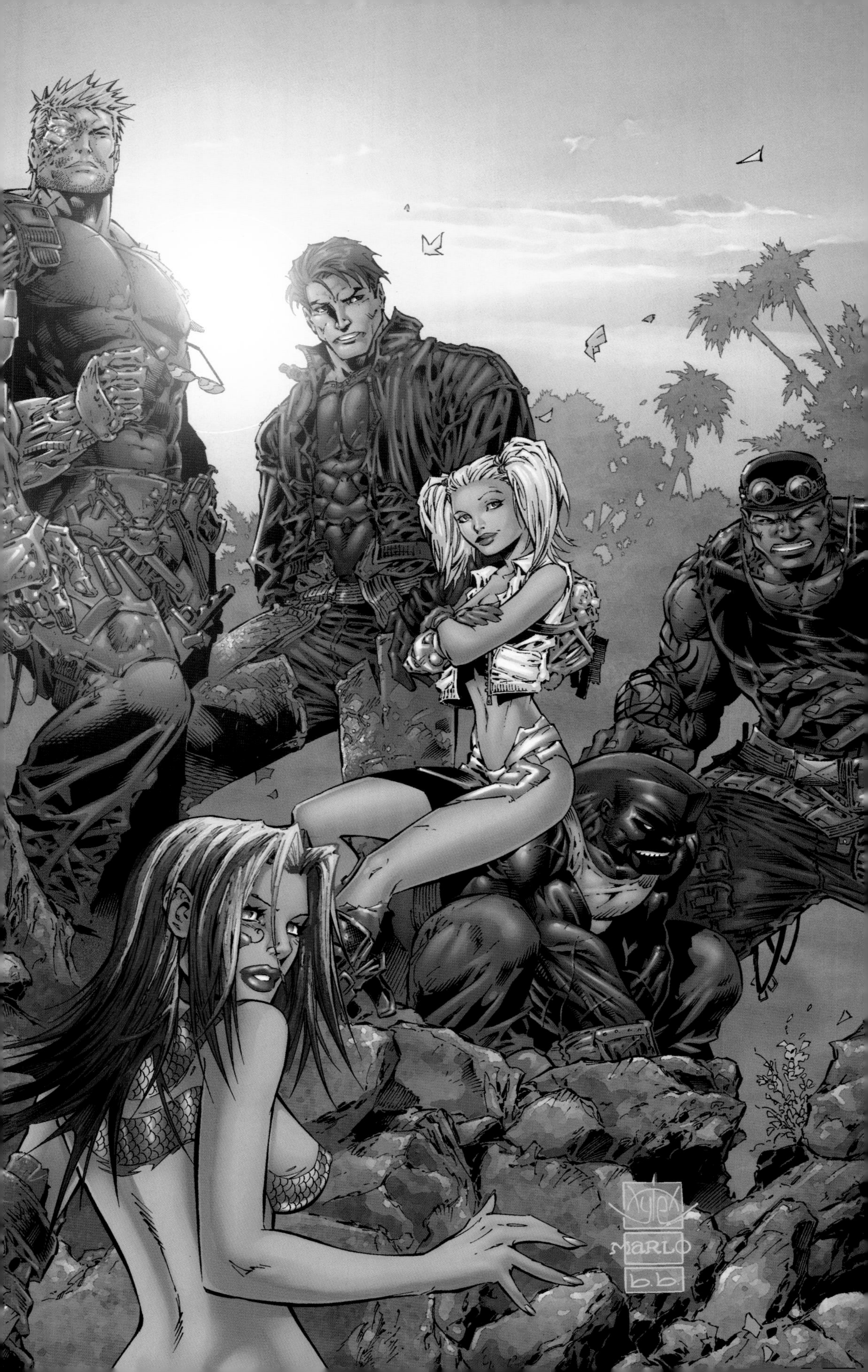

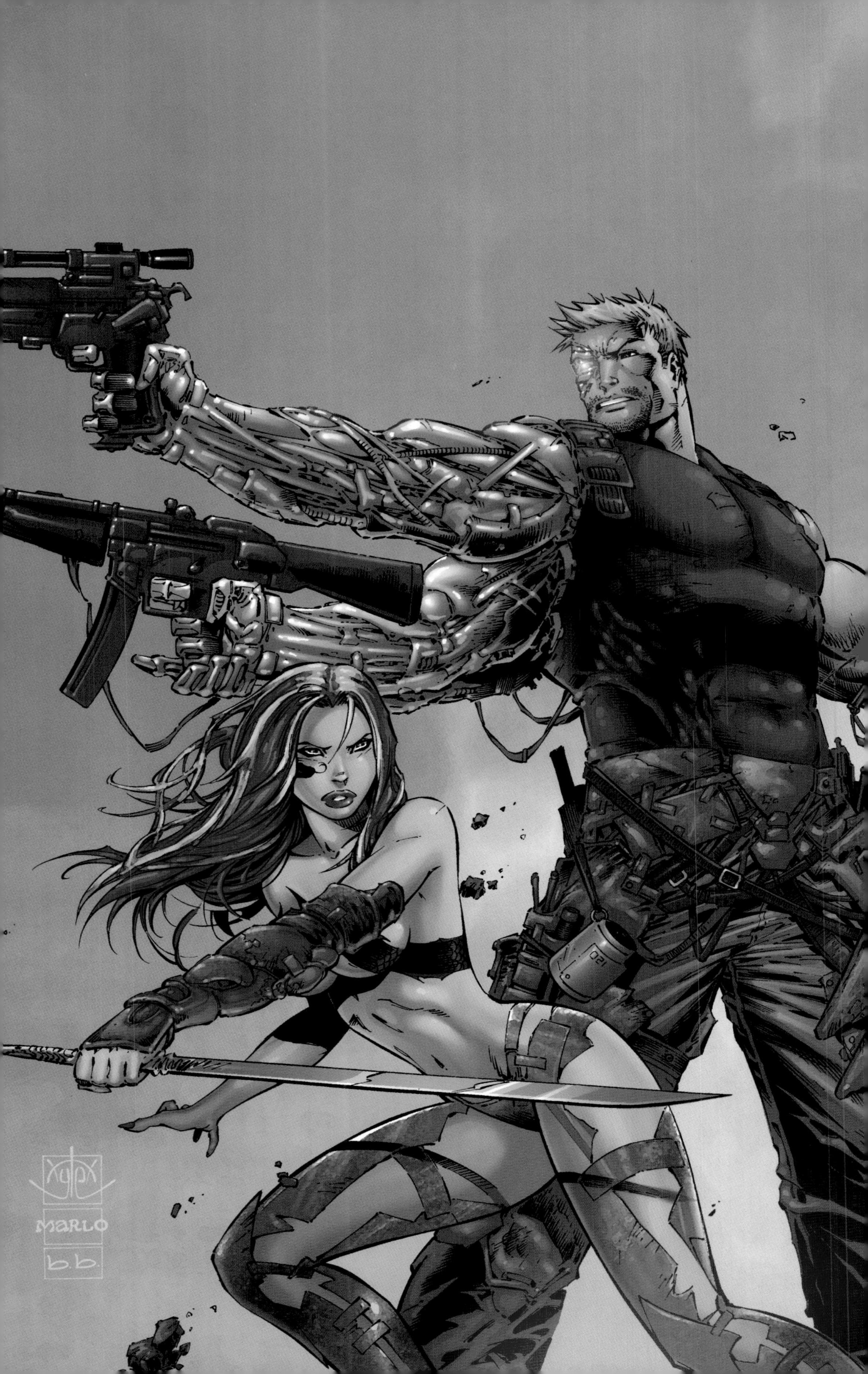
MARLO
b.b.

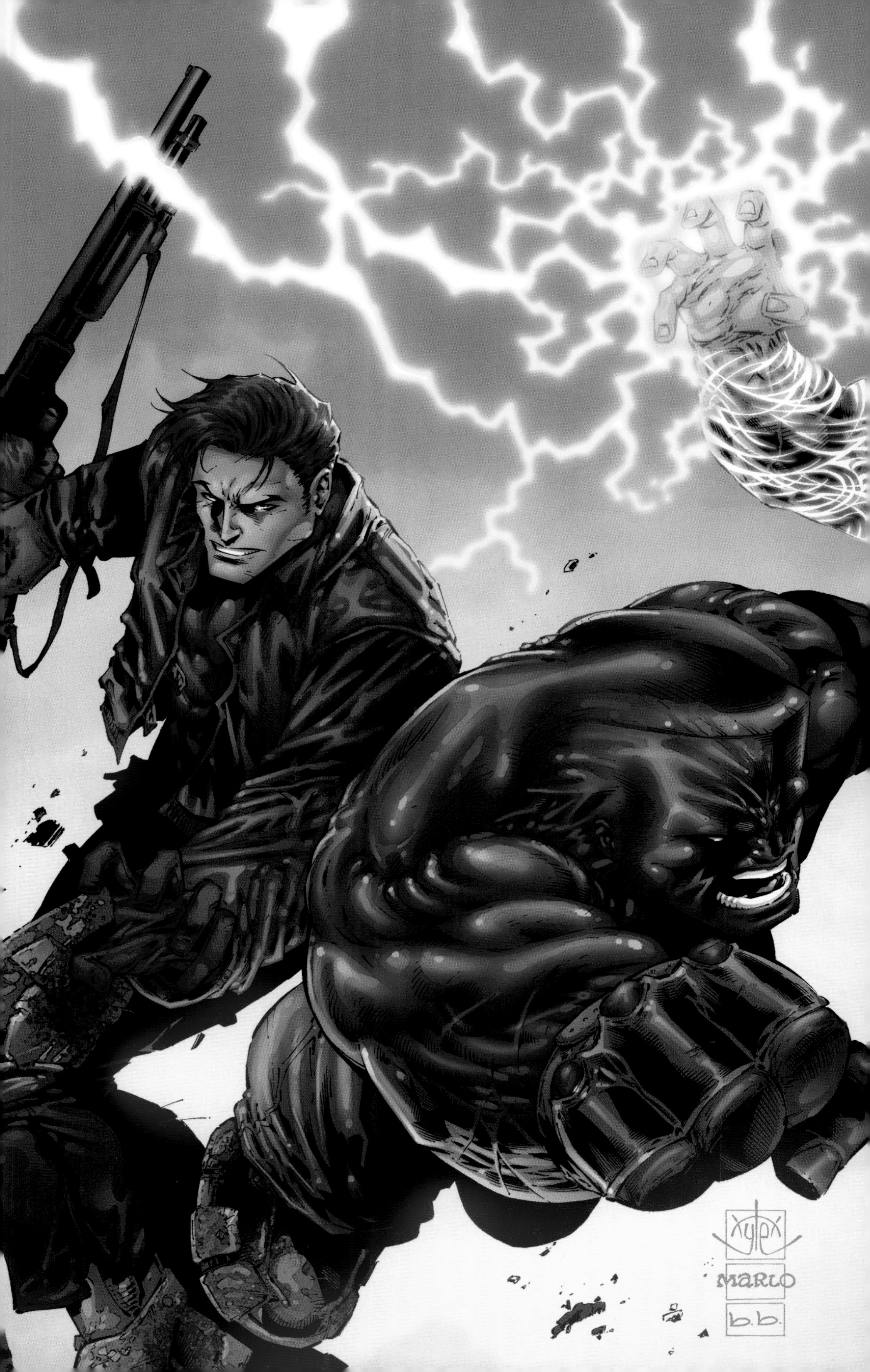
MARLO
b.b.

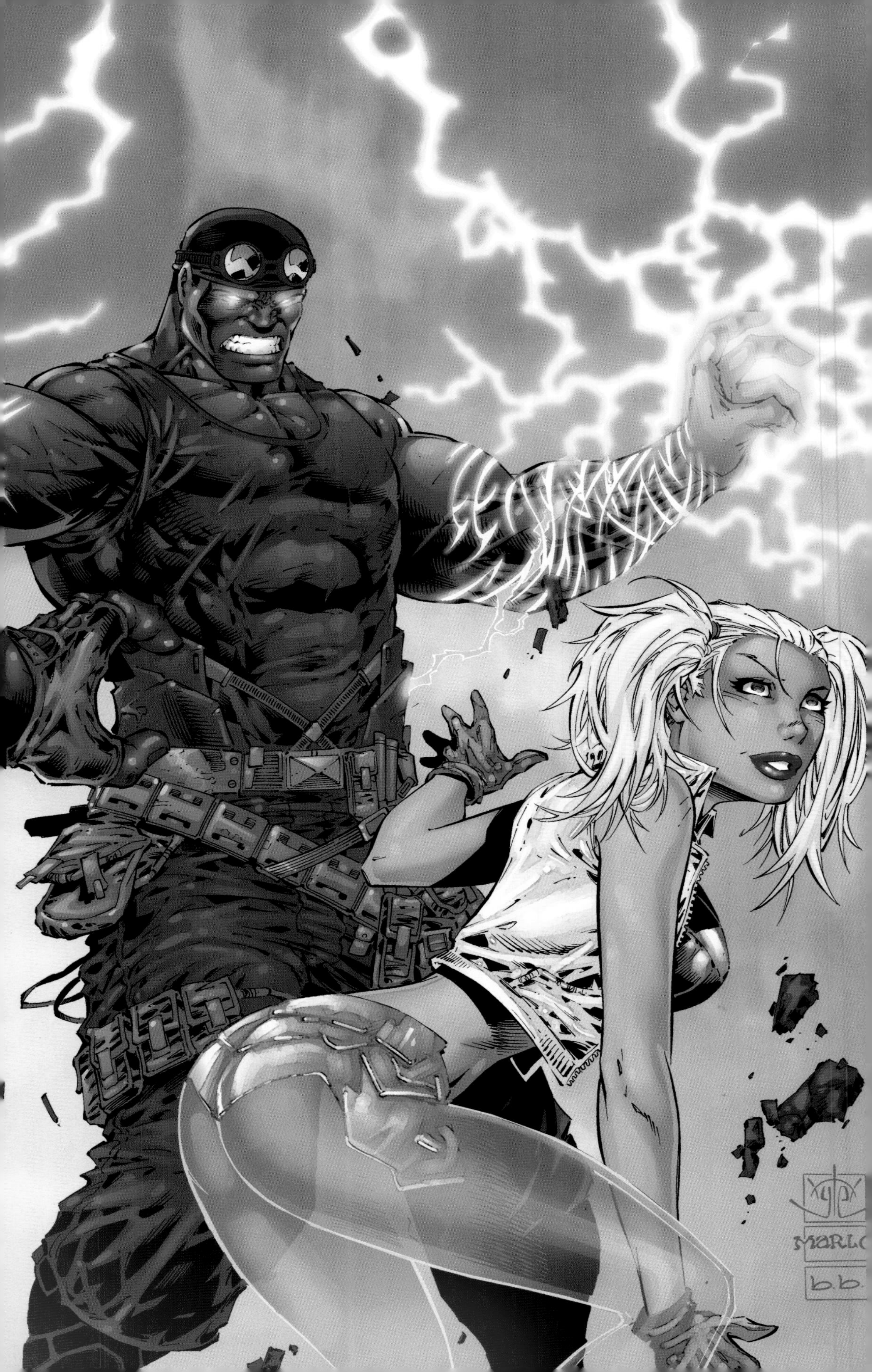
MARLO
b.b.

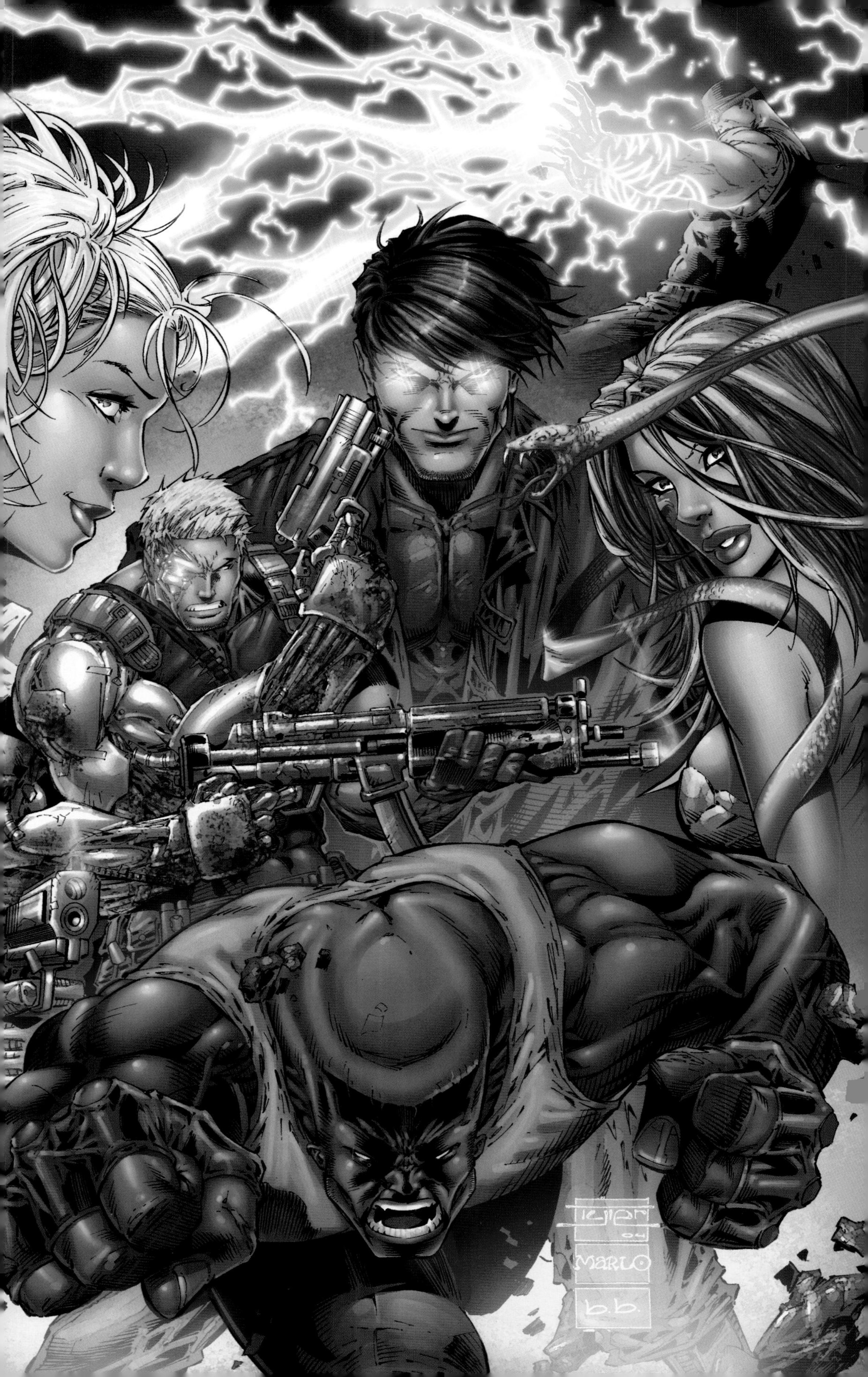
MARLO
b.b.

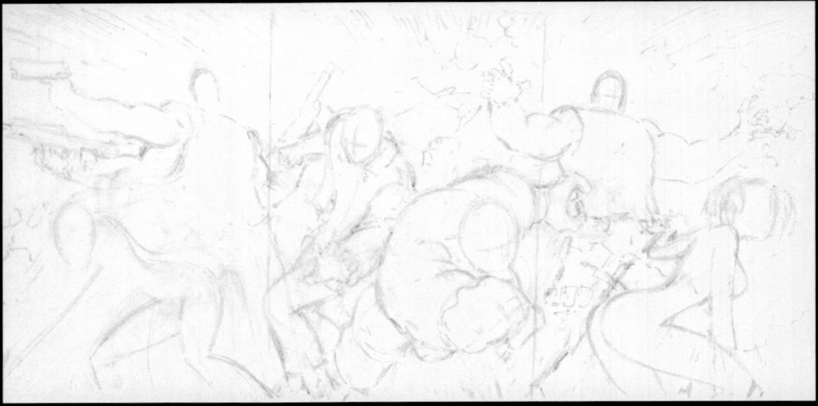

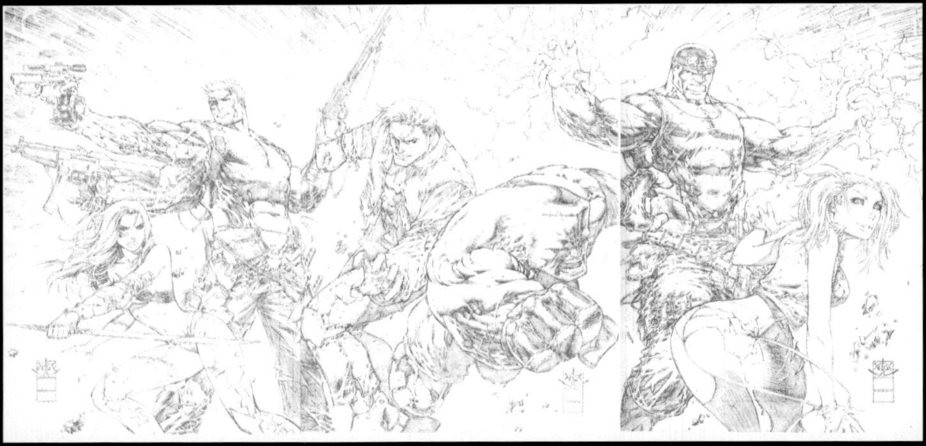

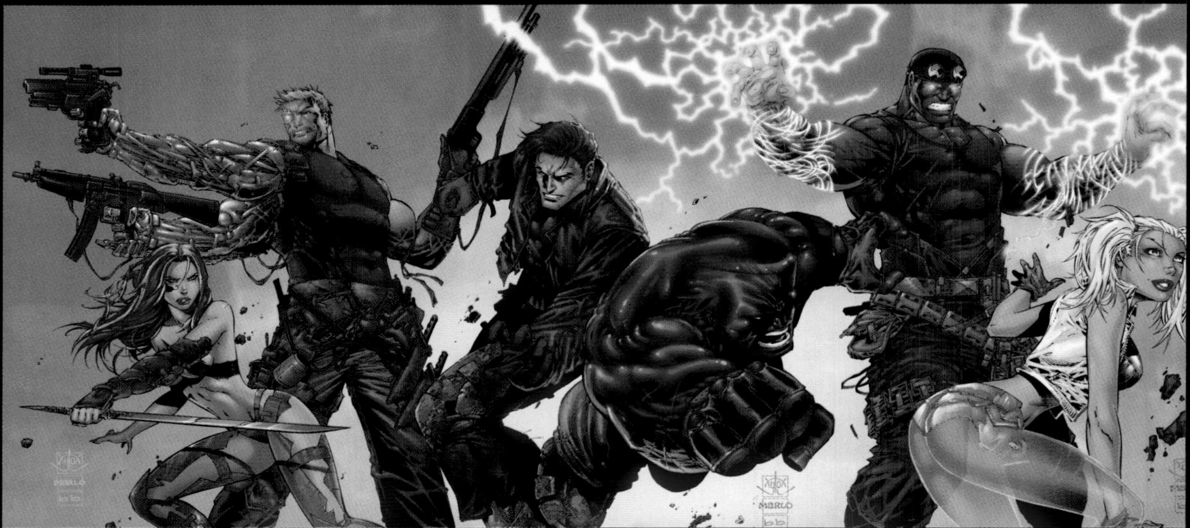

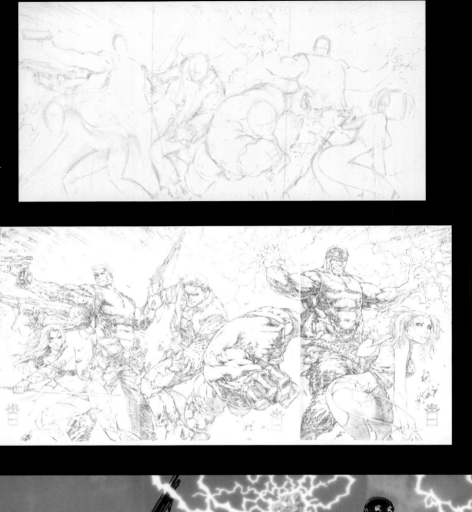

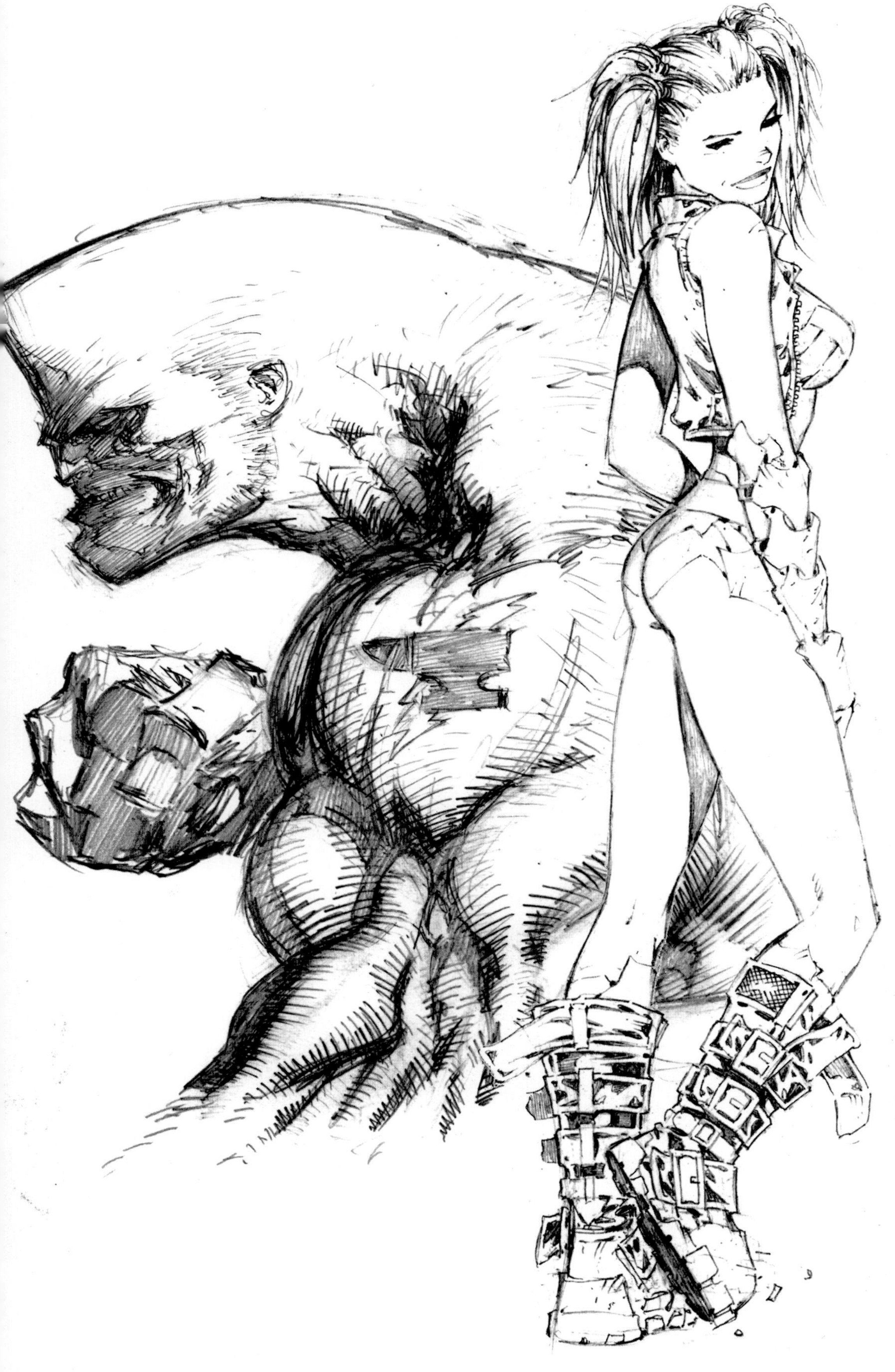

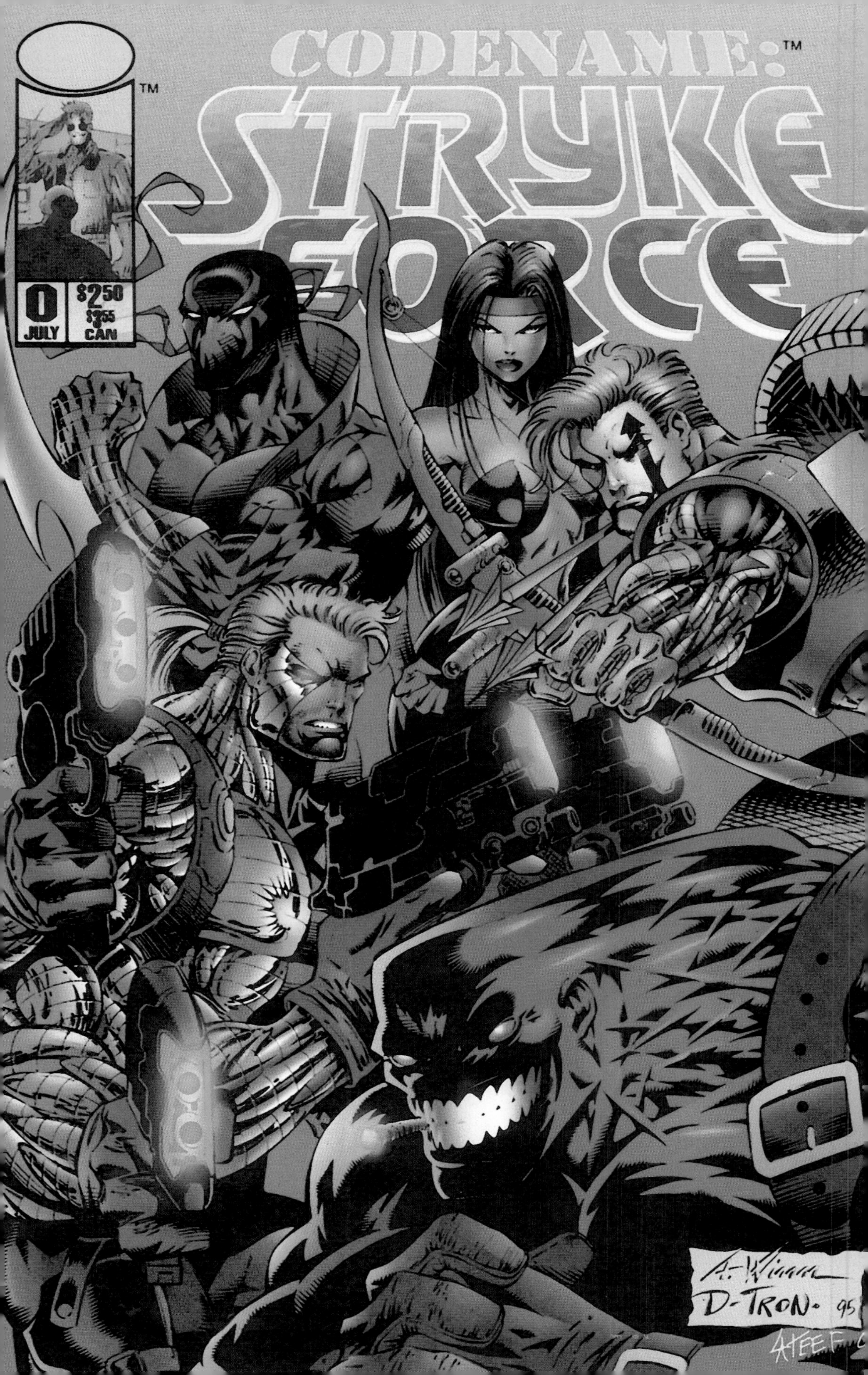
CODENAME:™
STRYKE FORCE
™
0
JULY
$2.50
$3.55
CAN
A. Winn
D-TRON 95

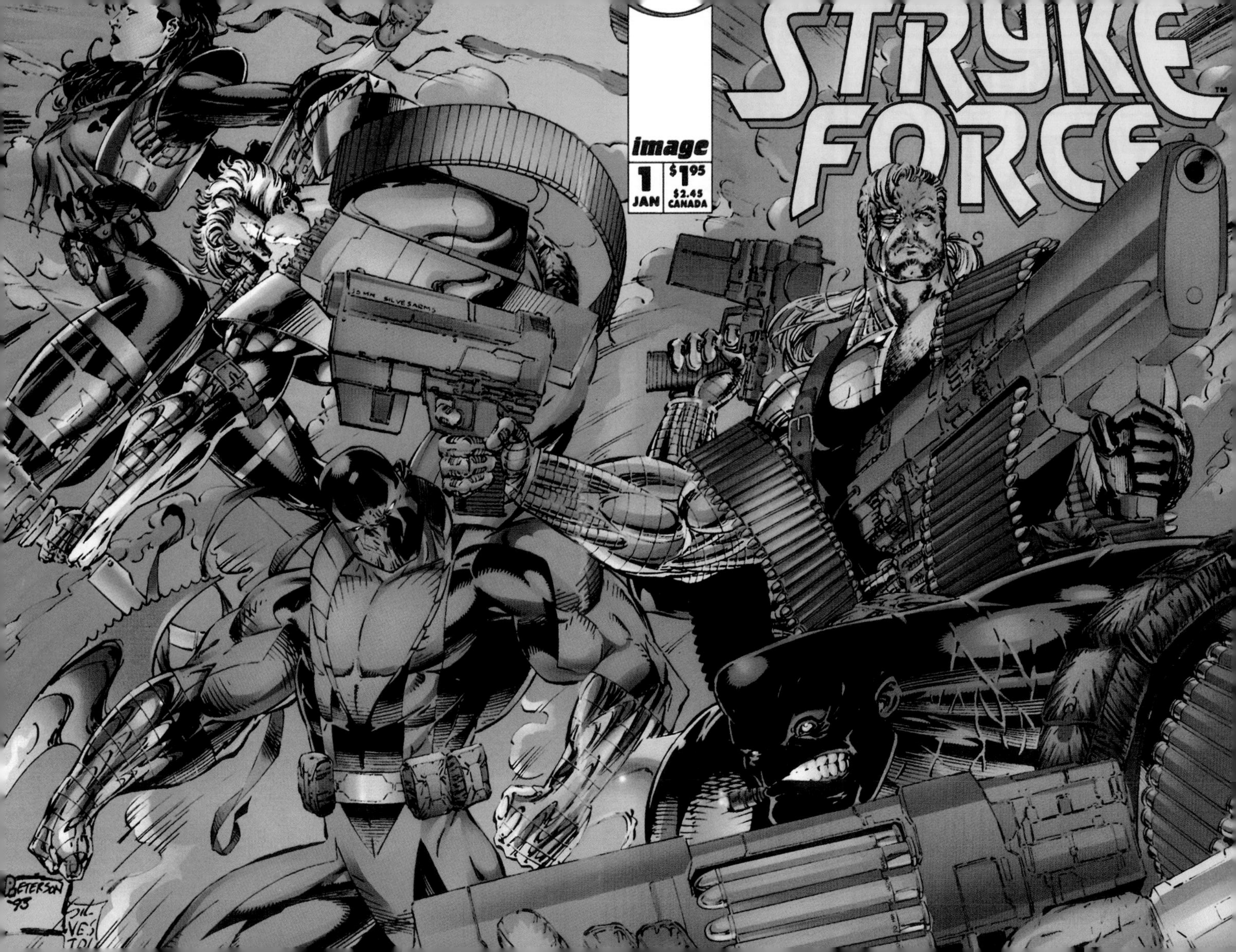
STRYKE FORCE™
image
1
JAN
$1.95
$2.45 CANADA
JOHN SILVESARMS
PETERSON '93
SILVESTRI

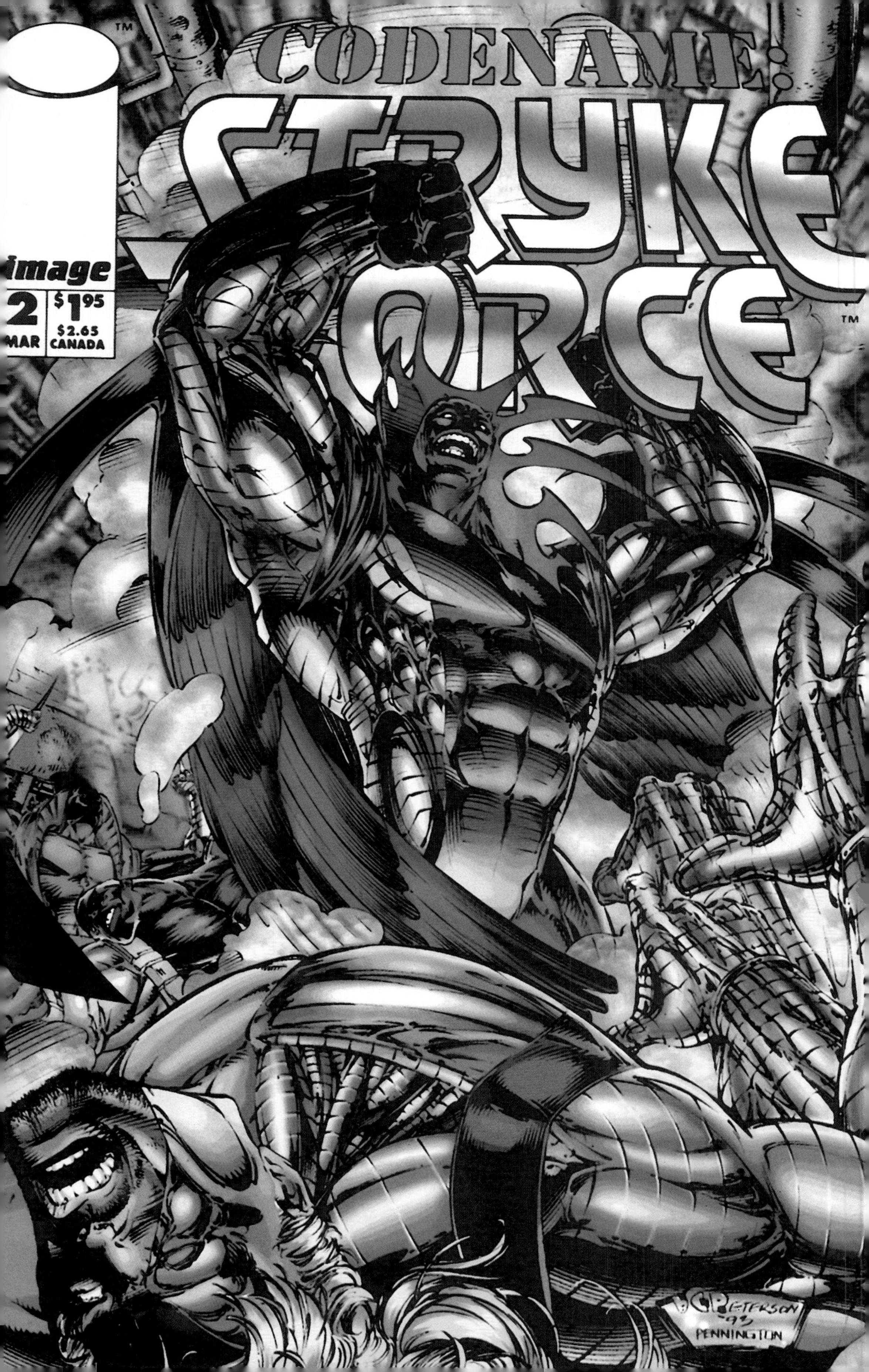
CODENAME: STRYKEFORCE
image
2 MAR
$1.95
$2.65 CANADA
PETERSON '93
PENNINGTON

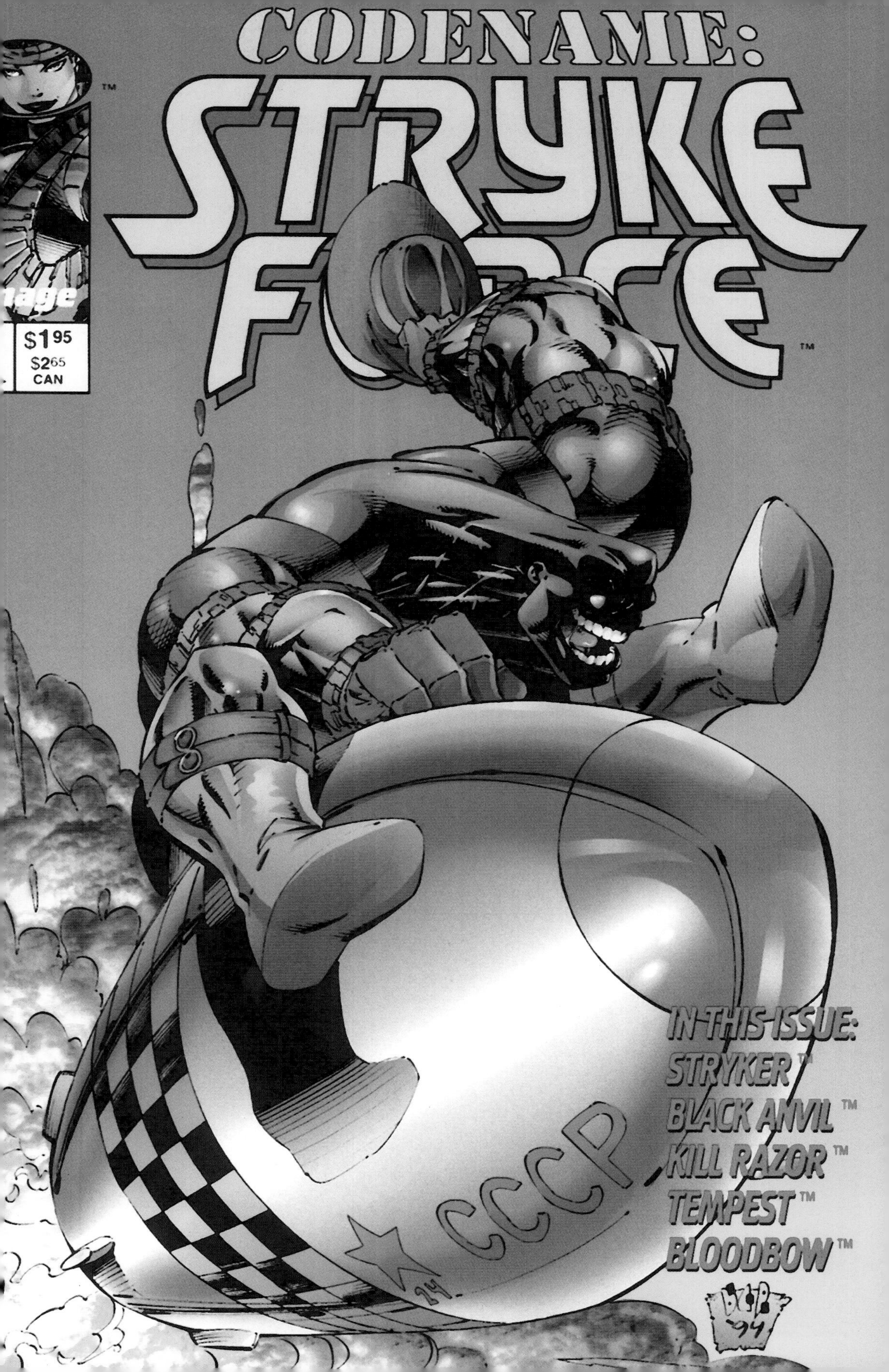
CODENAME:
STRYKE FORCE
$1.95
$2.65 CAN
IN THIS ISSUE:
STRYKER
BLACK ANVIL
KILL RAZOR
TEMPEST
BLOODBOW
CCCP

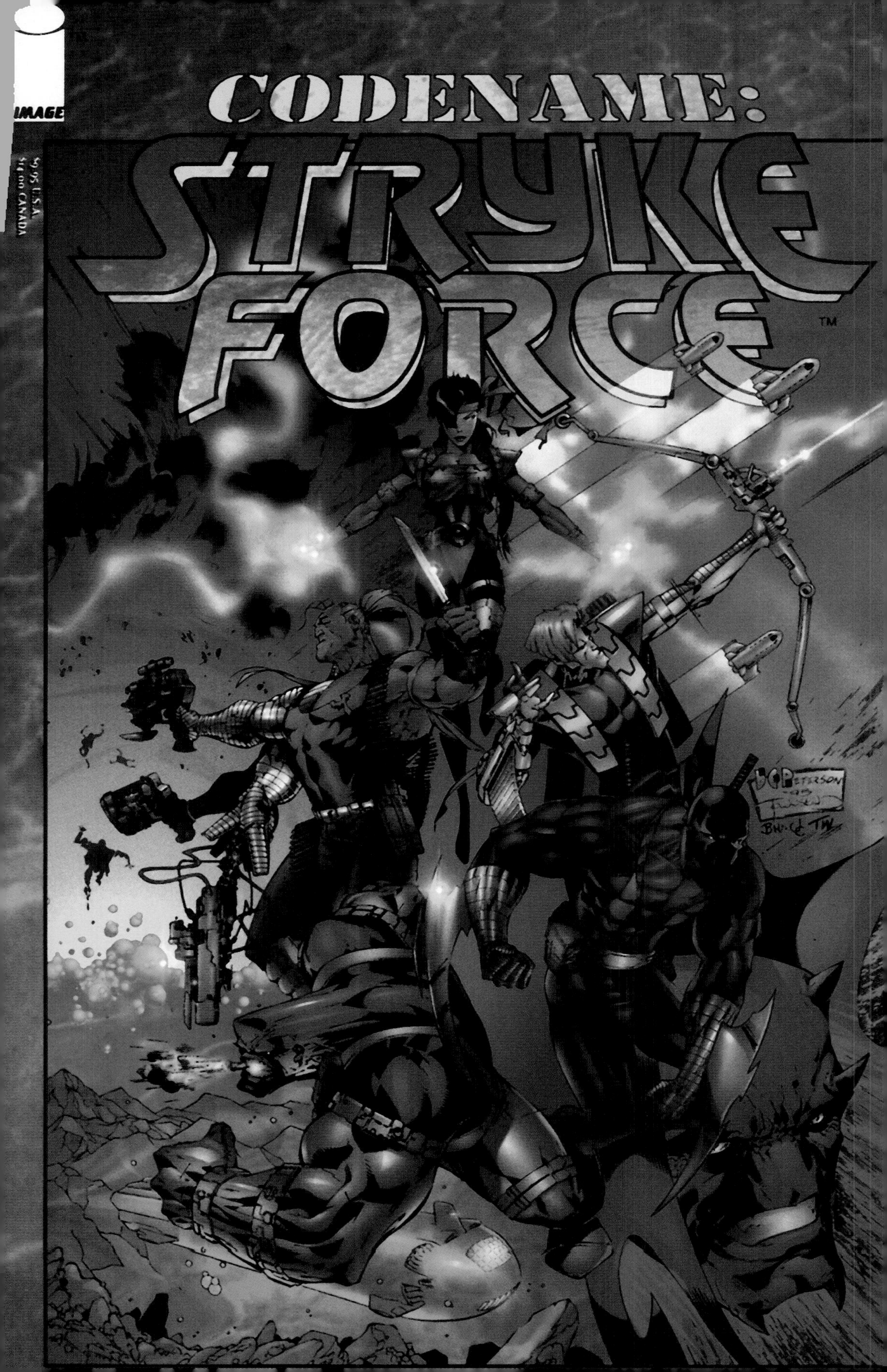
IMAGE
$9.95 U.S.A.
$14.00 CANADA
CODENAME:
STRYKE FORCE
TM

BEHIND THE SCENES OF

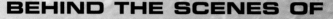

STRYKE FORCE

With series writer **Jay Faerber** and series artist **Tyler Kirkham.**

THE FOLLOWING PAGES are an inside look into some rare, and in some cases previously unseen, works that went into the making of the *Strykeforce* relaunch.

HERE IS WHERE THE ART FOR THE STRYKEFORCE RELAUNCH BEGAN, WITH ARTISTS DOING PROMOS AND CONCEPT DESIGNS...

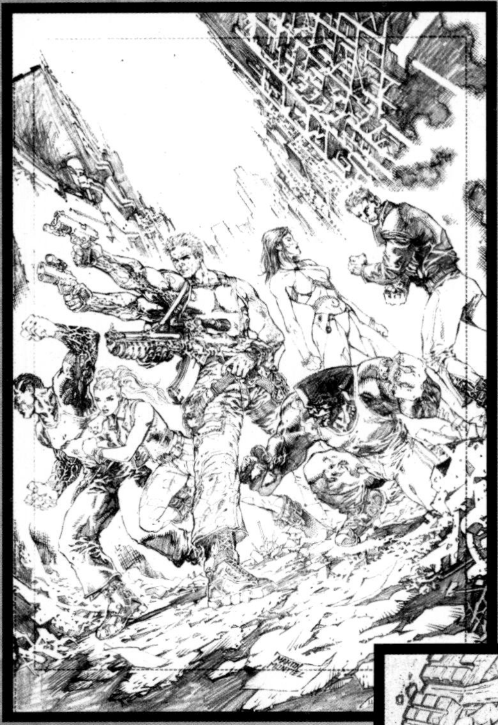

Martin Montiel *(Magdalena/Vampirella, The Darkness)* submitted this fantastic splash page of the new *Strykeforce* line-up. Around this time, Martin was handed a run on *The Darkness* Vol. II with writer Ron Marz.

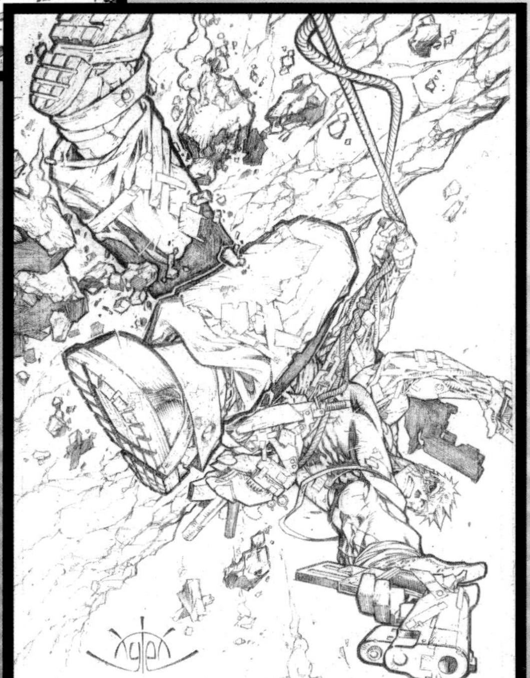

Tyler, who was interning at the Cow at the time, submitted this dynamic shot of Stryker which got the attention of Top Cow editorial and Jay Faerber.

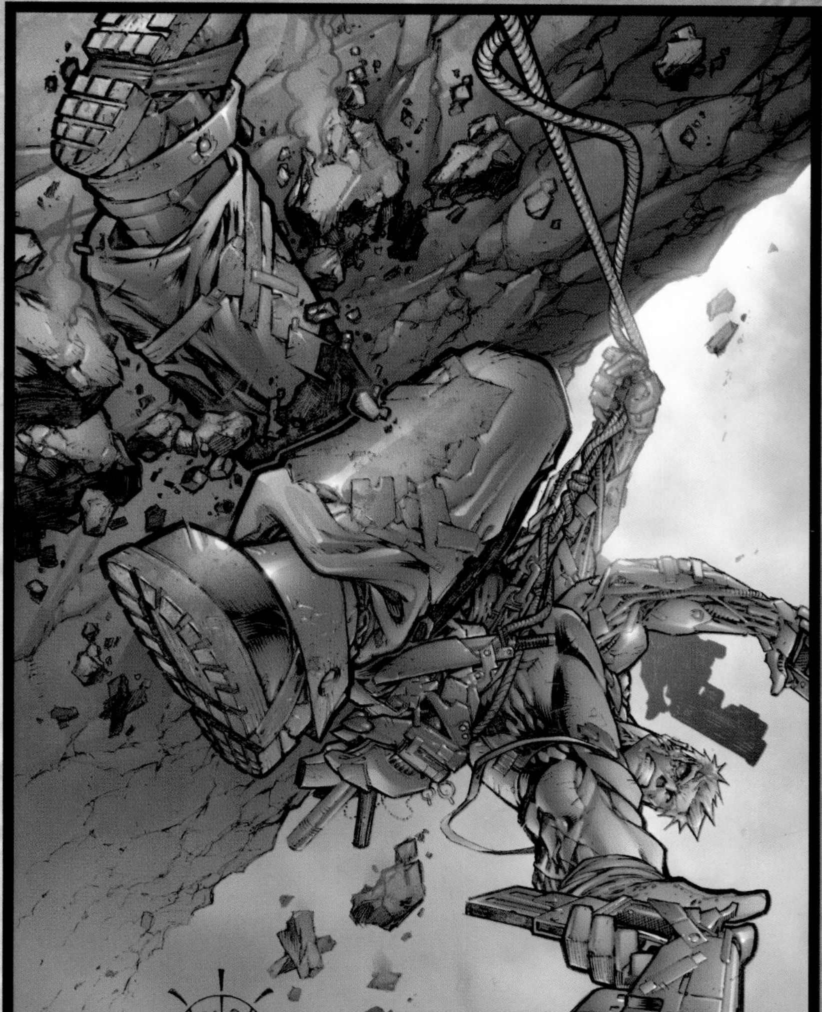
FGD

And here is the finished piece in full color!

HERE ARE SOME WORDS FROM SERIES WRITER JAY FAERBER AND ARTIST TYLER KIRKHAM ON THE CONCEPTS AND ART THAT WENT INTO THE *STRYKEFORCE* RELAUNCH.

How did you end up with the gig drawing ***Strykeforce?***

TK – Well, I was working on another project and I was just sketching and doing pinups of different Top Cow characters. I did a Stryker pinup and got a really good response. Next thing I know, I'm being told that they want to use it as a promo piece and they would like me to draw the mini-series relaunch.

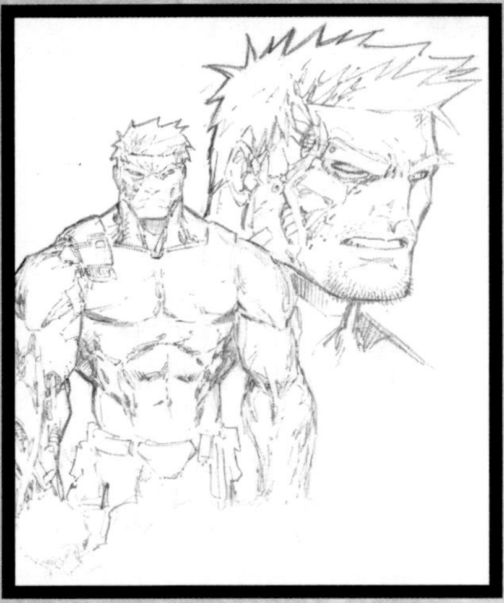

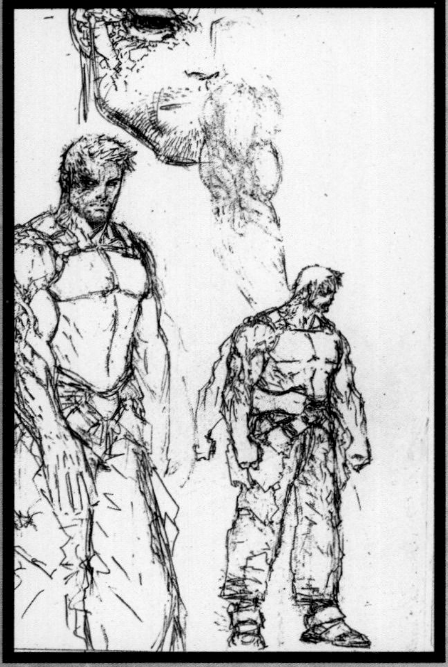

Looking at your 5-issue run as a whole, what did you most like/dislike about the experience?

TK – I really enjoyed the beginning because it was all so new and exiting, and I got to create a lot of things throughout the series. It was also my first "big" gig at Top Cow.

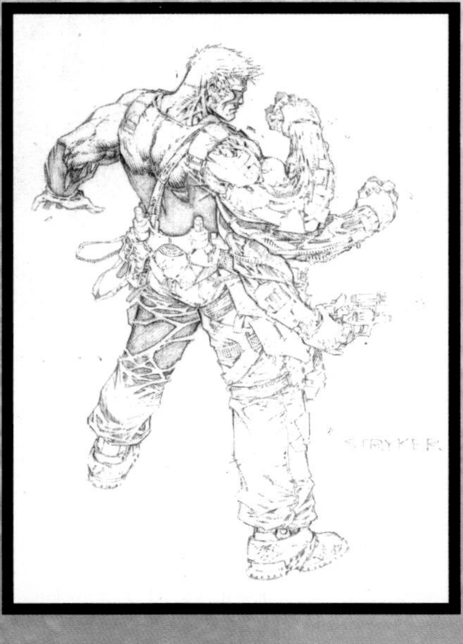
STRYKER

Stryker used to have three cybernetic arms, yet the number seemed to fluctuate in the updated ***Strykeforce.*** *How did that come about?*

JF - I thought it'd be cool if Stryker's arms were customizable. If he was just doing recon, and wasn't expecting trouble, he'd just hook up one of his robotic arms. If he was going to war, he'd hook up all three. That's also why I gave him the "grappling hand" device. It only makes sense that Stryker's cybernetic parts were continually upgraded.

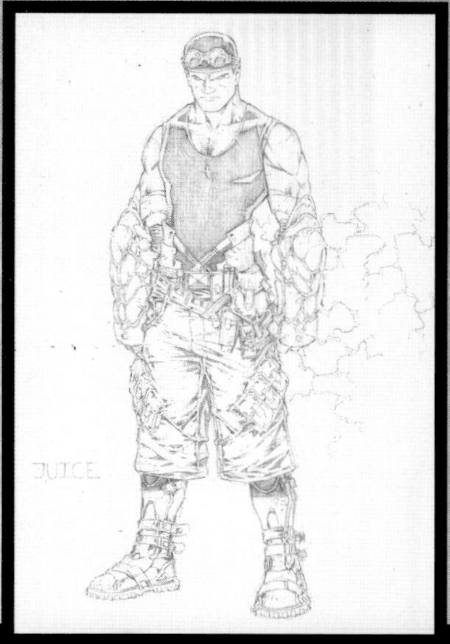
JUICE

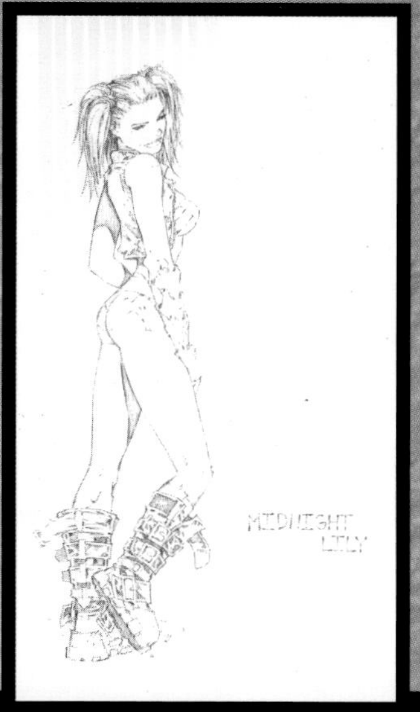
MIDNIGHT
LILY

Killawatt and Sly went through both design and name changes early in the conceptual process. "Juice" became Killawatt, and "Midnight Lily" became Sly.

Was it intimidating relaunching a series as your first official assignment?
TK – Oh yeah, I was scared out of my mind before I started. I felt like there was a lot to live up to. I didn't want to disappoint anyone, because this was my chance to prove myself to not only the fans but to Marc and the editors at Top Cow. We all stayed late nights to make it the best it could be and to put it out on time.

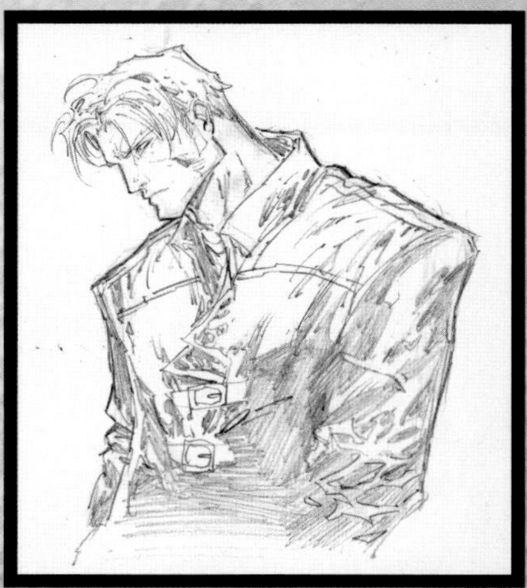

Who is you favorite Strykeforce character to draw?
TK – My favorite would have to be Lift. He's just an all around smooth guy. Stryker is also fun but he's way hard to draw because all the arms and gear.

Why did Sly always take her clothes off?
JF – I like characters whose powers have limitations, or take some sort of toll on them. Even the original Invisible Man had to go around naked, since his clothes didn't turn invisible. I thought by keeping that limitation, it made Sly's powers more interesting. And sure, I admit - - it provided a nice excuse for Tyler to draw the beautiful female form!

No complaints, Tyler is quite skilled.

What is your dream gig? If you could draw any already established character/s who would it/they be?
TK – That's a tough one. I have been drawing Superman, in the *Darkness/Superman* crossover which has been a total dream gig. But I would have to say that it would be Wolverine. It's always been Wolverine. He's my favorite. I Like the claws, ya know.

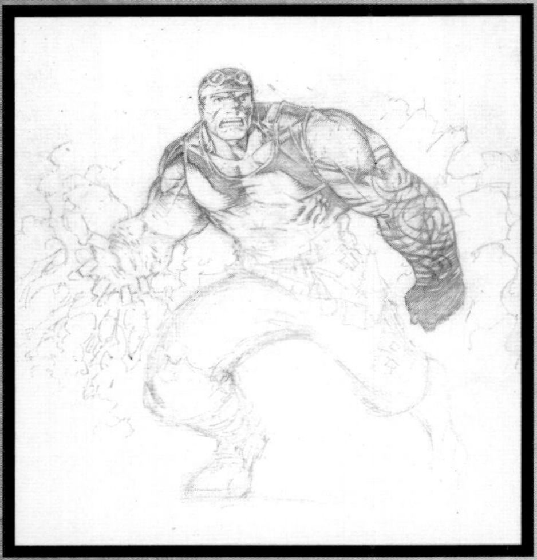

What's up with Killawatt's tattoos?
JF – Let's face it – anyone who's read comics for any length of time has seen plenty of guys who shoot lightning. I thought that, by giving Killawatt tattoos that glow when he's "powered up," it would create a more distinct visual, helping to set him apart from other characters.

Why did Anvil's name change?
JF – To be honest, I thought "Black Anvil" sounded a little goofy, and was a little more "super-hero"-y than I wanted this new team to be. I wanted their codenames to be more like nicknames. To me, "Anvil" just sounds cool.

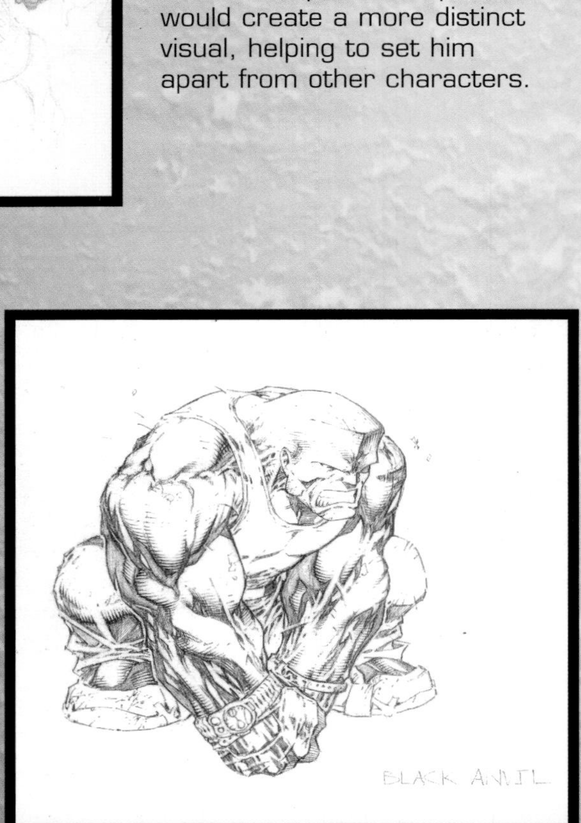
BLACK ANVIL

What was it like working with Jay Faerber? Was there direct interaction or were directions relayed through editorial channels?
TK – It was great working with Jay. He's really open to suggestions. We spoke a few times over the phone and at conventions. He's a really talented writer so it was pretty easy to work off his scripts.

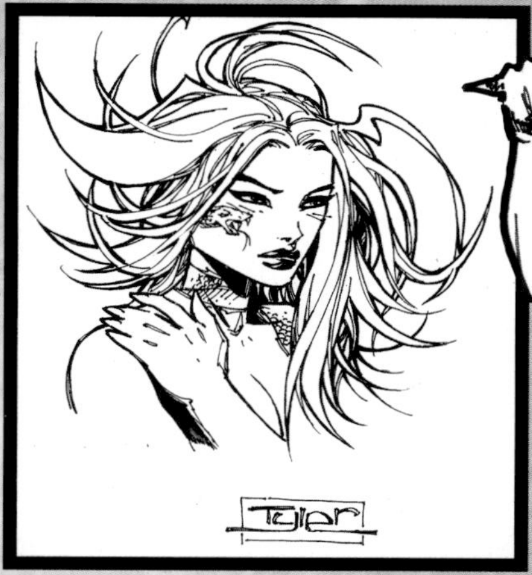
Tyler

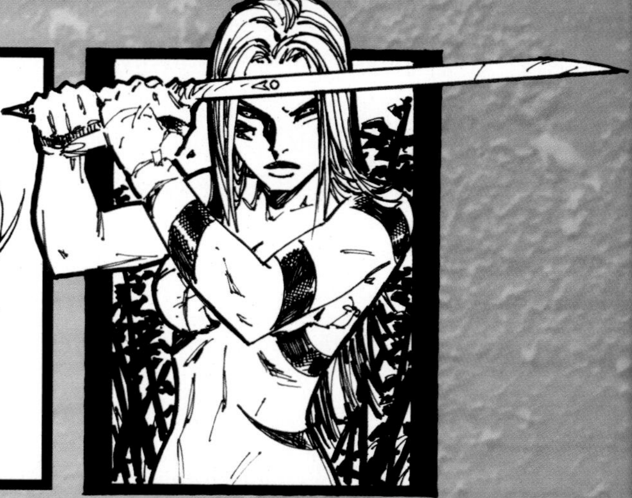

Previously unseen ink drawings by artist Tyler Kirkham

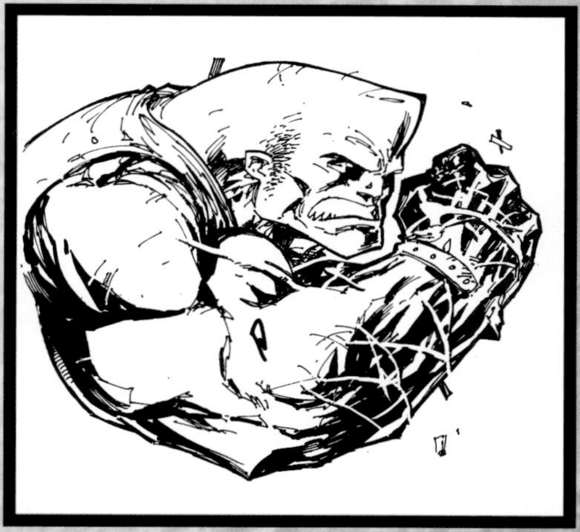

What was the best part about working with Tyler?
JF – The pillow fights.

If the book had continued, would Killawatt have betrayed the team to his boss at the F.B.I.?
JF – I have an answer for that, but I'm still holding out hope that we'll get to do more *Strykeforce* stories, someday in the future, so I don't want to reveal where that story was headed.

Tyler, you have the floor. Is there anything you want to throw out there to the audience?
TK – Well thanks for picking up this trade and I really hope you had as much fun reading it as we did working on it. And hopefully *Strykeforce* will return. Maybe bring back Killrazor. Oh yeah. I'm sure that Morgan Stryker and gang aren't finished yet.